MEN of MARK

WM. J. SIMMONS.

MEN of MARK

Eminent, Progressive and Rising

By
WILLIAM J. SIMMONS

EBONY CLASSICS

Johnson Publishing Company Inc.
Chicago, 1970

Publisher's Note

The Ebony Classics series has been designed for clarity and elegance in the hope of reaching a public outside the research libraries. The text has been entirely reset in a combination of Bodoni typefaces which echo the original editions, but are easier to read. Corrections of typographical errors and inconsistencies of style are the only amendments that have been made.

Other titles available in this series are:

Black and White by Timothy Thomas Fortune
The Narrative of Sojourner Truth
Autobiography of a Fugitive Negro by Samuel Ringgold Ward
My Bondage and My Freedom by Frederick Douglass
The Underground Railroad by William Still

Copyright Geo. M. Rewell & Co., 1887

Reprinted 1970 by Johnson Publishing Company, Inc.
Foreword by Lerone Bennett Jr. copyright © 1970

Library of Congress Catalog Card No. 78-102983
SBN No. 87485-035-5

*Printed in the United States of America
by the Rand McNally Company*
$12.50

FOREWORD TO THE 1970 EDITION

Although it was published more than eighty years ago, *Men of Mark* is still a basic text of black biography. It is a commentary on the state of American biography and a tribute to the vision of author William J. Simmons that this old and enduring classic contains more detailed biographical information on more figures of Afro-American history than any other single book.

Since it was first published in 1887, *Men of Mark* has been a standard reference work for all serious students of Afro-American history. But it is more than a reference book. A collection of dramatic and readable sketches of most of the great male leaders of Afro-American history, the book can and should be read as Simmons intended it to be read, i.e., as a testament to black resistance and persistence in the face of unparalleled adversity. Looking back on the years of slavery and oppression, Simmons paid tribute to the indomitable tenacity of the black spirit and asked: "Was ever such a thing seen in another people?"

A minister, teacher, and college president, Simmons wrote *Men of Mark* to define, defend, and illustrate the black personality. He also wrote the book to show that slavery did not crush the black spirit. He had noted, in his long experience as a teacher, "that many of my students were woefully ignorant of the work of our great colored men—even ignorant of their names." Simmons wrote the book to inspire students so that they might see "the means and manners of men's elevation."

Simmons cites what he calls a representative sample of distinguished black men. "Nearly all" of the subjects, he says, are former slaves. Many are ministers, but there is a full panorama of types: "The first Colored Judge in the United States," "Phenographer and Typewriter," "The Owner of a Street Car Railroad, a Race Track, and a Park," "Insurrectionist," "General," "Phrenologist," "Manufacturer of Telephones," "Lumber Merchant and Capitalist."

Simmons wrote out of a deep sense of identification with the struggles and achievements of his subjects. Born in slavery in South Carolina in 1849, he transcended his environment and became one of the leading men of his time. Like most of his subjects, he lived through the seminal experiences of slavery, Civil War, Reconstruction, and post-Reconstruction. With his family, he escaped and lived long years in harrowing fear of slave catchers. With other members of the Forty-First United States Colored Troops, he helped emancipate the slaves. After the war he was graduated from Howard University, and served as minister, teacher, and editor. Later he became president of the Kentucky Normal and Theological Institution, and participated in the major political and ideological struggles of the late nineteenth century. Simmons knew many of the great men of that period and some of them provided him with documents and research material.

Simmons was a man of his times and he writes with the full, rhetorical style of the nineteenth century. An unabashed partisan, he rejects the pseudo-objective approach and situates himself on the terrain of his subjects. He takes sides with them, rejoices in their achievements and bemoans their setbacks. The limitations of this approach (overemphasis of personal agencies and the failure to report negative factors) are obvious and Simmons was probably aware of them. At any rate, he said: "There is no great literary attempt made. I have not tried to play the part of a scholar, but a narrator of facts with here and there a line of eulogy." Despite this disclaimer, Simmons documents his statements with "copious extracts" from speeches, letters, and newspapers. On the debit side, it should be said that Simmons' enthusiasms lead him into some contradictions. In his zeal to combat the racist charges of the time, he repeats the erroneous story about the faithfulness of the slave population during the War.

Contradictions apart, Simmons demonstrates extraordinary breadth of view. He moves easily from the black conservative to the black radical, from the non-violent protestor to the violent protestor, from the integrationist to the nationalist, finding something to praise and admire in all positions. And he sent the book to the public with these words: "This writing has been a labor of love, a real pleasure. I feel better for the good words I have said of these gentlemen."

One observes with interest that the book was sold in 1887 by subscription and was not for sale in book stores. Simmons hoped thus to make enough money to finance a companion volume on black women. The response was apparently less than overwhelming for the book on black women never appeared. For all that, the reaction was interesting. Copies of the book were passed on from generation to generation and were soon circulating on the rare book market at premium prices. Now available at a modest price to the general public, *Men of Mark* validates the vision and hope of its author.

LERONE BENNETT JR.

Institute of the Black World
Atlanta, Georgia
December, 1969

CONTENTS

Author's Preface	1
Introduction by Henry M. Turner	19
I—Hon. Frederick Douglass, LL. D.	21
II—Rev. W. B. Derrick, D. D.	37
III—Phillip H. Murry	43
IV—Crispus Attucks	47
V—Granville T. Woods	51
VI—Hon. Jeremiah A. Brown	55
VII—William Calvin Chase	61
VIII—Rev. James W. Hood, D. D.	70
IX—Hon. Samuel R. Lowery	77
X—William Still	81
XI—J. W. Morris, A. B., A. M., LL. B.	91
XII—Hon. Robert Smalls	93
XIII—Henry Ossawa Tanner	105
XIV—Rev. Andrew Heath	108
XV—H. C. Smith	115
XVI—Rev. John Bunyan Reeve, A. B., D. D.	118
XVII—Thomas J. Bowers	120
XVIII—Rev. Nicholas Franklin Roberts, A. B., A. M.	122
XIX—Hon. Theophile T. Allain	125
XX—Demark Veazie	142
XXI—J. E. Jones, A. B., A. M.	145
XXII—John Wesley Terry	149
XXIII—William E. Matthews, LL. B.	153
XIV—Rev. James Alfred Dunn Podd	157
XXV—Hon. Henry Wilkens Chandler, A. B., A. M.	160
XXVI—Rev. Theodore Doughty Miller, D. D.	162
XXVII—J. D. Baltimore	167
XXVIII—J. R. Clifford	171
XXIX—Wiley Jones	175

XXX—John H. Burris, A. B., A. M. 179
XXXI—Henry F. Williams 183
XXXII—Rev. Edmund Kelly 186
XXXIII—Rev. Preston Taylor 189
XXXIV—Solomon G. Brown 193
XXXV—John Mitchell, Jr. 201
XXXVI—Rev. Loudon Ferrill 206
XXXVII—Richard Theodore Greener, A. B., LL. B., LL. D. ... 211
XXXVIII—Captain Paul Cuffee 217
XXXIX—Rev. Alexander Walters 221
XL—Benjamin Banneker 224
XLI—Rev. Richard DeBaptiste, D. D. 229
XLII—Hon. George French Ecton 234
XLIII—Newell Houston Ensley 237
XLIV—Rev. Christopher H. Payne 241
XLV—Peter Humphries Clark, A. M. 244
XLVI—Justin Holland 251
XLVII—William Hooper Council 255
XLVIII—Rev. James Poindexter, D. D. 259
XLIX—Richard Mason Hancock 261
L—W. S. Scarborough, A. B., A. M., LL. D. 269
LI—Rev. Solomon T. Clanton, Jr., A. B., B. D. 275
LII—John O. Crosby, A. M. B. E. 277
LIII—Hon. Francis L. Cardoza 281
LIV—Hon. John S. Leary, LL. B. 285
LV—E. S. Porter, A. B., M. D. 289
LVI—Rev. Augustus Tolton 291
LVII—William Wells Brown 296
LVIII—Walter F. Craig 298
LIX—Rev. Charles L. Purce, A. B. 301
LX—Alexander Dumas 303
LXI—Rev. William Reuben Pettiford 305
LXII—Hon. Robert B. Elliott 310
LXIII—Inman Edward Page, A. B., A. M. 315
LXIV—Rev. E. K. Love 321
LXV—J. A. Arneaux 323
LXVI—Rev. Richard Allen 329
LXVII—Hon. Samuel Allen McElwee, A. B., LL. B. 335
LXVIII—Rev. Lott Carey 342
LXIX—Hon. John Mercer Langston, A. B., A. M., LL. D. ... 345
LXX—Rev. William B. McAlpine 353

LXXI—Rev. Alexander Crummell, A. B., D. D. 357
LXXII—Hon. George H. White 362
LXXIII—Hon. Josiah T. Settle, A. B., A. M., LL. B. 365
LXXIV—William H. Gibson 369
LXXV—Hon. George W. Williams 371
LXXVI—William Eve Holmes, A. B., A. M., LL. D. 384
LXXVII—Rev. Randall Bartholemew Vandervall, D. D. ... 387
LXXVIII—Rev. Elijah P. Marrs 392
LXXIX—Rev. Daniel Jones 395
LXXX—Rev. Henry N. Jeter 399
LXXXI—Rev. J. T. White 401
LXXXII—Rev. G. W. Gayles 405
LXXXIII—Hon. Mifflin Wister Gibbs 407
LXXXIV—William H. Steward 413
LXXXV—Rev. Frank J. Grimke, A. B. 416
LXXXVI—Hon. Robert Harlan 421
LXXXVII—Dr. Anthony William Amo 423
LXXXVIII—Rev. Rufus L. Perry, Ph. D. 425
LXXXIX—Rev. Bartlett Taylor 430
XC—James M. Gregory, A. B., A. M., ... 433
XCI—Rev. Daniel Abraham Gaddie, D. D. 445
XCII—W. Q. Atwood 449
XCIII—Rev. Henry Highland Garnet, D. D. 453
XCIV—Rev. Leonard A. Grimes 457
XCV—Rev. James H. Holmes 460
XCVI—General T. Morris Chester 463
XCVII—Rev. Lemuel Haynes, A. M. 467
XCVIII—Hon. H. O. Wagoner 469
XCIX—Rev. Marcus Dale 473
C—Charles B. Purvis, A. M., M. D. 477
CI—W. H. Crogman, A. B., A. M. 480
CII—Hon. Blanche K. Bruce 483
CIII—J. D. Bowser 488
CIV—Rev. Jesse Freeman Boulden 491
CV—Rev. William T. Dixon 495
CVI—Rev. Matthew Campbell 501
CVII—Rev. C. C. Vaughn 505
CVIII—Rev. Harvey Johnson 509
CIX—Ira Aldridge 513
CX—Hon. George L. Ruffin, LL. B. 518
CXI—Augustus Straker, LL. B., LL. D. 521

CONTENTS

CXII—Rev. John Hudson Riddick 527
CXIII—Rev. J. C. Price, A. B. 529
CXIV—Hon. Pinckney Benton Stewart Pinchback 533
CXV—Alexander Petion 547
CXVI—Timothy Thomas Fortune 549
CXVII—Troy Porter 555
CXVIII—"Blind Tom" (Thomas Green Bethune) 557
CXIX—Rev. Henry Adams 561
CXX—James C. Farley 563
CXXI—Rev. Henry McNeal Turner, DD., LL. D. 567
CXXII—Rev. John W. Stephenson, M. D. 577
CXXIII—Joseph Carter Corbin, A. B., A. M. 583
CXXIV—Hon. James M. Trotter 587
CXXV—Rev. Allen Allensworth, A. M. 595
CXXVI—Rev. George Washington Dupee 599
CXXVII—Sameul C. Watson, M. D. 608
CXXVIII—Rt. Rev. Richard Harvey Cain, D. D. 613
CXXIX—Hon. John H. Smythe 617
CXXX—J. J. Durham. A. B., A. M., M. D. 622
CXXXI—Rev. Benjamin W. Arnett, D. D. 625
CXXXII—Olander Equiano or Gustavus Vassa 633
CXXXIII—John W. Cromwell 637
CXXXIV—Rev. E. M. Brawley, A. B., A. M., D. D. 645
CXXXV—James W. C. Pennington, D. D. 648
CXXXVI—Hon. Edward Wilmot Blyden, LL. D. 651
CXXXVII—Rev. B. F. Lee, D. D. 655
CXXXVIII—Hon. James J. Spelman 659
CXXXIX—Rev. Marshall W. Taylor, D. D. 662
CXL—Toussaint L'Ouverture 665
CXLI—Hon. Hiram R. Revels 672
CXLII—Rev. Harrison N. Bouey 675
CXLIII—Colonel James Lewis 677
CXLIV—Rev. E. H. Lipscombe, A. B., A. M. 681
CXLV—James C. Matthews 685
CXLVI—William Howard Day, D. D. 701
CXLVII—Rev. Benjamin Tucker Tanner, A. M., D. D. 705
CXLVIII—Geoffrey L'Islet 709
CXLIX—R. C. O. Benjamin 711
CL—Hon. John J. Irvine 713
CLI—George T. Downing 718
CLII—Major Martin R. Delaney, M. D. 721

CONTENTS

- CLIII—Rev. J. B. Fields 727
- CLIV—Robert Pelham Jr. 733
- CLV—Booker T. Washington 737
- CLVI—Rev. J. P. Campbell, D. D., LL. D. 741
- CLVII—Nat Turner 743
- CLVIII—Hon. Hilery Richard Wright Johnson 746
- CLIX—Hon. John R. Lynch 749
- CLX—Rev. P. H. A. Braxton 753
- CLXI—T. McCants Stewart, A. B., LL. B. 757
- CLXII—Hon. E. P. McCabe 761
- CLXIII—Rev. Charles Henry Parrish, A. B. 763
- CLXIV—Rev. John Jasper 767
- CLXV—James E. J. Capitein 775
- CLXVI—Rev. D. A. Payne, D. D., LL. D. 779
- CLXVII—Rev. Isaac M. Burgan, B. D. 785
- CLXVIII—Rev. W. J. White 791
- CLXIX—Hon. Alexander Clark 793
- CLXX—Hon. John C. Dancy 796
- CLXXI—Charles L. Reason 799
- CLXXII—Rev. John M. Brown, D. D., D. C. L. 805
- CLXXIII—Professor David Abner, Jr. 809
- CLXXIV—Rev. A. A. Whitman 812
- CLXXV—E. M. Bannister 816
- CLXXVI—Hon. C. C. Antoine 820
- CLXXVII—Rev. James Matthew Townsend, D. D. 822
- Index To Sketches 825

ILLUSTRATIONS

W. J. Simmons	Frontispiece
Frederick Douglass	20
W. B. Derrick	36
Granville T. Woods	50
Jeremiah A. Brown	56
William Calvin Chase	60
Samuel R. Lowery	78
William Still	82
Robert Smalls	94
H. C. Smith	114
Theophile T. Allain	124
J. E. Jones	144
William E. Matthews	152
J. D. Baltimore	166
J. R. Clifford	172
Wiley Jones	176
John H. Burrus	178
Henry F. Williams	184
Preston Taylor	190
John Mitchell, Jr.	202
Richard Theodore Greener	210
Alexander Walters	220
Richard DeBaptiste	230
Newell Houston Ensley	236
Justin Holland	250
James Poindexter	258
W. S. Scarborough	270
John O. Crosby	278
Francis L. Cardoza	282
John S. Leary	284
E. S. Porter	288
Augustus Tolton	290
Charles L. Purce	300
W. R. Pettiford	306
Inman Edward Page	316

ILLUSTRATIONS

J. A. Arneaux	324
Richard Allen	330
Samuel A. McElwee	336
John M. Langston	344
Alexander Crummell	358
Josiah T. Settle	364
George W. Williams	372
Randall Bartholemew Vandervell	388
Daniel Jones	394
Henry N. Jeter	398
J. T. White	402
G. W. Gayles	405
Mifflin Wister Gibbs	408
William H. Steward	412
Robert Harlan	420
Rufus L. Perry	426
James M. Gregory	434
Daniel A. Gaddie	444
W. Q. Atwood	448
Henry Highland Garnet	452
Leonard A. Grimes	458
H. O. Wagoner	468
Charles B. Purvis	476
Blanche K. Bruce	484
Jesse F. Boulden	490
William T. Dixon	496
Matthew Campbell	500
C. C. Vaughn	504
Harvey Johnson	508
Ira Aldridge	512
D. Augustus Straker	522
J. C. Price	528
Pinckney Benton Stewart Pinchback	532
Timothy Thomas Fortune	550
"Blind Tom" (Thomas Green Bethune)	558
J. C. Farley	564
Henry McNeal Turner	566
Joseph Carter Corbin	584
James M. Trotter	588
Allen Allensworth	596
George W. Dupee	600
Richard Harvey Cain	612
John H. Smythe	618
B. W. Arnett	626
Olaudah Equiano *or* Gustavus Vassa	632
John W. Cromwell	638
E. M. Brawley	644

EDWARD WILMOT BLYDEN	*650*
JAMES J. SPELMAN	*658*
TOUSSAINT L'OUVERTURE	*664*
HARRISON N. BOUEY	*674*
JAMES LEWIS	*678*
JAMES C. MATTHEWS	*684*
BENJAMIN TUCKER TANNER	*706*
JOHN J. IRVINE	*714*
MARTIN R. DELANEY	*720*
J. B. FIELDS	*726*
ROBERT PELHAM, JR.	*732*
BOOKER T. WASHINGTON	*736*
J. P. CAMPBELL	*740*
JOHN R. LYNCH	*748*
P. H. A. BRAXTON	*752*
T. MCCANTS STEWART	*758*
E. P. MCCABE	*760*
CHARLES H. PARRISH	*764*
JOHN JASPER	*768*
D. A. PAYNE	*778*
I. M. BURGAN	*784*
ALEXANDER CLARK	*794*
CHARLES L. REASON	*798*
DAVID ABNER, JR.	*810*

This volume is respectfully dedicated to the women of our race, and especially to the devoted, self-sacrificing mothers Who moulded the lives of the subjects of these sketches, laboring and praying for their success. It is sent forth with the earnest hope that future mothers will be inspired to give special attention to the training of their children, and thereby fit them for honorable, happy and useful lives.

The Author

AUTHOR'S PREFACE

To presume to multiply books in this day of excellent writers and learned book-makers is a rash thing perhaps for a novice. It may even be a presumption that shall be met by the production itself being driven from the market by the keen, searching criticism of not only the reviewers, but less noted objectors. And yet there are books that meet a ready sale because they seem like "Ishmaelites"— against everybody and everybody against them. Whether this work shall ever accomplish the design of the author may not at all be determined by its sale. While I hope to secure some pecuniary gain that I may accompany it with a companion illustrating what our women have done, yet by no means do I send it forth with the sordid idea of gain. I would rather it would do some good than make a single dollar, and I echo the wish of "Abou Ben Adhem," in the sweet poem of that name, written by Leigh Hunt. The angel was writing at the table, in his vision,

> *The names of those who love the Lord.*

Abou wanted to know if his was there—and the angel said "No." Said Abou,

> *I pray thee, then, write me as one that loves his fellow-men.*

That is what I ask to be recorded of me.

> *The angel wrote and vanished. The next night*
> *It came again, with a great awakening light,*
> *And showed the names whom love of God had blessed,*
> *And lo! Ben Adhem's name led all the rest.*

I desire that the book shall be a help to students, male and female, in the way of information concerning our great names.

I have noticed in my long experience as a teacher, that many of my students were wofully ignorant of the work of our great colored men—even ignorant of their names. If they knew their names, it was some indefinable something they had done—just what, they could not tell. If in a slight degree I shall here furnish the data for that class of rising men and women, I shall feel much pleased. Herein will be found many who had severe trials in making their way through schools of different grades. It is a suitable book, it is hoped, to be put into the hands of intelligent, aspiring young people everywhere, that they might see the means and manners of men's elevation, and by this be led to undertake the task of going through high schools and colleges. If the persons herein mentioned could rise to the exalted stations which they have and do now hold, what is there to prevent any young man or woman from achieving greatness? Many, yea, nearly all these came from the loins of slave fathers, and were the babes of women in bondage, and themselves felt the leaden hand of slavery on their own bodies; but whether slaves or not, they suffered with their brethren because of color. That "sum of human villainies" did not crush out the life and manhood of the race. I wish the book to show to the world—to our oppressors and even our friends—that the Negro race is still alive, and must possess more intellectual vigor than any other section of the human family or else how could they be crushed as slaves in all these years since 1620, and yet to-day stand side by side with the best blood in America, in white institutions, grappling with abstruse problems in Euclid and difficult classics, and master them? Was ever such a thing seen in other people? Whence these lawyers, doctors, authors, editors, divines, lecturers, linguists, scientists, college presidents and such, in one quarter of a century?

Another thing I would have them notice, that the spirituality of this race was not diminished in slavery. While in bondage, it may have been somewhat objectionable, as seen in the practices of our race, it must be remembered that they copied much from their owners—they never descended to the level of brutes, and were kind, loving and faithful. They patiently waited till God broke their chains. There was more statesmanship in the Negro slaves than in their masters. Thousands firmly believed they would live to be free, but their masters could not be persuaded to voluntarily accept pay from the government, and thus save the loss they afterwards bore through the "Emancipation." They went to war and fought "the God of battles," but the slaves waited, humbly feeding the wives and children of those who went to battle to rivet their chains. To my mind, one of the most sublime points in our history is right here. We never harmed one of these helpless women and children—they testified of that themselves. And yet they tell stale lies of ravishing now, when the war is over, and freedom gained, and when the men are all home. No, God has permitted us to triumph and through Him. He implanted in us a vigorous spiritual tree, and since freedom, how has this been growing? Untrammelled, we have, out of our ignorance and penury, built thousands of churches, started thousands of schools, educated millions of children, supported thousands of ministers of the Gospel, organized societies for the care of the sick and the burying of the dead. This spirituality and love of offspring are indubitable evidence that slavery, though long and protracted, met in our race a vigorous, vital, God-like spirituality, which like the palm tree flourishes and climbs upward through opposition.

Again, I admire these men. I have faith in my people. I wish to exalt them; I want their lives snatched from obscurity to become household matter for conversation. I have made copious extracts from their speeches, sermons, addresses, correspondence and other writings, for the purpose of showing their skill in handling the English language, and to show the range of the thoughts of the American Negro. I wish also to furnish specimens of Negro eloquence, that young men might find them handy for declamations and apt quotations. It was hard to draw the line in making many selections, and I do not claim that a better selection might not be made. Indeed I am aware that many are entitled to a place here, and the reader may think I did wrong in selecting some of my subjects; but I ask no pardon for the names I present. They may be the judgment of a faulty brain, and yet there is much to admire in all. The extent of our country makes it impossible to secure all who may be "eminent, progressive and rising." I trust I have presented a representative of many classes of those who labor. The book may therefore be a suggestion for some one to do better.

The illustrations are many, and have been presented so that the reader may see the characters face to face. This writing has been a labor of love, a real pleasure. I feel better for the good words I have said of these gentlemen. There is no great literary attempt made. I have not tried to play the part of a scholar, but a narrator of facts with here and there a line of eulogy. The book is full; and has already passed the limit of first intentions. I am in debt to many gentlemen for their kindness—especially to Rev. Alexander Crummell, D.D., for the use of books; Hon. James M. Trotter for the loan of cuts taken from his work *Music and Some Highly Musical People;* Rev. R. DeBaptiste for assistance in securing sketches; Rev. B. W. Arnett, D.D., loan of books; Hon. John H. Smythe for assistance in sketches and pictures of E. W. Blyden and President W. W. Johnson; General T. Morris Chester, for picture of Ira Aldridge and facts on his life; Professor W. S. Scarborough for many kind helps; Rev. J. H. Greene, for cut of Augustus Tolton and facts in his life; William C. Chase, John W. Cromwell, T. McCants Stewart, Hon. D. A. Straker, Marshall W. Taylor, D.D., Hon. P. B. S. Pinchback, Hon. H. O. Wagoner, Rev. Rufus L. Perry and many others, and pre-eminently do I feel grateful to Bishop H. M. Turner, my distinguished friend, who trusts his own good name by associating it with this poor effort. May God bless him for this kind act to a beginner in book-making. This book goes out on the wing of a prayer that it will do great good.

WILLIAM J. SIMMONS

May, 1887

INTRODUCTION

Accompanied by a Sketch of the Life of Rev. W. J. Simmons, A. B., A. M., D. D.

It is a historic fact that Virginia soil has been rife with Presidents, but truly South Carolina has given to the world more men of note than any other State in the Union. In Charleston, South Carolina, June 29, 1849, Edward and Esther Simmons, two slaves, added to their fortune the subject of this sketch, who though born in poverty, shrouded by obscurity, was destined to make for himself a name honored among men. At an early period in his life, interested parties hurried the mother with three small children northward, without the protection of a husband and father, to begin a long siege with poverty. When the steamer landed at Philadelphia they were met by an uncle, Alexander Tardiff, who left the south some time before. This uncle, a shoemaker by trade, displayed the virtues of a generous nature in caring for the mother, William, Emeline and Anna as well as he could, with prejudice to fight. These were days of hardships and anxieties so keen for the little family that even now the survivors speak of them in hushed tones and with misty eyes. While in Philadelphia they were harassed by slave traders who seemed determined to burrow them out of their hiding place. At this time disease laid his hand upon them.

> *Disasters come not singly;*
> *But as if they watched and waited,*
> *Scanning one another's motions.*
> *When the first descends, the others*
> *Follow, follow, gathering flock-wise*
> *Round their victim, sick and wounded,*
> *First a shadow, then a sorrow,*
> *Till the air is dark with anguish.*

Huddled together in the garret of the three-story brick house where they lived, stricken with the small-pox, almost destitute of food, and fearing to call in medical attendance lest by attracting attention they would be carried back into slavery; while death stared them in the face, fugitive slave hunters rapped at the door of the front room which the uncle used as a workshop. These beasts in human flesh, after many inquiries and cross-questionings were so misled by the shrewd uncle that they went away. Shortly after, the uncle finding it impossible to earn a living at his trade, decided to go to sea. The family was left at Roxbury, Pennsylvania. Here for two years the faithful mother toiled morning, noon and night, at washing and other hard work to support the children and keep them together. At the expiration of this time the uncle returned and carried them to Chester, Pennsylvania, where he was able to do a good business; but the same old trouble arose. The slave traders were on their track again! The family was smuggled away to Philadelphia and remained long enough for the uncle to secure employment, by answering an advertisement inserted in the papers by George and Arthur Stowell, Bordentown, New Jersey, for a journeyman shoemaker. At this place it was a daily contest with poverty and a struggle for bread; however, the children were kept together, and none were ever hired out. During the entire boyhood of William, so hard pressed were they because of sickness, dull seasons of work and other difficulties, that never a toy, so dear to childhood, brightened his life; and for days and weeks, milk and mush were his only food. He never attended a public school in his whole school life. The uncle having attended school in Charleston under D. A. Payne, now Bishop Payne of the A. M. E. Church, was a fair scholar and undertook the education of the children, laying a foundation so broad and exact, that in after years college studies for the boy were comparatively easy.

William was by no means a good "Sabbath-keeping-boy" such as we read of in books. He gave considerable trouble at home and abroad. In 1862 he was apprenticed to Dr. Leo H. DeLange, a dentist in Bordentown, New Jersey. So far as giving him necessary instruction, the doctor was kind to him. William had learned so thoroughly all there was to be learned in the profession, that when the doctor was absent he was able to do a large part of the work. Though often rebuffed by white patients, he operated on some of the best families in the city. He endeavored to enter a dental college in Philadelphia, and was refused largely on account of color. Unwilling to enter the profession without a thorough knowledge, such as could be given only in a training school, he decided to abandon the profession, but remained with the doctor until September 16, 1864, at which time, becoming disgusted at the treatment received at the hands of the doctor, he ran away and enlisted in the Forty-first United States colored troops.

His army life was not uneventful; he took part in battles around Petersburg, Hatches Run, Appomattox Court House, and was present at the surrender of Lee, the crisis out of which our own happier cycle of years has been evolved. He was discharged September 13, 1865, and in 1866 and 1867 worked as journeyman at his trade for Dr. William H. Longfellow, a colored dentist of Philadelphia, after which he returned to Dr. DeLange.

He was converted in 1867 and joined the white Baptist church in Bordentown, pastored by Rev. J. W. Custis, a brilliant man, under whose influence about one hundred and fifty joined the church that spring.

Although the only colored man in church, he was treated with much kindness; and when his call to the Gospel ministry was made known, they rallied to his support, defraying his school expenses three years. The New Jersey State Educational Society aided him to attend Madison University of New York, from which he graduated in 1868, taking the academic course. Both students and teachers were his warm friends and are to-day. The dark-skinned youth, though alone, never felt the sting of injustice at their hands. September, 1868, found him matriculated at Rochester University, having been led to make the change by an offer of additional aid by laboring in a small Baptist church in Rochester, and because there he found colored people among whom he could associate and do missionary work. At this early date we see cropping out the love for the race which in after years became one of the ruling passions of his life.

One pleasant year slipped by, and the freshman year completed, when his eyes became seriously affected. The trouble was brought on by continuous night study of Greek during his academic year. This prevented school attendance until the year 1871 when he entered Howard University, Washington, District of Columbia, and graduated as an A. B. in 1873. His graduating oration treating of the Darwinian theory, a subject then very popular in literary circles, attracted much attention and newspaper comments. Extracts were printed in a paper in England devoted to science and literature.

At many periods, his school life was a sequel to the days of deprivation of childhood. Time and again he would be forced to stay indoors while having his only shirt laundered. Poor shoes and patched clothes were the rule, not the exception. During his entire course he did not have a whole suit until reaching the senior year. Once he ate cheese and crackers three weeks. During the senior year, September, 1872, to June, 1873, he walked seven miles a day, and taught school; came home and drilled the cadet company from four to five; recited at night, and graduated with the salutatory of the class. That was a happy day; by frugality he had saved three hundred dollars. Commencement day for him ended many deprivations and sacrifices in one sense. Both have come since, but of a different character and easier to bear. In the world one can find means of replenishing his purse, and many opportunities of changing his circumstances; but with a student it is different. He must in a degree be stationary, and cannot move around for the purpose of getting benefits.

During these years his mother lavished on him the devotion and pride of a loving heart. She washed, ironed and labored in other ways to help him. In this she was greatly assisted by one Bunting Hankins and his devoted wife of Bordentown, New Jersey, in whose family she labored. General O. O. Howard, president of Howard University, and General E. Whittlesey, dean of the college department, showed him many kindnesses during and after college days. While a student, he showed such aptness to teach in conducting a school at a place called Bunker's Hill, rebuilding it almost from nothing, that the school-board promoted him to the principalship of a much larger building, with several hundred scholars. This was the Hillsdale Public school, District of Columbia. Here he boarded in the house of Hon. Solomon G. Brown, one of the ablest scientists in this country.

Immediately after graduating, he took Horace Greeley's advice, and went west, to Arkansas, with the idea of making it his home; was examined and secured a State certificate from the Honorable Superintendent of Education, J. C. Corbin, but soon returned to Washington and taught at Hillsdale until June, 1874.

After marrying Josephine A., the daughter of John and Caroline Silence, in Washington, District of Columbia, August 25, 1874, he went south. By this union they have had the following children: Josephine Lavinia, William Johnson, Maud Marie, Amanda Moss, Mary Beatrice, John Thomas and Gussie Lewis. Desiring to better his financial condition he went to Florida, September, 1874, and invested in lands and oranges, but the investment did not prove a paying one. While in Ocala (in 1879) he was ordained a deacon, and was licensed to preach without asking for it. Pastored at a small station a year before ordination, after which time, he was ordained the night before leaving the State.

He was principal of Howard Academy, deputy county clerk and county commissioner. Here, too, his political tendencies received an impetus. He was chairman of the county campaign committee, and a member of the district congressional committee. Stumped the county for Hayes and Wheeler, and when it is remembered that the State went only 147 majority for Hayes, it is quite a material thing that the county in which he lived raised its quota from 525 Republican majority to 986. After this he returned to Washington and taught public school until 1879, when he left to accept the pastorate of the First Baptist church, Lexington, Kentucky. To do great work, God raises up great men.

September, 1880, he was called to the presidency of the Normal and Theological institution (as it was then called), a school conducted under the auspices of the General Association of Colored Baptists of Kentucky. At that time the school had but thirteen pupils, two teachers and an empty treasury. Says *The Bowling Green Watchmen,* a State paper edited by Rev. Eugene Evans:

Few men of Professor Simmons' ability and standing would have been willing to risk their future in an enterprise like the Normal and Theological Institution; an enterprise without capital and but a few friends. But it can be truly said of Professor Simmons, that he has proven himself master of the situation. The school had been talked of for nearly twenty years but no one ever dreamed of its being a possibility. When he was elected president, every cloud vanished, and the sunshine of success could be seen on every side. Some of his students already rank among the foremost preachers, teachers and orators of the State.

As an educator, he has likely no superiors. Discarding specialism in education, he claims that ideal manhood and womanhood cannot be narrowed down to any one sphere of action, but that the whole being—every faculty with which we are endowed—must receive proper development. No boy or girl comes under his influence without feeling a desire to become useful and great. He infuses inspiration into the least ambitious. He has a knack of "drawing out" all there is within. No flower within his reach "wastes its sweetness on the desert air." If there are elements of usefulness in those around him, he trains and utilizes them. As a president, his executive ability is excellent. Students admire, respect and stand in awe of him; his teachers are proud of him, trust his judgment and abide by his decisions. For poor students he has the tenderest sympathy, especially for those who most desire an education and struggle hardest for it. He rewards those who are faithful in discharge of duty, and for those who accomplish something he has words of cheer, but for idlers nothing.

September 29, 1882, he was elected editor of the *American Baptist,* and at this time is President of the American Baptist Company. As an editor, Dr. Simmons brings before the public every live issue of the day. His editorials are racy, versatile and logical. He contends for rights and cries down wrongs. He is extensively copied, and has the personal respect of every editor and prominent man in the country. A man of forcible character and deep convictions must reveal himself in his writings, and the subject of this article is such a man. His pen pictures are characterized by a rugged strength which takes hold of the reader and fixes the thought in memory more than by elaboration and flourishes which soothe and please, but pass from the mind as water through the seive. In regard to the duty of colored citizens to existing parties he believes "that committed as both parties are to the pernicious doctrine of State Rights, colored people should pay less attention to national politics than to State affairs." He says:

The days are slipping by and our children are growing into manhood and womanhood—we are fast passing away. Shall we live deluded with the hope that the general government will bring to us a panacea for all our ills? No; we must court the favors of the people of the State. We must be for progress wherever found. We must act wisely. Indeed the Republican party could not, if it would, help us. They are debarred by statutes, and sentiments, stronger than statutes. Let us study State interests, its schools and its development in every direction. Let us cast our votes for liberal men who will help us. We cannot expect those against whom we vote to do so. Take Kentucky; who has secured all the school advantages for the colored race? Why, the colored people themselves. The Republican party did not do it—not a bit of it. The white men of the party and their children were all right. When did they offer to make a special fight for us? Never. When, then, did we secure a change of the forty-eight per cent per capita tax to an equalization of the tax for all children alike? By petition of our own and by favor of Democrats, even when put to a popular vote, and by the act of a Democratic legislature. Is it not queer, too, that we never thought to demand of our party that they made the fight for us? The answer is, the colored man is such a slave to party that his blind obedience has befogged his reason so that he has fought the white man's battles, secured office for him, and fought for his own rights unaided in "Negro Conventions." White men would have made a broad open fight and demanded the Negro votes. After the convention was over the Negroes would petition the very legislature members whom they had fought and voted against in every county. Negroes attempt to do in convention what they ought to do with their votes, and are driven to it by the policy of the Republican party in the South. We should change this thing.

Dr. Simmons' activities are prominently identified with the most important affairs of the race. Several years he has been chairman of the executive committee of the "State Convention of Colored Men of Kentucky." At the meeting in Lexington, November 26, 1875, he was reelected. The call of the said meeting, a document enumerating in a few words the long catalogue of injustices practiced upon the colored citizens of the State, shows a high degree of statesmanship. It begins thus:

FELLOW-CITIZENS:—When a free people, living in a body politic, feel that the laws are unjustly adminstered to them; that discriminations are openly made; that various subterfuges and legal technicalities are constantly used to deprive them of the enjoyment of those rights and immunities belonging to the humblest citizen; when the courts become no refuge for the outraged, and when a sentiment is not found sufficient to do them justice, it becomes their bounden duty to protest against such a state of affairs. To do less than vigorously and earnestly enter our protest is to cringe like hounds before masters, and to show that we are not fit for freedom. We are robbed by some of the railroad companies who take our first-class fares and then we are driven into smoking cars, and, if we demur, are cursed and roughly handled. Our women have been beaten by brutal brakemen, and in many cases left to ride on the platforms at the risk of life and limb.

We are tried in courts controlled entirely by white men, and no colored man sits on a Kentucky jury. This seems no mere accident, but a determined effort to exclude us from fair trials and put us at the mercy of our enemies, from the judge down to the vilest suborned witness.

When charged with grave offenses, the jail is mobbed, and the accused taken out and hanged; and out of the hundreds of such cases since the war, not a single high-handed murderer has been ever brought before a court to answer. Colored men have been deliberately murdered, and few if any murderers have been punished by the law. Indecent haste to free the criminal in such cases has made the trial a farce too ridiculous to be called more than a puppet show.

The penitentiary is full of our race, who are sent there by wicked and malicious persecutors, and unjust sentences dealt out by judges, who deem a colored criminal fit only for the severest and longest sentences for trivial offenses.

In all departments of the State we are systematically deprived of recognition, except in menial positions. In our metropolitan city, and even cities of lesser note, we are not considered in the appointments in fire companies, police force, notary public, etc. In fact, we are the ruled class and have no share in the government.

Dr. Simmons was chairman of the committee appointed by the convention to lay before the Legislature the grievances of the 271,481 colored citizens. His speech on this occasion was a masterpiece. Says the *Soldiers' Reunion*, a paper published at Lexington:

The speech of Rev. W. J. Simmons, D. D., before the Kentucky Legislature, was one of the ablest efforts ever made in the interests of the colored people. They (the Legislature) have ordered two thousand copies printed.

Said he:

Only the history of the two races in our beautiful country could give birth to such a scene as this. That we, born Americans, finding distinctions in law, should be driven to appeal to a portion of the same body politic for rights and equalities; and though American sovereigns ourselves, because too weak, bend the suppliant knee, craving that we might be given that which appears rightly ours without contest. We feel some pride and are consequently jealous of the good name of the State and of the United States. We also feel humiliated that a foreigner who has never felled a tree, built a cabin, or laid a line of railway, seems more welcome to this shore, and is accorded every facility for himself and children to make the most of themselves, even BEFORE NATURALIZATION; while we, seeing them happy in a new-found asylum, and knowing you from our youth up—our mothers washed your linen and nursed you, our fathers made the soil feed you, and kept the fire burning in your grate—are compelled to beg, in the zenith hour 1886, your favors. Two generations are before you; the one born in the cradle of slavery, the other born in the cradle of liberty; the one saw the light mid the discussions of your fathers; the other mingled their infant's voice with the retreating sound of the cannon. We belong to the South—the "New South." Your own progress in the questions of human liberty and our own thirst for draughts from higher fountains, and, indeed, in obedience to the demands of our constituents, we venture to lay before you in a manly, honorable way, the complaints of 271,481 as true hearted Kentuckians as ever came from the loin of the bravest, truest and most honored of women, sired by the most distinguished fathers. As Kentuckians we meet you with the feelings and aspirations, common and peculiar to those born and sorrounded by the greatness of your history, the fertility of your soil, the nobility of your men and the beauty of your women. We come, plain of speech, in order to prove that we are men of judgment, meeting men who are really desirous of knowing our wants.

At the meeting of the Colored Press convention in St. Louis, Missouri, July 13, 1883, he was nominated for its president, but was beaten by Hon. W. A. Pledger of Georgia by one vote. When said convention met in Richmond, Virginia, July 8, 1885, he was made chairman of the executive committee and at the next meeting, August 3, 1886, Atlantic City, New Jersey, he was elected president by a majority of four over Mr. T. T. Fortune, editor of *The Freeman*.

Dr. Simmons is very much interested in the education of the hand. He has written a pamphlet on *Industrial Education* which has had a wide circulation. A sample of it will be seen below.

If the industrial craze be not watched, our literary institutions will be turned into workshops and our scholars into servants and journeymen. Keep the literary and industrial apart. Let the former be stamped deeply so it will not be mistaken. We need scholars. All men are not workers in the trades, and never will be. If we cripple the schools established, by diverting them largely from their original plan, we shall have no lawyers, doctors, professors, authors, etc. And again, the money in the schools will be divided and neither end will be reached; we will be like clowns trying to ride two horses, and as they get wider apart, we drop in a ditch, and our horses run away from us and break their own necks. Keep these schools apart, and attempt not the task of grinding scholars out of industrial, nor finished workmen from literary schools. Each has a legitimate sphere and let each stick to it. In the colleges, universities and higher schools of the South, not less than a thousand white men are teaching our youth; it is not intended that they will do so forever. I would, therefore, prepare the professors to take their places in the same manner that they were prepared—in literary institutions. In plainer words, let the student be free from industrial trade work when he has made certain grades in his classes. We want good workmen and good scholars, not deluded smatterers in either department. Gingerbread work, fiddling with tools, frittering away time, is not seriously making a mechanic. Industrial work as a sentiment must be crystallized into a profitable reality.

Hence, this feeble effort in Southern schools will only be the means of deceiving many into the notion that they are "workmen," when they are only botchers, and will furnish another poor class of mechanics to supplement a class of which we now complain. It would be wiser to spend ten thousand dollars on a single school per year, and make a first class industrial department, than two thousand dollars on each of five schools. Many will learn to do things for which they can give no reason.

The people, the masses, the boys, the girls, the rank and file, must be taken through a thorough English course and made master of a trade. I said this school was needed as a corrective; that is, to teach the dignity of labor. They must learn the gospel of manual labor; not simply as a means of bread and butter, but an honorable calling and duty. Let the buzz of the saw, the ring of the hammer, the whistle of the engine, the spinning of the wheel, the low of the ox, the bleating of the lamb, the crow of the rooster, all be music and inspiration to the rising race. Labor is honorable, but it is fast becoming unfashionable for the colored boy or girl to seek manual labor, and rather than work, many become loafers, dissipates and wrecks. Let us start a current large enough to meet the mental tide and mingling, find the happy medium. Parents must give their children trades. Teachers and Preachers must see to this matter.

This school should have a large farm attached, where agriculture in every form should be taught, and by means of which living could be made cheap to poor students. To sum up the words of another, here in this school, the farmer should be educated in science, elementary engineering, mechanics and agriculture; the miner, mineralogy geology, chemistry, and his own work, the merchant in geography, history, foreign language, political economy and laws; the machinist must master all the known powers of material nature—heat and cold, weight and impulse; matter in all conditions—liquid, solid and gaseous, standing or running, condensed or rare, adamantine or plastic—all must be seen through and comprehended by the master of modern mechanics. Architects, engineers, teachers and all classes of workers require a technical education.

I mean to take the female along too. They must be taught domestic economy, household ethics, home architecture, cookery, telegraphy, photography, printing, editorial work, dressmaking, tailoring, knitting, fancy work, nursing, dairying, horticulture, apiaculture, sericulture, poultry raising, stenography, type-writing, practical designs, painting, *repousse* work, etc., for if men must make money, the women must know best how to save it, or what is better, help get it. A saving wife is worth her weight in gold and earns her own board and is entitled to have her washing done from home.

Before I leave this subject, let me say that it may prove the best thing after all that our youth cannot get into the workshops and factories as readily as white youths. The latter class have the blessings of good homes and the amenities of a social life beyond that of a colored child. Every library, lecture hall and art gallery is open, and the finest music, sculpture, books, magazines and journals fall as thick around them as autumn leaves. But our youths need to have the moral training which comes from the school-room as well as the skill that comes from the workshop. They need practical drill in habits of industry, care in business, punctuality in dealing with the world, and, in fact, they need the moral bracing up that makes good citizens and square business men and women. Perhaps Providence has so hedged us that out of trials and darkness may come pleasure and light. So now we are driven to do perhaps the best thing for our race by putting our children where head, hand, eye, ear, and in fact the whole man, must be trained.

The great National Convention of colored men held at Louisville, September, 1883, enrolled him as a member. His love for the people is shown in the following little incident. While serving as a member of the committee on education and labor, a proposition was made to ask Congress to pass a bill giving the monies which had been left in the treasury from the unclaimed bounties of colored soldiers to the high schools of the South, which would of course have included the denominational, and excluded the public schools. Against this he protested, notwithstanding he was at the head of the denominational school which would have received benefits, on the grounds that the masses should be aided and not the few, and because it was a lack of statesmanship and knowledge of the laws governing the land to ask aid for denominational schools. The committee voted him down solidly, but when the matter was called up in the convention, he took the platform and made a speech so convincing that the chairman, Hon. D. A. Straker, LL. D., of South Carolina, was called upon to change the report, which was done with good grace. At the convention of the Knights of Wise Men, held in Atlanta, Georgia, he took an active part in the deliberations. He has delivered several addresses before the American Baptist Home Mission Society. At the fiftieth anniversary held in New York, May 24, 1872, his oration, "What are the Colored People Doing?" was much spoken of and published in the Jubilee Volume. He delivered another before the same body, May 26–27, 1885, at Saratoga, and has been invited to address the next meeting, May 29, 1887, at Minneapolis. In 1884, he was appointed by Hon. B. K. Bruce commissioner for the State of Kentucky in the colored department of the World's Industrial and Cotton Exposition held at New Orleans, Louisiana, and succeeded in giving a splendid representation, thereby reflecting credit on the State. The school over which he presided made a creditable exhibit. The trustee board, in making the annual report to the General Association of Colored Baptists, said:

> At the suggestion of our worthy president, who was also the commissioner for Kentucky for the World's Exposition at New Orleans, an exhibition of our

University, of both the literary and industrial work, was sent to the Exposition. To say that the display was complete and satisfactory is but to state it mildly. It has done much to advertise our University, and shows the capacity of our people for both education and industrial pursuits.

In September, 1883, Dr. Simmons called together and organized the Baptist women into a convention, for the purpose of raising money for the educational work of the denomination in the State. The body known as the "Baptist Women's Educational Convention" has met every year since, and has and is doing a noble work in paying off the indebtedness of the State University.

Were you to ask me Dr. Simmons' motto, I would say, "God, my race and denomination." While holding tenaciously his own religous views, he is willing for other men to hold theirs. Among his strongest friends are eminent preachers, scholars and laymen of every demonination in the United States with which colored people are allied. The fact that the Wilberforce University conferred upon him the degree of D. D. is an ample evidence of the friendliness existing between him and the brethren of that faith. The faculty of said school ranks with the most eminent men of America, among whom are Rev. B. W. Arnett, D. D., Professor W. S. Scarborough, LL. D., Bishops D. A. Payne, D. D., LL. D., John M. Brown, D. D., C. L., and others of like grace and eminence.

Being impressed with the idea that colored Baptists were not doing what they should for the support and influence of their peculiar views, he suggested, through the *American Baptist*, April 5, 1886, that a convention be held. This suggestion was heartily endorsed by Baptists throughout the United States. He issued the call at their suggestion, and the result was the organization of the American National Baptist Convention, which met, August 25, 1886, in St. Louis, Mo., and of which he was unanimously elected president, and chairman of the executive committee. He preached the denominational sermon which was published in the minutes. It was rich in statistics and history, pregnant with the faith as handed down from the Apostles. He concluded by saying:

> The work of the colored Baptists is marvelous, aye, stupendous. When we remember our elevation today, it is not with undue pride; no! no! no! with thanksgiving and humiliation, with self-abasement and lowliness, and with an earnest prayer for more faith, we lift our eyes to the Great Father of souls and pray His righteous benediction, that we bow our heads because we have been unprofitable servants. Yet it is with astonishment that we have reached such lofty heights, and with remarkable pleasure do we look back upon the depths from which we came. Driven out, Hagar-like, we have, Ishmael-like, still become a people and dwell in the presence of our brethren, and to-day, in figures bright and glowing in the ending of the nineteenth century, we count fully

1,071,000—every sign of progress. It might be remarked, if we can rise to this point with a few learned men, what shall be the result in the next twenty years? Books, papers, magazines and pamphlets shall be as plentiful as the maple leaves in full blown spring.

The Baptist host is like a cube; throw them aside and they always land on an equal side, and you need never despair when in your trials and doubts in your several churches; remember the God of battles is on your side and that the ages have only increased His glory.

His knowledge of the tenets of the denomination with which he is identified is marvelous. In this direction his research has been thorough and extensive as is shown in an article on "Baptism'" published in the *A. M. E. Review*, October, 1886, in reply to Rev. B. W. Williams.

As an orator Dr. Simmons is pleasing to his audience. A quick thinker, and possessing a rich and ready flow of choice language, a figure that can be seen, and a voice that can be heard at a distance. At times, in the heat of debate, the whole grandeur of his soul is transfused into his countenance; and his hearers are electrified as only true eloquence can electrify.

He was invited to address the students of three different colleges in one year. At Selma University, May 28, 1885, his subject was "True Manliness." The *Baptist Pioneer* commented as follows:

> For nearly an hour and a half the speaker held the large audience spellbound. He was eloquent and inspiring. Rarely have we listened to a more practical oration. At times the audience was convulsed with laughter at the wit, and then immediately made to reflect under the solid words of wisdom which fell from the speaker's lips.

His address before the Berea College students, subject "The Great Text-Book of the Ages," received much comment. June 18, 1885, after delivering an oration before the Wilberforce Literary Society, subject "Leaders and Followers," he had conferred on him the degree of D. D., by that venerable institution. In 1881, he had received the degree of A. M., from Howard University. During the educational movement in Kentucky, in 1885, I think, Dr. Simmons delivered a speech before the Inter-State Educational Convention, which was held in the white Baptist church, subject "The Education of the Negro Race." In this convention were found the most eminent educators, State superintendents and the most noted thinkers in America. Favorable criticism was made by the *New York Journal of Education*, the *Courier-Journal* of Louisville, and other State papers.

He delivered an oration at the Lexington Emancipation celebration, January 1, 1887. Urging the hearers to greater efforts, he said:

> The warm blood of the Negro that haunts the channels of his veins with ancient Egyptian and Ethiopian fires has been tempered in the climate of the South and reduced to that proportion which robs it of its sluggishness, sub-

dues it of wild passion and holds it by reason, while the trials of the past have been the friction that brightens, the winds that toughen, and the frosts that ripen. No great song, or poem, or book, or invention has yet seen birth south of the "Mason and Dixon Line." It has been reserved for us. The only American music was born on the plantations and wrung from aching hearts as wine from the luscious grape. It has touched the heart of the learned and engaged the attention of the scientific musician. As the Indian faded in the North, before the white man, so the white man of the South must yield to us, without, however, a bloody conflict. We shall gather wealth, learning and manhood, and occupy the land. This is the asylum of the world; and the tramp of hurrying nations warns us that this is the "Valley of Decision." On this soil are settled the great questions of the earth. Already the march of empire has bathed its weary feet in the Pacific, and with the exception of watery waste has arrived at its home, and it is possible that He who made all nations of one blood, will here in our land, marry and intermarry, and reduce this conglomerate mass to one distinct nationality, with all the blood made one, and the highest type of consecrated manhood being realized, reduced back to the Adamic color through us; or He may out of the aggregate develop each to its highest type, and let them live to the end of time, carrying out His divine plans, and unerringly accomplishing His decrees. Here in this new South the Negro shall shine in the constellation of the nations, and by his words and deeds hand down to unborn ages the glittering pages of our history. We shall in some prominent way mount the ladder of difficulties, scale the cliff of prejudices and hide our heads among the stars.

Dr. Simmons, in his modesty, does not claim for this work any special literary excellence, but his aim is simply to embalm in some place the lives of these men for future historians, who may take isolated cases' and do justice to each. He also wishes to inspire the youth of the land, giving the many trials through which these men have had to pass, and have them further influenced by the great degree of promotion which has been granted to them. His talents, developed by cultivation, are also enriched by the love of God and man which reaches beyond the boys of to-day who are trying to be somebody, to the boys of the future, who will inquire into the deeds and achievements of their fathers. As a man, Dr. Simmons is loyal to his convictions, sympathetic, independent, far sighted, therefore a wise counselor, methodical and liberal. He regards money as a trust from God, to be invested in every cause relative to bettering the condition of his fellow men and advancing the cause of Christ. His hand is shut when those who do not want, come to him; but when the really needy and friendless come to him, it is like a strainer full of holes, letting all he possesses pass through. To friends he is faithful; to enemies he shows a steady resistance, but no aggressiveness.

Thus far, I have sketched a few of the prominent phases in the life of the doctor, more in a biographical outline than in analysis of his true worth, reserving for the conclusion a few facts adumbrated in the preceding remarks.

I regard Dr. Simmons as one of the most replete scholars to his age in the country, for all the invincibility that attached to his boyhood and youthful days, enabling him to triumph over every obstacle that confronted him, still incites him to literary research, so that almost every subject within the circle of learning has been pierced by his intellectual prowess. Yet it could not be expected that a man of his age could be the master of every branch, for such exalted attainments only come by years of laborious application, which a young man has not had time to accomplish. The doctor has a large, symmetrically developed head, elevated in the centre at the organ of veneration, with a brain texture of the highest type, attesting marvelous powers, when, even in many instances the head is oblong, but infinitely more so when rightly shaped, thus giving the doctor giant powers to use while employed in ferreting out the deep things of science, philosophy and theology, which will, if the doctor lives fifty years, culminate in making him one of the most mighty men of our race upon the globe.

As has been said of liberty, vigilant application is the price of profound scholarship; and this being the charm of his life, nothing but premature death can avert it. Too many of our young men after reaching literary distinction forget the rock from whence they were hewn, and waste their lives in endeavoring to become white, or expend it in worshiping white gods. But this charge cannot be made against the doctor. He is as true to his race as a needle is to the pole, and no stronger evidence is required than the work that will contain these sketches of eminent colored men. The future historian will ponder these pages, glean their contents as he traces the great men of this age, and wonder at the achievements made by them, in the face of so many environments that militated against them. Negro giants now sleeping in the womb of the future, will come forth an Armada that will defy the powers of earth, trample colored prejudice in the dust, write glory, honor and immortality itself upon the brow of black; frown thunders at race distinctions, fire the citadels of manhood discriminations and burn them to the ground; hurl defiance in the face of our defamers and contemners, and with pens of lightning write up the history of our ancestry, and present them before earth and heaven as no one now ever dream.

When that time comes, as it will, unless God ceases to reign, this work of Dr. Simmons' will form the foot-base of the mighty superstructure that will be reared with chancel, dome, spire and minaret, to the undying worth, merits and fame of the Negro. The abominable heresies set adrift by pseudo-philosophers, pseudo-scientists, and other figureheads as ignorant as they were mean and low, that the Negro race were naturally inferior, and nothing great could ever be evolved from them, will be remembered in the grand hereafter as the overflowing slag or dross which precedes the incandescent rocks dashed from the volcano's fiery jaws, while hurtled thunders shook the ground as though the gods were in battle arrayed. The Indian represents the past, the white man the present, but the Negro the future. The Indian is old, decayed and worn out; the whites are in the prime of life and vigor; but the Negro is a boy, a youth at school, a mere apprentice learning his trade. When the white race reaches decrepitude, as races are periodical as well as worlds, the Negro will have reached his prime, and being in possession of all he has and will acquire from the whites, and his own genius and industry to manufacture more and lift him to a higher civilization, he will stand out the wonder of the ages. The earth will tremble beneath his tread, while nature opens her bosom and pours into his lap her richest treasures. With mystic keys he will unlock her coffers, and her very arcana will divulge the secrets which she never whispered before into inquiring ears. Then, if not before, the name of Dr. Simmons will be as familiar to the millions as that of Herodotus, Josephus, Pliny, Plutarch and other historians enshrined in the gratitude of the world. For him the world will have to look largely for a true narrative of the merits of the men who came upon the tapis at the death of our enslavement, and directed affairs while we were in a transitional state, rather while we were bursting the chrysalis that bound our intellectual and moral pinions, and barred our development until we had thrown off the slave forms, slave ears, slave doubts, as to our ability to live by merit and claim rank among the more favored of earth.

Little as the common observer may regard it, we men who gather up the fragments of our labors, acts, achievements, sayings, songs, oddities, peculiarities, fun, speeches, lectures, poems, war struggles, bravery, degradation and sufferings, and preserve them for the future, now while they are within reach, will stand out as heroes in the day to come. The future orator, statesman, minister, poet, journalist, ethnologist, as well as the historian, will from these gather materials to build towers heaven-reaching that will monument the grandeur of our race, and still grander struggles that lifted them from the barren plains of the contempt of the world, to the majestic heights that we are destined to scale in God's Providence. To this book, when Dr. Simmons will be numbered with the dead for centuries, will come the men above described, and others in countless scores, to light their torches, inspire their young, encourage the doubtful, animate the faltering and forward the tide of elevation till the last Negro boy and girl on the globe shall be proud of their color, their hair, their origin and their race.

Henry M. Turner.

FREDERICK DOUGLASS

CHAPTER I

Hon. Frederick Douglass, LL. D.
Magnetic Orator—Anti-slavery Editor—Marshal of
the District of Columbia—Recorder of Deeds of the District
of Columbia—First Citizen of America—Eminent Patriot
and Distinguished Republican

———•◆•———

Who can write the life of this great man and do him justice? His life is an epitome of the efforts of a noble soul to be what God intended, despite the laws, customs and prejudices. That such a soul as Douglass' could be found with the galling bonds of slavery is the blackest spot in the realm of thought and fact in the whole history of this government. But such a man as he would not remain in slavery, could not do so. Aye! it was impossible to fetter him and keep him there. He was a man. He was not going to remain bound while his legs could carry him off, and, as he facetiously remarked, he prayed for freedom, but when he made his legs pray, then he got free. He shows himself a man of works as well as faith. And these go together. But eulogy is wasted on such a man. His life speaks, and, when he is dead, his orations will keep his memory fresh, and his name will stand side by side with Webster, Sumner and Clay.

Frederick Douglass was born about the year 1817, in Tuckahoe, a barren little district upon the eastern shore of Maryland, best known for the wretchedness, poverty, slovenliness and dissipation of its inhabitants. Of his mother he knew very little, having seen her only a few times in his life, as she was employed on a plantation some distance from the place where he was raised. His master was supposed to be his father.

No man perhaps has had a more varied experience than the subject of this sketch. During his early childhood he was beaten and starved, often fighting with the dogs for the bones that were thrown to them. As he grew older and could work he was given very little to eat, overworked and much beaten. As the boy grew older still, and realized the misery and horror of his surroundings, his very soul revolted, and a determination was formed to be free or die attempting it.

At the age of ten years he was sent to Baltimore to Mrs. Sophia Auld, as a house servant. She became very much interested in him, and immediately began teaching him his letters. He was very apt, and was soon able to read. The husband of his mistress, finding it out, was very angry and put a stop to it.

This prohibition served only to check the instruction from his mistress, but had no effect on the ambition, the craving for more light, that was within the boy, and the more obstacles he met with the stronger became his determination to overcome them. He carried his spelling book in his bosom and would snatch a minute now and then to pursue his studies. The first money he made he invested in a *Columbian Orator*. In this work he read "The Fanaticism of Liberty" and the "Declaration of Independence." After reading this book he realized that there was a better life waiting for him, if he would take it, and so he ran away.

He settled in New Bedford with his wife, who, a free woman in the South, being engaged to Douglass before his escape, followed him to New York, where they were married. She was a worthy, affectionate, industrious and invaluable helpmate to the great Douglass. She ever stood side by side with him in all his struggles to establish a home, helped him and encouraged him while he climbed the ladder of knowledge and fame, together with him offered the hand of welcome and a shelter to all who were fortunate enough to escape from bondage and reach their hospitable shelter; and never, while loving mention is made of Frederick Douglass, may the name of his wife "Anna" be forgotten.

In New Bedford he sawed wood, dug cellars, shovelled coal, and did any other work by which he could turn an honest penny, having the incentive that he was working for himself and his family, and that there was no master waiting for his wages. Here several of their children were born.

He began to read the *Liberator,* for which he subscribed, and other papers, and the works of the best authors. He was charmed by Scott's *Lady of the Lake,* and reading it he adopted the name of "Frederick Douglass." He began to take an interest in all public matters, often speaking at the gatherings among the colored people. In 1841 he addressed a large convention at Nantucket. After this he was employed as an agent of the American Antislavery Society, which really marks the beginning of his grand struggle for the freedom and elevation of his race. He lectured all through the North, notwithstanding he was in constant danger of being recaptured and sent to the far South as a slave. After a time it was deemed best that he should for a while go to England. Here he met a cordial welcome. John Bright established him in his house, and thus he was brought in contact with the best minds and made acquainted with some of England's most distinguished men. His relation of the wrongs and sufferings of his enslaved brethren excited their deepest sympathy; and their admiration for his ability was so profound, their wonder so great, that there should be any fear of such a man being returned to slavery, that they immediately subscribed the amount necessary to purchase his freedom, made him a present of his manumission papers, and sent him home to tell his people that

> *Slaves cannot breathe in England;*
> *If their lungs receive our air, that moment they are free;*
> *They touch our country, and their shackles fall.*

Returning to America he settled in Rochester, New York, and established a paper called the *North Star,* afterwards changed to *Fred Douglass' Paper,* also *Douglass' Monthly.* These were all published in his own office, and two of his sons were the principal assistants in setting up the work, and attending to the business generally.

There has been a great deal of speculation as to what connection Frederick Douglass had with the John Brown raid. The two great men met, and Brown became acquainted with Douglass' history. They became fast friends. They were singularly adapted to each other as co-workers, both being deeply imbued with the belief that it was their duty to devote their lives and means to the cause of emancipation. They lived frugally at home that they might have the more to give. Their families caught their inspiration, and their lives were all influenced by the one motive-power—the cause of freedom. Many men and women who successfully escaped into Canada, and thence to other places, will tell how, after they had been well fed, nourished and made comfortable by the mother, one of Fred Douglass' boys had carried them across the line and seen them to a place of safety. When other boys were enjoying all the comforts of pleasures their parents could provide for them, Douglass' sons were made to feel that there was only one path for them to walk in until the great end for which they were working had been attained.

Brown's first plan was to run slaves off, and in this Douglass heartily joined him; but when he found Brown had decided to attempt the capture of Harper's Ferry, he went to him at Chambersburg, Pennsylvania, a short time before the raid, and used every argument he could to induce him to change his plans. Brown had enlisted a body of men to accompany him who felt as he felt, that their lives were nothing as weighed against the lives and liberties of so many who were suffering in bondage. His arms and ammunition were ready, his plans were all laid, and to Douglass' argument he answered: "If we attack Harper's Ferry, as we have now arranged, the country will be aroused, and the Negroes will see the way clear to liberation. We'll hold the citizens of the town as hostages, and so holding them can dictate our terms. You, Douglass, should be one of the first to go with us."

"No, no," replied the latter, "I can't agree with you and will not go with you—your attempt can only result in utter ruin to you, and to all those who take part in it, without giving any substanial aid to the men in slavery. Let us rather go on with our first plan of the 'Underground Railroad' by which slaves may be run off to the free states. By that means practical results can be obtained. From insurrection nothing can be expected but imprisonment and death."

"If you think so," replied Brown, "it is, of course, best that we should part." He held out his hand. Douglass grasped it. "Goodbye! God bless you!" they exclaimed, almost in the same breath, and then parting forever, were soon lost to each other in the darkness.

It was soon discovered that Douglass and Brown were in sympathy, and that Douglass, besides harboring Brown, had furnished him money to defray expenses, and thus making his safety a matter of great doubt. His friends advised him to leave the country for awhile. They were willing to stand by him, even to fight for him, but felt that it would be wiser to avoid the danger if possible. After much hesitation he was induced to abide by their advice, and the result proved the wisdom of his having done so. He went first to Canada and from there to England. Only a short time after his departure a requisition for his arrest was made by Governor Wise of Virginia. The requisition read as follows:

[Confidential]

RICHMOND, VIRGINIA, November 13, 1859.

To His Excellency, James Buchanan, President of the United States, and to the Honorable Postmaster-General of the United States—

GENTLEMEN:—I have information such as has caused me, upon proper affidavits, to make requisition upon the Executive of Michigan for the delivery up of the person of Frederick Douglass, a Negro man, supposed now to be in Michigan, charged with murder, robbery and inciting servile insurrection in the State of Virginia. My agents for the arrest and reclamation of the person so charged are Benjamin M. Morris and William N. Kelly. The latter has the requisition and will wait on you to the end of obtaining nominal authority as postoffice agents. They need to be very secretive in this matter, and some pretext of traveling through the dangerous section for the execution of the laws in this behalf, and some protection against obtrusive, unruly or lawless violence. If it be proper so to do, will the Postermaster-General be pleased to give Mr. Kelly for each of these men a permit and authority to act as detectives for the postoffice department without pay, but to pass and repass without question, delay or hindrance?

Respectfully submitted by your
Obedient Servant,
HENRY A. WISE

Mr. Douglass did not feel it necessary to hasten his return on account of this interesting document, and so remained abroad till it was safe for him to come home. This adventure did not in the least dampen his ardor in the great cause. Wherever and whenever he could do or say anything for it, he never failed to do so. When the first gun was fired at Sumter, he was among the foremost to insist upon the enrollment of colored soldiers. In 1863 he, with others, succeeded in raising two regiments of colored troops, which were known as Massachusetts regiments. Two of his sons were among the first to enlist. His next move was to obtain the same pay for them that the white soldiers received, and to have them exchanged as prisoners of war; in fact, that there should be no difference made between them and other soldiers. His work did not end with the war. He recognized the fact that a new life had begun for the former slaves; that a great work was to be done for them and with them, and he was ever to be found in the foremost ranks of those who were willing to put their shoulders to the wheel. His means, as well as his time, he largely gave to the cause. He was one of the most indefatigable workers for the passage of the amendments to the Constitution, granting the same rights to all classes of citizens, regardless of race and color. He attended the "Loyalists' Convention," held in Philadelphia, in 1867, being elected a delegate from Rochester. Some feared his presence would do more harm than good, knowing how radical he was; but he felt that it was his duty to go, and nothing could change him. It has been conceded that it was due principally to his persistent work in that convention, that resolutions favoring universal suffrage were passed. A little incident in connection with this convention shows the value of his work in that meeting, by disclosing the feeling of the men he had to deal with. As the members assembled proceeded to fall in line, on their way to the place of meeting, every one seemed to avoid walking beside a colored delegate. As soon as Theodore Tilton noticed it, he stepped to Douglass' side, and arm in arm they entered the chamber. This act has made them life-long friends, and these two are both brotherly in their devoted friendship. In Mr. Douglass' recent visit to France, he met Mr. Tilton, who resides in Paris, and had a glorious time.

He established the *New National Era* at Washington, D. C., in 1870. This paper was edited and published principally by him and his sons, and devoted to the cause of the race and the Republican party. In 1872 he took his family to reside in the District of Columbia. In 1871 President Grant appointed him to the Territorial Legislature of the District of Columbia. In 1872 he was chosen one of the Presidential electors-at-large for the State of New York, and was the elector selected to deliver a certified statement of the votes to the president of the Senate.

He was appointed to accompany the commissioners on their trip to Santo Domingo, pending the consideration of the annexation of that island to the United States. President Grant in January, 1877, appointed him a police commissioner for the District of Columbia. In March of the same year President Hayes commissioned him United States marshal for the District of Columbia. President Garfield, in 1881, appointed him recorder of deeds for the District of Columbia. This last position he held till about May, 1886, nearly a year and a half after the ascendancy to the national administration of the Democratic party.

No man has begun where Frederick Douglass did and attained to the same giddy heights of fame. Born in a mere hovel, a creature of accident, with no mother to cherish and nurture him, no kindly hand to point out the good worthy of emulation and the evil to be shunned, no teacher to make smooth the rough and thorny paths leading to knowledge. His only compass was an abiding faith in God, and an innate consciousness of his own ability and power of perseverance.

Harriet Beecher Stowe, in her book entitled *Men of Our Times*, says: "Frederick Douglass had as far to climb to get to the spot where the poorest white boy is born, as that white boy has to climb to be President of the nation, and take rank with the kings and judges of the earth." Again, in the Senate of the United States, in a recent important case under consideration, the following statement formed part of a resolution submitted by that body in reply to the President of the United States: "Without doubt Frederick Douglass is the most distinguished representative of the colored race, not only in this country, but in the world." To-day he stands the acknowledged peer in intellect, culture and refinement of the greatest men of our age, or any age; in this country, or any country. His name has never been written on the register of any school or college, yet it will ever be written on the pages of all future history, wherever the names of the ablest men of our times appear, side by side with those of the more favored race. His relations with such men as John G. Whittier, Oliver Wendell Holmes, Wendell Phillips, William Lloyd Garrison; and such women as Lydia Maria Child, Grace Greenwood, and Harriet Beecher Stowe, have ever been cordial and pleasant. Some men who never graduate from a college have more sense in five minutes than many a conceited graduate who has all his knowledge duly accredited by a sheepskin, but is not the real possessor of an education. The trustees of Howard University honored themselves and their institution, more than they did Mr. Douglass, when they conferred upon him the title of LL. D., and when also they gave him a seat in their board.

Mr. Douglass in *His Life*, written by himself, gives the following account of his visit to his old home:

The first of these events occurred four years ago, when, after a period of more than forty years, I visited and had an interview with Captain Thomas Auld at St. Michaels, Talbot county, Maryland. It will be remembered by those who have followed the thread of my story that St. Michaels was at one time the place of my home and the scene of some of my saddest experiences of slave life, and that I left there, or rather was compelled to leave there, because it was believed that I had written passes for several slaves to enable them to escape from slavery, and that prominent slaveholders in that neighborhood had, for this alleged offense, threatened to shoot me on sight, and to prevent the execution of this threat my master had sent me to Baltimore.

My return, therefore, to this place in peace, among the same people, was strange enough in itself; but that I should, when there, be formally invited by Captain Thomas Auld, then over eighty years old, to come to the side of his dying bed, evidently with a view to a friendly talk over our past relations, was a fact still more strange, and one which, until its occurrence, I could never have thought possible. To me Captain Auld had sustained the relation of master—a relation which I had held in extreme abhorrence, and which for forty years I had denounced in all bitterness of spirit and fierceness of speech. He had struck down my personality, had subjected me to his will, made property of my body and soul, reduced me to a chattel, hired me out to a noted slave breaker to be worked like a beast and flogged into submission; he had taken my hard earnings, sent me to prison, offered me for sale, broken up my Sunday-school, forbidden me to teach my fellow-slaves to read on pain of nine and thirty lashes on my bare back; he had sold my body to his brother Hugh and pocketed the price of my flesh and blood without any apparent disturbance of his conscience. I, on my part, had traveled through the length and breadth of this country and of England, holding up this conduct of his, in common with that of other slaveholders, to the reprobation of all men who would listen to my words. I had made his name and his deeds familiar to the world by my writings in four different languages; yet here we were, after four decades, once more face to face—he on his bed, aged and tremulous, drawing near the sunset of life, and I, his former slave, United States marshal of the District of Columbia, holding his hand and in friendly conversation with him in his sort of final settlement of past differences preparatory to his stepping into his grave, where all distinctions are at an end, and where the great and the small, the slave and his master, are reduced to the same level. Had I been asked in the days of slavery to visit this man, I should have regarded the invitation as one to put fetters on my ankles and handcuffs on my wrists. It would have been an invitation to the auction block and the slave whip. I had no business with this man under the old regime but to keep out of his way. But now that slavery was destroyed, and the slave and the master stood upon equal ground, I was not only willing to meet him but was very glad to do so. The conditions were favorable for remembrance of all his good deeds and generous extenuation of all his evil ones. He was to me no longer a slaveholder either in fact or in spirit, and I regarded him as I did myself, a victim of the circumstances of birth, education, law and custom.

Our courses had been determined for us, not by us. We had both been flung, by powers that did not ask our consent, upon a mighty current of life, which we could neither resist nor control. By this current he was a master, and I a slave; but now our lives were verging towards the point where differences disappeared, where even the constancy of hate breaks down, where the clouds of pride, passion and selfishness vanish before the brightness of Infinite light. At such a time and in such a place, when man is about closing his eyes on this world and ready to step into the eternal unknown, no word of reproach or bitterness should reach him or fall from his lips; and on this occasion there was to this rule no transgression on either side.

As this visit to Captain Auld had been made the subject of mirth by heartless triflers, and regretted as a weakening of my lifelong testimony against slavery by serious minded men, and as the report of it, published in the papers immediately after it occurred, was in some respects defective and colored, it may be proper to state exactly what was said and done at this interview.

It should in the first place be understood that I did not go to St. Michaels upon Captain Auld's invitation, but upon that of my colored friend, Charles Caldwell; but when once there, Captain Auld sent Mr. Green, a man in constant attendance upon him during his sickness, to tell me that he would be very glad to see me, and wished me to accompany Green to his house, with which request I complied. On reaching the house I was met by Mr. William H. Bruff, a son-in-law of Captain Auld's, and Mrs. Louisa Bruff, his daughter, and was conducted by them immediately to the bedroom of Captain Auld. We addressed each other simultaneously, he calling me "Marshal Douglass," and I, as I had always called him, "Captain Auld." Hearing myself called by him "Marshal Douglass," I instantly broke up the formal nature of the meeting by saying, "Not MARSHAL, but Frederick to you as formerly." We shook hands cordially, and in the act of doing so he, having been long stricken with palsy, shed tears as men thus afflicted will do when excited by any deep emotion. The sight of him, the changes which time had wrought in him, his tremulous hands constantly in motion, and all the circumstances of his condition affected me deeply, and for a time choked my voice and made me speechless. We both, however, got the better of our feelings and conversed freely about the past.

Though broken by age and palsy, the mind of Captain Auld was remarkably clear and strong. After he had become composed I asked him what he thought of my conduct in running away and going to the North. He hesitated a moment as if to properly formulate his reply, and said: "Frederick, I always knew you were too smart to be a slave, and had I been in your place I should have done as you did." I said, "Captain Auld, I am glad to hear you say this. I did not run away from YOU, but from SLAVERY; it was not that I loved Caesar less, but Rome more." I told him that I had made a mistake in my narrative, a copy of which I had sent him, in attributing to him ungrateful and cruel treatment of my grandmother; that I had done so on the supposition that in the division of the property of my old master, Mr. Aaron Anthony, my grandmother had fallen to him, and that he had left her in her old age, when she could be no longer of service to him, to pick up her living in solitude with none to help her; or in other words, had turned her out to die like an old horse.

"Ah," said he, "that was a mistake; I never owned your grandmother; she, in the division of the slaves, was awarded to my brother-in-law, Andrew Anthony; but," he added quickly, "I brought her down here and took care of her as long as she lived." The fact is, that after writing my narrative, describing the condition of my grandmother, Captain Auld's attention being thus called to it, he rescued her from destitution. I told him that this mistake of mine was corrected as soon as I discovered it, and that I had at no time any wish to do him injustice, and that I regarded both of us as victims of a system. "Oh, I never liked slavery," he said, "and I meant to emancipate all my slaves when they reached the age of twenty-five years." I told him I had always been curious to know how old I was, that it had been a serious trouble to me not to know when was my birthday. He said he could not tell me that, but he thought I was born in February, 1818. This date made me one year younger than I had supposed myself, from what was told me by Mistress Lucretia, Captain Auld's former wife, when I left Lloyd's for Baltimore in the spring of 1825; she having then said that I was eight, going on nine. I know that it was in the year 1825 that I went to Baltimore, because it was in that year that Mr. James Beacham built a large frigate at the foot of Alliceana street, for one of the South American governments. Judging from this, and from certain events which transpired at Colonel Lloyd's, such as a boy without any knowledge of books under eight years old would hardly take cognizance of, I am led to believe that Mrs. Lucretia was nearer right as to my age than her husband.

Before I left his bedside, Captain Auld spoke with a cheerful confidence of the great change that awaited him, and felt himself about to depart in peace. Seeing his extreme weakness I did not protract my visit. The whole interview did not last more than twenty minutes, and we parted to meet no more. His death was soon after announced in the papers, and the fact that he had once owned me as a slave was cited as rendering that event noteworthy.

His life has been marked by a purity of purpose from its beginning. He has filled many offices of trust, yet in not one position has he ever betrayed his trust. He has been largely, deeply engaged in politics, yet has been no politician. That is, he understood and practiced none of the tricks of politicians. His work has always been honest and conscientious, because he believed in whatever cause he worked for, and did not, as most of our public men, have an eye to a personal reward. All the recompense he sought was a consciousness of having accomplished some good. Whatever has been given him in the way of office has been unsolicited by him. Some of our public men have wavered in their fidelity to the Republican party, when after long waiting they fail to see a substantial reward laid at their feet; but not so with Mr. Douglass. He believed implicitly in the Republican party and realized that being composed of human beings it might sometimes err; but he would say, "The Republican party is the deck and all outside is the sea." Another saying of his is, "I would rather be with the Republican party in defeat, than with the Democratic party in victory." By such expressions may be seen his faithful adherence to what he believed to be right.

He is generous and forgiving, almost to a fault. On the friendliest terms with Lincoln, Grant, Sumner and many of their compeers, his opinions on public matters were always heard with deference and often adopted. His clear, forcible, yet persuasive way of presenting facts, always carries conviction with it.

And now, after a long and well fought battle of seventy years, we find him still erect and strong, bearing gracefully and unassumingly the laurels he has so nobly won. No one who visits him in his beautiful home at Cedar Cottage comes away without being richer by some gem of thought, dropped by the genial host.

A few years ago Fred Douglass married a white lady, who was a clerk in his office while recorder of deeds. This was much objected to by many of his race, but on mature reflection, it has been about decided that he was no slave to take a wife as in slave times on a plantation—according to some master's wish—but that it was his own business, and he was only responsible to God. He has been invited to the President's levees and he and his wife shown every mark of consideration. His travel in foreign countries has in no way been embarrassed by this act. If any one thought he was so foolish as to not know what would be said of his marriage, they have mistaken the man. But Douglass did as he thought was right as he understood it. It showed he had the courage to brave popular opinion as he had done on other occasions.

Frederick Douglass enjoys a joke as well as any man I know. I was traveling with him recently from Atlantic City, New Jersey, to Washington, District of Columbia. We had been traveling on the territory of Maryland. Near Havre de Grace, a rather officious white gentleman was particularly attentive to Mr. Douglass, and after introducing himself to the eminent orator stood up and called out to the people in the car: "Gentleman and ladies, this is Frederick Douglass, the greatest colored man in the United States." The people flocked around him for an introduction. One white gentleman who was a Marylander, said "Let me see, Mr. Douglass, you ran away from Maryland, did you not, somewhere in this neighborhood, I believe?" "No," said Mr. Douglass, with that grand air and good humored laugh which is his own property, "Oh, no sir, I did not run away from Maryland, I ran away from slavery."

There are three great orators in this country, Frederick Douglass, John M. Langston and George W. Williams, the first two are a couple of as magnificent speakers as ever heard on an American platform; the last is a gifted star ascending the zenith. Douglass and Langston are ripe with age and mellow with experience. The young man is now vigorous and full of strength and handles the less exciting subjects of the day. The older men had the subjects of slavery and reconstruction; two greater themes, can and may never engage our minds in this broad land of swift passing events. They showed their zeal and inspiration against wrong; Williams shows his learning, research, and brilliant oratory.

God grant, when in the course of nature the mantle shall fall from his shoulders, that one may spring up to wear it, to guard it as vigilantly as he has, and as lovingly and carefully protect its folds from pollution.

If the extracts here given should be long, let it be remembered that Mr. Douglass, by length of service, by preeminence in public office, by his standing not only in America, but in the world, is entitled to large space. I want the young people also to declaim these extracts. I am tired of hearing every man's good works repeated and no Negro's eloquence chain an audience when, too, there are such elegant specimens.

The following is taken from his great speech in the National Convention of Colored Men held in Louisville, Kentucky, September 25, 1883.

The speaker addressed the greater part of his remarks to the white citizens of the country in the nature of a rebuke for their shortcomings towards the colored race, and said:

Born on American soil, in common with yourselves, deriving our bodies and our minds from its dust; centuries having passed away since our ancestors were torn from the shores of Africa, we, like yourselves, hold ourselves to be in every sense Americans. Having watered your soil with our tears, enriched it with our blood, performed its roughest labor in time of peace, defended it against enemies in time of war, and having at all times been loyal and true to its highest interests, we deem it no arrogance or presumption to manifest now a common concern with you for its welfare, prosperity, honor and glory.

WHAT THE NEGROES WANT

Referring to the antagonism experienced in calling the convention, he said:

From the day the call for this convention went forth, the seeming incongruity and contradiction of holding it has been brought to our attention. From one quarter and another, sometimes with argument and sometimes without argument; sometimes with seeming pity for our ignorance, and at other times with fierce censure for our depravity, these questions have met us. With apparent surprise, astonishment and impatience, we have been asked: "What more do the colored people of this country want than they now have, and what more is possible for them?" It is said they were once slaves, they are now free; they were once subjects, they are now sovereigns; they were once outside of all American institutions, they are now inside of all, and a recognized part of the whole American people. Why, then, do they hold colored national conventions, and thus insist upon keeping up the color line between themselves and their white fellow-countrymen?

Mr. Douglass then proceeded to answer these questions categorically, and took occasion to administer a basting to those of his people who were too mean, servile and cowardly to assert the true dignity of their manhood and their race, and referred the existence of such creatures to the lingering remains of slave caste and oppression.

To the question "Why are we here in this National Convention?" he answered:

Because the voice of a whole people, oppressed by a common injustice, is far more likely to command attention and exert an influence on the public mind than the voice of simple individuals and isolated organizations: because we may thus have a more comprehensive knowledge of the general situation and conceive more clearly and express more fully and wisely the policy it may be necessary for them to pursue. If held for good cause, and by wise, sober and earnest men, the result will be salutary. The objection to a "colored" convention lies more in sound than substance. No reasonable man will ever object to white men holding conventions in their own interest when they are once in our condition and we in theirs: when they are the oppressed and we the oppressors.

In point of fact, however, white men are already in convention against us in various ways, and at many important points; and the practical structure of American life is in convention against us. Human law may know no distinction between men in respect of rights, but human practice may. Examples are painfully abundant. The border men hate the Indians; the Californian, the Chinaman; the Mohametan, the Christian, and vice versa, and in spite of a common nature and the equality framed into law, this hate works injustice, of which each in their own name and under their own color may complain.

The apology for observing the color line in the composition of our State and National conventions is in its necessity, and because we must do this or nothing.

CIVIL RIGHTS OBSTRUCTIONS

In vindication of the convention and its cause, the speaker continued:

It is our lot to live among a people whose laws, traditions and prejudices have been against us for centuries, and from these they are not yet free. To assume that they are free from these evils, simply because they have changed their laws, is to assume what is utterly unreasonable and contrary to facts.

Large bodies move slowly; individuals may be converted on the instant and change the whole course of life; nations never.

Not even the character of a great political organization can be changed by a new platform. It will be the same old snake, though in a new skin. Though we have had war, reconstruction and abolition as a nation, we still linger in the shadow and blight of an extinct institution.

Though the colored man is no longer subject to barter and sale, he is surrounded by an adverse settlement which fetters all his movements. In his downward course he meets with no resistance, but his course upward is resented and resisted at every step of his progress. If he comes in ignorance, rags and wretchedness, he conforms to the popular belief of his character, and in that character he is welcome; but if he shall come as a gentleman, a scholar and a statesman, he is hailed as a contradiction to the national faith concerning his race, and his coming is resented as impudence. In the one case he may provoke contempt and derision, but in the other he is an affront to pride and provokes malice. Let him do what he will, there is at present no escape for him. The color line meets him everywhere, and in a measure, shuts him out from all respectable and profitable trades and callings. In spite of all your religion and laws, he is a rejected man. Not even our churches, whose members profess to follow the despised Nazarene, whose home when on earth was among the lowly and despised, have yet conquered the feeling of color madness; and what is true of our churches is also true of our courts of law. Neither is free from this all-pervading atmosphere of color hate. The one describes the Deity as impartial and "no respecter of persons," and the other shows the Goddess of Justice as blindfolded, with a sword by her side and scales in her hand held evenly balanced between high and low, rich and poor, white and black, but both are images of American imagination, rather than of American practice. Taking advantage of the general disposition in this country to impute crime to color, white men color their faces to commit crime, and wash off the hated color to escape punishment.

Speaking of lynch law for the black man, he says:

A man accused, surprised, frightened and captured by a motley crowd, dragged with a rope around his neck in midnight darkness to the nearest tree, and told in terms of coarsest profanity to prepare for death, would be more than human if he did not in his terror-stricken appearance more confirm the suspicion of his guilt than the contrary. Worse still; in the presence of such hell-black outrages the pulpit is usually dumb, and the press in the neighborhood is silent, or openly takes sides with the mob. There are occasional cases in which white men are lynched, but one swallow does not make a summer. Every one knows that what is called lynch law is peculiarly the law for colored people and for nobody else.

He next referred to the continuation of Ku-klux outrages, and said generally this condition of things is too flagrant and notorious to require specification or proof.

Thus in all the relations of life and death we are met by the color line. We cannot ignore it if we would, and ought not if we could. It hunts us at midnight, it denies us accommodation in hotels and justice in the courts; excludes our children from schools; refuses our sons the chance to learn trades, and compels us to pursue such labor as will bring us the least reward. While we recognize the color line as a hurtful force—a mountain barrier to our progress, wounding our bleeding feet with its flinty rocks at every step—we do not despair. We are a hopeful people. This convention is a proof of our faith in you, in reason, in truth and justice, and of our belief that prejudice, with all its malign accompaniments, may be removed by peaceful means. When this shall come, the color line will only be used as it should be, to distinguish one variety of the human family from another.

THE REPUBLICAN PARTY'S ATTITUDE

Our meeting here was opposed by some of our number, because it would disturb the peace of the Republican party. The suggestion came from coward lips and misapprehends the character of that party. If the Republican party cannot stand a demand for justice and fair play, it ought to go down. We were men before that party was born, and our manhood is more sacred than any party can be. Parties were made for men, not men for parties. This hat (pointing to his big white sombrero lying on the table before him) was made for my head; not my head for the hat. (Applause.) If the six million of colored people in this country, armed with the Constitution of the United States, with a million votes of their own to lean upon, and millions of white men at their backs whose hearts are responsive to the claims of humanity, have not sufficient spirit and wisdom to organize and combine to defend themselves from outrage, discrimination and oppression, it will be idle for them to expect that the Republican party or any other political party will organize and combine for them, or care what becomes of them.

The following is taken from an anti-slavery speech delivered many years ago:

A PERTINENT QUESTION

Is it not astonishing that while we are plowing, planting, and reaping, using all kinds of mechanical tools, erecting houses and constructing bridges, building ships, working in metals of brass, iron and copper, silver and gold; that while we are reading, writing and ciphering, acting as clerks, merchants and secretaries, having among us lawyers, doctors, ministers, poets, authors, editors, orators and teachers; that while we are engaged in all manner of enterprises common to other men, digging gold in California, capturing the whale in the Pacific, breeding cattle and sheep on the hillside; living, moving, acting, thinking, planning; living in families as husbands, wives and children; and, above all, confession and worshiping the Christian's God, and looking hopefully for immortal life beyond the grave; is it not astonishing, I say, that we are called upon to prove that we are men?

In the *Negro,* a monthly magazine, published in Boston, Massachusetts, of date August, 1886, under the head of

"MISNOMER,"

Mr. Douglass wrote as follows:

Allow me to say that what is called the Negro problem seems to me a misnomer. The real problem which this nation has to solve, and the solution of which it will have to answer for in history, were better described as the white man's problem. Here, as elsewhere, the greater includes the less. What is called the Negro problem is swallowed up by the Caucasian problem. The question is whether the white man can ever be elevated to that plane of justice, humanity and Christian civilization which will permit Negroes, Indians and Chinamen, and other darker colored races to enjoy an equal chance in the race of life. It is not so much whether these races can be made Christians as whether white people can be made Christians. The Negro is few, the white man is many. The Negro is weak, the white man is strong. In the problem of the Negro's future, the white man is therefore the chief factor. He is the potter; the Negro is the clay. It is for him to say whether the Negro shall become a well rounded, symmetrical man, or be cramped, deformed and dwarfed. A plant deprived of warmth, moisture and sunlight cannot live and grow. And a people deprived of the means of an honest livelihood must wither and die. All I ask for the Negro is fair play. Give him this, and I have no fear for his future. The great mass of the colored people in this country are now, and must continue to be in, the South; and there, if anywhere, they must survive or perish.

It is idle to suppose these people can make any large degree of progress in morals, religion and material conditions, while their persons are unprotected, their rights unsecured, their labor defrauded, and they are kept only a little beyond the starving point.

Of course I rejoice that efforts are being made by benevolent and Christian people at the North in the interest of religion and education; but I cannot conceal from myself that much of this must seem a mockery and a delusion to the colored people there, while they are left at the mercy of anarchy and lawless violence. It is something to give the Negro religion (he could have that in time of slavery) : it is more to give him justice. It is something to give him the Bible; it is more to give him the ballot. It is something to tell him that there is a place for him in the Christian's heaven; it is more to allow him a peaceful dwelling-place in this Christian country.

W. B. DERRICK

CHAPTER II

Rev. W. B. Derrick, D. D.
Minister of the African M. E. Church—Pulpit Orator

The subject of this sketch was born on the Island of Antigua, in the British West Indies, July 27, 1843. Nineteen years after the boon of emancipation was conferred on those islands by the British Parliament, in 1834, Antigua, his native land, was the first island in the British West Indies which had the courage to ameliorate her slave laws, by affording the accused the benefit of a trial by jury; and an act of the assembly, February 13, 1834, decreed the emancipation of every slave without requiring a period of apprenticeship prescribed by the British Parliament. She refused to believe in the virtues of apprenticeship to prepare her bondsmen for freedom; if they were to be liberated, why not *at once?* And she has never had occasion to repent it.

His father, Thomas J. Derrick, belonged to the highly respectable family of Derricks who were large planters in the islands of Antigua and Anguila. His mother, Eliza, was of medium height, with regular features always lighted up with smiles, of genial disposition, and a mind well stored with witty and original thoughts, which rendered her conversation interesting, animating and devoid of monotony. Both parents are now slumbering, the former in the cemetery of the village church, the latter beneath the pendant branches of the mahogany tree in the public cemetery of the metropolis of the island. Mr. Derrick when very young was sent to a private school, and at the end of two years was admitted in the public school at Gracefield, under the auspices of the Moravians, and regularly attended from 1848 until the spring of 1856, when the head master of said school was removed to another charge. During these eight years, his progress at every stage in his studies was rapid and substantial, as if he had adopted for his motto *"I will excel."* His natural talent, especially for oratory, elicited general applause at the annual examinations, largely attended by the elite of the neighborhood, who took special interest in the cause of education. In his class, conspicuous for his uncommonly large head, high forehead and penetrating eyes, he stood *among the few* who could manfully grapple with the difficult questions put by the tutor. In the spring of 1856, he was sent to a select private high school in the metropolis, under the tutorship of J. Wilson, Esquire, a fine classical scholar, but a great disciplinarian. Here he remained three years. He was afterward sent to learn the trade of a blacksmith. His parents finally consented to let him go to sea, under the care of Captain Crane, with the understanding that he was to be taught the science of navigation, and at the end of two or three years to return home and embark in business. On the 6th of May, 1860, he was on his first voyage to the United States. The ship was soon enveloped in a violent storm, and driven ashore at Turk's Island, but saved from becoming a total wreck. She took in her cargo, however, and sailed to New York. After a voyage of fourteen days, the merchantman reached the back-waters and continued to glide until she reached Sandy Hook. On coming along the Jersey coast, some altercations, on the term "nigger" being applied to him, took place between an Irishman and himself, which ended in his convincing the young Irishman, pugilistically, that his complexion had nothing to do with his manhood. He did considerable sailing around in ships, visiting the coast of Massachusetts and other places, and finally came to Boston. On this trip he met with a serious accident, namely, the breaking of his leg in two places. The case was aggravated by not having a surgeon on the spot for treatment. After making several trips and being shipwrecked, he volunteered in the service of the United States government for three years, and was assigned to the flagship "Minnesota," of the North Atlantic squadron. He was thrown among five hundred other sailors, of all nationalities, who, like himself, were enlisted on the side of right. War absorbed his whole soul, yet with all this he could not repress the old idea, or smother the returning voice of the spirit which seemed to haunt him, urging him to enter the Christian ministry. When he met with the accident previously alluded to, he had had serious thoughts concerning this matter. Like a nail driven in a sure place by "the master of assemblies," there was no getting away from him who was determined to be heard amid the din and roar of artillery and the shrieks of shells. The hand of the Lord was upon him. He was formally enrolled in the list of sailors from 1861 to 1864 and contributed his quota to the gallant exploits and glorious achievements, and shared in the trials and triumphs of those brave ones in their struggles and conquests in the civil war.

Many incidents transpired while he remained on board his floating home, many of which beggar description, as, in the conflict between the "Merrimac" and "Monitor," and in the heartrending scenes of carnage and blood. He was an American citizen now, and having been dismissed from the United States navy, took two steps, one in leading to the altar of matrimony Miss Mary E. White, the only daughter of Edwin White, Esq., of Norfolk, Virginia, and the other to take the initiatory to enter the ministry of the African M. E. Church by joining the church at Washington, District of Columbia, under the pastoral care of Rev. [now Bishop] J. M. Brown, who, after the usual preliminaries, licensed him to preach and at the same time to act as missionary agent, both of which offices he held until 1867. He was then admitted to the regular traveling connection, appointed by the Rt. Rev. D. A. Payne, D. D., LL. D., to Mt. Pisgah chapel, Washington, District of Columbia, where he labored for one year as preacher and teacher. In the year 1868 he was ordained deacon, and transferred to the Virginia conference, which closed before he arrived. His only alternative was to accept one of the most impoverished missions in the district, situated in the Allegheny mountains, almost on the border of the Tennessee line. At the annual conference at Portsmouth, he was elected elder and was ordained by Bishop J. P. Campbell, D. D., LL. D., after which he was appointed pastor and presiding elder of the Staunton church and district. From this time he may be said to be firmly established in the Christian ministry. He was reappointed presiding elder, pastor and conference secretary at the annual conference held in Norfolk in 1870; Staunton, 1871; Richmond, 1872; Portsmouth, 1873; Danville, 1874; Richmond, 1875; Portsmouth, 1876; Wytheville,1878; Farmville, 1878; and Hampton, 1879; as a delegate to the general conference held in Nashville, 1872, at Atlanta, Georgia, 1876, and at Baltimore, Maryland, 1884, serving on all important committees in the sessions. In politics he has taken an active part. In Virginia, when the question of readjusting the State was agitating the country, and was submitted to the people to be voted upon in the November elections of 1879, he took sides with the party that was in favor of paying the debt as had been contracted. This party was known as the "Funders." His attitude was in perfect harmony with the platform of the National Republican party insomuch that the administration at Washington sanctioned his course again. As the colored people were considered dangerous and willing tools in the hands of ambitious men, who were unscrupulous and always ready to make use of them in furthering their own ends, regardless of consequences, he publicly denounced the faction known as "Readjusters," who repudiated the payment of an honest debt. This controversy was considered the most vindictive political war ever waged in that section, and lasted several months, terminating in the triumph of the "Readjusters." Mr. Derrick was disgusted, and knowing full well that as leader of the opposite faction he would have to suffer, he resigned his charge, left the South again, and took a trip to the West Indies in company with his wife. In this tour he traveled in the Bermudas, Jamaica, St. Thomas and Antigua, his native land. After twenty years absence he first visited the home of his oldest sister; then the graves of his departed parents and other members of the family. He preached and lectured to almost all the churches, on popular subjects. Returning to the United States, he resumed his ministerial duties. He has since served churches in Salem, New Jersey; Albany, New York, and Sullivan street church, New York City, where he continues to enjoy the confidence of the members of his church and the community at large.

The doctor has many personal admirers and they will read with interest a book of over three hundred pages, in press at this writing, which will contain a "Tribute to the Life and Labors of Rev. W. B. Derrick, D. D., Minister of the A. M. E. Church." The contents will be about as follows:

Preface; Dedication to the Sons and Daughters of Liberty in the United States and the West Indies; Recommendatory Letters from Bishop H. M. Turner, D.D., Rev. Dr. B. T. Tanner, Rev. J. A. Handy, D.D., Professor T. McCants Stewart, LL.B., Rev. W. H. Thomas, A.M., Rev. T. T. B. Reid, B.A.; Outline History of Antigua, Dr. Derrick's native land; Notices of some of the leading men in the A. M. E. Church—the whole work of his life covering four periods, viz:

PERIOD I.—His Childhood and Youth.
PERIOD II.—Life Abroad; or, The Young Man from Home.
PERIOD III.—In the American Navy during the Civil War.
PERIOD IV.—Twenty-three years in the Ministry of the A. M. E. Church; Sermons and Orations and Contributions to the Press.

His sermons, addresses and speeches are noticed in the *New York Tribune, Sun, Herald, Times,* the *Evening Telegram,* the *Christian Recorder* and the leading colored journals in this country, such as the *New York Freeman* and the *Boston Advocate.* He is a staunch Republican in politics, a progressive and evangelical preacher of the gospel, filled with the broad benevolence of Heaven and unwearied in his efforts to save immortal souls. The Wilberforce University conferred upon him the title of D. D., in 1885. He is an honorary member of the I. O. G. Templars, the Masonic Body, Odd-Fellows and Good Samaritans, the Publication Board of the A. M. E. Church and trustee of Wilberforce University. He has succeeded in accumulating about five thousand dollars worth of property, and was also the executor of the late lamented Bishop R. H. Cain, D. D., who died at his residence in New York City. He has paid an elaborate tribute to the virtues of the deceased in that city recently. He has been offered the superintendency of the church work in the West Indies, but respectfully declined. He is a diligent student of the Bible and as a pastor is ever solicitous that his flock should be fed with the "bread of life." His church is justly proud of his works, which show wisdom and care on his part. No man has a higher standing in this country, for his power is felt among all classes. His rich voice and personal magnetism make him powerful in the field of oratory. His qualities of head and heart, his sound patriotism and sturdy manhood mark him a progressive man of the age.

The *Evening Telegram,* New York, gave "Sketches of Some of the Prominent Divines," had the following, among other good things, to say of Rev. Dr. Derrick:

After leaving Albany, Dr. Derrick became pastor of the Sullivan Street Church, which is situated in the heart of the largest colored colony in this great metropolis. His church is a low-browed and plain brick structure, but it is roomy inside, and is generally well filled with a class of worshipers much more devout than are to be found in many churches frequented by white persons. Dr. Derrick is a short, stout, full and smooth-faced man of light color, with great command of language and exceeding felicity of illustration to suit the plain understanding and comprehension of the people with whom he labors. Outside of the pulpit, he exercises a shrewd business supervision of the personal affairs of his flock, and serves them as legal adviser and political leader. He is an ardent Republican.

As presiding elder, his district embraces Fleet Street Church, Brooklyn, and the African Methodist Episcopal churches at Williamsburg, Flushing, Melrose, Albany, Chatham, Kinderhook, Catskill, Coxsackle, White Plains and Harlem Mission. The church which Dr. Derrick has charge of is valued at $80,000, and the adjoining parsonage is worth $10,000 more. He is paid $2,000 per annum, a furnished house included. They also support a paid choir, under Professor Savage, one of the best musicians of the race. The church membership is 1,000, and the seating capacity of the building 1,500, but frequently more than 2,000 worshipers stand within its walls and listen to the eloquent appeals of its pastor in behalf of human progress.

In June, 1884, he was nominated as a Presidential elector-at-large by the Republican State Committee, at the instance of Fire Commissioner Van Cott. There was considerable opposition among his own race to the nomination. It was headed by John J. Freeman, the then editor of the *Progressive American.* The opposition alleged that Dr. Derrick was not a citizen, and, therefore, could not serve as an elector. W. H. Johnson, ex-janitor of the State Senate, made affidavit that once after a ward meeting, in Albany, which Dr. Derrick had attended, he asked why Dr. Derrick did not vote, and that Dr. Derrick said he was not a citizen, having been born in the West Indies, and never having taken out naturalization papers. When asked why he had not been naturalized, he replied that he did not wish to gve up his allegiance to Her Gracious Majesty, the Queen, as he had intended to stay in this country only until he had amassed sufficient means to live like a gentleman at home, where living was cheap.

A CITIZEN

On July 1 Dr. Derrick declined the nomination. He took this action, however, before he knew of the Albany affidavits, his reason being that he had been chosen by his church to assist in arranging for the centennial celebration of American Methodism, and, therefore, had not time to be an elector. This was the first time his citizenship was called in question, although he had exercised his rights and privileges as a citizen. He proved at the time that he had come to this country when he was seventeen years old, and that when he enlisted in the navy he had taken the oath of allegiance to the United States.

CHAPTER III

*Philip H. Murry, Esq.
Phrenologist—Editor and Philosopher*

———•◆•———

One of the brightest and most gifted men among the editors is P. H. Murry. He was born in Reading, Pennsylvania, in 1842. His parents, Samuel and Sarah Murry, were anxious that their boy should have opportunities to make a man of himself. His father was born on the eastern shores of Maryland, in Kent county, and living in a slave State, he found that he would not be able to place such advantages before his son. He never was a slave, but as far back as he could trace the genealogical tree, his ancestors were pure, unadulterated Negroes, who came from Africa to America through the British West Indies. The mother is a mixed Negro, Indian and Irish. On the paternal side of his mother's ancestry, the grandfather half Negro and Indian, bought, during the colonial times, an Irish woman for her passage and made her his wife. It will be remembered in the history of the Virginia colonists that many women were sent over for wives to the fortune seekers, and they were purchased for one hundred and fifty pounds of tobacco apiece. She was born in Schuylkill county, Pennsylvania, and Jack, her husband, was free born. On account of the inferiority of colored schools in Reading, at the time of his youth, his father only permitted him to attend school about a week. Afterwards he was placed under Father Patrick Keevil for private instruction. Father Keevil was at this time a castaway, but was nevertheless a scholar, having graduated at Minonth College, England. After passing through the rudiments young Philip entered into a series of scientific and philosophical studies, embracing natural science, natural philosophy and the more liberal works on theology, especially physiology, and the brain as a physical instrument of thought and feeling. This was when he was about the age of fifteen, and these studies no doubt laid the basis of his future investigations. He has studied the whole realm of science and philosophy, going deeper than the surface, inquiring into the "whys" and "wherefores" with patient zeal and unremitting toil. One can scarcely converse with him without seeing and feeling that his thoughts are drawn from a deep well and that the fountain is pure. Later on he was absorbed in the abolition movement, and was an attendant and promoter of the movements which were prevalent before the war. He came frequently in contact with Douglass, Garnet, H. Ford, the Shadds and Watkins, Bishop Payne, Rogers, the Negro historian, Wolf and Hamilton, the journalists, and other leading Negroes, including Dr. Martin R. Delancy, who then were foremost in that work. He delivered a series of able, comprehensive and learned lectures on "Cerebral Physiology" throughout New England, and made some useful and important investigations, experiments and discoveries on the temperaments, and the cranium as a continuation of the spinal development. As a phrenologist he is a perfect success. The writer remembers when quite a boy he met Mr. Murry in the city of Burlington, New Jersey. At that time examining his head, he accurately told the characteristics so plain to him, but at the time so undeveloped and unknown to the writer that he has been astonished in later years to find that the very things he predicted would be developed, were developed unconsciously, and are recognized as a verification of his deductions. In 1864 he was a delegate to the famous Negro convention which met at Syracuse, New York, and was chosen chairman of the Pennsylvania delegation. When Lee first invaded Pennsylvania, Mr. Murry, anxious to serve his country in the capacity which would do the most good, organized a company of soldiers and offered their services to Governor Curtin, but was refused because Negroes were not then needed to suppress the rebellion. But in after days when the Southern armies had shattered the Northern forces, and doubt was overhanging the country as to which side would win, the government found out that a Negro could stop a bullet as well as a white man. At the age of twenty-one, he bought the homestead of which his father was about being deprived, and deeded it to his mother; said property being worth about three thousand dollars. In conjunction with J. P. Sampson, he published the first colored journal in Kentucky, *The Colored Kentuckian*. He taught school in Pennsylvania, Kentucky, Virginia and Missouri, and took conspicuous and active parts in securing colored teachers for the colored schools in St. Louis and throughout Missouri. This idea was projected by him in a convention of teachers which met at Jefferson City, Missouri, in 1876, and for which he made speeches in St. Louis, which were published in all the dailies verbatim, and drew editorial comments as well as universal discussion among the citizens of the city and State. He published the *Colored Citizen* at Washington, District of Columbia, in 1872, and held the inspectorship of public improvements under a board of public improvement at the same time. During the war he traveled in the South and corresponded for several Northern journals. In 1880, Mr. Murry established the *St. Louis Advance*, and this paper has for its primal mission the industrial education of the Negro. He was for several years clerk in the Money Order Department of the St. Louis Post Office, also held positions of trust and honor in the comptroller's office of St. Louis. He has been a delegate to the various State and National conventions during the nine years he has lived in that city. He is now chairman of the Colored State Committee, Missouri. In 1879, he organized the St. Louis Colored Men's Land Association, which is now a success. As a writer, Mr. Murry is one of the most brilliant in the country. His editorials are always fresh, vigorous, far-seeing and progressive; bristling with argument and backed with facts. His aim in life is to press home the importance of industrial education. His remarks on the subject at the National Press convention, Atlantic City, July, 1886, are worthy to be kept, and as many may read this book we give here a few of the sentences which ought to be read by every colored man, woman and child. Said he:

"I would rather see a colored man on 'change than a colored man in Congress. We have produced a Fred Douglass, now we want a James B. Eads. We are in a large degree a landless, a tradeless and a homeless race. We are too much absorbed by politics; the best talent of the Negro is engaged in political machinations, scheming to elect some white man to office, or praying for the "New Jerusalem" to descend down out of Heaven. Emigrants from the most fecund blood of Europe are marching by our doors in platoons of ten thousand deep, to the possession of the fertile lands of the West. They create a "New Jerusalem" for themselves, but the "New Jerusalem" for the Negro never comes. We loiter about in the big cities, living on the offals of the wealthy that overawes and overshadows us at every turn. But we stay until some great city springs up in the West and the trains are burdened with the commerce of the new lands, then we go West with the broom and white jacket. We should have gone West with the hoe and the plow. This is the age of material progress; the engineer has replaced the scholar; the mathematician instead of puzzling his brain over the problems of Euclid, is wrestling with the 'Bulls and Bears on 'change.' The Greek grammarian has been supplanted by the machinist, and the man who would hunt for a hundred years to find out the meaning of a Hebrew dot only illustrates the intellectual fool of our modern times. Railroads, big farms, manufactories, steam engines, electric lights, cable cars and the telegraph, are the text books of today; and if the Negro will not study to understand, control and take possession of these, he cannot keep pace with the progress of the age.

On the subject of emigration he said:

Stop this crying of emigration; lay hold where you are; get together, put your dollars together like you put your votes and see if the result will not bring more lands, houses, and offices too, for the enjoyment of the colored people. Financial unity will establish that bond of interest that brings better social, personal and political harmony and power. Our oath-bound organization may be a strong tie, but an organization bound together by "Dollars," welded by business, girded by houses, trades, lands and manufactories, forms a bond of general, political and personal, as well as financial union to which the obligations of secret organizations appear but as a rope of sand.

In a recent editorial upon the same subject he has said:

Aside from all political considerations, whether the Negro should be Democrat, Republican or Independent or become equally divided among all factions seeking to elevate the national policy or control government, the great need of the race today is a thorough knowledge and the skillful training in the various fields of mechanism and labor. If the energies wasted among the Negroes in trying to reach great political prominence, were directed toward acquiring a knowledge of the necessary and useful arts, the next generation of American Negroes would come forth full-fledged and equipped as artisans, and thrifty business men, skilled carvers in wood, iron and stone structures, and whatever enters into the convenience, comfort and facilities of our organization.

Such doctrines as these are calculated to be of immense value to the people. He has vigorously taught and insisted on industrial institutions, and his paper is sound on all questions touching the progress of the race and upbuilding of waste places.

He has a wife and four children, one dead, and his possessions are valued at about five thousand dollars.

CHAPTER IV

Crispus Attucks
First Martyr of the Revolutionary War—A Negro Whose Blood
was Given for Liberty—"Blood the Price of Liberty"

———•◆•———

The subject of this sketch was born in slavery in 1723, and died in 1770. He ran away from his master, William Brown of Farmingham, Massachusetts, on the thirtieth of September, 1750, at the age of 27. He was a mulatto, six feet and two inches high. His master advertised for him in the following description: "Short, curly hair, his knees nearer together than common; had on a light colored bearskin coat, plain brown fustian jacket, or a brown wool one, new buckskin breeches, blue yarn stockings and a checked woolen shirt. Whoever shall take up said runaway, convey him to above said master, shall receive ten pounds, old tenor reward, and all necessary charges paid. And all masters of vessels, or others, are hereby cautioned against concealing or carrying off said servant on penalty of the law. October 2, 1750."

Only after much meditation and thought, he had broken away from the cruel chains that bound him, and was determined to be a free American citizen. He learned to read at odd times, and he used this accomplishment in understanding the fundamental principles that underlie all regulated forms of governments. A fiery patriotism burned in his breast. He was anxious to avenge oppression in every form, not by fighting alone, but by the sacrifice of life, if necessary. Twenty years later, Crispus' name once more appeared in the journals of Boston. This time he was not advertised as a slave who had run away, nor was there a reward for his apprehension. His soul and body were beyond the cruel touch of master. The press had paused to announce his death and write the name of the Negro patriot, soldier and martyr to the ripening cause of the American Revolution, in fadeless letters of gold.

On March 5, 1770, the Boston massacre occurred. The people had been oppressed by British tyranny, they had been treated as inferiors; they were taxed without representation and their souls galled until they were maddened. When British troops, to add insult to injury, encamped upon their grounds, they could withhold no longer. They were greatly exasperated; they formed themselves into clubs and resolved to avenge themselves and gain their rights. They ran toward King street crying "Let us drive out the ribalds. They have no business here." The rioters rushed fearlessly towards the custom house. They approached the sentinel crying, "Kill him! Kill him!" It has been said that Crispus Attucks led one of these clubs, which has not been denied, but rather assented to. Botta speaking of it says: "There was a band of the populace led by a mulatto named Attucks, who brandished their clubs and pelted them with snowballs." The scene was horrible. The populace advanced to the points of their bayonets. The soldiers appeared like statues. The howlings and violent din of bells still sounding the alarm, increased the confusion and the horrors of these moments. At length the mulatto and twelve of his companions pressing forward environed the soldiers, striking their muskets with their clubs, cried to the multitude, "Be not afraid, they dare not fire. Why do you hesitate? Why do you not kill them? Why not crush them at once?"

Inspired by his words, his followers rushed madly on, and the soldiers, incensed by this act of insolence, answered the war-like cry by discharging their guns. Attucks had lifted his arm against Captain Preston and fell a victim to the mortal fire. Three were killed and five were severely wounded. The cry of bloodshed spread like wild-fire. People crowded the street, white with rage; the bells rang out with alarm, and the whole country was aroused to battle. Attucks was buried from Fanueil Hall with great honor. He had led the people and made the attack. He was the first to resist and the first slain. His patriotism was the declaration of war. It was liberty to the oppressed; it opened the way to modern civilization and independence. It has blessed and will continue to bless generations yet unborn. He is rightly claimed as the savior of his country. No monument has ever been reared to his name. Repeated efforts have been made before the Massachusetts Legislature, and notwithstanding the various testimonies and the histories going to show that he was entitled to the honor we have here accorded him, upon a flimsy testimony the honor has been given to one Isaac Davis of Concord, a white man. George Williams, the historian of the race, in his very excellent work, uses these words in regard to Crispus Attucks:

Attucks had addressed a letter to one Thomas Hutchinson, who was the Tory governor of the province, in which he had used these words: "Sir, you will hear from us with astonishment. You ought to hear from us with horror. You are chargeable before God and man with our blood. The soldiers are but passive instruments, mere machines, neither moral nor voluntary agents in our destruction, more than the leaden pellets with which we were wounded.

"You were a free agent; you acted coolly, deliberately, with all that premeditated malice, not against us in particular, but against the people in general, which, in sight of the law, is an ingredient in the composition of murder. You will hear from us further hereafter."

CRISPUS ATTUCKS

This letter is taken from *Adams' Works,* Volume II, page 322. Said Williams:

This was the declaration of war and it was fulfilled. The world has heard from him, and more, the English speaking world will never forget the noble daring, the excusable rashness of Attucks in the holy cause of liberty. Eighteen centuries before He was saluted by death and kissed by immortality, another Negro bore the cross of Christ to Calvary for Him. And when the colonists were struggling wearily under their cross of woe, a Negro came to the front and bore that cross to the victory of glorious martyrdom!

A sketch also will be found of his life in the *American Encyclopedia* and in William C. Nell's books on the colored patriots of the Revolution.

GRANVILLE T. WOODS

CHAPTER V

Granville T. Woods, Esq.
Electrician—Mechanical Engineer—Manufacturer
of Telephone, Telegraph and Electrical Instruments

———•◆•———

"Some men are born great; some have greatness thrust upon them; and some achieve greatness." To the last class belongs G. T. Woods, who was born in Columbus, Ohio, April 23, 1856. He attended school until he was ten years of age, when he was placed in a machine shop where he learned the machinist and blacksmith trades. In the meantime he took private lessons and attended night school, and exhibited great pluck and perseverance in fitting himself for the work he desired to undertake. He pursued with assiduity every study which promoted that end. November, 1872, he left for the West, where he obtained work as a fireman and afterwards as an engineer on one of the Iron Mountain Railroads of Missouri. While in the employ of the railroad company he had a great deal of leisure, and as saloons had no attractions for him, he took up the study of electricity as a pastime. In December, 1874, he went to Springfield, Illinois, where he was employed in a rollingmill. Early in 1876 he left for the East, where he received two years special training in electrical and mechanical engineering at college. While obtaining his special instructions, he worked six half days in each week in a machine shop, the afternoon and evening of each day being spent in school. February 6, 1878, he went to sea in the capacity of engineer on board the "Ironsides," a British steamer. While a sailor, he visited nearly every country on the globe. During 1880 he handled a locomotive on the D. & S. Railroad. Since then he has spent the major portion of his time in Cincinnati, Ohio, where he has established a factory for the purpose of carrying on the business, as indicated at the head of this sketch. A company has been formed recently for the purpose of placing Mr. Woods' Electrical Railway Telegraph on the market. Mr. Woods says that he has been frequently refused work because of the previous condition of his race, but he has had great determination and will and never despaired because of disappointments. He always carried his point by persistent efforts. He says the day is past when the colored boys will be refused work only because of race prejudice. There are other causes. First, the boy has not the nerve to apply for work after being refused at two or three places. Second, the boy should have some knowledge of mechanics. The latter could be gained at technical schools, which should be founded for the purpose. In this respect he shows good sense and really prophesies the future of the race, and these schools must sooner or later be established, and thereby we shall be enabled to put into the hands of our boys and girls the actual means for a livelihood. He is the inventor of the "Induction Telegraph," a system for communicating to and from moving trains, and is intended to diminish the loss of life and property, and produce a maximum of safety to travelers. In the United States patent office, in the case of *Woods* v. *Phelps' Railway Telegraph Interference*—L. M. Hosea, attorney for Woods, and W. D. Baldwin, attorney for Phelps—it will be shown that the patent office has decided that Mr. Woods was the prior inventor of this system. His rights having been questioned, he secures this verdict which gives him triumphal possession of a great discovery. The following is taken from the *Scientific American:*

The public prints give us almost daily accounts of railway collisions in one section of the country or another. Every effort has been made to avert these. The general introduction of the telegraph has unquestionably done much in this direction; but in thick weather the operatives at the railway stations could scarcely be looked to to guard points of the road beyond their ken, and the railway switchman or signalman, as in other walks of life, is fallible. If railway signalmen could be found who require neither sleep nor rest, who are not subject to fits or spasms or spirituous excesses, and, above all, having eyes to pierce the fog, then railroad travel would indeed be divested of its greatest terrors. But, taking human nature as we find it, we learn that so grave a responsibility as the care of human life should never be thrust upon the shoulders of a single man.

The "Block System" recently introduced would, it was believed, prove a reliable means of preventing accidents on the rail, and it is but fair to say that it has made an excellent record; but that it is not, under all conditions and circumstances, to be relied upon, there is abundant evidence. Only last week it failed to prevent a collision between two freight trains at New Brunswick, New Jersey, on the line of the Pennsylvania railroad, in which two lives were lost and property to the value of half a million dollars destroyed. It was of course only by mere chance that these trains were not carrying passengers. From this it may be inferred how pressing is the demand for some system in which the safety of the traveling public is not made to rely on an unthinking and not always reliable automaton, or, still worse, upon the action of an overworked and irresponsible employee, whose perception of colors may be defective.

Many able electricians have believed the solution of this problem to lie within the domains of the electrical science; and those who have followed the drift of recent electrical endeavors are aware of the contrivances, all looking towards the same goal, that have made their appearance. The general principle on which all these have been based was electrical communications between all trains, while en route, and the train despatcher; most of these systems have shown a certain degree of efficiency when tested under favorable conditions, but the best of them were subject to interruptions, and this, from the very nature of the work they were called upon to perform, has been rendered more or less uncertain, owing to the fact that they relied upon a direct contact with the conductor, either by a wire, wheel or brush.

Now comes forward a practical system of train signaling, which does not rely upon contact at all; the electrical induction coil upon the moving train being distant from the conductor, lying between the track at least seven inches.

The future possibilities of these new inventions appear to be very great; just how far the system can be extended and applied it is impossible to foretell. But this appears to be certain; the risk of disaster on railways will be greatly reduced from this time onward.

Mr. Woods claims that his invention is for the purpose of averting accidents by keeping each train informed of the whereabouts of the one immediately ahead or following it; in intercepting criminals; in communicating with stations from moving trains; and in promoting general, social and commercial intercourse. The following appeared in the *Cincinnati Sun:*

Granville T. Woods, a young colored man of this city, has invented a new system of electrical motor, for street railroads. He has invented also a number of other electrical appliances, and the syndicate controlling his inventions think they have found Edison's successor.

The *Cincinnati Colored Citizen,* in its issue of January 29, 1887, says:

We take great pleasure in congratulating Mr. G. T. Woods on his success in becoming so prominent that his skill and knowledge of his chosen art compare with that of any one of our best known electricians of the day.

The *Catholic Tribune,* January 14, 1886, said of him:

Granville T. Woods, the greatest colored inventor in the history of the race, and equal, if not superior, to any inventor in the country, is destined to revolutionize the mode of street car transit. The results of his experiments are no longer a question of doubt. He has excelled in every possible way in all his inventions. He is master of the situation, and his name will be handed down to coming generations as one of the greatest inventors of his time. He has not only elevated himself to the highest position among inventors, but he has shown beyond doubt the possibility of a colored man inventing as well as one of any other race.

The following appeared in the *American Catholic Tribune,* April 1, 1887 (Cincinnati, Ohio):

Mr. Woods, who is the greatest electrician in the world, still continues to add to his long list of electrical inventions.

The latest device he invented is the Synchronous Multiplex Railway Telegraph. By means of this system, the railway despatcher can note the position of any train on the route at a glance. The system also provides means for telegraphing to and from the train while in motion. The same lines may also be used for local message without interference with the regular train signals.

This system may be used for other purposes. In fact, two hundred operators may use a single wire at the same time. Although the messages may be passing in opposite directions, they will no conflict with each other.

In using the devices there is no possibility of collisions between trains, as each train can always be informed of the position of the other while in motion. Mr. Woods has all the patent office drawings for these devices, as your correspondent witnessed.

The patent office has twice declared Mr. Woods prior inventor of the induction railway telegraph as against Mr. Edison, who claims to be the prior inventor. The Edison & Phelps company are now negotiating a consolidation with the Woods' Railway Telegraph company.

It is recorded that a very distinguished preacher said: "If everything the Negro had invented was sunk at the bottom of the sea, the world would not miss them, and would move on as before." This was not true then, is not true now, and will be less so in the future. Hundreds of slaves invented instruments which have been taken by their masters and patented, and many others for want of means to put their inventions through the patent office and manufacture them, have sold their knowledge for almost a "mess of pottage." The future will bring forth men who will yet astonish the world with inventions of labor-saving character, and add materially to the wealth of the nation, by producing those instruments which will decrease manual labor, multiply articles more rapidly, facilitate communication and benefit mankind.

CHAPTER VI

Hon. Jeremiah A. Brown
Legislator—Carpenter and Joiner—Clerk—Deputy Sheriff —Turnkey and Letter-Carrier

---

Hon. Jeremiah A. Brown, or as he is familiarly called "Jere," was the first child of Thomas A. and Frances J. Brown, Pittsburgh, Allegheny county, Pennsylvania. In that city on the fourteenth of November, 1841, the subject of our sketch first saw the light of day. His younger days were spent in that city where he attended school, having among his classmates such men as the Rev. Benjamin T. Tanner, D. D., Hon. T. Morris Chester, James T. Bradford of Baltimore, Maryland, and many other distinguished men, who are now prominently before the people. He continued in the pursuits of knowledge with these until about his thirteenth year, when he accompanied his father as a steamboatman on our Western rivers. This avocation engaged his attention until his seventeenth year, when he became very much imbued with the importance of the advancement of himself in such a particular as to secure to him the possibilities of a livelihood. To this end he learned a trade, choosing that of a carpenter and joiner. At the close of his seventeenth year he entered the shop of James H. McClelland, Esq., as an apprentice. This gentleman was the foremost builder in that city at the time and a gentleman known far and wide for his interest in the advancement of the colored people. Upon his entrance into this shop, it was the immediate signal for a number of the employees quitting work, such was the prejudice existing against a colored boy entering upon any of the trades; but Mr. McClelland promptly filled their places, with the remark: "that that boy will stay in this shop until he learns the trade, if I have to fill it with black mechanics from the South." Thus was the backbone of prejudice broken by this bold stand, and our young man remained and finished his trade with honor to himself, his race, and his friendly employer. After finishing his apprenticeship, his parents decided to remove to Canada West, believing that it would be beneficial to the children, of whom they had six, to be under a government that did not sanction human slavery. They desired to take their children

JEREMIAH A. BROWN

away from its blighting and withering effects; not as practiced in its enormities, but as sanctioned by the laws of Ohio, which were then known as the "black laws," and against which he has had an opportunity to battle in the Legislature of Ohio. These black laws were very obnoxious to the colored citizens and have constantly provoked unlimited antagonism from them and their ardent white friends. Young Brown accompanied them to Canada and settled near Chatham, Ontario. Upon the inauguration of the Civil War he returned to the United States and located in St. Louis, Missouri, and again returned to steamboating, but from time to time paid visits to his parents.

January 17, 1864, he was married to Miss Mary A. Wheeler, of Chatham, Ontario, a sister of Hon. Lloyd G. Wheeler, of Chicago, Illinois, and the Rev. Robert F. Wheeler, of Hartford, Connecticut. Returning to St. Louis, he remained there a short time and then decided to settle in the State of Ohio. With that end in view he went there in 1869 or 1870, stopping at Wilberforce, Ohio, to which place his parents had removed for the purpose of educating their youngest children. After prospecting in several cities in the southern part of Ohio, he determined upon Cleveland as the place where he would locate and lay the foundation for a useful and happy life; and here he has remained ever since. A few years' residence found him an active participant in the political field. His first political position was a baliff of the probate court of that county; then he was deputy sheriff and turnkey of the county prison for four years, and clerk of the "City Boards of Equalization and Revision." Then he obtained a position in the postoffice as letter-carrier and remained in the employ of the general government until the fall of 1885, when he secured the nomination on the Republican ticket as a representative in the Ohio Legislature from Cuyahoga county, being elected by nearly three thousand majority over the highest competitor on the Democratic ticket— an honor by no means small. His career has been short, and yet long enough to show that he has made due effort to wipe out those prescriptive laws of the State which we have spoken of above. He made a telling speech on the subject March 10, 1886, a bill having been introduced by the Hon. Benjamin W. Arnett. Said he:

All the colored man desires, Mr. Speaker, is that he be given the same legislation that is accorded to other men. No man can deny that we have proven ourselves other than true, patriotic and honorable citizens. Going back to the early days of the history of our country, where the picture is presented of the black man, in person of Crispus Attucks shedding his blood, the first spilt in the great American war for freedom, we are forced to stand appalled at that country's ingratitude. When, again, I bring in this galaxy of bright lights, Benjamin Banneker, the great mathematician, and those brave men of my race who fought, bled and died for my country in the War of 1812, I ask you, gentlemen, is such ostracism the reward for that heroism and devotion? But when I contemplate the actions of the American Negro on the battlefield of the South—at the many scenes of carnage in which he was engaged during the late War of the Rebellion—with what heroism he performed deeds of valor, showing and demonstrating his ability even at the cannon's mouth, my very heart bleeds for the foul blot heaped upon the countless thousands of black men, who laid their lives upon their country's altar for the establishment and the perpetuity of this government. In that Southland my race put on the blue, shouldered their muskets, and today their bones lie bleaching on dozens of battlefields, where they were massacred by those who sought to destroy this fair land. What, gentlemen, I ask you, is the reward Ohio gives those of her black sons whose bones are scattered there?

Further on, in reference to these black laws, he says:

Repeal them, and to your ensign will cluster the friendship of my race—redress our grievances with that power delegated to every American citizen. Defeat this bill, and the wrath of the colored voters will bury you beneath their ballots cast by as loyal citizens as the sun of Heaven looks down upon. Repeal them, and in after years when we show our children these obnoxious and pernicious laws, explaining to them the disadvantages we were subjected to, by and under them, we can teach them to love and venerate the memories of those who were instrumental in giving us equal facilities with our more than favored brethren.

Mr. Brown is connected with the Masonic fraternity of Ohio, by whom he is highly honored and respected, as is readily shown by the numerous positions he has held. For a number of years he has held, and is at this time holding, the grand secretaryship of the Grand Lodge F. A. A. M. of the Grand Chapter R. A. M.; Grand Recorder of the Grand Commandery of Knights Templars and of the order of High Priesthood; he is also a member of the Carpenters' and Joiners' Brotherhood of America; believing that organization, if good for white men, is equally, if not more, beneficial to the black men. His early education was acquired in the common schools of his native State, with a short course in the Avery College of Allegheny, Pennsylvania. At the time the facilities and opportunities for acquiring an education were far below what are now in vogue. There were no opportunities for black men other than situations of a menial and degrading character to be obtained; but he, imbued with the firm determination to enter the race of life, succeeded in arriving at a point where he can be called a successful man, and has indeed risen from the carpenter's bench, and a common laborer on a steamboat, to the distinguished position of a lawmaker of the State of Ohio. His religious training was under the A. M. E. Church while a youth, but he is not connected with any denomination now, but attends the Congregational Church, the Sabbath school of which is and has been under the superintendency of his wife for about eight years. In financial affairs he has succeeded moderately, being worth probably five thousand dollars. May his life and success be some encouragement for those who find life hard and labor become unprofitable.

WILLIAM CALVIN CHASE

CHAPTER VII

*William Calvin Chase, Esq.
Editor of the Washington* Bee—*Vigorous and Antagonistic
Writer—Politician—Agitator*

———•◆•———

Whatever may be said for or against Mr. Chase, it can well be remarked that he is a true friend, an untiring enemy, a defender of his race, and a lover of his home. Mistakes he has made, no doubt, and yet they were in behalf of his convictions or when he has been mistaken as to the justice of the cause which promoted him to act. He has led a life of agitation, turmoil and combats, and has taken and given many blows, and, like the "Black Knight" of Scott's matchless *Ivanhoe*, he has unhorsed many a Front-de-Boeny and Athelstane—using both sword and battle-axe. Relying as I do on his written views, newspaper articles and other material before me, I have attempted to furnish the facts with little comment. But let it now be said that while Mr. Chase may differ from any one, yet he is a pleasant and agreeable companion at any time, and those from whom he has differed are all distinguished friends of his. His paper has a motto which greatly interprets the man, viz: "Honey for friends and stings for enemies." The next birthday of Mr. Chase will occur on February 2, 1888, when he will be thirty-four years of age. He is still a very young man. His father, William H. Chase, was a blacksmith, and one of the leading citizens of Washington, District of Columbia, during his day. He was shot by a man named Charles Posey, in 1863, who called at his place of business, pretending that he wanted him to examine a revolver, claiming that it was the one that was used by a man who killed a woman in the southern section of the city. Posey said the revolver was not loaded; but as soon as Mr. Chase was handed, he refused it, and told him to take it away, it might do harm, and before he had finished this remark the deadly weapon went off and he was shot through the heart. His own brother (Chase's) immediately asserted that it was an accident. Very soon after his death, and before any of Mr. Chase's immediate family arrived, he was robbed of every cent he had in his pockets. The death of Mr. Chase left his widow with six small children. Young Chase being the only boy, had many hardships to encounter, as will be seen in the history of his life. His mother was a Lucinda Seaton of Virginia, a daughter of one of the most aristocratic colored families of that State, and who is at this time one of the leading citizens of Washington. She is a woman of determined will, who has succeeded in educating her children. One is married to Rev. E. W. Williams, principal of Ferguson's Academy, which she established, and lives in Abbeville, South Carolina; two are teaching in the public schools of Washington; another is employed in the government printing office at Washington, and has the reputation of having excelled a steam folding machine in folding papers.

During the struggle of Mrs. Chase to educate her children, she met with opposition on all sides, mainly from her husband's relatives, some of whom brought suits, aggregating eight thousand dollars, against her. William H. Chase was also a musician, and it is said that he performed skillfully on the violin and bass violin, the latter of which was the cause of a lawsuit in the Orphan's court. The instrument was left to his son, and at the time of the death of Mr. Chase, his nephew had it in his possession, and declined to give it up until forced to do so by order of the court. Young Chase did not take to music; his ambition was journalism. To be successful in that, he knew that it was necessary to acquire a good education. He was only ten years old at the death of his father, and knowing that his mother had a heavy responsibility on her, he began to sell newspapers. The prejudice against colored newsboys was so great that they were not allowed by the white newsboys to come where they were. Chase managed to receive his papers through a colored gentleman who was employed by the Star Publishing Company, by the name of George Johnson, who did all in his power to aid him. Young Chase always knew how to ingratiate himself in the good graces of those who had charge of newspapers, so much so that he succeeded when others failed. He was well known around every newspaper office of any prominence in Washington, and became one of the most popular newsboys in the city. Before the death of his father, he attended the private school of John F. Cook, present collector of taxes in the District of Columbia. Leaving this school after the death of his father, he began his noted career as a newsboy. He would sell papers before school in the morning, and after it in the afternoon. While so doing, he met a white lady who became impressed with his manners, and she asked him if he did not want a place; he said he did. She gave him her card and requested him to call at her boarding place the next day. Calling as requested, he was given a pen and ink to write his name; he could not do so, but in less than three days he accomplished the task. He was but eleven years old then. Still more impressed was the lady; she secured him a place with Holley & Brother, wholesale hat manufacturers in Methuen, Massachusetts. Not caring much for the business, he attended a white school taught by a lady named Mrs. Swan. He remained there some time, and finally wrote to his mother to allow him to come home. So appealing was his letter that his mother consented. It was in this town that Chase conceived the importance of an education; there, too, he got an idea of the printing business, and his ambition continued to force him to get an education to enable him to become a useful man. He declared when a boy, that he would some day become an editor.

On returning home he took up selling papers again, making himself a kind of utility boy around newspaper offices, and got a good idea of newspaper business. He left the public school and entered the Howard University Model School, "B" class, and remained in that department two years, passed a successful examination, and was recommended by his teacher as qualified to enter the preparatory department. During his stay in Howard University I was his teacher for a short while, and found him one of the brightest in the class. His wife was also a pupil of mine. Just as he was about to enter college he received an appointment in the government printing office, at which place he remained two years. He did not get the place promised by the public printer; for this, and injustice to the colored employees in the office, he assigned as good reasons for denouncing the public printer, which he did. This was his first public act, although prior to this he had made himself prominent in politics and was recommended for a consulship, having been endorsed by the most prominent Republican campaign organizations in the city, by members of Congress, and Senator Thomas W. Ferry of Michigan. After leaving the government printing office he filed charges with the President against the public printer, A. M. Clapp, and introduced a resolution in the Hayes and Wheeler campaign club, of which he was secretary. Colored men under Clapp called a meeting for the purpose of denouncing Chase and refuting his charges against Clapp; but Chase arrived at the hall just as the resolution was about to pass, and told them that if such a resolution was adopted he would expose all those who had urged him to denounce Mr. Clapp on account of his injustice to the Negro. The resolution did not pass. He gives the following account of the rupture between himself and Mr. Douglass:

> Mr. Frederick Douglass, who had been appointed United States marshal by President Hayes, heard that I was to be given an appointment, said to me that he would like to have me in his office, "and as the President is to give you an appointment," said Douglass, "tell him if he (President Hayes) will send me a letter, I will appoint you." I called on President Hayes and informed him of what Mr. Douglass had said. The President, after looking over my papers, wrote a personal letter to Mr. Douglass. The letter was handed

to him by me. The "Old Man Eloquent" said, "Ah! Mr. Chase, you have caught me on the fly. Come in and I will see what I can do for you." After entering Mr. Douglass' office, he said, "Chase, call in, in a few days; I am going to discharge a man and put you on." In the meantime Mr. Clapp, who had been requested to resign his office, wrote to Mr. Douglass and informed him that he had heard that the President had recommended me to him for an appointment; that the charges I made against him were false. In reply Mr. Douglass wrote to Mr. Clapp and said: "Although the President has requested me to appoint Mr. Chase, I don't know whether I shall do it or not." I was informed of the letter of Mr. Douglass by a colored man and a friend of his, employed in the press room of the government printing office, to whom Mr. Clapp read the letter. I called on Mr. Douglass and informed him of the letter written to Mr. Clapp, and before Mr. Douglass replied, his son Lewis, then deputy marshal, denied it. I said that such a letter was written, and any one who attempted to deny it was a liar. L. Douglass said: "I won't appoint you now, any way." I said it made no difference to me, and demanded that the letter sent to Mr. Douglass by the President be returned to me, and said that I would inform the President that he refused to appoint me, after having promised. Mr. Douglass said "No, as the President's letter was a personal one to him." I then asked for a copy of the letter, at the request of ex-mayor Bowen. Mr. Douglass declined. I had become somewhat noted as a newspaper correspondent, and in every letter to the *Boston Observer* I remembered Mr. Douglass, and would paragraph him in the most pointed manner, and they would appear weekly, greatly to the discomfort of Mr. Douglass and much to my gratification. I returned to President Hayes, but before seeing him talked with his private secretary, Mr. W. K. Rodgers. I was given a card to the President and related to him the actions of Mr. Douglass. The President seemed to be somewhat indignant, and said that Mr. Douglass had nothing to do with the action of the Invincible Club against Mr. Clapp. He gave me a letter to the postmaster-general. Six months later Mr. Douglass met me in the presence of Captain O. S. B. Wall, and seemed to be greatly aggrieved at the letters written by me to the *Boston Observer*, and asked me what I was doing. I told him; whereupon he invited me to call and see him. I called and told Mr. Douglass that the President had given me a letter to Postmaster-General Key. Douglass volunteered to endorse the President's recommendation. While my appointment was pending, some of my enemies heard that the postmaster intended to appoint me to an important position. To defeat this, an anonymous letter, denouncing the President's "Southern Policy," was written and the name of the secretary of the Hayes and Wheeler Invincible Club signed. The letter stated that I denounced the President's policy and was organizing a new African party, which would prove detrimental to the President and the Republican party. This letter was sent to the postmaster, and I failed to get the appointment.

Although the *Boston Observer* had suspended, a new paper had been started, known as the *Washington Plaindealer,* edited by Dr. King, a West

Indian. Mr. Chase was made reporter and the "Chit-Chat" editor. He was considered a valuable news and society editor. Not being satisfied with the policy of the paper, he resigned and turned his interest over to A. St. A. Smith and A. W. DeLeon. Mr. Douglass became a supporter of the *Plaindealer*. Mr. Chase turned his attention to the management of the public schools and endeavored to reform them. He claimed to know of immorality existing in the schools and prepared several specifications of charges against certain trustees. Commissioner Dent requested the trustees, against whom these charges were made to answer them. They were all denied, but were proven by Mr. Chase. One of the trustees was removed, but the other was retained, owing to some doubt on the part of the commissioners, as this trustee had offered the Colored Normal School bill which would have benefited the colored people. Chase called a public meeting and charged these men openly with having corrupted the schools. The meeting was packed by the friends of the trustees with society friends. These were charged by Mr. Chase with attempting to hide corruption and keeping a set of corrupt men in office. The meeting was taken from Mr. Chase and his friends, and resolutions adopted endorsing the trustees. Notwithstanding this, Mr. Chase filed his charges and proved them. Previous to this Mr. Douglass had made up with Mr. Chase, but Mr. Douglass had been informed by one of the trustees that Mr. Chase was using the letter sent by Mr. Douglass to Postmaster-General Key in connection with the charges against the trustees. Mr. Douglass came out in the following card in the *National Republican* of Washington:

WASHINGTON, DISTRICT OF COLUMBIA, September 25, 1876
To whom it may concern:
Whereas, one William C. Chase, is using a letter of mine in connection with certain charges against the trustees of the public schools, I desire to say that I have lost confidence in said Chase and withdraw my letter of endorsement of him.

Very Respectfully, etc.
FREDERICK DOUGLASS

Mr. Chase said in a public speech "that Mr. Douglass knew that he was using no letter of his." The letter referred to was on file in the postoffice department, and was not withdrawn until after the appearance of Mr. Douglass' card, which was certified to by General O. P. Burnside, the disbursing officer of that department. During this fight President Hayes had given Mr. Chase another letter, this time to the district commissioners, for an appointment. Captain Phelps, one of the commissioners, opposed Mr. Chase's appointment on representations made to him by the friends of the trustees, while Commissioner J. Dent favored it and would listen to nothing said by his enemies. Mr. Chase, however, did not secure the appointment. Presuming that he would give the President a rest for a while, he accepted the editorship of the *Argus,* which was offered him, at that time edited by Charles N. Otey, one of the brainest men known to the colored race. The *Argus* was controlled by a board of directors. Mr. Otey retired and Mr. Chase appointed to succeed him, with Captain G. W. Graham, business manager. He changed the name of the paper to that of the *Free Lance.* The change of the name excited great feeling among the people, as they knew of the vindictiveness and determination of Mr. Chase to expose fraud and get even with those whom he considered enemies. Nor did he disappoint them. His first attack was made on Senator John Sherman, then the secretary of the treasury; "the schools," "police force," and the National Republican committee for not appointing colored men in the campaign. So great was the feeling of the Republicans against him, that the board of directors, who were all office holders, while *they* dared not remove Mr. Chase, sold out the paper to L. H. Douglass, H. Johnson, M. M. Holland, and others, office-holders, claimed by Mr. Chase to be his enemies. The sell out of the *Argus* Publishing Company greatly pleased his opposers, for the name of Chase was becoming a household word, and notwithstanding his many defeats, he conceived the idea that he would sink or swim in his next attempt.

He went to the President and asked for another appointment; this time the President put him off; he left, got additional endorsements from prominent Republicans in Virginia, among whom was one of Colonel Sampson P. Bailey, in whose interest he canvassed the Eighth Congressional District, Colonel John F. Lewis and many others. He returned to him and presented a letter which was referred to his private secretary, who was very favorably disposed towards Mr. Chase. When asked where he wanted to go, Mr. Chase replied, "Back to the government printing office; foreman of the lower paper warehouse," a position then held by a white man. Mr. Chase called on Mr. John D. Defrees whose nomination was pending. He promised to appoint Mr. Chase, but as soon as it became known that Mr. Chase was to return to that office, the friends of Mr. Clapp commenced to work on Mr. Defrees' prejudice. After his confirmation by the United States Senate, a minor place was offered him, which he declined. At this time an investigation against Defrees, and Clapp was instigated by Hon. Ebenezer B. Finley of Ohio, chairman of the sub-committee on expenditures. Mr. Chase was subpœnaed by that committee, which became known at the government printing office; he was sent for by H. Robert, foreman of the bindery. After this subpœna he was appointed in the government printing office, but remained only one week, as the place was not what he desired. Before Douglass was transferred from the marshalship to recorder of deeds, a public meeting was called by the friends of John T. Johnson to endorse him for the place of Douglass. Mr. Chase opposed the resolution, and asked that Douglass be retained and Johnson be endorsed for recorder of deeds, to which Mr. Douglass was subsequently appointed.

Although Mr. Douglass had been requested not to appoint Mr. Chase in his office, he did so eventually. This was considered a victory for Mr. Chase after the publication of Mr. Douglass' card. While in this office Mr. Chase wrote a severe criticism on the *History of the Negro Race* by Colonel G. W. Williams, of which Mr. Douglass was accused; it was in this office that Mr. Chase was accused of being inspired to criticise and condemn the political course of Hon. R. Purvis. He was editing the *Bee* at the time. He denied all accusations against Mr. Douglass. A heated correspondence passed between Messrs. Douglass and Purvis. Mr. Purvis requested the discharge of Mr. Chase, but Mr. Douglass refused to comply, and suggested that Mr. Purvis meet him on equal grounds and not ask him to do that which would not be honorable. Mr. Purvis became very indignant at this, and instigated a criminal libel suit against Mr. Chase, which was subsequently withdrawn.

Mr. Chase was not satisfied with the position in Mr. Douglass' office, and Hon. B. K. Bruce, who was a staunch friend of his, was accompanied by Mr. Douglass to see the secretary of war, Hon. R. T. Lincoln, to obtain a better place. It is said that instead of Mr. Douglass recommending Mr. Chase, he recommended some one else, which greatly embarrassed Mr. Bruce, who requested Mr. Chase to go with him to see Mr. Lincoln. Two weeks later Mr. Chase was notified to appear in examination, after which he received a probationary appointment for four months, at the end of which, his appointment was made permanent. Then his thoughts were turned to the law department of Howard University, where he remained one year, when he was asked to enter the Virginia Republican canvass, which he did, and which necessarily compelled him to give up the study of law. He took an active part in the campaign of '84, both in person and with his paper, the *Bee*. In 1885, he went as one of the delegates from the convention of colored citizens to President Cleveland, to request him to review the Emancipation Day parade. At the conclusion of remarks by Mr. Chase, the President produced a copy of the *Bee* containing the following article:

MURDER AND ASSASSINATION

We are constrained to say that the time has come when murder and the assassination of black Republicans in the South must cease. The time has come for the Negroes and loyal white people of this country to show to the world that there is purity in American politics. In the State of Louisiana, a few days ago, the most cowardly and bloody murders were committed. Innocent colored Republicans were shot down by Democrats like dogs. The same was a repetition of the past brutalities, when helpless colored female virgins and babes were snatched from their beds and murdered. The scene in the South on last Tuesday has raised the indignation of over five millions of true black American citizens. It is time for every American Negro in the South to make an appeal to arms and fire every Democratic home where Negro-killers live, from a palace to a hut, in retaliation for the foul and dastardly murders that were committed in the South. We speak without fear and in defense of the helpless Negro. It is far more noble to die the death of a freeman than an ignominious slave. The hundred and fifty-three electoral votes from the South were obtained through theft and assassination; schemes of the most outrageous character were resorted to; Negroes murdered; ballot boxes stuffed; peaceable citizens were imprisoned to prevent them from exercising the rights of elective franchise. Under these circumstances it will cost the lives of millions to inaugurate Grover Cleveland.

Mr. Chase informed the President that he was the author of the article; that it was written in the heat of the Presidential campaign; that the Copiah, Danville, and Louisiana massacres were the causes of the publication of the article; but since it was decided that he was the legally elected President, no paper had been as conservative as the *Bee*. Mr. Cleveland said that his life was in danger when the article appeared; he condemned it and called upon all other citizens to do likewise. Nearly every paper in the country had something to say. The Democratic papers were loud in their condemnation of Mr. Chase, and in all directions of the city, groups of persons could be seen discussing "Chase and the President."

Many Republicans who knew that what Chase said was true, were among those who condemned him. At the request of the President, Mr. Chase sent him different copies of his paper, and it was thought that this would tend to appease him, as Mr. Chase had supported him after his inaugural address, which contained some kind words in behalf of the Negro. On the twenty-fifth of April, about ten days after Mr. Chase had called on the President, he received his discharge from the War Department, by order of the President and W. C. Endicott, secretary of war. Long before the ascendency of the Democratic party, attempts had been made to have Mr. Chase discharged. These charges had no effect with Secretary Lincoln as Senator Bruce frustrated them. Mr. Chase was elected one of the vice-presidents of the Louisville convention, and was first to nominate Rev. W. J. Simmons, president of the National Press convention, to which he was elected, and was himself elected historian of said association, August 4, 1886. General Logan said that "Mr. Chase was one of the brightest young men he knew, and one who will succeed."

Mr. Chase has been indicted for libel five times and convicted once, the fine being fifty dollars. He was married January 28, 1886, to Miss Arabella V. McCabe, a very accomplished lady in music and literature. His wedding was one of the grandest that ever took place in Washington. Presents were received from all parts of the country. He is now editor of the Washington *Bee*, which is flourishing. His office is fitted up in style, all the material of which is his own. Although the fights between Messrs. Chase and Douglass were bitter, they subsequently became friends, and for three successive years Mr. Douglass was elected Emancipation orator through the influence of Mr. Chase. He had become so popular that a young lady, Miss Susie Brown, named her school for him. On account of his great height and massive form, he is often called a "long, narrow, slender slice of night." This name was given him by the *Sunday Capital*. In the press convention of 1880, held in Washington, he was the only editor North who read a paper favoring separate schools; when he had finished, his address was endorsed by the entire Southern press, without one exception.

His report at the Press convention, on Southern outrages, was highly commended by the *Philadelphia Press*. Mr. Chase is a determined man and has an undaunted disposition, and will never give up as long as there is a fighting chance. He delights to have a broil on hand, and seems never happier than when he hears the shouts of battle and the clash of arms. The *Bee* was foremost in the fight concerning the Matthews-Recorder-of-Deeds-muddle. Mr. Chase made a gallant fight, which, while it did not secure the nomination of Mr. Matthews, whipped the Senatorial children soundly and compelled them to confirm Mr. Trotter. They did not dare furnish the occasion for another battle. They dared not go home with the *Bee* behind them. They had felt its sting already and did not care to continue to need it further. A full statement of the case will be found under the name of Mr. J. C. Matthews. Truly did he furnish "stings for the enemies" of the race.

CHAPTER VIII

Rev. James W. Hood
Bishop of the A. M. E. Zion Church—Church Organizer
and Builder—Assistant Superintendent of Public Instruction—
His Many Contests For Civil Rights on Steamboats and Cars

One of the most influential men in this country is Bishop Hood. His labors have been crowned with abundant success, and his acknowledged ability marks him as a special favorite. He has a large amount of what is called character. He is the son of a preacher, and his life shows that all "preachers' sons" are not bad. The names of his parents deserve to be mentioned. The family constituted one of the thirteen families who founded the separate Methodist church in Wilmington, Delaware. He was born in Kennett township, Chester county, Pennsylvania, May 30, 1831. At the age of twenty-five, being converted, he felt a call to preach the gospel. In 1859 he was received on trial in the New England conference of the A. M. E. Zion church. In 1860 he was ordained deacon and sent to Nova Scotia missions. The year 1863 found him stationed at Bridgeport, Connecticut. This same year he was sent to North Carolina, where he now lives "as the first of his race appointed as a regular missionary to the Freedmen in the South."

He has founded in North Carolina, South Carolina and Virginia over six hundred churches, and erected under his supervision about five hundred church buildings. He was elected bishop of the General Conference which held its session in North Carolina, in 1872. He was elected a member of the Ecumenical Conference, in London, in 1881. He has published a volume of sermons, to which Rev. Atticus G. Haygood, agent of the Slater fund, has written a complimentary introduction in which he says:

These sermons speak for themselves; their naturalness, their clearness, their force and their general soundness of doctrine and wholesomeness of sentiment, commend them to sensible and pious people. I have found them as useful as interesting. Those who still question whether the Negro in this country is capable of education and refinement, will modify their opinion when they read these sermons, or else they will conclude that their author is a very striking exception to what they assume is a general rule. Bishop Hood entertains many broad and important views as to the wants, duties and future of his people. He believes that their best interests are to be conserved in preserving the race from admixture with other bloods. They should, he thinks, hang together, and he is persuaded that if his people are to succeed permanently and broadly in this country, they must largely work out their own salvation.

He has twenty-one very able and comprehensive sermons in the book, well worth the reading. Besides peculiarly striking sermons by Bishops S. J. Jones, J. J. Moore, J. P. Thompson, Thomas H. Lomax, some of the themes treated in Bishop Hood's book, are "The Claims of the Gospel Message;" "Personal Consecration;" "Divine Sonship;" "The Sequence of Wondrous Love;" "Why was the Rich Man in Torment?" "The Streams which Gladden God's City;" "The Glory Revealed in the Christian Character;" "David's Root and Offspring, or Venus in the Apocalypse."

Bishop Hood went to North Carolina in January, 1864. At Newbern, during that year, in the absence of the chaplain, he preached to the colored troops and was often called "chaplain," but he never held the commission as such. He went there as missionary, under General Butler's invitation to the churches to send missionaries into his department. Newbern was twice attacked after he went there, so that he understands what it is to be under Confederate fire. Among the "first" conventions, if not the first of them all, of colored men in the South, was the one in October, 1865, in Raleigh. In this meeting he was elected president as the "dark horse." Three other candidates had packed delegations as it appears, and thus defeated each other. The opening speech in that convention was the subject of much comment from the press, some not very complimentary to the speaker. He was reminded "that hemp grew in that part of the State." It was the first time that a black man had so publicly stated that the Negro was among those who came from one blood, and among those whom the Declaration of Independence included as endowed with inalienable rights, liberty and the pursuit of happiness; a right to the jury-box, cartridge box, and ballot box, were among the demands which he said the colored people would contend for, and that with the help of God. He was reminded in some of the bitter papers at the time that he would get all these in one box. In 1868 he demanded and obtained cabin passage on the Cape Fear steamers. The agents told him that nothing but the fact that the city was under military authority caused the company to yield to his demand. He advised the bishop not to attempt to take advantage of this, as it would be the worse for him when the military was withdrawn. The answer was characteristic of the man. He said he would enjoy it while he could, and trust the Lord for the balance. His right, however, has never been questioned on that river since. This proves what we have often said, that, if colored men would demand what belongs to them they could very many times get it, but because of their indifference and littleness of soul, they are often shoved into places wher it is a disgrace to go. He also broke the ice on the railroads in that early day, and in this respect stood foremost in the Southern States. To go a little back, he says:

I have been contending for my rights in public conveyances from boyhood. Time and again, between '48 and '63 did conductors try to put me out of the first class cars on the Pennsylvania railroad, but they never did it. Once I think they would have done it, but a Quaker lady called on the passengers to interfere in my behalf. I was carried out of the street cars five times in one night in 1857, and, after all, rode from the corner of Church and Leonard streets up to 28th street in time to preach, but of course I was a little late. I could give many instances in which I had to contend, but generally made my trip in the car. A thirty-eight years' fight with railroad conductors seems like a long contest, from which I have come forth without a scar.

Bishop Hood has always been a traveler, more or less, and has traveled 15,000 miles a year. It is doubtful whether any man living has had so many railroad contests. He is getting tired and worn out, and avoids the far South as much as possible on this account, but nevertheless he has opened the way and smoothed the path in these years for others, and has opened up to the traveling public better accommodations. In 1867 he was elected as a delegate to the Constitutional Convention of the State of North Carolina, and took such a prominent part that the Democrats called the constitution adopted "Hood's Constitution" until they amended it slightly about 1875.

In this convention he made a speech which was full of sarcasm and ridicule of his opponent, a gentleman who had opposed some measure in which he was interested. He says:

After all I am compelled to acknowledge that I feel myself to be under some obligation to the secessionists. I am compelled to acknowledge that to their folly, in a great measure, we owe our present enfranchisement. The gentleman from Orange remarked last night that his race has always occupied a position more elevated than the rest of mankind. I am astonished at that young man that he has no more regard for his reputation as a historian than to assert such a ridiculous fallacy in the hearing of intelligent gentlemen in the noonday splendor of the nineteenth century. Does he not know that his ancestors, the ancient Britons, were in bondage in ancient Rome, in the days of Julius Caesar, and ever since that day? Mr. Chairman, the worst that has ever been said of my people was that they were too ignorant to be anything but slaves; but of the Britons it was said that they were too ignorant even to be slaves. A friend of Julius Caesar, writing to him, urged him not to bring slaves from Britain, for they were so ignorant that they could not be taught music. Now I have never heard it said of colored people that they were too ignorant to sing. I admit that this is not very flattering to the ancestors of the gentleman from Cleveland and Orange. Ancestry is something that they should not go back into, except with their mouths in the dust; but I don't blame them for this. It is somehing they cannot help. I am sorry for them, but I don't blame them for springing from such a low origin. I only think hard of them for making mouths at me.

This speech was considered so valuable that it was used as a campaign document. It is full of such passages, and the comment of the press was very favorable, though the information was easily gained by any one who would take the pains to read, yet it was considered wonderful because a colored man showed such an acquaintance with the history of his race and turned with such grace and dignity and delivered such a clever shot into the ranks of his opponents.

The homestead and public schools in this convention claimed his especial attention, and he was allowed to have his own way pretty much in regard to these measures. He believed that a good homestead law would secure the ratification of the constitution, and he was not mistaken. It proved to be a very popular measure, and he used it for all it was worth in canvassing. The school law was free from any hint of condition on account of color. He canvassed at the time fourteen counties and carried them all for this constitution, although all but two were regarded as doubtful. He was associated with others, of course, in this canvass, but he enjoyed the lion's share of attention. Returning home from a meeting during the Presidential campaign in 1868, he received a commission as agent of the State Board of Education and assistant superintendent of public instruction. This appointment was made without solicitation from himself and friends and without his knowledge. The State Board of Education was composed of the governor and other State officers, and created the office and made the appointment, and the first information he had of it was the receipt of the commission, and an accompanying letter asking him to indicate at what time he could enter upon the duties of the office. His salary was fixed at $1,500 a year. He filled this position for three years, having his headquarters at Raleigh, and at the same time, with the assistance of a subordinate preacher, built up a strong church at Charlotte, North Carolina, out of which four others have been formed. He would leave Raleigh Saturday afternoon and go to Charlotte, one hundred and seventy-five miles away, preach three times a day and be back to Raleigh Monday morning. Sometimes he would not have his boots off from Saturday morning until Monday night. He generally filled the pulpit three Sabbaths in the month. One Sabbath in the month he would remain at Raleigh and divide the time among Methodist and Baptist congregations. There was no church of his branch of Methodists in Raleigh at that time, and he thought it was not fair to use the power of his office to establish one. During the time he was in office, he visited the greater portion of the State, lecturing and organizing schools. He received, unsolicited, a commission from General O. O. Howard, as assistant superintendent under the Freedmen's Bureau, without pay, except that he was allowed three dollars a day, when traveling in the interest of the Bureau, to cover expenses. In 1870 he had forty-nine thousand colored children in the schools, and had a colored department established for the deaf, dumb and blind, and about sixty of those unfortunates, under care and instruction, gathered from all parts of the State. Sometimes he had hard work to get parents to send their children. One blind boy, that he had to go for several times and who would hide when he heard that the bishop was in town, is now making his living traveling as Professor Simmons, the blind organist. The department formed at that early day has now a brick building worth $20,000, heated by steam and has every necessary convenience. It is the best institution for deaf mutes and blind of the colored people in this country, and yet there is only about the same number in the institution that he left when he gave up the office, while the statistics show about eight hundred in the State. He was about to establish a State University when the Democrats got control of the Legislature and legislated him out of office.

The only office he held under the State and National government was magistrate under a provisional government, and deputy collector for a few months. The latter position he resigned. He was the choice of the colored delegates for Secretary of State at the Republican State convention in 1872, as unanimously declared by the caucus, and declining it he was allowed to name a man who was nominated and elected. This gentleman promised to appoint a colored man as chief clerk and he did so. He never desired a purely secular office and did not regard his educational position in that light. He was made temporary chairman of the Republican State convention in 1876, and gave such satisfaction that the gentleman who was selected for permanent chairman wanted to decline in his favor. He was a delegate for the State-at-large to the National convention in 1872, which nominated Grant for his second term. He was Grand Master of the Masons in his State for fourteen years, and has twice declined unanimous election since. He was elected and re-elected Most Eminent Grand Patron of the Order of the Eastern Star, until he quit attending the annual meetings. Besides he held very many minor offices. He has ben High Priest, D. S. H. P. and D., inspector of the Thirty-third degree. At the great Centennial gathering of all branches of the Methodist church, black and white, held in Baltimore, 1885, he was elected to preside the first day. This body was presided over by one State governor, and one lieutenant-governor and a number of bishops in turn. He was elected to preside, but as he was not present, they sent a telegram for him, but he could not reach there in time. He was informed that an effort was made to get another colored man appointed, but a white bishop was finally selected. Notwithstanding his absence, when called for, another appointment was made for him, which he filled. Early in the day a couple of smart black men gave him an opportunity to show what he knew about parliamentary usage. His rulings were cheered and for the balance of the session both white and black tried to keep within the rules, and only made points of order when somebody was out of order.

He has been married three times. First, in his twenty-second year, he married Miss Hannah L. Ralph of Lancaster City, Pennsylvania, who died of consumption in 1855. In his twenty-seventh year he married Miss Sophia J. Nugent of Washington City. By that marriage he had seven children, four of whom are living, aged respectively fourteen, sixteen, eighteen and twenty. Three younger ones are at Zion Wesley College. His last marriage was celebrated in June, 1877, to Mrs. K. P. McKoy of Wilmington, North Carolina. By this marriage he had three children, two living, one five and one seven, and the youngest one dead. The bishop is a very liberal man, and in the building of the many churches over which he has had the oversight in the last twenty years, he has given over one hundred dollars to a single church and says he has no idea of the number of churches to which he has given the sum of twenty-five dollars and upwards. The bishop is a strict temperance man. From boyhood he has been an opponent of the liquor traffic, and has ever been ready to oppose intemperance and slavery. He says: "I have been called crazy on the subject of tobacco and whiskey. I have been able in some of the conferences over which I have presided to influence men who were not teetotalers to become such, and large numbers have discontinued the use of tobacco." Rev. Jacob Adams, leading minister of the New York conference, visited the Central North conference at its last session and said: "That for intelligence and sobriety, as well as in many other respects this conference was the banner conference of the church, as he knew that this was regarded especially as 'Bishop Hood's Conference.' It having been said that if he winked, the men in it would nod, it can be readily seen that he was paying a high compliment to said conference;

and that being a leading member of the oldest conference, he knew some of its history, and it was indeed a compliment that he should declare in open conference the superiority of this recently built up Southern work." The Bishop has been connected with many temperance societies, the most noted of these is the Good Templars, in a lodge of which he accepted a position of outside guard to encourage others to accept minor places. He was at the same time holding the position of Grand Worthy Chief Templar of the State, and Right Worthy Grand Chaplain of the Grand Lodge of the world. While in England he delivered many temperance speeches and received many notices of value from the temperance press. He has taken part in every temperance contest in the State of North Carolina.

Bishop Hood is a big man, and has nerves of iron and back-bone of steel; and, it may be well added, a face of flint which he constantly sets against error and wrong. May he live many years to continue his arduous labors for the bettering of his race.

CHAPTER IX

Hon. Samuel R. Lowery
Silk Culturist—Lawyer and Editor

No man in our broad country has exhibited more perseverance and pluck than this patient toiler. On December 9, 1886, he was fifty-six years old. A hard worker and earnest investigator and a courteous gentleman, he excites my admiration and challenges my good judgment, even when I think he has suffered enough privation and sacrifice to make him abandon his project. Nashville, Tennessee, has no other man exhibiting such a large amount of that self-sacrificing spirit as shown by Mr. Lowery. His mother was a free woman, a Cherokee Indian, and his father a slave, living twelve miles from the said city, and was purchased by his wife; God bless the woman. The old gentleman still lives in Nashville, aged seventy-six. Mr. Lowery lost his mother when only eight years old. The young man tried to get learning by working at Franklin College and studying privately under the Rev. Talbot Fanning, a famous Christian preacher, and who is of blessed memory now to Mr. Lowery. At the age of sixteen, our subject taught a school for the first time and had wonderful success for four years. In 1849 he united with the church of the Disciples and began preaching and continued till 1857. One year after this he pastored the Harrison Street church of that faith in Cincinnati, Ohio. He married in 1858, and becoming displeased with the country, went to Canada where he remained for three years, when he returned to this country, settling on a farm which was given him by his father in Fayette county, Ohio, near West Lancaster. In 1863, when Abraham Lincoln's Emancipation Proclamation was issued, he went to Nashville, preaching to the freedmen and colored soldiers, commanded by Colonel R. K. Crawford, of the Fortieth United States Colored troops. Not getting his commission as chaplain, he was transferred to the Ninth United States heavy artillery as chaplain, appointed by the officers, where he remained until the close of the war. Then he moved his family from Ohio to Tennessee, where he began preaching and teaching school. He commenced about this time the study of law in Rutherford county, Tennessee.

SAMUEL R. LOWERY

Political excitement was running very high at that time, and his school was broken up by the Ku Klux, and his affairs much disturbed. Being admitted to the bar he began the practice of law in Nashville, Tennessee. In 1875 he moved to Huntsville, Alabama, and continued practicing law and preaching. He also practices before the United States Supreme Court, having been admitted on the motion of Belva V. Lockwood. His daughter Ruth, then a girl fifteen years of age, living in Nashville, visited with her father and sister, Annie L. Lowery, ten years of age, an exhibition, of silkworms, given by one Mr. Theobald, and she persuaded her father to purchase her some silk-worm eggs, which he did. She hatched them in Huntsville, Alabama, and by the aid of the leaves of the white mulberry tree, succeeded in starting the enterprise in which Mr. Lowery is now engaged. After her death, which occurred in 1877, her father took up the enterprise. He now became disgusted with politics and began to devote his whole time to the silk-worm culture. He visited Paterson, New Jersey, and there met John Kyle, the pioneer silk manufacturer in the United States, who encouraged him to plant trees and raise the silk cocoons. He also visited South Manchester, Connecticut, and met Mr. Frank Cheney, the largest silk manufacturer in the United States, who also encouraged him, giving him ten years to succeed in the enterprise. Returning home, he imported some white mulberry seed from France, from which he has a fine nursery of mulberry trees in Huntsville, Alabama. The seedlings grown from this seed have produced the largest leaves of the kind in the world, and received the highest prize at the World's Exposition at New Orleans. Mr. Lowery has received but little encouragement from the people of Huntsville, Alabama, but there are a few noble exceptions to this rule. Our government paid a Frenchman a thousand dollars for making his exhibition, while Mr. Lowery, poor and unaided, made his display, and triumphed without aid from any source whatever. We give below an extract from the Birmingham (Alabama) *Manufacturer and Tradesman*. As the facts are known by me to be true, they only add additional weight to my own statements:

Mr. Lowery has visited, the last two seasons, at the Southern Exposition in Louisville, and received the first medal over several competitors from other nations. At new Orleans he took a premium over eighteen competitors from China, France, Japan, Italy, Mexico and other exhibitors in the United States, and was the only successful propagator, raising over 100,000 worms and cacoons on the grounds, while his competitors were unable to raise one. He has had forty acres of land given him near the city of Birmingham to go into the silk culture on a large scale, and has formed a company composed of the following leading citizens:

William Burney, Dr. H. M. Caldwell, W. A. Handley, C. C. Brenemen and himself, directors; with W. A. Handley, as president; C. C. Brenemen, secretary; William Burney, treasurer, and himself superintendent. He is an intelligent, conservative man, steadily refusing to mix up in any way with the disturbing element of his race. He is a lawyer by profession, and also publishes the *Southern Freeman*, and he constantly devotes his time to the advancement of the colored people of the South, and is very well respected by the people of that city and at his own home in Huntsville. His past experiments in the silk worm culture, with the strong backing he now has, assures success in the present enterprise. He owns shares of stock in the undertaking. Birmingham will be known well as a silk manufacturing center.

Mr. Lowery has an idea that the culture of the silk worm will take the place of cotton, and give to the women and children a refining and remunerative employment, which only takes six weeks in a year, and at the same time gives two- and three-fold more pay than they could earn all the year in their present employment.

I have never failed to have him address the students of the institution over which I have the honor to preside, and his enthusiasm has made a profound impression on his hearers; his genial manners, fund of information, knowledge of men and places, make him a welcome visitor and agreeable talker. He is yet destined to rank as a great benefactor to his race. He has had the faith of Columbus and the perseverance of Barnard Pallissey. Although famous, yet he has nothing. In conversation with me he said: "My read sir, I am very poor. I have not yet struck a bonanza, but I still hope for a competency yet ahead. Hope is a large faculty in my organization. I have tried to abandon it and become indifferent to its inviting fields. When I do, I am really not myself; yet I know I do not hope vainly or recklessly." Let us pray that he will yet realize his hopes, and that his cherished plans may be the means of furnishing to the race the sure road to wealth and refinement. When success shall fully crown his labors, may the trademark of the firm be his daughter Ruth's picture, as an honor to the humble girl, who died and did not live to see the success of her plans. She is worthy of this distinction.

CHAPTER X

Willam Still
Philanthropist—Coal Dealer, and Twenty Years Owner
of the Largest Public Hall Owned by a Colored Man

This distinguished gentleman, who made himself prominent during the dark days of slavery, by helping escaped fugitives at the peril of his own life, was born October 7, 1821, in Shamong, County of Burlington, New Jersey. He was the youngest of eighteen children of Levin and Charity Still. Mr. Still worked at farming and wood chopping until he was twenty-three years old, at which time he left New Jersey, the home of his birth, to stem the current of life alone. He had no education except what he had acquired when the weather prevented his working out of doors, and what he could pick up here and there from observation, conversation and other odd means.

Being a stranger, he was thrown wholly on his own resources, as he entered the city of Philadelphia with less than five dollars in his pocket. This was in 1844. While quite a boy he had pledged with himself never to touch intoxicating liquors, which pledge he ever kept; and it was, no doubt, the corner stone of his prosperity, and the means by which he has made a man of himself, thereby set an example for many of those fast young men who hope to succeed in life, and yet indulge in intoxicating drinks and riotous living.

He professed Christ many years after. In 1847 he obtained a clerkship in the office of the Pennsylvania Anti-slavery society, and occupied this position for fourteen years. He had seen so much of the cruelties of slavery that his heart was full of sympathy for the oppressed, and he determined to spend his time and his life in securing liberty for all over whom his influence might be exerted. His house was known as a safe and convenient refuge for all who were making their way to a land of liberty. Two of his brothers were left in bondage by the flight of their mother, and were lost to their parents for forty years. This seemed to have deepened his interest in the slaves, and yearly hundreds of escaped bondsmen found in him a friend. He was chairman and corresponding

WILLIAM STILL

secretary of the Philadelphia branch of the "Underground Railroad" for the last decade of slavery. He wrote out hundreds of narratives from the lips of fleeing fugitives and kept them secreted in the loft of the Lebanon Seminary till emancipation, when privacy was no longer a necessity. These same narrations make up his famous book, which bears the name of the corporation for which he labored. He, alone, of all the thousands who aided the fugitives, succeeded in preserving anything like a full account of the workings of the "Underground Railroad," as it was called, before emancipation.

His book, *The Underground Railroad*, which is well known by all readers, was published in 1873. This volume of eight hundred and fifty pages, was highly commended by the leading men of the nation and reviewers of the country. It had a large sale and will continue to sell for many years to come. It is a valuable book, and every colored man ought to have it in his library. We cannot do better than frequently recur to its pages for the purpose of measuring our present greatness by looking back on the path through which we have come, filled with thorns and precipices. It might not be out of place here to give one of the narratives which he has recorded in his book. It will show the character of the work, and revive in some measure the memories of those days of bitter persecutions and trials. The narration which is here selected is that of prominent personages whose history is largely familiar to the older people, and cannot fail to be interesting to the younger ones.

A quarter of a century ago, William and Ellen Craft were slaves in the State of Georgia. With them, as with thousands of others, the desire to be free was very strong. For this jewel they were willing to make any sacrifice, or to endure any amount of suffering. In this state of mind they commenced planning. After thinking of various ways that might be tried, it occurred to William and Ellen that one might act the part of master and the other the part of servant.

Ellen being fair enough to pass for white, of necessity would have to be transformed into a young planter for the time being. All that was needed, however, to make this important change was that she should be dressed elegantly in a fashionable suit of male attire, and have her hair cut in the style usually worn by young planters. Her profusion of dark hair offered a fine opportunity for the change. So far this plan looked very tempting. But it occurred to them that Ellen was beardless. After some mature reflection, they came to the conclusion that this difficulty could be very readily obviated by having the face muffled up as though the young planter was suffering badly with the toothache; thus they got rid of this trouble. Straightway, upon further reflection, several other very serious difficulties stared them in the face. For instance, in traveling, they knew they would be under the necessity of stopping repeatedly at hotels, and that the custom of registering would have to be conformed to, unless some very good excuse could be given for not doing so.

Here they again thought much over the matter, and wisely concluded that the young man had better assume the attitude of a gentleman very much indisposed. He must have his right arm placed very carefully in a sling; that would be a sufficient excuse for not registering, etc. Then he must be a little lame, with a nice cane in his left hand; he must have large green spectacles over his eyes, and withal he must be very hard of hearing and dependent on his faithful servant (as was no uncommon thing with slaveholders) to look after all his wants.

William was just the man to act this part. To begin with, he was very "likely looking," smart, active and exceedingly attentive to his young master—indeed, he was almost eyes, ears, hands and feet for him. William knew that this would please the slaveholders. The young planter would have nothing to do but hold himself subject to his ailments and put on a bold air of superiority. He was not to deign to notice anybody. If, while traveling, gentlemen, either politely or rudely, should venture to scrape acquaintance with the young planter, in his deafness he was to remain mute; his servant was to explain. In every instance when this occurred, as it actually did, the servant was fully equal to the emergency—none dreaming of the disguises in which the underground railroad passengers were traveling.

They stopped at a first-class hotel in Charleston, where the young planter and his body-servant were treated as the house was wont to treat chivalry. They stopped also at a similar hotel in Richmond, and with like results.

They knew that they must pass through Baltimore, but they did not know the obstacles that they would have to surmount in the "Monumental City." They proceeded to the depot in the usual manner, and the servant asked for tickets for his master and self. Of course the master could have a ticket, but "bonds will have to be entered before you can get a ticket," said the ticket master. "It is the rule of this office to require bonds for all negroes applying for tickets to go North, and none but gentlemen of well known responsibility will be taken," further explained the ticket master.

The servant replied that he knew "nothing about that"—that he was "simply traveling with his young master to take care of him, he being in a very delicate state of health, so much so that fears were entertained that he might not be able to hold out to reach Philadelphia, where he was hastening for medical treatment;" and ended his reply by saying, "My master can't be detained." Without further parley the ticket master very obligingly waived the old "rule" and furnished the requisite tickets. The mountain being thus removed, the young planter and his faithful servant were safely in the cars for the city of Brotherly Love.

Scarcely had they arrived on free soil when the rheumatism departed, the right hand was unslung, the toothache was gone, the beardless face was unmuffled, the deaf heard and spoke, the blind and the lame leaped as a hart, and in the presence of the few astonished friends of the slaves, the facts of this unparalleled underground railroad feat were fully established by the most unquestionable evidence.

The constant strain and pressure on Ellen's nerves, however, had tried her severely, so much so, that for days afterwards she was principally very much prostrated, although joy and gladness beamed from her eyes, which bespoke inexpressible delight within.

Never can the writer forget the impression made by their arrival. Even now, after a lapse of nearly a quarter of a century, it is easy to picture them in a private room, surrounded by a few friends—Ellen in her fine suit of black, with her cloak and high heeled boots, looking, in every respect, like a young gentleman; in an hour after having dropped her male attire and assumed the habiliments of her sex, the feminine was only visible in every line and feature of her structure.

' Her husband, William, was thoroughly colored, but was a man of marked natural abilities, of good manners, and full of pluck, and possessed of perceptive faculties very large.

It was necessary, however, in those days, that they should seek a permanent residence, where their freedom would be more secure than in Philadelphia; therefore they were advised to go to headquarters, directly to Boston. There they would be safe, it was supposed, as it had then been about a generation since a fugitive had been taken back from the old Bay State, and through the incessant labors of William Lloyd Garrison, the great pioneer, and his faithful coadjutors, it was conceded that another fugitive slave case would never be tolerated on the free soil of Massachusetts. So they went to Boston.

On arriving, the warm hearts of Abolitionists welcomed them heartily, and greeted and cheered them without let or hindrance. They did not pretend to keep their coming a secret or hide it under a bushel; the story of their escape was heralded broadcast over the country—North and South, and indeed over the civilized world. For two years or more not the slightest fear was entertained that they were not just as safe in Boston as if they had gone to Canada. But the day the Fugitive Bill passed, even the bravest Abolitionist began to fear that a fugitive slave was no longer safe anywhere under the stars and stripes, North or South, and that William and Ellen Craft were liable to be captured at any moment by Georgia slave hunters. Many Abolitionists counseled resistance to the death at all hazards. Instead of running to Canada, fugitives generally armed themselves and thus said: "Give me liberty or give me death."

William and Ellen Craft believed that it was their duty as citizens of Massachusetts to observe a more legal and civilized mode of conforming to the marriage rite than had been permitted them in slavery, and as Theodore Parker had shown himself a very warm friend of theirs, they agreed to have their wedding over again according to the laws of a free State. After performing the ceremony, the renowned and fearless advocate of equal rights (Theodore Parker), presented William with a revolver and dirk knife, counseling him to use them manfully in the defense of his wife and himself, if ever an attempt should be made by his owners, or anybody else, to re-enslave them.

But, notwithstanding all the published declarations made by the Abolitionists and fugitives, to the effect that slaveholders and slave-catchers in visiting Massachusetts in pursuit of their runaway property would be met by just such weapons as Theodore Parker presented William with, to the surprise of all Boston, the owners of William and Ellen actually had the effrontery to attempt their recapture under the Fugitive Slave laws.

His reasons for writing this book are given in the preface of the edition of 1886, and I cannot but give his own words as his apology for placing such a book before the reading people. There are many of our people who are so foolish as to desire to rub out all the traces of our past history, and would do away with all emancipation celebrations and everything that reminds us of a past, which though painful and full of bitterness, cannot yet but be remembered with praise to God that he has permitted us to pass through these trials and come out more than conqueror. He very happily refers to the fact in this preface that the bondage and deliverance of the children of Israel will never be allowed to sink into oblivion. The world stands, and the Jews do not hang their heads in shame because of their bondage, but tell it with some pride, that God, though they were in bondage, did not forget them, but finally brought them forth and made a people of them. Quotations are here given because it is in the line of instruction that is badly needed and which should be heeded by our people, and he does well to send these thoughts through the country in each of his books, that they might influence at least the readers of that section in which he says:

Well conducted shops, stores, lands acquired, good farms managed in a manner to compete with any other, valuable books produced and published on interesting subjects—these are some of the fruits which the race are expected to exhibit from their newly gained privileges.

This gains our highest approval. It is the very thing for our people to consider. But let me without further elaboration give a passage in this preface, which one, in the reading, will find full of truth and instruction.

And in looking back now over these strange and eventful providences, in the light of the wonderful changes wrought by emancipation, I am more and more constrained to believe that the reasons which years ago led me to aid the bondmen and preserve the record of his sufferings, are today quite as potent in convincing me that the necessity of the times requires the testimony. And since the first advent of my book, wherever reviewed or read by leading friends of freedom, the press, or the race more deeply represented by it, the expressions of approval and encouragement have been hearty and unanimous, and the thousands of volumes which have been sold by me on the subscription plan, with hardly any facilities for the work, makes it obvious that it would, in the hands of a competent publisher, have a wide circulation.

And here I may frankly state that but for the hope I have always cherished, that this work would encourage the race in efforts for self-elevation, its publication would never have been undertaken by me.

The race must not forget the rock from whence they were hewn, nor the pit from whence they were digged.

Like other races, this newly emancipated people will need all the knowledge of their past condition which they can get.

These scenes of suffering and martyrdom, millions of Christians were called upon to pass through in the days of the Inquisition, are still subjects of study and have unabated interest for all enlightened minds.

The same is true of the history of this country. The struggles of the pioneer fathers are preserved, produced and reproduced, and cherished with undying interest by all Americans, and the day will not arrive while the Republic exists when these histories will not be found in every library.

While the grand little army of Abolitionists was waging its untiring warfare for freedom prior to the rebellion, no agency encouraged them like the heroism of the fugitives. The pulse of the four million of slaves and their desire for freedom was better felt through "The Underground Railroad" than through any other channel.

Frederick Douglass, Henry Bibb, William Wells Brown, Rev. J. W. Logan and others, gave unmistakable evidence that the race had no more eloquent advocates than its own self-emancipated champions.

Every step they took to rid themselves of their fetters, or to gain education, or in pleading the cause of their fellow-bondsmen in the lecture room, or with their pens, met with applause on every hand, and the very argument needed was thus furnished in a large measure. In those dark days previous to emancipation, such testimony was indispensable.

The free colored men are as imperatively required now to furnish the same manly testimony in the support of the ability of the race to surmount the remaining obstacles growing out of oppression, ignorance and poverty.

The angels have recorded the deeds of this noble-hearted man, and God will reward him. It is impossible to do justice to those men and women who held their lives as nothing when the cries of the slaves reached their ears. There was never greater heroism than that shown by William Still. Think, reader, of the pain his heart has undergone. Think of the moments of intense agony he bore. Think of a life of care, suffering and prayer; then tell me we are destitute of the finest feelings held by any other race.

They said we were not men, but if not men then we have been angels.

For indeed the history of our sufferings and the manner in which we have borne them without revolution and bloodshed, without falling to the depths of infidelity, but still holding to a trust in God, mark our career as more than marvelous.

Is it not a wonder that in all these dark shadows we did not lose our faith in God and cry out, "There is no God"? Is it not a wonder that in all these years there was not stamped out of us every feeling of mercy, generosity and manhood?

What could have been expected of a race that was deep in the well of ignorance, hidden from the light of day? What could have been expected of us and our children, except that we would be brutalized and destitute of all the finer feelings of our nature.

It does seem as if we were made of finer material than others, that even so many good men, philanthropists, strong Christian men, preachers and faithful workers in every missionary department of life, could have been gotten out of this race so cruelly treated, so badly despised. Here is an example in the life of Mr. Still worthy of record. In the 'Book of Ages' how many look back and thank him for succor, for comfort, for food, for clothing, for money, and for liberty? This is a wonderful record. The deeds which were done in his office, the acts of charity, would almost form, as it would seem, a special volume among the records of Heaven.

O God! We thank Thee for such a man as William Still. Men who, like their Master, went about doing good. Men who fulfilled the teachings of the Scriptures and who shall be on the right hand and hear these words: "Come, ye blessed of my Father, inherit the kingdom prepared for you from the foundation of the world. For I was an hungred, and ye gave me meat: I was thirsty and ye gave me drink: I was a stranger and ye took me in: naked and ye clothed me: I was sick and ye visited me: I was in prison and ye came unto me. Then shall the righteous answer him saying, Lord when saw we Thee an hungred and fed Thee? or thirsty and gave Thee drink? when saw we Thee a stranger and took Thee in? or naked and clothed Thee? or when saw we Thee sick or in prison and came unto Thee? And the King shall answer and say unto them: Verily I say unto you, inasmuch as ye have done it unto one of the least of these, my brethren, ye have done it unto me."

Mr. Still's name should be in the mouths of all lovers of philanthropic deeds, and his name is fittingly placed here that he might be known by the rising generation. His work is no less eminent than those who were partners in the labor of love, and yet extreme danger, namely, Abagail Goodwin, Thomas Garrett, Daniel Gibbons, Lucretia Mott, J. Miller McKim, H. Furness, William Lloyd Garrison, Lewis Tappan, William Wright, Elijah F. Pennypacker, Dr. Bartholomew Fussell; Robert Purvis,

John Hunn, Samuel Rhoades, William Whipper, Samuel D. Burris, Charles D. Cleveland, Grace Anne Lewis, Frances Ellen W. Harper and John Needles.

In 1859, when old John Brown with one bold dash opened fire for freedom at Harper's Ferry, Virginia, several of his officers who were with him in the hottest battle at the Ferry, escaped with heavy rewards hanging over their heads, and sought shelter under the roof of William Still, who kindly received them. He also comforted and ministered unto the wife, daughter and sons of Brown who had come, utter strangers, to Philadelphia while the old hero was in prison waiting his execution. All this was cheerfully done while conscious of the fact that his deeds of charity were imperiling his own life. In 1850 he recognized one of his brothers who had been separated by slavery from his mother, when a child of only six years. In 1860 he left the Anti-slavery office with the most hearty sympathy and confidence of his Anti-slavery friends and at once turned his attention to business of his own. Having some knowledge of the stove business, he opened a new and second hand stove store. In less than three years he was well established and quite successful. In the meantime, the civil war broke out and the curse of slavery ended unexpectedly. The secretary of war furnished him with a post sutler's commission at Camp William Penn, at which point colored soldiers were stationed for Pennsylvania. In 1865 he purchased a large lot, built an office and entered the coal business, and for over twenty years he has successfully conducted this branch of business, amassing quite a fortune. He is the owner of Liberty Hall, the largest public hall in the country owned by a colored man; and to the credit of the race, be it said, that it is well patronized.

He still keeps up his philanthropic work; always ready to help the needy and to contribute of the world's goods which God has given him in order that others might have their suffering lessened. He was a member of the Freedmen's Aid Union and Commission, organized at the close of the war by the leading philanthropists of the country to prosecute educational work and aid the newly emancipated generally.

For many years he has been vice-president and chairman of the board of managers of the "Home for the Aged and Infirm Colored Persons" in Philadelphia; also for many years he has served as a member on the board of trustees for the "Soldiers and Sailors Orphan Home" and "Home for the Destitute Colored Children." His interest in the educational work has been so manifest that he has been selected, and has served for many years, as member of the board of trustees of Storer College. He has served as an elder of the Presbyterian church, which position he has held for quite a while, and was sent by the Presbytery of Philadelphia as commissioner to the General Assembly at Cincinnati, Ohio, which convened in 1885. He was one of the original stockholders to the amount of one thousand dollars in the stock company of the *Nation*, a member of the board of trade of the city of Philadelphia, and the corresponding secretary to the "Social and Civil Statistical Association" of Philadelphia. His literary labors have not been confined to the underground railroad. He has also published a pamphlet entitled *Voting and Laboring*, and another *The Struggles for the Rights of the Colored People* of Philadelphia. In 1884 the centennial and general conference of the M. E. church which convened in his city, honored him with a vote of thanks for entertaining the colored delegates from the South.

He still lives in Philadelphia, a quiet and honored citizen, an upright business man and a devoted friend of his race. May his last years be crowned with honor, and may he go down to his grave with the best wishes of the nation on account of the manner in which he has lived and served his God and his people.

CHAPTER XI

Professor J. W. Morris, A. B., A. M., LL. B.
President of Allen University, Columbia, South Carolina—
Professor of Languages

The subject of this sketch was born in Charleston, South Carolina, August 26, 1850. His parents were John B. Morris and Grace Morris. He was born of free parents and enjoyed early advantages for education. In early childhood he was sent to a private school taught by Simeon Beard, then a distinguished teacher in the city of Charleston. After the close of the late war he entered the public schools of his native city, passing through the various grades of the same, until he left the high school, to take a collegiate course at Howard University. While attending the public schools he was sent in the afternoons to learn the printing trade, which he completed under that celebrated scholar and printer, the late Hon. R. B. Elliott, who was at that time editor of the *Charleston Leader*. Afterwards this paper was merged into the *Missionary Record*, edited by the late Bishop R. H. Cain. He was elected principal of a parochial school, and while in this capacity he worked as a compositor on the *Missionary Record*, which was a weekly paper.

While a pupil of the Normal school of Charleston he was twice awarded a prize for proficiency in Latin by that eminent scholar and instructor, Professor F. L. Cardoza, now of Washington, District of Columbia. Young Morris evincing, in early life, so great a tact and aptitude for learning, was sent to Howard University, which institution he entered in the fall of 1868. After spending six years at the university, he graduated in June, 1875. While at the famous seat of learning he was regarded as an excellent student. At the Junior exhibition of 1874, he took the first prize awarded his class for oratory.

After graduation he returned to his home in Charleston, South Carolina. In the fall of 1875 he entered the law department of the South Carolina University, Columbia, South Carolina, under the tuition of that celebrated judge and jurist, Chief-Justice F. J. Moses. He graduated with distinction from this department, December, 1876. He applied for admission to the Supreme Court of his native State, and, after passing a most critical and searching examination, was admitted to practice in all the courts of the State. His first case was an interesting and prominent one; he won it. He was elected in 1876 one of the commissioners of public schools for the city of Charleston, but as this office would interfere with his law studies, he refused to accept the position. He also received in the county convention of Charleston, the nomination for the legislature, but, again for the same reasons, refused to accept.

After much persuasion and the earnest solicitation of personal friends, he was induced to abandon what promised to be to him a very lucrative practice, to accept the principalship of Payne Institute, the educational work of the A. M. E. church in the State. He served for four years as principal of this institution, until it was merged into Allen University, a demand being made for a more central location for the work. While principal of Payne Institute, he was a lay delegate to the Ecumenical Council, which met in London, England. While in Europe he visited Paris and Geneva, Switzerland.

He was now elected professor of mathematics and ancient languages, principal of Normal and Preparatory departments, also secretary and instructor of the law department of the Allen University, which positions he held until elected president—the position he now holds. The writer was impressed with the quiet unassuming manners of President Morris while in college at Howard University. His position is only the reward of faithful toil and well directed effort. He was always in earnest; he enjoys fun as well as any man, but his "Life is real; life is earnest." He is a fine student, a gifted writer and a man of high standing.

CHAPTER XII

Hon. Robert Smalls
Congressman—Pilot and Captain of the Steamer "Planter"

This daring and cool headed man was born in Beaufort, South Carolina, April 5, 1839; and being a slave was of course limited in the opportunities for gaining book knowledge; but some men can no more be bound than the waves of the ocean, and despite all opposition he learned to read and write. "Where there's a will there's a way." In 1851 he moved to Charleston, where he worked as a "rigger" and thus became familiar with ships and the life of a sailor by actual experience. He first became connected with the "Planter," a steamer plying in the harbor of Charleston as a transport in 1861. His further connection with the steamer is given in the following, taken from the record of the House of Representatives, Forty-seventh Congress, second session, Report No. 1887. The document was a "Bill authorizing the President to place Robert Smalls on the Retired List of the Navy:"

JANUARY 23, 1883.—RECOMMITTED TO THE COMMITTEE ON NAVAL AFFAIRS AND ORDERED TO BE PRINTED.

MR. DEZENDORF, FROM THE COMMITTEE ON NAVAL AFFAIRS, SUBMITTED THE FOLLOWING

REPORT
[To accompany bill, H. R. 7059.]

The Committee on Naval Affairs, to whom was referred to bill to retire Robert Smalls as captain of the Navy, beg leave to report as follows:

This claim is rested upon the very valuable services rendered by Robert Smalls to the country during the late war. The record of these has been very carefully investigated, and portions of it are appended, as exhibits, to this report. They show a degree of courage, well directed by intelligence and patriotism, of which the nation may well be proud, but which for twenty years has been wholly unrecognized by it. The following is a succinct statement and outline of them:

ROBERT SMALLS

On May 13, 1862, the Confederate steamboat "Planter," the special dispatch boat of General Ripley, the Confederate post commander at Charleston, South Carolina, was taken by Robert Smalls under the following circumstances from the wharf at which he was lying, carried safely out of Charleston Harbor, and delivered to one of the vessels of the Federal fleet then blockading that port:

On the day previous, May 12, the "Planter," which had for two weeks been engaged in removing guns from Cole's Island to James Island, returned to Charleston. That night all the officers went ashore and slept in the city, leaving on board a crew of eight men, all colored. Among them was Robert Smalls, who was virtually the pilot of the boat, although he was only called a wheelman, because at that time no colored man could have, in fact, been made a pilot. For some time previous he had been watching for an opportunity to carry into execution a plan he had conceived to take the "Planter" to the Federal fleet. This, he saw, was about as good a chance as he would ever have to do so, and therefore he determined not to lose it. Consulting with the balance of the crew, Smalls found that they were willing to co-operate with him, although two of them afterwards concluded to remain behind. The design was hazardous in the extreme. The boat would have to pass beneath the guns of the forts in the harbor. Failure and detection would have been certain death. Fearful was the venture, but it was made. The daring resolution had been formed, and under command of Robert Smalls, wood was taken aboard, steam was put on, and with her valuable cargo of guns and ammunition, intended for Fort Ripley, a new fortification just constructed in the harbor, about two o'clock in the morning the "Planter" silently moved off from her dock, steamed up to North Atlantic wharf, where Smalls' wife and two children, together with four other women and one other child, and also three men, were waiting to embark. All these were taken on board, and then, at 3:25 A.M., May 13, the "Planter" started on her perilous adventure, carrying nine men, five women and three children. Passing Fort Johnson the "Planter's" steam-whistle blew the usual salute and she proceeded down the bay. Approaching Fort Sumter, Smalls stood in the pilot-house leaning out of the window with his arms folded across his breast, after the manner of Captain Relay, the commander of the boat, and his head covered with the huge straw hat which Captain Relay commonly wore on such occasions.

The signal required to be given by all steamers passing out, was blown as coolly as if General Ripley was on board, going out on a tour of inspection. Sumter answered by signal, "all right," and the "Planter" headed toward Morris Island, then occupied by Hatch's light artillery, and passed beyond the range of Sumter's guns before anybody suspected anything was wrong. When at last the "Planter" was obviously going toward the Federal fleet off the bar, Sumter signaled toward Morris Island to stop her. But it was too late. As the "Planter" approached the Federal fleet, a white flag was displayed, but this was not at first discovered, and the Federal steamers, supposing the Confederate rams were coming to attack them, stood out to deep water. But the ship "Onward," Captain Nichols, which was not a steamer, remained, opened her ports, and was about to fire into the "Planter," when she noticed the flag of truce. As soon as the vessels came within hailing distance of each other, the "Planter's" errand was explained. Captain Nichols then boarded her, and Smalls delivered the "Planter" to him. From the "Planter," Smalls was transferred to the Augusta, the flagship off the bar, under the command of Captain Parrott, by whom the "Planter" with Smalls and her crew were sent to Port Royal to Rear Admiral DuPont, then in command of the Southern squadron.

Captain Parrott's official letter to Flag Officer DuPont, and Admiral DuPont's letter to the secretary of the navy are appended hereto.

Captain Smalls was soon afterwards ordered to Edisto to join the gunboat "Crusader," Captain Rhind. He then proceeded in the "Crusader," piloting her and followed by the "Planter" to Simmons' Bluff, on Wadmalaw Sound, where a sharp battle was fought between these boats and a Confederate light battery and some infantry. The Confederates were driven out of their works, and the troops on the "Planter" landed and captured all the tents and provisions of the enemy. This occurred some time in June, 1862.

Captain Smalls continued to act as pilot on board the "Planter" and the "Crusader," and as blockading pilot between Charleston and Beaufort. He made repeated trips up and along the rivers near the coast, pointing out and removing the torpedoes which he himself had assisted in sinking and putting in position. During these trips he was present in several fights at Adams' Rum on the Dawho river, where the "Planter" was hotly and severely fired upon; also at Rockville, John's Island, and other places. Afterwards he was ordered back to Port Royal, whence he piloted the fleet up Broad river to Pocotaligo, where a very severe battle ensued. Captain Smalls was the pilot of the monitor "Keokuk," Captain Ryan, in the memorable attack on Fort Sumter, on the afternoon of the seventh of April, 1863. In this attack the "Keokuk" was struck ninety-six times, nineteen shots passing through her. She retired from the engagement only to sink on the next morning, near Light House Inlet. Captain Smalls left her just before she went down, and was taken with the remainder of the crew on board of the "Ironside." The next day the fleet returned to Hilton Head.

When General Gillmore took command, Smalls became pilot in the quartermaster's department in the expedition on Morris Island. He was then stationed as pilot of the "Stono," where he remained until the United States troops took possession of the south end of Morris Island, when he was put in charge of Light House Inlet as pilot.

Upon one occasion, in December, 1863, while the "Planter," then under command of Captain Nickerson, was sailing through Folly Island Creek, the Confederate batteries at Secessionville opened a very hot fire upon her. Captain Nickerson became demoralized, and left the pilot-house and secured himself in the coal-bunker. Smalls was on the deck, and finding out that the captain had deserted his post, entered the pilot-house, took command of the boat, and carried her safely out of the reach of the guns. For this conduct he was promoted by order of General Gillmore, commanding the Department of the South, to the rank of captain, and was ordered to act as captain of the

"Planter," which was used as a supply-boat along the coast until the end of the war. In September, 1866, he carried his boat to Baltimore, where she was put out of commission and sold.

Besides the daring enterprise of Captain Smalls, in bringing out the "Planter," his gallant conduct in rescuing her a second time, for which he was made captain of her, and his invaluable services to the army and navy as a pilot in waters where he perfectly knew not only every bank and bar but also where every torpedo was situated, there are still other elements to be considered in estimating the value of Captain Smalls' services to the country, The "Planter," on the thirteenth of May, 1862, was a most useful and important vessel to the enemy. The loss of her was a severe blow to the enemy's service in carrying supplies and troops to different points of the harbor and river fortifications. At the very time of the seizure she had on board the armament for Fort Ripley. The "Planter was taken by the government at a valuation of $9,000, one-half of which was paid to the captain and crew, the captain receiving one-half of one-half or $1,500, Upon what principle the government claimed one-half of this capture cannot be divined, nor yet how this disposition could have been made of her without any judicial proceeding. That $9,000 was an absurdly low valuation for the "Planter" is abundantly shown by facts in the affidavits of Charles H. Campbell and E. M. Baldwin, which are appended. In addition thereto their sworn average valuation of the "Planter" was $67,500. The report of Montgomery Sicard, commander and inspector of ordinance, to Commodore Patterson, navy-yard commandant, shows that the cargo of the "Planter," as raw material, was worth $3,043.45; that at anti-bellum prices it was worth $7,163.35, and at war prices $10,290.60. For this cargo the government has never paid one dollar. It is a severe comment on the justice as well as the boasted generosity of the government, that, whilst it had received $60,000 to $70,000 worth of property at the hands of Captain Smalls, it has paid him the trifling amount of $1,500, and for twenty years his gallant daring and distinguished and valuable services which he has rendered to the country has been wholly unrecognized.

The following is the testimony in proof of the facts alleged in the bill:

REPORT OF FLAG OFFICER DUPONT

Flag-Ship "Wabash,"
Port Royal Harbor, South Carolina, May 14, 1862

Sir: I inclose a copy of a report from Commander E. G. Parrott, brought here last night by the late rebel steam-tug "Planter," in charge of an officer and crew from the "Augusta." She was the armed dispatch and transportation steamer attached to the engineer department at Charleston, under Brigadier-General Ripley, whose barge, a short time since, was brought out to the blockading fleet by several contrabands.

The bringing out of this steamer, under all the circumstances, would have done credit to any one. At four o'clock in the morning, in the absence of the captain, who was on shore, she left her wharf close to the government office and headquarters, with Palmetto and Confederate flags flying, passed the successive forts, saluting as usual by blowing her steam-whistle. After getting beyond the range of the last gun, she quickly hauled down the rebel flags and hoisted a white one.

The "Onward" was the inside ship of the blockading fleet in the main channel, and was preparing to fire when her commander made out the white flag. The armament of the steamer is a 32-pounder, or pivot, and a fine 24-pounder howitzer. She has, besides, on her deck, four other guns, one 7-inch rifled, which were to have been taken the morning of the escape to the new fort on the middle ground. One of the four belonged to Fort Sumter, and had been struck in the rebel attack on the fort on the muzzle. Robert, the intelligent slave and pilot of the boat, who performed this bold feat so skillfully, informed me of this fact, presuming it would be a matter of interest to us to have possession of this gun. This man, Robert Smalls, is superior to any who have come into our lines—intelligent as many of them have been. His information has been most interesting, and portions of it of the utmost importance.

The steamer is quite an acquisition to the squadron by her good machinery and very light draught. The officer in charge brought her through Saint Helena Sound, and by the inland passage down Beaufort river, arriving here at ten o'clock last night.

On board the steamer when she left Charleston were eight men, five women and three children.

I shall continue to employ Robert as a pilot on board the "Planter" for the inland waters, with which he appears to be very familiar. I do not know whether, in the views of the government, the vessel will be considered a prize; but, if so, I respectfully submit to the department the claims of this man Robert and his associates.

Very respectfully, your obedient servant,
S. F. DuPont,
Flag Officer, Commanding, &c.

Hon. Gideon Welles,
Secretary of the Navy, Washington, D. C.

United States Steamship "Augusta,"
Off Charleston, May 13, 1862

Sir: I have the honor to inform you that the rebel armed steamer "Planter" was brought out to us this morning from Charleston, by eight contrabands, and delivered up to the squadron. Five colored women and three children are also on board. She carried one 32-pounder, and one 24-pounder howitzer, and has also on board four large guns, which she was engaged in transporting.

I send her to Port Royal at once, in order to take advantage of the present good weather. I send Charleston papers of the 12th, and the very intelligent contraband who was in charge will give you the information which he has brought off.

I have the honor to request that you will send back, as soon as convenient, the officer and crew sent on board.

I am respectfully, &c., your obedient servant,

E. G. PARROTT,
Commander, and Senior Officer present

Flag Officer S. F. DuPont,
Commanding South Atlantic Blockading Squadron

WAR DEPARTMENT,
QUARTERMASTER-GENERAL'S OFFICE,
WASHINGTON, D. C., January 3, 1883

SIR: Your communication of the twenty-sixth ultimo, in relation to your services on the steamer "Planter" during the rebellion, and requesting copies of any letters from General Gillmore and other officers on the subject, has been received.

The records of this office show that the name of Robert Smalls is reported by Lieutenant-Colonel J. J. Elwell, Hilton Head, South Carolina, as a pilot, at $50 per month, from March 1, 1863, to September 30, 1863; and from October 1, 1863, to November 20, 1863, at $75 per month.

He was then transferred to Captain J. L. Kelly, assistant quartermaster, November 20, 1863, by whom he was reported as pilot from November 21 to November 30, 1863. He is reported by that officer in same capacity from December 1, 1863, until February 29, 1864, at $150 per month.

The name of Robert Smalls is then reported by Captain Kelly as captain of the steamer "Planter," at $150 per month, from March 1, 1864, until May 15, 1864, when transferred to the quartermaster in Philadelphia.

He is reported by Captains C. D. Schmidt, G. R. Orme, W. W. VanNess, and John R. Jennings, assistant quartermasters at Philadelphia, as captain of the "Planter," at $150 per month, from June 20, 1864, to December 16, 1864, when transferred to Captain J. L. Kelly, assisant quartermaster, Hilton Head, South Carolina, by whom he is reported to January 31, 1865.

From February 1, 1865, he is reported as a "contractor, victualing and manning the steamer "Planter."

I respectfully inclose herewith a copy of a letter, dated September 10, 1862, from Captain J. J. Elwell, chief quartermaster, Department of the South, in relation to the capture of the steamer "Planter," which is the only one found on file in this office on the subject.

Very respectfully, your obedient servant,

ALEX. J. PERRY,
Deputy Quartermaster-General, U. S. A.,
Acting Quartermaster-General

HON. ROBERT SMALLS,
Member of Congress, Washington, D. C.

OFFICE OF THE CHIEF QUARTERMASTER,
HILTON HEAD, SOUTH CAROLINA, September 10, 1862

GENERAL: I have this day taken a transfer of the small steamer "Planter," of the navy. This is the Confederate steamer which Robert Smalls, a contraband, brought out of Charleston on the thirteenth of May last. The Navy Department, through Rear-Admiral DuPont, transfers her, and I receipt for her just as she was received from Charleston. Her machinery is not in very good order, and will require some repairs, etc.; but this I can have done here. She will be of much service to us, as we have comparatively no vessels of light draft. I shall have her employed at Fort Pulaski, where I am obliged to keep a steamer.

Please find enclosed a copy of the letter of Rear-Admiral DuPont to General Brannan in regard to the matter.

I am, general, very respectfully, your most obedient servant,

J. J. ELWELL,
Captain and Assistant Quartermaster.

J. G. CHANDLER,
Deputy Quartermaster-General, U. S. A.

Personally appeared before me Charles H. Campbell, of the city, county, and State of New York, who, being by me duly sworn according to law, deposes and says as follows:

That during the year 1862, and from that time up to and including the year 1866, he was doing service in the department of the South, headquarters at Hilton Head, South Carolina; that he knows Hon. Robert Smalls, of Beaufort, South Carolina; that he was present when the steamer "Planter" of the city of Charleston, came into Hilton Head on or about the thirteenth of May, 1862; that he went on board the "Planter" and made a personal examination of her condition, and found she was built of live oak and red cedar, and a first-class coastwise steamer, well furnished and complete in every respect; that he was, and is, well acquainted with the value of steamers, and has been engaged in the business of steamboating, both as captain and owner, for the last fifteen years; that the steamer "Planter" was fully worth, at the time she came into Hilton Head, the sum of $60,000 in cash for the boat alone; that the United States government was paying at that time for steamers of her class $400 per day under a charter-party agreement with the chief quartermaster at that place, the government finding both wood and coal; that he chartered to the United States government at or about that time the steamer "George Washington" for $350 per day, which was only about half the size of the "Planter," and not more than half her value; that he executed seven charters for steamers with the government, and also had a valuation set on them in case of loss, and the above statement is made in accordance with the prices paid by the government at Hilton Head and elsewhere during the time the "Planter" was in the service; that, at the close of the war, and while the "Planter" was laying up in Charleston and in a very bad condition from the nature of her past services, I was commissioned by her former owner, Captain Ferguson, to purchase the "Planter" from the government for the sum of $25,000, which sum I did offer, and the same was refused on the part of the government of the United States; that the steamer "Planter" was an extra strong built boat, her frame was live oak and red cedar, and built as strong as possible; she was built expressly for the coastwise trade, and she is running out of the city of Charleston to-day, and is considered by steamboat men one of the strongest and best steamboats in the South.

CHARLES H. CAMPBELL.

Subscribed and sworn to before me the twenty-third day of March, 1876.
[OFFICIAL SEAL.] JAMES A. TAIT,
Notary Public.

Personally appeared before me, a notary public, E. M. Baldwin, of the city of Washington, District of Columbia, who was by me duly sworn according to law, deposes and says:

That during the year A. D., 1862, and afterwards was doing service for the Navy Department at Hilton Head, South Carolina, in the South Atlantic blockading squadron; that he was captain of the steam-tug "Mercury," and was one of the first persons that boarded the "Planter" at Hilton Head on the thirteenth day of May, A. D., 1862.

That he has been for years, and is now, engaged in the steamboat business as an officer and owner, and is familiar with the prices paid for charters by the quartermaster at Hilton Head, and the value of steamboats generally at that time and since; that he examined the "Planter" when she came into said harbor at Hilton Head, and found her a first-class steamboat, built of live oak and red cedar, and her outfit and findings complete in every particular; that she could have been readily sold at the time she arrived at Hilton Head for $75,000 in cash for the steamboat alone, or could have been chartered to the government for $400 per day, which at that rate would have paid the purchase money at the price aforesaid in less that one year, and would have left a large surplus to the purchaser; that she was considered by both the officers of the Army and Navy, on account of her light draft and great srength, by far the best steamer for that coast service in the Department of the South.

E. M. BALDWIN

Sworn to before me and subscribed by him in my presence this twenty-fifth day of March, A. D., 1876.
[OFFICIAL SEAL.]

JAMES A. TAIT,
Notary Public

For the services Mr. Smalls ought to have been rewarded. The bill did not pass on the ground that there was no precedent for placing a civilian on the retired list of the navy, but some other reward should be granted. This record is preserved in full for the benefit of history.

Exhibit of the estimated values of certain ordnance and ordnance stores on board the Rebel steamer "Planter," which came out of Charleston, South Carolina, to the United States blockading fleet on the fifteenth day of May, 1862.

Articles of ordnance and ordnance stores on board the *Planter*.	Estimated under the supposition that the guns and projectiles of value to the United States only as old material, the powder being considered as useful for saluting.		Estimated supposing that all the articles are valued at prices paid before the war, except the Brooks rifle and its projectiles, which are given at war prices.		Estimated supposing that all the articles are valued by the United States at war prices.	
1 long 32-pounder of 72,000 lbs.	At ¾ ct. per lb.	$ 54.00	At $5\frac{6}{10}$ cts. per lb.	$ 403.20	At 10 cts. per lb.	$ 720.00
1 short 32-pounder of 3,300 lbs.	At ¾ ct. per lb.	24.75	At $5\frac{6}{10}$ cts. per lb.	222.00	At 9 cts. per lb.	297.00
1 short 24-pounder of 1,476 lbs.	At ¾ ct. per lb.	11.07	At $5\frac{6}{10}$ cts. per lb.	82.66	At 9 cts. per lb.	132.84
2 8-inch Columbiads of 9,240 lbs. each	At ¾ ct. per lb.	138.60	At $5\frac{6}{10}$ cts. per lb.	1,027.49	At 11 cts. per lb.	2,032.80
1 7-inch rifle of 10,500 lbs.	At ¾ ct. per lb.	78.75	At 12 cts. per lb.	1,260.00	At 12 cts. per lb.	1,260.00
200 32-pounder shot	At 1¾ cts. per lb.	113.00	At 66 cts. each	132.00	At $1.00 each	200.00
150 8-inch 32-pounder shot	At 1¾ cts. per lb.	170.62	At 83 cts. each	124.50	At $1.25 each	187.50
200 32-pounder shell, loaded and fused	At 1¾ cts. per lb.	78.75	At $1.80 each	360.00	At $2.50 each	502.00
100 24-pounder shell, loaded and fused	At 1¾ cts. per lb.	29.26	At $1.40 each	140.00	At $2.00 each	200.00
200 7-inch rifle shell, loaded and fused	At 1¾ cts. per lb.	315.00	At $6 each	1,200.00	At $6.00 each	1,200.00
150 8-inch rifle shell, loaded and fused	At 1¾ cts. per lb.	131.00	At $2.33 each	349.50	At $3.39 each	508.00
400 32-pounder charges, 8 lbs. each, 3,200 lbs.	At 22 cts. per lb.	704.00	At 18 cts. per lb.	576.00	At 30 cts. per lb.	960.00
100 24-pounder charges, 2 lbs. each, 200 lbs.	At 22 cts. per lb.	44.00	At 18 cts. per lb.	36.00	At 30 cts. per lb.	60.00
200 7-inch rifle charges, 10 lbs. each, 2,000 lbs.	At 22 cts. per lb.	440.00	At 18 cts. per lb.	360.00	At 30 cts. per lb.	600.00
300 8-inch Columbian charges, 10 pounds each, 3,000 lbs.	At 22 cts. per lb.	660.00	At 18 cts. per lb.	540.00	At 30 cts. per lb.	900.00
1 32-pounder carriage, Army pattern	At 22 cts. per lb.	40.80	At 18 cts. per lb.	330.00		500.00
1 24-pounder carriage, Army pattern	At 22 cts. per lb.	10.00		20.00		30.00
Total		$3,043.05		$7,163.35		$10,290.60

After the "Planter" was put out of commission in 1866, Captain Smalls was elected a member of the State Constitutional convention. He was of course the hero of an important act in the drama of the late war, and his people always delighted to hear him tell, in his own style, the story of the capture. His zeal, good sense and pure disinterestedness, easily made him the idol of his people, whose faith in him was unbounded. Indeed, even to this day he is very popular. It was recently reported in the papers that two colored men, partisans of his, were talking on the corners. Said one to the other "I tell you, Smalls is the greatest man in the world." The other said, "Y-e-s, he's great, but not the greatest man." "Pshaw, man," replied the first speaker, "Who is greater than Smalls?" Said No. 2, "Why, Jesus Christ." "O," said No. 1, "Smalls is young yet."

This, though it may be only a joke on the general, illustrates his popularity with the masses. At the general election in 1868, he was elected to a seat in the House of Representatives of the State and signalized his efforts by the introduction of the Homestead Act, and introduced and secured the passage of the Civil Rights bill. He continued in this capacity until Judge Wright was elected as associate judge of the Supreme Court of the State, when he was elected to fill his unexpired time in the Senate in 1870, and, at the election in 1872 he was elected Senator, defeating General W. J. Whipper. His record here was brilliant, consistent, and indeed he led in all the most prominent measures. His debating qualities were tested, and he was acknowledged a superior and powerful talker. He was on the "Committee on Finance," chairman of the "Committee on Public Printing," and a member of many other leading committees. An old sketch says of him:

> His character is made up of some of the best traits of human nature. He is generous, daring and true. His mental faculties are acute, sensitive and progressive. He is, in fine, one of the most distinguished of his race, and may justly be deemed one of its representative men.

Taking much interest in the military affairs of his State, he was appointed lieutenant-colonel of the Third regiment, South Carolina State militia, in 1873. Afterwards he was promoted to brigadier-general of the Second brigade, South Carolina militia, and later major-general of the Second division, South Carolina State militia, which position he held until the Democrats came into power, in 1877.

He was a delegate to the National Republican convention at Philadelphia, in 1872, which nominated Grant and Wilson, and also to the National Republican convention, which met at Cincinnati, in 1876, and nominated Hayes and Wheeler; also delegate to the National Republican convention which met at Chicago and nominated Blaine and Logan; was elected to the Forty-seventh and Forty-eighth Congresses, and was re-elected to the Forty-ninth Congress as a Republican, receiving 8,419 votes against 4,584 votes for Elliott, Democrat, and 235 votes scattering. He was also a candidate at the last election but was counted out, not beaten, by the Democracy. He will contest the seat of the man holding the certificate. The general affiliates with the Baptist church, and is of a high spiritual tendency, and can be seen attending the Berean Baptist church, Washington, D. C., every Sabbath morning. His mother, wife and daughters are all members of the same faith.

CHAPTER XIII

Henry Ossawa Tanner, Esq.
A Rising Artist—Exhibitor of Paintings in the Art Galleries—
Illustrator of Magazines

The story goes that many artists die in garrets, poor, desolate and friendless; that unborn generations do justice to their works and pay high prices for their masterpieces; the merest daubs become highest specimens of art, and people go into rhapsodies over those pictures which are no better in after days than they were in the days they were made. The poor artist, perhaps, died for want of a meal, and was unable to get the necessary comforts for the sustenance of life. But in these days of activity, enterprise and speculation, meritorious work of every character secures good prices, and the man who has lived to make a good thing need not go far to find a market.

Says a distinguished writer:

The true artist does not begin his picture or statue as one does the brick wall of a house, laying it out by metes and bounds and erecting it with line and plummet, according to fixed mathematical rules; but, in the dream of the artist or artisan, a beautiful dome with all its elegant finish, is instantly brought into being and spanned above his head. A statue or picture comes to him like a dream, and the secret of art power is to hold those models in the memory until the faculties of constructiveness, form, size and order have wrought out and fixed the image in material form.

This is very largely true of this young man. His whole nature and temperament bespeak the artist. While by no means he is affected in his manner, yet his thoughts are of the finest character, and are delicately expressed on the canvas before him. His taste is somewhat on the order of that of Landseer and Bonheur, who love animals. These artists did not look upon them simply as so many bones, with hide, horns and other necessary parts thrown in, but they delighted to portray their nature, habits, affections, symmetry and beauty. This is indeed an exaltation of their Maker and the dignifying of God on canvas, by employing their genius in portraying the characteristics mentioned.

These and other thoughts engage the mind of the true artist. Pictures are to them the solidifying of the imagination, an embellishment of an idea, a thought made tangible. Indeed a picture is the impression of one's thoughts upon canvas in such a way that it leaves the thought fixed thereon and becomes a means of communication to others. Often so delicately expressed, and so very carefully presented, that pictures are sometimes said to almost speak, so faithfully do they convey the idea of the painter. It can be readily seen how, in ancient times, hieroglyphics were used for writing, and surely they were nothing more than pictures. Pictures are to the eyes, then, what the type is in the book to the same organ—a vehicle of thought, though of a much higher grade than writing.

"Boss Tweed" used to say, "Print what you please about me but spare me from the pictures of Tom Nast." So powerfully did his pictures portray the stealings and villainies of that New York alderman.

Abraham Lincoln told Nast, "Transfer your talents to me and you can take my place." It can readily be seen what power is in the hands of the man who controls the pen, pencil or brush.

This young man, then, will gain a widespread influence if he continues to supply illustrations to Harper Brothers, for the *Harper's Young People* and for Judge Tourgee's paper *Our Continent* as he has done. The firm of Harper & Brother does much to encourage colored men, and in employing Mr. Tanner, deserves here to be mentioned.

His services rendered in this capacity for so old and well established a firm, show that he is a talented young man and that brains will win every time. Young men need not mope around, smoking cigars, carousing, and whining about prejudice and proscription. Let them go to work; let them do something.

Mr. Tanner is the son of the well known Rev. B. T. Tanner, D.D., and has his father's talent and progressiveness. He was born June 21, 1859, at Pittsburgh, Pennsylvania. His school advantages have been good, and he is fairly fitted for life's work. He studied art at the Pennsylvania Academy of Fine Arts, in Philadelphia, Pennsylvania, where he has lived for many years. His pictures take high rank. No favoritism is shown in the selection to enter the academies and galleries of this country. Each specimen must pass the committee of eminent men, who are art critics of long standing. This is stated lest many might think he is patronized by rich men or through the influence of his father, or because some one takes pity on him, trying to help a colored man to rise. No! It is merit; let that be understood at once. Perseverance, pluck and brains is any young man's capital. Let him use them.

He has exhibited pictures, as has been said, at several galleries. He exhibited "The Lions at Home" in 1885, and "Back from the Beach" in

1886, at the National Academy of Design and at the Pennsylvania Academy of Fine Arts. This first named picture was sold at the National Academy of Design, New York City. He also exhibited "Dusty Road" at the Lydia Art gallery, at Chicago, where it was sold. Exhibited picture "The Elk Attacked by Wolves" at the International Exposition at New Orleans, in the department for the colored people. Being commissioner from Kentucky, I remember this picture very well. It attracted my attention at the time on account of its size and naturalness. He has also exhibited pictures at Washington and Louisville. At the last named place he exhibited "Point Judith." This picture I also remember and was very much pleased with it, though I did not know at the time that it was the work of a colored artist.

He is constantly engaged in furnishing work upon special orders. I visited his gallery and was shown quite a number of his pictures; especially was I pleased with one of a lion in his den, where it was shown that he was eating bloody meat. It was truly life-like and the lion's head with all its fierceness, seemed so natural that one would almost feel like looking toward the door for egress. The bloody meat, as it lay before him, seemed as if it lay upon the floor. Let me explain here that the picture was out of its frame and was standing upon its edge upon the floor, leaning against the easel. The lion's massive paw, seemed as if he were about to lift it and reach out for the meat, just before him.

Indeed, it was true and life-like as I have said. This artist has been encouraged by many of the leading men of his profession of the city, and his future seems brilliant.

I earnestly hope that those of our race who deal in pictures will not forget to encourage such men as Mr. Tanner. Mention is made of him not simply that the book might be filled and space employed, but that knowledge of him may extend throughout the country and he be encouraged by those who read of his ability. Be satisfied that the statements here made are true and his work as described.

CHAPTER XIV

Rev. Andrew Heath
A Minister of the Gospel, Eminent for his Piety

Rev. Andrew Heath, after a long illness, has gone where there is neither sorrow, pain nor death. He was born in Henderson county, Kentucky, February 20, 1832, and died February 19, 1887, at the age of fifty-five years. At an early period in life he became a Christian, and spent forty of the best years of his life working for the Master. In 1851 he was married to Miss Lucy Hamilton, who has worked bravely by his side. In 1867 a council, composed of Revs. Henry Adams, William Troy, R. De-Baptiste, R. T. W. James and Professor Green, ordained him to the Gospel ministry. In 1868 he became assistant pastor of Fifth Street Baptist church, Louisville, Kentucky, and in 1872, on the death of Rev. Henry Adams, became its pastor. The first Baptist convention ever held in the State, in 1863, enrolled him as a member, and in all the years since he has never withheld his hand from any work that would advance the interest of the race and the denomination. He has served the General Association in being a member of the Executive board and chairman of the same about sixteen years. During his pastorate about fifteen hundred persons have been baptized by him. We may safely say that no minister in the State held a higher place in the estimation of the people who knew him. Every charitable cause found a ready helper in him, the orphans a father and the Christan church a true leader. His character was pure; his reputation never received a blur in all the years of his ministry.

His death, though he had been ill a long time, was unexpected and created general and profound regret. The church appointed the assistant pastor, Rev. J. H. Frank, Deacons Thomas Parker, Shelton Guest, Q. B. Jones, Moses Lawson, Horace Crutcher, R. M. Hightower, R. Hamilton, and Messrs. William H. Steward, W. L. Gibson and George W. Talbott a committee to arrange for the funeral, and Mt. Moriah Lodge, F. and A. Masons, appointed Messrs. E. W. Marshall, Felix Sweeney, Edward Caldwell, Matthew Goodall and Enoch Maney. During Saturday, Sunday and Monday, thousands of people who had admired this noble man in life called at his late residence to view his remains and tender sympathy to the bereaved family. Sunday at the church was a sad day. The heavily draped building was a silent reminder of the mournful event. Monday morning the several meetings of the city pastors and the students of the State University passed suitable resolutions and agreed to attend the funeral services in a body.

Tuesday morning, long before the hour for the opening of the church, the street was literally packed with a mass of humanity, and when the doors were opened the church was instantly filled. So eager were the people to witness the ceremony that hundreds stood patiently for hours. While this interest was being shown at the church, sad and heartrending scenes were occurring in the home of sorrow, from which his body was soon to be borne. A few minutes before eleven o'clock the funeral cortege started for the church. So dense was the crowd that it was almost impossible to force an entrance. The funeral requiem on the great organ, in deep and solemn tones, announced the procession. No evidence more convincing of the love and esteem of this people for their lamented pastor could have been given than the spontaneous and unfeigned expressions of grief when the body entered the church in charge of the following pall-bearers: Revs. E. P. Marrs, A. Stratton and W. P. Churchill, Messrs. Q. B. Jones, Wm. Morton, Shelton Guest, Isaac Morton and Willis Adams. About two hundred ministers, representing the several ministers' meetings and associations, were present. The white Baptist clergy being represented by Rev. J. A. Broadus, J. P. Boyce and W. H. Whitsitt of the Southern Baptist Theological Seminary, and Revs. T. T. Eaton, H. Allen Tupper, C. M. Thompson and A. C. Caperton; also the presence of a large number of ministers from abroad, including Revs. G. W. Bowling of Elizabethtown; E. J. Anderson of Georgetown; S. P. Young of Lexington; E. Evans of Bowling Green; M. Allen of Shelbyville; R. Reynolds of Pee Wee Valley; M. Bassett of New Albany, Indiana; Willis Johnson of Bloomfield; J. Jacobs of Harrodscreek; J. W. Carr of San Antonio, Texas; Wm. Miller of Jacksonville, Indiana; J. M. Washington of Indianapolis, Indiana; and B. T. Thomas of Clarksville, Tennessee. The large audience, despite the uncomfortable surroundings, listened attentively and eagerly. Rev. J. H. Frank opened the services with a short introductory address, paying a deserved tribute to the deceased. Rev. H. Allen Tupper, pastor of Broadway Baptist church, read the favored hymn: "Is my name written there?" which was sung with much feeling by the choir of the church; Professor J. M. Maxwell read an appropriate scripture lesson and Rev. Lee Y. Evans, pastor of Quinn chapel, offered a fervent prayer.

The old familiar hymn—"Why Should We Start and Fear to Die?"—was lined by Rev. G. E. Scott, pastor of Zion Baptist church.

Resolutions of different organizations and telegrams of regret from friends and fellow ministers were read by Revs. C. H. Parrish, S. P. Young, R. Harper and Mr. William H. Nelson.

Mr. M. Lawson made a statement expressing the views of the deceased as related to him a few weeks prior to his death, bearing expressly upon the relative importance of masonry and the church.

Rev. William J. Simmons, D.D., then preached the funeral sermon from Acts, 20: 24–27. "But none of these things move me, neither count I my life dear unto myself, so that I might finish my course with joy, and the ministry which I have received of the Lord Jesus, to testify the gospel of the grace of God. And now behold, I know that ye all, among whom I have gone preaching the kingdom of God, shall see my face no more. Wherefore I take you to record this day, that I am pure from the blood of all men. For I have not shunned to declare unto you all the counsel of God."

The sermon was a warm tribute to the memory of a good minister of Jesus Christ and found a response in the heart of every person present.

At the close of the sermon, remarks were made by Revs. G. W. Ward and A. Barry by request of the family, and by Revs. A. C. Caperton representing the Baptist Ministers' meeting (white), by Rev. C. C. Bates, representing the Executive Board, and Rev. D. A. Gaddie representing the General Association.

Rev. T. T. Eaton, pastor of the Walnut Street Baptist church, gave out the hymn "Asleep in Jesus."

When the hymn was concluded the benediction was announced by Rev. Spencer Snell, pastor of the Plymouth Congregational church.

The floral offerings, which were profuse and beautiful, were removed from the casket and the march for the cemetery begun.

The streets were lined with people who, being unable to get into the church, waited patiently to pay the last tribute of respect to a faithful minister.

The procession, which was as large as ever followed a man to his last resting place in this city, reached the cemetery about four o'clock. The funeral service of the Masonic fraternity was rendered by William H. Steward, the Grand Master of the State, in the presence of an immense number of people, when the body was placed in the vault.

The following resolutions were passed by the church of which he had been pastor and by the Ministers' and Deacons' conference of this city.

CHURCH RESOLUTIONS

WHEREAS, It has pleased the Ruler of the universe, the great Head of the church, the Disposer of all things, to call, February 19, in the year of our Lord, 1887, at 7:53 A.M., our dearly beloved and worthy pastor, the most faithful and wonderfully wrought workman of the gospel ministry of our community, and

WHEREAS, But a few have, with such exemplary fidelity, exerted an influence for good in the Master's vineyard. A man of fair literary attainments, acquired under many disadvantages, strong, spiritual inclinations, sound and conservative doctrine, ardent and unostentatious in piety, spotless in character, unblemished in reputation, dignified in appearance and "faithful in his house;" therefore be it

Resolved, That we, the members of the Fifth Street Baptist church, believe he was truly a bishop of the description of 1st Timothy 3, "blameless, the husband of one wife, vigilant, sober, of good behaviour, given to hospitality, apt to teach; not given to wine, no striker, not greedy of filthy lucre, but patient, not a brawler, not covetous; one that ruled well his own house, not lifted up with pride and having a good report of them which are without." The church has indeed lost a good pastor, the Sunday school a strong support, his wife a kind husband, the children a devoted father, the widows and orphans a friend, the poor and needy a comforter, and missions an advocate. We mourn his death yet it is a consolation to know that our great loss is his eternal gain. We extend our sympathy to the bereaved family and a helping hand in time of need.

Resolved, That in token of our respect and esteem, the church be draped in mourning for thirty days, and a copy of these resolutions be presented to the stricken family, spread upon the records of the church and published in the city papers.

JOHN H. FRANK,
GEORGE W. TALBOTT,
Q. B. JONES,
MOSES LAWSON,
WILLIAM H. STEWARD.
Committee.

ANDREW HEATH

MINISTERS' AND DEACONS' CONFERENCE

The Fifth Street church and the Baptist denomination of this vicinity and State have met with a great loss in the death of Rev. Andrew Heath, which occurred in this city the nineteenth inst. We feel desirous of expressing ourselves as follows:

He was a devout Christian for nearly forty years, connected with the General Association since its origin, for fourteen years pastor of the Fifth Street Baptist church of this city and also a former member and exchairman of the Executive Board of the General Association. He has long resided in our midst, and here in this city achieved his honorable and noble success as a Christian pastor. With comparatively limited means and opportunity, he has woven his name into the inmost soul of this community. With a liberal heart he has promoted all the true interest of society and religion. A noble, honest and true man, an humble and consistent Christian has fallen. His counsel, kind and fair; integrity, clear; and fidelity, beyond reproach. In his home he was the model Christian, husband and father. Therefore be it

Resolved, That we sincerely deplore his death, for in it we have lost a true minister and exemplary Christian.

That in honor of his great worth, a memorial meeting be held at Fifth Street church next Sunday afternoon at three o'clock; that said meeting include all the ministers of the city, and such visiting ministers as may be present, of all denominations.

That our fullest and tenderest sympathies are hereby extended to his afflicted family and church.

That we attend his funeral in a body.

That we wear a memorial badge for thirty days.

That these resolutions be sent to the family, spread upon our minutes and published in the city papers.

>D. A. GADDIE
>T. M. FALKNER
>W. JOHNSON
>G. W. WARD
>G. E. SCOTT
>J. W. LEWIS
>C. H. PARRISH, Secretary
>Committee

Resolutions were also passed by the choir of the Fifth Street Baptist church, and by the State University, of which he was a former pupil, by the Lexington ministers and deacons in assembled meeting, by the Junior class of the State University, of which a daughter is a member, and by the Louisville Ministerial Association, composed of brethren of other denominations.

Telegrams were received from the following persons expressing grief and sympathy: E. W. Green, Maysville, Kentucky; G. W. Dupee, Paducah, Kentucky; R. Bassett, Indianapolis, Indiana; J. K. Polk, Versailles, Kentucky; O. Durrett, Clinton, Kentucky; Mrs. A. V. Nelson, Lexington, Kentucky; R. H. L. Mitchem, Springfield, Kentucky; James Allensworth, Hopkinsville, Kentucky; Peter Lewis, Louisville, Kentucky; M. Harding, Owensboro, Kentucky. All of these testified to his high standing as a Christian gentleman, a man of many virtues, of varied graces, and who seemed to have no enemies. Sunday, February 27, the memorial services, in honor of Rev. A. Heath, at Fifth street, were held and largely attended.

Rev. D. A. Gaddie presided and made the introductory address. The choir sang several appropriate anthems and hymns. Rev. W. J. Simmons, D.D., read the Scripture lessons. Revs. B. Taylor and J. Mitchell offered prayer; Rev. G. W. Ward portrayed him "as a preacher," and Rev. E. P. Marrs, "as a pastor."

Remarks were made by Revs. B. Taylor, M. F. Robinson, R. Hatchett, J. W. Lewis, and Messrs. Thomas Parker, Q. B. Jones, Albert Mack and Albert White. At the conclusion of the addresses, a committee, which had been previously appointed, submitted a tribute of respect which was approved as the sentiment of the meeting.

A touching tribute to this truly good man is given by J. C. Corbin, Pine Bluff, Arkansas, who was an associate with Elder Heath in his early life. He writes: "Elder Heath was modest, teachable and unassuming; that he succeeded was not due to extraordinary gifts of eloquence, scholarship or other talents. It must have been the result of his earnest piety, pure character and entire consecration to the work of his ministry. These secured for him the favor of Almighty God."

He was the "architect of his own fortune," and now he rests from his labors and his works do follow him.

Blessed are the dead who die in the Lord.

I might have said more in way of eulogy from my own standpoint, but I felt that his death brought forth the testimony sufficient to show how he lived, and this chorus of praise is far more telling than my own feeble utterances.

H. C. SMITH

CHAPTER XV

H. C. Smith, Esq.
Prominent Editor—First-class Musician—Deputy Oil Inspector of Ohio—Song Writer—Leader of Bands—Cornetist

---

Mr. Smith is what we might call a self-made man, as it is largely through his own energies that he has reached his present station in life; but he says he owes his education and training to the devotion of a faithful mother, assisted by his sister. He was born in Clarksburg, West Virginia, January 20, 1863. His parents were named John and Sarah Smith. It was twenty-eight days after the issuing of the Emancipation Proclamation by "Old Abe." He went to Cleveland with his widowed mother in 1865 or 1866, and there his mother and sister toiled very hard to educate him. After leaving the grammar schools of Cleveland, with the aid of his cornet, which he had learned to play without a teacher, having secured the rudiments of his musical education in the schools of Cleveland, he made much of the money so earned, by which he secured advantages. He was constantly employed in playing in orchestras and brass bands; by this means also he was able to assist in the support of his mother and sister. He attended the Cleveland Central High School, entering in 1878, and finished a four years course of what was known as the Latin and English course. In 1882, while at the high school, he corresponded for papers in Indianapolis, Cincinnati and Springfield; and at different times during the last year and a half he wrote for a weekly paper called the *Cleveland Sun*—a white journal. After leaving school he followed music as a profession for about a year and a half, directing a colored band and orchestral and vocal organization, at different times. The summers of 1881 and 1882, he spent at Lakewood, Chautauqua Lake, New York, playing the cornet in the orchestra. He was director of the Amphion male quartet; director of Freeman and Boston's orchestra, a well known organization in the northern part of Ohio, for two or three years; was president and director of the First M. E. and Central High School orchestras—white organizations, and leader of the famous Excelsior reed band of the city of Cleveland, and captain of several athletic organizations, the members of which were white persons, with the exception of himself. While at High School, in August, 1883, he was one of a company of four that started the *Cleveland Gazette*. He was general manager and editor, having a one-fourth interest in the venture. He soon bought out each of his partners and is now sole proprietor. His views, as expressed in the *Gazette,* are clear, concise and easily comprehended. He never fails to speak most earnestly for the race and its representatives.

Having been brought up in the mixed schools of the city, he has always antagonized the color line in the most fearless manner. Says Professor W. S. Scarborough.:

Mr. Smith has always wielded a fearless and able pen for right and truth. He has fought squarely in behalf of his race, demanding recognition wherever denied. No other proof of this is needed than the *Gazette* itself; though at times he has been severely criticised, he has never wavered from what he considered his duty. He believes that the Republican party can serve best the interests of the Negro, and thereupon he becomes its able and active defender. He also believes that mixed schools are best for all concerned, and especially for the Negro, as separate schools simply imply race prejudice and race inferiority, and, therefore, he becomes a relentless antagonist to the color line in the schools.

Read what the eminent colored divine, Rev. J. W. Gazaway of Ohio and Indiana, has to say of

THE CLEVELAND GAZETTE.

The most healthful signs of life and a highly useful career are indicated in the existence of the above named paper. That it is a paper of brain and culture cannot be doubted when the fact is remembered that in its columns are found communications from the wisest and best minds of our race. It is a paper for the people it represents, and it can be relied on as a friend of every colored man, though his face may be of ebony hue. The *Gazette* is a practical demonstration of what can be done by the young men of our race. The editor is a young man, who, by dint of industry and economy and fair dealing, has succeeded in giving to the colored people of Ohio and the country a paper worthy the patronage of all. Having been a reader of the *Gazette* since its first appearance, and having watched its course, I feel that, in justice to the paper, the editor and the race, I should urge upon the people generally to support the paper that is practically identified with the colored people, and is in harmony with the interests and success of all without regard to complexion.

His paper is now in its fourth year, and is one of the newsiest and most successful in the United States. He claims that it is not only paying its way but is actually making money; this can be said of but few colored journals in the United States, and marks his paper as popular and in demand. He has given constant attention to the questions which have arisen in Ohio. Besides being editor of this prominent journal, which has steadily assumed a powerful interest and influence, he is one of the two colored clerks who secured appointments in the city, having been appointed by a non-partisan board of electors; his appointment in the Thirteenth ward was a compliment to his journal, to himself and a recognition of his worth. Through the agency of Governor Foraker he was also appointed Deputy State Oil Inspector at a handsome salary. He not only is fitted to fill this position but he is thereby recognized as one of the factors in holding the party together, and he is especially deserving of it because of the noble manner in which he championed Governor Foraker's cause in the canvass. No other colored man holds a similar position in the State, and never has held such.

It should be mentioned here that as a musician he has taken very high rank, as has been shown by what has been written above. He has written several songs which are deservedly popular and can be found upon the pianos of thousands of homes. Among the most popular is the song, "Be true, bright eyes."

He is one of whom the race is justly proud and from whom we shall hear much in the future. Already he has been mentioned as a possible candidate for legislative honors, and he will be deserving of all the honors that might be thrust upon him. He is by no means one of those who seek to reap that which he has not sown, but is modest and retiring. His intellectual qualities, his goodness of heart and generous nature always bring him to the front among his friends, who are loyal and true to him. He is manly and in every way shows his superiority over the common man. May he continue to prosper in worldly goods and honors as he is now prospering. He has attained some wealth and delights to use it as a slight contribution to the loved ones at home, his mother and sister, who labored so hard to give him the opportunities to make the most of himself.

CHAPTER XVI

Rev. John Bunyan Reeve, A. B., D. D.
Distinguished Presbyterian Divine—Professor of Howard
University, Theological Department

———•·•———

In Philadelphia, Pennsylvania, lives one of the oldest and most respected Presbyterian preachers in America. One whose virtues and long life of devotion to the precious Gospel are known far and wide. A worthy nobleman of feeling so tender and sympathetic, that while he ever listens to you with deep and lasting interest, it pains you to see how keenly a tale of sorrow affects him. He is a man of large physique, commanding stature, and impresses one as a gentleman of strong convictions and earnest purpose.

He was born October 29, 1831, at Mattatuck, Suffolk county, New York. His parents and grandparents had long lived in that neighborhood, and in this place he had his home until he was seventeen years of age. He attended district schools while young, and worked on a farm. From 1848 till 1852 or 1853, he lived and worked in the State of New York, during which time he became a member of the Shiloh Presbyterian church, during the pastorate of the Rev. J. W. C. Pennington, D.D. His parents were Presbyterians, and his mother had early dedicated him to the ministry. A mother's prayers, personal conviction, and the pastor's counsel prevailed over him, and in 1853, after having taught school for a few months at New Tower, Long Island, and having been received under the care of the Third Presbytery of New York City, as a candidate for the Gospel ministry, he entered the preparatory department of the New York Central College, then at McGawsville, New York, where he spent one year in the preparatory and graduated from the college department in June, 1958. He then entered in September, 1858, the Union Theological Seminary of New York City, from which he was graduated in April, 1861, the same month was licensed to preach the Gospel by the Third Presbytery of New York City, and was then dismissed to the Fourth Presbytery of Philadelphia, Pennsylvania. June 14, 1861, he was ordained by the latter body and installed pastor of the Lombard Street

Central Presbyterian church, Philadelphia, where he remained until September, 1871. Then he resigned his pastorate to accept the invitation of General O. O. Howard, and the appointment of the American Missionary Association, to organize a theological department in Howard University, Washington, District of Columbia and teach therein.

He remained in this work, faithfully serving the institution until June, 1875, when he resigned to accept a recall to the pastorate in Philadelphia. He was reinstalled pastor of this church in September, 1875, where a kind Providence still permits him to serve.

He has never sought any high honors, and with extreme modesty and dignified deportment, he has gone through life thinking that his "highest honor was that of having had Godly parents; the Rev. Dr. Pennington, when in his prime, as the pastor and guide of his youth, and the late Hon. William E. Dodge and the Rev. Asa D. Smith, D.D., then his pastor, and later president of Dartmouth College, for his patrons when a poor student." He was made moderator of the Presbytery of Philadelphia in 1865, and a commissioner to several assemblies the same year.

His talents being of such a high order, his personal popularity so well known, and the purity of his life so marked, that Lincoln University, in Pennsylvania, in 1870, honored herself in conferring upon him the degree of D.D. He is beloved by his congregation, which he has served for many years, and with whom it is presumed he will end his labors and go to the haven of rest prepared for the people of God; and his lasting influence over the lives of those to whom he has ministered will be as a grateful incense ascending to God.

CHAPTER XVII

Thomas J. Bowers
The American "Mario," Tenor Vocalist

The American "Mario" was born in Philadelphia in 1836. In childhood he was very fond of music, and exhibited rare talent in that direction. His father, a man of considerable intelligence, and filled with anxiety to have his children learn this fine accomplishment, procured a piano and a competent instructor for his oldest son, John C. Bowers, thinking if he became proficient he should teach the others. This purpose was accomplished, and our subject was instructed by his brother to perform upon the pianoforte and on the organ. In a short time he became a master of the art and succeeded his brother as organist of St. Thomas church, in Philadelphia. He was restricted from becoming a public performer for a long time because of his parents. As a tenor vocalist he attracted the attention and excited the admiration of many persons. His voice was extraordinary in its power, mellowness and sweetness. At Samson Street Hall, in Philadelphia, in 1854, he was induced to appear with the Black Swan as her pupil. It was not on this occasion that he made his fame, yet the *Press* of Philadelphia spoke of his performance in flattering terms and called for a repetition of the concert. After this repetition, a critic, commenting upon the voice of Mr. Bowers, styled him the "Colored Mario." Colonel Woods, once manager of the Cincinnati museum, hearing of the remarkable singing qualities of Mr. Bowers, came to Philadelphia to hear him. He was delighted and entered into an engagement with him to make a concert tour of New York and the Canadas. Mr. Bowers was accompanied by Miss Sarah Taylor Greenfield, the famous songstress. They were highly applauded, and met with great success wherever they appeared. During this tour, Colonel Wood urged that he should appear under the name of "Indian Mario," and again under that of "African Mario." He hesitated for quite a while before he would accept either, but at last he consented to that of "Mario." As a lover of his race, Mr. Bowers engaged in public performances more for the purpose of encouraging colored persons to take rank in music with the more highly cultured of the fairer race, than for that of making a display of his rare abilities, also for the enjoyment which he derived from it. Writing to a friend, he says:

What induced me more than anything else to appear in public was to give the lie to Negro serenaders (ministrels), and to show to the world that colored men and women could sing classical music as well as members of the other race, by whom they had been so terriby vilified.

A love of filthy lucre nor his care for fame ever caused him to yield to that vulgar prejudice that compelled the colored persons to take back seats or go to the galleries. If they did not receive the same treatment as the whites he refused to sing, which was manly to say the least. He had an occasion to take this step and stood firm, and thereby broke down the prejudice that many encourage.

Mr. Bowers sang in many of the States, and even invaded the slavery cursed regions of Maryland. Many very favorable comments had he from different papers. He was ranked among the most cultured of his day, and as a tenor vocalist surpassed all of his contemporaries. As Mr. Bowers is dead, and we were unable to secure material for this sketch, we are largely indebted to *Music and Some Highly Musical People* for much of the above, and also for permission from the author to use the same.

CHAPTER XVIII

*Rev. Nicholas Franklin Roberts, A. B., A. M.
Professor of Mathematics—President of the Baptist State
Convention of North Carolina—Moderator of* 100,000
Colored Baptists

Among the rising young men of the old "Tar Heel State" is the one whose name is at the head of this article. He has reflected honor upon the State that gave him birth; he is a young man who has risen from the drudgery of farm life to the prominence of a professor in a university, and is therefore a representative of his people. There are many older persons, of course, who might be selected, and some may bring the charge of "young men" against some of the characters in this book, but if in early life they have placed themselves at the head of great enterprises, it seems fitting that they should be noticed for the encouragement of others who come behind them. Then the depths from which some people rise, and the heights to which they climb, is worthy of notice. Now is there reason for the farmer boy who reads this sketch to be discouraged because he has hard work, plowing, cutting and hauling wood, caring for the pigs, feeding the cows, and other laborious work? It seems not to me. The advantages of a farm life are many, though there may be rough spots and difficult passages. Indeed, the days of a farmer are well spent in being influenced by nature and thus being led up to nature's God. Boys in the country have their minds measurably kept pure and untainted by the things that destroy the purity of the mind, and many of these "young men" referred to are mentioned as a means of encouragement to those who still are behind in the race of life.

He was born near Seaboard, North Hampton county, North Carolina, October 13, 1849. At the age of twelve years he relates that he had a thirst for learning, which made him apply himself to his books very diligently. He would study very late at night, often all night. The young man was especially apt with figures, easily leading the other boys, with whom he was associated, in all efforts at mathematical calculation. With ease every problem was solved by him in common school mathematics before he ever attended school. His mathematical mind was the subject of much comment, and he has only accomplished in that sphere what was prophesied for him. October 10, 1871, he entered Shaw University, then known as the Shaw Collegiate Institute. Here he pursued an eminently satisfactory life, entering the lowest grade and passing up the line through a college course, eliciting the praise and commendation of the president and faculty. May, 1878, he graduated with much honor and received the applause of his fellow-students and the congratulations of his friends.

Having been converted March, 1872, and feeling a call to the ministry, he was ordained to the work of a gospel minister May 20, 1877. Rev. Roberts' ability as a mathematician has steadily promoted him in this department of educational work, and the professorship of mathematics has been held by him in his *alma mater* ever since graduation, except one year when he labored as general missionary for North Carolina, under the auspices of the American Baptist Home Mission Society of New York, and the Baptist State Convention of North Carolina. God has thus given him an extended field of usefulness where he might develop into a powerful man. Blount Street Baptist church, Raleigh, North Carolina, called for him to serve them as their pastor on July 2, 1882. This pastoral work has been done in connection with his work as professor, and they have been of mutual help to each other. There is great love existing between the pastor and the people, and the church has prospered, adding year by year to their numbers "such as shall be saved." As a Sabbath-school worker, earnestness and love to God has characterized his life. From 1873 to 1883, a period of ten consecutive years, he has held the position of president of the State Sunday School convention, and in October, 1885, he was unanimously elected president of the State Baptist convention, which position he now holds, esteemed by all the brethren of the State. His position makes him the representative of 100,000 colored Baptists, and as such he is recognized and respected. His position in the university gives him prestige among the educated, and his indorsement by the convention shows the people are in favor of education.

THEOPHILE T. ALLAIN

CHAPTER XIX

Hon. Theophile T. Allain
State Senator of Louisiana—Agitator of Educational Measures
and Internal Improvements—Contractor for Repairing Levees

———•◆•———

After the battle at Salamis, the generals of the different Greek states met in council to vote to each other prizes for distinguished individual merit. Were the task mine to pick from the ranks of Louisiana's sons those who have in the face of opposition towered head and shoulders above their fellow men, shedding lustre on the name of the sons of Ham, the subject of my sketch would take front rank. Having passed through forty-one years of the most eventful period of the Nation's history, it is but natural that he should have from boyhood thought on and traced the struggles to which the race has been subject, and that his heart would be stirred with that patriotic devotion which sacrifices luxurious idleness on the shrine of duty. Opposition calls forth resistance, and it may be well that the Africo-American has prejudice to fight, otherwise Mr. Allain, with scores of other noble men, would be quietly performing personal duties, letting the world surge in at their windows, but never going out to meet it. October 1, 1846, on the Australian Plantation Parish of West Baton Rouge, was born Theophile, a boy who evinced at an early age those signs which point to future usefulness. His mother, "a pretty brown woman," possessing all the taste and attractions found among those of more fortunate circumstances than falls to the lot of a slave, attracted the attention and affection of her master, a millionaire of culture, who was the father of this son. Mr. Sosthene Allain, in the prime of life, was surrounded by all the comforts which taste and a princely income can give. Setting at naught the sentiments of the land, he shared these comforts with the mother and his dear "Soulouque," often refusing to take his meals unless the boy ate with him. Mr. Allain always spent his summers North or in Europe, but not without taking Theophile, who received the same accommodations. When he was ten years old his father, who was in Paris, sent for him, and he was sent in charge of Madam Boudousquie, an accomplished actress, who treated him with love and kindness. When the ship landed at Havre, ten thousand people were there to welcome the Emperor Soulouque of Hayti, but instead it was the "Soulouque" of our sketch. These yearly visits, the contact with other customs, was a more liberal education to the observing boy than could have been acquired by years of application to books. He was present at the christening of the Prince Imperial at the church of Notre Dame de Paris, attended bathing school and accompanied his father everywhere he went. Returning to America he entered school in 1859 under Professor Abadie, New Orleans, Louisiana, and in 1868 entered a private school in New Brunswick, New Jersey. In 1869 he returned home and went into the grocery business in West Baton Rouge and Iberville and remained until 1873, when he invested largely in sugar and rice cultivation. Genius in one man may run in the line of literature, in another, art, but in this man business seems to be the ruling passion. For twenty years he has been a successful shipper of sugar, syrup, molasses and rice, and every day brings him in business contact with the leading commercial men of the South. Every Exchange in the city of New Orleans is open to him. In 1883 the total crop on his plantation was estimated at four hundred barrels of syrup. Although living in competency, his sympathies are all with the laboring class. At the Sugar Planters' convention which met in New Orleans, August 20, 1884, a resolution was offered for the appointment of a committee to collect "data as to the cost of land, labor, food, stock, fuel, etc., with the idea of producing cheaper sugar. Hon. Allain opposed it on the ground that it meant simply the cutting down on wages for the laborer." At another time in the Legislature, he said: "I tell you, gentlemen, that when you cultivate any spirit of animosity between the tillers of the soil on one hand and the proprietors on the other, you cut your own throats. Nature and nature's God have so arranged it, that labor and capital are mutually dependent upon each other." Besides this business he is giving work to more laborers than any colored man in the "public works of the country," being under bond and contract with the State of Louisiana to put up within three years one hundred and fifty thousand yards of levee. When the levees of the Mississippi were in a deplorable condition, the Republican Executive and Financial committee of the Third Congressional District of Louisiana, of which Hon. L. A. Martinet was secretary, met April 8, 1882, and adopted the following resolutions. We give the full statement and all the immediate outgrowth thereof. Mr. Allain counts the following as the champion record of his life. He desires this record handed down to his children.

RECORD

The credentials below were furnished him in Louisiana, and he went to Washington, District of Columbia, and appeared before the committee on commerce:

Mr. Allain, upon being introduced by the Hon. R. L. Gibson of Louisiana, presented to the committee the following credentials:

Resolved, That Hons. T. T. Allain and George Drury be appointed a committee to proceed to Washington to lay before the President and those in authority, the deplorable condition of the Mississippi levees, and urge the necessity on the part of the National Government of taking early action toward building and maintaining the same, and also to ask a continuance of government aid to the sufferers from the present overflow.

Resolved further, That the said committee is hereby authorized to present to the President the condition of political affairs in this State, so far as the Third Congressional district is concerned.

NEW ORLEANS, LOUISIANA, April 8, 1882

To all whom it may concern:

I hereby certify that the foregoing is a true copy of resolutions adopted at a meeting of the executive and finance committee of the Third Congressional district of this State, held in this city March 27, 1882.

L. A. MARTINET,
Secretary Republican Executive and Finance Committee,
Third Congressional District, Louisiana

NEW ORLEANS, April 5, 1882

To the honorable Senators and Representatives in Congress from the State of Louisiana:

The undersigned Republicans and Federal officials here regard with great pleasure the selection and appointment of Hon. T. T. Allain, a sugar planter, and representative Republican of the parish of Iberville, by the Republican committee of the Third Congressional district of Louisiana, to proceed to Washington, District of Columbia, and endeavor to enlist the services of our Representatives and Senators and the National administration for the purpose of rebuilding and maintaining of the levees of the Mississippi river by the National Government, and we commend him to the attention of the authorities, and trust his mission may be eminently successful.

Very respectfully,

DON. A. PARDEE
EDWARD C. BILLINGS
A. J. DUMONT
T. B. STAMP
M. V. DAVIS
A. S. BADGER
JACK WHARTON
P. B. S. PINCHBACK
SAM'L WAKEFIELD
JAMES LEWIS
L. A. MARTINET
ROBT. F. GUICHARD

NEW ORLEANS, April 8, 1882

To the Senate and House Committees on the Improvement of the Mississippi River:

Mr. T. T. Allain having informed me of his intention to visit Washington, and as a sugar-planter interested in the reparation and maintenance of the levees in this State, and as a Representative of the colored people of this State, it gives me pleasure to indorse and recommend his mission as one of much importance.

I regard the colored laborer as well adapted to the cultivation of sugar and to the diseases of this climate, and should consider it as a misfortune if it should be discouraged and driven away by the inability of the planter to restore the levees.

Congress, in protecting the great American interest of sugar, may incidentally provide employment for a great number of her colored race, estimated at more than one hundred thousand.

Mr. Allain deserves approval for his public spirit in urging upon Congress the importance of promptly assuming charge of the levees of Louisiana, and will be entitled to the gratitude of the planters and laborers for any influence he may exercise in securing the adoption of a system which will prevent Louisiana from the calamity of an overflow, and the public from the abandonment, and possibly the destruction of the sugar crop, which now retains at home more than $25,000,000, otherwise exported for the purchase of foreign sugar.

Your obedient servant,
R. S. HOWARD,
President Chamber of Commerce

NEW ORLEANS COTTON EXCHANGE,
NEW ORLEANS, April 6, 1882

Hon. T. T. Allain, Louisiana State representative, is entitled to full encouragement and assistance from our Senators and Representatives in Congress, as a delegate from the suffering people of the overflowed section of Louisiana.

We therefore recommend him to their good offices, and earnestly request that he be granted such hearing as the importance of his mission warrants, which mission is to show fully the dire necessities of our people and their claims upon the general government for assistance in protecting themselves from a recurrence of the terrible disasters through which they are now suffering.

Very respectfully,
THOMAS L. AIREY,
President New Orleans Cotton Exchange

NEW ORLEANS STOCK EXCHANGE
NEW ORLEANS, April 8, 1882

The New Orleans Stock Exchange cordially indorses the mission as represented by Hon. T. T. Allain to succor the distressed sufferers from the overflow, and trusts that his efforts to bring influence to rebuild our levees will be successful.

T. S. BARTON,
President

A. A. BRINSMADE, Secretary

NEW ORLEANS, April 6, 1882

To Hon. W. P. Kellogg, U. S. Senator from Louisiana, and Hon. C. B. Darrall, Representative Third Congressional District of Louisiana, Washington, D. C.

GENTLEMEN: The undersigned, members of the Americus Club of this city, beg to commend to your favorable attention Hon. T. T. Allain, representative from Iberville Parish in our present State Legislature, who has been appointed to visit Washington, District of Columbia, by the Third Congressional District Committee of the State of Louisiana, with the view of obtaining National aid in rebuilding and maintaining the levees of the Mississippi river.

We ask that your aid and influence be given him in accomplishing this desirable object, and thanking you for your joint and individual effort in behalf of these interests, subscribe ourselves,

Yours respectfully,

WM. A. HALSTON,
    Secretary Executive Committee

P. LANDRY, Corresponding Secretary

JAS. E. PORTER,
    First Vice, Acting President

GEO. H. WALKER,
    Secretary Americus Club

FRED. SIMMS,
    Treasurer Americus Club

F. MOSS, Vice-President
    Chairman Executive Committee,
    Americus Club

THOMAS J. BOSWELL
A. P. WILLIAMS
GEO. G. JOHNSON
W. SILVERTHORN
J. E. MARTINEZ
W. S. WILSON
JAMES D. MACARY

C. A. PHILIPPI & CO.,
COTTON FACTORS AND COMMISSION MERCHANTS,
No. 48 UNION STREET, NEW ORLEANS, April 6, 1882

To our Senators and Representatives in Congress:

GENTLEMEN: Hon. T. T. Allain, a prominent representative of the parish of Iberville, is delegated by a large number of planters and business men of Iberville and this city to proceed to Washington, to intercede with our Senators and Representatives in Congress, in asking the National government to build and maintain the levees of the Mississippi river. We desire to state that we furnished him on and for making his sugar crop about $4,000 within the last two years, all of which he has paid.

We therefore take pleasure in recommending Mr. Allain to our delegation in Congress, and ask a favorable consideration for the cause he advocates, and commend his statements.

Very respectfully,
C. A. PHILIPPI & CO.

OFFICE OF RENSHAW, CAMMACK & CO.,
COTTON AND SUGAR FACTORS, No. 32 PERDIDO STREET,
NEW ORLEANS, LOUISIANA, March 28, 1882

To whom it may concern:

We have had business relations with the Hon. T. T. Allain, of Iberville parish during several years, and feel satisfied that any statement he might make concerning the condition of the levees and the consequent needs of the river parishes may be confidently relied on.

Very respectfully,
RENSHAW, CAMMACK & CO.
AR. MITTENBERGER & POLLOCK
E. B. WHEELOCK
STAUFFER MACREADY & CO.
HANSELL & WEBSTER
J. W. BURBRIDGE

I fully and cheerfully indorse all that is said above, and commend Mr. Allain to the Louisiana delegation in Congress, and respectfully request their thorough co-operation in his patriotic purpose.

I. N. MARKS

CITIZENS' BANK OF LOUISIANA,
BANKING DEPARTMENT,
NEW ORLEANS, April 8, 1882

To the Hon. Senators and Representatives of the State of Louisiana in Congress, Washington, D. C.:

GENTLEMEN: The bearer, the Hon. T. T. Allain, a sugar planter of excellent repute, from parish Iberville, in our State, and no doubt known to most of you, comes to Washington accredited as a delegate from his parish and district, to intercede with members of Congress for an early and ample appropriation toward rebuilding the Mississippi river levees for the future protection of agricultural interests against a repetition of the disastrous and ruinous flood which has this year desolated so large a portion of our State.

We earnestly solicit from yourselves and associates in both houses a favorable consideration and prompt action toward the desired end, never so indispensable as now.

Very respectfully, your obedient servants,

E. L. CARRIERE,
President,
JAS. J. TARLETON,
Cashier

OFFICE OF TERTROU & PUGH,
COTTON AND SUGAR FACTORS,
NEW ORLEANS, March 28, 1882

HON. R. L. GIBSON, Washington:

DEAR SIR: We take pleasure in introducing to your acquaintance Hon. T. T. Allain, a prominent planter of the parish of Iberville, in this State, being a neighbor to a plantation whose owners are in Paris, and of whom we are the agents. Mr. Allain is from a parish in which are many large plantations and wealthy planters, and is personally known to us. He intends visiting Washington for and on account of levee purposes.

We therefore recommend him to your consideration and any bid or information which he may need, and extend to him, will be appreciated by,

Yours respectfully,

TERTROU & PUGH,

I cordially indorse Hon. T. T. Allain as worthy and intelligent. Any courtesy extended him will be appreciated.

Respectfully,

CYRUS BUSSEY

OFFICE OF THE MANHATTAN LIFE INSURANCE COMPANY,
156 AND 158 BROADWAY, NEW ORLEANS, LOUISIANA, March 28, 1882

HON. B. F. JONAS, Washington, D. C.:

DEAR SIR: Hon. T. T. Allain, of Iberville parish, visits Washington in the interest of levee protection for the State at large, and has the influence of our best citizens to aid his mission. As Mr. Allain represents the combined political elements of his parish, doubtless his visit will result in great benefit, just at this condition of distress arising from present high water.

I have the honor to be, respectfully, etc.,

H. M. ISAACSON

THE SPEECH

Mr. Allain said:

MR. CHAIRMAN: The papers and documents which I have had the honor to present to you from the New Orleans Chamber of Commerce, the Cotton Exchange, and a number of prominent, wealthy, and deeply interested merchants and other business men of that city, together with the indorsement and recommendations of the Republican committee of the Third Congressional district of Louisiana, are the sanctions of authority and the credentials on which I venture to appear before you; not, however, without a profound sense of my inability to do full justice to a subject of such vast importance as the preservation of the levees of the Mississippi river by the National government, the advocacy of which I am charged with.

And, cheerfully as I respond to the obligations thus imposed, my diffidence is not at all diminished, and especially, when I remember how frequently, fully, forcibly—and, we had hoped, conclusively—it has been shown by facts, figures, arguments, and demonstrations that it was—and as it now is—the interest and the duty of the National government to build and keep in repair the levees of its mighty river, the Mississippi.

It is mine today, sir, to once more tread this beaten path, and if it be true that there is no evil without its corresponding good, it is mine to seize the lamentable opportunity, the moment when millions of acres of cultivable and cultivated cotton, sugar, and rice lands are many feet under water; when thousands of families are flooded out of their homes, and taking refuge everywhere, anywhere from the angry flood; when a hundred thousand laborers, driven by the waters, have fled in every direction, to the utter demoralization of labor; when horses, mules, oxen, and innumerable, but valuable lesser animals are destroyed or sacrificed in one way or the other; I say that at this moment of our deepest affliction I am commissioned to come here and appeal to you and to the government to use every exertion, to relax no effort to save our section (as far as human agency and human effort can rescue us) from the periodic recurrence of these calamitous overflows.

I may state, as an absolute fact, that the States whose lands are periodically overflowed by the Mississippi river are utterly unable to build and maintain the levees to meet these occasional emergencies.

This argument in itself would not, I know, constitute any valid basis for our claim that the National government should therefore assume the task of efficiently providing against the disasters.

I have, therefore, been at some pains to prepare my statements to fortify the position I now assume, and that is, that it is the *interest* and the duty of the United States Government to construct and maintain an efficient system of levees along the banks of the Mississippi river, and that upon it must rest the enormous moral responsibility, at least, of the incalculable suffering and losses which are entailed by the overflows.

It is not necessary for me to labor to show you that the United States possessing and exercising the powers and prerogatives of absolute ownership of this mighty inland sea, is placed thereby under obligation to adopt every necessary precaution to keep it within bounds.

I take it that this branch of the subject having been so well and so frequently set before the government I need not dwell on it here.

I cannot resist the temptation, however, to quote the following forcible language from the speech of Hon. James B. Eustis, late United States Senator from my State:

"We know, Mr. President, that the jurisdictional authority of the United States Government is exclusive over that river throughout its length, and we know how that jurisdictional authority was acquired. It was acquired by the statutes of the United States and by the decisions of the Supreme Court. In the early period of our history there was a conflict going on between the Federal authority and the State governments, with reference to the jurisdiction over nagivable streams, a controversy which was as acrimonious upon the bench of the Supreme Court as was the slavery question. It was finally determined, after twenty-five years of contest, that the maritime and admiralty jurisdiction over those streams was exclusively vested in the Federal government; and only a short time ago, as high up as Shreveport, on Red river, it was decided that the admiralty and maritime jurisdiction over that stream was exclusively vested in the United States government. That jurisdiction is an exhaustive jurisdiction. It denies to the States any authority, or any power, or any responsibility, or any obligation whatsoever touching the Mississippi river. The United States Government can bridge it; the United States Government can determine what commerce shall be carried on that river, what shall be the means of transportation on that river, who shall have the privilege of navigating that river; and it is even said in one of the decisions of the Supreme Court that it has the authority to change the channel of that river.

"Now, I ask, Mr. President, why is it, if every individual in this land, every corporation, is obliged to discharge the obligations and the responsibilities and the duties arising from the mere tutorship or control of property—I ask upon what ground can the United States absolve itself from that obligation and from that responsibility, particularly when we consider the immense loss and devastation and ruin which result from omitting to discharge that obligation? And I do not understand that there is any such thing as degree in national duties and national obligations. If I can convince the Senate that it is the duty of the United States Government, that it is an obligation of the United States Government, it then follows that it is as much a question of national faith to discharge that duty, to discharge that obligation, as for the Government of the United States to pay the interest on its public debt."

Passing from this branch of the subject to the *ability* of the government, I presume that there is not one well-informed citizen of this great Republic that raises this question.

Then, if all these things be true, the only essential lacking is the *willingness* of the government to recognize the propriety, the *justice*, and the *obligation* to undertake *this work*.

And I hold that it is as much to the *interest* as it is the *duty* of government to undertake the task of protecting the lands of both sides of its river from incursions by its occasionally turbulent stream.

It is the interest of the National Government because of the enormous revenue—the support—which it derives from the section of country which suffers from overflows.

I am aware that this is an appeal to the Nation on the lowest plane—the sordid motive of self-interest, but the argument I hold is sound and the conclusions I shall draw most just.

Taking Louisiana as the illustration, look at our production and the revenue which the National Government derives as the necessary direct result of our agricultural products.

Not to be tedious, Mr. Chairman, I will offer the tabulated statement of Hon. R. L. Gilson, one of our congressmen, in his recent speech on the Hawaiian treaty and sugar.

I give you our production of sugar from 1870 to 1880, and rice from 1877 to 1880:

Year	Sugar		Molasses	Rice
	Hogsheads	Pounds	Gallons	Pounds
1869–70	87,090	99,452,946	5,724,256	
1870–71	144,881	168,878,592	10,281,419	
1871–72	128,461	146,906,125	10,019,958	
1872–73	108,520	125,346,493	8,898,640	
1873–74	89,498	103,241,119	8,203,944	
1874–75	116,867	134,504,691	11,516,828	
1875–76	144,146	163,418,070	10,870,546	
1876–77	169,331	190,672,570	12,024,108	
1877–78	127,753	147,101,941	14,237,280	35,080,520
1878–79	213,221	239,478,753	13,218,404	36,592,310
1879–80	169,972	198,962,278	12,189,190	20,728,520

In the matter of cotton it is as important as it is interesting to note a few particulars.

The Southern country produced in 1880 the enormous amount of 2,770,000,000 (two billions seven hundred and seventy millions) of pounds of raw cotton, which is nearly four-fifths of the entire cotton crop of the world.

During the war we had no production to speak of; but after that dreary period, and when we had resumed cultivation under the new and improved order of things, the increase in the production of this staple became marked.

Every year since 1866–67, except in overflow years, we have increased our cotton production until 1880, when we reached the magnificant figures of 6,611,000 bales, as will be more fully seen by the following extract from the report of "Louisiana Products," by Commissioner W. H. Harris, to the Legislature of 1881:

COTTON CROP OF THE SOUTH

Year	Crop	Year	Crop
1872–73	3,930,508	1877–78	4,773,765
1873–74	4,185,534	1878–79	5,074,155
1874–75	3,832,991	1879–80	5,761,252
1875–76	4,669,283	1880–81	6,611,000
1876–77	4,485,423		

The value, sir, of these staple productions of our lands, which are largely subject to overflow, make an aggregate value that to me, at least, is perfectly bewildering.

I have heard it declared the conception of a million was an overtax on an ordinary mind. But, sir, when we figure up the annual value of our sugar, cotton, and rice crops, we cannot but be astounded to find that we run up into hundreds of millions of dollars.

This year, sir, unfortunately we shall find no difficulty in computing and comprehending the value of our production.

But when it is taken into account that we pay cheerfully into the National treasury our proportion of the taxes for the support of government, and that from such an exhibit, brief and incomplete as it is, it can be readily seen that in this matter we are not paupers, and that we need feel no hesitancy in coming up here urging and demanding that the National Government, which so generously, but not always wisely, donates millions upon millions to railroads, should return to us a modicum of our contributions in the shape of the preservation of the levees of the great Father of Waters.

The loss in revenue to the United States Government this year will be greater than the few millions we are asking and which we deserve to have.

Again, the expenditure of over a million of dollars in rations, which have been hurried to our rescue so promptly and so cheerfully, is an expenditure that might have been better utilized.

Build the levees and keep them in order, and then we shall not need to appeal for bread and meat, and tents and medicines.

Demoralizing as we know these things to be, we earnestly desire to dispense forever with the reliance on charity for food and shelter. But driven by our extremities, we have been compelled to once more tolerate the call for and dependence on "rations."

It seems to me, Mr. Chairman, that where so many important channels of profit are neglected that there must be some *duty* in the matter, and hence I say that it is the *duty* of the National Government to undertake without further delay the construction and keeping in order an efficient system of levees along the Mississippi banks.

For years we have had river committees, and river conventions, and Mississippi Valley conventions, and public meetings, and public speeches, and monster petitions, all in the direction of urging on Congress the duty of undertaking this work, but up to this date all of our appeals have been unavailing.

I say, sir, that we hold it to be the constitutional prerogative and duty of Congress to provide "for the welfare of the United States."

We form, in the relations we have alluded to, no inconsiderable portion of the United States, and our welfare is materially injured by the trespass of the river, and when we observe Congress recognizing the loud and just clamor raised against the imprisonment abroad of American citizens, and dealing with the question as suits a free republic; when we see the interest taken in projects to check the influx of Chinese, even to the practical abrogation of a solemn treaty with China, without the consent of "the other party"; when we see Congress undertaking the laudable, if gigantic, task of even regulating the polygamists of Utah; when we see, last, but not least, the beneficent propositions seriously made by a revered Senator to provide for the education of the aboriginal Indians of our country, and I reflect that the warrant and the authority for the accomplishment of these diversified objects, and that these all are regarded as *duties* of the United States Government, I wonder whether the *interests* of a million of people in Louisiana, a people who feel that by every just and patriotic consideration should—are entitled to have their "welfare" considered by the government to the extent we are seeking.

A continued neglect of the performance of the duty cannot but result in permanent disaster to the sections periodically overflowed, and the responsibility for the decay, the ruin, the bankruptcies, and the neglected fields will rest on the shoulders, on the only proper, the only competent, and the only efficient power to avert them—the Government of the United States.

I present you the following statement, made by one of the best informed men in the State, on the overflow, Major E. A. Burke, who has personally visited and inspected the crevasses, the condition of the levees, river, and the cost that the State would incur in rebuilding the levees. He says:

"Eighty-one crevasses in State, from 300 to 1,500 feet each. Say an average of 900 feet in length of each levee washed away, making a running length of 72,900 feet, or say 1,043,000 yards of levee swept away—costing $260,750. To reconstruct the same levees, owing to the effect of the crevasses on the land requiring extra wings to gulches, etc., would require earthwork of at least double that quantity, or say an expenditure in Louisiana of $521,500, as a result of the flood of 1882, and without estimating the crevasses previously in existence. Those crevasses were the Bonnet Carré, in Saint John Parish, Morganza, in Pointe Coupee, Diamond Island, in Tensas, and Ashton, in East Carroll, all large crevasses broken a length of about nine miles of extra large levees, seventeen and eighteen feet in height, or 1,800,000 cubic yards. Owing to the great height of levees, the cost of rebuilding would be fully fifty cents per cubic yard, or $900,000 to reconstruct old levees. Thus we find that it would cost over $1,400,000 to reconstruct the levees broken by crevasses in Louisiana, a sum utterly beyond our ability."

Add loss cotton, sugar, miscellaneous, fences, stock.

I speak of demoralization, scattering of people, rising of water, under the head of crevasses.

But, sir, my vocabulary is too limited to express to you what "crevasses" in the banks of the Mississippi mean. I will therefore again borrow from the speech of Mr. Eustis. He says:

"Now, sir, a crevasse in the levees of the Mississippi river is something of which the imagination, unaided by observation, can scarcely form any accurate conception. At first it may be but a slender thread of water percolating through a crawfish hole, or a slight abrasion in the upper surface caused by the waves set in motion by a passing steamer or by a sudden storm, but in a few hours the seemingly innocent rill is swollen to a resistless torrent, the great wall of earth has given way before the tremendous pressure of the mighty river, and the waters rush through the opening with a force which soon excavates it to a depth of thirty or forty feet, with a roar which rivals the voice of Niagara and with a velocity which is great enough to draw an incautious steamer into the boiling vortex.

"The effect is not simply that of an overflow, which may subside in a day or two. The level of the river, at its flood, is above that of the surrounding country; and, consequently, when the embankments break, it is as if an ocean were turned upon the land. In a short time the neighboring country is converted into a sea. Cattle and horses are swept away and drowned, or forced to seek refuge on the few dry spots which remain among the seething waters; the crops are destroyed, and the people in many cases are forced to abandon their homes. Sometimes, indeed, the land itself is greatly injured by these inundations; for, while the floods which come from the Red river, or the Ohio, or even the Arkansas, bring some compensation in the fertilizing character of the deposits which they leave behind, those of the Missouri, being charged with sand and alkaline earths swept down from the great deserts of the west, have a pernicious and sometimes even a ruinous effect on the lands which they invade.

"In the year 1874, the phenomena which I have feebly described occurred on so extensive a scale that the catastrophe may well be regarded as a national calamity. Through the thirty Louisiana crevasses and the permanent openings in Arkansas, and through the breaks on the left bank a vast body of water overspread a district of country more than three hundred miles in extent from the north to the south, and averaging fifty miles from east to west. I take no account, sir, in this statement, of the vast tracts inundated by the overflows of tributary rivers. I limit myself to the direct influence of the Mississippi waters from the Arkansas southward, and within this region, more than three hundred miles in length by fifty miles in width, as I have said, about 22,000 square miles, much of it arable and cultivated land, much of it the most productive portion of the southwest, was laid under water for many weeks."

And strong and pointed and forcible as is this description, it is but a faint representation of the present condition of affairs in Louisiana. I have here, sir, a map of the State showing the overflowed districts of 1882.

There are a million of acres of the richest and most productive sugar, cotton and rice lands under water.

There are a hundred and twenty thousand human beings driven from their homes to seek shelter anywhere from the ravages of the flood.

Conjure up the picture, sir, if you can; look down the river as far as the eye can reach, every curve, every bend straightened; look on the right hand and then on the left as far as the eye can reach, and see the vast and apparently illimitable ocean of water.

Water, water everyhwere.

Remember, now that underneath this vast body, this "crevasse," lay buried the seed cane, the cotton-seed, the rice, the cereals, the homes, the all of over one hundred thousand people.

The picture of calamity can not be depicted by human pen or tongue. And remembering that these dire afflictions are of periodical recurrence, I am the more impressed with the necessity of using every legitimate appeal to the justice, and philanthropy, if you please, of this great Nation to come to our rescue.

And I cannot let this opportune moment escape me, as the representative of a class who, born and held in bondage until the utterance of the ever-living, ever-abiding decree of the immortal Lincoln gave them unconditional liberty, to specially invite consideration to an important feature of this question.

By this overflow, for the third time since freedom, our country has been flooded and desolated.

For the third time a hundred thousand stalwarts, yeomen, to the manor born, inured to toil, and living and laboring equally safe in the burning suns of August, the epidemic period of September, or the genial season of March and April.

For the third time, sir, this large, this necessary, this indispensable class, starting with nothing of this world's goods, but with "heart within and God o'erhead," assumed their new relations, determined to justify the act of their enfranchisement, determined to vindicate their title to the exalted position of equal citizenship in our great country, determined to erect homes, acquire property, build up their families, establish churches, support schools, cultivate the arts of peace, and so rise in the scale of humanity, and all the while contributing to the material prosperity of the section in which they reside.

But they cannot continue living and laboring under the apprehension of having their all remorselessly swallowed up every four or five years.

It requires no gift of prophecy to foretell that if this government persists in its refusal to keep its river confined to its regular channel (and we don't care how you do it) and thus prevent these overflows, there will be an exodus, a serious and permanent change of abode by a vast number of our laboring population, who cannot continue to endure the losses entailed by the disastrous overflows.

And in these days of railroads and enterprise, of openings up of sections of our common country not subject to overflow, and with climates as genial for us as our own, the danger of the loss of this element is considerably increased.

So speaking for this element, I say to the representatives of that glorious party which enacted the Thirteenth, Fourteenth and Fifteenth amendments to the Constitution of the United States, come once more to our rescue and save us from the necessity of abandoning our homes, the land of our birth, the clime and the products to which we are suited and which are suited to us, and the sympathy and increased loyalty of every black man, woman and child in Louisiana, yes, and in the United States, will be cordially given to you for this act of justice and humanity.

We are all, in Louisiana, "without regard to race, color, or previous condition," solicitous to avert the damages from overflow, and hence the unanimity among the representatives of the business and the wealth of our State, and of the two great parties, with which I have been authenticated to you, to all of whom I extend my humble and heartfelt thanks.

Finally, sincerely thanking you for the patience and attention with which you have honored me, I have but to say that if you keep the Mississippi out of our lands and homes we will in the near future turn 7,000,000 bales of cotton; we will send to market 250,000 hogsheads of sugar, 20,000,000 gallons of molasses, 25,000,000 pounds of rice, and develop a new industry dawning upon us; we will sent to the North in March our early cereals, our spring poultry, and Southern home products, while the snow and the ice of winter remain on your lands and fields.

Sir, we make three appeals for protection.

We appeal against the ravages of the mighty waters of the Mississippi; we appeal against the admission of foreign sugars to our markets free of duty; and, thirdly, we, the Negroes of the South appeal to you to protect us, our properties, and our lives against the annual overflows of the great river, in order that we may enjoy the benefits of liberty, husband the fruits of our industry, educate our children, and continue to increase our productions, and protect the fruits of our labor, which now is two-thirds of the cotton crops, four-fifths of the sugar crops, and very near all the rice crops.

We appeal to the National Government, which, in the name of Almighty God, we thank for all that we have, to take charge of the levees of the Mississippi river, and under the direction and supervision of officers of the

Finally, again thanking those who commissioned, and you who so patiently listened to me, I rejoice above them in the proud reflection that, in the sublime language of Frederick Douglass, I appear here "in the more elevated character of an American citizen."

government to maintain them.

This speech was made Tuesday, April 18, 1882, at eleven A.M., before the following committee on commerce: Hon. Horace F. Page, of California, Chairman; David P. Richardson, of New York; Amos Townsend, of Ohio; Roswell G. Horr, of Michigan; William D. Washburn, of Minnesota; John W. Candler, of Massachusetts; William Ward, of Pennsylvania; John D. White, of Kentucky; Melvin C. George, of Oregon; Richard Guenther, of Wisconsin; John H. Reagan, of Texas; Robert M. McLane, of Maryland; Randall L. Gibson, of Louisiana; Miles Ross, of New Jersey; Thomas H. Herndon, of Alabama.

It will be remembered that the question of levees affected more directly the prosperity of the State than all the others combined. It is not a small matter that this colored man should be selected by the most prominent business men of the section. President Arthur said: "No man can present papers from any part of the country that could say more." He pleaded well for his constituents, telling the true state of affairs and giving a reason for every demand made. Hon. Allain possesses a large amount of perseverance. Ten years before this, 1872-74, while serving his first term in the Legislature he agitated this question. In 1875 he was elected to the State Senate and remained until 1878. 1879 finds him a member of the Constitutional convention, and from '79 to '86 in the House of Representatives again. Sixteen years of public life is no short time for one who is still young. Hon. Allain is a strong advocate of popular education, and is second to no man in the State when it comes to educational matters for the colored people. He was the first man after the war to organize public schools in West Baton Rouge for both the white and colored children. In 1886, Mr. Allain introduced a bill in the Legislature asking for an appropriation of twenty thousand dollars and secured fourteen thousand dollars for the purpose of erecting the College buildings of the "Southern University." In a speech at the laying of the "corner stone" he said: "I look forward to a period not far distant, when Louisiana will be able to have a white and colored school-house dotting every nook and corner in the State of our birth, the home of our choice, with a public sentiment advocating for high and low, for white and colored popular education." January 27, 1877, he offered at the "Farmers' State Association," a resolution requesting the association to recommend the passage of an act by the Legislature to establish an Industrial school for the education of colored people. Under the caption "A Good Move," January 15, 1887, the *Weekly Iberville South* quotes from the *Louisiana Standard:*

> Hon. T. T. Allain has succeeded in having designated as Depositories for Public Records the four institutions in our city which are attended almost exclusively by colored children, viz: Straight, Southern, Leland, and New Orleans universities. Mr. Allain deserves credit for the interest he takes in educational affairs, and as a business man is a success. While a member of the Republican party, he has always advocated unification between the two races.

The *Terrebonne Times* in the September 18, 1886, issue, accused him of drawing the color line, to which he replied:

I propose to issue a plan for "Unification" in 1888, and will ask the colored people in each of the fifty-eight parishes of Louisiana—including the city of New Orleans—to stand solid and support the nominees of the National Republican party for President, Vice-President, and for the members of Congress, but when it comes to State and local offices the colored man in Louisiana must not allow himself to be bulldozed by newspaper "Scarecrows." We know, much better than you can tell us, Mr. Editor, as to who among the "white Republicans" in "Louisiana" that have been "pure" and "true" to us—and God knows that the graves of thousands of our "best" men in the South, because of our support to "white Republican" candidates, should settle and put at rest forever the question of "gratitude." We must look to the peace, quiet and wellbeing of our people. We must have Normal and Industrial schools for our children, and more public schools in the parishes of the State, and we will go in and vote for the white men in Louisiana in 1888, who have the moral courage to give to their colored fellow-citizens a fair living chance, and the "enjoyment" of "full American citizenship."

Hon. Allain is an acute thinker, a man of sympathetic and benevolent nature and large culture. He is known as one of the "Colored Creoles" of Louisiana, and speaks French fluently, better than English. He has six children; the family affiliates with the Catholic church; the children are being educated for future usefulness at Straight University.

CHAPTER XX

Denmark Veazie
"Black John Brown"—Martyr

Nineteen years before the opening of this century, on the island of St. Thomas, was born a child who was destined to become a martyr for his race. Men may differ as to what makes a martyr, and believe it comes through the flesh or the wicked one; but martyrs are made of such material as fit men to attempt great things for what they believe to be right. Denmark was purchased by a man named Veazie, after whom he takes his name. He was fourteen years old when he was purchased. In 1800 he drew a prize of fifteen hundred dollars in a lottery. Of course we do not approve of his playing lottery by any means, but he made good use of six hundred dollars of the money, securing his freedom thereby. He was a carpenter by trade, and was the admired of all his companions, because of his strength and activity. Twenty-two years later he formed a plan to liberate the slaves of Charleston, South Carolina. His plan was to put the whole city to fire and the sword on June 16. He had particularly objected to any slave joining the conspiracy who was of that class of waiting men who received presents of old coats, etc., from their masters, as such slaves would be likely to betray them. At 10 o'clock at night, the governor having been informed of the conspiracy by the treachery of some of the Negroes, had military companies thrown around the city, and no one was allowed to pass in or out.

The slaves who were to come from Thomas Island, and land on the South bay, and seize the arsenal and guardhouse, failed to do so. Another body that was to seize the arsenal on the Neck, was also thwarted in its plans. All the conspirators, finding the town so well protected, did not attempt that which they intended. On Sunday afternoon, Denmark Veazie, for the purpose of making preliminary arrangements, had a meeting and dispatched a courier to inform the country Negroes what to do, but the courier could not get out of the city, and thus the project was a failure, but the leader died a martyr upon the gallows, and the slave who had betrayed him was purchased by the Legislature, thus putting a premium upon the betrayal of any one who should attempt an insurrection of this kind. From William C. Nell's *History of the Colored Patriots of the American Revolution,* we take the following:

The number of blacks arrested was 131; of these 35 were executed, 41 acquitted, and the rest sentenced to be transported. Many a brave hero fell, but history, faithful to her high trust, will engrave the name of Denmark on the same monument with Moses, Hampden, Tell, Bruce, Wallace, Toussaint L'Ouverture, La Fayette and Washington.

I have stood in the arsenal yard and seen the place where these men were executed, and the memory of their attempt will never fade from the history of the Negroes of South Carolina.

J. E. JONES

CHAPTER XXI

Professor J. E. Jones, A. B., A. M.
Professor of Homeletics and Greek in the Theological
Seminary, Richmond, Virginia—Corresponding Secretary
of the Baptist Foreign Mission Convention

Professor J. E. Jones was born of slave parents in the city of Lynchburg, Virginia, October 15, 1850. He remained a slave until the surrender. Against the earnest protestations of his mother he was put to work in a tobacco factory when not more than six years of age. This was in that period of the country's history when the question of human slavery was agitating the minds of the people from Maine to the Gulf. Then, when the feelings of the people of both sections of the country had almost reached their limits, the Southern States deemed it expedient to enact some very stringent laws with respect to the Negro. Therefore, the State of Virginia passed laws that prohibited anyone from teaching Negroes how to read and write, and if anyone was caught violating this law he would be imprisoned. Young Jones' mother believed, with all her heart, that the time would come when the colored people would be liberated. She did not hesitate to express that belief; she not only expressed it to her colored friends, but, on one occasion, went so far as to tell her owners the same thing. They regarded this as simply madness; but the idea took such hold on her that she, though ignorant herself, determined that she would have her son taught to read and write. At once she secured the services of a man who was owned by the same family as herself. This man agreed to come several nights each week to give this boy lessons. At this time—during the year 1864—things were getting to a desperate state in the South. Soon, Joseph's teacher began to think that he was running too much risk in giving these lessons at the boy's home. He decided that he could not continue. However, after some reflection another plan was tried. It was arranged that the pupil should go once a week to the room of his teacher. The time chosen was Sunday morning between the hours of ten and twelve o'clock. It was selected because the white people usually spent this time at church, praying(?) for the success of the Confederacy and the continuance of human slavery. Toward the close of the war, the master of the teacher discovered that he could read and write, and sold him. But this did not discourage the mother, she was determined, more than ever, to have her boy taught. After some time she succeeded in getting a sick Confederate soldier to teach him. She paid this man by giving him something to eat. The instruction by this man was cut short after several months by the surrender of General Lee. Immediately after the surrender, young Jones' mother placed him in a private school that had been opened by his first teacher, the late Robert A. Perkins. Up to this time, while the boy had made some progress, it could not be said to have been satisfactory. His was of a fun-loving, mischievous disposition. On account of this fact, combined with the irregularity of his lessons and other circumstances, he had not been impressed very seriously of the importance of an education. But when he commenced going to school after the surrender, his progress was more marked. He continued in this school for two years. The most of this period he stood head in his classes. The winter following he spent as a pupil in a private school taught by James M. Gregory, now a professor in Howard University, Washington, District of Columbia. He was one of the best scholars in this school. In the spring of 1868, Joseph was baptized and connected himself with the Court Street Baptist church of the city of Lynchburg, Virginia.

In October of the same year, he entered the Richmond Institute now Richmond Theological Seminary, with a view of preparing himself for the gospel ministry. He spent three years there, taking the academic and theological studies then taught. In April, 1871, he left Virginia for Hamilton, New York, and entered the preparatory department of Madison University, from which he graduated in 1872. The following fall he entered the university and after a successful course of study, graduated June, 1876. The same year the American Baptist Home Mission Society of New York appointed him instructor in the Richmond Institute, and entrusted him with the branches of language and philosophy. In 1877 he was ordained to the ministry. In 1879, his *alma mater* conferred upon him the degree of Master of Arts "in course." For two years Professor Jones has occupied the chair of Homeletics and Greek in the Richmond Theological Seminary. He has not only performed well his work in the class room, but has taken an active part in all the denominational movements as well as other questions relating to the welfare of his people. He is a member of the Educational Board of the Virginia Baptist State convention. November, 1883, Professor Jones was elected corresponding secretary of the Baptist Foreign Mission Convention of the United States of America. This convention has grown considerably since he has occupied this position. The *Religious Herald* of Richmond, Virginia, in speaking of the subject of this sketch says:

Professor Jones is one of the most gifted colored men in America. Besides being professor in Richmond Theological seminary, he is corresponding secretary of the Baptist Foreign Mission convention. He has the ear and heart of his people, and fills with distinction the high position to which his brethren North and South have called him.

Professor Jones has constant demands made upon him both to speak and to preach. He took an active part in getting colored teachers into schools, both in his native city and the city of his adoption. He has corresponded considerably for newspapers, and at one time was one of the editors of the *Baptist Companion* of Virginia. He was six years president of the Virginia Baptist Sunday School convention. In June, 1880, he was requested by the corresponding secretary of the American Baptist Home Mission Society of New York, to deliver an address at the society's anniversary at Saratoga, New York. His subject was, "The Need and Desire of the Colored People for these Schools." He spoke in the public hall to a vast audience which seemed to be perfectly spellbound as he told the tale of the Negro's condition and surroundings. The *Examiner* of New York, in commenting on the address said:

Mr. Jones is a young colored man, prepossessing in appearance and manners, and his address would have been creditable to any white graduate of any Northern collope. It was sensible, witty and eloquent.

The *Watchman* of Boston, in speaking of the same address, said:

The speech of the evening was that of Professor Jones, a colored man. His manly, strong, and sensible address made a stronger appeal for the education of his race than the words of the most eloquent advocate.

Two years later, on the twenty-first of June, Professor Jones was married to Miss Rosa D. Kinckle of Lynchburg, Virginia, a graduate from the Normal department of Howard University, and was then a teacher in the public schools of her city. This young man is doing a most excellent work for the general advancement of his race. He is very hopeful as to the future of the race. He holds, however, no utopian ideas respecting them. He believes, he says, "If the race would rise in the scale of being, they must comply with the same laws that conditionate the rise and development of other people." He points with pride to not a few of the young men who have gone out from the Institute since he has been connected with it. Some of them are succeeding admirably well as doctors, lawyers, teachers, and ministers of the gospel. Dr. Cathcart, in the *Baptist Encyclopædia*, says:

Professor Jones is an efficient teacher, a popular and instructive preacher, and a forcible writer. In 1878 he held a newspaper controversy with the Roman Catholic Bishop Keane of Richmond, in which the bishop, in the estimation of many most competent to judge, was worsted. Professor Jones is regarded as one of the most promising of the young colored men of the South.

In following the career of Professor Joseph Endom Jones, and observing and marking the changes in it, we can but say that it was simply marvelous—it must have been divinely ordered and superintended. In his manners he is princely and attractive. He is never excited, and, while an enthusiast in his work, is never more careful than when discussing or planning the preparatory part thereof. Nothing overthrows him. With great consideration, careful and accurate information, he seldom makes a mistake. It might seem to one that his interest might be lacking in any given affair—for he can sit all day and show no desire to speak, and when all are through he will pointedly show that no thought was wasted on him, but that he had given strict attention to the whole matter. Such is the man.

CHAPTER XXII

John Wesley Terry, Esq.
Foreman of the Ironing and Fitting Department of the Chicago
West Division Street Car Company—Director and Treasurer
of the Chicago Co-operative Packing and Provision Company—
Director of the Central Park Building and Loan Association

———◆———

John Wesley Terry is only about forty-one years of age, having, as near as can be ascertained, seen the light of day in Murry county, Tennessee, in 1846, and began life a poor, miserable slave, owned by William Pickard till emancipated by the war of the Rebellion. His mother's name was Mary, and his father's name was Hayward Terry. When he was but a crawling babe, and needed a mother's tender care, he with his dear brother, but little older than himself, were put into a pen that had been fenced off in one corner of the lot, and there, on the bare ground with no covering or shelter, had to crawl around on the ground, unattended from early morning, when his mother had to go out into the field to work, till it was too late to continue, when she had to come to the house and spin "ten cuts" of yarn or cotton before she was permitted to go to her children and take them from the pen. The only attention they received through the day was a pan of food placed in the pen by their mother to which they could go and eat.

In 1863, while the Federal army was in possession of Columbia, Tennessee, his mother took him and his brother and started for the Union lines. She succeeded and found protection for herself and her two boys. Henry, the older, being of sufficient age, enlisted in the army, leaving his mother and brother at Columbia. John remained with his mother till a Colonel Myers was placed in command at that point, and who delivered all slaves in his lines to their masters when they came for them. John and his mother were unfortunate in being carried back to Murry county by their old master, who came in search of them. Colonel Myers had been superseded in command at Columbia, and the Union forces had advanced and taken possession in Murry county, at which time John says: "I proclaimed to the old master, Pickard, my freedom, and at the same time threatened him with the Union army for harboring and feeding 'Rebel soldiers' as he had threatened me with the Secession army for attempting to gain my freedom." The old man begged him not to inform them against him and proposed to hire him for wages if he would not leave him. He worked two years for the old man for wages, who said he thought it was "hard to have to pay wages to a 'nigger' he had owned." After this he worked one year with his father on the "Terry farm," on Tennessee pike, near Sandy Hook. The latter part of 1866 he went to Nashville, Tennessee, to look for his mother, who had made her second attempt of escape before the Union army took possession of the country around the old farm in Murry county. Finding her, he worked on the steamboat in 1867, during which time his mother kept house for him.

In 1868 he took charge of the farm department known as the "Younglove Fruit Farm," on "Paradise Hill," and remained till 1869. Returning to Nashville, he and his brother Henry opened a "Tailor, Dye and Repair shop," and worked at it for about one year; then he entered the employ of P. J. Sexton, contractor and builder. Remained at the trade with him in Nashville till he went with him to Chicago, in 1872—the year after "the great fire." In 1873 he professed a hope in Christ, united with the Olivet Baptist church, in Chicago, and was baptized into its fellowship by the pastor, Rev. R. DeBaptiste. March 11, 1873, he was united in marriage to Miss Catharine Brown of Nashville, Tennessee, in Olivet Baptist church, Rev. DeBaptiste officiating. In 1875 he entered the employment of the Chicago West Division Street Car company, in their "car shops," and worked with them for two years, purchased a house, but leased the ground. Having a neatly, though not a costly, furnished little cottage home, he began to reflect upon his duty to the Saviour and perishing souls. He soon decided to enter some institution of learning and take a higher and more extended course of studies than had before been his privilege. His faithful wife consented to go with him and aid him in the accomplishment of his noble aspirations so far as she was able. They "stored" their furniture, broke up housekeeping, rented their house, and, in 1877, entered Wayland Seminary, Washington, D. C. He remained there four years, finished the normal course and received his diploma. He took the theological course of studies there, and returned to his home, in Chicago, 1881, and was ordained to the work of the gospel ministry by a council composed of pastors and delegates from the churches of the city and vicinity, called by the Olivet Baptist church. Having contracted some debts in the prosecution of his studies, and his house having been sold to meet a part of this indebtedness, and not obtaining a support from his ministerial work, he sought and very readily obtained employment again in the shops of the West Division Street Car company.

After one year he was promoted to be foreman of the ironing and fitting department. He was the only colored man in this department, or indeed in the shops, and he had from seven to twelve mechanics under him and subject to his orders—all of them whites, of various nationalities.

The superintendent and master mechanic of the shops said to him: "You have attained your position in these shops by your merit, and not from having any individual influence or backing, or from any consideration of sympathy. Your color is not considered here, but your skill and ability, and if any of the men of your department refuse to respect and obey your orders, send them to the office." He had no occasion to do this, for the men of the shop respected him and stood ready to resent any indignity that might be offered him on account of his color. Some one was heard once to say something about him and used the word "nigger" in the shops, and there was raised in all the shops such a feeling of indignation, and the inquiry from one to another, "Who said it?" that whoever it was that used it was considerate enough not to let himself be known.

He united with the Knights of Labor in 1866, and was chosen by the men of the shops to represent them on the committee to settle the great Chicago strike of that year at the "stock yards," and was elected judge-advocate of the Charter Oak Assembly of Knights of Labor, March 29, 1886. Being the only colored man in the organization, he was elected only because of his ability, and was re-elected at the end of the year. During the stock yard strike he was one of those who suggested the formation of the "Chicago Co-operative Packing and Provision Company," which held its first successful meeting January 2, 1887, and he was elected a director of the same. In February he was elected treasurer of the organization and gave up his position in the car shop. This organization has in running now a main office and a wholesale department, and several flourishing markets in different parts of the city. In 1886 he was elected a director of the Central Park Building and Loan association. December, 1886, he was sent as a delegate to the Cook County Political Assembly of the United Labor party; at the first assembly of the same, was chosen one of the executive committee. Was a delegate to the city convention of the United Labor party which met February 26, 1887, and was then put in nomination for alderman for the Thirteenth ward, to be voted for in the spring election.

I am proud of such men. What a hellish curse was slavery that a mind so strong, so ingenious as his should be stunted and crippled by such treatment as was dealt out to the infant Terry, penned like a hog, neglected all day by a mother who labored in the field with an aching heart. Let the boys and girls of today thank God that slavery has been wiped from the face of our country and condemned by our statutes.

WILLIAM E. MATTHEWS

CHAPTER XXIII

William E. Matthews, LL. B.
Broker—Real Estate Agent—Financier and Lawyer

Mr. William E. Matthews, the subject of this sketch, was born in the city of Baltimore, July, 1845. His father died when he was a boy at the age of twelve, and he at once assumed the responsibilities which devolved upon him as filling the place of a father. While in the city of Baltimore he was a prominent member of the literary institutions, especially the Gailbraith Lyceum, which wielded a wonderful influence at times. He was the agent of this society, which had been organized by the loyalists of Maryland, for the purpose of assisting in the education and training of the colored people of the South, and especially of that State. As such, he traveled through the State, organizing schools and addressing the people on all questions which were intended to improve their morals, and encourage them to establish homes and enlighten them upon the duties of the new citizenship, which they had just received. In 1867 he became the agent of another body which was organized by Bishop D. A. Payne and others for the purpose of founding schools and building churches in the South among the freedmen. This work he continued for three years, being engaged most diligently, speaking in many of the wealthiest and most refined churches in the East, such as Dr. Bellows', Dr. Chapin's, Rev. Dr. Adams', Mr. Frothingham's and Dr. Vincent's and others of New York, and Drs. Cuyler, Storrs and the Plymouth church in Brooklyn. At Mr. Beecher's church on one occasion, after speaking a few minutes he secured fourteen hundred dollars. His subscription book contained the names of such men as Henry W. Longfellow, James Russell Lowell, Oliver Wendell Homes, William Cullen Bryant, James G. Whittier, which show to a great extent the appreciation of his efforts. In 1870 he severed his connection with the society and was appointed to a clerkship in the post office department by Hon. J. A. Cresswell. He is the first colored gentleman ever appointed in that department. In 1873 he graduated from the Law Department of Howard University. Previous to this he had devoted much of his spare time after office hours to business in real estate, mortgages, loans, bonds, etc., amassing considerable wealth, and gaining a great experience which befitted him for larger operations which he undertook in after years. He is a prominent man in the community, being one of the most liberal supporters of the 15th Street Presbyterian church, and has been a long time chairman of its board of trustees. Mr. Matthews is a gentleman of pleasing address and entertaining manners—a leading man, whose opinions weigh, and are always sincerely sought for in the interest of right. His devotion to the race is shown in his liberality and earnest efforts to improve their condition, and benefit the poor in any and every way. Few things are discussed or attempted for good that they do not receive his cognizance. It is said that his first effort as a speaker was made when he was quite a boy, at a great meeting of the State loyalists held at the Front Street theatre, Baltimore, 1863, to discuss the question of abolition in the border States, Hon. John Minor Botts of Maryland, presiding. On the stage were a large number of leading Republicans of the South, including Hon. Horace Maynard of Tennessee; Thomas H. Settle of North Carolina; J. A. Cresswell, Judge Bond and others of Maryland. The theatre is said to have been packed by an audience of three thousand. When Mr. Matthews was called on to speak, he carried the house with a brief but enthusiastic speech, which was noted for the boisterous and enthusiastic manner in which it was received. He has some distinction as an orator, though of later years he has done very little speaking. In 1880 he was invited by a prominent gentleman of Boston to deliver a eulogy on the life and character of Rev. John F. W. Ware, an eminent Unitarian preacher (white). He was pastor of the church in Baltimore during the war, and did much by his sterling work and great ability to strengthen the new cause and aid the colored people in emancipation and education. On this occasion the meeting was presided over by the Hon. John D. Long, Governor of the State. The audience was a notable one, including Edward Everett Hale, James Freeman Clark and Dr. Rufus Ellis, Dr. Foote of King's Chapel, and the late Judge George L. Ruffin. An excerpt from that speech will show his estimate of this gentleman and also his style as a writer and speaker. Said he:

You know of his patriotic work for the soldiers in tent, field and hospital; of his sermons at our beautiful Druid Hill Park, where thousands of all climes, tongues, colors and conditions would hang on his words as he outlined some grand thought in a way which was charming and captivating to the simple as to the educated, on noble living, high thinking, or passionate devotion to one's country; of his theatre preaching on winter nights, when he would, week after week, hold his audiences of two thousand spellbound, from newsboys and shoeblacks who sat in the gallery of the gods, to the solid merchant or eminent judge who sat in orchestra chairs. All this you know, but I am not so certain that you know that to the colored people of the city and State he was our William Lloyd Garrison, because he was our emancipator; our Horace Mann, because he was our educator; our Dr. Howe, because a philanthropist; our Father Taylor, because a simple preacher of righteousness; and our John A. Andrew, because of his inflexible patriotism. All this he was, and, I might also add the Charles Sumner, for statesman he was also, braver and greater than many who held seats in the great hall at Washington.

This speech was put in pamphlet form by a vote of that meeting. In 1881 the private business of Mr. Matthews grew to such proportions that he severed his connections with the post office department, in which service he had been for eleven years, and opened a real estate and broker's office in Le Droit Building, Washington, District of Columbia, in which business he has met with great success. Few men among us understand so well as Mr. Matthews the true handling of money and the way to make it pay, as was shown in his able article in the A. M. E. Church Review for April, 1885, which the editor, Dr. B. T. Tanner, declares the most finished and exhaustive article on economic subjects that has ever yet appeared. The subject treated was, "Money as a Factor in the Human Progress." The business integrity of Mr. Matthews is one of which any man might be proud. His best indorsement is, that his check is good for ten thousand dollars at any banking house in the city of Washington. Since he has been in business he has handled one hundred thousand dollars belonging to colored gentlemen, among whom might be named Hon. Frederick Douglass, Bishop D. A. Payne, D.D., LL.D., James T. Bradford, Dr. C. B. Purvis, Dr. Samuel L. Cook, Dr. William R. Francis, T. J. Minton and Bishop Brown. Mr. Douglass on his recent departure for Europe closed his account with Mr. Matthews. It was then shown that he had handled over forty-nine thousand dollars of Mr. Douglass' money. As an evidence of his appreciation of his business talent and strict honesty, he writes in these words:

WILLIAM E. MATTHEWS, ESQ.

MY DEAR SIR: It gives me pleasure to inform you and all others, that in all the pecuniary transactions in which you have handled my money, you have given entire satisfaction, and I take pleasure in commending you to all my friends who may have occasion to loan money through your agency.

Very truly yours,
FREDERICK DOUGLASS

Washington, District of Columbia, September 3, 1886.

The office of this gentleman is visited by all persons of national celebrity who sojourn in Washington, and as he himself is widely known, we do not hesitate to say that the future has much in store for the man who began without a penny and today can be considered one of our wealthiest men, and besides this he has never been known to enter into a questionable business transaction of any kind, maintaining his integrity, though many men have fallen far short of the expectations of their friends.

He is a natural financier, easily understanding all financial combinations; and were he a white man he would readily be classed with Sherman of America and Rothschild of England. It is indeed gratifying to have the name of so distinguished a financier and broker, with such eminent abilities as a business man, to present to our readers. Success in business has not marked the pathway of many colored men, for lack of training while young. Had he depended on this, he too would have fallen by the wayside. In this respect we claim that his ability is natural more than acquired. It is refreshing to notice the high grade of intellect he possesses in this department of life.

CHAPTER XXIV

Rev. James Alfred Dunn Podd
Superintendent of Schools—Editor—Brilliant Pastor

Rev. James Alfred Dunn Podd was a native of Nevis, a West India island belonging to Great Britain, leeward group, latitude 17 degrees, 10 minutes North, longitude 62 degrees, 40 minutes West. It is a little one, area 20,000 square miles, separated from the south end of St. Christopher's by a channel two miles across. Its population about the time of his birth was 10,200 souls. He was born March 16, 1855. His parents moved to the island of St. Christopher when he was yet quite young. His father, a leading minister of the gospel in the Wesleyan Methodist church, in addition to a careful home training, endeavored to give him a liberal education. He was given the advantage of the best schools in the island where he was born and raised. In St. Kitts he pursued a preparatory course, graduating from his academic course quite young, and gave promise at a very early period of becoming a brilliant scholar.

With the view of preparing himself for the ministry in the Episcopal church, he went to England to take a more extended course of studies in the venerable and highly cultured educational centers of the mother country. Being admitted into a collegiate school under the patronage and management of the Church of England, he received a literary and classical education that shone brilliantly in his life as a scholar, and adorned so beautifully the work he did in the pulpit and on the platform. He was strongly attached to the institutions and forms of service in the Episcopal church (from cultivation, no doubt, while pursuing his studies in the institutions of learning under the Church of England, and from being in constant attendance upon its services), and this would assert itself often in his manner of conducting his pulpit services, even after he had connected himself with a church whose simpler rites and plainer forms of service showed such a marked contrast.

Leaving England he returned to his home in the West Indies, seeking a field for his future labors. He was tendered and accepted of appointments under the civil government of his island home, in connection with the department of education, being at one time superintendent of schools for the island. His inclination and taste for literary work induced him to accept of the editorship of a journal that was published on the island in the interest of education, literature and religion. In these various capacities he showed aptitude and ability, and gave to the interests of his people, the islanders, the vigilance and care his talents and education so well fitted him to do.

However useful he may have been in these spheres of service, God had a higher calling for him, and so ordered his providence toward him that he should find that to "go preach the gospel" was for him the life work.

The death of his mother, and other unfortunate occurrences in his home life, so completely upset all his cherished plans that he could no longer content himself to remain at home in the West Indies. Thus unsettled, he turned his eyes toward the continent of North America, and leaving his island home and the scenes and associations so familiar and dear to him, he came to Canada. There he connected himself with the British Methodist Episcopal church, and entered its ministry, served in the pastorates of several of its congregations.

Having undergone a change of view upon the ordinance of baptism, he united with the Baptist church at St. Catherines, Ontario, and received from the church a call to its pastorate. Having served that church for a short time, his talents soon attracted the attention of other churches, and the Baptist church of London, Ontario, was the next to extend him a call. Having been previously recognized as a minister of the Baptist denomination by a regularly constituted council called for the purpose, he accepted the call to the pastorate of the London church, and served it two years. December, 1881, he received a call from the Olivet Baptist church, Chicago, Illinois, which he accepted on February 1, 1882. The Bethesda Baptist church having been organized in the south part of the city, a new field and a new congregation was opened for him, and in February, 1883, he took charge of the congregation that had been organized for him. Under his leadership its membership commenced immediately to increase, and his preaching attracted large congregations to its services. His pulpit ministrations were of marked ability. The increased interest in his ministry, and the growth of his congregations occasioned several changes of location and removal to more spacious quarters for accommodations to meet their demands, for his preaching, polished in literary finish as it was, was yet clear and forcible in its presentations of the truths of the Bible, and continued to increase in popular favor.

The financial strain occasioned by the expensiveness of the temporary occupancies, determined the pastor and his little flock to begin the purchase of property and the erection or purchase of a house for a permanent church home. This enterprise drew out and put into exercise his fine pastoral qualities as an organizer, and resulted, after an heroic struggle, in the settlement of the church in its neat and well furnished quarters, in the pretty little chapel at the corner of 34th and Butterfield streets.

The strain on both pastor and flock was very severe, and hastened his death. The last time I saw him was at the Baptist National convention, where he read a paper on the subject of African mission. It was evident that his heart was filled full of the work, and indeed his remarks impressed the convention, because of his earnestness and zeal in this department of Christian labor. At the close of his remarks he made a very strong appeal to the convention to contribute to the cause through Rev. T. L. Johnson, the missionary. Mr. Podd would impress one as intellectual from his personal appearance. His classic countenance was interesting, and his health being at the time very feeble, he gave one the impression of a man able to meet the demands of any occasion when in full health. It could be seen then that he was near the end of life, and his words for this reason had the more weight and secured careful attention.

He was not narrow in the exercise of his gifts and talents, but with a large heart and generous nature, he laid his hand to every good work for the uplifting of his race and the cause of humanity.

Death cut short his earthly labors at Jacksonville, Florida, on Thursday, December 23, 1886, in the thirty-second year of his life.

CHAPTER XXV

*Hon. Henry Wilkins Chandler, A. B., A. M.
Member of the State Senate of Florida—Capitalist—
Lawyer—City Clerk and Alderman*

Ocala, Florida, is proud of the Hon. H. W. Chandler, whom she honors so often in sending him to the State Senate.

Reared in a State in which there was little or no discrimination, he enjoyed excellent school advantages. His father has been for many years a deacon in a white Baptist church and superintendent of the Sunday school; it can be seen, therefore, that he has had little of the embarrassments of life which go to make difficulties for young colored men.

He was born in Bath, Sagadahock county, Maine, September 22, 1852. He pursued the usual course of studies in the common schools of his native city, graduating from the College Preparatory Department of the High School in June, 1870, and the following September entered Bates' College, Lewiston, Maine, where he graduated, in 1874, with the title of A. B. September, 1874, he entered the Law Department of Howard University, Washington, D. C., and at the same time became instructor in the Normal Department of the same institution. He pursued his law studies at the university and privately till June, 1876. He went to Ocala, Marion county, Florida, in October of the same year and engaged in teaching. In 1878 he was on examination, admitted to the practice of law. In 1880, was nominated and elected State Senator for the Nineteenth Senatorial district, comprising the county of Marion. At the expiration of his term, in 1884, he was renominated and elected for a term of four years.

Mr. Chandler was a delegate to the Republican National convention in 1884, and has been prominently connected with the Republican State and Congressional committees. Since he entered politics, in 1878, he has held various positions of honor and trust—clerk and alderman of his adopted city, Ocala; delegate to the recent State Constitutional convention, in 1885.

October 2, 1884, he was married to Miss Annie M. Onley, a teacher in the Staunton Grammar school, Jacksonville, Florida, and the daughter of the Mr. John Onley, a prominent contractor and builder in that city.

Mr. Chandler still resides in Ocala, Florida, where he wields a very large and powerful influence, politically and socially. He is deacon of the Mount Moriah Baptist church of that city, and was baptized by Rev. Samuel Smalls, now deceased.

He had the good fortune of meeting true and staunch friends in the persons of Watson Murphy, F. C. W. Williams, Reuben S. Mitchell and others, who have always been devoted to his interests. The writer was a resident of Florida, and was largely instrumental in Mr. Chandler's settlement in that State. Having gone there first, he invited Mr. Chandler, with another friend, to make their homes in that State, and here, in this volume, I wish to testify to the generosity, the whole-souled respect, which these gentlemen have shown, not only to Mr. Chandler but to himself, as they are men made in uncommon moulds. No better men live; they are as true to a friend as the needle to the pole, and can only be spoken of with tenderness and love.

Mr. Chandler had only two dollars and one-half in his pocket when he settled in Florida, but by hard work, honest methods and kind treatment to all with whom he came in contact, he has been enabled to secure a vast amount of property, and today his real estate is worth probably twenty thousand dollars.

Senator Chandler is a man of fine scholastic taste, discriminating in his choice of books and of the subjects which he treats. He is already a successful lawyer. As a politician he is shrewd, calculating and far-seeing. His speeches are specimens of eloquence, rhetoric and polish; in every case a subject is exhausted by him before dropped. He generally anticipates his opponent's argument, and so presents them that he would be ashamed to use them afterwards. His style is both analytical and synthetical. His life is an inspiration for those who come after him.

CHAPTER XXVI

*Rev. Theodore Doughty Miller, D. D.
The Eloquent Pastor of Cherry Street Baptist Church,
Philadelphia, Pennsylvania—A Veteran Divine,
Distinguished for Long Service*

The subject of this sketch was born of Henry and Sarah Miller, in the city of New York, September 19, 1835. He was a very bright and active boy, whose winning ways won him many friends, who have maintained their pleasant relations for many long years. When he began studying he was a pupil of the well known teacher, John Patterson, of colored school No. 1, where he remained for ten years and secured an excellent common school education. In July, 1948, he was examined, passed and received a certificate as a teacher, and at once entered upon his profession, becoming first assistant in the Public High school. He was brought up in the Episcopal church (St. Phillips), was confirmed and became a member of the choir for many years. Though privileged, he was conscientiously opposed to accepting communion, and left that organization to form a part of the newly organized church of the Messiah, also Episcopal, under the rectorship of Alexander Crummel, D.D., who is now rector in the City of Washington, District of Columbia. His father died when he was an infant, and his mother was very suddenly called away when he was about sixteen years of age, leaving him alone in the world to fight the battle of life. He had an older brother, but he had gone many years before to California when the popular rage for gold was at its height, and never returned, being lost in the wreck of the steamer "Golden Gate."

From 1849 to 1851 he spent his evenings and Saturdays as a pupil of the St. Augustine Institute in the study of the classics, determined to thoroughly equip himself to make a mark in life. During a revival of religion at the Baptist church he was converted and brought to the knowledge of the Lord Jesus Christ. Through uniting with no church, not being able then to reconcile the Baptist views of baptism and church fellowship with his own, he determined to study all the creeds and compare them with the Bible so as to stand on a Bible platform and defend himself in his religious views against all encroachments and entreaties from the many who were seeking his services, both in the church and Sunday-school. In the year 1851 he left New York City to assume charge of the public school in Trenton, New Jersey, which he held for years, during which time he united in marriage with Miss Elizabeth P. Wood of that city. He made himself useful in the formation of a young men's association, and in the choir and Sunday-school of the Mt. Zion A. M. E. church, his religion being of that liberal nature which constrained him, regardless of their names, to aid in any way the onward march to Christ. In the year 1856 he left Trenton, New Jersey, and took charge of the public school at Newburgh, New York, during which time, as a result of much study and prayer, he decided to accept the views of the Baptists, believing them to be in accordance with the Bible; and his wife, also having just been brought to a saving knowledge of Christ, accepted the same views, and they were both baptized February 22, 1857, in the Hudson river. He at once felt impressed to do something to advance the interests of his Master's kingdom. Having felt keenly the loss of several years service in a decision as to Bible views, he joined the Shiloh Baptist church, but they having a white pastor, and he being naturally jealous of his abilities, which were noticed and which led to frequent invitations to participate publicly in their services, every obstacle to advancement was put in his way. But despite the pastor's opposition he was chosen as a teacher, then superintendent of the Sabbath-school, then a trustee of the church, then a deacon of the church. But here the pastor determined must be the limit; he was rising too fast. But Mr. Miller was determined not to be outdone. He opened his own house Sabbath afternoons and preached each Sunday night, or rather exhorted, for they had refused to license him. He was sent by the church as its messenger to the American Baptist Missionary convention, held at Philadelphia, Pennsylvania, with the request that they hear him preach, and if they approved, license him. They gave him a hearing, which was highly satisfactory. It being out of their province to license him, they sent back a unanimous recommendation to that church to at once grant him the license, and stated to the candidate that if they refused to do so, that he should sever his connection and unite with the First Baptist church (white), who, knowing his abilities and prospects of usefulness, had promised to give him a license. Fearing to rebel, they granted the license. He continued speaking and teaching in all the churches until 1858, when he received a call from the Zion Baptist church of New Haven, Connecticut, which he accepted. He was ordained to the gospel ministry January 19, 1859, at the Concord Street church, Brooklyn, New York, by the unanimous decision of a large council, composed of many white men, who sought, though vainly, to retard the progress of the rising young colored man. His fame spreading, reached Albany, where the field being barren and long a desert, they desired an active young man; so they extended him a call, which after deliberation and prayer he accepted. Bringing the church up by gracious revivals, he remained over five years, a longer period than any preceding pastor for twenty years, and leaving only against a strong and united protest and tears. During this time he fortified himself with a full course of theological studies, under the tutelage of that noted scholar and preacher, Dr. E. L. Magoon, whose pulpit, with those of several others (all white), he often occupied, often exchanging pulpits.

In 1864 he was invited to visit Oak Street Baptist church, West Philadelphia, with a view to their pastorate. While there the Pearl Street church, the old mother church organized in 1809, which has had but four regular pastors, situated on Cherry street, also invited him to spend a Sabbath with them with the same view, after which calls were extended to him from both churches, and he accepted that of the latter, beginning services with them August 1, 1864, in whose service he still remains, the oldest pastor in continued service in the city, but one. During his pastorate, the membership has been quadrupled, he having baptized over six hundred in the successive revivals, the largest of which, in the history of the church, occurred in the spring of 1886, in his twenty-second year of service, among whom were two of his own children, a son and daughter having previously been baptized, making four of his children in the church, a blessing accorded to but few pastors. His oldest son is a very eminent musician and is the organist of the church, and also clerk in Wanamaker's great clothing establishment, his oldest daughter being accomplished in the manufacture of fancy hair work and a dressmaker, while the other two are fitting themselves for positions of usefulness. During his long pastorate many calls have been extended to him, some with larger salaries, among them the Nineteenth Street Baptist church and a position in the Howard Theological Seminary, all of which he declined. His progress has been really wonderful and crowned with success. Crowded audiences greet him every Sabbath morning to catch inspiration from his thoroughly prepared discourses. The other many offices he has filled prove the just appreciation of his gifts. He was for many years corresponding secretary of the American Baptist Missionary convention and is now recording secretary of the New England Baptist Missionary convention. On every occasion of note his services and voice have always been demanded. He has occupied more white pulpits than any other colored pastor in the city, and the first and only colored man that by their own appointment was privileged to occupy the high position of preaching the introductory sermon for the Philadelphia Baptist Association—the oldest in the country, three years ago. By the united request of the Sunday school and church, he assumed, though reluctantly, owing to his own pastoral duties, the charge of the Sunday school. The wisdom of the choice was manifested in the large revival breaking out in the school, from which over ninety were baptized and united with the church. He has also organized a church at Princeton, New Jersey, and has a branch of his own church at Germantown, and rendered them valuable assistance.

During his pastoral duties he has licensed and sent forth to the work of Christian ministry, Milford D. Herndon, missionary to Africa, Benjamin T. Moore, Ananias Brown, James Banks, Henry H. Mitchell, Benjamin Jackson and others. Our subject is admired by his flock, and faithfully upholds the doctrine of the Lord Jesus Christ. Who can count the good of this man's life; twenty-two years of true teachings has not failed to bless both teacher and pupils. The writer remembers a sermon which he heard him preach in 1870. The text was "God is Faithful," and to this-day it is just as distinct in his mind as it was the day he heard it. He is a man of oratorical powers, a clear reasoner, forcible writer and elegant talker; a man highly respected for scholarly attainments, strictest integrity, honor and common sense.

Recognizing the good qualities in him, a university conferred on him the title of D.D. A sketch of his life appears in the *Baptist Encyclopedia* by Cathcart, which pays him the following compliment:

Mr. Miller was appointed to preach the introductory sermon before the Philadelphia Baptist Association in 1879, the first colored man that ever occupied that position, and he was not placed in it by political power, but as a simple recognition of his Christian work. His sermon showed the propriety of the choice.

Mr. Miller is a man of scholarly taste. He is one of the best colored preachers located in Philadelphia, and his piety is of a high order. May he ever live to proclaim the riches of "His mercy" and the truth of that Saviour of souls and bring to his kingdom those who have wandered away.

J. D. BALTIMORE

CHAPTER XXVII

J. D. Baltimore, Esq.
Chief Engineer and Mechanician at the Freedmen's Hospital—
Engineer—Machinist—Inventor

Jeremiah Daniel Baltimore first saw light in Washington, District of Columbia, April 15, 1852. His parents, Thomas and Hannah Baltimore, were free, the former a Catholic and the latter a Methodist. The boy, following the goodly walks of his mother, adopted the same faith, joining the Wesley Zion church and filling every position in the Sabbath school, from pupil to superintendent; also secretary of the board of trustees of the church, having united with it in 1866. He was a scholar in Enoch Ambush's school for quite a while, but when he left could neither spell nor write his own name. He then attended the district public school. Prior to this he spent most of his time planting old tin cans and coffee pots in the ground for steam boilers. He would make so much steam and smoke that his mother would often be compelled to shut herself up in the house. After he had worked with the tins for a year or longer, he weighted the tea-kettle lid down with a flatiron, and succeeded in generating sufficient steam to raise the lid and produce a noise by its escape that caused everybody in the house to predict that he would soon blow his head off, if he didn't stop such dangerous pranks.

One day he told his mother that he would get to be an engineer, but she said, "No, my son, it takes a smart man to fill that position. I am sure there is no way for us to get you through school." He said he could go through, though his skin was dark.

His further experiments consisted of a piece of stove pipe and old brass bucket hoops, etc. With these he made a steam boiler, to which he attached an engine that he had constructed, but it would not work. It was highly spoken of by all who saw it. The Rev. William P. Ryder placed it upon exhibition in the Wesley Zion Sabbath school. It was then placed on exhibition in the United States Treasury department, and was examined by the officers and employees, who pronounced it the work of a genius. This so encouraged him, he tried to make a better one; he took a piece of soft brick, cut the shape of the wheel and of other details deep enough to hold the molten metal. Then taking an old flower pot and lining it thickly with clay, he thus succeeded in melting his brass with an ordinary fire in the kitchen stove. With the aid of a file, a pair of old shears and an old knife used for a saw, he finished his engine, which was a horizontal high pressure one with a tubular boiler. The engine was first placed on exhibition in the public school, in the room of which he was then a pupil. It was carried to the patent office, and by the aid of Anthony Bowen, a very distinguished colored member of the City Council of Washington, the attention of the public and the press was called to it. One morning soon after, an article appeared in the *Sunday Chronicle*, headed like this: "Extraordinary Mechanical Genius of a Colored Boy." This boy desired to do something to further his own cause, and one day seeing the people going into the President's house, he was bold enough to send the paper with the sketch in it to the President. When the usher returned he announced that, as it was "Cabinet day," the President could not be seen. Not having any idea that the President would become interested in the matter, the boy had started out with the crowd. Soon, however, the usher called him and said: "The President wants to see you, young man." He went in and found General Grant with his feet on the desk and a cigar in his mouth. He turned to him and inquired if he was the young man of whom he had just been reading. To this the boy, being put at ease by the kindly manner of the general, replied, "I am, sir." The general said: "You must have a trade," and handed him a card with these words on it:

Will the Secretary of the Navy please see the bearer, J. D. Baltimore. I think it would be well to give him employment in one of the United States Navy yards, where he can be employed on machinery. Please see statements of what he has done without instruction.

U. S. GRANT

This card he presented to the Secretary of the Navy and was immediately appointed as an apprentice in the department of steam engineering at the Washington Navy yard, where the prejudice was very strong, and after standing it a few months, he complained of his treatment, and Professor John M. Langston interviewed the Secretary of the Navy who said to him: "Young Baltimore shall go to another navy yard if you desire it." He was transferred to the Navy yard at Philadelphia, where he studied very hard. He was ostracized by the men, who told him that the President might send him there, but couldn't make them show him anything; and there were very few of the men who would have any friendly dealings with him. But he would arise at 4 o'clock in the morning and study until it was time to go to work. He would study all the dinner hour and late at night. He was admitted to the Franklin Institute at Philadelphia, being the second colored man enjoying that privilege. The chief assistant engineer noticed his close application to the duties of the shop and scientific studies, and on one occasion, when lecturing to the apprentice boys, Chief Engineer Thompson of the department of steam engineering, asked this question. "How many of you can tell the strength of a steam boiler by mathematical computation? Can you, Baltimore?" He answered "Yes, sir," and from that moment the hatred of the men and boys increased. They would nail his coat to the wall, steal his tools and destroy his books, and do everything that would make it unpleasant for him, but he still held out. He graduated from this department obtaining his certificate, which contained these words:

UNITED STATES NAVY YARD

To all whom it may concern:

This certifies that Jeremiah D. Baltimore of Washington, District of Columbia, has served as an apprentice to the United States in the Machinists' Department at the Navy yard at Philadelphia, Pennsylvania, for the term of three years and six months, and until he had arrived at the age of twenty-one years. During that time his general character has been *very good*. His proficiency in both trades very good. His term of apprenticeship is hereby honorably closed.

JAMES W. THOMPSON, JR.
Chief Engineer

Given at the Navy yard at Philadelphia, this fourth day of December, 1873.

G. F. E. EMMONS, Commandant

J. W. KING, Chief of the Bureau of Steam Engineering
September 6, 1873

He was then detailed to go to the Naval station at League Island on the Delaware river, to assist in repairing four of the United States monitors. When it became necessary to reduce the force, he was placed in the front ranks. He then took a position in charge of a large mill, receiving twenty-seven dollars per week, but after awhile the work was stopped, and the firm paid him ten dollars per week, which he accepted for a few weeks and then concluded to seek employment in one of the machine tool manufacturing establishments in Philadelphia. He tried Cramp & Sons, who did a great deal of work for the government. They said, "Mr. Baltimore, we have heard of you and would like to employ you, but if we do, all of our men will leave us, as they refuse to work with colored mechanics." It can be seen that prejudice existed in the North as well as in the South, for a colored man can find work in the South. He then went to Sellers & Brother six times, and five times he was put off with all sorts of excuses. The sixth time he was refused at first, but insisted that he wanted work, not because he was a colored man, but because he could do the work. After some deliberation they concluded to give him employment. He held this position until he resigned on account of ill health. Returning to Washington, May 29, 1872, he was married to Miss Ella V. Waters, to whom he owes much of his success. In a private letter to a friend he said once: "She is to me what the governor is to a steam engine, or the helm to the ship." After he was married he opened a general repair shop, which he carried on for twelve years. He has been employed as engineer of the United States Coast Survey at Washington, District of Columbia, and at this writing holds the position of chief engineer and mechanician at the Freedmen's Hospital, Department of the Interior, Washington, having been appointed August 2, 1880.

Mr. Baltimore has realized from his labors about five thousand dollars. He is the inventor of a pyrometer, which was on exhibition in the colored department of the New Orleans Exposition. He is a member of the Mechanics' Union in Washington, and at a recent meeting, the two bodies came together, one which has only white members, and the other which has both. Mr. Baltimore at this meeting made a speech and criticized very severely the white class, which forced the president to say that one year from now the constitution of his Union would not have that clause in it. Mr. Baltimore is interested in every subject that touches his race, and has lectured very frequently for the benefit of churches, upon the subject of heat, steam, and other scientific subjects. His triumphal success over many severe difficulties marks him as a man of genius, firmness and talent.

CHAPTER XXVIII

J. R. Clifford, Esq.
Editor—Lawyer—Teacher—Orator

———•◆•———

There are but few names in West Virginia well known to the public; but among these stand prominent Editor Clifford. He is progressive, independent and ambitious. He is a native of the State, having been born at Williamsport, Grant county, West Virginia, September 13, 1849. When quite a lad he was taken to Chicago, by the Hon. J. J. Healy, and given a rudimentary education. In early life he followed the barber's trade, and not being satisfied with a little learning he received in Chicago, he went to Zeno, Muskingum county, where his uncle dwelt, who sent him to a school taught by one Miss Effie McKnight. In this place he attended a writing school taught by Professor D. A. White, from which he took a diploma in that art. In 1870 he went to Wheeling, West Virginia, and conducted a large writing school with nearly one hundred attendants; in the years 1871, '72 and '73 he taught a similar school at Martin's Ferry, Ohio. Not yet satisfied with his attainments, he attended Storer College, at Harper's Ferry, graduating in 1878. He was called to the principalship of the public school at Martinsburg, West Virginia, which he held for ten consecutive years, and only resigned to give attention to the *Pioneer Press,* a vigorous, influential journal which he so ably, fearlessly and consistently edits. The Republican party has had a strong friend in him. Being delegate to the State convention in 1884, he was elected a delegate to Chicago by a majority of fifteen, and the white delegates went around to the several delegations and persuaded them to withdraw their votes from him after the vote had been cast and counted, thus defeating him. This outrage was not forgotten, and the metal of the man is shown, who, when he had an opportunity, paid these men back in their own coin. Mr. N. H. W. Flick, a white Republican, was leader in the defeat of Mr. Clifford, and in the last congressional election he was nominated by the Republican party, but was bitterly opposed by the *Pioneer Press,* which defeated him. They have indeed cause to fear such a man, who not only has power and influence to back him, but who will

J. R. CLIFFORD

stand up for his rights and accept nothing which reflects upon his race. As a delegate to all the conventions of the State, he has many opportunities to give as well as to take defeats. I first made the acquaintance of this gentleman in the Knights of Wise Men Convention, held at Atlanta, Georgia, where he delivered the oration of the day. In that body were Hon. F. L. Cardoza, Bishop H. M. Turner, D.D., LL.D., Hon. Richard Gleaves, J. W. Cromwell, the eloquent R. P. Brooks, now dead, and some of the most gifted men of the country. Mr. Clifford was but little known to many of us. On the cars going from Nashville, Mr. Brooks said to Mr. Cromwell, "Who is that over there?" pointing to Mr. Clifford. Mr. Cromwell answered it was the orator. Brooks laughed in his hearty way and replied it would be a hard oration, and he wanted to be absent when it took place. Brooks himself was totally unassuming, however, and was also one of the most polished orators of the Old Dominion, yet when the speech was heard, the house was electrified, and Brooks led the movement in securing a contribution to present Mr. Clifford with a goldheaded cane, which was presented in the State house by Lawyer William H. Young of Nashville, Tennessee, in a very elaborate and complimentary speech. Mr. Clifford has delivered many orations since. As honorary commissioner of the colored department of the New Orleans Exposition he served his State faithfully and did all in his power to aid the general work. When only sixteen years of age he enlisted in the United States heavy artillery (Kentucky), Company F, and served as a corporal, but finally appointed nurse in a hospital, serving there until the war ended, when he was mustered out at Louisville, Kentucky. He studied law under J. Nelson Wirner, in the city of Martinsburg, and has had some success as a lawyer. Fortunate in his marriage, he is now on the road to success, and has accumulated a little capital as a basis for competency. One John T. Riley of Martinsburg, West Virginia, editor of the *Herald,* and who is described by the *Independent* as "a young man with a downcast look and a pusillanimous nature," and having "a mean, uneasy countenance," saw fit to make an attack on Mr. Clifford. Some comic writer has said: "It pays to have a few redhot enemies, as it always develops a few redhot friends." It proved true in this case, as the following, taken from the columns of the *Independent,* July 25, 1885, conclusively proves:

Riley is envious of the good reputation and high standing of Professor J. R. Clifford, the brainy and intelligent principal of the colored schools; and for several years, through running a Republican organ, has endeavored to asperse his character and discharge him from his position. In every effort he has been defeated, although we are reliably informed, in the last proceeding, his associate, Tolliver Evans, threatened never to vote again for the members of the Board of Education, which is amusing. The truth is, Clifford's standing in the community is in advance of either Riley or Evans. Intellectually, and in the point of education, they will never reach his standard. Therefore, they envy this colored man and try to down him. It cannot be accomplished. His moral standing and his friendship with the leading men, best thinkers and most respected citizens cannot be assailed. We doubt if any man living in our midst can present a better certificate of character than the following, which, when handed the Board of Education, put to flight his accusers, viz.:

To the Board of Education of Martinsburg:

Gentlemen:—The undersigned bear willing and cheerful testimony to the good character, correct habits and unquestioned moral standing and quiet, law-abiding qualities of Mr. J. R. Clifford, as a man and citizen. On none of these essentials can he be successfully impeached.

Charles P. Matthaei	Joseph E. Berry
C. R. O'Neal	Z. T. Grove
William Gerhardt	Wm. McKee
J. Nelson Wisner	Henry Wilen
John N. Abell	Robt. Douglass Roller
F. M. Woods	A. R. McQuilkin
J. A. Hoffheins	J. S. Boak
R. H. Pitt	E. C. Williams, Jr.
A. S. Hank	R. A. Blondell
R. C. Holland	William Wilen
S. N. Myers	Kinsey Creque
J. W. McSherry	Cyrus H. Wayble
J. H. Bristor	N. D. Baker
C. W. Doll	S. L. Dodd
Jno. A. Boyer	George W. Feidt
S. H. Martin	G. A. Crisman
Blackburn Hughes	J. T. Picking
Geo. S. Hill	Wm. S. Henshaw
W. L. Jones	John C. Hutsler
Lee M. Bender	I. L. Bender
H. A. Frazer	J. W. Bishop
C. W. Wisner	W. H. Keedy
C. O. Lambert	J. W. Pitzer
George Knapp	W. A. Pitzer
J. H. Gettinger	Wm. H. Criswell

The above list has the names of the ministers of the Protestant churches, the magistrates of the town, the mayor, sergeant, constable, president of the county court, president and cashier of the National bank, physicians, lawyers, superintendent of the town schools, ex-county superintendent, teachers, teller of People's National bank, ex-sheriff, clerks of the county courts, and leading merchants. Such a certificate cannot be beaten in this town. The man who merits the esteem of such citizens is beyond the reach of the venomous pen of John T. Riley or his abettors.

CHAPTER XXIX

Wiley Jones, Esq.
The Owner of a Street-car Railroad, a Race Track and a Park—
A Capitalist Worth About $125,000

The amount of enterprise shown in the life of the gentleman of whom I now write, is worthy of commendation. That an uneducated slave-boy should amass such wealth, is a surprise to many. His business tact and steady perseverance is marvelous. There are those who believe in luck, but sometimes no such thing can be seen in our lives; strive we ever so hard, live we ever so honest, labor we ever so faithfully, we do not seem to have that good fortune which many term "good luck." Of course there is no such thing as luck; all success is the result of qualities within, labor expended or fortuitous circumstances, brought about, perhaps, by what might seem to be an accident, or because of circumstances over which we have little or no control. Mr. Jones can content himself with the thought that an over-ruling power has thrown this money into his hands that he may do some great and lasting good with it. Surely his name could live long after he is dead if he would contribute to the special aid of his race in some direct manner.

His young life began in that State which had such severe regulations for Negroes in slavery days, that it was considered the place where they should be sent when they were refractory. He was born in Madison county, Georgia, July 14, 1848. His parents, George and Ann Jones, are both dead. At five years of age he was taken to Arkansas, and waited on his master, Fitz Yell, and performed the duties of a houseboy, and drove the family carriage. This he did for two years or more. Then he followed his master into the Federal army during the war. After that he went to Waco, Texas, and drove a wagon from the Brazos river to San Antonio, hauling cotton to the frontiers. After a while he returned to Arkansas and worked on a farm at twenty dollars a month. By this time it was 1868, when he began working at the barber's chair, and continued thereat until 1881, when he went into the tobacco, cigar and other businesses, which realized him this very large fortune of which he is now possessed. His brother, who is faithful to his interests, managed the business for the

WILEY JONES

first two years, while he was working at his trade. Mr. Jones had no school training, and consequently his education was very limited. He had to rely entirely on what he could pick up through life, as he came in contact with men and things.

This school of adversity is often the best teacher for some men, for really good men are often spoiled by trying to give them what is vulgarly called education, and the truth of the matter is they would be much better and more properly educated if they felt the conflicts which come to those who battle with the world against the many adversities common to life. He extended his operations by securing the charter for the street car line in the city of Pine Bluff, where he now lives. This was secured August, 1886, and he had one and one-quarter miles completed and ran the first car on October 19, 1886, the first day of the annual fair of the Colored Industrial and Fair Association, of which he is also treasurer. He is also the sole owner of the grounds the fair was held on, and of the race track and park which covers fifty-five acres, located one mile from Main street. The street car stables, which cover forty by one hundred feet, are also located on the grounds.

He carries a stock of goods in his business of fifteen thousand dollars, and estimates his wealth at a figure not below one hundred and twenty-five thousand dollars, which consists of his business, real estate and cash. He is also a great fancier of fine blooded stock, and owns a herd of Durham and Holstein cattle, and is also breeding trotting stock, the best of which is the noted stallion "Executor," that has made a record of $2.24\frac{1}{4}$. On his farm he has about twelve choicely bred mares, and hires a professional driver to handle them, which insures him first-class handling and develops their speed to perfection.

Mr. Jones can be accounted as one of our most successful business men, and the only hope is that he will use his wealth wisely, and to the honor and glory of God. He has not yet seen fit to marry, and therefore has no one to whom he may look as the heir of the large property which he has accumulated.

JOHN H. BURRUS

CHAPTER XXX

Professor John H. Burrus, A. B., A. M.
President of the Alcorn University—Professor of Mental
and Moral Philosophy and Constitutional Law—
Teacher of Political Economy, Literature and Chemistry—
Attorney at Law

After many struggles as a waiter in hotels and at other hard work, Professor Burrus has attained prominence among men, and has been called to the head of a very flourishing institution. This gives him the endorsement of the State officers of Mississippi. Regardless of political bias, he has maintained his position from year to year under the scrutinizing eye of a Democratic Legislature. These things show that worth is being recognized wherever found. The surrender of 1865 found James B., John H., and Preston R. Burrus with their mother in Marshall, Texas, with the remnant of Bragg's Mississippi Confederate army. They were brought to Shreveport, Louisiana, thence to New Orleans, and afterwards to Memphis, Tennessee. Here John H., then a boy, found work as a cook on a stern-wheel boat. When opportunity presented itself for better things, he took advantage of it. About 1866 he removed to Nashville, where he worked hard as a hotel waiter, studying much of the time at night with the Misses Shadwell and Jameson, boarders at the hotel where he worked. Very zealous was he for an education, and every energy was devoted to this one purpose. The frugality and care of the mother was manifest in the son, for never did he indulge in the many extravagances of youth in dress or pleasure seeking, but every cent was carefully laid aside until the summer of 1867, when three hundred dollars had been saved, which was spent for school advantages at Fisk University. While in school no time was wasted; extra hours were spent in work and study, while the vacations were used for school teaching, until his eyes failed him from overwork, then he could study only by hearing others read his lessons to him. Thus he continued in school until 1873, when, being unable to teach, he bought a religious panorama, with which he traveled through parts of 1873 and 1874.

During the first year in Fisk University he was converted and united with the Congregational church of the university, of which church he is still a member. The president often related how he economized and struggled to keep in school. He is an illustration of "where there's a will there's a way." J. H. Burrus was engaged as teacher in a graded school in the suburbs of Nashville for the school year following his graduation, but was made principal before his year was out.

Before his school closed in 1876, he was selected by the Republican State committee as one of the delegates from the Sixth Tennessee Congressional district to the National convention. There he voted five consecutive times for Senator O. P. Morton for President, but when that distinguished son of Indiana was withdrawn, he voted for Rutherford B. Hayes, who was nominated on the seventh ballot.

After the convention he visted Harper's Ferry, Washington, District of Columbia; Niagara, Philadelphia, New York, Oberlin, and many other places. Not long after, returning to Nashville, he accepted the principalship of the Yazoo city school, of Yazoo, Mississippi. He was re-elected to the principalship of this school soon after closing in June, 1877, and he was also offered the position of instructor of mathematics in his *alma mater* in place of his brother, who had resigned. After due consideration he finally accepted this position and taught two years in Fisk University, till 1879, when he received the degree of A. M. During this year he resigned this position in favor of his younger brother, who had just graduated from this place.

Professor Burrus, who had been reading law to some extent, now gave himself to that study under legal advisers, and was admitted to the bar early in 1881. For the first year he did not make bread out of his law practice, but besides making use of his leisure to get more legal knowledge, he corresponded for several newspapers, getting some work looking up titles to property, and being enabled on several occasions to point out serious involvements of property where even the owner thought none existed. He made some reputation for that kind of work which promised to bring him handsome returns. At this time he was offered the presidency of Alcorn Agricultural and Mechanical College, in Rodney, Mississippi, in August, 1883. This will be remembered as the college where Hon. Hiram R. Revels presided for several years.

He was elected permanent secretary of the Tennessee Republican State convention in 1878; was secretary and treasurer of the State executive committee, for two years; he was also chosen alternate from the State-at-large to the National Republican convention which met in January, 1880, and was independent candidate for register in Davidson county, Tennessee, August, 1882, and a candidate on the Republican ticket for the

Lower House of the Legislature in the following November. The people in his district in the edge of Nashville, Tennessee, elected him one of their school directors in 1878. When his term of three years expired in 1881, he was re-elected, beating both of his competitors, a colored and a white man, although a majority of the citizens were white. Brains and character will win, no matter what the color of his face may be. There are many sitting down complaining about their color keeping them down in life and preventing them from succeeding. Ninety-nine times out of a hundred it is the man's lack of brains and character. There were then seventeen teachers in the district, of whom nine were white and eight were colored. The other two directors were white, still Mr. Burrus served as chairman of the board, in which capacity it was his especial duty to look after *all the schools* and see that the teaching was properly and faithfully done. Yet when he resigned the chairmanship of the board, upon his acceptance of his present position, he was on the pleasantest terms with both colleagues and teachers. While a member of the board he had succeeded in equalizing salaries of white and colored teachers, and effected some other measures of a progressive nature. He took part in the municipal elections of Nashville, and discussed the injustice of not employing competent colored teachers in the public schools, and for not furnishing enough school facilities for the colored children. This election was followed not many months after by an additional colored school, and for the first time a corps of colored teachers. He read a paper before the State Teachers' Institute, held in Nashville in 1880, in which he spoke of all the Congressional script from the act of 1862, belonging to Tennessee, having then been given to the East Tennessee University, and of the colored people of the State getting no benefit therefrom, although their numbers entitled them to more than six thousand dollars of the nearly twenty-four thousand dollars yearly interest. At the close of the paper he moved that the institute appoint a committee to meet the Legislature to convene January, 1881, and call the attention of that body to the wrong and ask that the injustice by remedied. A committee was appointed consisting of Mr. J. H. Burrus, Dr. John Braden, Central Tennessee College, and Professor L. B. Teft, of what is now Roger Williams University, Professor H. S. Bennett of Fisk University and several others. Mr. Burrus was made chairman, and the committee had several interviews with the Legislature educational committee. The result was the Legislature passed an act appropriating twenty-five hundred dollars annually for the next two years to be used as follows: Each of the State's twenty-five senators was authorized to select two colored persons, male or female, of suitable age and scholarship, who might be sent to any one of the five institutions specified and receive from the State fifty dollars a year, the board to pay his or her expenses. A number of the Republicans of the same Legislature were induced to appoint a number of young colored men as cadets to the University of Tennessee, who thereby for several years got their tuition in Fisk University paid by the aforesaid University of Tennessee.

Mr. Burrus quietly but firmly holds that the people ought to take as much pride in their respective States as do other citizens, that they may condemn the policy of the ruling party as do other citizens. He also holds that they ought to keep wide awake as to their rights, and demand their fair and just portion as American citizens of all public monies spent for educational purposes, and that wherever they are denied or defrauded out of the same, they shall unceasingly protest against the un-American, unpatriotic and unjust discrimination until the wrong is righted. Upon his urgent recommendation, the first Legislature of his adopted State that was elected after his acceptance of the Alcorn A. M. College, Rodney, Mississippi, appropriated in addition to the usual amount for running expenses eleven thousand dollars for additions to the library and apparatus, and for greatly needed repairs.

With the aid of his co-workers the attendance at the college has steadily increased until it is now shown by the catalogue to be two hundred and sixteen, about double what it was before his connection with the institution. President Burrus has a large heart and is ever full of plans for the benefit of his students. His duties are discharged with singular ability and extreme conscientiousness. His rough road in early life is having a fruitful end as well as a peaceful one. He knows how to extend sympathy to those who are climbing the educational ladder; he has been over the whole road and knows every foot of the way. His attachment for his brothers is really pleasant to behold. He is loving and affectionate, and he has very tenderly cared for his mother.

CHAPTER XXXI

Henry F. Williams, Esq.
Composer—Violinist and Cornetist—Band Instructor

———•◆•———

Mr. Williams forced his way upward in the face of all those difficulties, against which the Negro has to contend. The singular excellence which he reached in this art was mainly the result of careful study. He had the gift, which he faithfully cultivated. His aim was to become master of the situation, and he did this. At the Coliseum of Boston he figured conspicuously among voices, accompanied by an orchestra of two thousand musicians; with the exception of Mr. F. E. Lewis, he was the only colored performer. He was dignified and graceful, and his manly appearance caused much comment. His talent was put to a severe test, by his being required to execute on the double bass a very difficult piece—Wagner's *Tannhauser*. This was done, not because his ability was doubted, but for a protection to his color should objections to him arise. The gentleman who gave the test said he wanted to be able to point to his excellent results.

So proficient was Mr. Williams that men forgot his color and thought only of his excellent music. No man took offense because the orchestra contained a sable son of Ham, but all was union and harmony. He was far superior to many of the fairer performers. He could look back with pride on thirty years of very persevering energy, which was ripe with experience. He felt as did Beethoven, the barriers are not erected, which can say to aspiring talent and industry, "thus far and no farther." The way he did not find he made.

There are many who persevere in life, but continue only for a season, and then sit down discouraged and disgusted, because they have not reached the giddy heights of fame. Men must remember there is no royal road to learning; that fame must be attained by severe self-denials of many pleasures, and in this way only can man hope to achieve those exalted positions and undying fame which are so much cherished by noble souls.

Mr. Williams was born in Boston, August 13, 1813. He began his studies when he was seven years old, mainly by his own efforts. He pulled

HENRY F. WILLIAMS

himself up to the pinnacle of fame from obscurity and a very humble position. What he has done, others can do. His soul was filled with melody, and his hand was skilled with such an infinite touch that he has made his instrument a part of himself; it only caught the harmony within and gave utterance of love and vocalization with the insensible matter of which his instrument was made. I said insensible; but truly, nothing can be insensible to so delicate a touch and sympathetic nature. All things were friends to him that had music in them.

He is a skillful performer on the violin, double bass and cornet; and is also able to play the violincello, baritone trombone and pianoforte. He is also a skillful arranger of music for these instruments. As a composer, his music is attractive, soothing and captivating, and he has thereby secured the recognition of eminent publishers. Persons who so bitterly opposed him among the white, from the selfish prejudice of their natures, became his warm admirers.

His favorite instruments seem to be the violin and cornet. Upon these he produces charming music, which is quite varied, from the fantastic to the gravest. He gave much time to the formation and instruction of bands, and was often employed by the celebrated P. S. Gilmore. He is the author of many pieces, such as "Come Love and List Awhile;" "It was by Chance we Met;" "I Would I had Never Met Thee," etc. His productions have had good sales, from which he has realized a handsome profit. Many doubted his authorship, but were soon made to acknowledge his rare ability by the unmistakable powers of his genius.

Such a brief outline of the career of a master, an almost self-taught musician, whose life affords but another illustration of the power and force of courage and industry in enabling a man to surmount and overcome difficulties and obstacles of no ordinary character, is given here as a light to guide aspiring young musicians. A fuller sketch of him will be found in *Music and Some Highly Musical People*, by James M. Trotter, through whose kindness we have been permitted to use the cut which accompanies this sketch.

CHAPTER XXXII

Rev. Edmund Kelly
Christian Letter-Writer—Lecturer and Author

―――•◆•―――

This good man was born May 23, 1818. He is the son of a slave woman and Edmund Kelly, an emigrant from Ireland, who in early manhood settled in Tennessee. As the father was unable to purchase his family, the children all followed the condition of the mother and remained slaves. When young Edmund Kelly was but six years old, his mother was sold from her little ones and he with his sister were left to the mercies of the slaveholders. In 1883 Mr. Kelly was hired to a very well-to-do primary school-master, where he served as a table waiter, errand boy, and in whatever work he could be useful. He was always desirous of an education, and the opportunities offered the slave for mental improvement were scanty, generally none. In this family, however, young Kelly thought he could take advantage of little children who came to the house to attend school, and for a speller and a few lessons he gave the scholars *bon bons* from his master's table.

All this was a secret, as no one was allowed to teach the slave under penalty of the law. Mr. Kelly managed in this way. During the day he kept steadily at work and all his books were carefully hidden. Early each night he retired with a prayer that God would guide and direct him and wake him at eleven P. M.; thus he first learned how to pray.

At the appointed hour he awoke and studied and wrote until one A. M. For some time this was done entirely unknown to every one save the teacher and the taught, but at last the watchful eye of his mistress discovered some books in which was legibly written "Edmund Kelly." After some questioning and finding out that all concerned were minors, she gave up the investigation and did nothing against it. In the above way Mr. Kelly laid the foundation for after study, for he never had the privilege of attending school in his life.

In April, 1837, Edmund Kelly gave his heart to Him who had blessed him above many of his fellow slaves, and the first of May that same year, at Columbus, Tennessee, he was baptized and joined a Baptist missionary church in that place, composed of both white and colored members. This brother was a convert from the Catholic faith of his father to the Baptist principles, by private study of the New Testament, consequently his open declaration of a new faith created not a little stir and many persons witnessed his immersion.

On the nineteenth of May, 1842, he was licensed by the church of which he was a member to preach the gospel without an application for this privilege, and October 1, the same year, after a unanimous vote had shown the approval of the church and congregation, Rev. R. B. C. Harvell, D. D., pastor of the First Baptist church (white), of Nashville, Tennessee, ordained this brother to the Christian ministry as an evangelist. His first subsequent labor was the organization of the Mt. Lebanon Baptist church, in 1843, with only six members.

As Rev. Kelly always felt it his duty to lead men in the straight and narrow path, he never accepted any civil positions nor titles, though many have been offered him. With ardent soul has he worked for the furtherance of the blessed influence of gospel knowledge—

First. By introducing missions into the Southern plantations by the aid of zealous, humble Christian men and women.

Second. By writing letters on simple gospel themes to be read to the unconverted for their salvation, and for encouragement to the converted.

We were furnished by this brother with a little book written by himself showing the course he pursued in Bible study. This contains many questions and answers quoted from the divine word, which are to be committed by the persons taught. In this way he conducted Sunday school and Bible readings.

Said Rev. Daniel A. Payne, Washington, D. C., once, in speaking of this brother's method:

> I have had the happiness of being present at one of his exhibitions, and am, therefore, prepared to recommend it to you as one of the best I ever witnessed. The cause of our common Christianity and our common humanity will be greatly promoted by furnishing him with opportunities of demonstrating the utility and beauty of his method before your congregations.

He had the interests of the Negro at heart, and for forty years he steadily plead for and defended the cause of this deeply wronged race, and as an outgrowth of experience in mission work the following subjects were written on and sent to any one desiring them: 1. "Edmund Kelly's Key to the Work Among the Colored People of the South." 2. "The Colored People from the Flood, from a Bible Standpoint, Including Africa's *quota* to the American Nation." 3. "The Three Amendments to the National Constitution, with their Historic Sketches." 4. "The

Colored Race as Slaves in this Country from 1620, Commencing with Twenty Slaves and Endng with Six Millions, all Free now." 5. "A Light that is not Clear nor Dark." 6. "Indispensableness of Colored Organizations in this Country, in Order to their Full Development as a Part of One Great Whole."

As a temperance worker, too, for over thirty years throughout the North and South has this consecrated soldier upheld the banner of the Lord, and anywhere he may be called to do any labor for his Master he gladly goes.

During his life he has always been a successful minister, pastor and evangelist, and has accumulated much, though it has generously been expended in mission work and for the education of his family, which he bought from slavery, paying for a wife and four children twenty-eight hundred dollars. With these he went North, where his children were educated, among whom are Professor J. H. Kelly of Columbia and W. D. Kelly, who was a member of the Fifty-fourth Massachusetts regiment.

This aged soldier for Christ, though worn with many years of service, is still active and vigorous, writing for the benefit of mankind the results of his careful lifelong Bible study.

Many of his children have died and his companion is a constant sufferer, besides being deprived of her eyesight; but in all these afflictions he leans upon God and praises him for his goodness and love. He is an honored and faithful minister of the gospel in the city of New Bedford, Massachusetts.

CHAPTER XXXIII

Rev. Preston Taylor
Pastor of the Church of the Disciples, Nashville, Tennessee—
General Financial Agent of a College—Big Contractor

Our subject is the leading minister of the Church of the Disciples. He was born in Shreveport, Louisiana, November 7, 1849. He was born in slavery; his parents were Zed and Betty Taylor. He was carried to Kentucky when a year old; he was a promising boy and shed sunshine wherever he was. At the age of four years he heard his first sermon on the spot where the First Baptist church now stands, in the city of Lexington, Kentucky, and afterwards told his mother that he would be a preacher some day; so deep was the impression made on his young mind that years have not been able to eradicate it. He was affectionately cared for, and he grew up as Samuel of old—ripe for the duties of his life. When the war broke out he saw the soldiers marching, and determined to join them at the first opportunity, and so he enlisted in Company G, One Hundred and Sixteenth United States infantry, in 1864, as a drummer, and was at the siege of Richmond, Petersburg, and the surrender of Lee. His regiment also did garrison duty in Texas, then returned to New Orleans, where they did garrison duty until mustered out of the service. He then learned the stonecutter's trade and became skilful in monument work and also in engraving on marble. He went to Louisville, Kentucky, and in the leading marble yards found plenty of work, but the white men refused to work with him because of his color. He was offered a situation as a train porter on the L. & C. railroad, and for four years he was known as one of the best railroad men in the service, and when he resigned he was requested to remain with a promotion to assistant baggage-master; but as he could be no longer retained, the officers gave him a strong recommendation and a pass over all the roads for an extensive trip, which he took through the North. He accepted, on his return, a call to the pastorate of the Christian church at Mt. Sterling, Kentucky. He remained there fifteen years, and the Lord prospered him in building up the largest congregation in the State among those of his faith, besides building them

PRESTON TAYLOR

the finest brick edifice, as a place for the worship of God, in that section of the State. During these fifteen years he became known as the leading minister of his church in the United States. Not only in Kentucky has he been instrumental in organizing and building both congregations and meeting-houses, but he was unanimously chosen the general evangelist of the United States, which position he now holds, besides assisting in the educational work of his race. He very recently purchased the large, spacious college property at New Castle, Kentucky, which originally cost eighteen thousand dollars, exclusive of the grounds, and at once began the task of paying for it. The school is in operation with a corps of teachers, and has a bright future before it. He is still one of the trustees, and the financial agent of what is now known as the "Christian Bible College," at New Castle. Some idea can be given of this man of push and iron nerve and bold undertakngs by giving a passage in his life. When the Big Sandy railroad was under contract to be completed from Mt. Sterling to Richmond, Virginia, the contractors refused to hire colored men to work on it, preferring Irish labor. He at once made a bid for Sections 3 and 4, and was successful in his bid; he then erected a large commissary and quarters for his men, bought seventy-five head of mules and horses, carts, wagons, cans and all the necessary implements and tools, and, with one hundred and fifty colored men, he led the way. In fourteen months he completed the two miles of the most difficult part of this great trunk line at a cost of about twenty-five thousand dollars.

The president of the road, Mr. C. B. Huntington, said he had built thousands of miles of road, but he never saw a contractor who finished his contract in advance; and so he then was requested by the chief engineer of the works to move his force to another county and help out some of the white contractors; this he did not do. Afterwards he was offered other important contracts, but declined. A syndicate in Nebraska offered him the position of superintendent of their coal mines, but knowing it would take him away from his chosen calling, he declined the offer. For a number of years he was editor of "Our Colored Brethren," a department in the *Christian Standard,* a newspaper published as the organ of his denomination at Cincinnati, Ohio, with a circulation of 50,000 copies a week. He has written for many books and periodicals. He is a member of both Masonic and Oddfellow lodges and was State Grand Chaplain of the former and State Grand Master of the latter, and held that position for three years and traveled all over the State, speaking and lecturing. Especially do the Oddfellows owe much to him for their rise and progress in the State of Kentucky, and the order conferred upon him as a mark of honor, all the degrees of the ancient institution. He has represented his lodge in many of the National conventions of the B. M. C., preaching the annual sermons for a number of years. His headquarters are at Nashville, Tennessee, and he lives in considerable style, with a handsome office and library worth one thousand dollars. The pastoral oversight of the Gay Street church at Nashville, Tennessee, increases his labors. This is one of the largest, wealthiest and most influential congregations in the city. I will give another incident that will show the character of the man, how he loves his race, and with what respect he treats them. While serving the church in Nashville, in 1886, the choir of the church gained great reputation by taking a prize over every other church choir in the city, in a musical contest. The *Nashville American* gave a very flattering account of the results which caused forty-two leading citizens of the white race to petition the pastor of the church, for a concert to be given in the opera house for the special benefit of their friends. When Mr. Taylor met this committee, they informed him that on the night of the concert the colored people would be expected to take the gallery as usual. Mr. Taylor refused deliberately to have anything further to do with the matter and publicly denounced the whole crowd in his church, which was very satisfactory to the colored citizens who urged him to give a concert nevertheless, and he consented. On the night of the concert there was scarcely standing room for the people, who said they desired to show their appreciation of this manly stand in resenting such overtures, and the result was an increase to the treasury of over two hundred dollars. He is one of the leading men in the community where he lives, commanding the respect of all who know him. A slight idea may be given of his popularity by stating that once when a gold cane was voted for in some entertainment in the city of Nashville, his name was submitted by his friends to be voted for. He opposed the suggestion, but, nevertheless, when the votes were counted, out of the three thousand votes in that large city, he got over two-thirds of the number. A quotation from the *Christian Standard,* Cincinnati, Ohio, March 3, 1886, will give some estimate of how he is held by the editor of that paper. A grand party was given for his benefit, and the editor used these words in reference to his absence.

We have just received an invitation to a tea party at Nashville, Tennessee, to be given in honor of Ed. Preston Taylor. We would go all that distance, were it possible, to show our respect for the zeal, ability and untiring energy of Preston Taylor. As we cannot go, we take this method of atoning for our absence.

Mr. Taylor is a man who will impress you when you meet him as thoroughly in earnest. He is never idle, always with new plans, warm hearted, generous, sympathetic and a true brother to all men who deserve the cognizance of earnest, faithful workers for Christ.

CHAPTER XXXIV

Hon. Solomon G. Brown
Distinguished Scientist—Lecturer—Chief Clerk
of the Transportation Department of the Smithsonian Institution,
Washington, District of Columbia—Entomologist—Taxidermist
—Lecturer on "Insects" and "Geology."

Solomon G. Brown was the fourth son of Isaac and Rachel Brown. He was born of free parents in the city of Washington, District of Columbia, February 14, 1829. He was deprived of the common school education by the loss of his father in 1833, when his mother was left a widow, and had at that time six children. They were very poor. His father's property was seized for pretended debts in 1834, leaving the family penniless and homeless. Solomon was early placed under the care of a Mr. Lambert Tree, assistant postmaster in the city post-office. He received an appointment under Mr. Tree in one of the departments in the post-office in 1844, from which he was detailed to assist Professor Joseph Henry, Professor Samuel F. Morse and Mr. Alfred Vail in putting the new magnetic telegraph system in operation in 1845, and he remained with them until the enterprise was purchased by the Morse Telegraph company, when he accepted a situation as battery tender from the new company, and served until appointed assistant packer to Gillman & Bros. manufactory, in their chemical laboratory.

This is quite an incident in Mr. Brown's history, for he was present when the first wire was laid from Baltimore to Washington. It will be remembered that Mr. Morse had conceived the idea of a magnetic telegraph system in 1832, and had exhibited it to the Congress in 1837, and had vainly attempted to get a patent in England, as Professor Wheatstone in England had claimed a prior invention over the American. He struggled on with scanty means until 1843, and just as he was about to give up the whole matter Congress, at midnight in the last moment of the session, appropriated thirty thousand dollars for the purpose of making an experiment with the line between Baltimore and Washington. After the success of this line Mr. Morse was voted testimonials, orders of nobility, honors and wealth, but the Negro who assisted materially has been almost forgotten. Mr. Brown was a natural scientist, and coming in contact with these learned men only increased his thirst for knowledge. He is a man of rare scientific acquirements, very unassuming in his appearance, and yet his intelligence would astonish one on making his acquaintance. Mr. Brown is very handy with the brush, for while he was in this chemical laboratory he mounted and colored maps for the general land office as well as prepared colors in the Gideon company's bookbinding establishment, where he remained until 1852, when he was appointed to the foreign exchange division of the then new Smithsonian Institution where he has remained until this time, filling acceptably all positions that he has been honored with. Few men in the city of Washington are better known, and certainly none stand higher in the estimation of the people. He has filled very many honorary positions and has done great good for his race. He has been a trustee of Wilberforce University, and trustee of the 15th Street Presbyterian church, superintendent of the North Washington Mission Sunday school, and active member of the Freedmen's Relief association. He was elected to the legislature for the District of Columbia in 1871, and re-elected twice, overcoming at one time four candidates. He was trustee of the public schools, grand secretary of the District Grand Lodge of Masons, commissioner for the poor in the County of Washington, and one of the assistant honorary commissioners of the colored department of the New Orleans Exposition for the District of Columbia. In 1866 he was elected to the office of President of the National Union League; was a member of the executive committee of the Emancipation Monument erectors, and honorary member of the Galbraith Lyceum; corresponding member of the St. Paul Lyceum, Baltimore; director of the Industrial Saving and Building Association of Washington, District of Columbia; Washington correspondent of the *Anglo-African Christian Recorder* when it was under the management of Bishop H. M. Turner; also assistant in the organization of the Pioneer Sunday school association, Hillsdale, District of Columbia, presiding as superintendent from 1868 to 1887, and is again re-elected to serve another year. He is also editor of the "Sunday school Circle" of the *Christian Index*, at Jackson, Tennessee, and a frequent lecturer on scientific questions before scientific societies in Baltimore, Alexandria and Washington. Mr. Brown's connection with the Pioneer association deserves to be especially mentioned.

In early days, directly after the war, when General O. O. Howard had charge of the Freedmen's Bureau, through it, in some way, a little town now known as Hillsdale was purchased and many families secured homes for themselves in that neighborhood. Mr. Brown was one of these, and through his direction, encouragement and advice many happy homes have been established, to which the Pioneer association with its very large Sunday school work, its brilliant concerts, its Bible readings, lectures and other entertainments, has added materially to the moral, spiritual and intellectual and financial condition of the people. Only judgment day will be able to tell the good that Solomon G. Brown has accomplished in that neighborhood. Personally acquainted with him, living in his house for several years, I can speak from knowledge. His whole life seems devoted to the people. He spends his money freely in providing those things for the intellectual culture and the moral training of the Sunday school attendants, male and female, young and old, and he was never weary in well-doing. No period of my life was more pleasantly spent than in his house. Surrounded as he is with musical people, with the choicest library, pictures and other evidences of culture, one could not but enjoy life. His home is indeed a pleasant one, because his amiable wife, whom he married June 16, 1864, has been to him truly a helpmeet and has contributed largely to the carrying out of his plans. Mr. Brown is a poet, and has in press a book of poems which will show to some extent his genius and literary taste. Never having been blessed with children of his own, he has adopted several and trained them to useful womanhood.

Solomon G. Brown began his public lecturing on the sciences about the year 1855. His first lecture was delivered January 10, 1855, before the Young Peoples' Literary society and lyceum, at Israel church, Washington, District of Columbia, south of the Capitol building, to a large, fashionable audience; this lecture was called out by the request of several prominent citizens of Washington, as will be shown from the following letter:

Mr. Solomon G. Brown

Dear Sir: A number of your personal friends who were present at the last meeting of the Young Peoples' Club, at Israel (presided over by Dr. Enoch Ambush), were somewhat surprised at certain pleasing and instructive remarks, made by you in *explanation of society*, especially when you so graphically described the social habits of insects, etc., and in order that we may hear you more fully, we beg to request that you will at some early date consent to give us a lecture on insects, at such place as you may select.

We are yours very truly,
Sampson Nutter
Anthony Bowen
Andrew Foote
William Slade
Alfred Kiger
James Wright
Andrew B. Tinney
James Wormley
Alfred Barbour

Washington, District of Columbia, November 24, 1854

A reply was made and forwarded, and January 10 was named as the time. Mr. Brown was introduced by Mr. Enoch Ambush. He was greeted by a large, intelligent audience, among whom were several white citizens.

The lecturer, after thanking the audience for their flattering ovation and Dr. Ambush for his fine introduction, said that we are now introduced as a race to a new and rich field of thought, quite different from that in which we have been accustomed to engage, for from all the facts that he could gather, he, S. G. Brown, was the first to enter the field as a lecturer and student of natural science, and more especially zoology, and for that reason he begged of the hearers a patient sympathy in his feeble efforts. He then began thus:

But before I proceed, and I cannot consent to do so without first paying a living compliment to those profound, eminent thinkers who have, after years of labor, study, investigation and research, added so much to our stock of knowledge, in that department of zoology called insects.

The scientists I will name in the order that they have fixed themselves in my mind as follows: Say, Melsheimer, Harris, Fitch, LeConte (father and son), Randall, Haldman, Ziegler and others, who have for years pursued industriously the study of entomology, and have many of them, departed and left their labors on record in so many scientific memoirs as a record. And I am here to-night to say, that to them the world owes much for our present stock of knowledge of these little animated creatures, both as a benefit and rare benefit to human economy.

The word "Insect" is derived from the Greek and means *cut into*. A living creature whose form is articulated, having a sensitive body composed of three distinct parts; the head, the thorax and the abdomen. Legs, six in number; the first two act as maxillary; the second two as super-maxillary; the third two as lifters or props to an overhanging oblongated abdomen. Two, and sometimes four wings, attached to the thorax and abdomen. Along the sides are openings or spiracules lined with ferruginous hairs, through which they breathe or carry on respiration.

The word "Insect" is sometimes used in a sense of derision, as something small, insignificant, mean, low and contemptible. This we think is a grave error, for in nothing created (except man) has God in His infinite wisdom and goodness, displayed so much grandeur and wonder as is found in these minute, delicate and wonderful creatures. And we do this evening come to the defense of the insect and claim for it a high place in the great kingdom of zoology, and class it as the head of the articulates, forming a distinct branch, yet a zoological unit, and a thing worthy of the best and most costly investigation and thought, for no man can boast of a complete knowledge of zoology without at least some acquaintance with entomology.

I am truly proud to say that among the branches studied to inclose a liberal education now encouraged, that natural history is incorporated, and some attention and even respect is being paid to the study of entomology; and the most flattering demonstration of that fact is this gathering tonight.

The earlier students have carefully collected and arranged all known families of insects into groups, families, varieties, genus and species, naming each class according to some well-defined characteristic. Then again subdividing them into two grand roots: First, insects which are beneficial; second, insects which are injurious to man.

A further investigation was found necessary when it was discovered that the identical species were not found all over the globe. Then a geographical distribution was fixed; this and many other difficulties were met with, among the earliest naturalists, and after a systematic study of food, habitation, habits, arrival, departure and climatic situations considered, they finally arrived at a proper philosophical data.

The lecturer dwelt for some time, and spoke of many amusing incidents of superstition and of association, industries, union, affections, offenses and defenses, deceptions and profanations, their mode of communications, their song and language, their destructiveness, friendship and enmity to man, their presence and absence at various seasons of the year, their Providence, unity, obedience to authority and communism. He then named those which benefited man, such as bees, silk-worms, house-fly and numerous others; and among those which injured man, he named fleas, chigoes, ticks, bed-bugs, horse-flies, wasps, hornets, mosquitoes, lice, ants, scorpions, etc.

In the concluding portion of the lecture, the social order of insects was again referred to at some length, and it was proven very clearly and logically, as well as wittily, that insects in very many cases had been men's closest and nearest companions, more so than any other known animal, following him through all departments of life, at times even his bed-fellow and constant bosom friends.

The lecturer was applauded very heartily at the conclusion, and, indeed it was a decided success, as may be judged from the many times this lecture has been repeated—each time by request.

This lecture was fully illustrated by forty-nine large drawings or diagrams, and was repeated in Georgetown, District of Columbia, for Rev. W. H. Hunter, Alexandria, Virginia; Rev. Clement Robertson, Baltimore, Maryland. Three times at different places: at Zion, Wesley, South Washington. The following lectures followed this: "Geology," "Water," "Air," "Food," "Coal," "Mineralogy," "Telegraph," "Fungus," "Embryo Plants," "Man's Relations to the Earth," "Straight Lines, its Product, Circles and its Waste," "God's Providence to Man," "Early Educators of D. C.," and six others.

In connection with his own diagram, Mr. Brown has prepared or assisted in preparing nearly all the important diagrams for the grand scientific lectures which have been delivered in the famous Smithsonian course for the past thirty-five years.

The following is an outline of a lecture by the Hon. Solomon G. Brown, and shows in a great measure his interest in these matters.

The first lecture on geology before the annual conference of the A. M. E. church, Bethel church, Baltimore, April, 1863, by special invitation of a committee. The immense building was filled when Rev. Henry M. Turner [now Bishop] introduced the lecturer. After being introduced to the vast audience, the lecturer began by saying that the selection of the subject to be discussed was not left to him, but had been called out by an invitation from a special committee appointed by the conference. Then he proceeded by saying that geology is the science which treats of the constitutional crust of the earth; its object is to describe the mineral matter and its organic remains, both animal and vegetable, that have lived and held a place upon the globe, many of which are now extinct. It also marks the successive changes that have passed over with time, also the laws that have governed these changes.

Geology is divided into three distinct departments, as follows:
1. Descriptive geology.
2. Theoretical geology.
3. Practical geology.

The descriptive exhibits the facts of science; the theoretical attempts to account for them; and the practical shows their practical application to practical purposes.

Subservient to geology is chemistry, which treats of the ultimate parts of matter and their modes of combination; mineralogy, which characterizes and classifies the various rocks and minerals of which the earth is composed; botany and zoology, which describes plants and animals; and physical geography, which relates the facts concerning the general distribution of matter at the surface of the earth, the form and extent of continents and islands, rivers and mountain systems, together with the changes now occurring in them. And in order to get a more complete knowledge of geology we will necessarily have to consider the chemistry of the earth. In doing this we recognize sixty elements or simple bodies which combine to produce all the varieties of matter with which we are acquainted. Many of them occur in small quantities and are rarely seen. Fifteen or sixteen of these elements enter largely into the compositions of rocks.

These substances, however, very rarely present themselves in their elementary state; but combined with each other they make the greater portion of the earth's crust.

The most prevalent of these is oxygen, which forms eight-ninths of water, one-fifth of the atmosphere, and constitutes one-half of all the matter known to us.

With silicon it forms silica; with potassium it forms potassia; with iron, the oxide of iron, etc. There are but few minerals or fossils that do not contain oxygen.

Hydrogen forms a portion of minerals, especially bituminous coal, and enters into the composition of water.

Nitrogen is not so abundant, but is found in the bones of animals, living and fossils, in vegetables and in the atmosphere.

Carbon is the most abundant ingredient in coal, and enters into the composition of limestone, which is carbonate of lime.

Sulphur exists in the sulphurets of the metals; sulphuret of iron, iron pyrites, sulphuret of lead, galena or lead ore; also in sulphates, as sulphate of lime, gypsum or plaster of paris.

It is thrown out extensively by volcanoes. Chlorine is one of the constituents of rock salt (chloride of sodium) and is widely diffused in the ocean.

Fluorine occurs in fluoride of calcium (fluor spar) and other minerals.

Phosphorus enters into the composition of many minerals and of animal bones, as the phosphate of lime.

Silicon exists in most of the rocks, combined with oxygen, as silica quartz, which constitutes about forty-five per cent of the crust of the earth, and form the walls of nearly all vegetable matter.

Oxide of aluminum—aluminia forms one-fifth of the mineral feldspar, and abounds in clay and slate rocks; it is estimated at ten per cent of all the rocks.

The oxide of potassium also enters largely into feldspar and clay.

Sodium forms a part of rock salt and other minerals.

The oxide calcium (lime) occurs chiefly in carbonates (limestone, marble), which is estimated to form one-fourteenth part of the globe's crust.

Magnesia—The oxide of magnesia enters into the composition of many rocks, and abounds in magnesium limestone.

Iron is very widely diffused in the various forms of its ores, oxide, carburet, sulphuret, etc., and by these the geologist is enabled to discover the various changes that have taken place by the agency of chemical affinity for many thousands of ages.

The lecturer then took up at length the following agencies which had modified, reduced and changed the surface of the earth from away back into millions of years, as follows: Atmospheric, aqueous, igneous and organic. The lecturer then concluded with practical geology.

The lecture was illustrated by twenty-nine large, well executed diagrams. No. 1 of the set showed the geological formations of strata in their geological order. All the other twenty-eight were fully explained.

WORTHY THE LAMB THAT WAS SLAIN

BY HON. SOLOMON G. BROWN

*On the mountain tops the beacon lights are kindled
By the rosy flush that tells the day is born;*

Height to height replies as up to the waiting heavens
    Comes the rising sun that heralds Easter morn;
Smiles the earth arrayed in robes of living verdure,
    Sing the birds on leafy bough a joyous strain,
Nature joins with man in praise and adoration,
    Saying: Worthy is the lamb that was slain!

In their channels leap the streams with throbbing pulses,
    Life renewed is in each whisper of the breeze,
All the little twigs and shoots are stirring softly
    With the life that animates the waving trees;
Overhead the cloudless sky is brightly bending,
    Sunbeams rest alike on grassy hill and plain,
Earth and heaven are lighting up their glad thanksgiving,
    Saying: Worthy is the lamb that once was slain!

Bring no spices to anoint the dead, ye mourners,
    From the grave the stone of grief is rolled away;
Over death and hell the Saviour rose triumphant
    On the morning of the Resurrection day;
Seek him not within the tomb for he is risen;
    Jesus is not here, behold where he has lain!
Look above while angels swell the joyous anthem,
    Saying: Worthy is the lamb that once was slain!

Hallelujah! for the crucified is risen,
    Let the earth rejoice, the mountains clap their hands,
Let the floods be glad and offer up thanksgiving,
    Hallelujah! oh, be joyful all ye lands,
Sing aloud for joy all nations and all people,
    Angels and archangels swell the loud refrain,
With the blood-bought millions cast your crown before him,
    Saying: Worthy is the lamb that once was slain!

CHAPTER XXXV

John Mitchell, Jr.
The Gamest Negro Editor on the Continent—A Man of Grit and Iron Nerve—A Natural Born Artist

---

Men are brave often from experience with arms and the scenes of war, others because of a recklessness of life and a dare-devil spirit, and still others are born for deeds of bravery and glide as easily to places of danger as if led by unerring instinct; they are bold, aggressive, determined and venturesome. Such a man as the last is John Mitchell, Jr., and it remains yet for history to say for certainty what good July 11, 1863, had in store for the Nation, for on this day he first raised his infant voice. It was when his parents lived in Henrico county; they were slaves. His mother was a seamstress and his father was a coachman. From the day of his birth it will be observed that he, too, was a slave. But little does he know of those dark and "cruel slavery days." The sound of cannon, the roar of musketry, the hissing of grape and canister did not go unheeded by his infant ears. At this time the "Fall of Richmond," the Union sentinels passing back and forward on the streets of the city did not *slightly* attract his attention. Little fellow that he was, their presence has as much terror for him as they had for the rebels. The "blue coats' " mission, however, he could not then understand. His mother taught him his a, b, c's, a-b ab's and e-b eb's and the other monosyllabic beginnings, in that old antiquated method, now a long time out of date. Many times has he felt the full force of her hand on his young face to enable him to have a better appreciation of his lessons. As he grew older, he coupled with his school duties that of the duties of a newsboy, peddling the evening daily papers on the streets of the city, with all the strength of his young life crying out "*State Journal,* here's your *State Journal.*" He soon became carriage boy for James Lyons, a rich, aristocrat lawyer; he was a typical Southerner who had owned young Mitchell's parents before the war, and consequently had been his "master." The boy often accompanied him to his farm in Henrico county.

It was this Southerner who tried to instil in him the idea that there

JOHN MITCHELL, JR.

were no colored gentlemen, the same having been told him when, upon answering the door bell, he would inform Mr. Lyons that a colored gentleman wished to see him. His mother had so taught him, and it could be readily seen that she had different ideas from that of the "blue blood" on that score. It was here he had the recollection of seeing Jefferson Davis, the ex-President of the Confederate States, and he was reminded that he had a glass eye, a thing that remains fresh in his mind to the present day. He also waited on the table at Mr. Lyons' residence on the corner of Sixth and Gray streets, the place now being the palatial quarters of the Westmoreland Club.

He bitterly opposed young Mitchell's being educated, but despite all this his mother kept him at school, taught by Rev. A. Binga, Jr., now of Manchester, Virginia. What ability he had, if any existed at that time, seemed latent within him. In 1876 he entered the Richmond Normal High School. In 1877 he received the silver medal for having stood the highest in a class of thirty pupils. This so encouraged him that he was successful ever after in this direction for years. A competition in map drawing at the Fair Grounds of the State Agricultural Society, at Richmond, took place, and a gold medal was offered for the best map of Virginia, and he lost, though he tried very hard. He thought that he lost unjustly. He was careful as to details and was sure if accuracy was called in question he would win.

This defeat but spurred him on to greater efforts; he felt convinced that he could win, and he was determined to make others have the same opinion. January 1, 1881, he brought into the school-room a map of Virginia, on which he had spent his Christmas holidays to make it ornamental as well as accurate. His surprise was great when teachers and pupils gathered round and gazed in wonderment upon the production. This he donated to the school upon the suggestion of the principal, and then proceeded to draw another which would render insignificant the work they had taken the pains to praise.

In May, 1871, this production was exhibited. Crowds of pupils gazed thereon; it was taken from him and he heard nothing more of it until at the graduation exercises, Hon. A. M. Riley, who was minister to Austria, and now one of the judges of the Court of the Khedive of Egypt, saw it and said it was worthy of a special gold medal, and he would be the one to present it. This he did June 5, 1881, stating that it was the best production ever executed by any pupil, white or black, in the State.

Young Mitchell stood at the head of his class and won a gold medal offered for that accomplishment. In 1881 he won another gold medal in an oratorical contest in which there were five competitors. He has since drawn a map of Yorktown, surrounded by dignitaries of the Revolutionary War. All this was done with lead pencils which usually cost two cents each. The work resembles the finest steel engraving, and would be readily taken for such. Mr. Mitchell has never received any lessons in the work and this makes it the more surprising. So imbued were his friends with the fine character of the work that they endeavored to secure for him an apprenticeship in the Bureau of Engraving and Printing at Washington, District of Columbia.

Addressing Mr. M. E. Bell, supervising architect at Washington, Senator William Mahone, of Virginia, said: "I wish you would give a moment to this young colored man. See his drawings, they will interest you. There is talent here which ought to be encouraged."

Hon. B. K. Bruce, then register of the treasury department, wrote: "I cordially concur with the sentiments expressed by Senator Mahone, and hope Mr. Mitchell may receive the encouragement he so richly reserves."

Senator John A. Logan wrote, after seeing the drawings: "I most cordially concur in what has been said of Mr. Mitchell. He is a wonderful young man in his line."

August 15, 1881, when Hon. Fred Douglass wrote to Mr. J. W. Cromwell, by whom Mitchell had been sent: "I am much obliged to you; I am glad to have the evidence of the talent and skill afforded in the map of Virginia by your young friend, John Mitchell, Jr., with the industry, patience and perseverance which he has shown in this work, I have no fear but that young Mitchell will make his way in the world and be a credit to our race."

In May, 1878, young Mitchell professed religion and joined the First Baptist church, Richmond. He became an active member of the Sunday school, and was made chairman of the executive board of the Virginia Baptist State Sunday school convention. In 1883 and 1884 he was the Richmond correspondent of the *New York Freeman.* December 5, 1884, he assumed the editorial charge of the *Richmond Planet,* since which time the journal has become the most influential in the State.

Mr. Mitchell is a bold and fearless writer, carrying out to the letter all he says he will. He has given his attention particularly to Southern outrages of the colored people. His exposure of the murder of Banks, a colored man, by Officer Priddy (white) attracted wide-spread attention. The jury brought in a verdict that the deceased came to his death by some unknown disease and no one was to blame. Mr. Mitchell condemned the crime and declared the officer guilty of murder. He was summonded before the grand jury, an attempt being made to indict him for making such a charge. The case was dropped. He discovered that the man had been unmercifully clubbed by the officer; so he consulted four colored physicians in order to have the body exhumed and the head examined. After much inquiry, he discovered that the body had been sent to the dead-house of the University of Virginia, Charlottesville. He boarded a train for that place and went into the dead-house; he saw portions of a body which were covered over as he entered. He did not know the victim. He was locked in the dead-house himself, by parties present, but got out, and after hunting for the physician in charge without success, hurried back to Richmond to appear at court the next morning. The officer was never punished; this was a specimen of Southern justice.

The lynching of Richard Walker, in Charlotte county, demonstrated Mr. Mitchell's courage again. This colored man was lynched by a mob of white men at Smithville, about eighty-six miles from Richmond, Virginia. Mr. Mitchell condemned the affair and declared that his murderers should be dangled from a rope's end. This occurred in May, 1886. The editorial appeared on a Saturday, and on the following Monday he received a letter containing a piece of hemp, abusing him and declaring they would hang him, should he put his foot in the county. Mr. Mitchell replied that he would visit the county, adding: "There are no terrors, Cassius, in your threats, for I am armed so strong in honesty that they pass me by like the idle winds, which I respect not."

Later on he armed himself with a brace of Smith & Wesson revolvers, went to the scene of the murder, which was five miles from any railroad station, and was locked in the jail for the purpose of inspecting the place where Walker had been found, and then returned to Richmond and published an account of his trip.

A short account of him appeared lately in the *New York World* February 22, 1887, where these words depict clearly his character. Said this journal:

> One of the most daring and vigorous Negro editors, is John Mitchell, Jr., editor of the *Richmond Planet*. The fact that he is a Negro and lives in Richmond, does not prevent him from being courageous almost to a fault.
>
> He is a man who would walk into the jaws of death to serve his race; and his courage is a thing to be admired. Mr. Mitchell is one of the intensest lovers of his race. His pen seems dipped in vitriol and his words are hurled with the force of Milton's Satan, whom we find described as having such strength "that his spear, to equal which, the tallest pine hewn on Norwegian hills to be the mast of some great admiral, were but a wand."

CHAPTER XXXVI

Rev. Loudon Ferrill
Pastor of a Church Incorporated by a State Legislature—
An Old-Time Preacher—Hired by Town Trustees to Preach
to the Colored People

One of the most wonderful men who ever lived on the soil of Kentucky was the second pastor of what is now known as the First Baptist church in Lexington. He was the slave of Mrs. Anna Winston, in Hanover county, Virginia. His youth was spent about as boys usually spent their time; but at eleven years of age a singular thing happened to him, which made him think of a future life. He was bathing with a companion and they were saved from drowning only by the help of a woman, who caught them by the hair of the head and drew them ashore. After recovering, he received severe punishment and strict orders were given him to keep away from the river. In a sketch written at the time of his death, it is said that both of the boys were of the opinion that had they died they would have gone to the lake of fire and brimstone; they covenanted together that henceforth they would serve God only.

He served an apprenticeship as a house-joiner. Ferrill was faithful to his promise, while his partner was recreant throughout. After baptism he felt that he was called to preach the gospel, but he was disobedient to the promptings of his heart. At that time no slave was permitted to be ordained. Ferrill was permitted, however, by his brethren, to preach, so far as their power extended, in these words: "To go forth and preach the gospel wherever the Lord might cast his lot, and the door should be open to him." Fifty persons were soon converts under his ministry. When his old master died he became free, and he and his wife (for at this time he was married) came to Kentucky in search of a new field of labor.

When he arrived at Lexington he found a preacher known as "Old Captain" laboring among the people; however, his days were numbered and the people desired Ferrill to preach to them, which he refused to do because of the organization not being in fellowship with the Baptist denomination, although they held the faith and general practice of

Baptists; but he entered into the constitution of the First Baptist Church (white) in 1817. The colored people then applied to the white church for his services. The church being in doubt as to what to do, proposed to the Elkhorn association, in 1821, the following queries: First, "Can persons baptized on a confession of faith by an administrator not ordained be received into our churches under any circumstances whatever without being again baptized?" Second. "Is it admissible for the association to ordain free men of color ministers of the gospel?" The queries were taken up by a committee, consisting of Jeremiah Vardeman, James Fishback, John Edwards, Edmund Waller and Jacob Creath, who were appointed to consider the matter. They reported, first, that it is not regular to receive such members; second, that they knew no reason why free men of color could not be ordained ministers of the gospel, the gospel qualification being possessed by them. This first resolution referred to those colored people who had been baptized by "Old Captain," and the second to Ferrill's ordination. However, they were all received without re-baptism, and Ferrill was ordained. Ferrill took regular charge of the church and served it thirty-two years, during which time it increased from 280 to 1,820 members, and became the largest church in Kentucky. Ferrill was a remarkable man; he was descended from a royal line of Africans. Dr. William Bright, a white pastor in the State, said of him: "He had the manner of authority and command, and was respected by the whole population of Lexington, and his influence was more potent to keep order among the blacks than the police force of the city."

In 1883, when the cholera was raging in Lexington, he was the only minister that remained faithful; nursing his wife, who died at this time, and at whose funeral the largest number attended, which was thirteen, of any of the funerals of that dreadful day.

There has been many a dispute as to the length of time it takes to baptize any number of candidates. It is recorded in *Spencer's History of the Baptists,* from whence we get many valuable facts, that he baptized at one time 220 persons in 85 minutes, and at another time 60 in 45 minutes.

So popular was Loudon Ferrill that the trustees of the town of Lexington employed him to preach to the colored people. It is a singular fact that all good men have enemies, and his endeavored to destroy his church. Solomon Walker, his oldest deacon, advised him to discontinue his meetings, but Ferrill said: No, by the help of the Lord he was going on and believed that he would see so many people there that the house would not hold them. And this vision was fully realized, for under his preaching the attendance at his church was always a very large one, frequently his church was filled to overflowing.

Harry Quills, "whose heart was said to have been as black as his face," spread a report that Ferrill's character was not good in Virginia, but upon some of the white elders writing to persons living in the neighborhood in which he was born and raised, they were informed that his character was unspotted. He made another attempt to injure Ferrill; knowing that the law was such that no free colored person could remain in this State over thirty days, unless a native of the State, thought he would drive Ferrill away in this manner. He had warrants gotten out; a number of free people was sold and a number went away. The white people got Dr. Fishback to draw up a petition to the Legislature to give Ferrill permission to stay in the State, which was granted, and his church at length was incorporated by the Legislature under the name of the "Old Apostolic Church."

In his will he left his property to his two adopted children, and left the following prayer, also, as a legacy for Kentucky:

O! Great Father of Heaven and earth, bless the citizens of Richmond, Virginia, for their kindness toward me in my youthful days; but more particularly, O Lord, be merciful to the citizens of Lexington, Kentucky, and may it please Thee to bless, preserve and keep them from sin. Guide them in all their walks, make them peaceable, happy and truly righteous; and when they come to lie down on the bed of death, may thy good spirit hover around ready to waft their ransomed souls to Thy good presence. Lord, grant this for Christ's sake; and, O! God, bless the church of which I am pastor, and govern it with Thy unerring wisdom, and keep it the church as long as time shall last; and O, my Maker, choose, when I am gone, some pastor for them, who may be enabled to labor with more zeal than your humble petitioner has ever done, and grant that it may continue to prosper and do good among the colored race. O, merciful Father, bless the white people, who have always treated me as though I was a white man. And bless, I pray Thee, all those who through envy or malice have mistreated me, and save them, is my prayer. Bless the Church of Christ, everywhere; bless the Christians in every land. Bless, O Lord, my two adopted children and keep them in Thy way. Bring all sinners in all countries to feel their need of a Saviour, and pardon all their sins, and when they come to die, take them unto Thyself, and the glory shall be to the Father and Son and the Holy Ghost forever and ever. Amen.

The author of this book feels grateful that he shares especially in this prayer, as he pastored this same church so nobly established by this servant of the Most High. At the death of Mr. Ferrill, October 12, 1854, the *Lexington Observer* said "that he rests from his labors and his works do follow him." He had justly acquired an immense influence among the colored people of this city and surrounding country, and he always exercised this influence with prudence and for the furtherance of good morals and religion.

The *Kentucky Gazette*, March 6, 1878, speaking of his death, said:

The colored people of Lexington are under a lasting debt and obligation to Brother Ferrill; for he did more for their elevation and instruction than all other agencies combined, and we know that the masters of his people regarded him as a most useful and valuable assistant in governing and controlling them, and often averted harsher means. It is well to familiarize the generation that has sprung up since his death with the history of his blameless and useful life, for the lessons that it teaches can hardly be lost upon them. This good man is remembered by persons now living in Lexington, who worshiped him almost as a saint, and are never weary of telling of his good deeds. It is said, that in marrying slaves he used a very sensible ceremony. He pronounced them "united until death or distance do them part." Long may he be remembered, and his example of holiness and faithfulness be an inspiration to the rising generation.

RICHARD THEODORE GREENER

CHAPTER XXXVII

*Professor Richard Theodore Greener, A. B., LL. B., LL. D.
Chief Civil Service Examiner—Lawyer—Metaphysician,
Logician and Orator—Prize Essayist—Dean of the Law
Department of Howard University*

———◆◆◆———

Without doubt the gentleman whose name stands at the head of this page is one of the most accomplished scholars in polite literature among us. In this statement not an adjective is wasted, nor is it misused. His studies range over a vast field of learning. His taste is aesthetical, and can be compared to the eagle in its flights. He was never known to produce a poor article from his pen. He is an orator of the finest kind, differing from Douglass and Langston only in the degree in which they differ from each other. As we shall show his career, it can easily be seen that he has spent his life among books and has had the good judgment to use Bacon's advice when writing of studies: "Some books are to be tasted, others to be swallowed and some few to be read and digested; that is some books are to be read only in parts, others to be read but not curiously, and some few to be read wholly and with diligence and attention. Reading maketh a full man, conference a ready man, writing an exact man." All three of these characteristics belong to Mr. Greener, who has risen to his present status from a poor boy, for he supported a widowed mother by working as a porter while quite a lad. He was born in Philadelphia, Pennsylvania, and lived in Boston from the time he was five years of age. He was educated at the grammar school of Cambridge, and then spent two years preparing for college at Oberlin, Ohio, and finished his preparations at Phillips Academy, Andover, Massachusetts, the oldest in this country. He graduated from Harvard University as a Bachelor of Arts in 1870, when he was about twenty-six years old, and was immediately made principal in the male department of the institute for the colored youth in Philadelphia, Pennsylvania, from September, 1870, to December, 1872. He followed in this position the highly cultured and distinguished Octavius V. Catto, who was shot in a riot in 1871. Mr. Greener was the first one to be with him after his assassination. From January 1 to July 1, 1873, he was principal of the Sumner High School, Washington, District of Columbia, and was also associate editor of the *New National Era*, from April to October of that same year. September, 1873, found him at work in the office of the United States attorney for the District of Columbia. Two months later, in the same year, he was elected professor of metaphysics and logic in the University of South Carolina at Columbia, which chair he accepted and filled with great credit until March, 1877, when the university was closed by the Hampton Legislature. While he was a professor in this university he assisted in the departments of Latin and Greek, and also taught classes in International law and the Constitution of the United States. He was active in politics, though he never held a political office. At the same time he was librarian of the university from May 14 to October 31, 1875, when he rearranged the thirty thousand volumes and prepared a catalogue. He also wrote an interesting monograph on the rare books of the library, which he read before the American Philological Association, in June, 1877, at the Johns Hopkins University, Baltimore, Maryland. For his labors at the library even the *Charleston News and Courier* found words of praise. In 1875 also he was chosen by a concurrent resolution of the General Assembly of South Carolina a member of a commission whose duty it was to revise the school system of the State. In this commission he was the only one who had not been the president of the college. He also found time to complete his law studies, which he had begun in Philadelphia and had continued in the office of the attorney for the District of Columbia, by graduating from the law school of the South Carolina University, under Judge Moses, at the head of his class, and was admitted to practice in the Supreme Court of South Carolina, December 20, 1876, and the Bar of the District of Columbia, April 14, 1877. In 1877 he became instructor in the Law Department in Howard University, and on the death of John H. Cooke, Esq., in 1879, he was elected dean. September, 1880, he resigned the deanship and became a law clerk of the first comptroller of the United States treasury, Hon. William Lawrence of Ohio, which position he held until February 28, 1882, and then begun the active practice of law. He was an associate counsel with A. K. Brown, Esq., in the defense of J. M. W. Stone, indicted for wife murder, and made the opening speech for the defense in the argument for a new trial, and assisted in the general conduct of the case. It will be remembered that Stone's head was cut off by the rope, clean from his neck, when he was hung, one of the few instances of the kind on record. In preparation of his law cases, Mr. Greener is as careful as he would be in the preparation of an oration on any literary subject. His researches are indicative of his breadth of learning and acquaintance with text books in the matter at hand.

He was associate counsel with Hon. Jeremiah Wilson in the famous extradition case of Samuel L. Perry, one of those who had been originally exodized from North Carolina, and whose extradition was demanded by Governor Jarvis on the trumped up charge of forgery. Mr. Greener made the argument before Justice Wiley, of the Supreme Court of the District of Columbia, on the habeas corpus hearing, going over all the cases of extradition from 1791 down to the present time. In this argument he was opposed to Hon. R. T. Merrick, Tilden's counsel in the electoral commission, and counsel for the Government in the Star Route cases. Mr. Greener won the case and Perry was released from custody. He was also associated with Hon. Martin I. Townsend, United States district attorney, in the Whittaker court of inquiry, in April and May, 1880, and made the legal argument before the secretary of war, Hon. Alex. Ramsey, for the release of Whittaker and the granting of a court-martial. Whittaker was the colored student noted at West Point as the one whose ears were mutilated, and it was charged that he had tied himself and then mutilated his own ears, which seems to have been impossible. The result of his argument was that indefinite leave was immediately granted and a court-martial was ordered by President Hayes, December 28, 1880. He was also associated as counsel with ex-Governor Daniel H. Chamberlin, from January 20 to June 15, 1881, in defense of Cadet Whittaker during the court-martial. Mr. Greener was also secretary of the original exodus committee, with Senator Windom president, and was chairman of the first delegation that waited on Senator Windom after his speech, and stated the grievances of the colored people. He debated the exodus question with Hon. Fred Douglass, Washington, District of Columbia, and at the Social Science congress, at Saratoga, New York, September 13, 1879. In that year, also, he lectured all through the Western States and wrote many articles to the newspapers on the different phases of the movement. Professor Greener has had a large experience in political speaking, and has done a great deal of political work. In 1876 he also canvassed the Third Congressional district of South Carolina for Hayes and Wheeler and Chamberlin. His experience is enrolled on the Senate miscellaneous documents, Number 48, Senator Cameron's (Wisconsin) report, pages 223 to 228, Volume 1, and he was the only man who made the entire circuit of the district and spoke at every advertised place. After the overthrow of the Republican government in that State, he returned to Washington and has attended to his profession ever since. In every campaign his services have been in active demand, and he has spoken since 1877 in Virginia, Maryland, Pennsylvania, New Jersey, Ohio and New York.

He was a member of the Republican conference of one hundred, held in New York City, August 4, 1880, and represented South Carolina. He has represented that State in the Union League of America from 1876 to 1879, and is at present president of the South Carolina Republican association, Washington, District of Columbia.

This charming talker took an active part in the Republican campaign of 1884, speaking in seven States for Blaine and Logan. July, 1885, he was appointed secretary of the Grant Memorial association, in the State of New York, and October 9, 1885, he was appointed chief examiner of the municipal civil service of New York City by Mayor Grace. He now holds both positions, having been re-appointed to the latter by Mayor Hewitt. Mr. Greener has filled a very large place in the affairs of this country, and has risen so fast in the minds of the people that his name is linked with the names of Douglass and Langston, though a much younger man than either of them. In Masonic circles he has been active for the union of the colored Masonic bodies. He was initiated, passed, and raised, in Philadelphia, Pennsylvania, in 1872.

He has served as E. C., Gethsemene Commandery of Knights Templars, District of Columbia, 1873, and Grand Commander of the Supreme Council of Ancient Accepted Scottish Right, 33d degree, South and Western jurisdiction. He was one of the committee of thirty on the inaugural ceremonies of Garfield and Arthur. The title of LL.D. was conferred upon him by the College of Liberia, Monrovia, West Africa, January 13, 1873. We furnish here a list of the subjects of the many addresses which Dr. Greener has delivered, and which will in some measure show the range of his mind as well as the variety of subjects over which he roamed with such ease. The elegance and charm of their diction, together with the profound reasoning and extensive research have made them ever pleasing to those who have had the good fortune to hear them.

We have briefly portrayed in some feeble way the rise and progress of Professor Greener, but we cannot do justice to the brilliant career he has so far had, nor can we predict how large a place he will yet fill in the affairs of his race. Though born free, he has met the same difficulties which others have met who were born slaves, because he was identified with that downcast and humble race which suffered because of their color and their condition.

Mr. Greener is a gentleman of much literary taste, and has the knack of getting hold of many relics—some of great value. Among them may be mentioned *Banneker's Almanac,* in 1792; *facsimile* copy of his letter to Thomas Jefferson, which sold at a recent sale in New York for $18. *Walker's Appeal,* (Garnet edition) ; an original bill of the sale of a slave; *Gregorie's Histo de la litt. des Negres,* presented to Angelina Grimke by John Rankin; a copy of the *Freedom's Journal,* published in New York City, 1827–28, the first colored paper in the United States; very many rare papers on colonization; *Negromania,* by Campbell, of Philadelphia; the list of the original documents for the abolition of slave-trade, etc.

I append here a list of the subjects of his best orations. They can be judged from their titles, and show that his reading has been over a very wide range, and that he has the taste of an exceedingly high and cultivated mind:

1. "Fifteenth Amendment Celebration," at Troy, New York, April 28, 1870.
2. Celebration of Emancipation in the District of Columbia, April 15, 1873.
3. "Charles Sumner, the Idealist, Statesman and Scholar," an inaugural address, University of South Carolina, Columbia, June 24, 1874.
4. "The Public Life and Political Writings of John Milton," a lecture at Charleston, South Carolina, March, 1874.
5. An oration pronounced at the celebration of Saint John the Baptist, June 24, 1876, at Savannah, Georgia.
6. "The Library of the University of South Carolina, its Rare and Curious Books," prepared for the American Philological Association, June 11, 1877.
7. "The Missionary Work of Education among the Colored People of the South," an address delivered at the dedication of St. Mary's Protestant Episcopal Academy, Baltimore, Maryland, September 17, 1877.
8. "The Great Pyramid, its Age, Builders, and Purpose," a lecture, Washington, District of Columbia, April 29, 1878.
9. Address at the emancipation celebration, Washington, District of Columbia, January 1, 1879: "The Political Condition of the Colored People of the South."
10. "The Academic Life," an address before the students of the *Alpha Phi* Society, Howard University, November 26, 1878.
11. "The Life and Services of William Lloyd Garrison," a eulogy before the colored citizens of Baltimore, Maryland, June 19, 1879.
12. A Masonic address in honor of the union of the craft in Maryland and Virginia; Washington, District of Columbia, June 24, 1878.
13. "Socrates as a Teacher," a lecture delivered at Washington, District of Columbia, April 5, 1880.
14. "The Intellectual Position of the Negro," (a reply to James Parton), *National Quarterly Review* (New York City), July, 1880.
15. Decoration Day address before Lincoln Post No. 7, G. A. R., Department of Maryland, May 30, 1880.
16. "The Educational and Industrial Progress of the Colored People," an address before the citizens of Philadelphia, Pennsylvania; Musical Fund hall, January 4, 1881.
17. An address at dedication of Lincoln statue, Prospect Park, Brooklyn, New York, at invitation of Devins Post No. 148, G. A. R., Department of New York, May 30, 1881.
18. Celebration of the Fifteenth Amendment by the colored citizens of Frederick, Maryland, August 24, 1881.

19. An address before the students of the Garnet Literary association, Lincoln University, Oxford, Pennsylvania, June 6, 1881.

20. "Success, a Duty," at Bethel church, New York City, a lecture, December 28, 1880.

21. Masonic address at laying of corner-stone of Calvary Baptist church, Columbia, South Carolina, December 14, 1875.

22. "The Gospel of Work," a lecture before the Progress Workingmen's club, Philadelphia, Pennsylvania, December 1, 1881.

23. "Free Speech in Ireland," address at the Irish Land League, Washington, District of Columbia, October 28, 1882.

24. "Benjamin Banneker, the Negro Astronomer," a lecture, Washington, District of Columbia, February 1, 1882.

25. The twentieth anniversary of emancipation in the District of Columbia, April 17, 1882.

26. "Henry Highland Garnet," a eulogy delivered at Cooper Institute, New York, at the request of the colored citizens of New York City, May 10, 1882.

27. "The African Roscius," an essay on Ira Aldridge, the Negro American tragedian, read at the closing exercises of the Monday Night Literary club, Washington, District of Columbia, June 9, 1882.

28. Address at Tuskegee Normal school, Tuskegee, Alabama, June 29, 1884.

CHAPTER XXXVIII

Captain Paul Cuffee
Sea Captain—Wealthy Ship Owner—Petitions
to the Massachusetts Legislature against "Taxation Without
Representation"—Petition Granted

It takes recognized skill for a man to be commander of a vessel. Ship owners seldom run the risk of ignorant management, for they cannot well afford the losses which would probably follow such a line of conduct, but in this case the son of a slave became the captain and owner of his own vessel. His boldness is, therefore, remarkable, and yet not so when we remember that he is the son of a native African on his father's side and of Indian blood on his mother's side. He inherited, from his father, some land and other property which was not profitable, but he determined to make a man of himself, and to that end was diligent and industrious. He became efficient in mathematics and navigation. His intellect was very vigorous and the power of concentration was so great that his knowledge of the latter subject was gained in two weeks, and with it he commanded Negro crews for many years, in his voyages to England, Russia, West Indies, Africa and the whole coast of North America, especially its eastern coast. He was only fourteen when his father died. He was born in 1759, in Cutterhunker, one of the Elizabeth islands, near New Bedford, Massachusetts. At the age of sixteen he was a deck-hand on a vessel destined to the Gulf of Mexico; his second voyage was to the West Indies. On his third voyage he was captured by the British, and detained in prison in New York three months. At this time the Revolutionary War was in progress. Paul and his brother John having been called on to pay personal taxes by the collector, they both refused to do so. They were given so much trouble about it, that finally they agreed, in the language of Oliver Goldsmith, "to stoop to conquer." They paid the taxes, as it was a trifling sum, and determined to make an appeal to the Massachusetts Legislature, believing in the doctrine that they had heard all of their lives, that there should be "no taxation without representation."

In defiance of the prejudice of the times, their appeal was heard and a law was enacted by the Legislature rendering all free persons of color liable to taxation according to the ratio established for the white men, and, at the same time, granting to them full privileges that belonged to any other citizen of Massachusetts.

What a glorious result! See what a strong man can do by using that power which he has. Let us emulate his example. The right of petition is still ours. There are still many rights denied us which we could get by simply reaching out our hands to take them. Let the colored people of that State honor this grand man; and we trust that yet some testimonial to his memory shall be reared. It is with this hope that we have given him a place in this book. Let no one despise youth. We are so apt to think that young men are extravagant and indiscreet when they are bold enough to oppose what might seem, or what is,"popular opinion." Do right if you stand alone, remembering there are blows to take as well as to give. There were many colored people at that time who thought these colored men were fools, and said they were violating the law because they didn't obey what was an unjust law. Be discreet and attempt much, if but little be gained. There is honor even in a righteous effort.

Paul was only about twenty-one years old when he accomplished this result, scarcely able to vote when the privilege was granted. He made many trips with his vessel to Connecticut and traded all along her coast; sailed as far as the Banks of St. George, and secured large cargoes of codfish, opening up an extensive fish trade, which gave employment to great numbers. In 1797 Paul tried to establish a school, but the people quarreled over the location and many other things, and he finally built a school-house at his own expense on his own grounds, and allowed everybody to attend that desired, thus establishing a "public school" in Massachusetts. He owned several vessels, of 12, 18, 25, 42 and 60 tons burden, respectively. The last one was called the "Ranger." He had a half interest in one of 162 tons burden, and three-fourths interest in one of 268; this was called the "Alpha," which was built in 1806. He had a half interest in one called the "Traveler," of 109 tons burden.

A book written by William C. Nell, a colored man, in 1855, gives the following description of Cuffee:

He was tall, well-formed and athletic; his deportment conciliating yet dignified and prepossessing; his countenance blending gravity with modesty and sweetness, and firmness with gentleness and humanity. In speech and habit, plain and unostentatious. His whole exterior indicated a man of respectability and piety, and such would a stranger have supposed him to be, at first sight. He was a Quaker in his religious views. He carefully maintained a strict integrity and uprightness in all his transactions in trade, believing himself to be accountable to God for the mode of using and acquiring his possessions. On these grounds he would not deal in intoxicating liquors or slaves, though he might have done either without violating the laws of his country, and with great prospects of pecuniary gain.

The *American Encyclopedia* has this to say of him:

In the latter part of his life, Cuffee encouraged the emigration of free people to Sierra Leone. He corresponded with prominent friends of this enterprise in Great Britain and Africa, and in 1811 visited the colony in his own vessel to determine for himself its advantages. In 1815 he carried out to Sierra Leone thirty-eight colored persons as emigrants, thirty of them at his own expense, and on his arrival furnishing them with the means of subsistence, spending in this enterprise nearly four thousand dollars.

This good man terminated his labors and his life ended in the seventh day of the ninth month, 1817.

ALEXANDER WALTERS

CHAPTER XXXIX

Rev. Alexander Walters
Financier and Pulpit Orator

———•◆•———

He is the oldest son of Henry and Harriet Walters. His birthplace was Bardstown, Nelson county, Kentucky, August 1, 1858. Early in life he showed signs of piety, and was afterwards heard to say, "I was born to preach the gospel." This was the constant theme of his youthful days, and is the business of his present life. He entered a private school taught by Mrs. Amanda Hines, at Bardstown, Kentucky, in 1866, where he remained about eighteen months. The following year Mr. William Lawrence, a more efficient teacher, opened a pay school, which Alexander entered at once and continued in it until 1869. This teacher was succeeded by Miss Addie Miller of Louisville, Kentucky, who, teaching for a short time was succeeded by Mr. Rowan Wickliffe of Lexington, Kentucky. Soon after he took charge of the school he made a proposition to the Methodist and Baptist churches (they being the only two colored churches in the town) to teach a young man of each congregation free of charge. This proposition was accepted by the officers of each congregation, and the officials of the A. M. E. church chose Alexander Walters, the subject of this sketch. He remained in this school for two years, and, in the fall of 1870, having professed a hope in Christ, he united with the A. M. E. Zion church, Bardstown, Kentucky.

In 1871 he left his home for Louisville, Kentucky, and for two or three years was employed as a waiter in private families, hotels and on steamboats. In 1876 he went to Indianapolis, Indiana, and here he began the study of theology under the Rev. D. P. Seaton of the A. M. E. church, and was licensed to preach by Rev. Anthony Bunch of the A. M. E. Zion church, May, 1877.

He married Miss Katie Knox of Louisville, Kentucky, August 28, 1877. Joined the Kentucky annual conference of the A. M. E. Zion church, at Indianapolis, Indiana, September 8, 1878, and was sent to the Corydon circuit, Corydon, Kentucky, by the same conference, and remained there two years. He taught the public school the last year of his pastorate, and was ordained deacon at St. Louis, July 10, 1879. He was then sent to Cloverport circuit, Cloverport, Kentucky, April 10, 1880, and remained there sixteen months; he also taught school at this point during his stay. He was stationed at the 5th Street church, Louisville, Kentucky, in 1881, and was ordained elder at Louisville, Kentucky, September 8, 1882. Then he was transferred to the California conference, and was stationed at San Francisco, California, in 1883.

The church here was built at a cost of eighty thousand dollars, and is considered the finest and largest church in the Zion connection.

Rev. Walters has a fine open face, and by his pen and upright moral life made his mark—for he has ever been considered one of the brightest stars of the Zion connection. He was sent by this church as a delegate to the general conference of the Zion connection, which met in New York City, May 3, 1884. He was elected first assistant secretary of the general conference. While east he visited Washington, D. C., and had an interview with President Arthur, also Governor Patterson of Pennsylvania. It was by his aid and influence that Professor J. C. Price, President of Zion Wesley College was enabled to raise, while on the Pacific slope, in 1885, eighty-six hundred dollars.

While West he was made a member of several white associations (notable among them were a Biblical class, taught by Professor J. P. Ferguson of the Presbyterian church, which was taught daily at the Adelphia theatre, on California street, near Kearney), the Young Men's Christian Association, and a class which met every Saturday for the study of Sabbath school lessons; this class was taught by Rev. M. M. Gibson, D.D. He was also elected a member of the Executive Board of the Ministerial Union, San Francisco, California, being the only colored member of the board.

He was transferred to the Tennessee conference in 1886, and is now stationed in Knoxville, Tennessee, in charge of one of the finest churches in the South. Elder Walters bears a spotless reputation, and is honored and loved by all who know him. He is a close student, an indefatigable worker for the upbuilding of his race. As an orator, he is superior to most of the young men, and even the old ones in his church. He is affable, kind and gentlemanly, winning by his elegant manner all those who come in contact with him. His habits of life are plain, his methods of work practical, and his success is always of the highest order. His plan has always been in entering a new work, to secure at once a first-class instructor to help him in his studies, and thereby he has become familiar with the classics and the realm of ancient literature. As a historian, he deals largely in those phrases which lead toward the cultivation of race-pride, and the demonstration of those facts and principles which go to encourage enterprise and self-pride among his own people. He has wonderful faith in the future of the race, being by no means discouraged on account of present difficulties, and promotes with most earnest zeal every effort made in his church and community that looks toward the amelioration of the condition of colored people. As a pastor, revivalist and a church financier, he has had great success.

To such young men the future looks for great things.

CHAPTER XL

Benjamin Banneker
Astronomer—Philosopher—Inventor—Philanthropist

In the darkness there was light, and the fire of his intellect attracted universal attention to himself and made for him undying and imperishable fame. This remarkable genius and devoted son was born in Baltimore county, Maryland, November 9, 1731, near the village of Ellicott's Mills. It is thought that his parents were full blooded Africans, but George W. Williams, the historian, says his grandmother was a white emigrant who married a Negro whose freedom she purchased; and of the four children born to them, one was a girl who married Robert Banneker, of whom Benjamin was the only child.

His parents accumulated sufficient means to buy a few acres and build a small cabin. The son was sent to school in the neighborhood, where he learned reading, writing and arithmetic. When Benjamin reached a suitable age he was compelled to assist his aged parents in their labors, but every spare moment found him "ciphering" and storing his mind with useful knowledge. His mother was active enough to do the work of the house, and when seventy years old caught her chickens by running them down without apparent fatigue. The place of his location was thickly settled; though he was known as a boy of intelligence, yet his neighbors took but little notice of him. He was determined to acquire knowledge, and while his hands worked hard, his brain was planning and solving problems in arithmetic. His observation extended to all around him, and his memory was retentive and he lost nothing. But the little education he had acquired was all his parents, who were poor, could give him. Yet little by little he stored it all up, and in the course of time became superior to most of his white neighbors, who had more favorable opportunities and were in better circumstances than he was. His fame had spread so rapidly that they began to say to one another: "That black Ben is a smart fellow. He can make anything he sets out to; and how much he knows! I wonder where he picked it all up?"

In 1770 he made a clock which was an excellent timepiece. He had never seen a clock, as such a thing was unknown in the region in which he lived, but he had seen a watch which so attracted his attention that he aspired to make something like it. His greatest difficulty was in making the hour and minute hands correspond in their motion, but by perseverance he succeeded, though he had never read the Latin motto, "Perseverentia omnia vincet," yet he did persevere and succeeded. This was the first clock ever made in this country, and it excited much attention, especially because it was made by a Negro. Mr. Ellicott, the owner of the mills, became very much interested in the self-taught machinist, and let him have many books, among which was one on astronomy. This new supply of knowledge so interested Banneker that he thought of nothing else. This kind gentleman, who had allowed him to use his books, for some reason failed to explain the subject of the books when he gave them to him, but when he met him again he was surprised to find Banneker independent of all instruction. He had mastered all the difficult problems contained in them.

From this time the study of astronomy became the great object of his life. Soon he could calculate when the sun or moon should be eclipsed, and at what time every star would rise. In this he was so accurate that mistakes were never found. In order to pursue his studies he sold his land his parents had left him and bought an annuity on which he lived, in the little cabin of his birth. As he was never seen tilling the soil, his ignorant neighbors began to abuse him. They called him lazy when they peeped into his cabin and saw him asleep in the day-time. They were ignorant of the fact of his watching the stars all night and ciphering out his calculation. Banneker, instead of resenting all this bad feeling, endeavored to live in such a way as to demand their respect. His generous heart made him always kind and ready to oblige everybody.

A sketch of his life is found in the *History of the Negro Race in America*, by the Hon. George W. Williams, from which the following extract is taken:

The following question was propounded by Banneker to Mr. George Ellicott, and was solved by Benjamin Hollowell of Alexandria:

A cooper and vintner sat down for a talk,
Both being so groggy that neither could walk.
Says cooper to vintner, "I am the first of my trade,
There is no kind of vessel but what I have made
And of any shape, sir—just what you will—
And of any size, sir, from a ton to a gill!"
"Then," says the vintner, "you are the man for me;
Make me a vessel, if we can agree.
The top and the bottom diameter define,

> *To bear that proportion as fifteen to nine;*
> *Thirty-five inches are just what I crave,*
> *No more and no less, in the depth will I have;*
> *Just thirty-nine gallons this vessel must hold—*
> *Then I will reward you with silver and gold—*
> *Give me your promise, my honest old friend?"*
> *"I'll make it tomorrow, that you may depend!"*
> *So the next day the cooper, his work to discharge,*
> *Soon made a new vessel, but made it too large;*
> *He took out some staves, which made it too small,*
> *And then cursed the vessel, the vintner and all.*
> *He beat on his breast; "By the powers," he swore,*
> *He never would work at his trade any more!*
> *Now my worthy friend, find out if you can,*
> *The vessel's dimensions and comfort the man.*
>
> (Signed)   BENJAMIN BANNEKER

The answer to this question is as follows: The greater diameter of Banneker's tub must be 24.746 inches, and the lesser diameter 14.8476 inches.

In 1792, though limited in means and scanty education, he prepared an excellent almanac, which was published by Goddard & Angell of Baltimore. In the preface they expressed themselves as highly gratified with the opportunity of presenting to the public such an extraordinary effort of genius calculated by a sable son of Africa. This was the first almanac ever published in this country. Besides astronomical calculations, it contained much useful knowledge of a general nature and interesting selections of prose and verse. Professor R. T. Greener owns a copy of this almanac. Banneker sent a manuscript copy in his own handwriting to Thomas Jefferson, then secretary of state and afterwards President of the United States. In addressing him he said:

Those of my complexion have long been considered rather brutish than human—scarcely capable of mental endowments. But, in consequence of the reports that have reached me, I hope I may safely admit that you are measurably friendly and well disposed toward us. I trust that you will agree with me in thinking that one universal Father hath given being to us all; that he has not only made us all of one flesh, but has also, without partiality, afforded us all the same sensations and endowed us all with the same faculties; and that, however various we may be in society or religion, however diversified in situation or color, we are all of the same family and all stand in the same relation to Him. Now, sir, if this is founded in truth, I apprehend you will readily embrace every opportunity to eradicate the absurd and false ideas and opinions which so generally prevail with respect to us.

Suffer me, sir, to recall to your mind that when the tyranny of the British crown was exerted to reduce you to servitude, your abhorrence thereof was so excited that you publicly held forth this true and invaluable doctrine, worthy to be recorded and remembered in all succeeding ages: "We hold these truths to be self-evident, that all men are created equal, and that they are endowed by their Creator with certain inalienable rights; that among these are life, liberty, and the pursuit of happiness."

Your tender feelings for yourselves engaged you thus to declare. You were then impressed with proper ideas of the great value of liberty, and the free possession of those blessings to which you are entitled by nature. But, sir, how pitiable it is to reflect that, although you are so fully convinced of the benevolence of the Father of mankind, and of his equal and impartial distribution of those rights and privileges which He had conferred upon them, that you should at the same time counteract His mercies in detaining, by fraud and violence, so numerous a part of my brethren under groaning captivity and cruel oppression; that you should at the same time be found guilty of that most criminal act which you detested in others with respect to yourselves.

Sir, I freely and most cheerfully acknowledge that I am of the African race; and in that color which is natural to them I am of the deepest dye. But, with a sense of the most profound gratitude to the Supreme Ruler of the universe, I confess that I am not under that state of tyrannical thraldom and inhuman captivity to which so many of my brethren are doomed. I have abundantly tasted of those blessings which proceed from that free and unequaled liberty with which you are favored.

Sir, I suppose your knowledge of the situation of my brethren is too extensive for it to need a recital here. Neither shall I presume to prescribe methods by which they may be relieved, otherwise than by recommending to you and others to wean yourselves from those narrow prejudices you have imbibed with respect to them, and to do as Job proposed to his friends—"put your souls in their souls' stead." Thus shall your hearts be enlarged with kindness and benevolence toward them, and you will need neither the direction of myself or others in what manner to proceed.

I took up my pen to direct to you, as a present, a copy of an Almanac I have calculated for the succeeding year. I ardently hope that your candor and generosity will plead with you in my behalf. Sympathy and affection for my brethren has caused my enlargement thus far; it was not originally my design.

The Almanac is a production of my arduous study. I have long had unbounded desires to become acquainted with the secrets of nature, and I have had to gratify my curiosity herein through my own assiduous application to astronomical study, in which I need not recount to you the many difficulties and disadvantages I have had to encounter. I conclude by subscribing myself, with the most profound respect, your most humble servant,

B. Banneker

To this letter Jefferson made the following reply:

Sir, I thank you sincerely for your letter, and for the Almanac it contained. Nobody wishes more than I do to see such proofs as you exhibit that nature has given to our black brethren talents equal to those of the other colors of men, and that the appearance of a want of them is owing only to the degraded condition of their existence both in Africa and America. I can add, with truth, that no one wishes more ardently to see a good system commenced for raising the condition, both of their body and mind, to what it ought be, as fast as the imbecility of their present existence, and other circumstances which cannot be neglected, will admit. I have taken the liberty of sending your Almanac to Monsieur Condorcet, Secretary of the Academy of Sciences at Paris, and to members of the Philanthropic Society, because I considered it a document to which your whole color had a right, for their justification against the doubts which have been entertained of them. I am, with great esteem, sir, your most obedient servant,

THOMAS JEFFERSON

In 1803 Mr. Jefferson invited the astronomer to visit him at Monticello, but the increasing infirmities of age made it imprudent to undertake the journey. His almanacs sold well for ten years, and the income, added to his annuity, gave him a very comfortable support; and, what was a still greater satisfaction to him, was the consciousness of doing something to help the cause of his oppressed people by proving to the world that nature had endowed them with good capacities.

After 1802 he found himself too old to calculate any more almanacs, but as long as he lived he continued to be deeply interested in his various studies.

He died in 1804, in his seventy-second year; his remains were buried near the dwelling that he had occupied during his life. His mode of life was regular and retired. He was kind and generous to all around him; his head was covered with thick white hair, which gave him a venerable appearance; his dress was uniformly superfine drab broadcloth, made in the old, plain style, coat with straight collar, a long waist and a broad-brimmed hat. His color was not quite black, but decidedly Negro. In his personal appearance he is said to have borne a striking resemblance to the statue of Benjamin Franklin, at the library at Philadelphia.

Banneker's abilities have often been brought forward as an argument against the enslavement of his race, and ever since he has been quoted as a proof of the mental capacity of Africans. Surely the smoldering embers of the latent fires of their ancient greatness was awakened in him, and the thousands of camp-fires of an intellectual revival can be seen now on the highest hilltop, climbing the mountains, at its base, down the valley and in its darkest shade.

CHAPTER XLI

Rev. Richard DeBaptiste, D. D.
Corresponding Secretary and Beloved Disciple

———•◆•———

One of the humblest and most devoted Christians I ever knew is Rev. R. DeBaptiste. A very unostentatious servant of God is the man of whom I now write. Many have enjoyed the sunshine of his life and yet failed to recognize the cause of their growth and prosperity. Personally, I can bear testimony to his interest in young men, and his fatherly, tender advice to even the "stranger within his gate." Of Old Virginia's sons, none have given to the West a better life of honest toil for the people than he. Fredericksburg may well be proud of him. He was born November 11, 1831. William and Eliza DeBaptiste sought to educate their children, and though they had many difficulties to encounter, they nevertheless succeeded in giving them a fair education, in the State of Virgina, under the regime of slavery. The father made his own residence a school-house, his own children and a few of those of his relatives were pupils, first taught by a colored man and then by an educated Scotch-Irishman, who had been a teacher in Scotland, the police officers often watching the premises to detect some incidents leading to evidence that a Negro school was being conducted there. Fines and imprisonment would have followed the discovery. Mr. DeBaptiste was ordained to the ministry in the Baptist denomination at Mount Pleasant, Ohio, by a council called by the Union Baptist church, Cincinnati, Ohio, of the First and Ninth streets white churches, and the Union and Zion colored churches of Cincinnati, and the church at Lockland were represented in the council. He taught the public schools for colored youth and children of Springfield township, at Mount Pleasant, three years. He organized and pastored the colored Baptist church at this place from 1860 to 1863; baptized twelve converts as constituent members, took pastoral charge of Olivet Baptist church, Chicago, August, 1863; held it continuously till February, 1882. In the meanwhile, purchasing two building sites at a cost of $16,000, built two church edifices, both brick, with a seating capacity, the one of 800 and the other of 1,200, costing respectively, $15,000 and $18,000. Received

RICHARD DeBAPTISTE

over seventeen hundred persons to membership—about forty-eight per cent by baptism. The net increase for the first five years averaged one hundred per year, and over fifty per cent of that number by baptism. He was elected corresponding secretary of the Wood River association in 1864; has held it ever since, being re-elected every year, though absent at three or four sessions. He was also elected recording secretary of the Northwestern and Southern Baptist convention at its organization in St. Louis in 1865; was elected corresponding secretary at the annual meeting, 1866. He was elected president of the consolidated American Baptist Missionary convention at its first meeting, held in Nashville, Tennessee; was re-elected every year successively for four years. At Wilmington, North Carolina, in 1870, he was not present, but was, nevertheless, re-elected. In 1871, being absent from the meeting at Brooklyn, New York, he was not re-elected. In 1872 was again elected president and held the office by re-election at every meeting til 1877 at Richmond, Virginia, and was then elected corresponding secretary of the Foreign Mission department of this work, continued in that office until the meeting in Cincinnati, 1879, but it was no longer a consolidation.

In 1870 he was elected president of the Baptist Free Mission society (white) at its anniversary meeting in Cincinnati, Ohio, and corresponding secretary of the American Baptist National convention, which met August 25 to 29, in St. Louis, Missouri, at which time he read a paper of the greatest importance to the denomination. The American Baptist Publication Society of Philadelphia, in its annual year book, has hitherto enumerated only eight hundred thousand colored Baptists for the United States, but it was left for Richard DeBaptiste to give the larger final results. It will not be out of place to give here the remarkable statistics which he furnished, though, of course, much condensed: "Three hundred and eleven associations, 9,097 churches in 255 associations, ordained ministers 4,590 in 218 associations, with a total membership of 1,071,902 colored Baptists," without any baptisms having been gathered for that year from the States of West Virginia, New York, California, Colorado, Delaware, Maryland, Minnesota, Nebraska, New Jersey, Pennsylvania, Massachusetts, Rhode Island, Connecticut, Alabama, Arkansas, Georgia, Louisiana, Mississippi, South Carolina, Tennessee and Virginia.

During his lifetime he has been a frequent contributor both to religious and secular journals, white and colored, and held the position of editor of one secular and one religious journal, and corresponding editor of two others. He held the first position conjointly with Rev. G. C. Booth, on the *Conservator* of Chicago, for a year or nearly that time, the second or third year after it started, and on the *Western Herald* from September, 1884, to December, 1885. He was corresponding editor of the *Monitor*, a short-lived paper started by the Rev. H. H. White of St. Louis, Missouri, and for several years on the *National Monitor* of Brooklyn, New York, Rev. R. L. Perry, editor.

Having had only an English education in his youth, he has not failed to take advantage of the opportunities presented him for a thorough knowledge in the many branches of learning. He attended school about three years after removing from Virginia to Michigan, receiving in this school only instruction in English branches. The first teacher he had was Richard Dillingham, a Quaker, who was afterwards apprehended for helping several families to escape from slavery. He received such rough and cruel treatment that he died from the effects of it in prison, at Nashville, Tennessee. His second teacher was Rev. Samuel H. Davis, the pastor of the Second Baptist church of Detroit. In this city he also studied German, French, Latin, Greek and theology. He attended the lectures at the University of Chicago during the first two years, at what is now known as the Morgan Park Theological Seminary. He was married in the fall of 1855 to Miss Georgiana Brische of Cincinnati, Ohio, who died November 2, 1872. He was married again August, 1885, and this wife died April, 1886. He has three children, two of them members of the church and very proficient in music. None of them are very healthy, which has caused him much grief and sorrow; "Truly he is a man afflicted with sorrows and acquainted with grief."

This man has devoted his life to the ministry. In a private letter to the author he once said:

Beginning my manhood in a mercantile business, I had a fair prospect of success, carrying on the business of bricklayer and plasterer's trade. This mode of living I inherited from my father and uncles, William and Edward DeBaptiste, they being in their days the largest contractors and builders of the city of Fredericksburg, Virginia, and the surrounding country; but I unreservedly gave up all my worldly prospects and projects in obedience to the call of my Master to enter his vineyard, to "occupy till he comes." He has said: "He that forsaketh homes, lands, brothers and sisters for my sake and the gospel's, shall have homes, lands, brothers and sisters."

With very little worldly goods he is still cheerful and willing to spend and be spent for the Master's cause. At this writing he is pastor of a small church, declining many larger fields that he might secure a home and better prospects for the future of his children. It might be well to say that Mr. DeBaptiste comes of a historic family. There has been a representative of his family in each of the great wars of this country. His grandfather, John DeBaptiste, was in the Revolutionary war; his uncle George, in the War of 1812; and two brothers, George and Benjamin, in the war of the Rebellion.

The Rev. R. DeBaptiste is a man of whom the denomination is proud, and the State University, Louisville, Kentucky, recognizing his great services to the cause of Christ, as well as his many gifts and attainments, conferred on him the degree of Doctor of Divinity, May 17, 1887, an honor he will wear with dignity.

The name of Richard DeBaptiste will always linger in the memory of those who know him as a man of Chesterfieldian manners and rare attainments in literary affairs, and a man "full of the Holy Ghost."

CHAPTER XLII

Hon. George French Ecton
Representative from the Third Senatorial District, Chicago.
Cook County, Illinois—From the Plowhandles
to the Legislature—From the Capacity of a Waiter
to that of a Legislator

In presenting this sketch we have given some of the events which have taken place in the life of the Illinois colored Legislator. His position, from that of slave to public office holder, was not attained by a single jump, but by a series of repeated struggles and endeavors to remove hindering causes to become a respected man and public-spirited citizen. He first saw the rays of light at Winchester, Clark county, Kentucky, in 1846, and is the eldest of three living children. His father's name was Antonio Ecton, and his mother's, Martha George. His childhood and youth were spent in slavery. When yet a mere babe he was sent with other boys of his age, and older, to weed the crops. As he grew older he became a full hand at the plow and any other laborious tasks he was called upon to do. No matter what his occupation, he prided himself on doing whatever he did well, and herein lies his success. At the age of fifteen or sixteen the war came and his native State was soon made a thoroughfare for the contending armies. At the close of the war, about June, 1865, George and a friend determined to "make way for liberty," having received a set of "free papers," written for them by a white Abolitionist, which even at that late date were necessary to every traveling Negro to insure recognition of freedom, as slaves in Kentucky were not liberated until some months after the Emancipation Proclamation. With the amount of thirty or forty dollars which they had saved up, they started. The nearest railroad station being Paris, Kentucky, they reached it after walking nearly the entire distance of eighteen miles. The sight of a steam car was novel to them, and their astonishment can well be imagined. They boarded a train bound for Cincinnati, Ohio, and here found their "free papers" necessary, as on entering a car the white passengers demanded a sight of their passes. Arriving at their destination they were taken as deck hands on the steam packet "Sherman," plying in the pig-iron and salt trade between that port and Wheeling, West Virginia. George left this work after one trip, and on the return of the packet to Cincinnati he found employment at the old Broadway House, where he worked and saved one hundred dollars. He afterwards worked at the "Walnut Street House," the "Burnett House," and the "Spencer House." While at the "Walnut Street House" he became a victim to small-pox. He speedily recovered, however, owing to kindness from one of his nurses. On returning to work he began to attend night school, taught by Miss Luella Brown, who teaches at present on the suburbs of Cincinnati. He made rapid progress, and what learning he acquired he has been adding to ever since. On leaving Cincinnati, October 28, 1873, he went to Chicago and took charge of a dining room at the "Hotel Woodruff," where he remained up to his nomination and election to a seat in the Thirty-fifth General Assembly. As a legislator he will reflect credit upon his constituency. Mr. Ecton is no orator, but as a good listener, intelligent voter and close student he has few to surpass him. By strict application to business and economy that marked his earlier days, he has saved sufficient to purchase property worth ten thousand dollars. He wedded Miss Patti R. Allen of Winchester, Kentucky. The union is childless, but their home is thronged by a brilliant set of intelligent people, and both he and his wife take a great interest in passing events. He is a member of Bethesda Baptist church, and is identified with the Prudence Crandall Club, and has taken "master" degree in masonry. If his word be given, he can be relied upon to do as he says. He will win for himself the credit in the Legislature that he has hitherto won.

NEWELL HOUSTON ENSLEY

CHAPTER XLIII

Newell Houston Ensley, A. M.
Professor of Rhetoric and Sciences—Hebraist—Musician

One of the bright lights that beamed forth from the State of Tennessee and first shed its rays into a little Negro cabin in Nashville, August 23, 1852, was when a son was born to George and Clara Ensley.

The chains of slavery held this child, and although its grasp was not so painful as in many cases, yet he was a victim to its cruelty. His maternal grandsire was his master, and he desired his slaves to read and write, and at one time he purchased books and employed a man to teach the slave children to read.

Mr. Ensley does not remember when he could not read the Bible, and both his parents were good readers. When he was old enough he became body servant and buggy boy for the reserved, dignified old man, with snow white locks, who owned him. To Mr. Ensley it was always a problem how he could be a grandchild with his white playmates, who too were grandchildren of the same old man, and be treated so differently, and why he must say "Old Mass" while his mates said lovingly "grandpa." Notwithstanding all this, Mr. Ensley was treated remarkably well for a slave lad, and often was he commended for his capabilities. On one occasion he was ordered to water his master's cows in the pasture till noon. This command he disobeyed and for his disobedience his master attempted to whip him, but he ran away to the Yankee camps hard by, and remained hidden under empty cracker boxes for some time until the old man had abandoned the search. He remained in camp until the division moved away to Murfreesboro and advised him to return home to his mother.

He went home secretly and hid in his mother's room under the bed, where his master found him and gave him the whipping he had escaped so long, and exacted from him the promise never to run away again. His master owned large estates, and to this lad was given the responsibility of collecting rents and depositing the same in the bank. Thus Mr. Ensley worked on as slave until the Southern cause was lost. Then he continued in the employ of the same old gentleman, who paid the young man and all his slaves for the service rendered him; besides, he gave to each of his men employees two fine young mules and a cow and a calf. The cow and calf were taken home, and the mules left on the plantation. Soon the old man died and his estate went to his son, and the Negroes who had been in his employ were left poor. Mr. Ensley attributes his fame now and all he is to his devoted Christian mother, whom his grandsire had settled on an excellent estate of thirty acres and left comfortably fixed. This was in 1866. At this time the free schools opened about four miles from Mr. Ensley's home, and a happy day it was for this lad, who now had a slight opportunity to slake his insatiable thirst for learning; but this was for a short time only. His mother married and his step-father would not let him attend school and live at home. Because young Ensley went to school one day against his step-father's will, he was sent from home, notwithstanding the tears and pleadings of a loving mother. After he left, his mother sought and brought him home, where he was obliged to work for this new master and go to school with his permit when he had nothing else to do.

"Notwithstanding all this," said Mr. Ensley, "I worked and studied, and not only kept up with my classes but ahead of them." Benjamin Holmes, one of the original famous jubilee singers, was his teacher, and, when he resigned to go on his mission of song, Mr. Ensley was installed as his successor. But the labors as teacher, where only yesterday he was a pupil, were hard. The children left school, and only by indefatigable labor in the Sunday school and day school did he succeed, but the success was indeed a victory wonderful and worthy of note. The day school grew to its former size, and the Sunday school never was so large before. Soon Mr. Ensley professed a hope in Jesus, and was baptized and joined the church, where he was made deacon, which position he held for several years. Although in earlier years he had felt called to the ministry, he feared he might be mistaken, but his doubts were not confirmed by the words of a good brother who now dwells above. This brother laid the matter before the brethren, and the church sent a committee to tell him that he ought to preach. Mr. Ensley felt the need of preparation, and in February, 1871, entered Roger Williams University, under the guardianship of that venerable man, Dr. Phillips, where, with his usual application, he toiled and toiled until he was almost a physical wreck and his future was less bright. Quite to his surprise he learned that his church had licensed him to preach. Mr. Ensley was filled with ambition and a burning desire to be a man worthy of the love of God and the respect of his fellowmen.

Music had a charm for him and he had devoted much time to this art.

He always had a love for oratory, and, though he has never given himself to this, yet he has been very successful in his many lectures throughout the country, where the music of his voice and his graphic style have held audiences spell-bound. Many letters of appreciation are in his possession from friends and hearers who have listened to his instructive words. With Dr. Phillips he made his first tour to the North, where he, with this good man, represented the work in the Home Mission schools, and in that visit the centennial at Philadelphia attracted his attention. In June, 1878, he graduated from Roger Williams University, third in his class, and immediately went North, where he entered Newton Theological Seminary, Newton Centre, Massachusetts. After three years toil he graduated, one of the favored seven from a large class to give an oration graduation day, and he was the only colored one. After graduating, Mr. Ensley was offered many situations and the chosen one was Raleigh, North Carolina, where he was professor of theology and Latin.

After a year he went to Howard University, at a salary of one thousand dollars, where he enjoyed his work very much. At this time he was married to an estimable and most accomplished young woman, who has supported him in every work to which he has devoted his time. Alcorn University now called him, and there he and his family removed, and to him was assigned the honorable position of professor of rhetoric, natural sciences and vocal music. This young man is a scholarly Hebrew student, and has a brilliant future before him, and well may the race be proud of Newell Houston Ensley.

The professor is a man of many fine traits of character. His manners are polished, his whole demeanor dignified and courtly, and his conversation witty, even brilliant. In his lectures he does not follow old stereotyped phrases nor hackneyed expressions, but his humor bubbles up like a pure rill at the foot of a mountain. His voice is musical, his gestures graceful and his whole appearance captivating. An audience is at once taken with his earnestness, breadth and depth of thought, the extended reach after truth, and the skilful presentation of his facts and arguments. Among the themes he delights to dwell upon are "Toussaint L'Ouverutre," "Pluck *verus* Luck," "The Rights of Women," "Temperance" and "The Rights of the Negro." In his advocacy of women, he insists that they are entitled to "Life, Liberty and the Pursuit of Happiness," and he would brush away every custom and barrier that prevents the gaining of these objects. In this I certainly agree with him. Yet he is very cautious that he does not appear ridiculous, but advances solid argument for all he claims for them. In this respect he is at once progressive and aggressive, for this is a subject that is gaining more and more attention—while it has its antagonists even among women.

The professor has a funny way of putting some things, and so I end this sketch with an extract from a speech made in St. Albans, Vermont, in 1880. It has an amusing turn which for quaintness and *point* rather causes a smile when read.

THE BENEFIT OF THE NEGRO'S COLOR

He denied the statement that the Negroes were not an original race; they were largely imitative, he admitted, but there were three of the white men's vices which his people did not imitate—they were not skeptics, they were not infidels, and they did not commit suicide. Then he quoted a certain bit of philosophy, illustrating the advantages the race had on this question of suicide, namely: White reflects light, and therefore the face of the white man *reflects* the light, and he goes through life a melancholy creature; while the face of the black man *absorbs* light, which penetrates to his soul and makes him a glad, careless, jolly creature. Just here Mr. Ensley applied this same bit of philosophy to Whittaker, the West Point cadet. Now Whittaker, says the speaker, is three parts white and two parts black; if he had been a black man, he would never have injured himself—as the court, you remember, decided that he did mutilate himself; if he had been a white man, he would have hung himself; but as he was neither white nor black, why he hurt himself just a little.

The professor aspires to the poet's chair, and communes occasionally with the muses. I give here a short poem, simply to show the trend of his mind. It was written for the Roger Williams' *Record*, April, 1886.

WRITE THY NAME

Write your name upon the sand,
The waves will wash it out again.
Trace it on the crystal foam,
No sooner is it writ than gone.
Carve it in the solid oak,
'Tis shattered by the lightning's stroke.
Chisel it in marble deep,
'Twill crumble down—it cannot help.

Seeker for the sweets of fame,
On things so frail, write not thy name.
With thee 'twill wither, die, rot;
On things so frail, then, write it not.
Would'st thou have thy name endure?
Go, write it in the Book of Life,
Engrave it on the hearts of men,
By humble deeds performed in love.

CHAPTER XLIV

Rev. Christopher H. Payne
Preacher—Editor and Soliciting Agent

———•◆•———

Rev. Christopher H. Payne was born near the Red Sulphur Springs, Monroe county, Virginia, now West Virginia, September 7, 1848. His parents were free. His father was free-born, and his mother, who had been brought up a slave, was set free by her old master, James Ellison. After her freedom she was married to Thomas Payne. These two persons were among the first colored people who were lawfully married in the county of Monroe.

The subject of this sketch was the only child born to their union. When he was very young his father went to Baltimore, Maryland, with a drove of cattle, caught the smallpox and died, leaving his wife a widow, and his little son fatherless. Mrs. Payne finding herself alone in the world, with none to comfort her but her aged mother and her infant son, decided to devote her entire time to the rearing and training of the boy who was the idol of her life. Having received the rudiments of an English education at the hands of her old master, who is supposed to have been her father, she set about teaching the little boy, and so zealous was she in her work that he does not remember when he could first read. When he was quite young the war began, and because he was a free Negro, and his mother having no protection, she had to see the little child go into the army as a servant. Here he remained, except when at home on a pass, until 1864, when he left the service and went down on New river, in the southern part of Monroe county (now Summers county), and obtained employment from a Mr. Vincent Swinney, where he remained until the Confederacy was broken up by the victorious armies of the United States.

It was at this place he made the acquaintance of Miss Ann Hargro, whom he married while yet a mere boy. This union has been a very peaceful one. In 1866 he left home and walked through the mountains to Charleston, on the Kanawha river, where he took a steamboat and went to Ohio and spent some time traveling in that State and in the State of

Kentucky. Finally he returned to Charleston and he remained for more than a year, working in the day and attending school at night. After an absence of about fifteen months he returned to his home and began teaching in Monroe, Mercer and Sumner counties in the winter, and farming in the summer. In 1875 he was converted and baptized in Indian creek, near where he was born, on the fourteenth of October, by Rev. G. W. Deskins. On the twenty-second of February, 1876, he was licensed to preach the gospel, and on the twenty-ninth of May, 1877, after a very rigid examination, he was ordained to the full work of the gospel ministry by a council composed of five of the most intelligent and influential brethren who belonged to the Greenbrier association.

In September, 1877, he entered the Richmond Institute in Richmond, Virginia, and began a course of study. Passing the examinations in many of the primary studies, he entered the senior class in the Preparatory Department, and pursued his studies with such energy and success that he soon gained the confidence and respect of all his teachers and fellow students. At the close of the sessions, in the spring of 1878, he went back to his field of labor in West Virginia, and found the Baptist cause in such a bad condition that he remained out of school, working, preaching, and organizing churches and Sunday schools until the fall of 1880, when he returned to school at Richmond, Virginia, and remained three years. Soon after entering school he accepted a call to the Moore Street Baptist church, and preached Sunday, after doing his class work all the week. Notwithstanding this double work, he maintained a very respectable standing in all his classes, and succeeded in giving satisfaction to his congregation, which steadily increased during the entire time of his pastorate.

He is regarded as possibly the best preacher the school ever turned out. He is a fine speaker, pointed and logical; possessing a fine flow of language, he never fails to impress his hearers favorably. He was appointed by the American Baptist Publication Society of Philadelphia as Sunday school missionary for the Eastern district of Virginia, and after his graduation he attended the anniversaries of the denomination, which were held in May, 1883, at Saratoga Springs, New York, and there delivered an address before the Publication Society which was highly praised by many of the leading journals of the land, both religious and secular. As soon as the meeting closed, he returned to Virginia and entered upon his work. His district embraced all the largest cities in the State, and the most densely populated counties, and for nine months he labored most earnestly among the people, preaching, lecturing and delivering Sunday school addresses, organizing Sunday schools and Sunday school unions, until from Staunton to Norfolk, and from Alexandria to Danville, Sunday schools, churches, associations and individuals became familiar with his labor and success. Many persons were led to Christ by his efforts, but in January, 1884, on account of failing health, caused by overwork, he tendered his resignation to the society, which was accepted to take effect the first of March. After winding up his affairs with the society he returned to his native State, West Virginia, and in April, 1884, took charge of the First Baptist church of Coal Valley. Since he has became pastor, the church has added about one hundred to its membership, and is now one of the most prosperous in the State. It was chiefly through his efforts that the West Virginia Baptist State convention was organized, and he was made its first president. For many years he was moderator of the only association of the State. He has been among the principal leaders of all the work of the denomination in the State. He was one of the founders of the *West Virginia Enterprise*, the only weekly newspaper published by colored men in the State. He conceived a plan last year for putting on foot a school of higher grade in the State with an industrial department attached; and now his energy is being bent in that direction, having been appointed by the Executive Board of the West Virginia Baptist State convention, corresponding secretary and agent. The work of raising means, securing the property and starting the school rests largely upon him, so that he is now preacher, editor and soliciting agent.

About five hundred persons have been converted through his efforts, about three hundred of whom he has baptized. Nine churches and two Sunday schools have been organized by him, and in his eleven years of ministerial labors he has preached more than fifteen hundred sermons, delivered more than five hundred lectures and addresses, and during all his struggles and labors he has come out more than conqueror. His noble wife has stood by him in every effort, and by her energy, pluck and discretion, rendered him such aid as only a true wife can.

He feels a deep sense of gratitude towards Rev. C. H. Corey, D.D., president of the Richmond Institute, and Charles J. Pickford of Lynn, Massachusetts, and many others for aid and encouragement given him in times of his great need and severe struggles. For it was indeed a struggle for a man to spend four years in school, with a wife and five children, an aged mother and grandmother dependent upon him, and as he now expresses it, God alone led and raised him up to do the great work and has at the same time raised up the means whereby he could accomplish it. Difficulties only brightened him, and with a strong hold on the affections of the people much more may be expected of him.

His virtues are many and can never be forgotten, and his word is his bond. He is a vigorous and pointed writer, as is evidenced by his efforts through the paper. His aggressiveness is in the right direction and in behalf of his race and denomination.

CHAPTER XLV

Professor Peter Humphries Clark, A. M.
Educator—Editor and Agitator

Few men are better known than Professor Peter H. Clark, who began life March, 1829. He has accomplished very much in his career, and is a real student, with vigorous intellect and constitutionally well prepared for a great amount of mental labor. Until 1844 Cincinnati furnished him a very poor chance for education, but Rev. Hiram S. Gilmore opened a high school this year and he entered as one of the pupils. By the correctness of his habits, industry in his lessons and faithfulness in all things, he was given an assistant's place in the school, and at the same time he continued his own studies in the highest branches. Leaving school in 1848, he refused to take employment with his father, who was a barber, because it would make him move around at the dictates of every class of white men. He apprenticed himself to a liberal artisan, Thomas Varney, to learn stereotyping. It was strange at this day that a white man should take a colored boy, but Mr. Clark gives some prominent reasons for this line of conduct: First, he advanced two hundred dollars to Mr. Varney to assist him in his business; second, Mr. Varney's wife was a correspondent of the New York *Tribune*, and they were both naturally affected with the spirit of that paper, which Horace Greeley edited with so much ability; and in the same building was Stanley Matthews, who was editor of the *Herald*, a Freesoil paper. Just about the time Mr. Clark was able to do the work of a stereotyper, his employer sold out and went to California, and his successor in the business had no use for a colored man. In 1849 the Ohio Legislature passed a law allowing the colored people to organize schools and control them, which they did. Mr. Clark was employed as teacher. After three months the Council refused to pay him on the ground that the colored people, not being citizens and voters, could not be trustees, and their employing teachers was not legal. After a contest in the lower courts, the Supreme Court declared the law sound and the colored trustees were sustained. He was working in the barber shop when he was examined and appointed as a teacher. After his father died he had charge of the shop. He quarrelled one day with a white customer who wanted him to introduce him (the white man) to colored ladies at a fair. The white man being refused, declared he would not shave with him any more as he shaved "niggers." This shows that he was then running a civil rights barber shop. Mr. Clark threw the cup on the floor in rage and disgust, and declared he would never shave another white man, and, if he did, he would cut his throat.

In 1850 he started for Africa, disgusted as he was by the bitter prejudice of the times. But he never went any further than New Orleans. He returned to Cincinnati in a short time and in 1852 took an active part in the State convention in which the "emigration movement" was discussed. He advocated that America was the home of those who were born here. In 1853 we find him secretary of the National convention of colored men, held in Rochester, New York. The same year he had trouble with the school board, which now had no colored men on it. They charged that he commented on the scriptures contrary to law, because he selected different passages in reading the morning lessons. Mr. Clark is Unitarian in his religious convictions, and has been for many years. He has often been misunderstood as to his religious views, and it may be because many do not understand the Unitarian religion. The advocates of Unitarianism hold that each individual is responsible to God for the opinions which he entertains, and that where there is responsibility there must of necessity be perfect freedom of thinking and acting. Neither primitive fathers nor ecclesiastic councils, nor synods, nor established creeds possess any absolute authority for them. They hold to the absolute unity of the Supreme Being, thus necessarily denying the doctrine of the trinity or three persons in one God. They teach that Christ was the first and greatest of all created beings; that he was the wisest and best personage who ever existed on the earth; that His mission was divine, being what He Himself declared it to be, sent by God "to bear witness to the truth;" that the Holy Spirit is not a separate personal entity, but an *influence* which the Creator exercises upon the minds of men under such circumstances as may comport with His will and purposes. See statement of doctrines of this church in *History of all Religions*, by Schmucker, page 167.

He lost his place, however, and went clerking. He finally opened a grocery store for himself. In 1855 he tried the tempestuous life of an editor, by publishing the *Herald of Freedom*. It died early, but was, when alive, a very efficient organ, filled with vigorous matter. He was next called to fill the editorial chair on a Free-soil paper, printed at Newport, Kentucky. At this time it was unlawful for a freed colored person to enter the "dark and bloody ground," but no one disturbed him though he worked at his desk for several months; but William S. Bailey, who was the owner of the paper, was often mobbed for its sentiments. In 1856 he was on the staff of Fred Douglass' paper. In 1857 he was recalled to the public schools, to which was added later a high school known as "Gaines' High School," of which he was principal for thirty years, being relieved last year by the Republican board as payment, perhaps, for his independence in voting for the Democratic party and sustaining its principles. To his humanity and tender heart are due the laws which provided for the care of the colored paupers and insane of the State. He drew up the petition and personally visited the law-makers at Columbus, urging its passage. In 1853 the National convention of colored men met in Syracuse. He drafted a constitution of the "National Equal Rights League," which did so much to instruct and control our people.

As a politician he has had the varying fortunes incident to such a life. At Syracuse, New York, the Liberal party held their convention, and he then declared his faith in the Republican party, and from that date, sometime in 1856, to 1872 he was a devoted member of the party. No man could be more sincere and consecrated to his principles than he; and his brilliant talents as an orator and an organizer were felt in the movements in several campaigns. He was an important factor in the city, county, State and National affairs. Two years later he joined what was known as the "new departure," in company with such men as Hon. George Hoadly, Stanley Matthews, and others. Their principles were "universal suffrage and universal amnesty."

Mr. Clark is a man of great and liberal ideas. He believes that the colored man has not had his dues from the Republican party. Sure it is he has never received from any party, neither Republican nor Democrat, what his services merit. In 1878 he was a candidate for State school commissioner on the Workingman's ticket, receiving fifteen thousand votes. He is also trustee in the State University, appointed by Governor Hoadly, a Democrat. In 1882 he aided the Democrats in the county and State elections, and as soon as the Legislature was organized, being Democratic by his aid, they drew up and submitted to him the civil rights bill, which he approved. It was passed and signed by the governor. Many have judged him severely for the stand he has taken at times, but as he is so honest and manly, and labored for his race, why should free men find fault in a free country with a free man? No one ever charged him with corruption; no one ever appealed to him for aid that did not get it. Mr. Clark deserves credit for following his convictions. He is no trickster nor sneaking slave. If more colored men would refuse and resent the slights put upon them, and the kicks also, the race would be recognized more in party councils. Mr. Clark suffered more for his politics from his colored brethren than from the whites. He certainly made it possible for colored men now in position to get the honors they have. Had Mr. Clark been silent, Republicans would not have been so ready to accord honor to colored men, at least not in distinguished positions; had he submitted, the others would still be slaves with their noses on the grindstone, or holding little petty positions as "ward bummers." And many that bask in the sunshine that he prepared have spit upon him. He has frequently had small offices offered him, which he has declined. He will be no man's servant, to run at his beck and call. Without patronage to bestow, he would have to suffer many indignities which he would not take, hence his refusal. A white man of his ability and learning would be president of a State college or governor of the State.

We had already written this sketch when the following letter appeared in the *New York Freeman,* of March 29, 1887. It can only be fair to produce it here as his opinion touching the subject, especially since it rather harmonizes with my own. Of course there were others contending for recognition, but they made their fights *in the ranks,* and when denied stayed there. It took nerve for such men as Clark, Matthews, Trotter and Downing, to break away from the lash of white men and the aha! aha! aha! of black men. Men admire pluck even in bad men. They always applaud a deed that marks one as especially valorous—who does not admire Napoleon though his crimes were many? It is alleged that Milton so dignified Satan that, instead of hating him for his wicked rebellion, we sympathize with him and bemoan his fall. I confess to some of the spirit that delights in boldness, daring, pluck, and though not exactly in harmony with Mr. Clark's line of procedure, he has my respect for the manly stand he took in these matters. It is now becoming very fashionable, aye, popular, and he will cease to be lonesome. But here is the letter. His advice is good, and the Ohio prescription might serve as a remedy for National affairs.

WHO INSPIRED THE REPEAL OF THE BLACK LAWS

HAVING FORCED THE REPUBLICANS TO DO THEIR DUTY, BY SUPPORTING A DEMOCRAT FOR GOVERNOR, MR. CLARK THINKS THE TACTICS SHOULD BE TRIED ON THE FIELD OF NATIONAL POLITICS—THE NEGROWUMP AS A POWER.

To the Editor of *The New York Freeman:*

Frequently after a successful hunt the question is asked, "Who killed the bear?" In like spirit the question is being asked, "Who destroyed the Black Laws of Ohio, the 'knuckle close' colored Republicans or the 'kickers'?" A brief look at history will help us answer that question. For more than twenty years of Republican rule, beginning with John Brough and ending with Charles Foster, no governor of that party ever suggested the propriety of repealing those laws. And the colored people, by a strange neglect, scarcely seemed to be conscious of their existence and seldom asked for their repeal. There was a sort of notion prevalent that to ask the Republicans of Ohio to do justice to her colored citizens would embarrass the party in its alleged fight against wrong in the South. It is true that the resolutions of the Chillicothe convention, held in 1873, demanded the abrogation of all such laws, but most of the participants in that convention were soon whipped back into the ranks of the Republican party. Others, more stern in spirit, were so hounded by partisans, white and black, that they took refuge in the opposing party. In the course of that twenty years, colored voters of Ohio were rallied time and again to the support of the Republican party in the name of "Political and Civil Equality" for the colored people of the South; but oddly enough, the "Political and Civil" inequality of her own people was unnoticed.

But in 1883 there came into the governor's office, aided thereto by the votes of sundry thousands of colored "kickers," a man who, remembering the Scriptural injunction, "first cast out the beam out of thine own eye, and then thou shalt see clearly to cast out the mote of thy brother's eye," wasted no space in bewailing the condition of our brethren in the South, a condition beyond the control of the Ohio Legislature, but said concerning the laws which oppressed the colored people of his own State, "The existing legal discriminations on account of color are not based on character or conduct and have no relation to mental or moral fitness for civil usefulness, but are rather relics of prejudice which had its origin in slavery. I recommend their total repeal." That governor was George Hoadly and the thousands of colored men who, throwing off party shackles, had voted for him, found their reward in these noble words, so earnestly and honestly spoken in their behalf. Prompted by these words, there came a shower of petitions from colored men asking for civil equality in Ohio. The majority of these were honest petitions, but many were sent for the purpose of emphasizing what the senders supposed was difference of opinion between the governor and the Democrat Legislature that was elected with him. But the Legislature listened to the governor and enacted a law to guard the civil rights of all.

Thus challenged, the Republican managers did not dare to go into another election without bringing back those colored voters whose defection had given the State to the Democracy. They gave out political patronage with a free hand, they nominated three colored men to seats in the Legislature and were profuse in their promises that all laws making distinctions on account of color should be abolished, if colored men would again come unitedly to the aid of the party. The result was the election of Foraker. Hoadly in going out, and Foraker in coming in, advised that the remnant of the Black Laws should be abolished. And they were. If you ask the question of any "kicker," "who abolished the Black Laws?" he will slap himself upon the breast and say "I did it, with my free ballot." The "kickers" of Ohio are satisfied with the results of their plan and are prepared to recommend it to their brethren in other States. Indeed, some of them are asking if there is not a chance for the use of their tactics on the broad field of National politics.

PETER H. CLARK

Cincinnati, March 16, 1887

The Wilberforce University has conferred on him the title of A. M., and well does he deserve it. He is the leading Negro educator in America.

Mr. Clark has reared several children. His oldest daughter, Ernestine, is the wife of J. Street Nesbit, a letter-carrier; she graduated from the "Gaines' High School" and afterwards from the Cincinnati Normal School, being the first colored girl who, without denying her race, was admitted to that institution. Afterward obtaining the highest grade certificate granted to women, she taught for three years in the "Gaines' High School;" she is proficient in vocal and instrumental music and drawing. His second daughter, Consuelo Clark, graduated from the McMicken School of Art; she took a high school certificate, and also a certificate in drawing, and then studied medicine for four years, graduating at last from the "School of Medicine of the Boston University." She is now practicing her profession in the city of Cincinnati. His son Herbert is a graduate from the "Gaines' High School," and taught for three years at Alcorn, Mississippi. Was also deputy sheriff for two years, and gauger in the first Ohio collection district. It can be very well seen that there is talent of a high order in the family, and in his old age may he have the blessing and comfort of his children. He has saved but little, and can well reflect that he has spent his money judiciously in the education of his family and fitting them to take their places in the world.

JUSTIN HOLLAND

CHAPTER XLVI

Justin Holland, Esq.
Musical Author and Arranger—Performer on the Guitar,
Flute and Pianoforte

> *Music hath charms to soothe the savage breast,*
> *To soften rocks or bend the knotted oak.*
> —Congreve
>
> *His very foot hath music in it.*
> —Mickle

It so happens that the history of music furnishes some of the most remarkable talents found in the biography of art. Some of its greatest results are usually attained by simple means, and the exercise of ordinary qualities. Excellence in the art, as in everything else, can only be achieved by dint of painstaking labor. The subject of this sketch is a good example of what can be done by steady application.

Mr. Holland was born in Norfolk, Virginia, in 1819. His father was a farmer. In childhood his talent bespoke so much of a bright future, that he was determined to cultivate it. In a dense forest shut out from the noise and bustle of a busy town, he was afforded but few opportunities for either hearing or learning music. Yet nature taught him the purity of her tones, by the songs of the birds, and no doubt better fitted him for the greatness he achieved. He grasped every opportunity that came in his way, and used it to an advantage. When less than fourteen, he walked on Sunday to a log meeting-house, five miles away, to listen to, and also mingle his voice in such music as the place and people were able to produce. He often delighted himself with an old song book that came into his possession, and the tunes he gave them, while formed by himself, far surpassed those which really belonged to them. When fourteen he left the home of his birth and went to Boston from which he made his way to Chelsea, Massachusetts. At this place he earnestly began the study of music. He became acquainted with a distinguished musician, Signor Mariam Perez, whose performance upon the guitar he enjoyed very much. So charmed was he by the sweetness, tone and fine expressions which were brought from this instrument, by its skilled performer, that he determined to give his whole attention to the study, not that he thought of being looked upon as a master performer, as was Perez, but chiefly for his own amusement.

Mr. Simon Knaebel, an arranger of music, was his first teacher; he also took lessons from Mr. William Shubert, who was known as an expert in music on the guitar. Mr. Holland, in his eagerness to learn, made rapid progress and became a favorite pupil, on account of his ability to play duets with his instructor. He also evinced much skill with the eight keyed flute, taking lessons on this instrument from Mr. Pollock, a Scotch gentleman. Mr. Holland was poor, but poverty was no hindrance to his talents. He worked hard to defray his expenses, which were quite heavy, and the only time he had to practice, was part of his hours for sleep.

In 1841, he entered Oberlin College, for the purpose of obtaining a better education, where he diligently pursued his studies, and made rapid advancement. In the same year he was the author of a book of three hundred and twenty-four pages, on the subject of *Choral Reform*. In 1845, he went to Cleveland, Ohio, and while looking for something to do, his fame as a musician brought him applications, requesting him to teach music to the best people of the place.

James M. Trotter, in *Music and Some Highly Musical People*, a work of considerable merit and worthy to be in the hands of all intelligent people, says:

His character had not become finely formed, he being quite noticeable for his gentlemanly, scholarly qualities, and for the close attention he gave to the subject of music and with all that concerned the true advancement in the profession, in which he now resolved to remain for life.

As illustrating the principles by which he was guided, the following extract from a letter written to a friend will help to define some of his inner motives:

I adopted as a rule of guidance for myself that I would do justice to the learner in my efforts to impart to him a good knowledge of the elementary principles of music and a correct system of fingering (on the guitar), as practiced by and taught in the works by the best masters of Europe. I also decided that in my intercourse as a teacher I would preserve a most cautious, circumspect demeanor, considering the relation a mere business one, which gave me no claims upon my pupils' attention or hospitality beyond what any ordinary business matter would give. I am not aware, therefore, that anyone has ever had cause to complain of my demeanor or that I have been in any case presumptuous.

He headed the profession in the city, in which he was a proficient instructor; and, to make himself more perfect, he applied himself to the study of French, Spanish and Italian, in order to be able to read the systems of foreign musicians in their native tongue. By his persistent energy he found himself able to use the above mentioned languages with much self-complacency, and which were also of great benefit to him in his profession. His success was due to common sense application and unremitting perseverance. His gift came by nature, but he perfected it by self-culture. He took up a subject and pursued it with unflagging energy; he could not rest until he had reached the goal of his ambition. He did much in making the musical compositions of others for other instruments suitable for guitar practice by his skilful arrangement. In this country he was without equal, and stood on a level with the best foreign performers.

In 1848 he published many arrangements for the guitar, which were eagerly purchased by guitar students. It is said that most all of the music for that instrument has under it the name of Holland. He also wrote instruction books for the guitar, which were highly valued because of the simple methods and clearness of explanations, and are considered the best ever published. In 1876 Mr. Brainard, publisher, issued a volume known as *Holland's Method for the Guitar*.

All these years his pecuniary circumstances were embarrassing. Often he had not the means to buy food to sustain his body. At one time when this was the case he had some work to do for which he was to receive a good little sum. It was Sunday, and he began work at 7 P.M. and continued till 8 A.M. the next morning. He took the work and delivered it to his customer and returned with a light heart, for he had been well paid for his services.

His gentlemanly demeanor and true politeness towards his pupils caused them to entertain for him the deepest feelings of respect and the highest admiration.

Besides being a skilful guitarist, Mr. Holland was also regarded as a fine pianist and flutist. As a man of modest pretensions, he never sought public applause. He has very seldom appeared in public, and seemed to prefer a quieter and more sequestered life. His chief work is *Holland's Comprehensive Method for the Guitar*, written for and published by J. L. Peters & Company of New York, in 1874. It is noticeable that of all the musical firms for whom he has written, only one knew him personally, though he has written for J. L. Peters & Company, G. W. Brainard, D. P. Faulds of Louisville, Kentucky, and John Church of Cincinnati.

He was a distinguished Mason, and held many important offices in this order. He was the representative in this country of the Grand Lodges of France and Peru, each appointment being considered a very rare distinction. The Ohio Lodge presented him with a gold watch, as a token of their appreciation. Many such a noble life, full of good and earnest labor, inspires others of the race to strive for higher things, and to overcome difficulties to attain such. He died in the city of New Orleans very recently and the *Cleveland Plain Dealer* said of him:

The many friends and pupils of Professor Justin Holland will learn with great sorrow of his death in New Orleans, Louisiana, on Thursday, March 24. For several years he had been in delicate health, and late last fall went South in the hope of finding a cure by change of climate. But congestion of the brain, the result of a slight cold, set in, and in his exhausted physical condition, soon ended his life. He was sixty-seven years and eight months of age. Professor Holland has made Cleveland his home for years, and sought in this city to create and maintain a love for the guitar and guitar music such as had never been here before. Time can tell how great was his success, but he stood foremost among the members of his profession, as his name is more widely known than any other American guitarist. As a man, when one came to know him, the old professor possessed a heart flowing over with love for his pupils, and no favor was too great to be asked. He will be sadly missed in musical circles here, and it will be many years before Cleveland possesses another guitarist so gifted, so educated and so able to arouse a love for one of the noblest musical instruments.

CHAPTER XLVII

Professor William Hooper Council
President, State Normal and Industrial School,
Huntsville, Alabama—Editor and Lawyer

William Hooper Council was born in Fayetteville, Cumberland county, North Carolina, July 12, 1849, of slave parents. His father escaped to Canada in 1854, and made several unsuccessful attempts to procure the freedom of his family. The subject of this sketch, with all the other children, took the maiden name of their mother, who belonged to one of the largest and most influential families of the town. The family had never been separated, and, in 1857, when the two brothers were sent to distant parts of the South to be heard of no more, and the mother, with William and the younger brother, sold in the Richmond market, almost unbearable grief fell upon all hearts. This undermined the health of the mother and no other trader wanted her. It seemed that the two boys must be separated from her; but by some understanding no separation could take place without the consent of the two, and it was thought this could be easily obtained. So the boys were summoned to the office of the trader in Richmond, who offered them handfuls of gold and made many fair promises of a charming "life out west" if they would consent to leave their mother, who, it was promised, should join them later. Without any knowledge or warning of what was going on except such as only a mother's heart could know, at this juncture she mysteriously appeared upon the scene, and, seen only by the boys, was enabled to warn them by the expression on her face (for not a word was spoken) that told that the promises were of no account, and that the gold would be taken from them after they consented; consequently, all were sold and carried into Alabama together, where they remained until the close of the war, when the death of the younger brother was soon followed by that of the mother, and William was left alone. In 1863, when the Federal armies invaded north Alabama, the boys were carried into the back hills to keep them from the "Yankees." The mother was left in the city of Huntsville, thinking that her children would hold her, but she escaped with the army and sent back for the children, who, by the perfect system of grape-vine telegraphy well known to the colored people, and so long carried on while they were in slavery, learned of all these things, and were ever seeking an opportunity to be united with her. Finally the hour came, and, leaving home one Sunday afternoon, met each other in the forests, and, through swamps, over mountains, and wading two rivers, that Sunday night they reached the Federal lines, twenty-five miles away, and were united with their mother, to whom they were fondly attached. They entered the Freedmen's school at Stevenson, Alabama. Cicero soon died. When the war closed William waited on an officer for a year's food, clothing and schooling. However incredible it may appear, in 1866, at the age of seventeen years, he took charge of a county school, being the first to teach a colored school outside of a city in North Alabama.

His trials with the Ku Klux would require too much space for the relation, but he had many and severe difficulties. Closing his first session, he spent the following summer at service in a hotel on top of Lookout mountain, where he earned enough to defray his expenses in school the next session. He next worked in a restaurant in Nashville by day and attended night school. Afterwards he did night service at a restaurant and attended day school. He then undertook the task of teaching regularly, in which he has given abundant satisfaction, made much progress and developed into a professor. Desiring to advance, he procured chemical and philosophical instruments and walked eight miles once a week, paying one dollar, to hear a lecture on these branches. He also paid six dollars per month for private instruction in Latin and the higher mathematics. Unfortunately he took part in politics; he was enrolling clerk in the Alabama Legislature in 1872 and '74, and was associate editor of the *Negro Watchman* in the year 1874; also he was a nominee of the Republican party for the Legislature. In 1875 he was appointed by President Grant receiver of public monies for the northern district of Alabama, which position he declined, to accept a position as principal of the city school of Huntsville, to which he had been elected without solicitation. He was one of the secretaries of the Colored National Civil Rights convention, which met in Washington in 1873. He was elected president of the State Normal and Industrial school, and professor of sciences and pedagogics in 1876, which position he now holds. He has made of this school all that it is.

He has been highly honored by various societies of which he is a member; was appointed a notary public by Governor Cobb in 1882; he was editor and proprietor of the *Huntsville Herald* from 1878 until 1883, and was admitted to practice before the Supreme Court of Alabama in 1883. He is a minister in the A. M. E. church and a great Sunday school worker; for push and energy he has but few equals, and will surely accomplish more in his life.

In 1884 he was united in marriage with Maria H. Wheeden of Huntsville, since which time he has lived a pleasant and profitable life. He is highly respected by all who know him. His school has been a great success and receives the yearly commendation from the commissioners, Hon. A. S. Fletcher, Hon. J. R. Mayhew and J. D. Brandon. As a disciplinarian, he easily ranks among the most successful; for the students catch the spirit of the teacher and go forth into life filled with the high notions which ought to occupy the attention of the youth of this day. From the foregoing it will be seen that he is a self-made man, who wrung success from doubtful circumstances and brought himself into prominence. And he feels proud of his graduation from what he facetiously calls the "Pine Knot College." What men have done, others can do. Reader, take courage, go forward; you can and will win.

JAMES POINDEXTER

CHAPTER XLVIII

Rev. James Poindexter, D. D.
Advocate of Human Rights—Minister of the Gospel
and Agitator—Director of the Bureau of Forestry—Member
of the Board of Education of the City of Columbus, Ohio

The State of Ohio has had within its borders one of the strongest men in the United States, a man whose soul has been on fire on account of the outrages perpetrated against colored people, and who never lost an opportunity to speak and write with vigor against all species of outrages and to ally himself persistently with those elements that look toward the bettering of the condition of those for whom he advocated. His philanthrophy has not, however, confined itself to his own race; but those who know him have always done him the justice to say that his interest extended to all classes who are oppressed and downtrodden.

He was born in Richmond, Virginia, A.D. 1817. He attended school from the time he learned to talk and was instructed in common branches until he reached his tenth year, when he was apprenticed to the barber's business. His boss was barber for the most aristocratic class of citizens of Richmond, and he improved every opportunity afforded him for cultivating his mind by conversation and association with the customers. He was always ready to accept instruction from any who would take the pains to impart it to him.

After settling in Ohio he received private instruction from an Englishman, one of the ablest educators and ripest scholars in the city where he lived. As long as he continued the barber's business he had the good fortune to have as customers the cream of the intelligent people in the city of Columbus. His patrons comprised statesmen, scientists, men of all professions, professors of colleges, physicians, lawyers, merchants and capitalists. This sort of education is often more valuable than college training; it gives one the practical experience of life. Theory from books may assist in many enterprises in life, but to pursue life itself unto a successful end takes practical everyday experience—not only that which we ourselves gain, but through observation and contact with others. At the age of twelve he settled in the city of Columbus, where he now resides. He embraced religion and was baptized into the communion of the Second Baptist church of Columbus, Ohio, by Elder Wallace Shelton, in the spring of 1840. He was ordained an elder in 1849 and was chosen pastor of said church in 1862, and here he has labored continuously until the present time. He has served as trustee of the "Institute for the Blind" of Ohio by appointment of Governor Charles Foster for four years. He was appointed trustee of the Athens University of Ohio by ex-Governor George Hoadly, but was rejected by a Democratic Senate because they regarded him as an ultra-Republican. He has served four years as member of the City Council of Columbus, and was chosen vice-president of that body. He was unanimously appointed a member of the Board of Education to fill the vacancy on the board. And at the next election thereof was elected a member, which position he now holds.

He has just been re-elected to the position on the School Board by a majority of 512 votes over a Democratic opponent. This is very indicative of his standing in that city, for the issue of the daily *Ohio State Journal*, Columbus, Ohio, April 5, 1887, says:

The result of yesterday's election shows the success of the entire Democratic city ticket by majorities ranging from 400 to 800. When it is remembered that he is a stalwart Republican, his election is a subject of congratulation.

The following letter also shows a new appointment made by the governor of that State:

STATE OF OHIO, EXECUTIVE DEPARTMENT,
OFFICE OF THE GOVERNOR, COLUMBUS, MARCH 3, 1887
HON. JAMES POINDEXTER, COLUMBUS, OHIO.

DEAR SIR: I am directed by the governor to notify you that he has appointed you to be a member of the Board of Directors of the State Forestry Bureau for the term of six years, commencing April 28, 1887, and to say that a commission has been forwarded to you accordingly by this day's mail. I enclose herewith an official oath—which you will please execute and return to this office.

Very respectfully,
C. E. PRIOR, Ex-Clerk

In the early days of colored men's freedom he was the first colored man in Ohio nominated by the Republican party to a seat in the House of Representatives, but was defeated at the polls. He is a member of the Pastors' Union, where the ministers are all white except himself; nevertheless, he was president of said union. He was empanelled as a juror on the petit jury of the United States court at its last session and was unanimously chosen foreman of said jury, though, with the exception of himself, it was composed of white men taken from the best citizens of the State. He has the honor of being the only colored man in the State of Ohio who has been a foreman of a jury in a United States court. This may seem a small matter to mention in a man's life, and yet, because of existing prejudices, even such small honors have been withheld from colored men, and it is here related in order that those who read may see that character, honor and veracity will gain credence among all classes of people and a man be respected for what he is worth, that the color of the skin will not prevent men from rising mid the direst circumstances if they will be true to themselves. Rev. James Poindexter has been president of the society known as the "Sons of Protection" for thirty years of its forty-three years existence. The term of office when organized was only six months, but for the last twenty-five years the term has been twelve months. Thus he has been in many ways made the recipient of much confidence and esteem by his fellow-citizens of all colors, nationalities and conditions. As regards his aggressiveness, he might be called aggressiveness itself, but facts speak louder than words. No man in Ohio, even a regular employee of a daily paper, has contributed to the press or made more speeches on all matters relating to the rights, freedom, enfranchisement and elevation of our race, or on matters relating to the public welfare, than Mr. Poindexter. If he should be asked why he has not been further recognized by appointments to office, the answer could be readily given that he has esteemed his position as a minister of the gospel and the pastor of a kind-hearted, faithful membership of much more importance than official positions. Then, too, in his defense of an oppressed people, and in the utterances of such opinions as are even ahead of the times, I have no doubt he has played the part of a patriot, of a race defender, rather than a suppliant for small favors at the hands of petty politicians, who know not how to honor a man who is true to himself and the people. He never took his opinions from any man. His inspiration has been drawn from the word of God and his life has comported with his teachings, and thereby made him a power among men and one of the most vehement writers upon the subjects heretofore referred to. Specimens of his manner and style of speaking can be given and will verify the statement we have made. The Columbus *Capital and Dispatch* very frequently reports his addresses and sermons in full. On the subject of "Pulpit and Politics," delivered before the Pastors' Union, he spoke as follows:

Nor can the preacher more than any other citizen plead his religious work or the sacredness of that work as an exemption from duty. Going to the Bible to learn the relation of the pulpit to politics, and accepting the prophets, Christ, and the apostles and the pulpit of their times, and their precepts and examples as the guide of the pulpit to-day, I think that the conclusion will be that wherever there is a sin to be rebuked, no matter by whom committed, and ill to be averted or good to be achieved by our country or mankind, there is a place for the pulpit to make itself felt and heard. The truth is, all the help the preachers and all other good and worthy citizens can give by taking hold of politics is needed in order to keep the government out of bad hands and secure the ends for which governments are formed.

Speaking about the pulpit in connection with slavery he said some very keen things. It will be remembered that the Northern pulpit was often *silent* on the question of slavery; holding off with hypocrisy rather than respect for the proprieties of the pulpit; keeping their mouths closed for fear of losing their positions, rather than declaring the word of God. While on the other hand the South was *preaching* "Servants obey your masters" and holding the colored people in slavery and taking their earnings for themselves. It left the Negro at the mercy of those who bound them in slavery. Even the best, or what was supposed to be the best, element in the world, was either silent or against him. Said he:

Now it is a fact worthy of note in this connection that objections to preachers holding with politics generally comes from the thing assailed. Advocates of slavery never objected to the preachers who, in or out of the pulpit, maintained that the Bible sanctions slavery, or preached often from the text "Servants be obedient to your masters." Men who gave their sympathy to the rebellion never scolded the preacher who argued that the Constitution conferred no authority on the government to coerce a State or one who justified the legislator who said, "not a dollar and not a man to whip the South," nor would man pecuniarily interested in the whiskey and beer traffic utter a note of dissent if all preachers would unite in denouncing legislative intervention to control that traffic as a sumptuary legislation. It will not be denied that some good persons deprecate the presence of the pulpit in politics; that it is so unclean a thing that it cannot be touched without taint, unfitting one for spiritual usefulness. Such persons are deceived, as a careful perusal of the Bible with careful inspection of the lives, private and public, of the preachers referred to, will show.

As a preacher of the gospel, every subject within the range of human interest has received his attention. In a letter to the editor of the *Ohio State Journal* he shows how he has trained his people. This is a lesson to young ministers who have congregations and who desire their people to be profited and made strong in earthly things as well as heavenly. He says:

The colored people are a reading people; my charge comprises families of all grades of financial standing, and I visit the whole of them, every family, and where I find little else I find a newspaper; many of my people take from three to four dailies, *Ohio State Journal, Evening Dispatch, Commercial*

Gazette and not unfrequently *Cincinnati Inquirer* or the *Columbus Times*; and nearly every family one or more Sunday morning papers, and appear, as they are, a reading people; and as pastor of a church it is part of my religion to inculcate in all the rising generation the duty of making themselves as familiar with the Constitution of the United States and laws of their country as these relate to the rights and duties of the citizens, as with the Bible.

October 5, 1885, the *Ohio State Journal* gives a sermon in full which he preached to his congregation on "The Crime of Buying and Selling Votes." He thundered from his pulpit in most vehement and powerful language against the crime of selling votes, and held up to scorn and ridicule those who bought them as well as those who sold; and declared among other things, "that our votes are not ours in any such sense that we may dispose of them as we choose for our own pleasure or profit, as we may any other kind of property. They belong to the whole people; they are ours in trust to be conscientiously used by us to promote the safety, peace and prosperity of the whole. The trust itself is the highest, most important, most sacred ever vouchsafed by the Almighty God to a free self-governing people; in the exercise of it, it is the primary duty of the voter to see to it that the individual for whom he votes is an honest, capable man, one who knows how to discharge the duties of the office and has the integrity to discharge those duties in the light of an all-wise God." How much better our people would vote and what better rulers would be selected all over the country if the preachers would take the opportunity of telling them how to live as well as talking about the "Gold-paved streets of the New Jerusalem" so much. Some are content in preaching if they can get up a shout of hallelujah, and constantly keep mens' minds off the transitory things of life, as they choose to call it, and turn their attention *entirely* above. Thousands on top of thousands are made to *think* of heaven and are never directed how to live within the four walls of their own rooms; and they delight to deal in the rhapsodies and joys of the eternal world and are eminently careless about showing them how to get there.

Mr. Poindexter further referred to the fact that there are colored men mean enough to sell their votes, but not many of them; and that there are white men mean enough to sell their votes as well as black ones; and worse than all, that there are white men recreant enough to buy the votes of both white and black. He says:

When the bad men of the South wanted to defeat all the results of the war, they brought to bear on the colored people the persuasiveness of the revolver, bowie knife, shotgun and halter, and when the world stood aghast and cried shame, shame, the South responded, "No, no, not at all, not at all; if the North was in our place it would do as we do; it would be compelled to do as we do. The Negro is ignorant and as a consequence he is vicious, cannot tell the truth, steals everything he puts his hands upon, and must be scourged to his work, is insulting to white people; our women shudder when they meet him on the highway and have a right to; and above all and worse than all, he won't vote with his old masters."

And then with all the vigor of his soul, with all his wrath aroused, he continued his sermon with this vigorous question:

This self-evident damning lie was exhibited as a true bill against the Southern people by too many good people of the North, and as a consequence they were left to the tender mercies of the men whom they had helped to defeat in their cherished object, and that to destroy the only free government on the earth. I denounce this charge against the colored people of the South. A self-evident lie, because the men most entitled to be believed—men, who, when the fight was over, accepted the situation and went to work to rebuild their prostrate South—say it is a lie: say the Negro is a good citizen: say that when the strong men of the Confederacy were in the army, their women and children were undisturbed and safe in the hands of the Negro, and no single case of the outrages now so lavishly attributed to them, and so readily believed in the North, was known to occur. I denounce the charge as a damning lie on the colored man, because it does not present him as he is, but does present him as the monster two and a half centuries of barbarous oppression would seem calculated to make him, and thus obtained that credence in the North, which, to its shame, leaves the poor creature in a condition worse than when he was a slave.

These extracts can better epitomize the life and character of Mr. Poindexter than any words of comment which might here be given. To show the estimation in which he is held by the citizens of Columbus, the following letter is given. The writer was solicited by Mr. Poindexter to accept the position on the bench of the Supreme Court of the State, which had been tendered by Governor Foraker, and to this solicitation he replied in the following words:

Rev. James Poindexter,

My Dear Sir:—Your favor of yesterday came to my hand in the evening.

I received many letters and telegrams urging me to accept the appointment tendered by the governor, but I assure you in all sincerity that none of them had the persuasive influence on my judgment which your favor would have had if it had been received before I determined, and had communicated my determination to the governor. The considerations you urge upon my attention are very cogent, and the sentiment and tone of your entire letter show that you have a just appreciation of the judicial office. When I may happen to meet you I will communicate to you the reason which influenced my mind in declining to accept, as they relate to my personal affairs.

With great respect,

Richard A. Harrison

Mr. Poindexter has succeeded in surrounding himself with many comforts: he has a good home and a fine library, and many other comforts which go to make a home happy, and he dwells, as we have said, with a people who know how to appreciate his years of hard service for Christ and the race. No man is better known and honored. In the United States he has been a wall of fire against wrong, a generous supporter to every cause that needs assistance.

Faithful to every trust, careful, painstaking, and noble-hearted, though obliged to disagree with many, he has yet maintained friendly relations with all classes who respect manhood wherever it is possessed. If this sketch preserves a little of the history of his life, we trust that it will inspire some other to give a more extended history of this man whose deeds have entered into the affairs of the last half century.

Much has been said about the black laws of the States. Mr. Poindexter has been fighting that mountain of iniquity all his life, and younger men have arisen, and the opportunity having been presented, brought about largely by just such men as Mr. Poindexter, who were pioneers in these matters, they have had the opportunity by position and learning to do much which he could not accomplish. Had Mr. Poindexter lived in a Republican county, things which have existed could not have possibly remained to this day, for he would have been in the Legislature warring against these things years ago. No man has done more in the State to arouse the feeling and popular sentiment against the outrages of these laws than Mr. Poindexter, and that finally through the Ely-Arnett bill his past labors will be a fitting reward. No matter who may have a place against men, he must not be forgotten.

This eminent agitator, Rev. James Poindexter, delivered the baccalaureate sermon before the graduating class of the State University, Louisville, Kentucky, May 15, 1887. The old veteran of sixty years' service thrilled every heart, and the vast congregation in the Calvary Baptist church—Rev. C. H. Parrish, pastor—felt the powerful effects of his arguments, and were stirred to do greater works for Christ. On Tuesday night, May 17, 1887, the degree of Doctor of Divinity was conferred on him.

CHAPTER XLIX

Richard Mason Hancock, Esq.
Foreman of the Pattern Shops of the Eagle Works
Manufacturing Company, Chicago, Illinois. Mathematician—
Carpenter—Draughtsman—Foreman of the Liberty Iron
Works Pattern Shop

To speak of one who has made a success in this department is indeed a pleasure, for in this work he has had the honor of showing Negro talent and also overcoming those obstacles that defeat success in many men. It used to be that only white men could do the "bossing," but the bottom rail is on the top, and Mr. Hancock is now doing such work as guides over seven hundred white employees and gives satisfactions to his generous employers. We have said elsewhere that brains will tell, and here is an indisputable evidence. Do you think he would be employed if he could not do the work? No, indeed, not a bit of it. He is competent, and that indeed is the reason. Why should the firm trust him with the disposition of their thousands unless he could make them thousands? The truth is they do not know his superior, and hence employ him. It is a praiseworthy thing that his employers could see the man, the artist, the draughtsman, and be influenced neither by the color of his skin nor the drops of blood that may be in his veins attributable to black parents. I am indebted to a sketch, which appeared in the columns of the *Detroit Plaindealer,* May 14, 1886, for many of the facts which appear here.

Mr. Hancock was born of free parents at Newberne, North Carolina, November 22, 1832. His father, William H. Hancock, is a hale old gentleman, still alive, residing at Chicago, Illinois. At an early age Richard was sent to a private school in his native town, the public schools of which, and indeed the laws of the "Old North State," being then opposed to the education of Negro children. Here he mastered the rudiments of a common school course, and when thirteen years old began as a carpenter's apprentice under his father. He worked nine years at the bench; by that time having gained a thorough knowledge of the trade, and attained his majority, he left North Carolina and went to New Haven, Connecticut.

He soon found employment at his trade with Messrs. Atwater & Treat and Doolittle & Company, two white firms that were not slow in recognizing him as an efficient workman. "Joinering" was the particular branch of the trade at which he had been engaged up to this time.

He finally drifted to Lockport, New York, where he followed ship carpentry two years, building canal boats, after which he was taken into the employ of the Holly Manufacturing Company, with whom he remained four years. While with them he learned pattern-making, a branch of the trade that requires first of all a complete mastery of carpentry, besides an acquaintance with higher mathematics, a knowledge of draughting and the constant exercise of the very best judgment. For four years he worked and studied to make himself proficient, and at the end of that period had mastered all the theory and much of the practical details of that branch of the trade.

In 1862 he came to Chicago, and shortly after was given employment as a pattern-maker in the shops of the Eagle Works Manufacturing Company, whose president, Mr. P. W. Gates, was a true and tried friend of the Negro, when all the law and nearly all the public sentiment of the land was in favor of keeping him in slavery. At that time this company had the largest machine and boiler ships and foundry that was in operation in the West.

After working as a journeyman two years, he was promoted to the foremanship of the pattern department, and had in his charge fourteen men, all of whom were white. To serve under a Negro foreman, no matter if he did know more about the business than they did, was too much for their Northern blood, so they "struck." For three days Mr. Hancock was "monarch of all he surveyed." But the prospect was not a pleasing one, for the shop was crowded with orders and there was more work to get out than he could perform unaided. So fearing that its delayed execution might injure him with his employers, he went before the president and tendered his resignation. After hearing him through, Mr. Gates quietly said: "Oh! go back to work. It will all come right in an hundred years." He obeyed. Other pattern-makers to fill the places of the strikers were soon engaged, and ten years subsequent service with the same firm showed that less than a century could make all things right.

While with the Eagle Works Company, he was instrumental in teaching two colored young men trades—Mr. Beverly Meeks as a machinist, and Mr. John Johnson as a pattern-maker. The former is now in the employ of the C. & N. W. Railroad Company at their shops in Detroit, while the latter is plying his trade at Denver, Colorado. He also used his influence with good effect to secure work at their trades for other colored men in the foundry and blacksmith shops of the works.

In 1873 the firm for which he worked went out of business, and a new firm, composed of two of his former superintendents, Messrs. Fraser and Chalmers, started the Liberty Iron Works in this city. They showed their confidence in his ability by immediately placing him at the head of their pattern shops. Their business soon reached large proportions, requiring now the constant services of over seven hundred skilled employees, fifteen of whom are kept busy making patterns. The firm makes a specialty of manufacturing intricate mining machinery, and in the course of a year gets out an almost infinite variety of indescribable work, for most of which new patterns have to be made. All of the work must conform strictly to the drawings in every particular. This will show the importance of the position held by Mr. Hancock in the second largest establishment of the kind in this country. He has been with his present employers fifteen years, commands a good salary, and is held in high esteem by them and his fellow workmen. In the same shop with him is his son George, who is also regarded as an efficient pattern-maker.

In private life Mr. Hancock is a public-spirited and progressive citizen; a member of several societies, in some of which he holds a high rank, notably the Masonic fraternity; a vestryman of St. Thomas' Episcopal church, and an interesting talker at the literary sessions of the Prudence Crandall circle. He has a cosy home on Fulton street, where, assisted by his wife, an amiable and intelligent lady, his many friends are made welcome.

CHAPTER L

Professor W. S. Scarborough, A. B., A. M., LL. D.
Author of a Greek Text Book—Scientist—Lecturer—Scholar—
Student of Sanscrit, Zend, Gothic and Luthanian Languages

The names of the parents of the subject of this sketch were Jesse and Frances Scarborough. His father was set free by his old master about fifteen years before the war began, and three thousand dollars were left in the hands of his guardian, so that if he should desire to leave the South, he might do so. Further, it was stipulated with the railroad authorities, in whose employ he was for forty years, that half of the money he received as wages should be given him and the other retained by them to meet his doctor's bills and other demands, should he get sick. If he left the South, the half retained by them or as much of it as was not spent should be given to him. He remained in Georgia, as his wife was nominally a slave and could not accompany him if he went North. The conditions above stated were never fulfilled and he received none of the money.

Young Scarborough was born, February 16, 1852, in Macon, Bibb county, Georgia. Of course, under the circumstances stated, he was nominally a slave, and his early days were spent in Macon, where he began to go to school as early as six years of age. He would go out day after day, ostensibly to play, but with his books concealed under his arm. He spent six or eight hours each day in school till he could read well, and had gathered a good knowledge of geography, grammar and arithmetic. At the age of ten he took regular lessons in writing under an old South Carolinian and rebel of the bitterest type; despite the strict laws then existing against Negro education, it was miraculous that a man hating the Negroes as this white man did, would take such an interest in a colored youth, and would even go to the extent of teaching him the art of penmanship. But "God works in a mysterious way his wonders to perform." This man's name was J. C. Thomas, and he is now dead; it would be a pleasure indeed if he were living to see his young pupil so distinguished for his learning, and so prominent in the educational councils of the Nation.

Young Scarborough was also taught by his playmates, who were white

W. S. SCARBOROUGH

boys, receiving much instruction directly and indirectly. His parents having had a common school education were able to assist him very much by way of direction in his studies, in secret, until the war closed. He was put to the study of books by his parents as soon as they were able to do so.

He remembers one or two narrow escapes he had during his early life, which, when seen in the light of his present career, shows that God preserves those for whom he has special work. He was eight years old, on a fourth of July day. When he was returning from seeing a military parade, he had to pass through a long bridge; here he met two men very drunk, who seized him and held him through the window over the rushing waters below, from which terrible fate he was rescued by passers-by. During the war, friends would come to see the family without passes. Though a boy, he used to give them a safe permit home, signing their master's name. Many colored people would run the gauntlet with no other passport than that given by him. He began the study of music when he was twelve years old, and as there was no law against this, he used to practice twice a week openly. At the age of ten he had been elected secretary of one of the most prominent organizations among the colored people in Macon, Georgia. Such meetings were allowed during the war by the whites, provided the members got a permit. He received a slight fee for such services. During this period when not engaged in study, he worked at the shoemaker's trade, and just before the war closed he spent one year at the trade as a regular apprentice. Even in those days his intellect gave him advantages over many, and his services were always in demand, for he was called on to read the papers every morning by the men at work, and talk about and explain the movements of the two contending armies. When the war closed he passed from grade to grade in the schools, until 1867, when he entered the Lewis High School and finished in 1869. With this preparation, and with studious habits, a lad of seventeen he entered the Atlanta University, to prepare for Yale College. He remained at this institution two years and then entered Oberlin College, in Ohio, and graduated in 1875. Immediately after graduation he returned to Macon and accepted a position offered by the American Missionary Society to teach Latin, Greek and mathematics in the Lewis High School; but in September he returned to Oberlin, and gave several months study to theology in the seminary, devoting himself especially to Hellenistic, Greek and Hebrew. During the winter he was called to the principalship of Payne Institute, located at Cokesburg, South Carolina, now merged into the Allen University of Columbia, South Carolina.

While he was studying, he always taught during the summers to aid in his support, having positions at Albany Enterprise Academy, Albany,

Ohio, and district school at Bloomingburg, Ohio, Howard Normal school at Cuthbert, Georgia, and two selected schools at Macon, Georgia.

He was called to his present position in the fall of 1877, and established the post office at Wilberforce, Ohio, and was commissioned its first postmaster in 1879. Here he organized the first reading-room for young men, and was its president until he resigned in 1881. He assisted J. W. Fitch in editing the *Authors' Review and Scrap-book*, printed in Pittsburgh. His duties were such that he could not do justice to his work, so he sold out his share in the firm. This periodical succeeded well in its intent—to fill a need in the school-room.

Professor Scarborough is one of the brightest lights in the colored race. He has a masterly mind and a comprehensive grasp of all subjects which he investigates. His forte is the classics, more particularly Greek. He has been acknowledged as a scholar, more by his authorship of a Greek textbook and on account of his associations in eminent scientific societies and his association with learned men, than perhaps any other thing. He has read several papers before the Philological Association on the themotic vowel in the Greek verb, in Homer and Virgil, etc. He is a member of the American Philological association, elected at Harvard University, Cambridge, Massachusetts, July, 1882, and also a member of the American Spelling Reform Association, elected at Dartmouth College, July, 1883, Hanover, New Hampshire. He is a member of the Modern Language Association of America, elected at Johns Hopkins University, Baltimore, Maryland, December, 1884; a member of the American Social Science Association, elected at Saratoga, New York, September 1, 1885; member of the American Foreign Antislavery Society, elected in 1883, in New York; a member of the I. O. Good Templars. He is also connected with the A. M. E. church. Was brought up in part a Presbyterian, and his mother is still a Presbyterian, while his father when living was an African Methodist.

This church is justly proud of this eminent and progressive scholar, and there seems to be no jealousy among the older members that this young man should take such a prominent stand in the literary affairs of the times. He was a delegate to the Centennial of Methodism at Baltimore, December, 1884, and was very useful in said meeting. He has held various positions in his church, that always delights to honor him. He has been trustee and Sunday school superintendent several times, and at this writing fills both positions. He is in constant demand to deliver orations and lectures upon various subjects. He was invited to read a paper upon "Industrial Schools," before the colored teachers convention in Missouri; had a similar invitation to read a paper on the "Sphere of the Colored Teacher," before the colored teachers of Springfield, Ohio; read a paper before the Georgia Colored Teachers' Association on "The Importance of Union in Works of the Colored People of the Cuntry." He has lectured on various topics at various places. Many of these lectures have been published. He has written much for the press, and his articles are always acceptable.

After the death of Professor Wiley Lane of Howard University, he was prominently spoken of as his successor in the chair of Greek at said university. In the trustee board he was beaten by the votes of the white men who voted for a white man, while the colored men voted for him. He was the choice of Frederick Douglass, Francis J. Grimke, William Waring, Bishop John M. Brown, and Mr. Cook, who were trustees at the time. This was in April, 1885. Letters of indorsement were sent him from New York, Philadelphia, Boston, Chicago, Washington and Baltimore, in fact from all parts of the country. This proved that he was recognized as a specialist in the department of Greek by the leading colored people of the United States, especially the scholars of them. He has been invited to take a position in the Brooklyn school, but did not accept. After graduation he was solicited to go to Africa and engage in literary pursuits, that of learning and translating the languages, with a salary of $1,800. This he refused, preferring to make his mark in this country. He was invited to give, in the form of a paper, his views on the study of the classic languages in a course of liberal education before the convention of teachers in the State of New York, in 1884.

His career has been unusually brilliant, and should he live long will leave behind him a course of life worthy of emulation. He received the degree of A.B. from the Department of Philosophy and the Arts at Oberlin College in 1875; his degree of A.M., *in course* in 1878, and the degree of LL.D. from Liberia College, West Africa, 1882.

In 1881, A. S. Barnes & Company of New York, placed upon the market his *First Lessons in Greek,* of which Professor Greener said: "It is no small degree of praise to say that he has done just what he undertook. Amid the number of books of this class there is none more accurate or complete." Professor Gregory of Howard University said: "He has succeeded in avoiding the mistake made by so many authors of presenting many unnecessary complications in a first book, which serve to mislead and confuse the beginner." Professor Alexander Kerr of the University of Wisconsin, said: "Professor Scarborough has shown good taste and good judgment in avoiding long and complex sentences for translation, and in holding himself to a clear and concise statement of the rudimentary forms of the language." He sent a copy of his book to John F. Slater, who gave a million dollars to educate the colored race, and received the following reply:

NORWICH, CONNECTICUT, June 28, 1882
PROFESSOR WILLIAM S. SCARBOROUGH
DEAR SIR:—Your book entitled *First Lessons in Greek*, has been duly received by me. If I may hope that what I have tried to do for the promulgation of education among your race should result in any more such publications I shall feel that my efforts have been amply rewarded.

Very truly yours,
JOHN F. SLATER

He has also published several pamphlets, one called *Our Civil Status*, forty pages, in 1884. This was read at the Inter-State convention of colored men held at Pittsburgh, in April of that year. Another thirty-six page pamphlet on the *Birds of Aristophanes: A Theory of Interpretation*, published by D. C. Health & Company of Boston. This was a paper read before the American Philological Association at Cornell University, Ithaca, New York, July, 1886. He also has in manuscript, "Questions on the Latin Language with Appendix;" also the twenty-first and twenty-second books of Livy, based on the German editions of Weissenborn and Oölfflin. It will probably be published in 1887 by the University Publication Company of New York. He is also preparing other Latin and Greek works which will be revised and annotated by Professor W. B. Frost of Oberlin college, as soon as ready.

Professor Scarborough's range of studies is very wide, including a knowledge of the modern languages, also Sanscrit, Zend, Gothic, Luthanian, Old Slavonic, which he uses as aids in his special labors. He is at home in all kindred studies. While giving much attention to these matters, he has several times been elected to various positions in his county and State. Was one of the signers of a call for a convention which met in Columbus, Ohio, December, 1883, to consider the civil status of the colored men in Ohio. He was appointed by the State Central committee to organize "Equal Rights Leagues," in the Seventh district of Ohio.

In 1883 he was married to Miss Sarah C. Bierce. She is a very intelligent woman and cultivated writer, who secures opportunities for exercising her gifts at good pay. She is a graduate of the Oswego Normal school of New York, and filled a principalship of the Normal department of Wilberforce for three years. The ceremony was performed by the lamented Bishop W. F. Dickerson.

In worldly goods Professor Scarborough is worth anywhere from seven to ten thousand dollars, and his fame and fortune are both on the increase.

CHAPTER LI

Rev. Solomon T. Clanton, Jr., A. B., B. D.
Instructor of Mathematics—Secretary of the American National
Baptist Convention—Agent of the American Baptist
Publication Society

The secretary is a native of the "Pelican" State; his parents lived at Cypremore, St. Mary's Parish, Louisiana. Their names were S. T. and Mary Clanton. They rejoiced at the birth of S. T. Clanton, Jr., March 27, 1857. The parents were anxious for the boy to be educated, and he labored faithfully to assist them by obedience and closely following their advice. In order to further accomplish their desires, the boy was sent to New Orleans, where he attended the Government school in 1862, when he was only about five years old.

When he passed the examination for the High school, he could not go to the white school, and there were none for the colored, so he entered the New Orleans University and graduated in 1878 with the usual title of A.B. In December of the same year he was appointed instructor of mathematics in Leland University of New Orleans. He resigned this position in May, 1880, that he might enter in the next September upon a course of theology in the Baptist Union Theological Seminary at Morgan Park, Illinois, from which in May, 1883, he graduated with the degree of B.D.

In June, 1883, he was elected Sunday-school missionary of the American Baptist Publication Society, and has been in that position ever since. He had, however, labored on several occasions for this same society and this permanent appointment was only the result of great confidence in him when he labored for them on previous occasions, in the summers of 1877, 1879 and 1880, in Louisiana and Illinois. In the summers of 1881 and 1882 he also labored faithfully in their employ.

He married one of the most discreet, amiable and accomplished women in the country, June 6, 1883, at the residence of her parents, John and Rebecca Bird, in Decatur, Illinois. She was then Miss Olive Bird, and educated in the Public and High school of her native city. Mr. Clanton began life as a bricklayer, and has made remarkable progress in this short time; he bids fair to accomplish much, being a man of perseverance and tact. In the councils of his brethren, his opinion has great weight. His father dying when he was about nine years old, left him and his sisters to the care of a hardworking, loving mother, who with her own hands, unaided, was enabled to educate three children—Solomon, of whom we write especially; Elvina A. Clanton, graduated from the Leland University, from the scientific course with the title of B.S., and P. A. Clanton, who graduated from the same school in classified course with the title of A.B. What a monument to one pair of hands! What a blessing is a good mother!

Secretary Clanton has filled one term as secretary of the American Baptist Foreign Mission convention, which is doing work in Africa, sustaining missionaries there; and was elected August 25, 1886, as secretary of the American Baptist National convention. As a writer he is fluent and yet cogent, smooth yet forcible, graceful and yet vigorous. He has accumulated some property and lives comfortably.

CHAPTER LII

*Professor John O. Crosby, A. M., B. E.
Principal State Normal School, North Carolina*

In the little village of Crosbyville, Fairfield county, South Carolina, on the twenty-second of December, 1850, the subject of this sketch, Rev. John Oliver Crosby, was born in slavery. His mother's name was Sylvia. She came from Richmond, Virginia, when she was only twelve years old, having been sold to a speculator at the sale of John Tinsley to satisfy his creditors. His father was Thomas Crosby. At a very early age John Oliver was apprenticed to the carpenter's trade, which he learned so rapidly that at the age of twelve he was made foreman and superintended the building of numerous small houses of from two to ten rooms each. In 1860 Thomas Crosby died, and the same year the Crosby estate was sold. Mary Q. Crosby bought the young carpenter for $1,260. His apprenticeship ending, he moved to Shelton's Depot and became the slave of William Stanton, who had married his young mistress, Miss Crosby. In 1864 Mr. Stanton was drafted into the Confederate service and sent to Florence, South Carolina, to guard Federal prisoners. In the summer Mr. Stanton came home on a furlough, and on his return took the boy John along as a servant. At Columbia, Stanton and all other reserved soldiers returning to their commands were stopped by order of the government and put on duty as a guard at a prison containing about fourteen hundred Federal prisoners. This prison was about three miles west of Columbia, across the Congaree river, and about half a mile from the Saluda river. General Means was in command, and being an intimate friend of Stanton's, Stanton was appointed by him sutler to the prisoners. From this time he made his headquarters in Columbia. John Oliver spent the greater part of his time at the headquarters of General Means, where he made himselm useful as a servant, and occasionally acting as drummer, beating the reveille and other signals.

The boy despised slavery, and had always studiously and artfully avoided addressing his owners as "master." He therefore resolved to assist the prisoners in every way possible. There were three ways in

JOHN O. CROSBY

which this could be done. First, some of the prisoners were allowed to go out on parol to get wood, and as John was well known at the camp and allowed to go everywhere he pleased, he would occasionally furnish a prisoner with sufficient provisions to last two or three days. In this way the prisoner could spend several days in accomplishing his escape from the neighborhood. Secondly, he could furnish some of the prisoners with an occasional newspaper, giving the Confederate movements. But the greatest services were rendered in a very different way. At the headquarters, in a tent next to the one occupied by General Means himself, and to which John Oliver had free access at all times, were two large baskets. These baskets were the recipients of all the mail brought from the "prison post-office" to be forwarded to wives and friends in the North. Three young men were daily occupied reading these letters; those deemed fit to be sent on were put into one basket, and those containing any objectionable matter were thrown into the other basket. More than two-thirds of the letters were thus rejected and went to the flames. John Oliver conceived a plan by which some of the "refused letters" could be forwarded to their destination. The mail would leave the camp at eleven o'clock daily, and as all the letters examined between this time and the next day were allowed to remain in the basket, he would transfer from twenty to thirty letters daily from the rejected basket to the one containing the "approved letters."

After the war he went to live with his mother on a farm in Chester county. He remained there about one year; but he and his stepfather could never agree, as the "old man" despised "larning" and said it was "spilin" all the boys on the place. John was also pretty expert at figures up to division, and could read well in the second reader. He was to the boys on the plantation what *Webster's Dictionary* is to the learned, and, notwithstanding his ragged condition, was a favorite with all the old people. His mother was a woman of fine sense, her greatest blunder being the selection of a husband. This is a common blunder with women who have children. How many young men would become useful but for this very thing; they are hedged in on all sides by men of blunt feelings, of rough natures and of a lack of appreciation that ought to be given to the aspiring hopes of children. With his mother's advice, he resolved to make his escape from this paternal slavery far worse than the other. Promising to return to his mother in due time, he started from home late one afternoon, carrying with him a smaller brother. They had no money and only a pound of bacon and a corn ash cake. Their mother was not a Christian, but they felt while on their journey that their mother was praying for them. After some hardships the boys reached Winnsboro, a town of fifteen hundred inhabitants, thirty-five miles distant. Being poorly clad, they found some difficulty in getting employment. On the second day, however, he got a place for himself and his brother. He was at this time in good circumstances, and completing a course in music at one of our leading colleges, Mr. Crosby entered school, working at odd times for support and paying for tuition by ringing a school bell. He soon got to be president of a debating club and teacher of the only colored Sunday school in town. Having joined the Union league, and becoming prominent in the county politics, he was appointed in the spring of 1869, by Governor R. H. Scott, the census taker for Fairfield county. He entered Biddle University in the fall of 1869 and the Shaw University in 1870, graduating from the latter in 1874. He has since graduated from the National School of Elocution and Oratory, being the first colored man who ever graduated from this famous institution. Mr. Crosby resolved to enter the ministry; his first work in this line was done in the summer of 1872 as a student missionary under the auspices of the American Baptist Home Mission Society of New York. He was assigned Mecklenburg county as a field of labor. During the four months after the commission was given him he raised two hundred dollars for the First Baptist church of Charlotte and eighty dollars for Shaw University, besides organizing a church at West Holly, North Carolina, which has now a large and flourishing congregation. In 1874 he was ordained and took charge of the first Colored Baptist church of Warrington, North Carolina. In 1875 Mr. Crosby was elected delegate from Warren county to the State Constitutional convention, which framed the present constitution of the State. He took an active part in the deliberations and vigorously opposed by speeches and vote every ordinance aimed directly or indirectly at his race. In 1880 he was called to the Dixonville Baptist church of Salisbury, and during the same year became principal of the State Colored Normal school, located at the same place. These two important positions he still holds. He has also been moderator of one of the largest Baptist associations in North Carolina since 1881. He is chairman of the Home Mission board of the North Carolina State convention and editor of the *Golddust,* the organ of the colored Baptists of the State. He is connected with numerous other positions, boards and business enterprises.

To name and give an account of all the honors conferred and positions bestowed upon this worthy son of the old North State would occupy more space than can be allowed in a book of this size. He has baptized more than twelve hundred persons. Mr. Crosby occupies a place in the front rank as a preacher. He is one of the most popular and successful men in his denomination, which numbers more than one hundred and ten thousand in this State. Notwithstanding his charitable habits, he is worth more than four thousand dollars—the fruits of his own toil. He has risen by degrees from poverty and obscurity to one of the most honorable stations in the State.

CHAPTER LIII

Hon. Francis L. Cardoza
*Secretary of State—State Treasurer—Professor of Languages
—Principal of the High School, Washington,
District of Columbia*

He was born at Charleston, South Carolina, January 1, 1837, and was sent to school at five years of age, where he remained until he was twelve. He was then apprenticed to the carpenter's trade for five years, after which he worked as journeyman for four years. When he was twenty-one years old he left the bench and with one thousand dollars, which he had saved as a journeyman, started for Glasgow, Scotland, to obtain a collegiate education, to which he aspired. His ultimate aim was to prepare for the ministry. He studied four years at the University at Glasgow, and three years at the Presbyterian seminaries at Edinburgh and London. The cost of his education was about three thousand dollars, in addition to one thousand dollars, which he had saved before starting. Notwithstanding he was pursuing these courses, he worked during vacations at his trade and other employments, making about one thousand dollars. In a competitive examination among the graduates of four colleges, he won a scholarship of one thousand dollars, and then removed to London, England, and finished the remaining two years of his course. This was a very remarkable feat, and in this respect I think he stands almost alone. But this was not all. While at the university at Glasgow, he won the fifth prize in Latin, among two hundred students in his class, and the seventh in Greek among one hundred and fifty students. He returned to the United States in the summer of 1864, and was settled as pastor of the Temple Street Congregational church in New Haven, Connecticut, August 1, 1864. The American Missionary Association of New York requested him to establish and take charge of a Normal school of colored pupils in Charleston, South Carolina, August 1, 1865, which he accepted and presided over for three years. In this time he was noted as a scholar of rare attainments, and though a very quiet, unassuming man, he was not neglected or overlooked by his friends, who elected him a member of the Constitutional convention of South Carolina in January, 1868, estab-

FRANCIS L. CARDOZA

lished under the reconstruction acts. August the first, of the same year, he was elected secretary of State and served four years. Now while he was serving his first term as secretary of State, he was elected professor of Latin at Howard University. He resigned the position of secretary and accepted the professorship. The governor of South Carolina protested against his resignation, and suggested that he retain the office and appoint a deputy secretary of State. As Mr. Cardoza had only fourteen months to serve, this was finally agreed upon. He then taught at Howard until March, 1872, and returned to South Carolina at the earnest solicitation of his friends, to accept the position of State treasurer, to which he was elected August 1, 1872.

After he had served out the first term of the treasurership, he was reelected in 1876, but the downfall of Republicanism at that time prevented the exercises of the duties of the office. The transfer of the Republican State government of South Carolina and Louisiana to the Democrats by a *coup d'état* is perfectly familiar to all. During his treasurership he handled between six and seven million dollars and eight million in bonds and stocks. His books were carefully and thoroughly examined by a committee of the Democratic Legislature after his term of office expired, with an expert accountant, and they reported his books correct. He was appointed to a clerkship in the Treasury Department at Washington, District of Columbia, by Secretary John Sherman, in 1878, and remained for six years, when he was appointed principal of the Colored High School of Washington, District of Columbia, which position he now holds. The school has an enrollment of about two hundred and fifty pupils—two hundred females and fifty males, nearly all of whom are preparing for teachers. The work is of very great importance; is far-reaching in its influence, as these shall go out from his care to manage schools in the several sections of this country. Mr. Cardoza was married to Miss Catherine Romena Howell of New Haven, Connecticut, December, 1864. They have been blessed with six children—four boys and two girls, both of whom died in infancy. Mr. Cardoza is an educator of very fine talent; is very dignified in bearing, and polished in his manner. He was my professor in Latin while a junior in college, and I remember him as a courtly gentleman who treated his classes with the greatest of kindness. It never occurred to me that I might publicly thank him for his kindness and patience with two fun-loving students, especially one.

JOHN S. LEARY

CHAPTER LIV

Hon. John S. Leary, LL. B.
Attorney at Law—Legislator—United States Deputy Collector

North Carolina is well represented by the intelligent, progressive and popular John S. Leary, who was born at Fayetteville in that State, August 17, 1845. His parents were named Matthew and Julia Leary. His father was born in North Carolina in 1797; his grandfather was Aaron Revels, who was a free colored man and a Revolutionary soldier in the American army. His mother was born in France, and was six years old when her parents came to this country in 1810. Mr. Leary had a brother by the name of Louis Sheridan Leary, who was with John Brown at Harper's Ferry and was killed there October 17, 1859.

The subject of this sketch attended school in his native town for a period of eight years prior to the civil war. During the time he was under the care and instruction of six different teachers, five of whom were white persons, and one a colored woman. After quitting school he learned the trade of a saddler and harness-maker in his father's shop, who was a manufacturer, and carried on that business for fifty years in Fayetteville. The steady habits and business qualities of Mr. Leary, combined with strict honesty, purity of life and fidelity to trusts, made him a very popular man among all classes of citizens; and in the year 1868 he was elected, from Cumberland county, a member of the Legislature of the State of North Carolina. Having served with satisfaction to all his friends for two years, and having the good will of the opposing party, showing great intelligence and deep foresight into the laws, and promptly attending to every duty connected with the office, made him a very strong candidate for the second term, to which he was elected and served with singular ability until the close of the session. In 1871 he went to Washington, District of Columbia, and entered the Law Department of Howard University, from which he graduated with the title of LL. B. Here he was a favorite with the members of every department of the institution; his gentlemanly manners, his politeness and high intellectual attainments gave him the confidence and good will of all. The writer remembers him at this period, being at that time a member of the university. After graduation, he returned home and was examined by the State Supreme Court, and admitted to practice in all the courts of the State, since which time he has continued in his profession. He was alderman in the town of Fayetteville for two years, namely, 1876–77. He was school committeeman for a period of four years, both for white and colored schools of the town, namely, 1878–79–80–81. He has attended as a delegate from Cumberland county every Republican State convention since the year 1867; was alternate delegate to the National Republican convention held at Chicago in 1880, and delegate to the National Republican convention held at the same place in 1884.

Mr. Leary was appointed United States deputy-collector for the fourth district of North Carolina, Internal Revenue Department, May 1, 1881, which position he held for four years, going out of office when Mr. Cleveland became President of the United States. In the book published for the benefit of the State in the way of bringing emigrants thereto, Mr. Leary is given mention as one of the leading men of the State. It says of him that he is a man of influence among a large circle of people in the city of Fayetteville and the State, and is well suited to hold positions of trust; and in the Legislature of 1868 to '70, he voted with the minority against the fraudulent bonds. He is president of the North Carolina Industrial Association; he is an Odd Fellow, having joined the order in 1875, and was a delegate to the A. M. C., which assembled in Richmond, Virginia, in 1880. As honorary commissioner for the State of North Carolina, for the colored department in the World's Cotton Exposition, held in New Orleans in 1884, he did much to show forth the industrial condition of the colored people. He is a member of the Protestant Episcopal church, having been confirmed in 1867. He has been married twice; his first wife was Miss Alice B. Thomas of Raleigh, North Carolina, who died October 13, 1880; the fruits of this union were two children, both dead. His present wife was Miss Nannie E. Latham of Charlotte, North Carolina, to whom he was married July 14, 1886. He has a comfortable home in the city, a splendid law library, and a small farm about two and a half miles from the city. With these surroundings he dwells in the midst of people who delight to honor him.

CHAPTER LV

E. S. Porter, A. B., M. D.
Physician on the Sanitary Force of Louisville, Kentucky—
Medical Attendant at the Orphans' Home and State University
—Lecturer

This quiet, unassuming gentleman has made his mark as a dispenser of wisdom in the line of the healing art. It was said of Æsculapius "that he was of a quick and lively genius, and made such progress that he soon became not only a great physician but was reckoned a god and inventor of medicine, and is said to have restored many to life. And Jupiter is said to have feared that men, being put in possession of the means of triumphing over death, might refuse honor to the gods; so he struck Æsculapius dead with a thunderbolt, for which Apollo, the father of Æsculapius, destroyed the Cyclops that forged the thunderbolt for Jove." It used to be the colored people who, taking the place of Jupiter, slew all colored physicians, so to speak. Though these men had enlisted themselves in doing good for mankind, their traducers would declare that there were none good; no, not one. There seems to be among the same class of our people a very foolish notion that nobody but a white man can be a competent doctor, lawyer or professional man of any kind. This may be owing to their training, but it is time that they had gotten out of such thoughts, for by holding such opinion they unwittingly confess judgment and attribute the lack of skill in these matters to the inferiority of the race and color rather than brains. And notwithstanding the difficulties which colored physicians meet in attempting to practice, or rather, I might say, had met (for many of these foolish prejudices are passing away), many have risen to eminence.

Dr. Porter has succeeded in building up an extensive practice, and still lives. The life of a doctor is full of instances worthy of record, and while their professional deeds of mercy are many, they go "unhonored and unsung." Their losses also are heavy, and they can never refuse to answer a call, for the ethics of the profession lead them to relieve suffering at all times, pay or no pay.

E. S. PORTER

He is the son of Jesse and Priscilla Porter, and was born in the State of Delaware, October 19, 1848. This was the place of his youthful days, for not until he was fourteen years of age did he leave that "little monarchy" to make his way in the world. Thence he went to New York. Through the influence of a lady who took much interest in him, he was led to undertake a classical course at Lincoln University, Oxford, Pennsylvania. He began at the bottom rounds and through seven years he made his way to the graduating platform, where he was awarded his degree of Bachelor of Arts. This was in 1873. Going back to New York, he entered the Brooklyn Medical College, completing the full course of medicine, anatomy, surgery and hospital practice, and graduated with some distinction in his class in 1876. While looking for some place to practice, he wandered to the west and settled in Tennessee for one year. Not finding it to his liking, he moved to Louisville in 1878, and has there made a splendid reputation and settled the question of lack of prosperity in the practice of medicine. Contrary to the usual way, we have yet to find a colored person who has no confidence in him as a physician. His practice is extensive and constantly increasing.

He was elected on the sanitary force of Louisville in the years 1882, '83 and '84. He was chosen physician to the Orphans' Home by the proper authorities in 1882, which position he still holds. He is also physician to the State University, and also lecturer on physiology and hygiene in the same university. This position he has held since 1881, and to the satisfaction of all concerned.

He was married to Miss Lucy Bohannon, March 20, 1884. She is one of the prominent members of the celebrated Fifth Street Baptist church choir, and contributes very much to his success by her amiable manners, and she presides over his home with dignity and grace.

The doctor himself is a genteel, refined man, and all who know him love him. He is a special favorite with the children, a thing to be commended—for no child ought to be afraid of a doctor or a minister. His ability has never been questioned by the practitioners in the city. He has sat in counsel with Drs. E. D. Foree, William M. Griffith, Thomas J. Griffith and P. G. Trunnell. It would not be an exaggeration to state that his future is very brilliant and his chances for wealth very favorable.

AUGUSTUS TOLTON

CHAPTER LVI

Rev. Augustus Tolton
The First and Only Native American Catholic Priest
of African Descent, through both Parents, on the Continent

A few months ago it was flashed over the wires that Augustus Tolton had been ordained to the office of priest in Rome. The papers took up the news and sang the praise of the man who had by perseverance climbed to a strange, new position for one of his nationality. Many men of note have simply drifted with the current into positions held by a father, but this man attracts us because the circumstances under which he achieved eminence were far from the beaten paths made by the steady tramp of hundreds who had gone before. The career of Rev. Augustus Tolton is one of difficulties surmounted.

The subject of our sketch was born in Ralls county, Missouri, April 1, 1854, of slave parentage. His father, Peter Tolton, enlisted in the Union Army when the civil war broke out, and died in the hospital in St. Louis. His mother, Martha Jane Tolton, a Kentuckian by birth, made a bold stroke for life and freedom shortly after. After much planning, the day of decision came. Taking the babe of twenty months in her arms, a daughter of nine years, and little "Gussie" of seven to trudge by her side, she journeyed night and day through almost desolate regions and over almost impassable roads, with the swift feet of a hunted deer. Having crossed two counties her feet almost touched free soil, when new danger arose. On the banks of the Mississippi at Hannibal, they were challenged as runaway slaves, but some Federal soldiers interposed and smuggled her across the river that night. Pausing long enough to draw one breath of free air, the pilgrims dragged their weary limbs twenty-one miles farther to Quincy, Illinois, the town in which he was reared and from which he was called to Rome. Cradled amid such events, schooled during such a period, drinking aspirations from such a mother, mighty energies and impulses were sown for future reaping. Mrs. Tolton found no hand to help feed the hungry mouths. She was surrounded by poverty so grinding that at the age of seven her boy was put in a tobacco factory and for twelve years filled his father's place in providing for the younger children.

During this period at odd times, when the factory would close, in winter, and nights when others were sleeping, he would be poring over books, mastering this and that study. In 1872 his health failed, and acting on the advice of friends he gave up the factory work, and devoted his time exclusively to study. The children were sent to St. Boniface's and St. Peter's schools (white), but some race trouble arising, they withdrew and entered Lincoln, a non-Catholic school. The pastor of the church of which Mrs. Tolton was a member, Father McGirr, hearing of the difficulty, ordered their withdrawal and opened his own school to colored children. This was about 1863. As time passed, a wild hope took possession of Augustus. His soul longed for the holy office of a priest, and on the day of his first communion, when Father McGirr, who had watched year after year the exceptional purity, talent and goodness of the poor boy up to that time, suggested the priesthood, his cup of joy was full—his mind made up. Rev. Father Astrop and Rev. Theodore Wegmann believing firmly that his vocation should be that of a priest, urged his Latin studies, and instructed him, together with two German students, in Latin, Greek, German, English, etc. He was considered the best in the catechism class when he first communed, and now reads and speaks German as fluently as English. All seemed smooth sailing when suddenly his instructors are called to new fields of labor. Are his hopes to be dashed to the ground? No; in the dispensations of Providence we get what is needed at the right time. A priest in Northern Missouri hearing that Mrs. Tolton would make him a suitable housekeeper secured her services, promising to keep the son in his studies. The bargain proved a bad one, and mother and son were soon back in Quincy, the latter hard at work with the soda firm of J. J. Flynn & Company, and studying before and after hours only as an ambitious youth can, assisted by Father Reinhardt, in charge of St. Mary's church and hospital, and two Franciscans, Fathers Francis and Engelbert. Although the Franciscan College threw open its doors to him, poverty prevented him attending except early and late, after school hours, and then it was always a race with time, first to the college, then to the hospital, and then to the rectory chasing knowledge. The heavens for him were again overcast. Rev. Reinhardt departed for another field; Father Engelbert could not keep the appointments any longer. With his feet in the path to Propaganda College, Rome, he could not turn back. An opening was soon made. Says the St. Joseph's Advocate:

All credited the Rt. Rev. Peter Joseph Baltes, late bishop of Alton, to which diocese Quincy belongs, as having sent Augustus Tolton to the Propaganda College; but Father Tolton himself speaks of a prior credit as due to the Franciscans, and as having the higher claim to his gratitude. He names first of all in this connection the Rev. Father Michael Richardt, O. S. F., formerly of Quincy, but now of Teutopolis, Illinois, who sends this valuable letter in answer to our inquiries:

St. Joseph's Diocesan College,
Teutopolis, Effingham County, Illinois, March 12, 1887

Rev. and Dear Sir:—

I am in receipt of your esteemed favor of the eighth inst., by which you solicit information about Rev. August Tolton, the first colored priest of this country. I made the acquaintance of Mr. August Tolton, at Quincy, Illinois, about the year 1877. I then had formed the intention to do something for the spiritual welfare of the colored people at Quincy. I found Mr. August Tolton to be a pious, modest and studious young man, and requested him to aid me in my undertaking, as I was not acquainted with any body of the colored population. Soon he had a number of children together, both of Catholic and Protestant parents, whom I commenced to instruct in the Catholic religion every Sunday. The first lessons I gave them in the parochial school-house of St. Francis' congregation; but, in a short time, for convenience sake, we located our Sunday school in the centre of the city. The colored children liked it so well that a proposition I made to them to open a free day school was hailed with joy. Always assisted by Mr. August Tolton and his worthy mother, an accomplished lady and devoted Catholic, I soon had a schoolroom in an abandoned schoolhouse of St. Boniface's congregation, both Rev. J. Janssen, the rector of St. Boniface's congregation, and good Catholics assisting me to furnish the same. At my request, the Rev. Mother Caroline, superioress of the Sisters of Notre Dame at Milwaukee, appointed, gratuitously, Sister M. Herlinde to teach the school, which we opened with twenty-one children. Notwithstanding the opposition and indignation meetings of the Methodist and Baptist colored congregations, we soon had forty children, and within the next year had, with the help of God, the happiness of solemnizing several times baptisms, first communions, confirmations and marriages. When I, compelled by overwork and nervous prostration, had to leave Quincy, the school was closed for some time, but was re-opened by Rev. Theodore Bruener, then rector of St. Boniface's church, and is ever since in existence, and yet conducted by the same faithful and zealous Sister M. Herlinde, assisted by a candidate. Rev. Bruener secured also, not without the help of the Franciscan Monastery of Quincy, Catholic worship for the little colored congregation in the same schoolhouse, which had been a Protestant church. Rev. August Tolton has at present charge of the whole little and difficult mission.

Here you wish to know how it happened to pass that Mr. August Tolton became a priest and who directed him to Rome. As far as I know, I conceived that idea first and communicated it to the (late) Right Rev. Bishop P. I. Baltes. When, soon thereafter, that prelate made his visit *ad limina Apostolorum*, he tried to get the young student, Mr. A. Tolton, into the Propaganda, but in vain. I then wrote to our Most Rev. Father General, Most Rev. P.

Bernardino, a Partu Rometino, who resides at Rome, and he succeeded in securing Mr. A. Tolton's reception into the College *De Propaganda Fide* where he soon thereafter began and finally ended his studies. I had last summer the happiness to see him a priest in New York City, just on his arrival from Rome. May it please Divine Providence to achieve much good through Rev. A. Tolton for the salvation of the colored race in this country.

With the greatest respect I am, Dear Sir, yours in Christ,

P. MICHAEL RICHARDT, O. S. F.

Rector of St. Joseph's Diocesan College, Teutopolis, Illinois

Spending several years there, he returned to the United States, after having finished the course of study, bearing the honors of priesthood and receiving a warm welcome from the inhabitants of Quincy, where he is laboring. Says the Washington *People's Advocate:*

The arrival in this country of an American-born black priest of the Roman Catholic church, marks an era in the work of this church for the evangelization of the Negro. To-day an ex-slave returns from Rome to perform the priestly office in his native land, an evidence that the Eternal church, whatever the popular belief as to its variable policy "all things to all men" has planted its foot firmly against caste in the priesthood. Father Tolton is but the advance guard. We look forward to see the day when the colored priests of the Catholic church will be as numerous, proportionally, as those of any other denomination, and when one in whose veins flows the blood of the land of St. Augustine, will chant the *pater noster* before the altar of his memorial, the St. Augustine church of this city.

When the ordination of Father Tolton was proclaimed, a few secular journals discredited the statement that he was the first native Africo-American set aside to the priesthood. They claimed that years previous Bishop England proclaimed the first colored priest at Charleston, South Carolina. The *St. Joseph Advocate*, a quarterly, of January, 1887, published by Father J. H. Green, Baltimore, Maryland, in the interest of the colored people of the United States, after much research says:

How easy to slip on historic ice! Not a shred of probability that a Charleston bishop with only one or two small churches at his See, would or could afford the expense and risk of educating one for the priesthood, who, by the constitution and laws of South Carolina, would not be allowed to cross the border! There is a tradition among Catholics in Charleston that a priest of color on board a vessel bound for South America, and which, by stress of weather was driven into that harbor, was spared the honor of a police escort to the felon's hotel by the great influence of Bishop England, who got permission to hold him in charge till his vessel got ready for sea. Even this is stoutly denied by one who ought to know a thing or two, who resided in the very house of the bishop at the time, and is still living, a nonagenarian in her perfect senses! Monsignor Corcoran does not believe one word of the Father

Paddington story in relation to Charleston; and who knows more about the past of his own city than the learned Dr. Corcoran? Certainly no other Catholic living, except it be the Rev. P. G. McGowan, now of Arkansas, who resided in Charleston sixteen years, dating back all the way to 1831, many years living with the great bishop on the banks of the Ashley, and there ordained by him. Here before us is a letter from this venerable priest dated the fifteenth instant, in which he says, "As to the ordination of a black priest by Bishop England of pious memory, in Charleston, and residing there, there was no such thing. So *nothing of the kind took place in my time nor since I left*. It seems to me that Bishop England ordained some colored priests in San Domingo or Hayt, while visiting there two or three times in the performance of legatine duties for Pope Gregory the Sixteenth, of pious memory, who held him in great esteem." Bishop England took possession of that new See on the last day of 1820, so our search for the needle in the bundle of straw which hadn't it, from the year of his return to Ireland, "on a visit to his native city, Cork," till the arrival of Father McGowan, is brought down to a pretty fine point indeed (a point of time wholly inadequate to the education and ordination of anybody) by this valuable letter, which covers every inch of the chronological space back to 1831. Will our contemporaries who have copied that fiction for history be good enough to make the *amende honorable* by sending this messenger in pursuit.

And then gives also the following notice:

... And so we have in our midst to-day a colored priest, a native American, once a slave and the son of slaves, one of the *ante bellum* "four millions" said to be incapable of education, moral habits and what not, upon which assumption their degradation was boldly justified; no hybrid, but the genuine article; a typical Africo-American, the very one of all others we long to see chosen; not your ideal octoroon if possible, quadroon at the most, Caucasian in chiseling, Semitic in coloring, a pinch-nosed, thin-lipped and straight-haired "look-at-me," as if picked out for a compromise because of his proboscis and not of his brains, to show well on a perch with that degree of gamboge which comes nearest to whitewash when the stubbles are removed, and he slips out like a peeled onion, spruce, tidy, oil-tongued, a "nice young man," slippery and sanctimonious, of course. Nothing of the kind is Father Tolton, as our *perfect facsimile* of his photograph shows; the *vivid and striking* likeness of a solid man, true as steel, without a shadow of pretension, well up in his sacred duties, able to converse and preach in more than one language, humble as a child, boasting of his African blood, and all aglow with devotion and love for his race. As he passes through the streets of Quincy, white gentlemen raise their hats, and priests at tables take back seats to give him the place of honor. We have seen it; not once or twice, but almost *every* time—MANHOOD! And on the part of the laity, what a plain *act of faith* in the power and wisdom of Christ's Spouse on earth, which *can* and *will* elevate the lowest above the highest and invest him with a dignity above that of the greatest earthly potentate!

CHAPTER LVII

William Wells Brown, Esq.
Author—Lecturer—Historian of the Negro Race—
Foreign Traveler—Medical Doctor

———◆•◆———

Lexington, Kentucky, has the honor of giving to the world one of the most illustrious and earnest men, who did much in his lifetime to distinguish himself as well as to make known the virtues of the race, their origin and history, and marked for special mention a few of its eminent sons and daughters. Born of slave parents in 1816, he was in youth taken to St. Louis, Missouri, and was hired to a steamboat captain. After a year or so he was put in the printing office of Elijah P. Lovejoy. Going off on a steamboat, he escaped North. In 1834 he took to boating again, and aided many a slave to Kansas while acting as a steward. In 1843 he accepted an agency to lecture for the Anti-slavery Society and continued his labors in connection with that mission until 1849, when he took a trip to England. When it was understood that he was going to England, the American Peace Society chose him to represent them at the Peace Congress held in Paris. The executive committee of the American Anti-slavery Society gave him strong recommendations to distinguished people in Britain. He set sail for England, July 18, 1849; arriving at Liverpool, proceeded at once to Dublin, where he was warmly received and given a public welcome. He spent many years in Europe and had considerable attention paid him. He was an admirable public speaker, and charmed large audiences at the Peace Congress in Paris and in many gatherings in London. At this congress Victor Hugo presided and Richard Cobden, Esq., and such distinguished men paid him flattering attention. Mr. Brown is known as an author and lecturer. On one occasion he visited his native State to speak in both of the National associations for the support of temperance, and on the schools among freedmen. After holding a meeting at Louisville he started on a trip to speak at Pleasureville and was met by a colored man who told him that the meeting was five miles in the country. Following the man, they started to walk the distance, having waited a long time for a conveyance that was said to be coming for them. After some time they heard horses coming before and behind them. He was finally captured by a number of Ku-Klux and carried to a house where a man, presumably one of their party, was afflicted with the *delirium tremens*. The doctor's wit not forsaking him, he said he could cure the man; that he was a dealer in the black art and well acquainted with the devil. Having his doctor's case with him, he asked if he might be permitted to go into a room by himself for a while, which was granted. While in there he charged his syringe with a solution of acetate of morphia, and put the instrument in his vest pocket. Returning to the room he requested the aid of these men to hold the sick man while he made passes upon him, as if mesmerizing him; very quickly injecting the solution with his needle syringe into the man's leg, it was but a short time before he was quiet. This produced a wonderful impression upon them and saved his neck. His power having already been displayed, the leader of the band, who was called "Cap," was also suffering from a pain in his thigh. The doctor offered to cure him, if he would retire with him to the other room, which was done. While in there he injected the solution into "Cap" who soon fell asleep. All but one went away, giving him but a few hours to live, and leaving one man, who was full of whiskey, on guard. This one soon fell asleep and the woman of the house knowing that they had set four o'clock as the time to hang the doctor, kindly called the dog in, which the doctor had been wondering how to dispose of, and told him to leave, which the doctor was not long in doing. He got to town and took the morning train to Louisville, and decided never to return to that neighborhood again.

The doctor is an author of many books, among which may be mentioned *Sketches of Places and People Abroad*, published in 1854; a drama entitled *Doe Face; the Escape or Leap for Freedom; The Black Man*, published in 1863, which ran through ten editions in three years; *Clotelle*, a romance founded on fact, one of the most thrilling that was ever written, the *Negro in the Rebellion*, published in 1866; *The Rising Sun* in 1874, and numerous other works. In this last work he has given a sketch of the race beginning with the Ethiopians and Egyptians, describing the slave-trade of Hayti and the republic of Liberia; John Brown's raid on Harper's Ferry; proclamation of Freedom; the blacks enlisted in battle; the abolitionists and representative men of the race. His services to the race cannot be estimated. Few men have done as much by their writings as he to elevate and instruct his people. His books were very extensively read and brought quite a large sum of money, many of them running through more than ten editions.

CHAPTER LVIII

Professor Walter F. Craig
Solo Violinist—Orchestra Conductor

He was born in Princeton, New Jersey, December 20, 1854. His parents, Charles A. and Sarah E. Craig, moved to New York City in 1861, where he entered the Grammar school No. 4, Mrs. S. J. S. Garnet, principal. He graduated in 1869. He was always apt and smart in school. He was especially bright in mathematics, grammar, history, drawing, etc., and was the leading singer of the school. He commenced the study of violin playing and music in 1868, and made his debut before a New York audience as a violinist at a concert in Cooper Union in 1870. From that time he rapidly improved, and organized the orchestra known as "Craig's Orchestra" in 1872. He then gradually worked his way to the rank of a first-class musician and conductor, and now enjoys the honor of being the representative colored violin soloist and musical director of the race. His orchestra is quoted as being second to none, and his fame as a soloist extends throughout the entire United States and also some foreign countries. He has performed and conducted in all the principal cities, such as Boston, Philadelphia, Brooklyn, Providence, Newport, New York, Trenton, Scranton, Pennsylvania; Wilkesbarre, Pennsylvania; Washington, D. C.; and Baltimore, Maryland; and all through the States of Maine, New Hampshire, Connecticut and other New England States. He has appeared in the most prominent concerts in the city of New York, and with all the greatest colored talent, such as Madame Selika, Mrs. Nelly Brown Mitchell, Adelaide G. Smith and Flora Batson; and with such eminent male voices as Mr. L. L. Brown, the famous basso; Mr. William I. Powell, the celebrated baritone and humorist; Thomas Chestnut, the famous tenor. Mr. Craig is also a composer of music, and has given great attention to harmony under the best teacher in this country, Mr. C. C. Muller, a German. He has a large number of compositions, and has arranged music in every form, both vocal and instrumental, and is concert master of the Mendelssohn School of Music, and is the first and only colored conductor who is a member of the Musical Mutual Protective Union of

New York City, of which such men as T. S. Gilmore, Dr. Damrosch, Cappa and Theo. Thomas are associate members. His orchestra and himself are unrivaled at present in the country. He is also a manager of some repute in New York City, and has given and managed some of the most noted musical affairs ever put upon the stage in the great metropolis. When he appeared in Lexington Avenue opera house, October 29, 1886, the New York *Freeman* said of this distinguished musician:

Professor William F. Craig, the young prince of Negro violinists, mounted the elevated platform and waved his bow over the twenty musicians, and his enthusiastic admirers let forth a perfect storm of applause. The music was of the very best, and judging from the constant applause the musical appetites of the audience could not be easily appeased.

When he appeared in Steinway Hall, January 20, 1887, the New York *Herald* said:

Mr. W. F. Craig, the violinist, is well known to New York audiences as a perfect master of his instrument. His performances of the *Fantaisie of Faust* and De Beriot's *Seventh Air Varie* were marked by exquisite harmony, firm yet delicate.

September 20, 1886, the New York *World* pays a compliment to Mr. Craig as follows:

Walter F. Craig, who is from home visiting a sick relative, is the musician of the race. He was the first colored man who joined the Musicians' Protective Union of this city. He is a composer and violinist and leads an orchestra reputed good.

He is about twenty-seven years old, and was graduated from the Seventeenth Street Grammar school. His orchestra furnished the music for the grand dramatic festival and full dress ball at the time when Mr. J. A. Arneaux appeared in the complete cast as Richard III, October 29, 1886, at Lexington Avenue opera house.

It can be seen from these testimonials that Mr. Craig has a reputation that is not without a true basis. Ranking very high in the scale of musical eminence.

CHARLES L. PURCE

CHAPTER LIX

Rev. Charles L. Purce, A. B.
President of the Selma University, Selma, Alabama

In 1856, at Charleston, South Carolina, Mrs. Ellen Purce, the wife of William Purce, gave birth to Charles L. Purce, the subject of this sketch. His mother was a slave and his father hired her time in order that she might be able to live with him. In youth Mr. Purce had very many trials and hardships, consequent upon his parents' poverty. At fourteen he learned a trade. In 1875 he was converted and immersed by the Rev. Jacob Lagare. In 1878 and '79, he attended Benedict Institute, under the tuition of Rev. Lewis Colby, D.D., and graduated from the Richmond Seminary after four years' study under the teaching of Rev. Charles H. Corey, D.D. His class numbered fourteen. Two of that number went to Africa as missionaries, the Rev. J. J. Coles and the Rev. J. H. Presley. After graduation, in 1883, he held the pastorate of a large church of eleven hundred members at Society Hill, South Carolina, which he resigned to accept the chair of Greek and Latin at the Selma University, at Selma, Alabama, November, 1886. Since his graduation he has studied Hebrew, and taken a supplementary Greek course through the Correspondence Bureau. He is a hard student, and has made it the aim of his life to be always studying and learning a portion of his time every day. His motto is naturally *Dies Sine Linea*. The most of his education he paid for himself by hard work, both in and out of school and often consoled himself with the thought that if he could, with the many hardships which he had, he would educate himself. Surely many of those young people who have more opportunities need not stay away from school or fall short of equipping themselves for life's battles. He delivered the Baccalaureate sermon at Lincoln Normal University, the State Normal, at Marion, Alabama, June, 1884. It was the best ever delivered there. The chairman of the board complimented him by saying it was "Bullion's Grammar," meaning thereby that it was a specimen of grammatical and literary excellence. He has a wife and one child. He was married in Philadelphia, by the Rev. William C. Dennis, January 7,

1885. On the resignation of E. M. Brawley, D.D., he was promoted to the presidency of the Selma University by the unanimous vote of the board, which was endorsed unanimously by the General Convention of the Baptists of the State of Alabama. The position which he now holds gives assurance of a wide field of extended usefulness both for himself and for the university. He is a man of strictly temperate habits, very quiet in his demeanor, earnest in his purposes and devoted to the causes which ought to be of interest to all. He has good influence over the students who admire him for the perseverance with which he has risen from poverty to a position of influence and usefulness. His life ought to be a lesson to every student. It ought to be an inspiration to every poor boy and none need despair. Though the road be hard, there is hope for all as is proven by the career of Mr. Purce. His scholastic habits, sound judgment and diligent application to business gives assurances of a magnificent future. Let Alabama take pride in her distinguished president who shall preside over the destinies of many of her future sons and daughters.

CHAPTER LX

Alexander Dumas
Distinguished French Negro—Dramatist and Novelist—
Voluminous Writer

Very few colored people know Alexander Dumas as one of the family, not being thoroughly acquainted with the absence of colorphobia in foreign countries. He has become so distinguished that his name enters into the ranks of the *litterati* without question as to color, and no one asks what his color is, but simply refers to his works. The prolific French novelist and dramatist was the son of Alexander, who was himself the son of Marquis Davy de la Pailleterie and a Negro girl, Louisa Dumas of San Domingo. The mother of Dumas was named Marie LaBouret, an innkeeper's daughter, who was very fair, and it is a fact that some of the most tender and touching lines of his memoirs are those which refer to the boyhood days when she cared for him. It is truly remarkable what part the mothers play in the history of men's lives. It is said that the father of Demosthenes was a blacksmith; Euripides, a dealer in vegetables; Socrates, a mediocre sculptor; Columbus, a woolcarder; Shakespeare, a butcher; Cromwell, a brewer; and of Linneus, a poor country minister; but the greatness of these men has been accorded by those who speak of them, to the gentility of their mothers.

The family was very poor, and about 1826 he entered Paris, where he was destined to do such marvelous literary work as would astonish its citizens. By looking at several authorities, there seems to be a difference of opinion as to what is bad among his writings, but it does not materially interfere with the facts, and does not, therefore, play much part in what I am about to say. At fifteen he was a clerk; at eighteen he began writing; he wrote much, but at first received no praise nor compensation for his work, but in 1826, when he was only twenty-four years old, his fame as an author began with the *Nouvelles*. In 1829 he put on the stage an historical play *Henri III, et sa cour,* which met the sharpest shafts of the critics because he disregarded all the stage proprieties of the times, but gained the applause of the populace and brought thousands to his purse.

The Duke of Orleans led the applause, and so pleased and interested was he in this play when put upon the stage that he appointed Dumas as his librarian.

Dumas was now on the topmost wave of success. His best known works are *Les Trois (The Three Musketeers)*, in eight volumes, *Monte Cristo*, twelve volumes, and *Le Reine Margot*, six volumes. Much of his literature is classed as immoral. It might be considered immoral in America, but certainly is not considered so in France, and perhaps the times in which he lived had something to do with the character of his writings. Whatever may be said of him, his name cannot be omitted from the triumphs of literature. It is said that his name is attached to over twelve hundred separate works. Says the *American Encyclopedia:*

> In 1846 he made a contract to furnish two newspapers with an amount of manuscript equal to sixty volumes a year, and this exclusive of his plays and other productions. Such fecundity raised the question whether he was really the author of the books attached to his name. A lawsuit in which he was involved in 1847 with the contractors of the *Presse and Constitutionnel*, brought to light the fact that he had engaged to furnish these journals with more volumes than a rapid penman could even copy. But though he made liberal use of the talents of assistants, he claimed sufficient share in the plan and execution of all the work to make it truly his own, and the judicial decision finally supported his claim. Herein the generosity of Dumas is shown, for it was his custom whenever a poor author with no reputation desired his assistance he often gave him a plot, drawing all the outlines and scenes, and permitted him to work it up, after which Dumas put his name to it and the poor author reaped the pecuniary benefit. There is another Dumas, the son of the distinguished dramatist, now living in France, who was born July 28, 1824, and who has inherited some of his father's talent. He was elected a member of the French Academy in 1875. He is the result of a union between his father and Ida Ferrier, an actress of Porte Saint Martin, in 1842.

Sketches of all three Dumas will be found in various places, but of the father of this younger Dumas see the *American Encyclopedia, Encyclopaedia Britannica, Chamber's Encyclopedia,* and a sketch of the *Life and Adventures of Alexander Dumas,* by Perry Fitzgerald, in 1873.

CHAPTER LXI

Rev. William Reuben Pettiford
A Successful Pastor—Trustee of Selma University

This popular and influential pastor deserves mention for the trouble he has had to overcome and make his life successful. Hard, persevering labor and strong faith in the Almighty has wrought miracles for him, and through him, many things. He was born in North Carolina, Granville county, January 20, 1847. His parents, William and Matilda Pettiford, were free, and consequently he followed the condition of his parents, and was free. While a boy, he had little opportunity more than getting a few lessons on Saturdays and Sundays; at ten years of age he could read very well. His parents sold their little farm and removed to Person county, North Carolina, where he had the benefit of private instruction, by which a fair knowledge of the common branches was obtained. Being the oldest child, a part of the burdens of the family were placed on his shoulders; but all the time he continued his studies and would get help here and there from individuals. The rigorous duties of the farm were indeed a heavy task, but, nothing daunted, only served as the means to rise in the hands of this struggling young man. Those days seem now as many of the best; they toughened his muscles, gave him confidence and patience. With all this he has become an ambitious and hard working minister. Converted July 4, 1868, and baptized August 3, 1868, by Ezekiel Horton, in Salisbury, North Carolina, that life was begun which made of the rude farmer boy an apostle of Christ and an upright, honest man. Soon the place of clerk to the Pleasant Grove church of which he was a member was vacant, and he was elected to the vacancy by unanimous vote. July 4, 1869 the young man was married to Miss Mary Jane Farley, daughter of Joseph Farley.

Scarcity of business forced him to change his place of residence from North Carolina to Selma, Alabama, December, 3, 1869, where his knowledge of farming and books secured him work near Uniontown, not only as a farm hand but as a teacher. Affliction came to him in the loss of the partner of his bosom on March 8, 1870, only about eight months of mar-

WILLIAM REUBEN PETTIFORD

ried life having been enjoyed. This determined his course in getting further education; with a slender purse but strong arms and a full heart, he entered the State Normal school at Marion, Alabama, and remained seven years, teaching in vacations to secure the necessary means to pay expenses the following year. Once illness came on and the term opening, found no money on hand with which to commence; but nothing daunted, a job of work was sought; a garden was found in which he worked hard two and a half hours before and after school at ten cents an hour. This enabled him to get through the year with only nine dollars debt. This seems a clear demonstration of the fact that if parents will teach their children some kind of work while young, it will help them to rise in the world. It is also evident that his knowledge of farming brought him from the barn-yard to the pulpit; from the "country school" to a membership of the Board of Trustees of a university.

His church membership was now with the Baptist church at Marion, Alabama, where he gained favor with the brethren by attending prayer meetings and conducting revivals, and was licensed to preach March 6, 1879. July 24, 1873, he was married to Mrs. Jennie Powell at Marion, Alabama, who died September 5, 1874. For the second time he was afflicted, for after a short season of connubial bliss she departed this life. As principal of the school at Uniontown, assisted by the Rev. John Dozier and Mrs. Florence Billingslea, his faithful laborers, the gentleman had great success, which, however, was resigned in 1877, so he might enter college and finish his education. Here his course was successful until 1878, when the trustees at Selma Institute, now a university, elected him a teacher at twenty dollars per month, with the privilege of studying theology under Brother W. H. Woodsmall, who was the president; this he accepted, but added to these duties the privileges of those of sub-agent. In November, 1879, the Board at the State Convention in its session at Opelika, elected him general financial agent; this was well done, for more funds were collected than ever before. During the first year, contrary to the unanimous wish of the trustees, he resigned to accept the pastorate of Union Springs, Alabama. November 23, 1880, he was again married, to Miss Della Boyd, a daughter of Richard and Caroline Boyd of Selma, Alabama.

He received a letter of dismission from the First Baptist church of Marion, Alabama, and united with the St. Philips Street Baptist church, at whose request he was ordained to the Gospel ministry, November 21, 1880. Rev. W. A. Burch, then pastor, preached the ordination sermon; Rev. W. H. McAlpine gave the charge. These took part also with Revs. H. Stevens and John Dozier in the laying on of the hands after a rigid examination, assisted by Brother H. Woodsmall. He then moved to Union

Springs, and here his first work was to release a church of a large debt and to repair and refit the edifice. The membership also was largely increased. At this place his first heir, Carry Bell Pettiford, was born, September 22, 1882. During this time he continued pursuing the study of theology under private tuition and was principal of the city school. On the last Sabbath of February, 1883, he resigned this charge to accept a call to the Sixteenth Street church at Birmingham, being urged to accept it by many of the leading men of the State, who represented to him that he could render the best service to the church in the larger field which this great progressive city afforded. The church at Union Springs refused to accept his resignation, and the pulpit was not permanently filled until the year after. When he took charge in Birmingham, there was only a membership of about one hundred and fifty, and the church was holding services in a down-town store room; while the debt amounted to five hundred dollars. His first effort was directed to canceling the debt and erecting a building suitable to present needs and to future growth. This was a work of no light undertaking. Being cordially received by all classes of citizens, he was much encouraged in the work. By August, 1884, the indebtedness was all paid off, and a building fund raised. August 18, the first stone for the new structure was laid, and on the ninth of November services were held in it. The collection on that day amounted to a large sum. The building is large, being 40 x 80, and substantially built, and when completed will prove an ornament to the architectural beauty of the city. Up to the present writing there has been seven thousand dollars paid upon the property, and on account of the recent rise in property in Birmingham, the building could not be purchased in its present locality for twenty-five thousand dollars. The total membership of the church is now four hundred and twenty-five.

His family consists of wife and three children. His wife is a lady of education, full of energy and push, and in all his labors contributes very largely by way of encouragement and material help. At present he is president of the Ministerial Association in Birmingham, and also a member of the trustee board of Selma University; president of the Negro American Publishing Company, publishing the *Negro American Journal* of that city.

Materially he has prospered; the wonderful growth of that city and rapid advancement in the price of real estate have benefited him so that his property on Sixteenth street is valued at eight thousand dollars. Besides this he has half interest in another piece of real estate of which the total valuation is placed at twenty thousand dollars. The reverend gentleman has always so comported himself as to gain the recommendation of the State officials and of all with whom he associates. Of him

Brother H. Woodsmall says, in a letter of recommendation to the American Baptist Home Mission Society:

I take special pleasure in commending Rev. W. R. Pettiford, pastor of the Colored Baptist church, Birmingham, as a minister worthy of the Christian regard and confidence of all whom it may concern. I have known him during the past eight years; he was assistant teacher and a pupil in the Alabama Baptist Normal Theological school at Selma about three years, during the time I had charge of that institution. He was for quite awhile financial agent of the school and collected a large amount of money. He not only made a successful agent but faithfully accounted for all monies collected. He was equally faithful as a missionary, and I have always found him a man of admirable spirit, as well as honest and trustworthy. His influence can but be good in any community where he may labor. I regard it as a specially fortunate thing for the Baptist cause that he is pastor of one of the leading churches in Birmingham at this time.

No man in the United States has better means of knowing the general worth of Southern ministers than the brother who writes the above letter. He has lectured to more colored ministers in the South in any one year than perhaps any other Southern missionary has in any five years, and his testimony is acceptable in every district in the South where he has labored.

CHAPTER LXII

Hon. Robert B. Elliott
Congressman—Eloquent Orator—Distinguished Disciple
of Blackstone

The most scholarly Negro in any of the United States Congresses was the Hon. Robert Brown Elliott. His fame has been heralded to all quarters of the globe. He was a man of ability and unquestionable intelligence. His eloquence and logic carried his hearers into transports of joy, and swept his enemies before him like chaff before the wind. South Carolina sent more Congressmen to Washington than any Southern State—Rainey, Ransier, Smalls, Cain, DeLarge—but Elliott was easily chief in learning, knowledge of law and the arts of debate.

This distinguished lawyer, orator and member of the United States House of Representatives, was born in Boston, Massachusetts, August 11, 1842. His parents were West Indians who had settled in this country. While a boy, he attended private school in his native city. Shortly after this he was sent to the Island of Jamaica, where he had superior advantages in the grammar schools. Thence he was sent to England, and in 1853 he entered High Holborn Academy, London. Three years later he was admitted to the celebrated Eton, one of the colleges of the University of London, from which he graduated with high rank in 1859. Adopting the law as a profession, he began study under Sergeant Fitz Herbert of the London bar. He soon returned to the United States and began the foundation of that illustrious career which made him the centre of attraction. His eminent teachers, travels in Ireland, Scotland, South America and the West Indies, had broadened his views of life and ripened his understanding.

Choosing South Carolina as his home, he commenced his life work there as a printer on the *Charleston Leader*, which afterwards became the *Missionary Record*, owned by the lamented and eminent Bishop R. H. Cain, D.D. Soon Mr. Elliott became editor, and his powers were shown in the masterly articles he produced. When Congress began the reconstruction of the South, Elliott's eloquence and wisdom was in demand in

South Carolina. He was elected to the convention from the Edgefield district. For fourteen days after the Constitutional Convention had met, he said not a word. This was his first public service under the election of the people, but when he did speak, it was the making of him. After the adoption of the Constitution he was elected from Barnwell county to the Lower House of the State Legislature, serving from July 6, 1868, to October 23, 1870. The governor of the State appointed him assistant adjutant-general of the State, March 25, 1869, which he held until elected a representative from South Carolina to the Forty-second Congress of the United States as a Republican, receiving 20,564 votes against 13,997 votes for J. E. Bacon, a Democrat. He served until March 4, 1871, when he resigned. During this sesion he made a most excellent impression on the country; nailed Beck, the member from Kentucky, to the wall, tingled the ears of Harris from Virginia, sent the following shaft full in the face of Alexander Stephens and drove him from the House. Said he:

I meet him only as an adversary, nor shall age or any other consideration restrain *me* from saying that he now offers this government, which he has done his utmost to destroy, a very poor return for its magnanimous treatment, to come here to seek to continue, by the assertion of doctrines obnoxious to the true principles of our government, the burdens and oppressions which rests upon five millions of his countrymen, who never fail to lift their earnest prayers for the success of this government, when the gentleman was seeking to break up the union of their States, and to blot the American Republic from the galaxy of nations.

I will give a passage taken from a very fine "Eulogy on the Life and Public Services of R. B. Elliott," delivered by Professor D. A. Straker, LL.D., Columbia, South Carolina, September 24, 1884. Mr. Straker was formerly a law partner of Mr. Elliott, and is competent to speak of his life:

There was none abler to defend the rights of the Negro race against the opposition of Georgia's famous son than Robert Brown Elliott. This legislative battle for equal rights was an event in the history of the United States—nay, of the world—never before witnessed. There stood in the halls of Congress the representatives of divergent principles and conflicting ideas about human rights. There stood slavery and freedom, the advocates of rights for the white man only and the advocate of equal rights for all citizens before the law. Face to face stood the Anglo-Saxon and the undoubted African. The issue was before them; the contest began. Mr. Stephens was brought in the House in the accustomed manner—in his chair. He was even in such a condition looked upon as a giant among the Democratic Philistines. He severely arraigned the constitutionality of the Civil Rights bill and its policy, as did Mr. Beck of Kentucky and Mr. Harris of Virginia, who indulged in great bitterness of speech. At the close of Mr. Stephens' speech in the House of

Representatives, now filled in every possible manner with United States Senators, who had suspended their labors to witness this sight, foreign ministers, judges, lawyers, clergymen, scientists, authors and the laity innumerable, all were there to witness the political miracle, and if God was God to worship Him, and if Baal was God to worship him. Eager eyes were fixed, doubting hearts pulsated with accelerated motion, when at last Mr. Elliott arose and in reply to Mr. Stephens, said: "Mr. Speaker: While I am sincerely grateful for the high mark of courtesy that has been accorded me by this House, it is a matter of regret to me that it is necessary at this day that I should rise in the presence of an American Congress to advocate a bill which simply asserts rights and equal privileges for all classes of American citizens. I regret, sir, that the dark hue of my skin may lend a color to the imputation that I am controlled by motives personal to myself in my advocacy of this great measure of natural justice. Sir, the motive that impels me is restricted by no such narrow boundary, but is as broad as your Constitution. I advocate it, sir, because it is right. The bill, however, not only appeals to your justice but it demands a response to your gratitude. In the events that led to the achievement of American independence, the Negro was not an inactive or unconcerned spectator. He bore *his* part bravely upon many battlefields, although uncheered by that certain hope of political elevation which voctory would secure to the white man. The tall granite shaft, which a gratified State has reared above its sons who fell in defending Fort Griswold against the attack of Benedict Arnold, bears the name of John Freeman and others of the African race who then cemented with their blood the corner-stone of your Republic. In the State which I have had the honor in part to represent, the rifle of the black man rang out against the troops of the British crown in the darkest days of the American Revolution." In these words every man saw the greatness, the ability, and the patriotism of the speaker. Mr. Elliott then continued his speech, addressing himself to the legal, constitutional, political and social features of the Civil Rights bill, in which he completely annihilated the Georgia statesman. He then paid his attention to Mr. Beck of Kentucky, who had during the debate endeavored to cast odium upon the Negro, and to vaunt the chivalry of his own State, little thinking that there was in a Negro's brain or intelligence a foeman in retort worthy of his steel. Mr. Elliott reminded the Kentucky statesman that in the second war of American independence General Jackson reported of the white Kentucky soldiers that "at the very moment when the entire discomfiture of the enemy was looked for, with a confidence amounting to certainty, the Kentucky reinforcements, in whom so much reliance had been placed, *ingloriously fled*." And, with the culture of a well-skilled debater, Mr. Elliott then turned to Mr. Beck and said: "In quoting this indisputable piece of history, I do so only by way of admonition, and not to question the well-attested gallantry of the *true* Kentuckian, and to suggest to the gentleman that *he* should not flaunt his heraldry so proudly while he bears this bar sinister on the military escutcheon of his State—a State which answered the call of the Republic in 1861, when treason thundered at the very gates of the Capital, by coldly declaring her neutrality in the impending struggle. The Negro, true to that patriotism that has ever characterized and marked his history, came to the aid of the government in its effort to maintain the Constitution. To that government he now appeals, that Constitution he now invokes for protection against unjust prejudices founded upon caste."

He was re-elected to the Forty-third Congress as a Republican, receiving 21,627 votes against 1,094 votes for W. H. McCan, Democrat, serving from December 1, 1873, to May, 1874, when he resigned to accept the very lucrative position of sheriff. In the second Congress of which he was a member, he delivered, April, 1871, his famous and long-to-be-remembered speech on the "Bill to Enforce the Provisions of the Fourteenth Amendment to the Constitution," or better known as the "Ku Klux Bill." May 30, 1872, he again wrestled with the giants and smote them "hip and thigh." Voorhees and Beck felt the sting of his words when he hurled the most fitting rebuke at them after they had made strictures on the financial condition of the State government of South Carolina. He returned home and was elected to the Legislature again. General Elliott made some mistakes in life in being easily deceived by men who used his talents to prop their tottering fortunes. Mr. Straker said:

But although himself unstained by any charge or charges by any court, he did not forget his political associates less fortunate, and whenever one was found in the coils of Democratic accusation, he freely gave what assistance he could to his release, both as a lawyer and a former political friend. In this service he did not stop to ask whether the Republican in trouble was his friend or not. Frequently it happened that he was his bitterest political foe and detractor of his just merits; yet he stood by him in his hour of trial, and gave him what advice he could. He was counsel in several cases in which these political trials occurred, and yet a few base detractors would rob him of his good name. And why, sir? Because "base envy withers at another's joy, and hates that excellence it cannot reach." When the din and roar of Democratic political persecution had ended, and the fire of their revenge had been quenched, General Elliott's public life still remained untouched by legal accusation. Mr. Elliott then ceased political life and continued the practice of his profession, contenting himself with the pleasant recollection of having done his public duty faithfully and impartially.

In 1881 General Elliott was appointed by Hon. John Sherman, secretary United States treasury, special agent of the treasury, with headquarters at Charleston, South Carolina. As a delegate to the National Republican convention at Chicago, June, 1879, he seconded the nomination of John Sherman for President of the United States. When, therefore, Garfield fell by the hand of the assassin, a change of administration threw him out of office, though he had been first transferred to New

Orleans, Louisiana. He re-entered his profession there, having a branch office in Pensacola, Florida, conducted by Messrs. DeTucker & Thompson. He was a very brilliant Mason, and did much to re-establish its societies in South Carolina. He laid down his life in the city of New Orleans, August 9, 1884, 11 P.M., and was buried with ancient rights and ceremonies, on Sunday, August 10, 1884. The *Plaindealer*, Robert Pelham editor, said of him:

With Robert B. Elliott has passed away one of the brightest types of American manhood and Negro capability. He was a model of the possibilities of a race; pushing against the tide of opposition, he reached an eminence in scholarship and oratory which is enjoyed by a few only. He was qualified to meet the demands of the times and grasp them. This he always did. In the halls of Congress he held the representatives spell-bound by his eloquence. In his social life he was affable and courteous. He was a born leader, made so by indomitable will and untiring energy. In his passing away, he leaves an influence that will inspire many to persevere, and his teaching will continue to develop nobler and truer conceptions of an exalted manhood, such as would be worthy to occupy the position before the American people that he has filled so creditably.

Eloquent men pay tribute to eloquent men, and hence "The Old Man Eloquent" pays the following tribute to General Elliott, in the *New York Globe:*

Living as I have done, in an atmosphere of doubt and disparagement of the abilities and possibilities of the colored race, early taught that ignorance and mental weakness were stamped by God upon the members of that race, Robert Brown Elliott was to me a most grateful surprise, and in fact a marvel. Upon sight and hearing of this man, I was chained to the spot with admiration and a feeling akin to wonder.

There was no doubt as to complexion, form or feature. To all outward seeming, he might have been an ordinary Negro, one who might have delved as I have done, with spade and pickaxe. Yet from under his dark brow there blazed an intellect worthy of a place in the highest legislative hall of the Nation. I have known but one other black man to be compared with Elliott, and that was Samuel R. Ward, who, like Elliott, died in the midst of his years. The thought of both men makes me sad. We are not over rich with such men, and we may well mourn when one such has fallen. I, with thousands who knew the ability of young Elliott, was hoping and waiting to see him emerge from his late comparative obscurity and take his place again in the halls of Congress. But alas! he is gone, and we can only hope that the same power that gave us one Elliott will give us another in the near future.

FREDERICK DOUGLASS

CHAPTER LXIII

Professor Inman Edward Page, A. B., A. M.
Principal of Lincoln Institute—Oratorial Prize Winner
at Brown University, Providence, Rhode Island

Professor Page was born under the yoke of slavery in the town of Warrenton, Fauquar county, Virginia, December 29, 1853. His parents were named Horace and Elizabeth Page. In early childhood he exhibited strong moral affections which have grown as he has advanced in years; although often placed under the control of persons who were in the habit of drinking intoxicating liquors, yet his invariable practice was to refuse when such liquors were offered him. This habit of total abstinence he has carried from childhood into manhood, and he has become a man of soberness as well as sobriety. Horace Page moved his family to Washington, District of Columbia, in 1862. The opportunity here presented itself to Inman, and he was sent to the private school of Mr. George F. T. Cook, which he attended a little over three years, and where he made a good record. He was hired out for several years, and in this way helped to support the family. During this time he attended night school taught by the later Professor George B. Vashon, from whom he obtained an elementary knowledge of the Latin language. Soon after the opening of Howard University, young Page resolved to enter it as a student. His father being unable to pay for him, he went to the university and applied for work which he obtained immediately. At that time the university grounds had not been graded and the authorities were willing to employ industrious students to do the work. Although quite young and unaccustomed to this kind of labor, Inman, nothing daunted, full of ambition, went to work as an ordinary laborer at the rate of fifteen cents per hour. He continued to work in this way until the beginning of the summer vacation, when he, with a few other students, decided to continue this work during the entire vacation. His zeal for study soon gave him a promotion to a janitorship, which he held until he was placed in charge of the university building. When General O. O. Howard was closing the affairs of the Freedmen's Bureau, Page was employed as one of his clerks.

INMAN EDWARD PAGE

In this way he was enabled to attend the university until 1873. In the fall of 1873 he entered Brown University, at Providence, Rhode Island, he and his friend George W. Milford being the first colored students to enter that institution. Although he met with considerable prejudice, both from students and professors, he continued to struggle and at the close of the sophomore year succeeded in winning a prize in an oratorical contest, which established his claim for recognition; and to emphasize their endorsement, his classmates selected him to write a history of the class in the junior year. Towards the close of that year he was selected by the faculty to deliver an oration at the junior exhibition, which was pronounced by the *Providence Journal,* a leading newspaper in Providence, Rhode Island, "the ablest oration of the day." The impression made upon his white classmates by his scholarship, his orations and the "History" of the junior year, made him a prominent candidate for the position of class orator at the close of the senior year. Although a member of a class of over fifty white students which contained many brilliant young men of the best New England families, yet Inman E. Page, the Negro, was unanimously chosen to fill the position for which the ablest students were accustomed to struggle every year. This was a triumph indeed. He delivered an oration which attracted general attention, not only because of the ability evinced, but also because he was the first young man of color who had been selected by white young men to wear such an honor. The subject of the oration was the "Intellectual Prospects of America." While he was delivering his oration, Professor D. W. Phillips, now of the Roger Williams' University, Nashville, Tennessee, was sitting in the audience. Soon after the exercises were over he stepped up to him and offered him a position in the Natchez Seminary, Natchez, Mississippi. Mr. Page graduated with the degree of A.B. in the fall of 1877 and entered upon the duties of his position in the Natchez Seminary, where he gave satisfaction to the American Baptist Home Missionary Society, which employed him, and the colored people of Mississippi who were interested in the institution. At the close of his year's work he went to Providence, Rhode Island, where he married Miss Zelia R. Ball, a young lady of fine promise, who had graduated in 1875 from the Wilberforce University of Xenia, Ohio.

In 1878 he was employed as a teacher in the Lincoln Institute, Jefferson City, Missouri. For two years he was the only regular colored teacher in the instittue, but at the close of his second session the board of trustees decided to place the school in the hands of colored teachers, with Mr. Page at its head. To those who thought the change an experiment, there was no confirmation of their opinions, nor were they made ashamed. Mr. Page succeeded in raising the enrollment from ninety-seven to one hundred and fifty-three the first year, and reduced the expenses to students by introducing the "club system." He secured appropriations from the Legislature with which to build a dormitory for young men, costing seven thousand eight hundred dollars, and one for young ladies costing nine thousand dollars, and other appropriations aggregating about three thousand dollars. He also secured biennial appropriations by his solicitations and addresses before the Legislature from ten thousand to sixteen thousand dollars.

In 1880 he received the degree of A. M. from his Alma Mater, Brown University. In 1883 Mr. Page was made president of a convention called to meet in Jefferson City for the purpose of organizing a State teachers' association in Missouri, and was afterwards elected president of the association for three successive terms.

A Springfield paper, published by white men, speaking of Mr. Page, says:

He is now only thirty-two years of age and ranks with the most scholarly and cultivated men in Missouri, white or colored. Lincoln Institute was never so prosperous as during his presidency. His addresses abound in happy hits and salutary advice to his race. Large audiences are not only edified but captivated by his scholarly eloquence and simplicity of speech. He carried in himself one of the finest illustrations of what a thorough education can do for a colored man.

On the fifth of January last he was elected president of a conference of leading citizens in Jefferson City for the purpose of memorializing the Legislature for an industrial school, and for more advanced educational facilities for the colored youth of the State. In the summer of 1885 he was invited to read a paper before the white teachers of Missouri on the educational needs of the Negro in Missouri, which made such a marked impression that he was unanimously elected an honorary member of their convention, receiving a vote of thanks and a pledge that the association would use its influence to promote the interest of Lincoln Institute. At the recent teachers' association held in St. Louis, P. H. Murry, of the *St. Louis Advance,* paid him the following compliment:

He succeeded in proving at this convention his eminent fitness, both in culture and moral force, to preside over the educational interest of colored youth of Missouri. Races do not produce great men in very rapid succession. There may be many brilliant men, but with defects so apparent that their brilliancy is overcast with a cloud, and men who are possessed with native ability, can bring their culture, their moral character and habits of industry bravely to the front, side by side, and evenly developed, have the elements of success and usefulness, which brilliancy alone cannot secure. What the Negroes need among the educators of the State is a man of deep convictions, high sense of duty, unswerving will force and eminent culture; a man whose presence commands respect, and such a man we verily believe is Professor Page.

I have known Professor Page for many years, and can bear personal testimony to his greatness of heart, to the generosity of his feelings, and his deep sense of responsibility to God. While a student in Howard University he was converted and united with the Baptist church, with which he has ever held pleasant relations; his manly bearing, dignified demeanor, and cultured mind bear rich fruits, and his personal enthusiasm impresses those under his care to such an extent that they cannot fail to become useful citizens and prominent individuals. This, however, can only be attained personally by those who have the privilege as well as the honor to sit at his feet and have at least a great blessing, and are considerably helped toward the attainment of those things which befit them for useful lives. But the best of men have their enemies, and Professor Page has had his trials like all men. The following, taken from the *Jefferson City Daily Tribune,* is as fine an indorsement as any man would need. It is an honorable document and deserves a place here, and it speaks more eloquently than anything I might say:

The following testimonial of the regard and high esteem in which the citizens of this place hold Professor I. E. Page, both as a private citizen and the head of Lincoln Institute, should serve as an ample refutation of all the false reports trumped up by mischievous and meddlesome people to injure his standing and that of the school among the colored people of the State:

"Inasmuch as certain false and injurious reports have been published concerning the management of Lincoln Institute, and derogatory to the high standing of Professor Page and wife, we, the undersigned, feel that some testimonial is due the public in this regard, and cheerfully subscribe to the following facts:

"Professor Page and his wife have resided in this city eight years, and for six years the institute has been under their management. During this time the work of the school has been improving from year to year and has been at all times better than under any former management.

"Professor Page has labored earnestly and with marked success for the upbuilding of Lincoln Institute. He has extended the couse of study, increased the attendance and secured from the State large sums of money for the support of the school. He is an educator of ability and high intellectual attainments, a gentleman of refined manners and a sincere and earnest Christian, possessing at once the respect and good will of the best citizens of this city. We see no cause for complaint either against Professor Page or his wife. Their influence has always been exerted for the best interests of Lincoln Institute and the elevation of the colored race.

NAMES

"Arnold Krekel, president board of regents; L. C. Krauthoff, vice-president board of regents; R. E. Young, M. D., board of regents; Oscar G. Burch, board of regents; Jesse W. Henry, board of regents; W. E. Coleman, State superintendent public schools; W. T. Carrington, editor Missouri *School Journal*; Fred Rommel, J. S. Fleming, banker; A. Brandenberger, pharmaceutist; H. B. Church, merchant; J. A. Thomas, George W. Dupee, G. Branham, Howard Barnes, A. McCreary, T. C. Capleton, August Kroeger, deputy county clerk; W. H. Lusk, clerk Circuit Court, Cole county; Nelson C. Burch, attorney at law; John T. Craven, merchant; Jacob J. Peets, Hiram King, Wm. G. McCarty, post-master; F. J. Fromme, Wm. W. Wagner, sheriff of Cole county; W. Q. Dallmeyer, Louis Wolferman, merchant; James Hines, Harry Collins, J. M. Tompkins, C. A. Dixon, John A. Lindhardt, merchant; Archie Drake, John Gordon, C. C. Branham, Henry Bolton, Harrison Ramsey, sr., board of trustees, A. M. E. church; W. H. Jackson, barber; Phil. T. Miller, Jr., D.D.S.; Warwick Winston, D.D.S.; Jas. E. McHenry, D. H. McIntyre, ex-attorney-general; Robert McCulloch, register of lands; Prosser Ray, Nathan C. Kouns, O. W. Gauss, pastor Presbyterian church; Hugo Monnig, Rudolph Dallmeyer, C. B. Oldham, J. H. Edwards, A. C. Shoup, R. E. Oldham, superintendent public school; Thos. M. Cobb, pastor M. E. church; J. M. Hays, J. L. Moore, J. W. Carter, C. W. Thomas, W. W. Hutchinson, S. W. Cox, H. Nitchy, S. P. Lewis, pastor Baptist church; John Delahay, John H. Dirck, J. A. Thomas, G. A. Fisher, J. T. Thorpe, physician; P. T. Ellis, L. C. Lohman, Jack Scott, H. M. Ramsey, Jr., D. W. Anthony."

CHAPTER LXIV

Rev. E. K. Love
From the Ditch to the Pastorate of Five Thousand Christians—
Editor of the Centennial Record of Georgia—*Associate*
Editor—Honored of God

He was reared a slave and had no educational advantages before the Emancipation; he worked on the farm until 1870. He was born July 27, 1850, in Perry county, near Marion, Alabama. Being very anxious for an education he quit the farm at the time mentioned, and in 1870 entered Lincoln University, Marion, Alabama. After studying one term he reached the highest class except one in the school. He found he had learned many things imperfectly. He left this school and returned to the farm in 1872, and from that to ditching, accumulating by this means enough money to leave home again; therefore, November 17, 1872, he went to Augusta, Georgia, where he entered the Augusta Institute, under the late Rev. Joseph T. Robert, D.D., LL.D. Previous to this he was licensed to preach, and December 12, 1875, at Augusta, Georgia, he was ordained. He was baptized into the fellowship of the Siloam Baptist church by the Rev. W. H. McIntosh, for whom he had a great attachment. In the Augusta Institute he gained the front rank in his classes; he entered the lowest, but soon reached the head of the first class which he led until he finished school in 1877. Under the auspices of the Home Mission Board of New York and the Georgia Mission Society he was appointed missionary for the State of Georgia; this position he filled to the entire satisfaction of all concerned. July 1, 1879, he resigned and took charge of the First Baptist church of Thomasville, Georgia. The house of worship was repaired during his stay there, and four hundred and fifty persons baptized. October 1, 1881, he left this church and accepted the missionary position of the State of Georgia, under the auspices of the American Baptist Publication Society. This position he held for some time and gave entire satisfaction. October 1, 1885, he resigned and accepted the postorate of the First African Baptist church at Savannah, Georgia. Since he has held that church he has baptized eight hundred and ninety-three persons. This church numbers five thousand members. He has held many positions of trust and honor among the brethren of his State, has been an assistant teacher at one time under Dr. Robert, and has taught three public schools. He has been appointed editor of the *Centennial Record* of the Negro Baptists of Georgia, which will be read at their first centennial meeting in 1888. He is also associate editor of the *Georgia Sentinel*, a Baptist paper printed at Augusta, Georgia. He is considered an eloquent speaker and deep thinker; has strong affections and is certainly persistent in pressing his views. He has the honor of holding perhaps the largest church in the United States, and perhaps in the world. To be able to do this great work is evidence conclusive of his possessing eminent power over men. His position is one that makes him as especially favored of God who has called him to this exalted station.

CHAPTER LXV

J. A. Arneaux, Esq.
Professional Tragedian, "Black Booth"—Editor—Poet—
Graduate of the French Institutions of Learning

———•◆•———

The father of J. A. Arneaux was Jean Arneaux, a Parisian by birth. His mother was named Louisa Bell before her marriage, and was of French descent. Young Arneaux was born in the State of Georgia in 1855, and is therefore only thirty-two years of age; he is still a young man and is destined to rise to a wonderful eminence in his profession. He is following fast in the footsteps of the late lamented Ira Aldridge, the great impersonator and remarkable actor. He is of hedium height, fair and handsome. He often in a joke says he was born handsome, traded it off for a fortune, and is now bankrupt of both. This is by no means true. His manner is winning and his conversation learned, filled with wit and humor. He is an enthusiast in his profession, and as he has the material which will develop greatness in any department of life, it would be strange if he did not accomplish very much should life be spared to him. His accent is slightly tinctured with a flavor of French, and one would imagine himself in the presence of a Frenchman who spoke English tolerably well. His movements are graceful and have the polish of a Parisian. No doubt he takes these qualities from his father and inherits them from his mother's blood. He attracts by his jovial good fellowship, but nevertheless is weighty in argument and as skilful with the pen as with the sword in his masterpiece (Richard III). Losing his mother early in life, when only twelve years of age, he lost the tender care of her faithful hand and the tenderness of her love.

In 1865 he attended the first public school in his native city where he only learned his a, b, c's; next attended a small private school where he learned the fundamental branches. Then entering Beech Institute, he graduated after close application for four years. Then it occurred to him to go North and seek a better education. His parents had owned some property, but it had not yielded very much, so he was forced to work and pay his own expenses. In New York he was a student in German, Latin

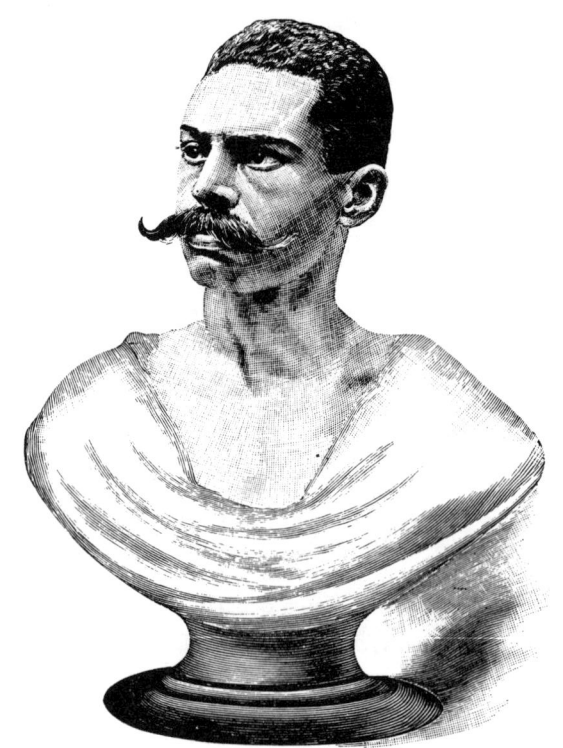

J. A. ARNEAUX

and other kindred studies. Being ambitious, he next went to Providence, Rhode Island, where he entired Berlitz School of Languages and mastered French.

While a school boy in the lower grades he had a reputation for special excellence in the English studies, and was a good speller, easily mastering hard words which troubled others. His success was phenomenal at the Berlitz school, for he secured the head of the class with ease, after only a short time. He then visited Paris, and took two courses, one in the Academie Royal Des Inscriptions et Belles Lettres et Morales et Politique. On his way to New York returning home, he stopped at London and saw many of the sights and scenes worthy of visitation. After much study he appeared as a song and dance artist, and filled engagements at the celebrated Tony Pastor's Metropolitan theater on Broadway, New York, as well as at the old Globe theater.

Mr. Arneaux's first appearance in legitimate drama was in 1876, at the Third Avenue theater, where he appeared as Tom Walcott, a Southern planter, in a drama of Southern life called *Under the Yoke,* or *Bond and Free.* Although he had read Shakespeare, it was not until the spring of 1884 he took to study for the stage. He began after being repeatedly urged by a theatrical manager, with the character of Iago, in which he made his debut at the Brooklyn Atheneum, June 17, 1884. The *New York Daily News,* commenting on his acting, said:

Mr. J. A. Arneaux, as Iago, surprised even his most ardent admirers with this difficult character to portray. He did what was his to do in a manner which proves beyond question that he possesses a keen preception of the cunning and craft necessary to a faithful copy of the accomplished villain. The whole play was Iago, and Mr. Arneaux's interpretation the best and truest in the entire cast.

Thus encouraged he formed the first Shakespearian troupe of colored tragedians, now known to fame as the Astor Place Tragedy company. Under Mr. Arneaux's management this company appeared at several of the leading theaters in the city, including the Academy of Music. But it was not until 1885 that Mr. Arneaux's ambition was triumphantly crowned, when he appeared for the first time to advantage in Shakespeare's tragedy of *Richard III.* His *debut* in *Richard III* was in a contest for a gold medal given to amateurs for excellence by the *New York Enterprise.* At this contest the prize was awarded to him by the *New York Sun,* the newspaper men being judges upon the occasion. His next appearance in *Richard III* was in Providence, Rhode Island. Shortly after returning to New York he was tendered a testimonial reception and a banquet by the leading men and women of his race. In this testimonial he played Richard III and was crowned by a committee of ladies with a wreath of laurels, and an address was made in his behalf by an eminent professor.

On the twenty-ninth of last October, Mr. Arneaux appeared in the Lexington Avenue opera house, and the following criticisms were made by prominent journalists. The Baltimore, Maryland, *Director*, says:

We have seen him in the difficult role of the Duke of Gloster, we have also seen Macready, Booth and Barrett in the same character, and we are free to say that Mr. Arneaux's conception of the character, his superb management of the part he assumed, were perfect.

The *New York Clipper* has said:

Mr. Arneaux is the rising star of the race.

The *New York Sun* said:

Mr. Arneaux scored success as Richard the Third and carried off the prize:

"Mr. Arneaux," said the *New York Daily News*, "merits the title of 'Black Booth.'" January 29, 1887, he played to a most refined and elegant assembly of people in the Academy of Music, in Philadelphia. *The North American* gave the following criticism:

In his conception of the title role, Mr. J. A. Arneaux followed in most respects that of the best of living exemplars of the part, Mr. Edwin Booth, and he could not have taken a better model; but Mr. Arneaux is evidently not satisfied with being a mere imitator, for there were certain features both in his reading and in his manner that showed originality. His walk, for instance, was something peculiarly his own, and if it apparently lacked the silent dragging of the foot of the generally translated morose and cruel Gloster, its rather flippant step was in accordance with his well-sustained theory that Richard was a villain whose humors rapidly changed from wicked to jocose. It was in this spirit of merriment that Mr. Arneaux made Richard take the audience in his confidence by a lightness of phrasing after each of his gravest deeds that showed the insincerity of Richard's good professions.

The idea is a novel one and most effective. The evenness of Mr. Arneaux's performance, and his accurate recital of the lines, deserve great praise and showed earnest and careful study.

A correspondent of the *Philadelphia Gazette* and special correspondent in Philadelphia for the *Cleveland Gazette* said:

The most effective and artistic scene given by Mr. Arneaux was the love-making with Lady Anne. In so passionate and natural a manner did he portray Gloster's well-concealed subtilty in his declaration to Lady Anne, and his supreme vanity upon his success in winning her, with such skill and pleasing inflection, that his ability as an actor was beyond question. But it was not until Richard was aroused from his dream by the terrifying visitations of the ghost of the murdered King Henry, that the audience were made fully aware of the wonderful talents of this brilliant young actor. It is useless to go into detail of this scene; suffice to say that his rendition of it stamped him a man of great promise.

Mr. Arneaux has been employed at different times as a writer on the staff of the *New York World,* and is at this time engaged in writing sketches of the leading editors and educators for the Sunday edition of *The New York Sun* and the *New York World.* In 1884 he was employed upon the last named journal, and resigned to take the associate editorship of the *Literary Enterprise.* He soon became the editor and changed the name to the *New York Enterprise,* when he became sole proprietor. His office was burned out December 14, 1886, since which time the paper has been suspended; but while it was alive it was one of the best and most ably conducted journals in the country. In this paper he advocated the total abolition of the word color, and the substitution thereof of the word Africo-American, and has induced many to adopt this word in their editorial work. He also advocated industrial schools, which can be seen in a pamphlet read at the Sailors' and Soldiers' Reunion, recently held at Dayton, Ohio. He also advocated an African Historical Society for the purpose of preserving the writings and deeds of the colored authors and prominent persons in the race. He has written several poems, one as a tribute to Wendell Phillips; also an epic poem upon General Grant at Appomatox. This poem was the subject of a prize which was offered in a contest among several young colored aspirants, and at the same time secured much praise and comment for its rhetorical composition as well as the subject matter. He has issued a pamphlet of *Richard III,* adapted for amateurs and the drawing room. He entered and graduated from the New York Grand Conservatory of Music and Elocution, where he gave diligent and ardent study for the purpose of completing his preparations for the stage. The future of Mr. Arneaux is in his own hands, and if he continues to succeed, will yet immortalize himself and bring credit and honor to the race.

We attach here a correspondence which will explain itself and show his immediate purpose:

MR. ARNEAUX AND THE MANHATTAN LEAGUE

J. A. ARNEAUX, ESQ.—ESTEEMED SIR: Being apprised of your intention of retiring from the stage for a period of two years for the purpose of studying—thus equipping yourself thoroughly for your noble calling—we, the undersigned members of the Board of Governors of the Manhattan League, beg to evince our appreciation for what you have already accomplished and applaud your resolution by tendering you a farewell testimonial and banquet and reception at any hall you may designate and any time that will suit your convenience. And beg to further request that you afford us the pleasure of witnessing upon the same evening a performance of a part or the whole of your favorite Shakespearean play. Hoping you may win your way to the realm of immortal fame, we remain yours admiringly, Rufus Hurburt, chairman; Charles Brodie, secretary; C. R. Dorsey, J. E. Garner, W. Landrick, Frederick Banket.

NEW YORK, April 5

To the Members of the Board of Governors of Manhattan League—Rufus Hurburt, Chairman:

DEAR FRIENDS:—It affords me the greatest pleasure of my life to accept the token of high esteem you so generously offer me, and hope ere my race of life is ended to fully merit the bounteous honors you have bestowed upon me. I shall be pleased to have the testimonial take place at Clarendon Hall on the evening of April 29, and, if it pleases your will, with the assistance of Messrs. Thomas T. Symmons, George Smith, J. W. Harris and Misses Henrietta Vinton Davis and Bertie T. Toney, who have generously made a similar offer, render several of the most important scenes, including the last act of Shakespeare's tragedy of *Macbeth*. Yours, with exalted fraternal regard,

J. A. ARNEAUX

NEW YORK, April 6

CHAPTER LXVI

Rev. Richard Allen
First Bishop of the A. M. E. Church—Founder of that Faith—
An Eminent Preacher—A Devout Man

The life and works of Richard Allen should now be read with much interest on account of the following notice that defines a very important epoch in the A. M. E. church:

EPISCOPAL ROOMS, AFRICAN M. E. CHURCH,
No. 1424 R. I. AVENUE,
WASHINGTON, DISTRICT OF COLUMBIA, February 4, 1887
TO THE BISHOPS, MINISTERS AND MEMBERS OF THE AFRICAN METHODIST EPISCOPAL CHURCH:

MY DEAR BRETHREN:—"Read, mark, learn and inwardly digest" the subject-matter of circular—the "Centennial of African Methodism." Its contents are more than a mere passing interest. "Remember the days of old; consider the years of many generations: Ask your father, and he will show thee; thy elders, and they will tell thee. Remember all the way which the Lord thy God led thee one hundred years in the wilderness!"

Next November will be one hundred years since Richard Allen and his compeers left St. George's M. E. church, in the city of Philadelphia, (1787) and the bishops of the semi-annual meeting adopted the following preamble and resolutions:

WHEREAS: November next, 1887, will be one hundred years since Richard Allen, Absalom Jones and others left the St. George's Methodist Episcopal church in Philadelphia, because "the colored people belonging to the Methodist Society of Philadelphia convened together in order to take into consideration the evils under which they labored, arising from unkind treatment of their white brethren, who considered them a nuisance in the house of worship, and even pulled them off their knees, while in the act of prayer, and ordered them to the back seats." (See preface to the *A. M. E. Church Discipline.*) And,

WHEREAS: This is the most decisive act of the religious colored people in the United States, and we know of none like it of the descendants of Africa in the world; if we except the resolve of the Haitians under Toussaint, Christophe Petiou and Boyer. These men were to Hayti and San Domingo, in a civil

RICHARD ALLEN

and political sense, what Allen, Jones, Tapsico and others were to the colored Christians of America; their act was manhood, freedom, and manhood Christianity. We must fully recognize their action a success—a republic we have—all therefore recognize their manhood because their acts prove it. To resist oppression in Church or State is manly. Toussaint and Allen are by us honored, revered and loved. The success of Allen and his compeers is demonstrated, for it has given us the largest colored organization in the world. It is therefore proper and right that we should commemorate an event so important and so full of interest to us as a race. Therefore be it,

Resolved, first, That the chief pastors of the African Methodist Episcopal church request that next November, a date in that month be hereafter fixed, to commemorate the one hundredth year since our existence commenced, and that services be held at all our churches throughout the connection. The order of exercises to be fixed by each conference, quarterly conference, and pastor and each church. A general arrangement to be fixed by a committee hereafter appointed.

Resolved, second, As our publishing interest has long suffered, because of her indebtedness, that a contribution be made by all of our churches, and whatever is collected to be appropriated to assist in the paying off of debts now resting on our publication department

Adopted.

Committee of Arrangements
J. M. BROWN
T. M. D. WARD
H. M. TURNER
R. R. DISNEY
B. W. ARNETT

The growth of the A. M. E. church is a splendid tribute to the Negro genius. Of all the denominations under the name of "Methodist," white or black, it has seemed to have touched the heart of the Negro and made him a man of power. Its institutions and laws are the result of Negro genius, and is also the exhibition of his executive ability and abundant wisdom.

When Richard Allen manifested his faith in the future and declared himself no longer willing to have the body and blood of Christ prostituted by being withheld from him until his white brethren(?) were served, he put his foot on the neck of hell-born prejudice and stamped it so hard that hell resounded with anger and a new song was given to the angels in heaven.

It was in the early days of 1816, when the times were not favorable to the expression of a dissent from anything a white man did in Church or State. And he is revered by the African Methodist Episcopal church as the founder of their faith. Says one of their scholarly writers:

If Luther was the apostle to mind freedom, and Wesley to soul freedom, then Allen was the apostle of human freedom, or liberty of mind and body.

If Luther's motto was, "The just shall live by faith"; and Wesley's, "The world is my parish"; Allen's was, "I perceive of a truth that God is no respecter of persons." The sons of Allen, through Bishop Payne, have formulated the sentiment of the three as follows: "God, our Father: Christ, our Redeemder; and Man, our Brother."

Many a time when a boy have I seen the tomb of Richard Allen in the little railing in front of the "Big Bethel" in the city of Philadelphia. This, the first church of the denomination, stands as a proud monument to the religious zeal of Richard Allen. It stands on the site of an old blacksmith shop where the first meeting was held, and as the generations pass this monument on the outside of the church, and go within the walls of "Big Bethel" they feel that Allen still lives. Often good men's "deeds are interred with their bones," but in this noble man's career we see a dignified manhood and religious zeal become the inspiration of four hundred thousand of those who follow in his footsteps. The Rev. B. W. Arnett has, in a graphic description of the times which I give here, shown how great was the cause for their separation from the white church:

The causes which led to the organization of the African M. E. church are numerous; but a few facts will give an idea of the principal reason of our origin. After the close of the War of the Revolution, while the world was rejoicing at the establishment of a government whose declared principles were universal, political, civil and religious liberty, and while they were singing the anthems of peace, there was another mighty conflict going on—not on the battlefield, with sabre and musket, but in the churches and the social circles of the land. Prejudice, the unrelenting enemy of the oppressed and weak, was asserting its power; and from the year 1787 to 1816, the conflict continued without cessation. The colored portion of the numerous congregations of the North and South were wronged, proscribed, ostracised and compelled to sit in the back seats in the sanctuary of the Lord. The sons of toil and the daughters of oppression remained on these seats for some time, hoping that some of the members, at least, would receive a sufficient amount of grace to enable them to treat these children of sorrow with Christian courtesy. But they were doomed to disappointment; for soon bad yielded to worse, and they were sent up into the dusty galleries. There, high above the congregation, they had to serve the Lord silently—for not an amen must come down from the sable band. These and other indignities our fathers bore with Christian patience for a number of years. They were denied the communion of the Lord's Supper until all the white members had partaken. This treatment continued until forbearance ceased to be a virtue, and our fathers drew out from among them; for the watchfires of soul-freedom were burning in their bosoms. These were kindled and fed by the sentiments of the age in which they lived; for on every side could be heard the watchword of the Nation—"All men are born free and equal, and endowed by their Creator with certain inalienable rights, among which are life, liberty and the pursuit of happiness."

Allen was a man of independent character, and was converted at the age of seventeen. His influence, though a slave, was so great that his master allowed him to preach and have preachers to preach for him, as he pleased. His master was converted under his preaching, and yet I have some doubt of his conversion, as he made poor slave Richard Allen purchase his freedom. This man may have been a Christian; "God," who "moves in a mysterious way," may have done something for his soul, but he took Allen's money when he should have set him free. How they can ever harmonize God's words with their conduct will take a "general judgment" to tell. If for no other thing it were needed, it will be good for that. However, he had three able, honest men to stand by him: Rev. Absalom Jones, William White and Downs Ginnings, and they determined to erect a building for the colored people. Says an article in the *Christian Recorder:*

This undertaking met with strong opposition from both white men in the Saint George's M. E. church and prominent colored men, while some of both classes encouraged him. Ministers of the M. E. church threatened to disown him and his followers, but with much sagacity he told them that if they turned him out otherwise than in accordance with discipline, he would seek redress. His own language is: "We are determined to seek out for ourselves, the Lord being our helper." He and his friends narrated to these brethren of the M. E. church the especial grievances suffered in their communion(?) He also told them: "If you deny us your name (Methodist), you cannot seal up the Scripture from us or deny us a name in heaven. We believe heaven is free for all who worship in spirit and truth."

With manly dignity and a clear indication that he knew he was cutting loose entirely from a great body of people, believing as he did on religious doctrines, he said, when told finally that he would be disowned: "This was a trial I never had to pass through, but I was confident that the great Head of the church would support us." He states that on the first day he and Absalom Jones canvassed for money with which to purchase. They raised three hundred and sixty dollars after he had been authorized by the committee. He bought a lot on Sixth street, near Lombard, the site of the present Bethel church, Philadelphia. The committee agreed to purchase a lot on Fifth street and threw the Bethel lot on his hands. Having the true grit of manhood in his moral constitution, he said: "I would rather keep it myself than forfeit the agreement I have made." This he did. He says:

As I was the first proposer for an African church, I put the first spade into the ground to dig the cellar (basement) for the same. The old blacksmith shop was made a temple in which to worship God. On canvassing the little society it was found that a majority preferred joining the Church of England, rather than force themselves upon the Methodist Episcopal society, by which they considered themselves badly treated. But Allen was a Methodist, and though but one other member of the society agreed with him, he stuck to the old church, again showing the true metal for a leader of the colored Americans.

Richard Allen was born in Philadelphia in 1760. At seventeen he united with the Methodist society in the State of Delaware. At twenty-two he commenced preaching, and traveled through the Middle States extensively. He was ordained a deacon in 1799, by Rt. Rev. Francis Ashbury, bishop of the Methodist church. At the organization of the A. M. E. church, A.D. 1816, he was elected and ordained the first African bishop in America. The following names were enrolled in the first conference held on this occasion:

Rev. Richard Allen, Jacob Tapisco, Clayton Durham, James Champion, Thomas Webster, of Philadelphia, Pennsylvania; Daniel Coker, Richmond Williams, Henry Hardin, Stephen Hill, Edward Williamson, Nicholas Gailliard, of Baltimore, Maryland; Peter Spencer, of Wilmington, Delaware; Jacob March, Edward Jackson, William Andrews, of Attleboro, Pennsylvania; Peter Cuff, Salem, New Jersey.

These men had faith in God and faith in themselves, and the splendid results of this day show that they did not miscalculate their calling. The power of this denomination is felt in the land; its leaders are courageous, bold and intelligent, and it has some of the ablest men in the country in its ranks. My personal relations with them have been of the warmest kind, and I give them credit for utilizing every man they can lay hold on, and they know how to nurse their young eaglets into strong eagles, and to put their best efforts at work for the spreading of their views.

CHAPTER LXVII

*Hon. Samuel Allen McElwee, A. B., LL. B.
Lawyer—Legislator—President of the Tennessee Fair
Association—Orator—Speech in the Legislature on Mobs*

It is wonderful how easy some men rise in the world and how hard others struggle to accomplish the same ends. Every step with some seems marked with bitter trials; severe hardships and apparently insurmountable difficulties; but when at last the goal has been attained the prize seems ever so sweet—aye, sweeter than it could possibly be without the conflicts and discouragements. Samuel Allen McElwee is a brave soul, who can wear on his forehead *ad astra per aspera* "through difficulties to the stars." The chains of slavery bound his body not half so tightly as ignorance his mind. Already his voice holds the Tennessee Legislature with fixed attention while he defends his race and advocates the bettering of their condition. When the war ended he could not read. His father moved from Madison county, Tennessee, to Heywood county, Tennessee, in 1866. He was a farmer boy for many years, going to school only three months in the year; yet the boy studied till midnight, burning patiently the light which would give him opportunity to read, and which in after years gave him a brighter light whereby he might see the condition of his race and find a remedy for their many ills. Though worn with the daily toils, he never neglected his studies, and at each examination day entered with his class and passed the test, from the year 1868 until 1874. He then taught school awile. He often tells how at the time he had been influenced by the *National Era*, Fred Douglass' paper, and how a thirst entered his soul for more education. He matriculated at Oberlin and waited on the table, picked currants and washed windows for his board. He then went to Mississippi at the end of that year, where he taught school for five years. After that he secured a school in Alabama for a time, and on one occasion, failing to secure employment, walked thirty miles to secure a school in Tennessee. He was often without money and even a place to sleep. Still anxious to get means for returning to college, he commenced selling Lyman's Historical Charts, Bibles, and medicines,

SAMUEL ALLEN McELWEE

from which he became known as a great "Chill Doctor." He, however, could not return to school, and determined to study Latin, German and algebra under a private teacher. After teaching a very large school in the day, he would walk ten miles two nights in the week to recite to a white student at Vanderbilt University, and in this effort meets some young man's eyes it is sincerely hoped that he will make the same effort as young McElwee. Victory awaits the daring, and reward always follows the persevering. His story of privations and sufferings, of the long tramps, selling maps, and his zeal for books so weighed upon the student teacher's mind that he told the president of Fisk University of the ambitious boy. He was invited by the president to enter the university. After one year in the senior preparatory class, for which he found himself prepared, he entered college and graduated thence May 26, 1883.

June 30, 1887, Mr. McElwee will only be twenty-nine years old, and yet he seems a natural born politician, having canvassed his county every year save one since he was fourteen years of age. In the campaign of 1882 he traveled over the Eighth and Ninth congressional districts for the Republican party, advocating a just settlement of the State debt. He took his seat in the Tennessee Legislature, January 1, 1883, while he was still a student. He has just completed his third term. He studied law in the Central Tennessee College in Nashville, and graduated thence in 1885. He was a delegate to the Chicago convention which nominated Hon. James G. Blaine, and with six others voted for him on every ballot. In the Republican State convention of 1886 he was elected temporary chairman. Mr. McElwee takes a deep interest in the moral, social and industrial future of his people, and is president of the West Tennessee Colored Fair Association and the Memphis Fair Association. He was a commissioner in the colored department of the New Orleans Exposition, placing his State in a very favorable attitude. Mr. McElwee is a very magnetic speaker, forcible debater and indefatigable worker, a manly man and a truly honest citizen. Under the caption of a "Remarkable Record," this was written by a Kentucky editor after hearing him deliver a party speech in Hopkinsville, Kentucky:

A biographical sketch of this gentleman reads like a romance. No colored man in the South ever rose as rapidly upon the rounds of the ladder of fame. In 1879, Mr. McElwee was an ignorant, friendless colored tramp, going over the country, disposing of maps and charts in order to put bread in his mouth, and keep body and soul together. In the summer of the year above mentioned he tramped from Hopkinsville to Nashville, a distance of seventy-two miles in three days, in order to attend school. He was elected to the Tennessee Legislature in 1882 without opposition, and was successful in having a bill passed appropriating sixty-six hundred dollars towards further protection, progress and prosperity of the Normal school. In 1884 he was again elected his own successor, beating his opponent, Mr. H. C. Nolan, a popular white Democrat, by a large majority. It was in this last session of the Legislature that this able colored man fought a hard and successful battle in passing a bill appropriating eighty-five thousand dollars to the West Tennessee Insane Asylum, and also fifty-five hundred dollars to the Deaf and Dumb Institution. He is a brilliant conversationalist and eloquent political orator; his countenance is pleasing and intellectual and the formation of his head favorable to the belief that he possesses a phrenological development of a very superior character; the dogmas of philosophy and crudities of theology are impaled by his humor, and his wit is so boundless that it crops out often in his more serious utterances.

A man's associates can generally give good testimony as to his standing, so we quote a speech of R. R. Butler, who was selected by the Republicans of the Legislature to nominate Mr. McElwee for Speaker of the House of Representatives of the State of Tennessee during his second term. He says:

Mr. Speaker: It affords me much pleasure to nominate a candidate for speaker, one who was a slave in the days of slavery, which I thank God have passed away. One that by his own strong arm and determined will, and being blessed with a splendid intellect, graduating a short time since at the Fisk University in this city with high honors, and those of us here who served with him in the last Legislature remember his gentlemanly bearing and industrious habits, always vigilant and active, looking after the interest of his constituents and especially his race. I mean the honorable S. A. McElwee of Heywood county. I am proud of this occasion, and it is but another evidence of where the race must look for recognition. Having been born in the midst of slavery, and a slave-holder myself, I am grateful to know that I state the feelings and sentiments of my party associates. I would not say a disparaging word of the gentleman nominated by the Democrats. I have served with him a long time, rating him to be an honest man and will preside over the deliberations of this house impartially and will treat the minority with fairness. While I say that much in justice to Mr. Hanson, I can say of a truth that S. A. McElwee is the peer of any member on this floor, and will make an excellent speaker, and it affords me much pleasure to vote for him.

The future is big with promises for Mr. McElwee, and if his course is as steady in the future as it has been in the past, much can be expected from him in the way of honors, and he will lend inspiration to those around him. *The Union*, published in Nashville, gives a two column extract from his speech delivered on the subject of "Mobs" in the Tennessee Legislature, the issue of February 23, 1887. The words are those of a scholar, an orator and a patriot. They are full of wisdom and statesmanship—full of courage and boldness.

Said he:

It is remarkable to note the sameness with which all these reports read. It seems as if some man in this country had the patent by which these reports are written. Statistics do not show the number of Negroes who have in the past few years been sentenced in Judge Lynch's court, but judging from the number coming under our observation we are convinced that the number is most astounding. So prevalent and constant are the reports flashed over the country in regard to lynching of Negroes that we are forced to seek shelter with the poets and cry, "O for a lodge in some vast wilderness, some boundless contiguity of shade, where rumor of oppression and deceit, of successful or unsuccessful mobs might never reach me more." My ear is pained, my soul is sick with every day's report of wrong and outrage perpetrated upon the Negroes by mob violence. I am not here, Mr. Speaker, asking any special legislation in the interest of the Negroes, but in behalf of a race of outraged human beings. I stand here today and enter my most solemn protest against mob violence in Tennessee. Hundreds of Negroes, yes thousands, from all parts of this Southland, are to-day numbered with the silent majority, gone to eternity without a tomb to mark their last resting place, as the result of mob violence for crimes which they never committed. As we to-day legislate on this question, the spirits of these Negroes made perfect in the paradisiacal region of God, in convention assembled, with united voices, are asking the question, "Great God, when will this Nation treat the Negro as an American citizen, whether he be in Maine, among her tall pines, or in the South, where the magnolia blossoms grow?" Mr. Speaker, Tennessee should place the seal of eternal condemnation upon mob violence. "Your sins will find you out." The spirit of God will not always strive with man. For years American slavery was the great sin of the Nation. In the course of time God made clear his disapproval of this National sin by a National calamity. Four years of destructive and bloody war rent our country in twain and left our Southland devastated. The war came as the result of sin; let us sin no more lest a greater calamity befall us. We have had several cases of mob violence in Tennessee within the past six months. The saying that "light itself is a great corrective," is as true as trite. What is the position of the public press on mob violence?

I stand here to-day, Mr. Speaker, as a member of this body and a lover of my people, and indict the public press of the State for condoning, by its silence, the wrongs and outrages perpetrated upon the Negroes of the State by mob violence. Who doubts for a moment but that the public press of the State could burn out mob violence in Tennessee as effectually as the mirrors of Archimedes burned the Roman ships in the harbor of Syracuse? Read the dailies and the majority of the weeklies, and you will find them on the mobs at Jackson, Dyersburg and McKenzie as dumb as an oyster. The mob at Dyersburg took place in broad daylight, and as the result of that mob hundreds of Negroes refused to attend the second annual exhibition of the West Tennessee Colored Fair Association, which was held at Dyersburg in October, 1886. The mob at Jackson is without a parallel in the annals of our State.

Go with me, Mr. Speaker and gentlemen, to Jackson and look at that poor woman, with that weakness and tenderness common to women, as she is taken from the jail and followed by that motly crowd to the courtyard. The bell is rung, they enter the jail and strip her of every garment, and order her to march—buffeting, kicking, and spearing her with sharp sticks on the march. "She was led as a sheep to the slaughter; and like a lamb dumb before her shearer, so opened she not her mouth." She was swung up, her body riddled with bullets and orders issued not to interfere with her until after nine o'clock the next morning, in order that she might be seen. Men who spoke against it and said it was an outrage, had to leave town. Others who thought of giving vent to their feelings *en masse* by series of resolutions, were told that they had not better attempt it. Mr. Speaker, society prepares crime, and the criminal is only the instrument by which it is accomplished.

I therefore again indict the public press and citizens of Madison county for the foul play upon the person of Eliza Wood, and hold them to a strict account before the bar of eternal justice for the wrong done. The mobs of Jackson, McKenzie and Dyersburg are mentioned because they are the most recent, not because they are exceptional or that we lack other examples. Grant, for the sake of argument, that these parties were guilty, does that make it right and accord with our principles of justice? When the citizens of Madison, Dyer and Carroll go to judgment with the blood of Eliza Wood, Matt Washington and Charles Dinwiddie on their garments, it will be more tolerable for Sodom and Gomorrah in that day than it will be for Jackson, Dyersburg and McKenzie. For two hundred and fifty years, Mr. Speaker, we were regarded as chattel. More than twenty years ago we were made citizens, and as such we ask at your hands that protection which is common to American citizens. The sainted Garfield told us to go home and make friends with our neighbors. We are here to-day knocking at your door and ask that you "entreat us not to leave you or return from following after you; for whither you go we will go, and where you lodge we will lodge; your people shall be our people, and your God our God; where you die will we die, and there will be buried; the Lord do so unto us, and more also, if aught but death part you and us." If this mob violence continues, its influence upon society will be worse than the malign influence which Cataline wielded over the reckless and abandoned youth of Rome. Mob violence is sowing in America a seed that will ripen in a conspiracy that will eclipse in gigantic proportions the great conspiracy of Cataline to lay Rome in ashes and deluge its streets in blood, for the purpose of enriching those who were to apply the torch and wield the dagger. Mr. Speaker, the time has passed in the history of this Nation for race wars. We cannot afford it. There are at present questions of very great importance demanding the attention of both races. They call for the united effort on the part of both. The labor question, tariff and public service are all important, the interest of the white man is the interest of the black man, that which hurts one will hurt the other; therefore, as a humble representative of the Negro race, and as a member of this body, I stand here to-day and wave the flag of truce between the races and demand a reformation in Southern society by the passage of this bill.

The bill was defeated, but great excitement was produced by the terrible lashing which they received. His style was impressive and they listened with no slight interest to his powerful arraignment. It will yet bear fruit and do good. All the members of the Legislature have a high respect for his ability, integrity and loyalty to his constituents. His popularity with the people of his race is unbounded, and he is careful to live honorably and with soberness, thus challenging their admiration and courting their friendship.

CHAPTER LXVIII

Rev. Lott Carey
First American Missionary to Africa—The God-sent Missionary

———•◆•———

Carey was an earnest disciple of Christ. He began life as a poor tobacco packer in a warehouse in Richmond, Virginia. Born about 1780, he lived a very profane and wicked life. About 1807, in the gallery of a Baptist church, he heard a sermon from the third chapter of John, and he was so impressed with the story of Nicodemus that he determined to learn to read, that he might know the story for himself, and be able to repeat it word for word as he heard it. A Testament was his first reading book. He was a prudent man, who made and saved money with which he purchased his freedom. While in a night school, to the astonishment of everybody he announced his intention of going to Africa as a missionary. His teacher, William Crane, had that night been lecturing to them on the Messrs. Burgess & Mills report of an exploration on the coast of Africa. The matter so stirred up Carey that it made him declare his intention as heretofore stated. He was worth about fifteen hundred dollars in real estate, and his employer not desiring to lose his services, offered to raise his salary two hundred dollars more per year; but Carey having fully consecrated himself to this service, accepted an appointment as missionary of the "Tri-ennial Convention" and set sail for Africa, accompanied by Rev. Collin Teague, who was the first American to go to that country on such an errand. Teague was a great admirer of Carey, and once said very enthusiastically to a white man, "I don't hear any of your white ministers that can preach like Lott Carey." He sailed on the twenty-third of January, 1820, and after forty-four days reached Sierra Leone. Says the story of *Baptist Missions:* "The agent of the Colonization Company had not yet purchased any land, and therefore could not receive him and his friend Teague as cultivators of the soil." Hence they were obliged for some months to work as mechanics. In 1824 he was appointed physician to the settlers in Africa, a position the duties of which his studies of the diseases of the country enabled him to discharge. In 1828 he became acting governor of Liberia. It is said that in 1823 Mr.

Carey and his fellow-colonists lost confidence in the administration of the colored society. They found its government oppressive and demanded reform. Some few of the malcontents took advantage of the general insubordination and seized a portion of the public stores. We have only Governor Ashmun's account of these transactions. However, Lott Carey declared that he acted only on principle in the matter, which was afterwards compromised, and on his death-bed Mr. Ashmun urged that he should be permanently appointed to conduct the affairs of the colony, expressing perfect confidence in his integrity and in his ability to discharge the duties of the office.

Sometimes they would have difficulties with the natives in Liberia, and it was necessary to do fighting as well as preaching. Carey was pretty good at both, and lost his life while making cartridges. An explosion took place in which he was badly injured, and after lingering some days he died, November 10, 1828, leaving many to mourn his loss, and besides, leaving as a legacy to the American people the life of a devoted missionary. It has been said the Negroes have no fine feelings and that they are but little above irrational animals, but here is a man with no circumstances to inspire him, bearing in his heart a tender love for the Africans who knew not Christ, even though he, himself, was fettered with the chains of American slavery, and could see something for him to do in relieving others who, while free in body, were chained in sin. It is a remarkable fact that Lott Carey is the namesake of William Carey, the "singing cobbler" of London, who first carried the gospel to the dark skinned races of India. The white and the black Carey shall forever live side by side in the hearts of those who sympathize with down-trodden people. It has been said that the race has not furnished sufficient great men for biographers and encyclopedists to take cognizance of them, but here is a man who was born before this century began its course, whose name is imbedded in the history of his time and solidly wedged in the great books of the age.

Fair sketches will be found of his life in the American Baptist Missionary Union literature, the story of *Baptist Missions, Encyclopedia of Missions,* by Harry Newcomb, *American Encyclopedia,* and in a sketch called "Africa in Brief," by the Rev. J. J. Coles, present missionary to the Vey tribes in Africa.

JOHN MERCER LANGSTON

CHAPTER LXIX

Hon. John Mercer Langston, A. B., A. M., LL. D.
Lawyer—Minister Resident and Consul-General—Chargé
d'Affaires—President of the Virginia Normal and Collegiate
Institute—Formerly Dean and Professor of Law
in Howard University

One of the greatest Negroes in America is the subject of this sketch. His name has become a household word, especially among the younger generation, and his deeds shine brightly alongside of those of even older men. My personal acquaintance with him dates from the time I was a student attending Howard University, in 1870, to the present day. I remember him well as a man who did not fear to speak his opinions. In those days there were many colored men who bowed and scraped to any kind of bloated, shoddy aristocracy. We all had faith in him, and I remember distinctly that of all the six hundred students at that time, not one could have been found who believed Langston thought himself less than the best citizen of the country. At present, however, we have to deal with his distinct acts which, developed him into the great man we now find him.

He was born in Louisa county, Virginia, December 14, 1829, and is, in blood, Indian, Negro and Anglo-Saxon. He has the fortitude of the first, the pride of the second and the progressiveness of the third. He was born in slavery and takes, since his father was his owner, the name of his mother's family, which was Indian and Negro mainly, and was closely related to the family of Pocahontas. In this he can make the boast that he belongs to the F. F. V's. Emancipated when a mere child upon the death of his father, by his will and testament he was sent to the State of Ohio, where he grew to manhood, and was educated and pursued a professional and official life to the year 1867.

In 1844 he entered Oberlin College, located at Oberlin, Ohio, and graduated after five years regular collegiate study in 1849. He then sought admission to a law school, conducted by Mr. J. W. Fowler at Ballston Spa, New York, but was refused admission on account of his color. He was advised to edge his way into the school, claiming he was a Frenchman or Spaniard coming from the West Indies, Central or South America, for he could well pass for either, but his open manly nature scorned a trick even for success. He next tried to gain admission to a law school in Cincinnati, Ohio, conducted by Judge Timothy Walker, but he was refused here too, with the kind assurance from the judge that he being a young colored man could not find himself at home with white scholars. That man never made a greater mistake in his life.

He was forced to seek a situation as a student in some lawyer's office, and his success in this direction was poor enough, as few white lawyers in our country were ready in 1849 to take a Negro law-student into their offices. Only the Hon. Sherlock J. Andrews of Cleveland, Ohio, would consent to furnish Langston books, with an occasional opportunity for explanation of law doctrines and principles, so that no interference was made in ordinary office business. Of course there was little accomplished in this way, and the attempt under such cruel embarrassments only served to discourage him, so he abandoned the study for awhile, and entered the Theological Department of Oberlin College, from which he graduated in 1853. Then he entered upon the study of law under the tuition of Hon. Philemon Bliss of Elyria, Ohio, at the time one of the first lawyers of the Ohio bar, distinguished especially for his excellent culture, and his Anti-slavery sentiments and utterances, as well as his large and commanding influence in the community. About one year later Mr. Langston appeared by order of the court for examination, with reference to his admission to the bar, before a special committee appointed by the court, composed of two Democrats and one Whig. The matter of admitting colored men to the bar was novel. No one of this class up to that time had the temerity to offer himself as a candidate for such an honor. Mr. Langston was in the lead so far as the western part of the country was concerned, but his erudition in law was so apparent, and his general knowledge, classic and scientific, so profound, that he at once won the favor of the committee; but here again was the ghost of color. "Shall a Negro or mulatto be admitted to the Ohio bar?" "*Can* he be, legally?" At once the answer was made to these questions in the negative and in the judicial phrase with emphasis. The old Whig member of the committee, a man of generous and manly sentiment suggested to his colleagues and the court composed of five distinguished lawyers, that it might be well in view of the late decision of the Supreme Court of the State of Ohio to inquire whether Langston was either a Negro or mulatto; "for," he urged, "Judge Bliss is taking care of his case:" whereupon the color of Langston was inquired into and when it had been decided that he had more white than Negro blood, as it was phrased, he was ordered to be sworn by the court as a lawyer, October 24, 1854. Constant and uninterrupted scholastic labors including school teaching during the winter season from 1844 to 1855, eleven consecutive years, had considerably disturbed Mr. Langston's health. At the suggestion of his physician, he went, therefore, as soon as he was admitted to the bar, upon a farm in Brownhelm, Lorain county, Ohio. This was a rich, popular, intelligent and progressive community of white people in one of the best sections of the Western Reserve. He was the only colored person residing in that part of Ohio, but he no sooner purchased his farm and settled among these good people, than he was cordially welcomed with opportunity for the employment of all the ability, legal and otherwise, which he possessed. One week, just after he had moved into this new home, a leading Democrat lawyer of the community called upon him to assist in a trial of a very important case involving several questions of possession and occupancy of land, requiring consideration and verdict of a jury. Mr. Langston was, of course, delighted with such a call, and he hastened to accept it. It was well he did so, for no man ever gained a greater advantage and more various than that which came to him from the call of his friend, Mr. Hamilton Perry. For the first time, in the fall of 1854, on a beautiful Saturday afternoon, a colored lawyer appeared in an important suit as the assistant of a white attorney. The court, the witnesses, the lawyers, except Langston, were all white. Such was the success of the colored lawyer in connection with this case that he found himself at once surrounded by numerous clients with fat retainers. From that time he grew in business and influence rapidly and solidly. The spring elections in 1875 in the State of Ohio was signalized for the first time by the nomination and choice to the clerkship of one of the most advanced townships of the State, of a colored man, upon a total white vote. For the first time, too, in the history of our country, a colored man had been elected to an office of responsibilities and emoluments upon a popular choice. This fortunate colored man was Lawyer Langston. He was immediately called in view thereof to take part as one of the orators of the May meeting of the American Anti-slavery Society, held in 1855 in New York City.

    The speech on that occasion was of such character in sentiment, delivery and effect as to secure its full report and publication in the daily papers of New York and the leading journals and periodicals of the Anti-slavery societies of the times. Those who heard the speech of the young orator never can forget how his first sentences were uttered. His words were these:

A nation may lose its liberties and be a century in finding it out.
Where is the American liberty?
In its far reaching and broad sweep, slavery has stricken down the freedom of us all;
And American slavery itself has gone glimmering into the things that were. A schoolboy's tale, the wonder of an hour.

In his capacity as clerk in Brownhelm township, Mr. Langston was given special opportunities in connection with his profession, but he was, by reason of his peculiar relations to the Board of Education of the township, given special duties as regarded its common schools. Indeed he was ex-officio school visitor. In the fall of 1860, Mr. Langston was engaged in looking after the school interests of the colored youth of Ohio, organizing schools among them and supplying teachers thereof, traversing the entire State from Lake Erie to the Ohio river. When the war came, Mr. Langston signalized his conduct by loyal patriotic labors in favor of maintaining the authority of the government, and although he did not go into the field as a soldier, he engaged actively in recruiting troops and did more, perhaps, than any other single man to recruit the Fifty-fourth and Fifty-fifth regiments, to the latter of which regiments he gave the colors. He also recruited the Fifth regiment of colored troops of Ohio, to which also he gave colors, and finally when he thought the colored American should be given the full recognition which he had won, as introduced to Secretary Stanton by General James A. Garfield, he asked of that great war officer a commission as colonel, with permission to recruit and command a colored regiment officered by colored men who had already won distinction in the service. Such proposition was taken under discussion by the government, but it was not decided in time to give Mr. Langston his commission before the war closed.

Moving to Oberlin in 1856, Mr. Langston was at once elected clerk of the township of Russia; next year a member of the council of the incorporated village of Oberlin for two years, and a member of the Board of Education in that village, successively for eleven years. In this time he became especially distinguished for his skill in examining witnesses and his eloquence and power in addressing courts and juries.

Mr. Langston was an able, bold, determined advocate, using tongue, pen, and all the force of his nature and learning in behalf of the enslaved and oppressed colored Americans, demanding for them freedom, legal rights, and educational advantages. In 1867 Mr. Langston was invited by General O. O. Howard, through the influence of the Chief-Justice of the Supreme Court, Hon. Salmon P. Chase, to act as general inspector of the schools of the freed people of the country. It was in July of the same year that he made his first trip southward on the errand indicated.

He went entirely through the State of Mississippi on this trip, visiting and speaking in every prominent place in the South. On his return he found President Johnson declaring at the White House and through the journals of the country, that he intended to relieve General O. O. Howard of the commissionership of the "Bureau of Freedmen, Refugees and Abandoned Lands," to which he had been appointed by President Abraham Lincoln, and that he would appoint thereto Langston, if he would consent to take the place. Langston would not consent to such a change, claiming that General Howard should be retained and supported in his position, going even so far as to tell General Howard all that the President held and said against him, and tendering his services in his support, to the extent of a call upon and an argument to General U. S. Grant in his behalf. He did call upon General Grant, then secretary of war, whom he found altogether ready and willing to hear all that could be said in General Howard's favor. In his interview with General Grant, Mr. Langston became enamored of him and made bold to say to him that the advocacy of such sentiments as he had so clearly and eloquently expressed with regard to the reconstruction, the rights, the education and the care of the newly emancipated classes, would make him the next President of the United States. General Grant was elected to the position. About this time President Johnson offered to Mr. Langston the mission to Hayti. This he declined, preferring to remain at home.

This same year, 1867, he was admitted to practice in the Supreme Court of the United States, on the motion of Hon. James A. Garfield. He continued to act as general inspector of Freedmen's schools, traveling throughout the South during the time, to 1869, when he was called to a professorship in the Law Department of Howard University. He at once became Dean of that department, organizing it, and for seven years he was at the head of what was recognized as one of the finest law schools in the country, and graduating therefrom many of the first white and colored male and female students of the law that ever went from such an institution. It was from this school, while under his charge, that the first female student of the law in the world, a young colored lady, Miss C. B. Ray of New York, was awarded a diploma. During the last two years that Professor Langston remained at Howard University he was, by especial request, made vice-president and acting president of the institution. He filled this position with such marked efficiency and success, that at the close of his first year of such service the Board of Trustees of the university conferred upon him by special arrangement and in an especial and impressive manner, with address by General Howard, the degree of LL. D. During this time he was appointed by President Grant a member of the Board of Health of the District of Columbia. For seven years he acted as attorney of the board and for one year as its secretary. As a sanitarist, he was able and efficient.

In 1877 Mr. Langston was appointed by President Hayes United States minister resident and consul-general to Hayti. In this position he served his country in an acceptable and conscientious manner, as the records of the State department will show, from September 1, 1877, to July, 1885, almost eight years. As a diplomat he was an entire success, and the citizens always found him ready to serve them, as well as the officers; and the people of the country, near whose government he resided, united in bearing testimony to the fact. Besides being the Dean of the Diplomatic and Consular Corps, he was most of the time while in Hayti, a personal and great favorite in general society. It was as the Dean of the Diplomatic Corps that, during the yellow fever in the country when the very popular representative of the French government died of such disease, he pronounced an eulogy upon him at his tomb, in the French language, of such character and order of elegance and beauty that it found its way into the public journals of Paris and brought to him, through the French government, the cordial acknowledgments of the family and friends of the deceased ambassador. In the government of San Domingo, Mr. Langston was *chargé d'affaires* of our government, and his relation with the officers of that government, though many of the matters he had to deal with were like most of those in Hayti, difficult and trying, he won the warmest respect and consideration from all parties concerned. On the thirtieth of January, 1885, Mr. Langston, of his own choice, resigned the position of United States minister resident to President Arthur, having resolved on the expiration of his administration to return to this country and enter again upon the practice of his profession. After considerable delay, in July, 1885, he returned, and was at once employed by one of the first business houses of the country to attend to its interests in the West Indies. He made a single trip in such services, when, upon his return in the same year, he found that he had been elected by the Board of Education of Virginia, President of the Virginia Normal and Collegiate Institute, which was founded by the government in 1882, and supported by popular appropriations of twenty thousand dollars annually. The faculty, as at present constituted, is composed of ten well educated, scholarly persons, four ladies and six gentlemen. In addition to the ordinary departments and courses of study established and pursued in the institute, covering all the branches of the higher mathematics, philosophical, scientific and classical studies, the law provides for and creates a summer school for the public school teachers, which was attended at the last session by over two hundred teachers. The estimate put upon President Langston in his present position by the officials of the educational department of the government of Virginia, is discovered in the following words of the late superintendent of public instructions of Virginia, Hon. J. B. Farr, in his annual report for 1885:

After considering the applications of all who presented their claims for the place, the board determined not to confine its selection to applicants, but to seek out a man that would add most dignity and weight to the position, and whether he had applied or not to tender him the appointment. After taking into consideration the education, intelligence, honesty, energy and general ability, Hon. John Mercer Langston, ex-minister to Hayti, was considered pre-eminently fitted for the great work, and the Board of Education, November 19, 1885, unanimously elected him President of the Virginia Normal and Collegiate Institute. This was done without solicitation on the part of Professor Langston or his friends. Indeed he knew nothing of it until the official announcement of the action taken by the board was made. This was one of the extremely rare cases on record where the office sought the man, and we believe the quest was well rewarded. Fortunately for his race and State, he is a Virginian by birth, and he had patriotism enough to accept the honor and assume the responsibilities of building up an institution which has in its compass the grandest possibilities, and which reaps a wide and untilled field of usefulness. President Langston's reputation is national, and he not only enjoys the highest esteem and confidence of his own people, but by his education and ability commands respect of all with whom he is thrown in contact.

The following resolutions show how the president is appreciated by those over whom he presides: At the close of his usual Thursday lecture, on the twentieth of January, 1887, Professor D. B. Williams, on behalf of the faculty of the institute and its two hundred students, presented the following preamble and resolutions:

Whereas, The Hon. J. M. Langston, LL.D., did at a very critical period in the history of the institute, accept the presidency unanimously tendered him without his solicitation by the Honorable Board of Education at much personal pecuniary sacrifice, and

Whereas, He has succeeded so well not only in placing it upon a solid foundation, but is rapidly making it one of the leading institutions of the country; therefore be it

Resolved, first: That we regard our president as being fully equipped for the great work in which he is now engaged, in everything that pertains to intellectual ability, high moral purpose and religious culture.

Resolved, That his coming into Virginia as an educator has proved a great blessing to the people of the commonwealth and is indicative of great future results for good.

Resolved, That in these resolutions we voice the sentiment of the people of the State by asserting that his administration of the affairs has been entirely successful, and has caused the sons and daughters of Virginia to turn their faces toward this fountain of learning.

Resolved, That a copy of these resolutions be handsomely engrossed by the committee and presented to the president.

He is amongst the most scholarly, refined and accomplished gentlemen of the race. Surrounded as he is by wealth, and even luxury, he is a good parent, and owes much to his charming wife, who has been a great help to him in reaching this eminence. She has made his home pleasant and entertained his guests well, all of which goes a great distance towards a man's promotion. He has many testimonials of all kinds, that show his standing among men and testify to the worth of his character. What a beautiful picture is the engrossed resolution of the Board of Health of the District of Columbia, awarded President Langston as he took his leave of it in 1877, as the same hangs upon the wall of the broad and magnificent passage of his residence, and his certificate of life-long membership as a fellow of the great English philosophical association, the Victoria Institute, composed of the distinguished scholars and thinkers of the world. Then still how beautiful and interesting to witness the fact that a great library, law, scientific, literary, commercial, industrial, in the French, Spanish, Hebrew, Greek, Latin and English languages, gathered by him during the thirty-five years of his student life, occupying cases located in every part of his house, inside and outside the library room proper—every available nook and corner thereof.

It seems only a question of time when Mr. Langston will be made member of Congress from Virginia, and may it be so. He would be heard from on the most important questions of the day, nor would the matters pertaining to the race be neglected.

Let me close with the opinion of the *Montgomery* (Alabama) *Herald,* concerning President Langston:

It is impossible for the Fourth Virginia Congressional District to elect a man that would reflect more credit upon his constituents and race, or American statesmanship, than Mr. Langston. He is undoubtedly the highest type of Africo-American citizenship. All through his long, eventful, venturous course, leaping with giant-like strides, from the valley of obscurity to the summit of human grandeur and manly excellence, not one act of his has tended to reflect dishonor upon himself, his people, or his country.

To which we add a comment from another Negro journal:

This country has never yet produced a more remarkable man than Hon. John M. Langston. He is a man of observation, and nothing escapes his keen and penetrating eye, with knowledge of human nature that it would be almost impossible to deceive him. The life and services of no man will fill a brighter page in history than his. The future historians will record the remarkable fact that he has been equal to every emergency, and used only honorable means to attain his ends.

CHAPTER LXX

Rev. William H. McAlpine
Baptist Divine—President of a College—Editor of a Weekly Journal

---

Rev. W. H. McAlpine was born in Buckingham county, Virginia, near Farmersville, June, 1847. He was carried to Alabama by a Negro speculator when about three years old, in company with his mother and younger brother. His mother, brother and himself were sold by the speculator to a Presbyterian minister by the name of Robert McAlpine, in Coosa county, Alabama. His owner died when he was about eight years old, and the property being divided William was separated from his mother and taken by one of the sons of the McAlpine family, who was a doctor, and lived in Talladega county, Alabama. Here William remained in the family of Dr. McAlpine until the close of the late war. As it was customary for young boys to be nurses to the white children, we are not surprised to find him a nurse in that family for about ten years. Mrs. Dr. McAlpine being a Northern woman and not well pleased with the way Southern people taught their children, would not send hers to the school, but had them taught at home, when she did not teach them herself. The young slave being the nurse, and required to be in the white people's house with the children, and not allowed to assemble with those of his own race, and even not allowed to eat and sleep with them, learned to read and write, and gained some knowledge of arithmetic, grammar and geography. He was separated from his mother from the time he was eight years old, in 1855, until 1874, and for sixteen years of that time didn't even know whether she was living or dead. He never saw his father to know him.

He was converted to Christianity and joined a white Baptist church in the town of Talladega, Alabama, just one year before the close of the war of secession, under Rev. J. J. D. Renfroe, D.D. In 1866 he worked at the carpenter's trade. In the summer of the same year he taught school in Mardisville, a little village about five miles from Talladega. In the winter of the same year he entered the Talladega College, and not being able to pay for his board and buy his books and clothing, and having refused proffered aid, hired out himself and worked mornings, evenings and Saturdays in order to pay for the same and go to school during school hours. In a few months after conversion he felt that he was called to the work of the gospel ministry, but refused for some years to accept a license from his church, as he believed in thorough preparation.

Mr. McAlpine remained in connection with the Talladega College, from 1868 to 1873, and only lacked six months of graduating in 1874. He was licensed in 1869 and ordained in 1871, being called to the pastoral charge of a colored Baptist church in the town of Talladega, Alabama, in the fall of 1871. The call was accepted. The present house of worship for the colored Baptists of Talladega was erected during the pastorate of Rev. Mr. McAlpine. He was also pastor of a Baptist church about seven miles from the city, when he gave up that church. He was called to the pastorate of the church at Jacksonville, Cannelton county, Alabama, where he also taught public schools for several sessions. He was instrumental in organizing the Rushing Springs, Mount Pilgrim and Snow Creek associations in North Alabama.

While pastor in Talladega, he attended the college there, and during vacation was employed by Rev. E. M. Cravath, field secretary of the American Missionary Association, to canvass the State for students for the institution. The following is a letter from him at the close of the term of canvass:

NEW YORK, March 2, 1871

WILLIAM H. MCALPINE; Talladega, Alabama

DEAR SIR: Yours with bill, March 14, is to hand. Mr. Safford will pay you the balance due on account, and I feel sure that you have done us good work in the State, that will tell in the results more largely in the future. I hope that you will succeed in your efforts for the church, and that a blessing may rest upon your labors.

Very truly yours,
E. M. CRAVATH

Rev. Mr. AcAlpine was in the first meeting held in Alabama, in 1868, for the organization of the Colored Baptist Missionary State convention, and has attended every time except two since its organization. In the session of the above named association, November, 1873, in the city of Tuscaloosa, Alabama, when the white and colored conventions had a meeting in the same city, and at the same time, Mr. AcAlpine framed and offered a resolution to attempt the establishment of the present Selma University; and while the same was pending before the colored convention, a committee was appointed from the colored body to bear the resolution to the white brethren in their convention and ask their advice on the subject. The white brethren appointed a committee to advise the colored brethren, said committee consisting of Revs. Drs. Tague, Cleveland and Winkler. The committee waited on the Colored convention and advised them to turn what money they had over to them, and they would send such young men off to school as they, the colored brethren, deemed fit, and not to undertake to establish a school, as such a thing would be folly. In the face of these gray-headed D.D.'s., Rev. McAlpine arose and asked to differ from them as having quite a different view, and succeeded in convincing the convention that it was their duty to attempt to establish said institution.

In the 1874 session of this convention, in the city of Mobile, Alabama, he was chosen to canvass the State six months of 1875, and try what could be done for raising money for the proposed school. During this time he raised two hundred dollars above expenses, and awakened such interest all over the State that the next session of the convention was fuller than ever before, and about four hundred dollars was in the treasury after adjournment. He was then employed by the convention for the whole year of 1876, and raised over five hundred dollars above expenses; there was left in the treasury about one thousand dollars.

Having been elected traveling and financial agent for 1877, and not thinking the prospects favorable for raising money, he resigned and took charge of the Marion Baptist church. Arrangements, however, were made with him by the State Board to conduct the agency and do what he could to raise money in the field. In the fall of 1877, in convention, in the city of Eufala, it was decided to locate the school, now called Selma University, in Selma, Alabama. The convention had at that time one thousand dollars to put into property, and with that amount purchased the old Fair Grounds of Selma, for which they contracted to pay three thousand dollars. It was through the efforts of this earnest laborer that the school has been established, and the colored Baptists own a school second to none in the State.

In 1881 his brethren, seeing his adaptability to the work, elected him president of the institution, which position he held for two years. Feeling that the school needed a more scholarly man at its head, against the advice of all the board of trustees, teachers and students, he resigned. As soon as the church at Marion heard of his resignation, he was forthwith called back to the pastoral charge.

When the Baptist Foreign Mission convention of the United States was organized in the city of Montgomery, Alabama, in 1880, he was elected president, and served two sessions, and could have filled the office a third term but refused to let his name go before them as a candidate, because the constitution prescribed two terms for the presidency; although the members would have then and there changed the constitution, he stoutly refused. When the *Baptist Pioneer* was started, in 1878, he was chosen editor, and held the position till 1882, when he resigned in favor of Rev. E. M. Brawley, D.D., who succeeded him as president of Selma University. For six years his services were given as a member of the Board of Trustees of Lincoln Normal University, at Marion, Alabama, he being the only colored member of the board. He was for three years pastor of a large country church near Marion, which church had eight hundred members, and was served in connection with the Marion church, which church he now serves.

He is a man of fine parts, genteel, intelligent, faithful and earnest. He is much respected and beloved by all who know him. As he grows in age, he grows in wisdom, and the work of Alabama Baptists is largely guided by his suggestions. He has arisen to many offices of honor and trust, because he is always on the side of right.

CHAPTER LXXI

*Rev. Alexander Crummell, A. B., D. D.
Rector of St. Luke's Church, Washington, District of Columbia
—Professor of Mental and Moral Science in the College
of Liberia—Author*

———•◆•———

Bishop Hood says Dr. Crummell is among the most scholarly black men of the age. He is prominently a representative man of the Protestant Episcopal church. He is the son of a royal paternity on the one side and a free born maternity on the other side. He was therefore born free in the city of New York. His father was the son of a king and was born on Timanee, West Africa, a country adjoining Sierra Leone. He lived till he was thirteen years in the usual manner common to boys, and yet when quite young he began to study in what was known as the Mulberry Street school in New York City. His classmates were such men of fame as George T. Downing, Patrick Reason, Professor Charles L. Reason, Ira Aldridge, Dr. James McCune, Samuel Ringgold and Henry Highland Garnet. In the year 1831, Rev. Peter Williams, a white preacher, established a high school for the purpose of giving an opportunity to the colored youth of New York City to study the classics. In this school also, were found Garnet, Sidney and Crummell, but its facilities were not the best, and after hearing of a new school started in Canaan, New Hampshire, the parents of these boys, who had formed a close intimacy with each other, decided to send them there, as no color line was drawn. On arriving at the school they were welcomed by the students, about thirty in number, in the most generous manner. Fourteen colored lads had gathered there seeking superior advantages. They had not been in the place more than three months when the people in the neighborhood decided to break up the "nigger school;" and the end came when the people brought ninety oxen and pulled down the building, and threw it in a swamp half a mile from the place. This was accomplished after two days hard labor. They then drove the scholars out of town. Mr. Crummell relates the circumstances in an eulogy on Garnet, which he delivered May 4, 1882, when he said:

ALEXANDER CRUMMELL

Meanwhile, under Garnet as our leader, the boys in our boarding house were molding bullets, expecting an attack upon our dwelling. About eleven o'clock at night the tramp of horses was heard approaching; and as one rapid rider passed the house he fired at it. Garnet quickly replied to it by a discharge from a double barrelled shotgun which blazed away through the window. At once the hills for many a mile around reverberated with the sound. Lights were seen from scores of houses on every side of the town, and villages far and near were in a state of great excitement. But the musket shot by Garnet doubtless saved our lives. The cowardly ruffians dared not attack us. Notice, however, was given us to quit the State within a fortnight. When we left, the Canaan mob assembled on the outskirts of the village and fired field-pieces charged with powder at our wagon.

This Canaan was not by any means the sweet Canaan that the good old colored people love to sing about. In 1836 Mr. Crummell attended the Oneida Institute at Whitesboro, a manual labor school which had been opened for colored boys by Beriah Green. Here our student triumphantly entered and spent three very happy and prosperous years. In 1839 Mr. Crummell was received as a candidate for Holy Orders, under the tuition of Rev. Peter Williams, rector of St. Phillip's church, of which he was a member. He applied for admission to the General Theological Seminary of the Episcopal church, but was not admitted on account of color. He was received in the diocese of Massachusetts, and in the established order and procedure of his denomination was ordained to the diaconate by Bishop Griswold. He was a hard student, and after much theological training he was admitted to the Priest's Orders by Bishop Lee of Delaware. He was enabled afterwards to take a course in the Queen's College, Cambridge, England, where he completed his studies and after graduation went as a missionary to Africa, where he was rector of a parish and Professor of Mental and Moral Science in Liberia. While in Africa he was a leading spirit in every public meeting, and was often called upon to use his pen and voice in addressing the people by special invitation. It will not be out of place to give some idea of the great preacher's style and thoughts by excerpts from his writings. On the subject of "The Responsibility of the First Fathers of a Country, for its Future Life and Character," delivered to the young men of Monrovia, Liberia, West Africa, the first of December, 1863, he said:

I ask you also, what will you do? Look around you, then, at the vast moral waste that surrounds us in this country and throughout this continent, and think of the multitudinous minds and the vast energies of the painful labors of the martyr-like self-sacrifice on the part of both Church and State, which are to be expended from generation to generation, ere the great work of God and humanity on this soil will approach its consummation. Open your eyes upon the deep vista of grand futurity; glance along the long alleys of coming times, crowded with the rising generations of both emigrant and native, coming up into life and falling into the ranks of society and the State; and then think of all the sober, earnest work that is to be done by us in our day to prepare them for the burdens and duties of their position. You will have to participate in this work, and, therefore, I entreat you, gird up your loins, young man, for duty. Serve God and serve your country just where you are, however lowly your position, however rugged your pathway, serve God and not the devil. Serve your country and not your lusts, and this, by meeting the duties of your sphere; not by leaving them, but by ennobling them by faithfulness and manhood.

In an address delivered at the anniversary of the Pennsylvania Colonization Society, in October, 1865, upon the subject "How shall the Regeneration of Africa be Effected," he said:

It is all God's work. To him be the glory. While for two hundred and forty years the brutal hand of violence has been at the black man's throat, God has been neither blind nor quiet. He has seen it all; He has been moving, too, amid it all, latent and restrained in power, although atrocious and repulsive as it has ever been to Him. To use the words of another, "the ways of God are not found within narrow limits." He hurries not Himself to display to-day the consequences of the principle that he yesterday laid down; He will draw it out in the lapse of ages when the hour is come.

Winding up that same address, he used these beautiful words, after having urged them to use every endeavor to go as missionaries to other countries, said:

And then, in a sense far deeper, more real than ever he thought of when he uttered them, will the words of Henry Clay be realized—that every shipload of emigrants to this country will be a shipload of missionaries, carrying the gospel to Africa, and even now, the time, it seems to me, has come; and "the day is at hand," and all the great obstacles to the redemption of Africa are well nigh removed; the wide door of saving opportunity is open; and now good men everywhere should seize the "staff of accomplishment," and enter in at once, and claim that continent for their Lord.

In 1862 he published a volume of addresses, most of them delivered in Africa. They are varied as to their subjects, full of learning and written with the intention to promote the cause of God and the people. Perhaps the most sublime and elegant thought is found in one delivered upon the subject of "God and the Nation," from which a short extract is given in order to show his confidence in the God of Nations. He said:

Our only safety under the moral governments of this world is in fastening our country upon the throne of God. Without Him there is no life, in the body nor in our souls, in the States nor in institutions, in nature in plants nor in trees, in the depths of the sea, amid the whirling hosts of the Heavens, and so there is no life in the Nation without God. "In Him is life," and there is none besides. All growth proceeds from Him, whether it be the tiny plant "beneath the mossy stone" or the spiritual vitality of the grandest archangel in the eternal Heavens. All fixedness, all endurance depend on Him, whether it be the firm seating of the hills around us, or the everlasting permanency of the eternal throne, . . . and therefore I say again—"God and our Country"—for if this idea, in all its true relations, governs the minds of this people, then shall our country be unto God forever for a people, and for a name, for a praise, and for glory. For happy is the people that is in such a case, yea, blessed are the people who have the Lord for their God.

In 1883 he published a volume of sermons to which an introduction is given by the Rt. Rev. Thomas M. Clark, D.D., LL.D., bishop of Rhode Island, and so far there seems to be only three colored men who have published volumes of sermons. The first was probably the Rev. William Douglas, formerly rector of St. Thomas church, in the city of Philadelphia; the second was Rev. Alexander Crummell, D.D., and the other was Bishop James W. Hood, D.D.

His writings are chaste, scholarly, instructive and entertaining. They flow from a heart full of tenderness and love toward mankind and show a simple faith in Christ, which is touching and tender. He longs for a higher spirituality himself, and seeks to impress the same earnestness of soul into the minds of others. In personal appearance the doctor is slender, very neat and trim. He is a true African in color, and his intellectual development is of the highest order. His retiring disposition, his earnest enthusiasm and kindly demeanor are all very noticeable and give him a commanding presence. One feels like venerating his frost-white hair and patriarchal style, to the extent that he would rather stand than sit in his presence, not because he overawes one by his sternness, but because you wish to honor him. He has had abundant success in all his undertakings. He has a fine church and congregation, and his affable, genial manners do much towards maintaining it, in the capital of the Nation, a place of public worship. His refined and ladylike wife assists him in her devotion to the cause of the church and seeks to aid his ministry by attention to the missionary labors incident to the life of a successful minister.

CHAPTER LXXII

Hon. George H. White
A Member of the House of Representatives and the only
Colored State Solicitor and Prosecuting Attorney

Among the representative men of our race, George H. White holds an important position. He is a young man, having been born in 1852, and is scholarly, dignified and powerful. In his *alma mater*, Howard University, Washington, District of Columbia, where he graduated from an elective course in 1877, he was known for his excellence in science and mathematics, and especially literary tastes which have characterized his life. As a teacher in the public schools and Presbyterian Parochial School, and the Normal School of North Carolina, he was most successful.

The Supreme Court granted him, in 1879, a license to practice law in the Courts of North Carolina after he had completed that study under Judge Clark. But not only as a lawyer has this young man made his mark, still in this, his chosen avocation, his achievements are unrivaled.

Such wonderful skill has Mr. White always shown in the management of famous cases, often winning against the ablest white lawyers of Newbern, North Carolina, that the last Republican convention chose to nominate him over many white lawyers for State solicitor of the Second Judicial District. By an overwhelming vote was Mr. White elected, and January 1, 1887, he entered into office.

Previous to this election he was a member of the North Carolina Legislature, and for two years he was an efficient worker in the House of Representatives at Raleigh. Later in the State Senate, for the good of his people and his State, he devoted his untiring energies, and he aided much in securing Normal schools throughout his native State. As a speaker, Mr. White is eloquent; as an advocate, clear-sighted, pointed and wise; and the persuasive address with which he holds audiences spellbound, has won for him many honors in public life.

During the Centennial celebration in Philadelphia, Mr. White served as assistant in charge of the United States Coast Survey.

He is not an active politician. His desire is to honor his profession and uplift himself and race by his sterling worth. Such men elevate the race and prove that they are susceptible of high culture and that they can rise amid difficulties and embarrassments. The law opens a wide field for eloquence, learning and fame, and it is an incentive to the young to be pointed to such examples. His *alma mater* has had much honor reflected on her by such men as the Hon. G. H. White.

JOSIAH T. SETTLE

CHAPTER LXXIII

*Hon. Josiah T. Settle, A. B., A. M., LL. B.
Eminent Lawyer—Assistant Attorney-General of Shelby
county, Tennessee—Eloquent Orator—Legislator*

This gentleman was born September 30, 1850, on Cumberland Mountains, while his father and mother were *en route* from North Carolina to Mississippi, and as his parents continued their journey as soon as circumstances would permit and settled in Mississippi, he claims this as his native State. His parents were named Josiah and Nancy Settle. His mother belonged to his father, who was one of the famous Settle family of Rockingham, North Carolina. He had no wife at the time he began raising a family by his former slave, being at that time a widower. Unlike a great many Southern men of his time, he was devoted to his children and their mother. After a few years residence in Mississippi, he manumitted his children and their mother. After he had made them free he was informed that they could not remain in Mississippi as the laws of the State forbade "Free Negroes" residing therein. In March, 1856, he carried them to Hamilton, Ohio, where he bought them a home and located them there, spending his summers with them, and the remainder of the year upon his Southern plantation. Soon another difficulty presented itself. His Northern neighbors told him that he could not continue his relations with his family unless he was married. His reply to this was: "That is what I have always desired to do," and in 1858 the mother of his children became his lawful wife in the presence of their children, whom the law, at the same time, in its beneficence, made legitimate. He then went backwards and forwards attending to his property in Mississippi. At the breaking out of the war, being a Union man, he came North and remained until he died in 1869.

There is not a nobler specimen of manhood in the history of the South than this Southerner, who dared to do right. "Joe," as he was familiarly called, first attended school near Hamilton, Ohio, where there were no colored schools and few colored people, and mixed schools were not very popular in the State of Ohio at that period. When he was finally allowed to enter a little country school, he had to commence fighting at the same time. Sometimes his teachers were so prejudiced that it was impossible for him to attend and stand the punishment of teachers and scholars combined. Finally a good Christian woman, and an excellent teacher, took charge of the school and gave the "odd sheep" a chance. He soon became deeply attached to her, and she took a warm interest in him, and it was not long before he became first in all of his classes. It was this kind woman who first inspired him with a desire for something more than a "country school-house." He went to Oberlin, Ohio, in the spring of 1866, where he prepared for and entered college in 1868. He was chosen one of the orators to represent his class when they entered college, an honor much coveted by the students. In the spring of 1869 his father died, and at the close of his freshman year he left Oberlin College and went to Washington city and entered the sophomore class of Howard University, where he pursued his college studies and taught in the Preparatory Department. He graduated from the College Department of the Howard University in 1872, together with J. M. Gregory and A. C. O'Hear, the class of 1872 being the first class that was ever graduated from the College Department.

During the last two years of his college course, he clerked for a white man in the educational division of the Freedman's Bureau; during the latter part of his Senior year, he was elected reading clerk of the House of Delegates, Washington then being under a territorial form of government; and at the time of his graduation was performing his duties as reading clerk, and teaching two classes a day at the University, and pursuing his own studies at the same time. Immediately after his graduation from college, he joined the Law Department. He took an active part in the district politics, and held many places of honor and profit. He was clerk in the Board of Public Works until its expiration, then accountant in the Board of Audits.

He was also trustee of the county schools for District of Columbia. During the presidential campaign of 1872, he canvassed several counties in Maryland, where his youth and brilliancy created quite a sensation. He also made speeches in Ohio, speaking at Dayton, Cleveland and other places. At Dayton, he spoke after Gen. John Harlan, and after the meeting was given a banquet, he being the first colored man at that time who had ever delivered a speech from the court-house steps of Vallandigham's home. Upon his graduation from the Law Department, he was selected as one of the orators to represent his class. He was admitted to the bar of the Supreme Court of District of Columbia, but he determined to locate in Mississippi. He left Washington for that purpose in March, 1875, and was admitted to the bar in Mississippi upon an examination at Vicksburg, but traveled over a considerable portion of the State before he found a favorable location. He finally located at Sardis, Panola Co., in the Northwestern part of the State, and formed a partnership with Hon. D. T. J. Matthews, under the firm name of Settle & Matthews. He returned to Washington, and married Miss T. T. Vogelsang of Annapolis, Maryland, a refined and cultivated lady, already distinguished for her superior mental qualities, and she has made him a faithful wife. He returned with his bride to the South, and commenced there the practice of law. In August of the same year he was unanimously nominated by the Republican convention for the position of District Attorney of the Twelfth Judicial District of the State of Mississippi, in which there was a Republican majority of 2,500. The result of the elections in Mississippi in the year 1875 was a revolution of the politics of the South, and the virtual death of Republicanism in that part of the country, and Mr. Settle was of course defeated with all the rest; but he made an active and vigorous canvass, filling his appointments wherever made, knowing that he did so at the risk of his life. In 1876 he was a member of the State convention, which sent delegates to the National Republican convention at Cincinnati, Ohio. He was elected as a delegate, and was also selected as Republican elector for the State-at-large, on the Hayes and Wheeler ticket, in that convention. He was the only delegate from Mississippi who voted for the nomination of Roscoe Conkling for President, and continued to vote for him as long as his name was before the convention. In this convention he was selected by the members of the Mississippi delegation to second the nomination of Stewart L. Woodford of New York, for Vice-President, and addressed the convention in a telling speech. In 1880 he was again chosen as Republican elector on the Garfield and Arthur ticket.

In 1882 he was strongly urged to become a Republican candidate for Congress from the Second Congressional District of Mississippi. At the time, Gen. Jas. R. Chalmers moved from the Shoestring district to the Second, and Mr. Settle only declined to do so at the earnest solicitation of some leading Republicans in Jackson and Washington City, District of Columbia. Being induced to believe the interests of the Republican party demanded the indorsement of Gen. Chalmers, and in the convention where he could have been nominated with ease, he withdrew, and himself in an eloquent speech placed the name of Chalmers before the convention. He was made chairman of the Republican Congressional Executive Committee, and made a thorough canvass of the district, and Chalmers was elected by a handsome majority. In 1883 some of the Republicans and Democrats made a fusion ticket for county officers and members of the Legislature. This, Mr. Settle vigorously opposed, and became a candidate for the Legislature on an independent ticket. It was during this canvass that he made the most brilliant efforts of his life; he was met by the ablest speakers of both parties on every stump in the country, and although he was single-handed, he was before the people irresistibly, and was triumphantly elected by more than twelve hundred majority.

During his term in the Legislature, he won golden opinions on every side, and was regarded as one of the ablest men in the House. The first time he rose to address the House he won all hearers, and ever after that he had no trouble in getting the eye of the speaker. He never addressed the speaker unless he had something to say, and possessed the happy faculty of knowing when he had finished. At the adjournment of the Legislature he was presented with a gold-headed cane, as a token of the esteem in which he was held. Upon his return to his home he determined to abandon active participation in politics and devote his time to the practice of law, and moving from Mississippi he located at Memphis. In the spring of 1885, about two months after his location at Memphis, he was appointed Assistant Attorney-General of the Criminal Court of Shelby county, which position he held until the expiration of General Turner's term of office. During this time he was left almost in entire charge of all the responsibilities and duties of the position, and so thorough and able was his management of the prosecution, that he was on several occasions complimented by the Court from the bench, and at all times enjoyed the unbounded confidence of the Attorney-General and the Court. During his term of office as Assistant Attorney-General, Mr. Settle built up for himself a good practice. He is now engaged in the practice of law at Memphis, where he enjoys the esteem and confidence of the entire bar. His practice is constantly growing, and as he is a comparatively young man, his prospects are very flattering. In religion he is inclined to the Episcopalian views. This orator did not disappoint the expectations of his friends. While in school, we all admired him and predicted a splendid career. I remember hearing him make a Sunday school address to the pioneer Sunday school in Hillsdale, District of Columbia, and his eloquence was such that it was never forgotten. "Joe" owes much to Theresa, as she was called in the Howard, when Mr. Settle courted her. It is hoped that he will yet live many days to fulfill the measure of honor that awaits so learned a disciple of Blackstone. While in Memphis once, we heard it said "that young man is too eloquent to be a prosecutor for the State, because the jury would be so blinded by his eloquence that the opposing counsel could not persuade them to give a verdict of acquittal."

CHAPTER LXXIV

William H. Gibson, Esq.
School Teacher in the Slavery Days—Musician—Mail Agent—
RevenueAgent—Grand Master U. B. of Friendship

The narrative here given of the career of William H. Gibson, Sr., is worthy of perusal. Beginning life humble, he has become one of the most respected citizens of Louisville, Kentucky. Philip and Amelia Gibson, free Negroes in the city of Baltimore, were the parents of this honored son.

They gave him all the advantages of an education, that the city of his birth offered to the Negro child, and in 1834, when he was but five years of age, he could read. Continuing his studies, he had for several years as instructor John Fortie, a prominent teacher.

His color prevented him from learning the printer's trade as his parents desired, but it did not close every avenue for advancement. He served for ten years as porter in the book store of the Lutheran Book Company, and the kindness of the clerks at that place enabled him to continue his studies. Bishop D. A. Payne, D.D., was one of his instructors in English and Latin grammar. Music was one study that possessed his soul, and he began its study in boyhood, under the best teachers of Baltimore in vocal music, and Professor James Anderson, violinist. The Sharpe Street choir and musical associations of that city were honored with his membership. In 1847 he moved to Louisville with Rev. James Harper, and with Robert Lane he taught in this city, opening a day and a night school, and a singing school in the basement of the Methodist church, corner of Fourth and Green Streets. His school numbered from fifty to one hundred pupils, many of whom were slaves whose masters gave them written permits to attend school. His singing classes were led by the violin.

He introduced the first instrumental music in the colored churches of this city, which was regarded by many as a sacrilege and intolerable. The study of the piano and guitar were added to his accomplishments, and he imparted to others of this knowledge, until the breaking out of the Rebellion, in September, 1862, which closed schools and churches in this city.

He then went to Indianapolis, Indiana, and taught a school partially supported by the "Friends," for the freed children of the soldiers in the war.

During his whole life he served on many important committees, and held many positions of trust. In May, 1863, he received a commission from Colonel Condee, recruiting officer of the Fifty-fifth Massachusetts Colored Regiment, to raise colored soldiers. He accepted the commission for Louisville, Charleston, Albany and Jeffersonville, Indiana. In Indiana he succeeded in recruiting, but the military authorities of Louisville decided that Massachusetts had no right to Kentucky recruits, and he was arrested and ordered to leave the State. He returned to Indiana and thence to Leavenworth, Kansas, where he taught partly under the supervision of the American Missionary Society until the close of the war, when he returned to Louisville, July, 1866, and his schools were reorganized under the Freedmen's Bureau. He taught day and night until 1874, when he resigned to accept the position of assistant cashier in the Freedman's bank. This position he held until it closed. In 1870 he received a commission from General Grant, as mail agent on the Knoxville branch of the L. & N. R. R. He was transferred at the expiration of eight months to the Lexington branch. On his second trip he was attacked by the Ku Klux Klan, and his life was so endangered that a military guard attended him for some months.

In 1874 he received an appointment in the Revenue Department as United States gauger, which position he retained until the defeat of the Republican administration. In 1847 he was initiated in the Masonic fraternity in Baltimore, Maryland. He organized Enterprise Lodge, No. 3, and Mt. Moriah Lodge, No. 1, of Louisville. In 1859 he was elected Grand Junior Warden of Grand Lodge of Ohio, and was Grand Master of Kentucky in 1872, and has taken all degrees to Knights Templars. In 1869 he was a delegate to the colored National Convention held in Washington, District of Columbia.

In the city of Louisville, W. H. Gibson, Esq., will always hold an exalted place in the hearts of its citizens, as no project has been on foot for the improvement of the minds and morals of its citizens that has not met his sanction. In the Sunday school he is an active worker, and for several years has been president of the Sunday School Union of the Methodist churches. In society and church, home and country, W. H. Gibson ranks as one of the most respected Christian supporters of right, liberty and union.

CHAPTER LXXV

Hon. George W. Williams
The Most Eminent Negro Historian in the World—An Author of World-Wide Reputation—Legislator—Judge Advocate of the Grand Army of the Republic—Novelist—Scholar—Magnetic Orator—Editor—Soldier—Preacher—Lawyer—Poet and Traveler

---

Among the intellectual stars which shine in the zenith of the Negro world, increasing in brightness day by day, dispensing its light to the dark corners of the world, is the Hon. George Washington Williams. He was born at Bedford Spring, Bedford county, Pennsylvania, on the sixteenth day of October, 1849. His mother's maiden name was Nellie or Helen Rouse, who came of Negro and German parentage. His father was of Welsh and Negro extraction. He was a man of large mould, standing about six feet high and weighing from one hundred and eighty to two hundred pounds. His mother was medium in size, of fair complexion, large dark eyes and black hair, and was a woman of rare intellectual power, speaking German fluently, and was well up with the times in current literature. She was noted for her dramatic and elocutionary powers, of which the son is possessed of a large share, no doubt inherited from his mother.

When young George was about three years old, his parents moved to Newcastle, Lawrence county, Pennsylvania, and his early education was obtained in that State and in Massachusetts, comprising two years with a private tutor, four years in the common and high schools, two years in an academy, and four years at Newton Center, Massachusetts.

He was enlisted in the United States volunteer army by Major George L. Sterns, and served until the close of the war. Being only fourteen years old he ran away from home and begged to be accepted, even against the advice of the examining surgeon. He didn't give his own name when he enlisted, but used that of one of his half uncles. By his intelligence and attention to the duties of a soldier, he rose rapidly from one grade to another, beginning as private and ending the war as a sergeant-major of

GEORGE W. WILLIAMS

his regiment. Having been severely wounded he was discharged from the service, but soon re-enlisted and was detailed on the staff of General Jackson in 1865, and accompanied him in May to Texas. While there he was ordered to be mustered out, and he immediately enlisted in the Mexican army, where he was at once made orderly sergeant of the First battery from the State of Tampico, and in just one week was made assistant inspector-general of the artillery, with the rank of lieutenant-colonel After the capture and death of Maximillian he returned to the United States and entered the cavalry service of the regular army, serving in the Comanche campaign of 1867 with conspicuous bravery. February, 1868, while at Fort Arbuckle, this hero was converted, and in late autumn left the army for civil life, having been convinced as a Christian that killing people in time of peace as a profession was not the noblest life a man could live. As soon as he completed his six hundred miles' journey across the plains, he went to St. Louis, Missouri.

His father was a Unitarian, and his mother a devoted member of the Lutheran church; but the son read the New Testament and came to the conclusion that the Baptist church, in practices and doctrines, came up to the New Testament standard. Not being acquainted with a single person in St. Louis, save a few officers at General Sheridan's headquarters, he sallied forth into the streets to inquire for a Baptist church. Singularly enough the first man he met was a deacon in a church of that denomination, and on the following day, which was the Sabbath, he told his experience in the First Baptist church and was that evening baptized into the fellowship of the Baptist communion by the Rev. H. H. White.

From 1868 to 1874 he devoted himself to study, and graduated from the Newton Theological Institution, June 10, 1874, delivering an oration on "The Early Church in Africa." Here at once can be seen the tendency of Mr. Williams. He always inquires into the history of some subject connected with the race. He early developed the power of search and the love for deep investigation, and thus laid the foundation for his present and future life, which has become so widely connected with historical subjects which materialized themselves into the great histories which he has written. He was licensed to preach June 1, 1874, as the following will show:

This is to certify that the Watertown Baptist church, having confidence in the Christian character and fitness of our brother, George W. Williams, did on the thirty-first of May, 1874, unanimously vote to give him license to preach the Gospel of Christ.

In behalf of the church,
WILLIAM BLODGETT,
Church Clerk

WATERTOWN, June 1, 1874

His ordination to the Gospel ministry took place at Watertown, Massachusetts, June 11, 1874, under the call of the First Baptist church in Watertown.

April 4, 1874, he received a call to the Twelfth Street Baptist church in Boston. He accepted this call, and the following services were held by way of recognition of the new pastor. Sermon by Rev. Dr. George Lorimer, from 1 Corinthians chapter i, 16–17 verses. Prayer of Recognition, by Rev. R. M. Neale, D. D. Charge, Rev. D. C. Eddy. Hand of Fellowship, Rev. J. T. Beckley.

While pastor of this church he wrote the history of its struggles and labors, for the purpose of calling the attention of the charitable to its pecuniary needs. The church had done excellent work among the colored people of the West End and deserved to be sustained. It was organized in 1840, with an original membership of only about forty, who withdrew from the First Independent Baptist church. The volume contains eighty pages and was published in a popular form, by James H. Earle, No. 11 Cornhill. While pastor of this church, he preached a memorial sermon before the Robert A. Bell Post 134, Grand Army of the Republic, Sunday, May 24, 1874.

Mr. Williams applied to the Massachusetts Legislature for the position of chaplain. The request was not granted, but he made an open and plain request for that which he desired.

He served the Twelfth Street Baptist church one year as supply before he was ordained, and was pastor one year. The Divine favor that was shown him was an evidence of the fruitfulness of his ministry. His relation was terminated with that church in August, 1875, by his own voluntary resignation. He then went to the city of Washington, and the following notice is given of his purpose for visiting that city, in a speech which he delivered in the Presbyterian church, at a meeting held for the purpose of taking steps towards establishing a journal in that city to be managed by colored men, and devoted to the interests of the colored people. The report says: "The Rev. George W. Williams delivered an eloquent address in which he stated that he proposed to establish a journal in the District of Columbia, devoted to the interests of colored people." There was no question as to the necessity of such a journal. It was offered in objection that the colored people were not a reading people, but educational statistics of the country show that within the last decade they have become a reading people.

Speaking of Horace Greeley, he said that he considered him the most remarkable man of the nineteenth century in every respect, and especially in journalism. He, Mr. Williams, proposed to edit a paper devoted to the colored people—politics, art, and the events of the day.

He had been waiting a long time for an opportunity and was willing to sacrifice everything in the enterprise, because duty urged him. Mr. Douglass, in this meeting, said that he had listened to Mr. Williams with great satisfaction, and was impressed with his range of vision and decided ability. A committee was appointed to draft resolutions; said committee consisted of Messrs. Frederick Douglass, J. B. Sampson and M. M. Holland. The following is one of the most important resolutions which they reported.

Resolved: That we have heard with satisfaction the proposition of Rev. George W. Williams to establish such a journal in Washington, and we will do what we can to make the proposed enterprise a success.

The following persons took part in this meeting: Those above mentioned and Messrs. Barbadoes, Wall, Smith, Matthews, Emerson, Wilson, Professor John M. Langston and C. C. Crusoe. The result was the establishment of the *Commoner,* which did good service during its existence.

December 22, 1875, he was appointed in the Post Office Department at Washington, District of Columbia. He accepted, but resigned this position February 15, 1876.

He was called to take pastoral charge of the Union Baptist Church of Cincinnati, Ohio, on Thursday, February 10, 1876, which he accepted, and preached his first sermon on Sabbath, February 20, 1876. He was installed as pastor of the Union Baptist church, Thursday evening, March 2, 1876.

July 21, 1876, at the forty-fifth anniversary of their church, he delivered an address, in which he reviewed somewhat the history of the church. An extract of the address is here given to assist in preserving the history of that church, and also to pay tribute to some distinguished men who have done service in founding and sustaining this old and substantial church:

From 1831 to 1835, the pulpit of the Branch of Enon Church was filled by supplies, as the brethren were able to serve them. Drs. Lynd and Patterson often administered the Eucharist, baptized and preached as they found opportunity. In 1832, the venerable Elijah Forte was chosen to take the temporary oversight of the church. He was a man of fervent piety, unabating zeal, wisdom and discretion. He was a successful business man, and the same system, energy and caution which distinguished him in business, made him a leader among his brethren—a leader at once safe and judicious. How much the church owes to the faithfulness of Elijah Forte can not well be estimated.

After the Church was re-organized as the African Union Baptist church, the same year, 1835, the Rev. David Nickens was called to take the pastoral oversight of the church. He was probably the first ordained colored minister in Ohio. He did not possess the culture of the schools, and yet he was no stranger to books, especially the Bible. He was not fluent in speech, but careful. He was faithful to every trust, and earnest in manner. He accomplished much, baptized many, was loved by his people, respected by all classes, and died in the midst of his labors, deeply lamented, in 1838.

His ministry was brief, though wonderfully successful. During these four years he had organized a day and Sunday school, which were flourishing at the time of his death, receiving, per annum, $300.

The church was casting about for a shepherd, and laid hands upon a young man by the name of Charles Satchell. He was a young man of promise, and the church gave him the splendid opportunities that made him one of the most eminent divines the Colored Baptists have produced during the last half century.

The Rev. Charles Satchell was every inch a general. He cast his eye over the field in which he was to marshal his little company, and carefully reviewed his troops. His policy was to make every member sensible of individual responsibility, and found something for every one to do. He soon had a working church, because he was a working pastor, and his example was contagious. His sick were well cared for, the dying received the consolations of Christianity from the lips of a faithful pastor, and the wayward were affectionately sought and brought back to the love and service of Christ.

As early as 1841, the church had grown under Satchell's administration, from forty-five to two hundred and seventy-five. And its strength was not to be found in its numbers, but in the intelligence and spirituality of its members. He was a teacher as well as a pastor. He continued to work successfully for eight years, when he resigned, to the regret of his charge, and was succeeded by the Rev. Allen Graham. He was the esteemed pastor of the church for two years, working successfully and acceptably.

In 1850 the Rev. W. P. Newman followed brother Graham, and resigned in 1852 to accept a call to Canada. The late Rev. Henry Adams became pastor of this church immediately upon the retirement of Newman, and remained until 1855. Rev. H. L. Simpson was the successor of Adams, and held the pulpit for a term of three years. Rev. H. H. White, the polished writer and graceful speaker, followed Simpson in a pastorate of three years, and did well.

The Rev. W. P. Newman was tendered the pastoral charge of the church again and accepted. He was a man of spotless integrity, scrupulously conscientious, and strong in his likes and dislikes. He was unostentatious and generous in his private relations, earnest, forcible, original, and, at times, rough and severe; he was no apologetical, but rather a polemical preacher. He had the spirit of a reformer, with boldness and severity not always judicious or praiseworthy. The sinner who sat under his preaching, felt his searching, burning language, and felt every word was directed at him. He was unsparing in his denunciation of every species of ungodliness, whether in or out of the church, and was feared by one and respected by the other.

He was just in the most successful days of his ministry, when on the third of August, 1866, he was cut off by a brief but severe sickness from cholera.

The Rev. H. L. Simpson was recalled, and served until 1869, three years, when he tendered his resignation as pastor.

The Rev. James H. Magee was called during the same year, and was pastor for four years.

The pulpit was vacant for some time, when it was supplied by Revs. Campbell, Emery, Sage, Stone, Early, Barnett, Thardkill and Darnell.

During the first ten years of the church's existence, it grew so large that there was no longer sufficient sittings in the small edifice on Central Avenue. The brethren were casting about for another location, when a proposition came from the trustees of the First Baptist church, to the effect that their building on Baker Street could be had for $9,000, its actual worth being $12,000, and thereby donating $3,000. The offer was accepted, and in 1839 this church began to worship on Baker Street, and continued there for a quarter of a century.

From 1864 to 1874, ten years, the church enjoyed great prosperity, in spiritual as well as temporal things. It paid all its debts, gave with an unsparing hand, and enjoyed many glorious revivals. She had a strong hold upon the young people of this city, and a reputation for intelligence and usefulness throughout the Southwest, and especially in Ohio.

This church has set apart to the Gospel ministry twenty of its members, many of whom are faithful workers. The reverend brethren Shelton, Scott, Fassitt, Webb and Early are the sons of this church, and earnest pastors in or near this city.

About twenty members of this church, led by our venerable brother, Elder Henry Williams, Senior, withdrew with their letters, and formed the Zion Baptist church, in 1842. The church grew in numbers, and became quite influential under the pastoral charge of Rev. Wallace Shelton.

Rev. G. W. Williams resigned December 1, 1877. September 2, 1878, he was appointed internal revenue storekeeper by the Secretary of the Treasury, and served also in the Auditor's office as secretary of the four million dollar fund to build the Cincinnati Southern railroad.

He studied law in the office of Judge Alphonso Taft and the Cincinnati Law School; and was admitted to practice in the Supreme Circuit Court of the State of Ohio in the city of Columbus, June 7, 1881; and admitted in the Supreme Judicial Court at Boston, within the aforesaid Suffolk county, on the second Tuesday in September, A.D. 1883. He began his political life in Cincinnati. At first he was averse to going into politics, as he said in a speech at Hopkin's hall when addressing an enthusiastic meeting of colored Republicans:

As a rule, I believe that ministers of the Gospel should remain as far from the political arena as possible. But when the storm clouds thicken and darken our National sky, when the hand of treason is at the throat of the Nation, when the temple of justice, humanity and equality is about to be desecrated by traitors; when the Constitution is about to be eliminated and the gracious, benign amendments thereof to be rendered nugatory; when the proud institutions of America—our joy at home, and our glory among the civilized powers of the earth—are imperiled, I would be false to the race to which I am bound by the ties of consanguinity, false to the flag under which I fought, false to the great issues of this hour, false to the instincts and impulses of my better nature and deserving of the execrations of God and man, if I did not lend my pen, my voice, my soul, to the cause of the illustrious Republican party.

September, 1877, he was nominated for the Legislature from Hamilton county, Ohio. At the ratification meeting of the colored Republicans, Mr. Williams delivered an address of which the following is an extract. Said he:

My friends and fellow citizens—I appreciate the high public spirit of which this large and enthusiastic meeting is born. I am deeply touched by the manifold expressions of kindly sentiment concerning myself, and am cheered by the pledges already made to support the Republican party in the approaching canvass. I would, indeed, be an ingrate if I were insensible to the honor conferred upon me by my party and race. I did not seek the nomination, did not ask it. The party and my friends bestowed it with lavish hands, and, as I believe, with honest intentions. I said to my friends, who urged me to be a candidate for legislative honors, that I would yield to their wishes if it were certain I would serve the whole people. The nomination was made with a heartiness that led me to believe that the leaders of the Republican party, at least, honestly desired to give proper representation to the colored people; and that when a colored man, representing the people, should come to the front, they would give him their unqualified support. Then, when I turned to my people and found them almost a unit as to my nomination, there was but one thing left for me to do, and that was to accept the nomination—this unsought compliment.

I was not a stranger to every person when I came to this beautiful Queen City. I was known to quite a number of the people, either personally or through the press. From 1863 till the present moment I have identified myself with the various interests of my race and country. Upon the field of battle, under the mellow and enlightening blaze of the student's lamp, in the wide and useful field of journalism, in the sacred pulpit and in the political arena, I have striven for all that is noble, just and of good report. I was welcomed to your city by white and black men, by Democrats and Republicans, by saints and sinners. And I now call you to witness that I have labored for my people and party with zeal and faithfulness. For this you have honored me with a foremost place in your midst, a warm place in your hearts and confidence. One could scarcely be affected by a spirit of vainglory, standing where I stand tonight. I stand here, not for myself, but for the three thousand loyal colored men in this county, not for the fifteen thousand colored voters in this grand old commonwealth; but I stand here as a representative of the sovereign people. I am before you, fellow citizens, as an exponent and defender of the immortal teachings of the Republican party, the party that represents the loyal sentiments and political conscience of the American people.

During his term as a member of the Legislature, he was chairman of the committee on library, special committee on railroad terminal facilities; second member of the committee on universities and colleges, and took part in all the legislation, and secured the passage of several bills referring to police, railroad legislation and school legislation.

He has been a member of the Grand Army of the Republic for many years, and has been a National delegate and officer from the beginning of his membership. January 26 and 27, 1881, the fifth annual encampment of the above order met at Columbus, Ohio, at which time he was appointed to deliver a speech in response to the welcoming address of the mayor. In the minutes of the session which met at Cincinnati, January 18 and 19, 1882, will be found his report as judge-advocate of the department of Ohio, Grand Army of the Republic.

Mr. Williams is a man who has delivered many orations upon many topics and is still in great demand as an orator. As an author he has written two standard works, *The History of the Negro Race in America from 1819 to 1880; Negroes as Slaves, as Soldiers and as Citizens, together with a Preliminary Consideration of the Unity of the Human Family. An Historical Sketch of Africa and an Account of the Negro Government of Sierra Leone, Africa.*

At this writing he has in Harper Brothers' press a voluminous work on the *Negro as a Soldier*. We will give two criticisms of his *History of the Negro Race*, simply to show how the work is estimated. The first will be from the *Westminster Review*, London, England, which was sent to him with the compliments of that magazine, July, 1883. It says:

A *History of the Negroes* (the author insists on the propriety of spelling the word with a capital) has just been brought out by the first colored member of the Ohio Legislature and late Judge-Advocate of the Grand Army of the Republic of Ohio. He gives no particulars about his own life, whether he was ever a slave or not; but to judge from the honorable position he has attained, he must have been born before the emancipation of his race, though his portrait shows him to be still a young man, probably not of pure African blood, with the face indicating clearheadedness and resolution. The materials have been collected with great care, official documents in most cases printed in full; and though a member of an oppressed race cannot be expected to write calmly about the wrongs of his people, there is no needless or offensive vituperation. The style is clear and straightforward, with a few Americanisms here and there, some of which will be new to many of his readers on this side, as the verb "to enthuse," meaning to inspire enthusiasm.

From the *Kansas City Review of Science* we give the following:

Having referred quite fully to the general scope of this work in the April number of the Review, it is unnecessary to recur to it or to repeat the favorable comments then made upon the ability and skill manifested by the author in handling his subject. The present volume is devoted to an account of the Negro race in America between the years 1619 and 1800. Commencing with the unity of mankind and considering the subject in the light of philology, ethnology and Egyptology, the author proceeds to discuss primitive Negro civilization, the Negro kingdoms of Africa, the Ashantee Empire, African idiosyncrasies, languages, literature and religion, Sierra Leone, the Republic of Liberia, etc.

In part two he considers the history of slavery in the Colonies of Virginia, New York, Massachusetts, Maryland, Delaware, Connecticut, Rhode Island, New Jersey, South Carolina, New Hampshire, Pennsylvania and Georgia, giving the laws regulating slavery in each, and many other facts which have been collected with great pains and carefully condensed.

Part three is devoted to an account of the services of the Negro during the Revolution, including their military employment, the legal status, the statutory prohibition against educating them; notices of Banneker, the Negro astronomer; Fuller, the mathematician, and Derham, the physician; slavery during the Revolution as a political and legal problem.

Mr. Williams, though a very dark-skinned and pronounced Negro, is a lawyer and has been a member of the Ohio Legislature. He is a vigorous writer and a hard student. In the preparation of these volumes he has consulted over twelve thousand volumes, besides thousands of pamphlets, and has succeeded in producing a work which will be authority on the subject treated until a better one is produced, which is likely to be a long time.

The honorable gentleman has traveled extensively in our own country, especially giving some attention to Mexico and New Mexico, and has visited nearly every country in Europe, and though quite a young man, he has distinguished himself so that with all justice the following titles can be given him: Reverend, Honorable, Colonel, Editor, Traveler, Legislator, Lawyer, Orator, Poet, Historian and Novelist. Space forbids us to give quotations from all of his writings, but we will content ourselves with giving some at the close of this sketch.

One matter we might refer to here, before we close the biographical part of this work, and that is his appointment at the expiring hour of the Congress just before the inauguration of President Grover Cleveland. It will be remembered that President Arthur appointed him to office very nearly, if not the last act of his administration as President of the United States, and Grover Cleveland found him in office confirmed as Minister to Hayti, and the following extract which I take from the *New York Tribune* will give sufficient explanation of the matter. It will be remembered also that he did not fill the position, but was removed and another substituted in his place:

WASHINGTON, April 20—Mr. Williams, United States Minister to Hayti, addressed to President Cleveland, on April 13, a letter of which the following is a copy:

"It is unnecessary for me to give you the history of my case. It is brief and a matter of public record. You will remember, however, that when I called to pay my respects a month ago, I informed you of my nomination and confirmation as United States Minister Resident and Consul-General to Hayti. When you expressed pleasure at this statement, which was news to you, I abandoned my avowed purpose of tendering my resignation. Several weeks later I learned that a fight was being made against my appointment. Vice-President Hendricks had told me that he wanted the position. I came to you, Mr. President, and told you that if the administration had a candidate for the Haytian mission I would resign. You told me that you had no candidate. I then told you that a fight was being made against me in the dark, and that I understood that an effort was being made to have me recalled. You told me that my recall had been suggested, but that the matter would be judicially considered. Your promise of fair play, Mr. President, gave me confidence. I had then, and have now, absolute confidence in your promise. I have sent two communications to the Department of State. I have received no reply. After waiting forty-two days since I took the oath of office, I called today to draw my pay for "waiting instructions." After waiting an hour in the public hall, I saw the secretary in a private room. I was informed that there were charges pending against me. I asked for a copy but was refused. I was subsequently informed by the chief clerk that I could have my thirty days' salary, provided I would write my resignation. He said the secretary had sent him to me. I declined. I declined to be bribed to resign with charges hanging over my head. This is a very brief statement of the case, but there are many more important matters that I cannot properly mention at this time.

"Mr. President, I appeal to you for justice and fair play. My case ceases to be a personal matter from today. I am on trial before the country for my race, and, as far as I am concerned as a young man now some time in public life, I cannot in justice to myself seek a back door. I am a public officer; let my case have the same open examination that every honest official should court; let the charges be made in the light; let my accusers face me, and if I shall be found unfit for public station, let me be dismissed. If I shall endure the test, let me have my rights. I make no claim to perfection, but I do honestly believe that I have striven to be a man and a gentleman. I have no apology to offer for my record as a Union soldier and Republican citizen. I have not always felt enthusiastic over the candidate of my party, and sometimes have wished that my party had pursued a different policy. But all parties are human, and party policy is dictated by what is necessary rather than by what is right in the abstract. I rejoice in the noble record of the Republican party, and yet sincerely and honestly wish the present Democratic administration abundant success. I am a citizen and a patriot first, and a partisan last. Your election was a personal promotion and triumph of an honest public officer, and the Democratic party is in power today on account of your personal popularity. It is natural, therefore, that the stout-hearted, clear-headed New Englanders who gave you their moral support should be solicitous about the position of your administration toward the Negro, for whom they have worked for three generations. Believe me, Mr. President, I have no personal ambition; I do not beg to be retained. I have good reasons to believe that I am sought as the victim of race malice. It is my duty to endure the fire like a man. I certainly shall.

"Mr. President, you will doubtless see the justice of an early decision in my case. I feel confident that whatever it may be it will be dictated by a high-minded, honorable man, whose highest ambition is to rule wisely and mercifully over all elements in our composite nationality, by a man who desires to be President of the blacks and whites of the Democrats and Republicans of the North and South."

Colonel Williams has adopted original and unique methods of literary investigation and composition peculiar to himself. He believes that a literary man should take the best care of his health and consequently is scrupulously careful in the selection and preparation of his food, in his dress, ventilation of his study and bed chamber, and the character and quantity of his exercise to be taken indoors and outdoors. While residing at Columbus, Ohio, and in New York City, during the years he was engaged on his work, the *History of the Negro Race in America*, he took a great deal of exercise. At Columbus he purchased the Young Men's Christian Association's Gymnasium and bath rooms, employed a business manager, and engaged a professional gymnast from New York and by giving his personal attention for thirty minutes a day brought the institution up to a high standard.

He does not go into society except on rare occasions and then proves himself a congenial and racy conversationalist. There is but one place in which he may be found regularly, except prevented by indisposition or inclement weather, and that is the Thursday evening prayer meeting. He is a member of the Baptist church, and during his Christian life has been an active Sunday school and Young Men's Christian Association worker, until a severe attack of pneumonia and increased literary duties admonished him to husband his strength.

Few persons have had the privilege of knowing him intimately, but those who have come in close contact with him socially have found him an intelligent and interesting gentleman. He is loyal to his friends, but pays little attention to his enemies, except they provoke and bring about war; then it may be said of him truly "Beware of the wrath of a patient man." He is the equal or the superior in general learning, information and originality of any of the representative colored men in this country. He is familiar with the classics, with several modern languages, and is well-informed upon all questions of domestic and foreign politics. He writes poetry with grace and unction and is authority on English classics. As an orator he takes first rank. He has written three novels and a tragedy; the last two productions are destined to create a profound sensation on both sides of the Atlantic and give him additional fame. Although a good lawyer, and, in the practice making a good deal of money, his real tastes are those of the scholar and literary man; and the rest of his life will be devoted to literary pursuits.

At the commencement of the State University, Louisville, Kentucky, May 17, 1887, the Hon. G. W. Williams delivered an oration on "Books and Reading: How to read, what to read, and when to read." The oration was a masterpiece and at the same time a voluminous index to the orator's reading, an epitome of the varied and extensive historical research after wisdom. At this time the degree of LL. D. was conferred on him by the authorities of the State University. The "Eureka," the society before whom he lectured, was especially proud of the honor conferred on him.

CHAPTER LXXVI

*Professor William Eve Holmes, A. B., A. M., LL. D.
Hebrew, German and French Scholar—Professor in the Atlanta
Baptist Seminary*

―――――•◆•―――――

In slave life there were many pleasant scenes, many lives that ran smoothly and presented pictures of a happy home, and it was the wont of American slaveholders to liken slavery to the patriarchal days of father Abraham.

It was under very favorable scenes that W. E. Holmes was born in the city of Augusta, Georgia, January 22, 1856. His parents were slaves, his father belonging to one family and his mother to another. Separated as they were, the care and responsibility of rearing him devolved upon his mother. Fortunately for her, in the immediate service of her master, who was a planter, she never spent a day. From early youth to the close of the war she was hired out, and the family in whose employ she passed the last fourteen years of her slave life, consisting of a father, mother and son, were very kind. The head of the family was a contracting carpenter and did business on a large scale, and as is characteristic with most Southern men, lived an easy and flowing life, never thinking of providing for the wants of his family. There being no children on his premises, he took a liking to young William at an early age, and made a pet of him. He ate at his table, slept in his bed, and accompanied him in his walks. In this kind treatment his wife and son vied with him. His home was indeed a pleasant one. Books and papers were not kept from him, or indeed anything which was elevating and ennobling in its tendencies. His mother being able to read, early inspired him with a love for books, and taught him to read simple paragraphs with some degree of ease. During the last years of the war she sent him every day to school, carefully concealing his books under his clothes to avoid arrest; for the elementary instructions of Negro youth in slavery was forbidden, and the authorities were ever on the alert.

All over the South they were preparing in this secret manner a host to go forth and raise up their people, for had not this been the case our race would never have made such progress in so short a time. The war closing in 1865, gave better opportunities for continuing her labors, which she did, until 1871. During those years he enjoyed the instruction of some of the best teachers from New England. On account of ill health, he suspended studies that year, and was hired out to a cabinet-maker and undertaker, in whose employ he continued two years, but he still kept up his studies. On December 10, 1874, he was converted and joined the Thankful Baptist church, at Augusta, and on the seventh of February following, was baptized in the Savannah river. That year he began school again at the Augusta Institute, prosecuting his studies for seven years without interruption—four years in the city of Augusta, and three in the city of Atlanta, after the removal of the school to that city, and its incorporation under the name of the "Atlanta Seminary," Dr. Joseph T. Roberts, President.

He was a trustworthy disciple of that good man to whom he owes much for his instruction. Shortly after he entered the institution, he was gradually promoted till graduation, when he was made a full professor. Besides doing the work of the prescribed course of literary and theological studies, he has had good instruction in branches not taught in the seminary. In addition to careful preliminary instruction in the Hebrew language, he has been favored with the personal training of Dr. William R. Harper, the learned professor of Oriental languages at Yale University, and for two years he pursued the study of German under a gentleman who completed his education in one of the German Universities, and French under a graduate of Colby University. He was licensed to preach on the twenty-first of June, 1878, and on the second of September, 1881, was ordained to the ministry. In May, 1883, he was elected to the corresponding secretaryship of the Missionary Baptist Convention of Georgia, a body representing more than one hundred and thirty thousand communicants. He held that position for one year. The pressure of business being so great as to require his full time for the school, he declined re-election. He is still however officially connected with the convention and attends it every year. The denominational and educational work—a work in which he feels a deep interest, and which to-day he is laboring to advance, attracts much of his attention. Recently he delivered a speech at Spelman's University, which probably epitomizes his views concerning the race, his subject being: "A Problem to be Solved."

He said:

The *National Baptist* of Philadelphia says: "Let the Negro alone." This is just where the trouble lies. He has been let alone and severely alone. George W. Cable thinks that *at once* the Negro should be admitted to mingle freely with those surrounding him. I don't think so. Bishop Dudley of Kentucky says that the Caucasian should help us. This is good. The sentiment of Fred Douglass, that inter-marriage with a dominant race will settle all difficulties, is of course out of consideration. Grady thinks that if the whole matter be left to the South, that she is able to settle it. The South has had time to do it, and she has not done it. Who, then, shall solve this problem? It must be solved by the colored people themselves; so said Charles Dudley Warner, and with his view mine accords.

In pointing out the steps to be taken in the solution of this problem, he said:

There are three, the first is to make *solid moral progress;* I want our people to recognize the fact that there is rottenness and evil in society, and to that remember, until this is remedied we must keep out mouths shut. Second step is to make *common social progress* as we are too free and familiar, though not wishing to underrate the kindly hospitality, not wishing that we should be social icebergs, yet dignity is to be cultivated. Much that is called politeness, is downright vulgarity. The third step is to make *sound mental progress.* We must have men of learning that are broad and deep.

Speaking of industrial education, he emphasized the importance of handiwork, saying that "the colored men and women must come to recognize the fact that if they are to hold their own in America beside the progressive Caucasian, they must learn to work, the training of head and hand must go side by side."

The degree of Master of Arts was conferred upon him by the University of Chicago, June 11, 1884. He is worth about five thousand dollars in property. He married Miss Elizabeth Easley, a graduate of the Atlanta University, July 15, 1885, who taught in the public schools of Atlanta. He is a man universally beloved and admired by all who know him.

CHAPTER LXXVII

Rev. Randall Bartholomew Vandervall, D. D.
A Self-Made Man— A Graduate from the School of Adversity

———◆●◆———

Knowing of the many difficulties through which the good man whose name stands at the head of this sketch has passed, and admiring his success, which has been wrung from the severest circumstances, and delighting to honor such, it is with marked pleasure that we introduce a few words concerning his struggles and the manner in which he has succeeded in compassing every trouble and arriving at the place where he has become an honored citizen, useful preacher, a man distinguished among the race and his brethren in the ministry.

He was born in 1832 at Nesley's Bend, on the Cumberland river, ten miles above Nashville. His mother's name was Sylvonia. She was the property of a Major Hall, who had brought her from Virginia when a baby in her mother's arms. His father's name was Lewis, and was the property of a man named Foster; and serving said owner as coachman, he was allowed to visit his wife only once a year. There were eleven children in the family. After the death of Mr. Hall, the mother and children became the property of his only daughter, Anna, who hired out all the children that were old enough to leave their mother. When seven years old, young Vandervall was taken on New Year's day to the hiring ground to be hired out. An old white man came to him, saying, "Come with me." He was afraid of white people, and then the thought of leaving his mother was terrible. He snatched him violently from his mother's arms and threw him on a sharp-backed horse and carried him twenty-two miles away from all that was dear to him on the earth.

He was compelled to sleep on the floor, with only one quilt in which he rolled himself as well as he could and cried all night. A white lady next day tried to comfort him, but he was broken-hearted and dreadfully homesick. After several months he became accustomed to the place and remembered the prayer that his mother taught him. He slept in the house with the white people, and every night after they had gone to bed, he would go down on his knees and say his prayers. Sometimes as he was

RANDALL BARTHOLEMEW VANDERVALL

doing so, it seemed as if his mother's hand was resting on his head; then the tears would flow down his cheek. Those were bitter days with the young boy. He stayed there three years and enjoyed one advantage of unspeakable importance: he was permitted to attend school, and the white boys at home taught him to spell. After this time he was taken to Nashville and hired to a man by the name of Garite, who was a minister of the gospel and also kept a boarding house. At that time all the children had reached maturity and the guardian, Mr. Steele, was released and the property was now divided. Mr. Charles Hall secured him as part of his share, and came out one night to get him to go to Kansas. He ran off and did not return while he was there. He was shortly bought by Mr. Vandervall, with whom he was living, for the price of five hundred dollars. When he was fifteen years old he was converted and became more thirsty for knowledge, which he gained by attending night school, being aided very much by John Vandervall, the son of his master. He paid for his lessons by splitting rails. His spare time was given to holding prayer meetings and doing other religious work. Having been immersed by Elder Peter Tuckenway, he began preaching at the age of sixteen, walking twenty miles to appointments, and feeding five hundred at times with the bread of eternal life. He was the only colored Baptist raised in the neighborhood since the split in the denomination which occurred at that time. The brother who baptized him and indoctrinated him, as was common at the time, was called very hard names, but he was strong in the faith. Sometimes he preached for what was called the "Old Baptists," who were greatly in the majority—especially when there were a dozen or more to follow him, their object being to tear him to pieces. They would say, "He is young, he doesn't know any better." He was the wonder of the day, on account of his being so young.

He was married to Miss Martha Nicholson of Hill Brook, by the Rev. Daniel Watkins, and was sent shortly after his marriage to work on a railroad, and was, by this arrangement, permitted to live with his wife; but the man who had hired him, finding he could read and write, abused him so that he ran away, went home, and persuaded his master to let him go to Nashville and work, which he did. For this privilege he paid $200 a year. In six months more, he had his wife living with him, having arranged to pay for her time also. Next, a horse and dray were bought, with which he made considerable money, but he was destined to more trouble. An old white man told him one day that his master was fixing to sell him to one Dr. Wallace, to go South and drive a team. He dreamt the night before that he was sold. On the Sunday following he went home to his owners, and when he arrived they were in the wood-lot and he told them his dream. Mr. Barter said it was not so, but his wife said it was.

After some conversation, he told them he could not believe that they could sell him, as they had promised not to do so. Mr. Vandervall said to him, "God is just, and every man shall have to give an account of himself to God. Now, Mr. Barter, how would you like it to be treated as you have treated me?" "I should not like it," said he. He threw the blame on his wife, and said she would not rest until it was done. He then asked Mr. Barter what he was to do, and then Mr. Barter swore that he would not sign the papers.

Vandervall then asked them to let him keep on paying for his time as he had started to do, and further asked if he had ever been untrue to them, or ever gave them any trouble. They answered "No." He then asked why he wanted to sell him from his wife. To this they made no reply. Mr. Barter then said that he was willing that Vandervall should have a chance to buy himself, if he could do so. This was agreed upon, and the price fixed at $1,800, $500 cash. With all his promises, Mr. Barter, before he was through paying for him, sent a "nigger trader" to see him. Mr. Vandervall mounted his horse, and stayed away from home day and night. He secured Mr. R. L. Bell to become his executor; to him he looked for all protection in money matters.

Amid great difficulties, however, he succeeded at last in raising the money, but in the meantime his troubles were aggravated by the loss of several horses. Grief and hard work began to show themselves on his health. All this time of great darkness his wife was a help-mate indeed to him. Finally, his health was restored, and he started out again full of hope and courage, to secure blessings for himself and family. God with his unerring hand upheld him.

Wherever he went to preach, large audiences greeted him. On account of his power over men, he was sent as an evangelist, and met with great success. It seemed for a while as if the clouds were breaking away, but this did not last long. His wife belonged to an old bachelor who died, and another trouble came upon them, and they were sore afflicted. There were rumors that his wife would be set free, but she was sold to a man named Nelson Nicholson, her own father's grandson. Mr. Vandervall again hired his wife from him. He had saved a little money and he deposited it in the bank of Tennessee, and when it broke he lost it, and thus had another fall. A short time after that, Mr. Nicholson, who bought his wife, called at the hotel where he was at work, and inquired to whom he belonged, saying that he did not want to separate him from his wife, but that he would have to leave town, and would either sell his wife to his owner, or he would buy them. It ended with the young man, whom his wife had partly brought up, buying him, but he had hardly finished paying for her when the war broke out. From that time until the war closed they both hired their time.

Mr. Nicholson, who owned his wife, was rather weak-minded, and allowed a Mr. McKenzie to persuade him to let him have Mr. Vandervall, his wife and child. It was a wicked plot to accomplish a selfish purpose. Both husband and wife moved away, but stayed, however, only a year, when they returned to the city. Several of their children were dead, but amid all these troubles he has given education to those who are now living. James N. Vandervall is a graduate of the Medical Department of the Central Tennessee College, and is now practicing medicine in Waco, Texas. His son and two daughters obtained their education at Roger Williams University.

He has been living in East Tennessee about fifteen years, and when he first settled in that place there was no Baptist church. The Lord has been with them and blessed their labors, and now there is a neat plain building and a membership of nine hundred. Some years ago his church made him a life member of the American Baptist Publication Society. For many years he was President of the State Sabbath School convention. Since the death of Rev. N. G. Murray, he has been President of the Baptist State convention. In the early days of reconstruction he was one of those who aided Dr. J. B. Simmons in selecting the place where the Roger Williams University now stands, serving as a trustee when the school was chartered and since that time. The degree of D. D. was conferred upon him by this institution during the commencement of 1886. His work in organization of churches is worthy of mention, for he has organized nine churches.

After freedom came, he was married to his wife under the laws by the Rev. D. W. Phillips, his staunch friend and adviser. He has succeeded in gathering around him many friends, a valuable home and a good library.

Thus ends the life of a man who suffered in the bonds of American slavery and yet has risen to prominence.

CHAPTER LXXVIII

Rev. Elijah P. Marrs
Preacher—Soldier—Treasurer—Author

In Shelby county, Kentucky, January, 1840, was born Elijah P. Marrs, the subject of this sketch. His mother and father were Virginians by birth, the latter of whom received his freedom from an indulgent master. When quite a boy, Mr. Marrs displayed such elements in his character for successful work in the things that developed the spiritual being, that the neighboring folks called him a "little preacher."

Although the laws of Kentucky forbade the Negro to acquire such knowledge as books give, yet Mr. Roberson, his owner, being a Christian, desired that he should know enough to read the Scripture, and accordingly secretly taught him when still very young. At the age of eleven he professed hope in Christ and was baptized at Simpsonville by Rev. Charles Wells. He says with all sincerity that he never uttered an oath or spent a cent for liquor in his life. The year Abraham Lincoln was made President, manhood in him asserted itself. He devoured the contents of newspapers and books, and being the only colored man, except his brother, H. C. (now deceased), in the neighborhood who could read, he kept the colored people in the community well informed on the state of affairs. At this time Shelby county was threatened with Confederate soldiers, and his former master warned him to be on the alert and not be captured; but though heeding the caution given, he mustered a company of twenty-seven men, Sunday night, September 25, 1864, armed them with clubs, and as their captain, armed himself with an old pistol which had long discharged its last shot, marched a distance of twenty-two miles to Louisville and enlisted in the United States army. Two days later he was made a sergeant of Company L, Twelfth United States Heavy Artillery. His army life was full of excitement, and his company took part in several important engagements. While at home on a furlough before being mustered out, in 1866, he was attacked by a mob of Confederates, but having his presence of mind he held his ground and dispersed his assailants.

August 3, 1871, he married Miss Julia Gray, of Shelbyville, who died April, 1876. He has been a very successful teacher in Shelbyville, La Grange, Louisville, Beargrass, and other places in Kentucky. June 16, 1873, he was licensed to preach at the New Castle Baptist church, thereby realizing his boyhood dreams, and was ordained to the gospel ministry August 22, 1875. He has held no small place in the estimation of his fellow men. He was a delegate to the first educational convention held in Kentucky in 1868, and in the first political convention in 1869, looking forward to the ratification of the Fifteenth Amendment. He enrolled himself as a member, and was appointed a committeeman of resolutions. He was a member of the convention which nominated Governor Harlan, and was also in the State convention of colored men that met in Lexington, Kentucky, in 1882, and the National convention of colored men which met in Louisville in 1883, and the great educational convention which met in Frankfort in 1884. He has been a member of the Executive Board of the General Association of Colored Baptists for six years; a member and secretary of the Executive Board of the Central District Association, and for twelve years secretary of the Central District Association, and is at present treasurer of the General Association. From 1879 to 1880 he was business manager for the State University, then known as the Normal and Theological Institute. March 16, 1880, he was called to the pastorate of the Beargrass church, which position he has held until this time, excepting an interval of three months. This is one of the most successful churches in the State, though by no means the largest.

He has published a book containing a sketch of his life, which has brought him considerable revenue. It treats of his army life, his life as a teacher, of his ministerial labors. He has assisted in setting apart to the work of the gospel ministry fifteen young men. He has amassed some worldly goods, in value to the extent of $3,500. Mr. Marrs is a man admired by all who know him. His quiet, gentlemanly deportment makes him beloved by all the brethren. Usually in earnest, he is no enthusiast, but when he undertakes a thing he goes through with it. He is a strong friend to the cause of education, and can be depended on to be on the side of temperance and against the cause of Satan at all times. Above all he is a true preacher of the Word and a friend in truth and sincerity to those who prove themselves worthy.

DANIEL JONES

CHAPTER LXXIX

Rev. Daniel Jones
Presiding Elder of the M. E. Church—His Hairbreadth Escapes

On June 30, 1830, our subject was born in Reading, Pennsylvania. His parents were Henry and Catharine Jones. His father was a slave on the eastern shores of Maryland, up to he age of twenty-five, when he made his escape into Pennsylvania, where he raised a family of eight children, five of whom are living. Daniel left home at ten years of age to learn the barber's trade in the city of Philadelphia, where he worked at this employment for seven years; but becoming disgusted with it, he concluded to go to sea. After quite a lengthy voyage he landed in Charleston, South Carolina, and being of a venturesome disposition he went ashore with the mate to see the sights, having been warned at the time of the risk he would run in so doing; nevertheless he thought he would try it. At nine o'clock a bell rang as a warning for all the colored people to get in the house; and as he did not understand the signal, of course he did not retire. Mr. Jones is so fair that at first the patrols did not discover that he was not a "simon pure;" and when they undertook to arrest him, then began a mighty race for the vessel, which was footed in dead earnest; being fleet of foot, he managed to make his escape, and never had a desire to repeat the expriment.

On the sixteenth of January, 1849, he started around Cape Horn for the newly discovered gold fields of California, in one of the first of a class of clipper ships, "Gray Eagle." After sailing four months and two days, passing into the Golden Gate he entered the harbor of San Francisco. He worked in the gold mines of California and Oregon for five years with good success, and concluded to make the latter place his home; and so he located at Jacksonville, for some years and then, on recommendation of physicians, he moved to Cresent City, California, on the seashore. He recovered his health and moved to Salem, the capital of the State of Oregon. Here he lived in the midst of the famous Oregon Indian War and had many narrow escapes from death. One especially, he says, he shall never forget. A white man with whom he was traveling on horseback requested him to leave the main road with him that he might talk with some Indians that he saw a few hundred yards from the roadside, and about half a mile from the Indian camp. He found an Indian whom he said had a short time previous killed a relative of his. He drew his revolver and quickly shot the Indian dead. He started up the mountain side at full speed, leaving Mr. Jones almost dumfounded at the side of the gasping Indian. The shot and screams of the poor fellow brought the entire Indian camp to the spot with cocked revolvers and rifles. They rushed upon him with the intention of slaying him. He thought surely his time had come and that his race had been run to the end. But, like the disciples at Pentecost, he talked different tongues very rapidly until they understood that he was not the man who did the cowardly deed. Lieutenant Underwood of the United States Army, had charge of the Indians, taking them to the reservation, and to him, under God, was his perservation largely due.

He taught school in Jacksonville and Salem, Oregon, at different periods. In the latter place he joined the M. E. church in 1869. He was converted really in the middle of the street in the city of Philadelphia at the age of twelve, but didn't unite with any church until the time mentioned. He was licensed to exhort soon after, attaching himself to the church, and soon admitted on trial in the Oregon Conference. He entered the Williamette University at Salem, being the first colored man ever admitted within its walls as a student. A young white man in the class refused to recite in the algebra class with him because of a dread of the contact. The teacher, Mr. O. Frambes, with his big, sympathetic heart, told him at once to pack up his little bundle and leave the institution; but a good night's rest and a cool reconsideration caused him to become reconciled, and the next morning found him working at the "minus and plus," for he had just discovered the unknown "quantity" in Jones.

In 1873 Bishop R. S. Foster gave Mr. Jones about as long a transfer as Methodist preachers usually get, four thousand miles, from Oregon to the Newark, New Jersey conference. He was stationed for three years at Newark, New Jersey, and then transferred to Cincinnati, Ohio, where he remained one year, and was sent to Indianapolis, Indiana, as pastor for two years, and was then appointed presiding elder of the Lexington, Kentucky, district, by Bishop Wiley. After serving four years, he was returned to the pastorate at Paris for two years, and then to Winchester, Kentucky, as pastor of Clark's chapel. He received the ordination of deacon at the hands of Bishop Edmund S. Jones, and as an elder at the hands of Bishop Edward Ames.

His intellectual qualities and goodness of heart made him a general favorite with his brethren, and he received a number of votes for bishop at the general conference in 1880, at Cincinnati, Ohio.

He was elected a delegate from the State of Oregon, to the Civil Rights convention, which met in Washington, District of Columbia, in 1873. Also a delegate from the same State, to the National Convention of Colored Men, which met in Nashville, in 1880. He was elected delegate to the Educational convention which met in the city of Lexington, Kentucky; was one of the committee to present the work necessary to the Legislature at Frankfort; though not present at Frankfort, on account of having to perform the funeral services of a valued friend, he was thoroughly interested in the work accomplished.

He was married at Jacksonville, Oregon, in 1862, and the fruits of the union are four children. Two of them sleep quietly on the shores of the Pacific, one waits in the cemetery at Paris, Kentucky, for the great reunion, the other is still spared to cheer and comfort the hearts of the parents, and in some measure supply the place of those departed. He canvassed the State of Indiana in 1878, on behalf of the State candidates on the Republican ticket; was president of the Blaine club at Paris, Kentucky, during the National campaign. He also delivered the Fourth of July oration at Greencastle, Indiana, at the Odd Fellows' celebration in 1878. Said oration received the highest compliments of the citizens and the press, and was published in full in the *Indianapolis Journal*. He also delivered a eulogy at the death of Senator O. P. Morton, the same year, which was published in the same paper. He has been an occasional correspondent of the *Cincinnati Commercial Gazette;* has edited a couple of papers of a local nature in Paris, Kentucky.

Rev. Daniel Jones is especially noted for his high degree of courtesy, politeness and intellectual culture. His daily walk and conversation is worthy of commendation, and makes for himself a host of friends. His quiet and unassuming manners, his graceful and elegant speech, his highly persuasive language, brings tears to sinner's eyes, and moulds the lives of God's people. He has been preserved by Him through the many dangers of an early life, and through the vicissitudes of travel to preach the gospel, and has been used by Him as an instrument of good. His pen and voice are never silent, and his excellent character and splendid reputation does much to give him influence for the purpose of elevating his race.

HENRY N. JETER

CHAPTER LXXX

Rev. Henry N. Jeter
Baptist Preacher

Rev. Henry N. Jeter, pastor of Shiloh Baptist church, Newport, R. I., was born in Charlotte county, Va., October 7, 1851. His parents, Riland and Mary Jeter, were slaves and consequently had much to undergo in the rearing of their family and the education of their children.

In 1862 his father was compelled by the rebels who owned him, to throw up breastworks to protect the Southern army (which was doing all in their power to keep the Negroes in slavery) from the shots of the Federal soldiers, and this same year as a recompense for the service he had rendered, he was shot by a Confederate soldier. After the Emancipation Proclamation, being yet a lad, Mr. Jeter served as a shoemaker apprentice, during which time he improved his mind, being always anxious for an education, by attending night school in the city of Lynchburg, Va. In 1868, he found Christ precious to his soul, and was buried with him in baptism, Rev. Sampson White, pastor of the First African Baptist church, Lynchburg, officiating. This same year he felt that he was called to proclaim the unspeakable riches of God, and to better fit himself for this calling, in 1869 he entered Wayland Seminary, Washington, District of Columbia, where, under the efficient teaching of Rev. G. M. P. King, D. D., for six years, he carefully prepared himself for subsequent labors.

His first charge was Shiloh Baptist church, Newport, Rhode Island, where he was ordained June 24, 1875. Here he labored, a single young man with all the ardor and zealousness of a devoted Christian minister. In 1878 he married Miss Thomasinia Hamilton of Brooklyn, a very cultured and accomplished young woman, the daughter of Mr. Thomas Hamilton, then editor and proprietor of the *Anglo-African*, a paper published in New York City.

With his helpmeet he returned to his church, where with renewed strength and new support, he continued his work, which is often extremely arduous and of much importance because of its location.

Newport, on the New England coast, is a summer resort, and thither people from all parts of the United States throughout the summer months go, to throw of the restraint of home cares and renew their vigor for the year to come. As spiritual and physical growth must go hand in hand, Mr. Jeter bends his efforts to influence for good, through the light of Shiloh church, the many visitors from far and near who come to that city. Extremely successful has he been in this his first and only pastorate, for nearly twelve years; and by his untiring energy, the church has been enlarged and has built a parsonage and made repairs to the amount of $9,000, and is now in a flourishing condition. Mr. and Mrs. Jeter are the parents of four children, one boy and three girls.

CHAPTER LXXXI

Rev. J. T. White
Divine—Editor—State Senator—Commissioner
of Public Works

———•◆•———

One of the leading spirits in the State of Arkansas is the Rev. J. T. White, pastor of the Second Baptist church of Helena, Arkansas, whose life began in New Providence, Clark county, Indiana, August 25, 1837. His parents, James and Catharine, were members of the Second Baptist church of Indianapolis, Indiana, from 1850 to their death in 1860.

He received a good common school education with which he started in life. Having professed a hope in Christ at the age of seventeen, four years later he entered the gospel ministry. In the spring of 1865 he was sent as a messenger from his church to the Consolidated American Baptist convention which met in the city of St. Louis at the First Baptist church. While there he received a call from Helena, and on the twenty-first of August, 1865, entered upon the pastoral work of the church.

He found things in a very confused state, as would naturally be the case just after the close of the war. It was as late as the fourth of July, 1865, that a hotly contested battle fought between the Federal and Confederate forces at this place, startled the people in the neighborhood. He found a handful of Baptists worshiping in the government stable, which had been appropriated to their use. Colonel Benzonia kindly permitted them to move into the old Cumberland church, where services were held for two years.

He then built a house 45 x 70 feet, and moved into it in 1867. This building cost eighteen hundred dollars, and still stands as a reminder of the past.

In this plain, unassuming place there were at least two thousand persons converted and baptized by the hands of the pastor. In the year 1868, the reconstruction of the Southern States took place under the direction of Congress, and Rev. White was induced to enter the canvass for reconstruction, and in the fall of 1868 he was elected to the State convention, to frame a constitution for the government of Arkansas. He assisted in

J. T. WHITE

the canvass for the ratification of the constitution, and was sent to the House of Representatives in the fall of the same year, to which position he was re-elected twice. He was then honored with a seat in the State Senate, in which position he served one full term, after which he was appointed by the governor to the position of commissioner of public works and internal improvements.

It was during this period that he built a two story brick church edifice for his people at Helena, Arkansas, at a cost of eighteen thousand dollars, and a frame church in the city of Little Rock, Arkansas, which cost two thousand dollars. One of the saddest afflictions of his life was the loss of this fine brick church by fire. However, he rallied his forces and again built a fifteen thousand dollar church which is about completed. The pulpit, gallery and assembly chairs, with which the house is seated, make it the handsomest church in the State. The audience room is 45 x 80 feet. The whole number that have been baptized during his twenty-one years ministry is at least five thousand.

The Rev. J. T. White also organized an Arkansas Missionary Baptist convention in 1867, assisted by many brethren in the city of Little Rock, which organization still lives. Later he organized the first District Association.

When the reaction took place and the State went into the hands of Democracy, a convention was called to frame a new constitution, and in 1874 Elder White was elected to this convention. He then entered upon a college project, raised five thousand dollars, which was expended on what was known as the Helena University; but it was too much for him, the project fell through, and the property still remains encumbered, and is valued at one thousand six hundred dollars.

For the last three years he has turned his attention to a society work known as the Benevolent and Church Aid Society. In connection with this work he edits the *Arkansas Review*, a paper devoted to the religious, political and educational interests of his race. This journal is a creditable one, and staunch in the defense of the race. Elder White is a man of fine personal appearance, rather tall and powerfully built. He is a true friend to progress; his most excellent traits are devotion to principle and steadfastness to friends; and no matter how he may choose to differ from one, he will always be given the credit of sincerity. His standing among the people of the State is good, and he is certainly deserving of all he has reaped in that line. His studies have been over a wide range, and have deepened and broadened his views of men and things. He writes with a facile pen, free thoughts, clear head and forcible style. He is often more vigorous than others profess to be; but he speaks often only what *they* think but are *too cowardly to whisper above their breaths*. Altogether he is a strong, capable and earnest man, with a large future before him.

G. W. GAYLES

CHAPTER LXXXII

Rev. G. W. Gayles
The last Colored State Senator in the Mississippi Legislature—
Moderator of the State Convention—Member of the Board
of Police

In the Black Belt of Mississippi lives one of the colored race who is very prominent in that section of the country, and his influence extends to all parts of the State and adjoining States. He was born in Wilkinson county, Mississippi, June 29, 1844. His owner was Emily Haile. His boyhood days were passed on the plantation until 1863, when he went into the army and remained until December, 1864.

Previous to 1862 Mr. Gayles had succeeded in having his letters taught him by the Miss Elizabeth Powell of New York, who was at that time employed as a school teacher by Mrs. Nancy Barrow, to teach her two girls. Young Gayles seemed to have a natural love for reading the Bible and hymn-book, and as he progressed in study they became his constant friends and companions.

November 21, 1867, he was called before an ecclesiastical council by the Mount Horeb Baptist church of Greenville, Mississippi, for ordination, with Rev. M. B. Black, moderator, Brother J. F. Gilmore, clerk, Rev. Thomas Epps and others of the council, who joined in the work of setting him apart for the work of the gospel ministry. He then went to Bolivar county, and organized a Baptist church that is known as the Kindling Altar church, of which he is pastoring still.

In 1872 he was appointed missionary for the counties of Bolivar and Sunflower, where he served for many years, after which he was appointed missionary for Coahoma county. On September 17, 1869, he was appointed member of the Board of Police for District Number Three, Bolivar county, by Governor A. Ames, brevet major-general of the United States army, and on the second of August, 1870, he was appointed Justice of the Peace for the Fifth district, Bolivar county, by Governor J. L. Alcorn. On the twenty-ninth of August, 1870, Rev. G. W. Gayles was appointed supervisor for the Fifth district, where he served until

November, 1870. He was elected a member of the Mississippi Legislature, and held that position for four years, being returned in 1877 as State Senator, representing the Twenty-eighth Senatorial district, composing the counties of Bolivar, Coahoma and Quitman, which position Senator Gayles has held ever since by re-election, and he is the only colored senator in the Mississippi Legislature, there being none other since 1875. In 1874 he was elected corresponding secretary of the Baptist State Missionary Convention of Mississippi, and in July, 1876, he was elected President of the Baptist Missionary State convention, and has held said position ever since by re-election. Under his excellent administration, the Baptist convention has been a success. They bought a printing press in 1880, and elected him editor of the paper known as the *Baptist Signal*. Also a college was bought in the city of Natchez, costing about six thousand dollars, which has been opened, and has been in operation for about three years. It is an honor to the State of Mississippi.

Rev. Mr. Gayles figured prominently in the National Baptist convention in St. Louis, held August 25, 1886, where the writer met him, and found in him a quiet, unassuming gentleman. His manners were winning, and it is indeed apparent that his upright life and his perseverance in the discharge of every duty has caused his election to the many positions he has held.

His people are remarkably proud of him; he is popular with all classes; ever ready to distribute favors, and delights to treat all men with becoming respect. Holding as he does this important position in the Mississippi Legislature, he has an opportunity for good, and surely his services must be considered of value to his constituents, or they would not have kept him there all these years. No taint has ever yet been brought against his name in connection with bribery or corruption in his legislative duties. He is universally respected by his associates, noted for his zeal and wisdom in the votes which cast upon all important measures; he has become the last of his line in so distinguished a position.

CHAPTER LXXXIII

Hon. Mifflin Wister Gibbs
Attorney-at-Law—*The first Colored Judge in the United States*
—*An Active Politician—An Advocate of Industrial Education*
—*Contractor and Builder*

———•◆•———

This gentleman was born in Philadelphia, April, 1828. His father was a Methodist minister and died when this son was not more than eight years old. His mother was an industrious, frugal woman, and devoted herself to her children. Young Gibbs, by earnest labors, remained in school until he had acquired a good common school education. At this time he was apprenticed to a carpenter and builder, and after thoroughly learning this trade, at the end of his apprenticeship became a contractor and builder on his own account. He improved all the time and made every opportunity tell by cultivating himself in literary matters. At the age of twenty-one he was a conspicuous member of the Philomatheon Institute of Philadelphia, a literary association in which Messrs Purvis, Douglass, Whipper, Weir, and other noted colored men were active members. Feeling keenly the degradation and oppression of his fellow men, and knowing some of the obstacles to success that barred their aspiration and progress on every side, he turned every attention to the relieving of the hardships that environed them, and to this end he became a member of the anti-slavery Society, and a shrewd, active agent and worker on the "Underground Railroad." William and Allen Craft, "Box" Brown, and many others well known in the Anti-slavery period, were aided by this man in their eventful escape. The narrow limits of his native city offered for Mr. Gibbs little chance for work. Near this time, 1849, Fred. Douglass and the late Charles Lenox Remond visited Philadelphia to take part in the Anti-slavery convention of that year, and being impressed with the advanced ideas of this young man, and with his earnest manner and general information on the anti-slavery work, they persuaded him to start on a lecture tour, in New York, Ohio and Pennsylvania. While thus engaged the fever for gold in California broke out, and as he learned from many the success that might be made in that new land, at the close of his

MIFFLIN WISTER GIBBS

lecture tour he attempted the then expensive and hazardous trip to the far West. He arrived at San Francisco the latter part of 1850, poor in purse but rich in manhood. In this city ordinary mechanics were getting from five to ten dollars a day, common laborers two and a half. At first he obtained work at his trade, but after two or three refusals of white mechanics to labor with him, he resolved to quit the business. He then formed a partnership with Nathan Pointer in the clothing business, in which he was very successful. In 1852 he entered into a larger enterprise with Peter Lester as partner, under the name of Lester & Gibbs. They did an extensive business as importers of fine boots and shoes, importing all their goods from first class firms in London, Paris, Philadelphia and New York.

Notwithstanding his flourishing business had made great demands on his time, he was ever mindful of his race, and in 1851, with the late Jonas H. Townsend, W. H. Newby, William H. Hall, and other prominent colored men of San Francisco, he drew up and published in the *Atla California*, a series of resolutions that clearly defined the rights of the American Negro and their determination to rise and resist encroachments on them. This was the first expression of the colored citizens in that State, and it fell with great power on the pro-slavery Democrats. Mr. Gibbs was one of the proprietors, publishers and contributors to the first colored paper published in California, *The Miner of the Times*. He was a member of the conventions of 1854, '55 and '57, and took prominent part in the deliberations and always served on important committees. When an attempt was made to enforce the obnoxious act of the Legislature, known as the "Voters' Poll-tax," levied upon the colored men of the State, although disfranchised, the heroic stand of such men as Lester and Gibbs made this poll tax in San Francisco so unpopular that it was finally abandoned.

In 1858 the gold discoveries on the Frazier river in British Columbia interested the aggressive Gibbs and he embarked for Vancouver Island, and in due time reached Victoria where he was successful in a mercantile life, until he amassed quite a fortune. He was so popular that in 1866 he was elected by a flattering majority to represent the most aristocratic ward in the Common Council in Victoria. The following year he was re-elected without opposition to the same office. The Governor of the colony and other official persons were his associates.

When the anthracite coal on Queen Charlotte's Island was discovered, he became a large shareholder in an English company, and was elected one of the directors. After expending about sixty thousand dollars in prospecting and surveys, with no substantial results, they advertised for tenders for buildings, railroads, etc. Judge Gibbs put in a bid and, although not the lowest, on account of his integrity and responsibility he secured the contract and in spite of many difficulties, in twelve months, the specified time, he sent the first cargo of anthracite coal dug on the Pacific coast to the directors and to the market. He shortly after returned to the United States, where he entered and graduated from the Law Department of a leading university, in 1870; then he went South and settled in Little Rock, Arkansas, entering the law firm of Benjamin & Barnes, in that place, where he continued his studies and was admitted to the bar. One year after, he was appointed county attorney of Pulaski county, the capital county of the State. In 1873, he was elected to the office of city judge, the first colored man ever elected to such a position in the United States. In 1872 Judge Gibbs was a delegate from Arkansas to the National Convention of colored men at New Orleans. He canvassed his state for Joseph Brooks for Governor, against Baxter the traitor, who betrayed Arkansas into the hands of the Democrats. He was a delegate to the National Convention of colored men at Nashville, Tennessee, of which body he became President. In 1876 he ran on the Republican ticket as Presidential elector-at-large for the State of Arkansas, and led by several thousand votes over every other candidate on the ticket. In June, 1876, he was appointed by President Hayes, register of the United States Land Office at Little Rock, Arkansas. To this position he was reappointed in 1881. The subject of industrial education and industrial schools has claimed much of his attention, and he was instrumental very largely in the calling of an industrial convention, during the Exposition at New Orleans, at which meeting he was unanimously elected president. Judge Gibbs with ex-Congressman James P. Rapier, was a committee to visit Kansas and report upon the condition of the exodusting freedmen. He was a delegate to the Republican National Convention at Cincinnati in 1876, and one of the "immortal 306" who voted for Grant in the convention at Chicago, November, 1880; was elected a delegate to the last Republican National convention; two other colored men and himself, only, voting for Arthur in opposition to the other three-fourths of the delegation. He was commissioner of the colored exhibits to the World's Exposition at New Orleans for the State of Arkansas. He is a member of the Bar Association of Little Rock, to which his brother attorneys unanimously elected him in 1882. He is a member of the Howard Association (the friend of the poor and needy of Little Rock), and also a member of the Board of Visitors of public schools. His wealth enabled him to become a partner in the Electric Light company and a large shareholder in several other manufacturing companies of Little Rock, and in that city lives in a handsome residence, besides owning a large amount of business and resident property there and elsewhere. In the various walks of life he has commanded respect and won golden opinions from those even from whom he differed politically.

He has had the pleasure of seeing his daughter Ida graduate from the Oberlin College and take her place among the educators of the country, being employed in the Huntsville Normal school. The judge takes a lively interest in everything pertaining to the improvement of the race; he is a good friend, an able lawyer and a distinguished man. He is brave, true and honest, having always the courage to adhere to his convictions.

WILLIAM H. STEWARD

CHAPTER LXXXIV

William H. Steward, Esq.
Grand Master—Secretary—Business Manager—Letter Carrier

One of the men in the State of Kentucky who has the clearest head and brightest mind is the subject of this sketch. He was born at Brandenburg, Meade county, Kentucky, July 26, 1847, and when quite a child was brought to the city of Louisville, where he has since had his residence. Born a slave, he had more privileges than was usual in those days, and was always ready to take advantage of every opportunity which gave him increased power in matters pertaining to the development of the mind. In Louisville he attended a private school taught by Revs. Henry Adams, William H. Gibson and R. T. W. James, and was considered a very bright scholar, always leading his classes. When he became a man he taught school at Frankfort and Louisville, and occupied several responsible positions with the railroads in Louisville, and was for several years messenger for the cashier and purchasing agent of the L. & N. Railroad company, and even to this day the agents of the company are his devoted friends, often doing him great favors. In 1876, in the month of February, he severed his connection with the L. & N. Railroad company, and was appointed a letter-carrier in the Louisville post office, being the first colored man to occupy such a position in the State. He has always ranked "first class," and besides receiving many recognitions at the hands of his associates, who are mostly white men, he was elected as their representative to the National Letter-Carrier's Association, held in Philadelphia in 1882.

No person in the post office knows more of the general character of the work, and can better interpret the laws than he. He has given strict attention to these questions, and instructs many of the new carriers who have been put on from time to time.

He professed religion in 1867, and was baptized at Frankfort, Kentucky, by Rev. R. Martin. He joined the Fifth Street Baptist church in Louisville shortly after, and has ever been an active worker in this church. He has been associated with every enterprise therein, and is truly one of the leading men, and contributes without stint his time and talents to make the church prosperous and secure for it all the blessings that can come from assiduous labors in its interests. He was secretary of the choir for many years, and has for many years past been its leader. This choir has a musical reputation that it has sustained for several years without question.

In the Sabbath school there is a large class known as the "Infant Class," the largest in the city and State, and usually has from one hundred to one hundred and fifty children in it. This class he has taught for seventeen years, mainly by blackboard lessons, in which he is well skilled and to which matter he gives daily attention, so that the lessons on the Sabbath can be well prepared. The children graduate from this class and enter the higher departments of this school. Many of the brightest members of this church have been instructed in this class, and have become useful members of society and well acquainted with the Scriptures. He has also been assistant superintendent of the Sabbath school since 1884. He has always been interested in public affairs, attending nearly all the conventions in the State, political and otherwise, and filled many important positions in them. In the last convention of the State, held for the purpose of petitioning the Legislature in regard to civil rights and the Normal school, he was temporary chairman and secretary of the permanent body. He is also at present secretary of the State Executive Committee and has been ever since November, 1885.

In denominational enterprises he is earnest and faithful. He was one of the secretaries of the National Baptist convention held in St. Louis, August 25, 1886, secretary of the Kentucky Baptist State convention for several years, and was also its secretary in 1873, and statistical secretary in 1876. He was also secretary of the General Association of Colored Baptists of Kentucky, holding said position from 1877 until the present time.

He has been identified with the State University at Louisville since its establishment, and has filled the position as chairman of the Board of Trustees. In this department of labor he has shown zeal, earnestness and self-sacrifice, and has labored most perseveringly for its success. In the early history of the public schools of the city of Louisville, he was secretary and subsequently chairman of the Board of Visitors, and to him much of the excellent condition of these schools is due. Many times it has been said that this one or the other white gentleman has done so much for the public schools, but it does appear that too much neglect has been shown in giving to the Board of Visitors the due meed of praise for their constant petitioning, and the consideration for the upbuilding of the schools; and perhaps it could be said with justice that no colored man in the city of Louisville has secured more appointments for colored teachers than W. H. Steward.

The American Baptist, the organ of several Baptist organizations, was issued in January, 1879, since which time he has been associated with it as city editor, associate editor, editor and business manager. He joined the Masonic fraternity in 1881, and has made rapid progress in that order, having been Worshipful Master of United Lodge No. 12, High Priest of Enterprise Chapter No. 4, Eminent Commander of Cyrene Commandry No. 1, and twice elected Worshipful Master of the Grand Lodge of Kentucky, which position he now fills acceptably to all the craft. He is a most liberal man, contributing freely to every cause that is presented to him. No one appeals to him without having the appeal granted, if it lies in his power. With these generous emotions in his heart, it is no wonder that he gives much attention to the Orphans' Home of this city. He is a member of its Board of Directors, and has endeavored faithfully to discharge his duty to this much neglected class. In all his undertakings, he is zealous, earnest and faithful. He encourages the younger men of the race, endeavoring to have them seek the higher walks of life and accomplish much that would at first seem to be difficult, but which ought to be accomplished with little effort. This is a constant care to him, to see that these men make use of the time which God has given to them. As a writer, he has great power of expression, and readily reaches the point he desires to make without any circuitous methods. As a speaker, he is eloquent, forcible and convincing. His language is smooth, elegant and persuasive, and succeeds in holding the attention of his audiences. His power with men is derived from the effort he makes to serve a friend and to be true to the vows of a true Mason and a worthy master.

CHAPTER LXXXV

Rev. Frank J. Grimke, A. B.
Learned and Eloquent Presbyterian Divine—Touching
Memorial on Leaving Washington, District of Columbia

———⋅•⋅———

Mr. Grimke's parents were named Henry and Nancy Grimke. He was born in Charleston, South Carolina, November 4, 1850. His mother was a slave. On the death of his father, however, a change took place, when he was only a few years old. The children were all left free and placed under the guardian care of his father's oldest son, E. Montague Grimke, who faithfully discharged his duty towards them until Frank was about ten years old, when his guardian undertook to enslave them, which made some complications of course. Although a boy, Frank determined that he would not submit to such an outrage. He ran off and went into the Confederate army as the valet to one of the officers, in which position he continued for about two years. On visiting Charleston one day with the regiment to which he was attached, and which was stationed in Castle Pinckney, a fort in the harbor, he was suddenly arrested just as he was about to step into a boat on his return to the fort, and thrown into jail, or what is known as the work-house in Charleston. Here he remained for several months, and was taken dangerously ill from exposure and bad treatment, and came very near losing his life. It was only by being finally removed to his mother's house and by very skillful treatment that he recovered from this dangerous illness. Having thus fallen into the hands of this half-brother and guardian, who feared that he would go away again, he sold him, before he was well enabled to go out, to an officer, and again he went back in the army, remaining until the close of the war. Through the influence of Mrs. Pillsbury, who was then in charge of Morris Street school in Charleston, which he attended for awhile, his brother and himself went North for the purpose of being educated. Frank went to Stoneham, Massachusetts, into the family of a Doctor John Brown. With this family he was to remain with a view of studying medicine, but his treatment by them was so different from what he had been led to expect that he left them. During the whole stay with them he was forced to sleep in an open barn in the hayloft, with no other mattress than the hay and no other bedstead than the floor. He very soon found warm friends with Mr. and Mrs. Lyman Dyke, who took him into their shoe factory, where he began to learn the shoe-making business. Soon, however, he was summoned by Mrs. Pillsbury to report at once to Lincoln University, in Chester county, Pennsylvania, where arrangements had been made for the prosecution of his studies. As a student he ranked very high, and received the approbation of the professors and was acknowledged superior among the students. He graduated from the College Department of this institution in 1870 as valedictorian of his class. Immediately afterwards he began the study of law in the Law Department of the university, which at that time, in 1871, was on the university grounds. The next year he acted as financial agent of the university. The year after, he resumed his legal studies in the same department, which in the meantime had been removed to West Chester, Pennsylvania. The next year he went to Washington, District of Columbia, and entered the Law Department of Howard University. While there he decided to turn his thoughts to the ministry. In the fall of 1875, therefore, he entered the Princeton Theological Seminary, from which he graduated in 1878, and immediately went to Washington as pastor of the Fifteenth Street Presbyterian church, where he remained until October, 1885. When he was about to leave his flock the following testimonial was adopted:

At a farewell reception tendered by the congregation and friends of the Fifteenth Street Presbyterian church, Tuesday evening, November 2, 1885, in behalf of the congregation, visitors and friends, who, Sunday after Sunday, and from time to time, have listened to the words of wisdom from the lips of Mr. Grimke, pastor of this church, we beg leave to express our deep regret at his departure from our midst. Circumstances over which we cannot exercise control, as well as the voice of his Master, call him to another field of labor and duty. He leaves behind warm hearts and devoted friends, whose affection for him and his helpmate is best known from the true enthusiasm manifested on the morning of his farewell sermon. The language of that occasion being, "May God be with you both, since it has been decreed that for a while we must be parted." The earthly activities of this life are circumscribed by time and space, but the divine and essential genius which informs and inspires that life is boundless in the sweep of its influence and immortal in the energy of its activity. If any fraction of this community may claim the right to do honor and reverence to our friend Mr. Grimke, it is as it should be, those of us who have profited by the words of wisdom that have fallen from his lips and the influence exerted by contact with him. His services here have been a vast accession to a cause already moving forward with assured success. Remembering his work and the good deeds left behind him, and how he has, by the measure of unselfish devotion taught us, by precept and example, the way to be lifted up and strengthened, we make this feeble attempt to pay reverential respects, and extend the meed and honor of praise and true regard of him whom we shall ever know as our friend and benefactor. In the language of another:

> For seven years, he, with a pulse that felt for human needs,
> And eyes that saw among the meanest weeds
> Plants that through civilization, yet might bless
> The world with flowers and fruit of usefulness,
> And all he spake accorded with his deeds.

We sincerely commend him to those to whom he goes, in the land of flowers and sweet perfumes, of generous and hospitable people. May he find warm hearts, devoted friends and helping hands, to remind him of those to whom he now says, "Good friends, for a while, farewell."

F. F. SHADD,
President of the Meeting

As a preacher, Mr. Grimke stands foremost in our country. He is an eloquent divine, and speaks with ease and grace. President James Mc-Cosh, of Princeton College, said of him: "I have heard him preach, and I feel as if I could listen to such preaching with profit from Sabbath to Sabbath; and I rejoice to find that the colored people of Washington have such a man to minister to them."

Mr. Grimke's reception in Jacksonville, Florida, as the pastor of the Laurel Street Presbyterian church, was commented upon in this wise by the *Southern Leader,* whose editor, J. Willis Menard, is himself scholarly and eminent. He said:

His sermons, always delivered from the manuscript, are models of force, perspicuity and elegant rhetoric; while his deep piety, correct life and earnest devotion to his work, have won him universal respect and love. The people of Jacksonville, in particular, and the people in the South, in general, are to be congratulated on securing this scholarly and eminent divine. The growth of his influence and usefulness is but a matter of time and opportunity. Recently he was called to Tuskegee, Alabama, where he lectured before a vast audience, and a letter appeared in the *Montgomery Herald,* which said: "The Rev. Mr. Grimke, the most learned and profound thinker of the race arrived here last Saturday morning, one day too late; however he came in time to do inexpressible good. Sunday morning he preached to the school and town friends from the sixth verse of Christ's Sermon on the Mount, 'Blessed are they which do hunger and thirst after righteousness.' Sunday night a lecture took place in the lecture room. He emphasized the very fact that in order for the race to make itself felt upon other races as a mass, it must have education, morals and wealth. We wish every colored man in this country could hear that able young man and distinguished divine. Mr. Grimke has probably one of the most valuable libraries owned by colored men in the United States, consisting of over one thousand volumes of well selected works on theology, philosophy, history, science, art and general literature, together with quite a number of choice pictures."

We could scarcely write of Mr. Grimke without referring to his distinguished wife, who was before marriage named Miss Charlotte Forten of Philadelphia, who was well known in the literary world. She has been a true minister's wife, and has done much to make his ministerial career successful. Mr. Grimke bids fair to raise the tone of ministerial life in Florida as he has in Washington. The purity of his character and the quietness of his demeanor affect all favorably who come in contact with him. South Carolina has a great reason to be proud of her distinguished son, who has reflected so much credit upon her.

ROBERT HARLAN

CHAPTER LXXXVI

Hon. Robert Harlan
Resident in England Ten Years—Legislator—Fugitive from Prejudice

———•◆•———

Colonel Robert Harlan was born in Mecklenburg county, Virginia, December 12, 1816. His father was a white man, and his mother three parts white. Coming to Kentucky when eight years of age, he was brought up by the Hon. James Harlan, father of the Hon. John M. Harlan, at present associate justice of the Supreme Court of the United States.

As a boy, Mr. Harlan was bright, intelligent, and ambitious; and although a slave under the law, he was allowed unusual freedom. There were no schools in Kentucky for colored people, and no provisions for their education; but he was taught the elements of an education by Mr. Harlan's older sons, and with this start he displayed an intelligence beyond what was usual with the better class of his race. Allowed to hire his time, as was not unfrequent in slave States, he learned the barber's trade in Louisville, and opened and conducted a barber shop in Harrodsburg, and subsequently a grocery at Lexington. In 1848 he went to California, where, in a short time he amassed a fortune of forty-five thousand dollars in gold, which he brought back and invested in Cincinnati, Ohio. With his new found wealth he built two beautiful stone front homes on Fifth street, east of Broadway, and became the owner of Bull's first class photographic and daguerreotype gallery, which he fitted up in a style surpassing any similar gallery in this country, and conducted the business for a time with success. During this period he visited the World's Fair in London, in 1851. About this time, notwithstanding since his early manhood he had with the consent of his owner traveled without restriction, visiting almost every State in the Union besides Canada and countries of the Old World and located in a free State, he voluntarily returned to Kentucky and arranged for a formal acknowledgment of his freedom, paying five hundred dollars for the same. Thus all his life, performing all his obligations, whether legally binding or not, he has been trusted, and never forfeited the confidence reposed in him.

As soon as he was settled in Cincinnati, Ohio, he took an active interest in all affairs tending to improve and benefit his race. He was trustee of the colored schools and was elected and served as trustee of the Colored Orphan Asylum. The first school-house erected in Cincinnati for the education of the colored youth was the result mainly of his efforts. To escape the prejudice existing against men of his color in 1858, he took his family to England, residing there until 1868, when he returned home. He was selected as "orator of the day" for the first celebration of the adoption of the Fifteenth Amendment, and was always prominent in the councils of his party, being the first and only colored man that ever was a member of the Republican State Central Committee of Ohio; he was also delegate-at-large to the National convention that nominated Grant, in 1872. He has been delegate of the city, State, and county conventions for ten years; and in all conventions called to consider the interests of the colored race he has been a prominent actor. He was temporary chairman in the National convention held at Nashville in 1876. He has frequently declined foreign counsulships tendered him. In 1875 he raised a battalion of four hundred men, being commissioned as colonel by Governor Rutherford B. Hayes. During General Grant's administration he was special agent-at-large of the Post Office Department. President Hayes offered him a position in Cincinnati which he declined. In 1880, as the Republican candidate for the Legislature, he came within three hundred and twenty votes, out of a total vote of fifty-seven thousand, of defeating his popular Democratic opponent, General Devereaux. In 1884 he was alternate delegate for the State-at-large to the National Republican convention. He was appointed in 1881 special agent of the Treasury Department by President Chester A. Arthur, which position he held until removed by President Grover Cleveland as "an offensive partisan." In 1886 he was elected on the Republican ticket a member of the State Legislature, which position he filled to the entire satisfaction of his constituents, both white and colored, and with credit to himself and profit to the State and county. He took an active part in the abolition of the "Black Laws."

Mr. Harlan is well posted in county, State and National affairs; is a close reader and a thorough student of political economy. He has been a life-long Republican and is a man of whom his race should feel proud, for he is a stalwart defender of their rights. The genial colonel has a big heart and enjoys sport as much as any one; indeed he is specially fond of horse-flesh, and can relish a fine animal as only a native Kentuckian knows how.

CHAPTER LXXXVII

Dr. Anthony William Amo
A Learned Negro—Student at Halle—Skilled in Latin
and Greek—Philosophical Lecturer—Received Doctorate
from the University of Wittenberg—Made Counselor of State
by the Court of Berlin

───◆───

Born in Guinea, was brought to Europe when very young, and the Princess of Brunswick took charge of his education. He pursued his studies at Halle, in Saxony, and at Wittenberg, and so distinguished himself by his talents and good conduct that the rector and council of the university of the last mentioned town gave a public testimony to them in a letter of congratulation. Amo, skilled in the knowledge of the Latin and Greek languages, delivered, with success, private lectures on philosophy, which are highly praised in the same letter. In an abstract, published by the dean of the philosophical faculty, it is said of this learned Negro, that, having examined the systems of the ancients and moderns, he selected and taught all that was best of them. Besides his knowledge of Latin and Greek, he spoke Hebrew, French, Dutch and German, and was well versed in astronomy. In 1774 Amo published dissertations on some subjects which obtained the approbation of the University of Wittenberg, and the degree of doctor was conferred upon him. The title of one of these was *Dissertio inauguralis philosophica de humanæ mentis Apatheia: sen sensionis ac facultates sentiendi in mente humanæ absentia, et earum in corpore nostro organico ac vivo praesentia, quam praeside, etc., publice defendit autor Aut. Guil. Amo Guinea—afer philosophiæ, ect. L. C. magister, etc., 1734, 4° Wittenbergae.*

Another was entitled *Disputatio philosophica continens ideam distiectam earum quae competunt vel menti vel corpori nostro viva et organico, qual consentiente amplissimorum philosophorum ordine praeside M. Aut. Guil. Amo, Guinea—afer defendit Joa. Theod. Mainer, philos., et J. V. Cultor, in 4°, 1734, Wittenbergae.*

At the conclusion of these works are letters of approbation from the rector of the University of Wittenberg, who, in speaking of one of them, said: "It underwent no change, because it was well executed, and indicates a mind exercised in reflection." In a letter addressed to him by the president, he styles Amo, "vir nobilissime et clarissime." The University of Wittenberg has not evinced a belief in the absurd prejudice which exists against the colored portion of mankind.

The Court of Berlin conferred upon Amo the title of Counselor of State, but after the death of his benefactress, the Princess of Brunswick, Amo fell into a profound melancholy, and resolved to leave Europe, in which he had resided for thirty years, and to return to the place of his birth at Axim, on the Gold Coast. There he received, in 1753, a visit from the intelligent traveler, David Henry Gallandat, who mentions him in the Memoirs of the Academy of Flessinque, of which he was a member. Amo, at that time about fifty years of age, led there the life of a recluse. His father and a sister were living with him, and he had a brother who was a slave in Surinam. Some time after, it appears, he left Axim and settled at Chama.

The Abbé Gregoire, from whose work the foregoing particulars are translated, says that he made unavailing researches to ascertain whether Amo published any other works, or at what period he died.

This sketch was taken from the work entitled *A Tribute for the Negro*, published in 1848, by Armistead.

CHAPTER LXXXVIII

Rev. Rufus L. Perry, Ph. D.
Editor—Ethnologist—Essayist—Logician—Profound Student
of Negro History—Scholar in the Greek, Latin and Hebrew
Languages

The father of Rev. Mr. Perry was named Lewis Perry. He was a preacher of the Baptist faith. His mother's name was Maria. She, too, was an adherent of the same faith. Both of them were the slaves of one Archibald W. Overton, Smith county, Tennessee. His father escaped to Canada when the boy was only seven years old. He was a very fine mechanic, carpenter and cabinet maker. He hired his own time from his owner, and was energetic enough to secure the means and carry the family to Nashville, Tennessee, where the boy ranked as a free child, attending the school for free Negroes, taught by Mrs. Sally Porter. After his father ran away, this temporary freedom was terminated, and the whole family were taken back to the plantation. The schooling which young Rufus had at this time and which he had received in Nashville, doomed him to the contempt of his fellow-bondsmen, and soon won for him among the white people the reputation of a "dangerous nigger." He became so "dangerous" that in August, 1852, he was sold to a Negro trader, to be carried to Mississippi, but he remained with this trader only three weeks. Before he got ready to take him to Mississippi, he brought his reputed "dangerousness" to writing into requisition. *He* also fled to Canada. Mr. Perry was converted in the year 1854, and feeling a call from God, he decided to enter the ministry. To this end he studied in Kalamazoo, Michigan, at the Kalamazoo Seminary, with the class of 1861, and was ordained as pastor of the Second Baptist church at Ann Arbor, Michigan, on or about October 9, 1861, by a council of which the Rev. Samuel Cornelius was moderator, and Professor James R. Boise was clerk.

As a preacher, he is fluent, graceful and earnest. He is a very logical, clear reasoner, close and active debater, deep thinker and an excellent writer. He is a man of splendid natural abilities, and goes at once to the bottom of any subject that he undertakes. His life has been full of success,

RUFUS L. PERRY

filling very many positions in his church. He was pastor at St. Catherine's, Ontario, and Buffalo, New York. In 1865 he entered upon the general missionary and educational work among the freedmen, and has until the present day labored for the education, evangelization and general elevation of his race, serving as superintendent of schools for freedmen, and as editor of the *Sunbeam,* co-ordinate editor of the *American Baptist,* now the *Baptist Weekly* of New York, editor of the *People's Journal* and publisher of the *National Monitor,* the last of which is still in existence, and is a spicy paper, full of matter of interest to his denomination, and such general literature as is elevating in its tone. He was for ten years corresponding secretary of the Consolidated American Baptist Missionary convention, and is at present Corresponding Secretary of the American Educational Association, and of the American Baptist Free Mission Society. He has given much attention to the study of ethnology and the classics. He has recently written a work entitled *The Cushite, or the Children of Ham as seen by the Ancient Historians and Poets.* In it he has exhibited wonderful research, and a more than ordinary grasp of the subject under consideration. After quoting very largely from many historians, he says:

From these come three great and distinctly marked streams of people, reaching to this time through a period of four thousand two hundred and thirty-four years; and presenting us, from the earliest ages of written history, a white Europe, a black Africa and a yellow Asia. In the race of life, the Cushite led the van for nearly fifteen centuries; and the Greek theatres in which he played the best, the regions of his noblest deeds and grandeur, were Egypt and Ethiopia.

But the enemies of the Negro maintain that the distinguished Ethiopians and the Egyptians of such frequent and favorable mention, in both sacred and profane history, were not black men. They ingeniously explained the black men away and cunningly substituted some other race. They seemingly forget that the ancient language is a constructive tale-bearer; that its roots are etymological indices, twinkling like the fixed stars to light up the pathway of the scholar engaged in historic research.

One very eloquent passage shows the truth of our assertion that he is very learned and that his knowledge of history is not superficial, but extensive, deep and varied. Speaking of the Hamites, he says:

He has had a checkered life it is true, but so have the Shemitic and the Japhetic families. He has been master and he has been slave; but this is no less true of Ham than of Japhet. In the world's history of the rise and fall of nations, no race, no color, can boast of exemption from misfortune. But no race can boast of a higher celebrity in ancient times than the Negro, then called Cushites by the Hebrews and Ethiopians by the Greeks.

We can be pardoned for giving another extensive quotation from this admirable work because we desire to show the ability of the man. Our statement as to his mental capacity and rare attainments might need endorsement did we not give specimens of his ability. We give this passage as much to show his eloquence and inform the reader as for any other purpose. We also hope that in doing this that it will cause the reader to view the whole work. He says:

On looking back over the centuries to the beginning of the Christian era, to Noah, and noting the rise and fall of great men and great nations, we see none more conspicuous than the children of Ham. Greece had her Athens and could boast of Homer, Herodotus, Plato, Solon, Socrates and Demosthenes, and a host of other poets, historians, philosophers and orators, and of her great Alexander. Persia had her Cyrus the Great, her Cambyses, her Darius, and her religious Zoroaster. China had her great cities walled in so that nothing could come in or go out but the theosopic philosophy of her deified Confucius. Rome had her noted patricians, and, like Greece, her poets, orators, historians and generals, and begat for herself a great name; but before all these is the land of Ham, of Cush and the Cushite; the land of the chosen of God in which to train his peculiar people, and as a city of refuge for his own son, when Herod sought to slay him. Africa had her Cushite; Meroe had her Thebes, her Memphis, her sciences and her wonderful works of art. She had a great commercial traffic with the nations of the East, borne from country to country by numerous caravans. She had her high priests, whose sacred hieroglyphics bespoke their reverence for their gods. She had a thousand thousand soldiers, infantry and calvary, with generals of unequaled prowess. She had her astronomers, physicians, and wise men—men of deeds, rather than words, actions rather than theory. She had her Sesostris, her Memnon, her Shishak, her Zerah, her Nitocris, her Queen of Sheba, her Candace, and her long line of great Pharaohs mentioned in Sacred Scripture. She had her Hannibal and her Terrence, the one distinguished for being the greatest general of whom the Romans ever measured swords, and the other for giving polish to the Roman tongue and for giving expression to a philanthropic sentiment for which even the Christian age produces nothing grander.

On the question which is so much agitated this day whether the Negro will be absorbed by the white people, whether he will be annihilated or entirely disappear in any form from our country, he says:

Though undoubtedly more susceptible to amalgamation with the families of Shem and Japhet with whom he has more or less mingled for three thousand years, the Cushite still preserves his identity. He has neither been absorbed by social coition nor destroyed by nefarious colorphobia. He is here to stay, for God has so willed it, and so fixed it, by endowing him with a superior and indestructible fecundity.

These specimens are sufficient to show the opinion of the Rev. Mr. Perry upon the Negro question in several phases. Sketches of his life may be found in the *Baptist Encyclopedia,* by Cathcart, and in the *Rising Sun,* by William Wells Brown.

Rev. Rufus L. Perry has long been recognized for his many valuable attainments in letters and deep philosophical research. At the commencement of the State University, Louisville, Kentucky, May 16, 1887, he delivered a learned scientific lecture on the subject "Light." On the following night the authorities, through the president of the university, conferred on him the title of Doctor of Philosophy—a title he well deserves.

Without doubt, Rufus L. Perry is one of the ablest men in the United States. He is a splendid type of the Negro genius. As an editor especial for twenty long years, he has filled among the Baptists the same position as B. T. Tanner, D. D., among the Methodists. His pen has never failed in all these years to warn the race of dangers ahead. He always puts God first and his race next. His genius is consecrated to God, and he finds ample scope for his rare, splendid talents in assailing enemies as well as aggressively attacking maligners of the race. He has had a sword sometimes apparently dipped in wrath, and with giant force driven in the vitals of those who dared assail him and his cause; but he did it not for self but for the cause. May the future give vast opportunities for the use of his powerful intellect, conquering error and planting truth.

CHAPTER LXXXIX

Rev. Bartlett Taylor
Financier and Church Builder—Christian Pioneer

The subject of this sketch was born in Henderson county, Kentucky, Feb. 14, 1815. He was a slave. His mother belonged to Jonathan Taylor, who was her master and his father. He treated them very kindly and showed him many favors which the other colored children were denied. His master became financially embarrassed and his slaves were taken for debt. Among a large number taken away by the sheriff was young Taylor's mother and her infant in her arms, and her four grown sons who were half brothers to him also. Bartlett was at that time about seven years old and has never seen or heard of his mother since.

At the age of nine his owners moved from Henderson county to Oldham county, taking his sisters and himself with them, and settled on a farm six miles north of La Grange. When twelve years old his sisters and himself were taken to Westport and sold for his master's debts. He was bought by his master's brother, who willed him to his former owners, the youngest four children to be sold when the youngest of these became of age, and the money to be divided among them. Fortunately he was returned to the same people, where he remained until he was nineteen years of age. Then one of his oldest daughters married a Mr. Berry, who became quite attached to him. He moved to Louisville and hired his time and learned the butchers' trade. Disagreeing with his master he was then hired to a Mr. Clisindoff, who was one of the largest beef merchants in the city. For his services he received three hundred dollars per year. Being in pretty good circumstances he resolved to purchase his freedom, being assured by the three young girls to whom he fell in the division of the property that he should have the privilege of buying himself. He then began saving money, which he made at odd times from the profit of pigs' feet and beef-tripe, and other articles which had the privilege of selling. He accumulated money rapidly. In a short period he had saved eighteen hundred dollars. A particular colored friend of his got into his confidence and learned that he had this sum and borrowed fourteen hundred dollars, and another borrowed four hundred dollars, each telling him that when he was ready to buy himself they would return the money with good interest, which each failed to do, and he had no proof that he had let them have the money, and thus lost it.

His associates were of the best at the time, and he endeavored to so deport himself as to gain the favor of all well disposed persons. He was determined not to take unto himself a wife until he was a free man; so having a desire to marry he wrote to his owners that he had a wish to purchase his freedom. The time, September 20, 1840, was set for the sale when he was to be sold to the highest bidder at La Grange courthouse. Mr. Brent, who was to manage the sale, was a debtor to one of the heirs, and he had never seen Bartlett. He wrote, however, for him to be sure to meet him at the appointed time. When Bartlett got there he was without a cent of money. Nevertheless, he went to La Grange to meet the sale, trusting in the Lord. He was sold upon the block for two thousand dollars, himself being the highest bidder. He informed Mr. Brent of being defrauded of all his money, which he had saved for the purpose, and he then became responsible for the money, and gave him his free papers, believing that he would receive the money, which he did in 1840. He then married Mrs. Jane McCune of Abington, Virginia.

Being destitute of learning, he began to go to night school to Robert Lane and took writing of different teachers, his last one being the late Rev. Henry Adams of the Fifth Street Baptist church, who kept one of the free schools permitted in the South in the times of slavery. There were not many such schools, perhaps four or five in the whole South. In this way he learned to read, write and cipher, never going to day school in his life. Immediately after he was freed he began butchering, wholesaleing and retailing beef, mutton and pork, also packing and shipping large quantities, trading and shipping live stock South. He accumulated money rapidly, and in two years was in possession of six houses and lots on East Market street, but going security for a man named J. A. Gray, he had to pay that man's debt in 1858, which took all the property he had besides a large amount of money.

He lost his first wife in 1846, leaving three daughters. Two of them lived to be grown and were engaged in school teaching. The oldest, Mrs. Mary F. Scott, is still living.

In 1848 he was married to his present wife, Mariam A. McGill of Vincennes, Indiana. He is blest with one son who is twenty-four years old. This young man stood the civil service examination in June, 1884, for the postal service of the United States, and received the second highest average and was offered a position but declined, having come to the conclusion that he would make school teaching a profession. He is now teaching, and principal of one of the branch schools in the public schools of Louisville. In 1858 Mr. Taylor bought and built in the southeastern portion of the city where he has his present home. His property and other valuables are worth not less than fifteen thousand dollars. Having been impressed for a considerable length of time to preach the gospel, he finally took up mission work and continued on that for about four years. In 1866 he was appointed by Bishop J. P. Campbell, D. D., LL. D., itinerant worker, which he has been for twenty years. He has been the founder of and built a great many churches. He was appointed and served as a delegate to the Fifth General Conference of the A. M. E. church, to which he belongs. He was made treasurer of Wilberforce University in 1864, and held the office for several years, and was a trustee of the institution for sixteen years.

In Bowling Green, Kentucky, he bought the ground and built a church in 1872 and paid over nine thousand dollars on it. In 1874 he was stationed at Cynthiana and found a church partly erected, neither the ground nor building paid for, and both in the hands of the sheriff. He raised money and paid the indebtedness and finished the church at a cost of $8,000. In 1881 he returned to Shelbyville, Kentucky, and while pastoring the church there he saw the great necessity for a building for a graded school. He laid the matter before the people, then met the trustees of the town, and with their approval, bargained and bought a brick building with eight rooms and nearly four acres of ground, for $2,150; was instrumental in establishing the school and the employment of four teachers. In 1884 he was sent to Ashbury Chapel, Louisville, and rebuilt the church which had previously been destroyed by fire, and was successful in raising $2,150, and paid it in the hands of the trustees.

At the close of the late war, he was appointed missionary at large for the states of Kentucky and Tennessee, and received into the connection a large number of churches and members, the exact number of which it would be impossible for him to give, as they are received into the country churches, but the number was many thousand. He lives in the city of Louisville, and is respected very highly for his earnestness in Christian work, and his faithfulness in every department of life.

CHAPTER XC

Professor James M. Gregory, A. B., A. M.
Dean of the College Department of Howard University—
Linguist

———◆●◆———

James Monroe Gregory was born at Lexington, Virginia, January 23, 1849. His parents were Henry L. and Maria A. Gregory. Within the year 1849 the family went to reside at Lynchburg, even then a flourishing manufacturing center, with superior business advantages. The sentiments here towards people of color—the free as well as the slave—was possibly more liberal than in any other part of Virginia. Evidence of this may be seen in the fact that to-day there is no city in the South of equal population, where the colored people have accumulated more property and conduct more business enterprises than in Lynchburg. In 1859 they moved to Cleveland, Ohio, where young Gregory entered the public schools, being among the first colored boys to avail himself of their superior system of training. He at first encountered considerable ill-feeling on account of color, but he was soon as great a favorite among the boys as he already was among the teachers.

Temporarily residing in La Porte, Indiana, he attended a private school. Afterwards he went to Chicago, and there remained a while in the public school. Returning after a while to his home in Cleveland, he entered first the grammar school of that city, and then the high school. In 1865 he entered the Preparatory Department of Oberlin College. In one of his public addresses, he pays it the following glowing and well deserved tribute:

Before the War of the Rebellion we find colored students here and there admitted to the colleges of the North, but Oberlin was the only college professedly a school that received and welcomed them. It is the only one whose officers and students were heartily enlisted in the Anti-slavery cause, which, under the leadership of such men as Garrison, Douglass and Gerritt Smith, had begun already to arouse the dormant sympathies in the North, and consequently to alarm the pro-slavery element of the entire country.

JAMES M. GREGORY

Among his most pleasing experiences was his life at Oberlin. He found in his associates an entire absence of the spirit of caste, a generous and humane sentiment pervading the whole place; and he made also the intimate acquaintance of several men of our own race, since grown prominent in the service of the people, viz.: John M. Langston, B. K. Bruce, C. B. Purvis, John H. Cook, O. S. B. Wall, George W. Mitchell and George Collins. An interesting feature of Oberlin at this time was the Equal Rights League of the town. Here students and townsmen met to discuss the vital questions relative to the oppressed and oppressor. Young Gregory could not live and move amid such surroundings without having his whole nature deepened, broadened and ennobled. Those years at Oberlin were, no doubt, most decidedly formative in their effect upon his mind and character. As a student, he was industrious and ambitious. He, with ease, mastered the studies of the preparatory course, and is spoken of by his teachers as a bright scholar, and one that gave great promise for the future. Though the only colored man in the class, because of his high class standing, affable manners, powers as a writer and ability as a speaker, he was selected from a class of thirty-six as one of the nine students to represent the class at the senior preparatory exhibition; chosen not by the faculty, but the class itself. While here, on request of General Benjamin F. Butler, he was selected by the faculty to recommend for a cadetship at West Point; but Andrew Johnson, then President, pandering to the prejudice of the race, refused to appoint him. Meanwhile, Gregory had employed his vacation teaching at La Porte, Indiana, Mt. Tabor, Maryland, and Lynchburg.

In the year following Gregory's admission to college, while on his way from Lynchburg to Oberlin, he stopped in Washington to get the papers forwarded by the faculty in which he was recommended to General Butler for a cadetship to West Point. He was sent to the war department where the papers were filed, and there for the first time he met General O. O. Howard. Something in the address and bearing of the young man impressed the general who entered into conversation with him and drew forth the salient points of his personal history and prospects. Upon parting Mr. Gregory was told that probably he would be sent for in about a year to come to Washington, but no explanation was given. Scarcely twelve months had elapsed when he received a letter offering, if he would complete his course at Howard University, to give him at the same time a position as instructor in the Preparatory Department of that institution. Mr. Gregory accepted and at once entered upon his double duties at Washington.

In 1872 he graduated with the valendictory of his class and was regularly made tutor of Latin and mathematics in the Preparatory Department. In the winter of the next year he married an amiable and accomplished lady, Miss Fannie E. Hagan of Williamsport, Pennsylvania, at one time a student under his instruction. Three years later he was appointed professor of Latin in the College Department, a position which he still holds. He is also dean of the college, having been chosen to this responsible place by the college faculty for a fourth term.

Professor Gregory is one of the most successful young men of the race. He is eminently a scholar and one of those to whom we may point with pride in vindication of the Negro's ability to receive collegiate training and to engage in intellectual pursuits.

Although Mr. Gregory is professor of the Latin language, with its literature, and has made it a specialty, he has not confined himself to this one channel and thereby rendered likely a one-sided development. He is unusually familiar with matters of general history, is learned in the principles of political economy, international law and the science of government. He is also a fluent speaker and a ready writer.

Professor Gregory is an indefatigable worker; industry is among his most prominent traits of character; if he may be said to pride himself upon the possession of any one virtue it is this. He is, therefore, a genius, for true genius consists in work. Perseverance does not always accompany energy. Another of his characteristics is tact. One sees evidence of this quality in every phase of his life, domestic, social, educational and political. It is this that lends a charm to his intercourse in the family circle, that makes him a delightful person with whom to meet and converse. Not least among the powers belonging to the subject of this sketch, is strength of will.

The ordinary professor is engrossed in the little world of the schoolroom, and has but slight concern for the tide of human affairs without; not so is Professor Gregory. Latin roots interest but do not absorb him. He is fully awake to all that transpires, and is well-informed concerning matters generally. On this account he is the more efficient as an instructor and the more useful as a citizen. A few years ago he contested the right to send his son to any one of the public schools in Washington. His interest in the school question was soon manifested in another direction.

When George T. Downing and himself discovered in the new code of laws for the district, which had been prepared and was before the House of Representatives, a provision sanctioning by law the separate school system, they were aroused to immediate action. Pursuant to a call by these gentlemen, a meeting was held at the house of Dr. C. B. Purvis, when a memorial was adopted, calling the special attention of the Senate and House of Representatives to certain clauses in the proposed code for the District of Columbia, which, contrary to the provisions of the Constitution, permits an unjust and odious discrimination against a large number of its citizens of the District of Columbia. The committee on memorial was as follows: Frederick Douglass, president, Richard T. Greener, secretary, Frederick G. Barbadoes, John F. Cook, George T. Downing, James M. Gregory, Rev. F. J. Grimke, Milton M. Holland, Wiley Lane, C. B. Purvis, M.D., and Wm. H. Smith. They fought manfully for the principle at stake, and with such effect as greatly to alarm the enemies of their cause. Newspapers took up the question and grew vehement in its discussion. All sorts of vile epithets were hurled at the originators of the memorial; and finally, when through their exertions the code containing the obnoxious laws was defeated, they were branded as "Obstructionists." Their success was largely due to Representative D. B. Haskell of Kansas, who was their able champion in the House.

Professor Gregory has been intimately connected with many of the leading events of the Nation's capital and elsewhere, and has shown himself possessed of much executive ability as well as patriotic zeal. He was one of the originators of the Civil Rights mass meeting held in Washington, October 23, 1883, to consider the late decision of the Supreme Court of United States, and was also the presiding officer of the evening. The occasion was memorable and important as a presentation of views on this subject of vital moment. The speakers of the occasion were Honorable Frederick Douglass, Colonel Robert Ingersoll, Judge Samuel Shellaberger, and Dr. J. E. Rankin.

He aims to establish in connection with Howard University what shall be known as the "Frederick Douglass Scholarship Fund." His views on the subject of scholarships are best told in his own cogent words. In his triennial address to the alumni to the institution he said:

We need a permanent fund that may be applied to scholarships which do not necessarily oblige the recipients to devote themselves to the ministry or any other particular calling, for many young men do not make a choice of profession until they have reached their junior or senior years. Many of the most useful men in this country and Europe, men eminent in church affairs, in law, in medicine, politics and literature are those who have been assisted through college by scholarships. Scholarships in a college are now a necessity; for first, they are a direct benefit to the students, they enable them to undertake a college course, inspiring them with the hope that by diligent application they can become educated men. They relieve pecuniary embarrassments, anxieties for the necessaries of life, hardships and humiliations. They give the student time to devote to his studies, so that the best portion of the day may not be taken up in outside work; they prevent students from borrowing money and consequently running in debt. Again, they are a direct benefit to the college, being a large source of revenue. They should not be regarded as a charity but as a reward of merit, and should be given to those who can be commended for their correct deportment and scholarly attainments. To put our College Department upon a permanent basis, to make her hold out a helping hand to the scores of deserving youth who are anxiously turning their faces Howardward, but are kept away from us on account of their poverty—we must secure permanent funds—we must found scholarships.

Frequently called to important and responsible positions, he has shown at all times an ability most creditable to himself and most pleasing to his friends. His political career began comparatively early. While at Oberlin he was known as one of her most public-spirited young men and he often did important service in many of the citizens' gatherings. Prior to that time he had made himself useful in a public capacity as secretary of the well-known Fugitives, afterwards Freedmen's Aid Society in Cleveland. For four years he was secretary of the Republican Central committees of the District of Columbia. He was also of the number who signed the call for a National convention of colored men. The call was responded to and the convention met at Louisville, Kentucky, September 24, 1883. The delegates sent from the district were Hon. Fred. Douglass, Professor James M. Gregory and the Rev. W. S. Laws. An equal distinction with being elected to so important a position was such association with Fred. Douglass. At the Louisville convention Professor Gregory was elected temporary and then permanent secretary over all the worthy aspirants for that office. On the twenty-seventh of February, 1886, Professor Gregory was appointed trustee of public schools. When the appointment was made public, much opposition was manifested by the Democratic and conservative press of the city and country. It was said that this appointment meant mixed schools for the capital. The vials of newspaper wrath were poured out upon him and also upon the commissioners who appointed him.

The howling of the press did no good. The commissioners retained Professor Gregory, and upon the re-organization of the board in September of that year the president of the board, J. J. Darlington, Esq., himself a Democrat, recognizing the scholarly attainments of the professor and his acquaintance with school matters, appointed him on some of the leading committees and chairman of the most impotrant committee, namely, committee on teachers and janitors.

On the occasion of the celebration of the Twenty-fourth Emancipation of slaves in the District of Columbia, Professor Gregory was chosen chairman of the meeting held in Israel church. One of the leading papers speaks of his remarks as follows: "The Emancipation address of Professor Gregory, recapitulating the progress of the Negro in the district since his emancipation in 1862, was terse, graphic and striking." This address has been put in pamphlet form along with the three great Emancipation addresses of Hon. Fred. Douglass and will repay a careful perusal by those who wish to learn of the progress made in the last twenty years by the colored people at the Nation's capital in the matters of business, property and education.

Professor Gregory is one of the best extemporaneous speakers in our race. A brief report of an impromptu speech made recently by him appeared in the *Cleveland Plain Dealer*, January 28, 1887.

On Monday night Lincoln Memorial church was crowded with the best citizens of Washington to hear the eulogies pronounced on the life and public services of General John A. Logan. Hon. John M. Langston presided; Colonel George W. Williams was the orator of the evening. After the oration was finished, distinguished visitors present were called upon, and among others who spoke were ex-Minister to Liberia Smythe, Mr. Botts from Virginia, and Professor J. M. Gregory, dean of the college of Howard University. Professor Gregory's remarks were especially happy. He related an incident of how when a student at Oberlin, then a mere youth, chancing to be in Washington he called on the great Sumner to get information on a topic he had for discussion. How he hesitated before knocking at the door of the senator's room; how finally summing up courage he knocked and asked for Mr. Sumner and was admitted to the presence of the great man. The professor spoke of the great courtesy shown him by Mr. Sumner; how during the conversation, several distinguished gentlemen called and finding no one present but a young colored boy, began at once to make known their business; but Senator Sumner interrupting them, said: "Gentlemen excuse me, I am engaged at present with this young man." Then he went on giving the information desired. Professor Gregory mentioned a similar incident that happened during a visit to Senator Logan. He said that Logan, like Sumner, was a man of magnanimous soul; a man who in the midst of his duties and engagements found time to see those who called upon him seeking information or advice. He was never too busy to say a kind word or lend a helping hand to those who needed his assistance. It was this element in his character that made him a friend of the soldier, the poor and oppressed. Concluding, he said:

"In the field Logan was bold among the boldest, and daring almost to recklessness; endowed with these qualities of courage and intellect that make cowards forget their fright and lead braver men to victory. When again he changed the trappings of a soldier for the garb of the citizen, his career was no less illustrious. On the stump or in the councils of the party, he was alike unquestionably great. But in private, as it has been my pleasure to see him, surrounded by his friends, in the bosom of his family, there he was pre-eminently great."

Unlike many eminent men, Professor Gregory's private life is as pleasing as his public course is inspiring. He has that greatest of all earthly possessions—a happy home. He is identified with the Congregational church.

That the reader may know something of the forcible, eloquent style of Professor Gregory, we add a few extracts from some of the best speeches:

NEW LEADERS

New leaders for the Negro race are needed. Not the time-serving lickspittle, not the self-seeking parasite, not the obsequious, cringing go-between, not swaggering insolence or skulking cowardice in leadership, nor any man who is either ashamed of being, or mean enough to deny that he is a Negro. We want, we demand leaders, first of all, who are not ashamed of the race; who are possessed of brains, character, courage, zeal and tact. We want leaders who know the history of the race's trials, struggles, and achievements, and who can from that history draw inspiration for the great work to be accomplished. We demand leaders who are the friends of mechanical education for the rising young men, and who are pledged to a system of thorough education for our young women. We demand leaders who will neither touch, taste nor handle, nor put to their neighbor's lips, in private or public, at home or abroad, or on land or sea the accursed cup of drink. Men they must be of noble instincts and generous impulses, who have a genius for hard, self-sacrificing labor to build up the race. Such leaders will have the skill to detect the condition of our people, and the genius and heroism to lead the way to the heart of the race's moral need. God grant that such men may be forthcoming.

MORAL EMANCIPATION

is what we most need now. Many salutary lessons are taught us by the bitter past. Let us lay them to heart, and, taking fresh courage, turn to the great work that awaits us on every hand. All that remains of this tempestuous state of things is but the rocking of a troubled sea to rest. For He whose chariot the winds are, and the clouds, the dust that waits upon His sultry march shall visit us in mercy, shall descend propitious in His chariot paved with love.

CUBAN EMANCIPATION

But whether the enfranchised people in Southern United States get justice done them or not, the emancipated slaves in the island of Cuba will henceforth find a shield of Spanish justice over them and freedom in its letter and spirit will be evermore fraught with significant meaning and glorious reality! Once Cuba sat as a dark spectre amid the deep blue waters of the gulf, but now she wears the diadem of liberty, and humanity the world over rejoices in her birth to a new and better life. Her long benighted and besotted slaves, rising from their chains, may stir the island with the song—

> *No more for traders' gold,*
> *Shall those we love be sold;*
> *Nor crushed be manhood bold,*
> *In slavery's dreaded fold.*
>
> *Huzzah! huzzah!*
> *Our song shall be;*
> *Huzzah! huzzah!*
> *That we are free.*

The moan of the Atlantic ocean and the high of the Gulf of Mexico have answered the piercing cries of separated children and disconsolate mothers; but now they will chant a *Te Deum* for the promise of "Forever free" that turn the lamentation of slaves into the exultation of free men!

Cuba, the pearl of the gulf, adds new radiance to the crown of human liberty on the brow of civilization, casting a peerless light upon the pathway of the nations of the earth. The island, so frequently disheveled and bedraggled in the carriage of revolution is now tranquilized by the boon of liberty. And the imperial Spanish throne, the lullaby to which was the shock of embattled arms, rests secure in the hearts of free, grateful and loyal subjects. No revolution will ever rock that throne or imperil its crown, except, perhaps, in behalf of still wider liberty of government—for a State without a king or nobles, a church without a bishop. But the friends of liberty here in this great Republic will ever cherish a sentiment of profound gratitude to the Spanish nation for this noble decree of Emancipation. It is with conscious pride that we remember the illustrious service rendered to mankind by two royal women of Spain—Isabella sent forth Christopher Columbus on a voyage that resulted in the discovery of America, and Martha Christina blotted out the last vestige of human slavery in North America. *Bravo! Espana!*

THE REPUBLICAN PARTY

I know what I have said. I believe what I have said. I feel in my heart of hearts what I have said. To any colored man who understands the origin, purpose, character and capacities of our party, argument is superfluous. It was by years of agitation that the war was brought about. The Republican party invited the Negro to share the perils and horrors of war. It was a grand thing for a white man to defend his liberties, but it was a grander thing for the colored man to fight for his liberty. The proudest moment of my life was when I wore the blue and held a sword as a Federal soldier. And when in the army of the James I saw thirty-five thousand colored soldiers under arms, well drilled, and lacking no attribute of bravery, skill or endurance, I asked myself: "What hath God wrought through the Republican party?" I was gratified to see with my own eyes, and hear with my own ears, a colored man who went to the United States Senate to fill the place of the arch-traitor, Jefferson Davis. The Republican party that invited the colored man to help save the Union, welcomed him to the responsibilities and duties of citizenship. And every office held by the colored people was obtained through the Republican party. Under the rule of the Republican party we have seen colored men hold office from the United States Senate down to a messengership in the departments. Could we expect more in such a short time? Who gave our people schools in the South when the Democrats refused? The Republican party. Every measure that has proven to be beneficial to the colored people in the country is the production of Republicanism. The Democratic party in State and National legislation voted against every law enacted for the well-being of the colored race. Everything—I make no qualification —we enjoy as citizens is the gift of the Republican party. Do you tell me that there are colored men who are going to vote for the Democratic party? On what ground, pray? I hear no answer. Do you say that colored people are dissatisfied? About what? The principles of the party are pure, humane and just. Some men may not like the way that politicians have treated them. Don't put them in office. Are you dissatisfied with the Southern policy? Don't break up the party; don't vote against the whole organization because you are displeased with a few men. Don't do like Samson and lean against the pillars of this noble structure and bury yourselves with your enemies under the ruins. Remember, my friends, that all human organizations are imperfect. There are many men in our party that I would rather see out of it. But I am going to bide my time, and then help them out to the best of my ability. After the war, when there was but one party, some bad men rushed into our party and pushed good men to the rear. We must get rid of them as soon as possible. For which party some men vote has become a matter of cents and dollars. Let no colored man flatter himself that he is so far removed from a condition of servitude that he may vote for the Democratic party with impunity. If the Democracy get the Federal government in their hands in 1880, they will not hesitate to impugn the amendments from the constitution and strip the colored voter of every vestige of citizenship. The Democratic party cannot be trusted in power, and the colored men who aid it by the suffrage the Republican party gave them, ought to get all that their conduct would merit. But I am sure that the intelligent voters of Ohio will rally to the support of the party they have trusted and the party that will always accord them all the rights and privileges that belong to every American citizen.

THE ADVENT OF THE COLORED SOLDIER

In the late war, the Negro proved himself an able and efficient soldier. By the ponderous and incessant blow of this battle-axe of liberty, he opened the gate to social, political and religious relations and activities. Slavery had closed all of these gates against him; these relations lay beyond the boundaries of the cruel institutions, in the fair land of freedom. The moment the

Negro enrolled under the "Stars and Stripes" he began an existence hitherto unknown to him. He took a part in a drama that was not to end in a war of arms, but in a war of ideas and principles, in which war he was to take on his characteristics as a free man, not as a slave; as a civilian, not as a soldier.

The world has blindly ascribed qualities to the Negro slave that will not belong to him as an educated citizen, and would as readily belong to any other class of men in the same condition in which the American slave was before the war. But the time is come when the test is being applied. It remains to be seen what the Negro will be. The war was only an initiatory step. It was then that four and one-half millions of human beings came up out of the Egypt of bondage to begin their march of citizenship. Before them lie the fields of science and learning, and the plains of culture invite their weary feet.

Some have thought the war ended, the victories all won; but the struggle begun in the ditches of Pillow and on the parapets of Wagner, under the eyes of the whole civilized world, is still going on. It has been extended into the common school, where ignorance is to be conquered and superstition vanquished. Into the temple of God and into the halls of Congress, this struggle, this conflict is pushed. The battle between conscience and passion, between selfishness and benevolence, between slothfulness and duty, all these battles are to be waged with all the vehemence of manly effort. For we must remember that the victories won in war are conditioned to us on the ground of our success in conquering moral conflicts. We have not a moment to spare. The heat of the battle is now; so let every man be at his post. The world is watching and waiting for results.

I am indeed glad, comrades, that slavery is dead. Its ghost will no longer render our land hideous. Slavery is dead! But, comrades, the evil influences of the institution linger among us. Its impress was made upon the souls as well as upon the bodies of its subjects. It will take years before this country will be able to outgrow the scars it received from slavery. The government is yet weak from the fierce and protracted struggle; but time will close and heal every wound; she will yet be strong in truth and justice.

Comrades, this is the formative period of our race. We will be susceptible to many impressions, and it therefore becomes us to know just what kind of material we are putting into our characters. Everything we do now will go into history, whether good or bad. If we fail to be industrious and virtuous, the future historian will record it. He will write that after the Negro was free, instead of becoming virtuous, he became licentious; instead of becoming industrious, he became indolent; instead of becoming wiser, he became more ignorant; turning liberty into license, his last sin was worse than the former.

Ah! comrades and fellow Christians, I wish I could write the language of my heart in plainer letters! I wish I could tell you in articulate words, how much I love you, and how anxious I am that my race march on until it takes its place by the side of an ancient Greek and classic Rome; yea, even by the side of England and proud America! You may think me a fanatic to-day, but fifty years hence, when our race has taken on a national character its panegyrist will call this no idle dream.

DANIEL ABRAHAM GADDIE

CHAPTER XCI

Rev. Daniel Abraham Gaddie
From the Blacksmith Shop to the Pulpit—Temperance Advocate—Moderator of Fifty Thousand Baptists

---

Rev. D. A. Gaddie, one of the strong men of Kentucky, has risen from the sledge hammer and the anvil to a commanding position among men. This he has done by persevering diligence and application to business. He was born May 21, 1836, and is still hale and hearty. A man of splendid physique, a very Ajax in bravery, a Hercules in strength. He may be called a handsome man in personal appearance, and he impresses one as a safe protector in trouble. To such men we seem to fly for refuge when danger is near. In his twenty-third year he gave his heart to Christ, and commenced in earnest to serve Him who ruleth the hearts of all men. He owes his conversion to one Robert Gardner, a white brother. He was ordained in the year 1865, and was at that time a member of Green Street church. At his ordination, Rev. Henry Adams, Rev. Richard Sneethen, Charles Edwards and Solomon Patterson took part. He was pastor of several churches in the State; among them may be mentioned Elizabethtown, Greensburg, Campbellsville, Rude's Creek, Glendale and Green Street Baptist church, of which he has charge at this writing. Elder Richard Sneethen died April 11, 1872, and the subject of this sketch was elected pastor in October of the same year. Under his wise administration of the affairs for the past fifteen years, much good has been done in the systematic organization of the work. He has added more than two thousand members to the church; fifteen hundred, perhaps, of this number were converts. He has married about five hundred couples and preached thousands of sermons and delivered many addresses. The Green Street church is one of the most faithful in the State, and under his leadership it has been trained to give, when called upon, for every object worthy of Christian benevolence. The General Association of Kentucky Baptists has for years honored him with various offices. He has been assistant moderator for many years, but in the last session held at Bowling Green,

Kentucky, he was chosen as moderator of 50,000 colored Baptists. This was one of the largest gatherings in the State, and shows the popularity and strength of Rev. Mr. Gaddie. In the National American Baptist convention, which was held at St. Louis, August 25, 1886, he was chosen treasurer by a unanimous vote. All the old brethren, Rev. DeBaptiste, Rufus L. Perry and a host of others, are well acquainted with him and hold him in high esteem. He was vice-president of what was known some years ago as the American Consolidated Baptist convention. He has been a member of the Board of Trustees of the State University, located at Louisville, for seven years, and was a member of the Executive Board for sixteen years. He has also been very prominent in temperance work, being a strong opponent of alcoholic liquors in every shape. He is eminently a friend of young preachers, and none have applied to him who do not receive abundant sympathy and material help. Herein lies his strength. For many years he has been secretary of the Ministers' and Deacons' meeting, held in the city of Louisville. He has a large office and the meetings are always held with his church. This meeting has exerted a wonderful influence upon the Baptist ministry in more ways than one, creating much social feeling and promoting brotherly love among them. As moderator for the Central District Association for the last ten years, he has given satisfaction to the churches and in like manner increased the membership materially, more than doubling the number of churches connected with the work. This association contributes more money for the support of the State University than any other association in the State except the General Association and the Baptist Women's Educational convention. Intellectually he is a strong man, and in the subject of theology and history he is well posted, and much deference is paid to his opinion upon such subjects.

Few men in the State have more earnest supporters and well-wishers. Though he has had in lifetime many severe troubles yet he has always controlled his temper; though he has often had the power to crush enemies who are disposed to do him injustice, he has had long patience and exhibited those Christian virtues which go to make a man strong and powerful with the people, and to overthrow the machinations of them who desire to injure him. His hand is ever ready to assist any and every enterprise calculated to benefit the people of the State. He is often elected to conventions which consider the educational and industrial affairs of the colored people and is therefore more prominent on account of his own advocacies of every measure which will elevate the race. Such men hasten "the good time a coming," add to the moral, religious and educational worth of the people. His life full of usefulness, piety and acts of charity, draw to him the affection of a loving people whose personal kindnesses are well known to the writer.

The Rev. D. A. Gaddie, long a central figure in the Baptist world and a man of earnest and untiring efforts in the cause of education, was given the degree of Doctor of Divinity by the State University at its annual commencement, May 17, 1887.

W. Q. ATWOOD

CHAPTER XCII

W. Q. Atwood, Esq.
Lumber Merchant and Capitalist—Orator

Mr. W. Q. Atwood, the subject of this sketch, was born on the first day of January, 1839, on the Shell Creek plantation, two and a half miles from Prairie Bluff, a small village on the Alabama river, in Wilcox county, Alabama. His father, Henry Styles Atwood, was born the twenty-sixth of March, 1798, in the State of Connecticut. He traced his line of descent back to Dr. Henry Skilton, a surgeon in Oliver Cromwell's army. His father had a good common school training, and was a natural lawyer, but a very successful business man. Starting from a poor boy, his estate was valued at several hundred thousand dollars. His sister, Mrs. Alice Northrup of Beloit, Wisconsin, now eighty-three years old, is the only survivor of a family of three girls and himself.

His mother was born on the eastern shore of Maryland, and partly raised in Philadelphia; went South to Alabama when quite a young woman, had charge of their home in the South, and came North with them in 1853. She was a member of the Methodist church in good standing. Among other things, she practiced medicine, carded, spun, wove, cut and made clothing, cooked and did most everything about the house. She learned to read and write after she was forty-seven years old, and died at Zanesville, Ohio, February 14, 1873.

W. Q. Atwood was born under the yoke of slavery; his father was his master, and with the usual kindness and care which parents generally give to their children, he did not feel the curse of slavery, except in the want of school training, and such association as would brighten and strengthen his mind and harmonize with his feelings. He was provided with nearly everything he wished, and in this respect was, perhaps, no more denied than is usual to children.

After the death of his father, by his will, with about twenty-one other persons, he went North, to Ripley, Ohio, where he landed May 15, 1853. He went to a colored school in Ripley about two years, but getting in that time not more than ten or twelve months schooling. He worked in the meanwhile, and when not at school was of course busily employed.

In the fall of 1856 he went to Iberia school, and continued there until the spring of 1859. In the fall of 1859, in company with his brother, John S., he went to California. While in California he followed steamboating, and still later opened a restaurant. He also did some mining. John returned to Ohio before he did. On this trip he did not make much money, but he did gain much knowledge of men and things. He returned to Ripley, Ohio, about the fall of 1861, the home of his mother, Julius, John, David, Olive, Kossuth, all his brothers. Then he began speculating; talked about the war by day and taught school by night.

The following spring he made a visit to East Saginaw, Michigan, and returned to Ripley in the fall of 1862. Ripley is on the northern bank of the Ohio river, and this was not at all times the boundary line of the rebel doings, and it was not quite pleasant for him to remain so near, or in the midst of the war, and not be a soldier and take a part.

He went to East Saginaw, Michigan, and in the summer of 1863 he took a compass, map and plats, and went into the woods and looked for lands. He has bought and sold lands and city real estate from that time until now. In 1863, he located sixteen hundred acres of land, and sold the same in the fall of 1863, clearing four thousand dollars in cash. This was his first land deal. He has never made but one or two bad purchases or sales in real estate. Being a very shrewd business man, and a very careful reader of newspapers, and familiar with all the details of the business, there is really no reason why he should not succeed.

In the winter of 1868, with thirty men and eight teams, he cut and put in three million feet of pine sawlogs, and manufactured the same into lumber the following year, and sold it at a profit of six thousand dollars. He continued lumbering each year, cutting from one to five million feet, until 1877, and has made from twenty-five dollars to ten dollars per thousand feet. The average cost of taking the timber from the tree to the milldock, in East Saginaw, ready for shipping, is about eight dollars per thousand feet. He lumbered again in 1880, 1881, 1882, and in 1885 and 1886. He is not lumbering any at the present time. He has found market for his lumber during his experience, at Toledo, Cleveland, Dayton, Cincinnati, Columbus, Chicago, Boston, Baltimore and other ports.

He has on hand about six million standing pine, and more hard wood, but he does not intend to lumber any more. He has given employment to large bodies of men, having worked from thirty to fifty at a time, and from six to fifteen teams, or from twelve to thirty horses. In all his business transactions he has endeavored to use his own capital, and has invested it very carefully, never borrowing at any one time over six thousand dollars.

After he went to East Saginaw he took from his own lands the following pine timber: cut and sold in the sawlog, 12,000,000 feet; cut and manufactured into lumber 25,000,000 feet; bought and sold pine timber lands containing 100,000,000 feet; located and sold farming lands to settlers, 6,000 acres; bought and sold city real estate worth twenty-five thousand dollars, and still owns more city property than he has sold.

His business is done in true business style, keeping his books accurately, so that he knows at any moment where he stands financially. He owes not a dollar to any man, and as a successful lumber merchant he is worthy of recognition. To-day he has a bank account of five thousand dollars in cash; four thousand dollars in stocks; and notes and mortgages which he holds to the amount of twenty thousand dollars. Besides he has property worth twenty-five thousand dollars in the city of Saginaw; two thousand acres of farming lands; also six hundred acres of stump lands and a farm of four hundred and forty acres. He also has some logs and lumber. His pine standing is valued at from two dollars to ten dollars on the stump. He is now principally engaged in the real estate business.

He has a pleasant home and a very amiable wife and five children. His oldest son, Willie, is twelve years old; the second, Freddie Stiles, is ten; the third, Oliver Kossuth, is eight; and his fourth child, a girl, Alice May, is 5 years old, and the fifth, Lottie, is two years old. He takes great pride in their education, and carefully notes their standing in their classes and encourages them when they do well.

His wife was born in Georgia, Wilkes county, and is a graduate of the Salam Normal school, and taught school in Philadelphia and Washington. He married her in Cleveland, Ohio, May 15, 1872.

Mr. Atwood is a leading spirit in political, social and commercial matters in his city. He is the only colored member of the Board of Trade, and being worth in the neighborhood of one hundred thousand dollars and perhaps more, is able to surround himself with comforts of no ordinary nature. His beautiful residence is surrounded by magnificent lawns, situated on the corner of Hyde and Jefferson Avenue, and is in quite an aristocratic neighborhood.

We deem his career a worthy example of what can be accomplished by one possessing the requisite qualities of patience, enterprise and foresight.

HENRY HIGHLAND GARNET

CHAPTER XCIII

Rev. Henry Highland Garnet, D. D.
Minister Resident of Liberia—Distinguished Minister
of the Gospel and a Brilliant Orator

———•◆•———

Henry Highland Garnet was born in slavery in Kent county, Maryland, December 23, 1845. Although his father, George Garnet, was a slave, his grandfather was an African chief and warrior, and in a tribal fight he was captured and sold to slave-traders who brought him to this continent where he was owned by Colonel William Spencer. With the love for liberty burning in his veins, George Garnet could not endure the chains that fettered his life, and he planned a scheme to save his whole family from the galling yoke of slavery. He obtained permission from his master to attend a slave's funeral in Wilmington, Delaware, and he took his wife, son and daughter to that place where they remained one night under the watchcare of Thomas Garrett, a Quaker, celebrated for his aid to fugitive slaves and aiding them to go to Bucks county, Pennsylvania. In 1825 Mr. Garnet removed his family to New York City. From the father the son received much of his strength of character and love of knowledge; from the mother, a notable candor, intellectual face, and the bright, keen laughing eye. With such an inheritance, together with physical greatness, the subject of our sketch could not but possess such traits as we find in him and made him beloved by all who had the pleasure of knowing him and feeling his power.

In New York Mr. Garnet entered the African free school on Mulberry street and became the schoolmate and friend of many distinguished colored men whose names shall live in history, namely: Professor Charles L. Reason, George T. Downing, Ira Aldridge, the great tragedian, and others whose names are equally familiar. The privations of his family compelled him to discontinue school for a time, and he spent two years as cabin-boy. On one of his visits home he found that his father's family had been scattered by the inroads of Maryland slave-hunters. This painful news, although at first it nearly broke the young man's heart, proved the turning point of his life. He sought and found refuge and strength in his crucified and risen Lord, and he joined the Sunday school of the First Presbyterian church, under the pastorate of the celebrated Rev. Theodore S. Wright. Soon after he was baptized by this minister and became an earnest worker for the cause of Christ.

In 1831 a high school was established by leading colored men in New York for the pursuance of the classics, and Garnet was one of the first pupils. In 1835 the Puritans in New Hampshire, desiring to enlarge the cramped facilities for Negro education, opened a High school in Canaan, New Hampshire, and Garnet, still eager to feast on what his mind had only tasted, although physically very weak and feeble, started with two other friends to find what he hoped would gratify his intellectual hunger; but alas, the few colored boys were too much for this New England State. The New England Democracy declared the school a nuisance, and after a few weeks the farmers in that vicinity moved the school a great distance from its original site, simply because it was, as they termed it, "a nigger school." This attempt at knowledge proving a failure, he returned home so infirm that his life was often times despaired of. After remaining for a few months at home, information was given that Oneida Institute at Whitesboro, the manual seminary, had opened its doors for colored youth. Thither Garnet went, and in 1839 he graduated with distinguished honor and began a public life. He first settled at Troy, all the time studying theology with Dr. Beman, and acting as secretary to the colored Presbyterian church. He was licensed to preach in 1842, and became the first pastor of the Liberty Street Presbyterian church of that city. This charge he held for ten years, during which time he published the *Clarion*.

Garnet was a remarkable man. In his school life he always led his mates, and through life he always desired to be in advance, notwithstanding the hindrances his feeble health caused, for he was a cripple at fifteen years brought on by white swelling. He was earnest however, in the prosecution of everything he undertook. He afterwards had his leg amputated in 1841, and it was owing to this that he survived so many years thereafter. He was a great sufferer, but patient under all. He perfected in himself a rigid and rare mind, teeming with brilliancy and wit, mingled with pathos. This man possessed wonderful ability for holding audiences spell-bound; his pure English, deep thought and manly dignity in Anti-slavery movements were often in demand. He was active and progressive in everything. His speeches were made with such powerful effect that their force could never be put in print. He was a man of strong feeling and a true heart, and in speaking reached the inner nature of men. Many of his speeches can never die, and it is a shame that they cannot be gathered up and preserved as English classics.

In 1850 he visited Great Britain and there, in assemblies, he won the hearts of the people and charmed them with his eloquent language. From England he went as delegate to the Peace Congress at Frankfort-on-the-Main, and thence he traveled through Prussia and France. For a brief time he went as Missionary to Jamaica, stationed at Sterling Grange Mill in that place, until ill health forced him to return home. In all he undertook he was successful, and every work flourished under his care. He was one of the first during the Rebellion to call young colored men to arms, and he became chaplain to a regiment of colored troops. He organized a committee for the sick soldiers and was almoner to the New York Benevolent Society for colored sufferers of the mob. It was only providential that he himself escaped the wild fury of this maddened crowd. During his life-time he was president of Avery College in Pittsburgh, for about three years. He was induced at one time to pastor a Presbyterian church in Washington, District of Columbia, and was the first colored man to preach in the capital of the United States. He returned to his early love, Shiloh church, in New York, however, and was pastor of it for twenty-six years. In 1842 Garnet was married to Miss Julia Williams, who had been a classmate at Canaan Institute. He had cherished for a long while a desire to visit Africa, and when an offer was made of position of Minister Resident to Liberia, notwithstanding the grief of parting with friends whom he never met again, he gladly accepted the offer, and on the sixth of Nevember, 1881, he preached his farewell sermon at Shiloh church, New York City, to the people he had loved so long and well, and whose hearts were stricken because of his retiring. On the twelfth of November, he sailed for England and arrived at Monrovia, December 28. He lived but a short time after he reached his fatherland; but his life will ever be an inspiration to the young men of the race, as a type of what a sainted life might be and how men may, by their own energy and personal efforts, rise to lofty stations among their fellowmen. He died in the land of his fathers and as Alexander Crummel, D.D., has said, "They buried him like a prince, this princely man, with the blood of a long line of chieftains in his veins, in the soil of his fathers. The entire military forces of the capital of the republic turned out to render a last tribute of respect and honor. The President and his cabinet, the ministry of every name, the president, professors and students of the college, large bodies of citizens from the river settlement, as well as the townsmen, attended his obsequies as mourners. A noble tribute was accorded him by Rev. E. W. Blyden, D.D., LL.D., one of the finest scholars and thinkers in the nation. Minute guns were fired at every footfall of the solemn procession. And when they laid him lowly in the sod, there was heard on the hills, in the valleys and on the waters, the tributary peal of instantaneous thunder which announced through the still air the closing of the grave. There he lies, the deep Atlantic but a few steps beyond, its perpetual surges beating at his very feet, chanting ever more the deep anthems of the ocean, the solemn requiem of the dead."

CHAPTER XCIV

*Rev. Leonard Andrew Grimes
Imprisoned at Richmond, Virginia, Jail for Assisting Fugitives
from Slavery—A Lovely Disciple of Christ, and Pastor
of a Boston Baptist Church*

Rev. Leonard A. Grimes was distinguished for his tenderness of heart and his abundance of sympathy with all who were in trouble. His life was pure, and full of acts of mercy. He was one of those, who, like his Master, "went about doing good."

He was born in Leesburg, Loudon county, Virginia, on or about the ninth of November, 1815, and died at Boston, March 14, 1873. He was taken very suddenly ill at his residence on Everett avenue, East Summersville; he had just returned from a board meeting of the executive committee of the Home Mission Society, of which he was a member. His death was very sudden; he had scarcely reached home and been in the house more than ten minutes before he died of apoplexy.

Though born free, and so light that he often passed for a white person, yet he had Negro blood in his veins, for which he had to suffer all the ills to which the Negroes of the South were subject. He went to Washington to live, and as he grew into manhood, he got clear views of the institutions of slavery. His entire being was shocked at its enormities and cruelties. His relations in the services of slaveholders brought him at times into immediate contact with the painful sufferings of his race; this begot in him a deep hatred for slavery, and he resolved to do all he could to aid the slaves in any attempt they might make to escape from bondage. This disposition was known, and the slave who wished to run away sought Mr. Grimes for advice, which he never failed to give. Slaveholders began to suspect young Grimes as an enemy to their traffic in human flesh and blood. He was watched, detected, arrested, tried, convicted and imprisoned. But his conscience never condemned him, and he bore his imprisonment without the least feelings of remorse, and stood his punishment with heroic fortitude. At the expiration of his imprisonment at Richmond, Virginia, Mr. Grimes returned to Washington, and embraced

LEONARD ANDREW GRIMES

religion, and was baptized in 1840, by Rev. William Williams. He then went North, and associated himself with the American Baptist Missionary convention, and went to New Bedford, where he resided about two years; and then in 1846 he went to Boston, Massachusetts.

After laboring for some time, the church was organized on the evening of the twenty-fourth of November, 1848, and he was ordained their first pastor at the same time.

He remained as pastor of the Twelfth Street Baptist church till the day of his death. His ministerial life was full of good works. He was not an eloquent speaker, but as a pastor he had no equals, and was powerful in prayer.

He could look up and move the powers of heaven, and did it in the interest of whatever good object he prayed for. His ministry was in every way successful, and he had the satisfaction of baptizing hundreds of persons who were led to Christ through his ministry. In disposition, Mr. Grimes was peculiarly amiable, and on this account, as well as for his great fruitfulness in good works, he was beloved by all who knew him. No minister in Boston, white or black, was more generally respected and beloved by all classes and all denominations than Rev. Leonard A. Grimes. Mr. Grimes was also one of the most effective agents of the Underground Railroad. Hundreds of escaping slaves passed through his hands en route to Canada. If under an "act respecting fugitives from justice and persons escaping from the services of their masters," the fugitive was apprehended in Boston and remanded to slavery, Mr. Grimes would drop everything, and collect money, pursue the captors, buy his man and let him go without fear of further molestation.

During the war he took a great part in enlisting colored soldiers, and says George W. Williams in his *History of the Negro Race,* "So highly were the services of brother Grimes prized, that the chaplaincy of the regiment was not only tendered him but urged upon him. But his multifarious duties forbade his going with the regiment he loved and revered." This reference is to the Fifty-fourth Massachusetts regiment.

He was for several years president of the American Baptist Missionary convention and of the Consolidated Baptist convention. The history of the colored Baptists of the North, from 1846 to 1873, is full of the spirit of the good works of Leonard A. Grimes. When he died, universal lamentation was heard in the city of Boston.

CHAPTER XCV

Rev. James H. Holmes
Pastor of a Flourishing Baptist Church in Richmond, Virginia—
One who has Come Down from the Days of Slavery

James Henry Holmes has often been quoted as the preacher who pastored the largest flock in the United States. In estimating the worth of a man who has been the spiritual adviser of so many souls, it would be impossible, from a human standpoint, to calculate his value.

We often admire great generals who command large armies, but a singular credit must be given to the preacher of a Baptist church, who, according to the government of his church, is not able to discipline a member, nor has he any other appeal in controlling than through the members of the church itself. Knowing this to be a fact, a man who can guide and govern a large number of people, who are held in check only by their own obligations to God and the simple church government, must have great credit accorded him; and this man, who has for many years held one position, is deserving of such.

He was born December 9, 1826, of slave parents, in King and Queen county, Virginia. He was owned by Judge James M. Jefferies and was cowboy on the farm. His mother's name was Dellphia Holmes, and his father's Claiborne Holmes. His mother had sixteen children. He went to Richmond in 1835 and was hired out in Samuel S. Myer's tobacco factory. In 1842 he joined the church in Richmond, being baptized by Rev. Robert Ryland. In April, 1846, he married a daughter of John Smith, a printer. Smith and his wife soon after escaped by the Underground Railroad and were carried to Massachusetts. He left two sons, and a daughter whom Mr. Holmes married. He wrote back to his children, the letter falling into the hands of parties who implicated Mr. Holmes; on this account he was put into the Negro traders' jail, it being charged that he was about to run away himself. For this reason he was bought and sold by a Negro trader named Silas O'Mahundro. He remained in jail twelve weeks and was sold in 1848 to a man in New Orleans named Pipkin. He left his wife and two children in Richmond when sold; one was a year and six months old, and the other three months old.

In New Orleans he worked on the levee. In 1849 a steamer blew up at the wharf. He was working on the next boat to it and had his arm dislocated and his head cut open by the explosion. Many were killed, but he was preserved by the hand of the Lord to do the great work which we find him doing. His companions found him lying on the deck; seeing he was alive, they started ashore with him. Some one cried out about there being powder in the hold of the vessel; thereupon they became frightened and threw him on an ash bank. Finding the report false, they returned and carried him to his quarters, where proper attention was given him. In 1849 he joined the Second Baptist church at New Orleans by experience, it not being the custom to have letters—colored people were not supposed to read then. In 1850 he was elected deacon of the church. In the following year he married his second wife.

Mr. Pipkin having committed suicide, Mrs. Pipkin's daughter married, and her husband came to New Orleans to settle up the estate. Mr. Holmes being a cripple, he agreed to sell him to Royal Parrish, who owned his wife, (that is, Holmes' wife) and who bought him. Mr. Parrish's health failing, he went to Richmond to reside. Mr. Holmes and his wife went with him in the fall of 1852. In 1855 his owner died. This same year he worked at William Robinson's factory on Nineteenth and Franklin streets.

When he returned from New Orleans he renewed his connection with the church in Richmond, of which he was a member before being sold away. In 1855 he was elected deacon of the First Baptist church in Richmond, and served in that capacity until 1865, when he served as church clerk. During the war he kept store for Richard Gregory, a colored man on Franklin street, near Fourteenth street.

In 1862 he lost his second wife. He bought himself from the widow of Royal Parrish, paying her $1,800 in Confederate money. He promised to pay Lawyer Sands $200 to get his papers. He paid him $100 in cash and promised to pay him the other $100 when he got his papers. At the close of the war he owed him this amount which he paid with a drink of cider, and the lawyer said that settled it.

In 1866 he was elected assistant pastor under Mr. Stockwell, a school teacher. In 1867 he was elected pastor of the First Baptist church. He baptized two hundred persons in his first year's administration; the membership was thirty-five hundred. In 1863 he married his present wife, by whom he has seven children. The oldest, John H. Holmes, is pursuing his studies at Worcester Academy, Worcester, Massachusetts. In 1870 the membership of the church was 4,683. A new registration was ordered and all members requested to report; up to May, 1871, 2,400 reported and the remainder were dropped. That year during the revival he baptized 600 persons. In 1878 another registration was ordered; up to that time the membership was 3,800, about 2,500 reported.

In two baptisms in 1878, in the month of June, 866 were immersed, and during that year he baptized altogether 1,100 persons. In 1880 a dissatisfaction arose; the membership being 4,000 a split occurred; a new registration was again ordered and 1,700 names dropped from the roll. In 1876 it was decided to pull down the old church, and the present edifice was erected at a cost of $35,000, every dollar of which has been paid. A new organ has also been purchased at a cost of $2,500. This is the largest organ in any church in the State for colored people.

The Rev. James Holmes is a man who is well beloved by his congregation; a man who preaches the plain practical truths of every day life, and is now enjoying the fruits of his arduous labors under the most favorable circumstances. During his administrations the church has seen its best days and his career has been remarkable. God has blessed his work with abundant favor, and manifested His pleasure in his preaching by the number of souls which He has given him as an evidence of the power and consistency with which he has preached the gospel for so many years.

CHAPTER XCVI

General T. Morris Chester
General—Phonographer and Type-writer—Lawyer

———◆◆———

General T. M. Chester is the second son and fourth child of George and Jane Maria Chester, and was born May 11, 1834, in the city of Harrisburg, Pennsylvania. While a boy he had an earnest desire to secure an education. After some preliminary training he attended Avery Institute, in Allegheny City, Pennsylvania, where he remained till 1853, and then went to Liberia in May of the same year. Arriving there he attended the Alexander High School in the city of Monrovia till September, 1854, when he returned to the United States and entered the junior class of Thetford Academy, in Vermont, in the winter of 1854. He graduated with the second honor of the class in 1856. After graduation he returned to Liberia where he was superintendent of the recaptured Africans from American slavers, instructing them in school and in the civilized methods of industry. He remained in Africa until the breaking out of the civil war, when he returned by way of England to the States. In 1862 he visited Liverpool and London, in England, for the first time. He assisted in the enlistment of colored soldiers in the Fifty-fourth and Fifty-fifth Massachusetts regiments. In 1864 he had given some attention to the writing of short-hand. He was led to do this, as he says in his own words, "because he had frequently heard colored ministers and representative men of our race deliver very able extemporaneous efforts which he thought would add to the literature of any people." Said he: "I felt that such thought ought to be preserved for the lessons they taught and the inspiration they would naturally quicken. I knew, constituted as we are into separated classes, that the whites would take no interest in perpetuating our utterances only so far as they were benefited, and so I concluded that if our people were to be profited by the art, some one must acquire a knowledge of it, which I felt would have a thrilling effect wherever practiced. In this respect my fancy has been fully realized." He reported the proceedings of the General Conference of the African M. E. church, in the city of Philadlphia, 1864, for the *Philadelphia Daily Press,* which was so satisfactorily done that J. Russell Young, editor-in-chief, conceived the idea of sending him to the front as the war correspondent for the *Press,* which was approved by Colonel John W. Forney, the proprietor. Being duly authorized and furnished with authority from the secretary of war for that purpose, he was the special and only war correspondent for the *Press* with the Army of the James and the Potomac until after the surrender. He was especially complimented by Colonel Forney for the manner in which he performed the duties, and especially for his letter on the capture of Richmond, which was twenty-four hours in advance of any other daily papers of the kind in Philadelphia through special correspondence. In 1866 he visited England, Paris, Brussels, Berlin, St. Petersburg and Moscow, and passed the winter in Russia, where he was received by the Russian Court as Captain Chester, a title received by courtesy because of his commanding a company of emergency men, hastily armed and hurried into service in front of Harrisburg when the rebel forces were threatening the capital. He was invited by the Emperor Alexander to accompany him on an occasion of a grand review of forty thousand troops of all arms. Being furnished with a horse by order of the emperor and especially attended by an aide-de-camp who spoke English, he was given a position of honor, riding near the emperor, and was afterward invited by him to *déjeuner* in the famous winter palace with him and the whole body of the male members of the imperial family and the imperial staff. He was afterwards received at the courts of Denmark, Sweden, Saxony and England, and visited the great exposition of Paris in 1867, and made the acquaintance of General Solomon, then minister to Hayti from the court of France, and now President of that Republic. At the same time he was introduced to the great Alexander Dumas, supping with him at a banquet given by the literary men of Paris at Versailles. Here also he met the famous Ira Aldridge, the tragedian, and was on intimate terms of acquaintance with him and his noble wife, a Swedish baroness.

After spending four years in Europe, most of the time in England, where he studied law at Middle Temple Inn, London, one of the four Inns of Court, he was called, after three years' attendance, to the English bar, on the thirtieth of April, 1870. Mr. Chester is an eloquent, painstaking lawyer, who will do justice to any case committed to his care, and has figured in many prominent suits. He practiced a little at the old Bailey and at the civil courts. He returned to America in 1871, and went South and settled in Louisiana; was admitted to the Supreme Court and practiced law in the civil and criminal courts with great success. He was appointed division superintendent of Public education in the first district in 1875, in which there were seven parishes, and afterward in the fifth, where there were thirteen parishes, in 1876, having the white and colored schools under this charge. In 1873 he was appointed aide-de-camp on the staff of Governor Kellogg, with the rank of brigadier-general, and afterward placed in command of the first brigade, Louisiana State National Guards. He was appointed United States Commissioner by Judge Billings, and so administrated the office, which was one of fees, as to gain the confidence and patronage of the Crescent City. The other two white commissioners in the custom-house were left without business, and combined effort was made against him by both Democrats and Republicans. He was asked by Judge Billings to resign, because he (the Judge) was in an embarrassed position, with the promise that he should be reappointed; but Mr. Chester refused to do so. The Judge revoked his commission, which he had a right to do, with or without cause. Concerning his official career, it is well to give a correspondence which took place. The *Daily Picayune*, on Friday morning, April 24, 1879, under the head of "Republican Martyrs," speaking of the Republican party, used these words:

We could say, and say with truth, that there never has been a prominent Negro killed in this State, for so-called political causes, who was not a scoundrel by profession and by practice, but if there is an exception to this rule let him be named. We challenge the Republican party of the country to produce an example. We have already said that during the reign of Negroism and carpet baggery in this State there never was a Negro official from high to low, from first to last, that did not sell his public functions for money.

To which Mr. Chester replied on the morning of the twenty-fifth, in these words:

I had the honor of being division superintendent of public education, serving in the first and fifth divisions, and am now discharging the important duties of United States commissioner, which brings me into frequent intercourse with a sensitive business element, and I challenge the *Picayune* to furnish an instance in which I sold my public functions for money. If the *Picayune* cannot establish the charge against me, I trust it will do me the justice to except me from its indiscriminate denunciations.

To which the *Picayune* replied that it would have to say on that point, simply this:

We were making a general indictment. We could not go out of the way to hunt up exceptions; they are few enough, it is true, but hard to find. In spite of their slender numbers, we knew very well if there was one to whom the charge would not apply, he would come forward to repel it. Mr. Chester has done so. We are glad to give him the full benefit of his disclaimer. He has been an honest Negro official. Very well, where is the next one? If there is any next one, let him show himself with as little hesitation in challenging public scrutiny as Mr. Chester has manifested. And now when the exception is made, and when all of the rest of the exceptions are made, the fact as we stated it will not be appreciably modified.

In January, 1884, he was elected president of the Wilmington, Wrightsville & Onslow Railroad, a corporation of citizens of African descent. Work has been suspended for some time, but it is expected that it will be resumed again under circumstances that will guarantee its completion. In the capacity of railroad president, great ability is required, and it shows that the company has great faith in their choice for that office. In 1875 he became a member of the Pride of Jefferson Lodge No. 1679, Grand United Order of Odd Fellows in America, and was elected a delegate to the general session of the Order—the annual movable committee—at New Orleans, in 1876, and was elected one of the grand directors in 1877, and again at Chicago in 1878, and again in Cincinnati in 1884. He is the author of the law providing for a Relief Fund Bureau, and also the publication of the history and the manual of the Order. He is connected with no church, but has good will for all, and no prejudice against any. His preference is for the African M. E. Zion connection. As grand scribe of the Triennial Council of the past grand masters of Grand United Order of Odd Fellows, he reported phonographically, September 24 and 25 of 1884, the proceedings of the tenth Grand Triennial Grand Assembly of the Patriarchial Order of past grand masters of the Grand United Order of Odd Fellows in America, which is a full and complete report of the convention of colored men, and was the first ever published in the United States.

CHAPTER XCVII

*Rev. Lemuel Haynes, A. M.
A Distinguished Theologian*

———◆———

Among the early popular preachers in the State of Connecticut was one who was born of an African father and a white mother. He enjoyed excellent advantages for improving his intellect and became a very distinguished scholar, an eloquent and forcible preacher, and maintained a reputation for over thirty years. It is said his fame was created from the preaching of a sermon from Genesis 3–4, and his discussion with the venerable Hosea Ballou. He received the degree of A.M. from Middlebury College, Vermont, and was the first of the race to receive a degree of the kind in this country. His birthplace was Hartford, Connecticut, and the date of his birth, July 18, 1753; he was also a "minute man" in 1774 at the battle of Lexington. He joined the army at Roxboro; he was a volunteer in the expedition to Ticonderoga. He lived to the age of eighty-one, and died the twenty-seventh of September, 1833. His memory is preserved, and we can with pride point to him as the first titled Negro in America. To-day we have scholarly Negroes on every hand who have *earned* their tiles by severe intellectual labor in colleges and universities. It is refreshing also to find amalgamation on the other side of the fence. A native African and a white woman. "Holy horror!" cries somebody, "How curious they did not hang him." They were honorably married and he was popular. The black face was a thing of beauty to his wife, who saw a man with an intellectual soul and loved him. Love laughs at locks and bars and even the color of a man's skin. Both parties will cross the line.

H. O. WAGONER.

CHAPTER XCVIII

Hon. H. O. Wagoner
Compositor—Deputy Sheriff—Clerk of the Legislature

The best known and indeed one of the most solid colored men of Denver, Colorado, is the Hon. H. O. Wagoner. My attention was first attracted to him by his association as one of the commissioners of the colored department in the great Cotton Centennial Exhibition held in 1884 at New Orleans.

His birthplace is the little town known as Hagerstown, in Washington county, Maryland, and February 27, 1816, was the date.

At the age of five years, he was taught the English alphabet by his grandmother on his paternal side; and then along at scattered intervals he was sent to a little select school, making in all nine or ten months, including some night schooling. The difficulties that many of the older men had to undergo in order to secure even the rudiments of the English education ought to be known by the rising generation, that in order that they might see at least the propriety of giving close attention to the studies set before them. With books, school-houses and competent teachers, what should be expected of the young colored boy of to-day? Nothing more or less than that he should fit himself for the higher duties of life. Mr. Wagoner learned to write with white chalk on board fences for his slate.

From his seventh year until he was twenty-two, he did every kind of work that was done on a farm. On the twenty-eighth of August, 1838, he went to Baltimore, Maryland, and remained there eleven days. On the first of September, his old friend, the Hon. Frederick Douglass, left for the North, and on the eighth day of the same September, Mr. Wagoner left for the West. He reached Wheeling, West Virginia, on the seventeenth, and stayed there six weeks. He then left for Cincinnati and Dayton, Ohio, where he taught school till the next spring. At this time he must have had very little knowledge to go upon, taught as he has been by self and adversity; yet having utilized everything at command, he was, in a very great degree, able to teach others.

He continued his journey in the spring and went to New Orleans, where he arrived April 11, 1839. Here he remained two weeks, and then went to St. Louis; after remaining a short time, he went to Galena, Illinois, where he arrived April 29, 1839.

He had not been there long before he worked his way into the *Northwestern Gazette and Galena Advertiser,* a Whig tri-weekly paper, where he learned to set type. In this office he remained for some years as compositor, and overlooking the local distribution. His business was also that of tending to the mailing of the outside circulation and the collecting of bills. It was here he first owned real estate which he sold to the Hon. E. B. Washburne, who had never owned any real estate previous to that time, a fact he often mentions. It was in Galena where they first met, and at that time a strong mutual friendship began which has never known a shadow.

The property he had in Galena was worth about six hundred dollars. In the latter part of 1843 he went to Chatham, Canada West, and secured employment on the *Chatham Journal.* Soon after he was employed by the school commissioners of Kent county, to teach a primary school of colored children. While in this work he married, August 7, 1844. In May, 1846, he went to Chicago with his wife and child—a daughter—and there settled down, securing, at the same time, employment on the *Western Citizen,* an avowed Anti-slavery paper of the period. Some time during the year 1846, he states that Mr. Douglass commenced the publication of the *North Star,* and he at once became a subscriber and occasional correspondent.

During all these years, as far back as 1835, he had been engaged more or less in the Anti-slavery movements and the Underground Railroad. In the latter part of 1847 he quit work in the printing office and engaged in various kinds of business. After that he gradually began to acquire property.

When Garrett Smith was one of the presidential candidates, he was named by a few Anti-slavery papers as one of his electors for Illinois. His family still steadily increased, until 1858, when the whole number, including deaths, had reached eight. At this date he was in the milling business, and had an establishment which cost him $7,000. In 1857 he had been introduced to "Old" John Brown and the Honorable Frederick Douglass, and after that, from time to time, John Brown never failed to call upon him whenever he went to Chicago. It was his habit to send many fugitives to him who were in transit from Missouri and Kansas to Canada. The last company that passed through Chicago was in March, 1859. The fugitives were fifteen in number, under the personal charge of the old hero himself, and four of his white assistants. Mr. Wagoner sheltered and fed these fugitives for three days, while an old time friend, John

Jones, entertained the white men. For harboring fugitives, of course he was liable, under the then existing fugitive slave laws, to one thousand dollars fine and six months in prison. But what did he care for this? He simply felt that he was doing his duty, and was ready to do it at any risk or cost. In the day when God shall come to make up the account of those who have lived and assisted the poor of the earth, what a record there shall be for those who gave food to the hungry, shelter to the shelterless and freedom to the captive.

His liability to arrest was so perilous that, to the credit of Allan Pinkerton, be it said, he went manfully and bravely to his assistance, and raised the necessary funds to pay the transportation of the whole party of fugitives and their protectors, bag and baggage, to Detroit.

Before the old hero left Chicago for the last time, he called at his house and thanked him for what he had done for those who had been in bonds, and then bade him a friendly farewell. The next communication that Mr. Wagoner heard of him was by personal letter from Chatham, Canada West, inviting him to attend the secret convention to be held there. Mention of this convention is made elsewhere in this book.

At one time during his many visits to his place, he importuned him with impressive eloquence to lay aside his work for a time and go with him and assist in the prosecution of his humanitarian mission. But duty to his family impelled him to decline; soon after this, two fires and two removals were about equal to financial prostration. At that time he was about ten years past the zenith of life, and as the Pike's Peak excitement was still in existence, he made his way to Denver, Colorado, where he arrived August 1, 1860.

In the fall of 1861, the war being on hand, a large portion of the men began to return to their several homes, and this brought stagnation to business, so he returned to his family in Chicago. Soon after, he went down to where the Western armies were in battle array. He soon became assistant to a sutler, and did from time to time various other services, until the colored men were being recruited for military service. He was then urged to take hold and recruit for the Twenty-ninth Illinois colored troops, and for that purpose secured a commission. As the colored troops began to increase and were gradually swelling the Union armies, he secured another commission from Governor Andrews of Massachusetts, to recruit for the Fifth cavalry of that State. After doing service for Massachusetts, he was then commissioned by Governor Yates of Illinois, to go down to Mississippi and recruit refugees and contrabands, under the act of Congress and order of the War Department, No. 227. This was nearing the close of the conflict, and when General Grant returned to Galena he sent Mr. Wagoner a letter of recommendation, dated September 1, 1865. That letter and his letter to him from Paris, France, about his son Henry, who died at Lyons, France, while acting as Consul there, are still held by him as souvenirs of the great soldier.

After this he returned to Denver, November 24, 1865, where he has resided ever since. In 1876 he was appointed one of the clerks in the first State Legislature of the Centennial State, and served through that entire session. In 1880 he was appointed one of the deputy sheriffs of Arapaho county, Colorado. His duties were chiefly as bailiff of the District Court and serving legal papers for that court. He held his position for three years, and has served as one of the election judges of the Ninth ward of Denver.

When his friend General Grant was in Denver for the last time, Mr. Wagoner was selected as one of the committee of reception. After many mishaps by fire, sickness and death, his property is now reduced to a probable cash value of about twenty thousand dollars. His success in life has been slow but steady, and in a large measure is owing to his strict integrity, correct business habits and gentlemanly deportment.

CHAPTER XCIX

Rev. Marcus Dale
Shrewd Fiancier and General Manager—Business
Capacity Shown

David and Synthia Dale though born in the State of North Carolina, were not slaves. They moved to Galliopolis, Ohio, where was born their son Marcus, in the year 1832. The family ten years later moved to Detroit, Michigan. The father died during these years, which made it necessary for Marcus to stop school and go to work, in order to assist his mother in raising four children that were younger than himself. He did this until they became old enough to earn their own support. He learned the cooper's trade about this time, but it did not bring in much money to his depleted purse, but it was useful in after days. He was converted in 1851, and admitted into the A. M. E. church, January, 1852. His mother died, and this left two sisters and one brother depending on him. The fall of 1852 found him hard at work. A singular thing happened in his life, and shows that a man can do many things if he only thinks he can. Hearing that the new pastor, the Rev. J. M. Williams, had been appointed by the conference, had a large family, the oldest a young lady of seventeen years, he determined if she were a Christian to offer his hand in marriage. This was certainly a strange freak, for he did not know whether she was pretty or homely, high tempered or harsh, short or tall, light or dark. When she came he found that she was not a Christian, but he did not give her up, he was only the more fixed in his purpose. A revival broke out in about three months, in which the young lady was converted. He then waited with patience until she had served out the usual six months probation of the Methodist church, when he proposed and was accepted and was united in wedlock with Mary L. Williams, in the fall of 1854.

He soon planned to go to Oberlin College to study and began to save money by doing over work, two whole nights in a week for three whole years. Is not this an honorable, praiseworthy effort to get an education? In this time his family was increasing, having two children to care for. Moreover he entered Oberlin College and kept the old rule of working two whole nights, but it was not a task. He did this one year, till his money gave out, when he hired an old barn and commenced making barrels in it. This he continued for three years, providing the means and affording him the opportunity for taking the four years' course. He was licensed an exhorter in 1856, as a local preacher in 1858, and ordained elder in 1861. The war coming on he enlisted in the first colored regiment of Michigan, afterwards in the One Hundred and Second United States. The regiment left Detroit, March, 1864; made a short stop at Annapolis, and then proceeded to Hilton Head, South Carolina. Learning that colored troops would only receive one half the pay of white troops, he resolved to receive no pay from "Uncle Sam," and give his service free, rather than accept less than white soldiers. He influenced the soldiers to refuse the pay unless they got the same amount. He urged them, however, not to refuse to do duty, and though the pay-master came, and had the money in his hands, they refused several times, and only took it when he came the third time with the same pay as that of the white soldiers. It was a day of rejoicing; perseverance and persistency had won the day. When the "onpleasantness" was over, he commenced teaching. In 1867 he went to New Orleans. He entered St. Mary's Parish and taught a Freedman's Bureau school for five months. An ex-slaveholder gave half an acre of land for a church and a school-house on which Mr. Dale put a building, 20 x 30; his church was organized, and used the building for his meetings, and in the week he taught school in the same place. In less than a year the place was too small, and he concluded to erect a brick building. No bricks, no land, no mules, no lumber could be obtained. The people were poor and unable to buy. It gave him an opportunity to display his great business tact, which he did in the following manner: Learning that a white man in the neighborhood intended to have 100,000 bricks made at eight dollars per thousand and furnish everything, he proposed to him this plan: the minister would furnish the labor, and the white gentleman the mules, land, lumber, etc. The colored people would make a kiln of 220,000 bricks, the church to have 120,000 bricks, and give the other 100,000 to him for two hundred dollars less than he intended to pay. As he would have furnished everything to others he agreed to do this, and the colored laborers got their pay, built the church, and the benefactor was gratified as well, and was two hundreds dollars better off. A fine church was built of brick, two stories high, with a school room down stairs and the church above. At that time the planters would sell no land to the colored people. Finding out that there were about one hundred and twenty acres of land near the church, belonging to a man who lived in another parish, that could be purchased, he sought out the owner and got the land. He advised his brethren to unite their moneys. He put in his own, and in this wise they paid for the land, which was divided pro rata. For several years he stayed among these people and united with the Louisiana Conference and brought in with him a church worth five thousand dollars and in a flourishing condition. His first appointment was in New Orleans, at Union chapel, a church with about five hundred members. There he served three years. He was then appointed to Wesley chapel, the same city, the largest church in New Orleans. He served this church two years. In 1884 he was appointed presiding elder, serving four years, of the North New Orleans district. He was appointed again to Wesley chapel, where he remained three years. He is now serving his first year at Mount Zion.

He has succeeded measurably in this world's goods, owning a piece of property which is worth at present about three thousand dollars, in a place on the Gulf coast of Mississippi, 58 miles from New Orleans. He is much beloved by all his people, stands high in the denomination, and in the future will obtain great eminence. His success has been owing to his perseverance, diligence, sobriety and strict attention to duty. It can be seen that he neglects no opportunity of doing good for his race. He will continue to rise in the denomination until he obtains probably the highest position in the gift of his people.

CHARLES B. PURVIS

CHAPTER C

Charles B. Purvis, A. M., M. D.
*Secretary and Treasurer—Professor of Obstetrics and Diseases
of Women and Children—Surgeon in Charge of Freedmen's
Hospital—Acting Assistant Surgeon—First Lieutenant*

Professor C. B. Purvis' father's name was Robert Purvis, and his mother's name, before marriage, was Harriet Forton. Mr. Purvis was born in Philadelphia, Pennsylvania, and has no slave blood in him. His father moved from Philadelphia when he was about two years old to a country place called Byberry, in the county of Philadelphia. He devoted his time to farming, and was one of eight children who grew up inured to farm life. This occupation he followed until quite a young man; the neighborhood was a pleasant one, and many of the farmers were interested in the Anti-slavery questions and admired his father's devotion and efforts in that direction. His educational advantages were not very favorable, but were about as usual among farmers' sons. He derived some advantages from public schools, however, that he attended, chiefly under the control of Quakers, who made up the majority of the inhabitants of the place. His brothers and sisters were at that time the only colored children attending this school. In 1860 he went to Oberlin, Ohio, to attend college; he stayed there for two years, but for various reasons was unable to complete his college course. While there he evinced great mental ability and stood very well in his class. In 1862, he entered the Medical College of the Western Reserve, Cleveland, Ohio, and graduated from this institution in March, 1865. Two months after his graduation he was offered a position in the army as acting assistant surgeon, with the rank of first lieutenant, which he accepted and was assigned to duty in Washington, District of Columbia. He held this position two years, when he was appointed assistant surgeon in the Freedmen's Hospital. While holding this position, in the fall of 1868 he was elected by the trustees of Howard University professor of materia medica and medical jurisprudence, and he delivered a course of lectures upon the subject during the winter of 1868 in the Medical Department of the university. This position he held five years, when he was called to the chair of obstetrics and diseases of women and children; and at the same time elected as secretary to the Medical Faculty, which positions he still holds. This is the largest and most thoroughly equipped college in the capital of the Nation, and the majority of the students are white. In 1882 he was appointed by President Arthur surgeon in charge of the Freedmen's hospital, which position he holds at this writing. Since he has been in charge of the hospital, it has grown very much and improved in every way; in 1886 over five thousand patients were prescribed for and of this number two thousand remained in the hospital for treatment. After many years of hard struggling he has compelled the white physicians by force of his position and ability to acknowledge a colored physician and agree to consult with him. He was selected by the faculty to deliver the charge to the graduating class of 1883. In the address he used these words:

Gentlemen: Medicine is a science, a progressive one. In some of its branches it is almost an exact one. Each year, however, brings us new ideas, new experiences, and new successes. Therefore, I want to enjoin upon you the importance of keeping abreast with the daily growth of your profession. No man or woman will ever reach to the top of the castle his or her youthful fancies lead them to build, if they content themselves with the acquirements of their embryotic medical life.

These words can well be addressed to any young man going out into life, and is an epitome of his own methods of rising to his present position. Another phase in this speech seems also to present his own efforts and the many embarrassments which young men meet in acquiring eminence. Said he:

As you enter the arena do not flatter yourselves into the belief that your pathway is to be strewn with roses; that you possess unusual gifts, that whether you acquire fame, wealth or success, depends only if you elect to do so or not; do not conclude that there are to be no cloudy hours, that all is to be sunshine and beautiful. Be prepared for disappointments; the early life of a physician scarcely meets with anything else.

It might be well also to give his position upon two of the most prominent evils of the day; and coming from such high authority is worthy of being placed here to his credit, though less able physicians of the race might say that it is necessary to recommend intoxicating liquors and to approve of the habit of using tobacco. Said he:

Hygiene, mental, moral and physical, is to-day receiving much attention, and I hope to see the scions of this school manifesting no ordinary interest on these subjects, especially that of intemperance. We trust upon this one you will assume a positive position, that your trumpet will have no uncertain sound. There is no other habit among people that is calculated to undermine, physically, intellectually and morally as this one. I call your attention to the growing abuse in the use of tobacco, especially among our children. It is a sad sight to witness the practices of the multitudes of little boys who go daily to and from our public institutions of learning. There can be no perpetuity for our institutions; there can be no future of the race if these practices, I may say crimes, go unchallenged and unchecked.

These are strong words and deserve the closest attention of those who read this work. Mr. Purvis is considered to rank among the very first of his class, excepting none, and is the only colored professor in the Howard University medical faculty, and in fact the only one in any medical college in the world, and the only colored surgeon in charge of a hospital of any kind in this country. It is hoped that the mention of this man and this short sketch of his career may be the means of encouraging some colored boy to reach after greater things.

CHAPTER CI

Professor W. H. Crogman, A. B., A. M.
Professor of Classics in Clark University

Not having the honor of a personal acquaintance with Professor Crogman, I am indebted to a friend who has known him for many years, and who can speak most truthfully concerning his talents. Yet his name is very familiar with all who are acquainted with the rise and progress of the younger men of the day, who have attained distinction as scholars and orators. He is a man of considerable learning, and holds a very distinguished place as professor of classics in Clark University, Atlanta, Georgia.

He was born on the Island of St. Martin, in the town of Phillipsburg, May 5, 1841. In his fourteenth year, he came to the United States, with a white gentleman named Mr. B. L. Boomer, who is still living in Campbells, Massachusetts. He had the privilege of attending a district school during the winter months for a number of years, and had rare opportunities for travel, visiting many of the principal ports in Asia, Europe, Australia and South America. With the start in knowledge gained in the district school, supplemented by observations in his journeys, he was able to turn his vast amount of information to good account; and the experience which he gained in this way proved of great value to him in broadening and strengthening his mind, and at the same time giving him mental drill, which fitted him for his present labors. Shortly after the closing of the war he entered Pierce Academy, Middleborough, Massachusetts, under the principalship of Professor J. W. R. Jenks. Here he took a thorough academic course under the best tutors, in preparation for the work in the South, to which field the voice of duty and the sympathies of a generous nature drew him. He entered upon this work in 1870, and served for three years as a successful teacher in the Claflin University, Orangeburg, South Carolina.

Feeling the need of a more extended course of study to meet the requirements of the work in his chosen profession, he entered Atlanta University, in October, 1873, and graduated in the first college class sent out from that institution in 1876. The same year he became connected with Clark University, where he still remains as senior professor. As a teacher, Professor Crogman is able and successful. By broad study of the Greek and Latin authors, his mind has become thoroughly imbued with the spirit of the classical writers, and his knowledge and enthusiasm as a teacher kindles a deep interest in his pupils. As a public speaker, Professor Crogman has gained considerable distinction. He is a master of a clear, elegant style; his delivery is easy and forcible, and a vein of natural humor running through his whole discourse gives him power to hold the close attention of an audience to his thoughtful and well balanced addresses. By special invitation he has given addresses before the American Missionary Association at Chicago, and at the anniversary of the Freedmen's Aid Society of the M. E. church at Ocean Grove. He has the distinction, as a layman, of having been invited to fill the pulpit of the late Rev. Henry Ward Beecher of Plymouth Church, Brooklyn, New York, which he did on two occasions with success, the morning and evening of October 14, 1883. The following extract is taken from his evening discourse, which shows his forcible style and fealty also to the Negro race, and at the same time presses home the fact that the Negroes are patriotic:

There has not been a single war waged in defense of this government in which the Negro has not periled—yea, given his life for the government. The battlefields of the Revolution and the Rebellion bear witness alike to his courage, his patriotism and his loyalty. The military leaders of this country bear witness. Washington bore witness. Jackson at New Orleans bore witness.

Scores of officers in the War of the Rebellion bore witness. The Negro fought in common with you to found this government. He fought in common with you to perpetuate this government. The Negro has been found on the side of liberty and good government. Hanged in the streets of New York by an infuriated mob; snubbed and mocked, buffeted and spit upon; put like a leper outside the gate of American society, he has never for a moment deserted the Union, but has clung to it with unyielding tenacity and unwavering devotion. The world furnishes no parallel to the conduct of the Southern Negro during the Rebellion. With a remarkable degree of that Christian-like spirit which could call down benedictions upon his enemies, which could touch and heal the ear cut off by the sword of Peter, the Negro, during the four years of that terrible struggle, when every man and boy able to bear arms had been forced to the front by stern necessity, remained at home and cared tenderly for the helpless wives and children, who were at that time fighting to fasten more tightly the fetters on his limbs, and to found an empire whose corner-stone should be his perpetual enslavement and degradation. Nevertheless, in the heated debates that arose a few years after over the Civil Rights Bill, a certain member of Congress referred to this very remarkable and very humane conduct of the black man as proof of his utter worthlessness, unmanliness and cowardice. I thank God for that cowardice. I thank God for that unmanliness. I thank God that the Negro was too much of a coward to cut the throats of the helpless women and children.

These two lectures have been printed in pamphlet form, and highly commended for the forcible manner in which he presents the wrongs and disabilities of the race.

At the National Association of Teachers, at Madison, Wisconsin, he was a delegate from Georgia, and his address gained high praise from the press, and was published in full in the report of the association. He has also delivered addresses before the great summer gatherings at Chautauqua Island Park.

Professor Crogman is above reproach; his integrity and Christian manliness have gained for him the respect and confidence of all with whom he associates. He has on two occasions represented the Savannah Conference in the general Conference of the M. E. church, in which body he is an honored layman. In 1884, he acted as one of the secretaries of the General Conference, rendering efficient service in that important position. He has been secretary of the Board of Trustees in Clark University since the organization of the board. His devotion to the chair of classics, led him to decline the presidency of an important institution in the South, which was urged upon him. He was appointed by the Board of Bishops of the M. E. church as a delegate to the Ecumenical Council of Methodism held in London.

A poor boy cast out upon the world in early life, he has, through the providence of God, the assistance of good friends, and application to the rules of honesty, industry and integrity, reached a high position, achieving for himself a position in the hearts of the people worthy of emulation, respect and honor. He has a future large with success, and with brilliant prospects laid out before him.

CHAPTER CII

Senator Blanche K. Bruce
United States Senator—Register of the United States Treasury

───•◆•───

When in Old Virginia, March 1, 1841, a little babe was born and named Blanche K. Bruce, it did not move the world; few knew of the little slave boy, and his childhood days were not marked with unusual brilliancy and wisdom, nor with the buoyancy that fills young minds. Hard and toilsome was the lot of this boy, and the mantle of slavery so enveloped him that he could not see beyond. His opportunities for education were very limited, for when a better day dawned on the four million souls in cruel bondage, B. K. Bruce was a young man. Still not ashamed to be striving for the privileges which previously had been withheld, Mr. Bruce entered Oberlin College and pursued there an elective course. This awakened in the young man the dormant thirst for knowledge and a desire for the practical application of such.

With this determination he gave himself up to improvements in every avenue of learning, and thus his life was passed in partial obscurity, until the year 1868, when he entered into public life in the State of Mississippi. He first went into the State as a planter and every material interest of that State was of interest to this young man. He displayed from the first of his sojourn there those qualities which so peculiarly fitted him for the positions of honor and trust that afterwards give him such marked prominence in his public career. In 1870 he was elected sergeant-at-arms of the State Senate of Mississippi, and he made use of this close contact with leading men of that State to better develop the "judgment, tact and executive ability which have so signally characterized his after life." In 1871, in Bolivar county, he was appointed assessor of taxes, and the following year he was elected to fill the office of sheriff and assessor which were consolidated. The same year he was elected a member of the Board of Levee Commissioners of the Mississippi river. In 1874, without the opposition of another candidate, he was re-elected to these same official trusts.

Soon, however, the country needed the services of this son in a more

BLANCHE K. BRUCE.

exalted station, and, in February, 1874, he was elected to represent, in the United States Senate, the highest good of his adopted State. On the fourth of March, 1875, he took his seat in the "highest council of the Nation." In this body he showed remarkable forethought and wisdom, always speaking to the point and saying the right thing in the right place, defending his race and advocating its rights with all the loyalty of a true American citizen.

His first address to the Senate was delivered in 1876, when this body was considering the resolution offered by Oliver P. Morton, concerning the appointment of a committee to investigate the election frauds in the South. His speech showed clearly his view of Southern politics and his disapproval of their workings. His duty to his country did not conflict with his duty to his race. Whenever the test came, with wonderful clear-sightedness did B. K. Bruce make a clean record and the whole six years of his senatorial life is without a stain.

Says the *Detroit Plaindealer:*

When the Chinese Immigration Bill was before the Senate, and all the party leaders on both sides of the Senate were taking their stand for and against the bill, all eyes were seemingly turned to the Senator from Mississippi, who it was thought would find it his duty as a statesman in conflict with his duty to his race, or at least would meet with some embarrassment on that question by having to play the difficult role of American and Negro. But when the test came and he was called upon to record his vote on that question, he made an impromptu speech of a single sentence, which silenced the solicitude that hung upon his choice. It was this: "Mr. President, I desire to submit a single remark. Representing as I do a people who but a few years ago were considered essentially disqualified from enjoying the privileges and immunities of American citizenship, and who have since been so successfully introduced into the body politic, and having a large confidence in the strength and assimilative power of our institutions, I shall vote against this bill."

Says the same paper:

This speech was wired to all parts of the country, and before he had taken his seat his fellow Senators crowded around him and congratulated him upon his significant remarks.

He often presided over the Senate, and was chairman of many important committees. His efficient services rendered in a committee to oversee the affairs of the Freedman's Bank are worthy of note, as his watchcare and diligence saved annually eight thousand dollars to the poor depositors, and he also provided a way for dividend payment in this same bank.

The twenty-fourth of June, 1878, Senator Bruce married Miss Josephine

B. Wilson of Cleveland, Ohio, and made a bridal tour through the principal cities of Europe, where marked attention were shown the young couple from foreign nobility and distinguished residents, among whom were Minister Welsh at London, and Minister Noyes at Paris. Mrs. Bruce is a remarkable woman, wonderfully fitted to command the dignity and respect of her position, and she presides over her capital residence with true womanly grace, making it a fit rendezvous for the distinguished circle of friends with which she and her husband have been so closely identified.

Senator Bruce was a delegate to the National Convention at Chicago and temporarily presided over that body, where was present, as a brother delegate, the lamented President Garfield. After the expiration of his Senatorial office, ex-Senator Bruce was offered the mission to Brazil and the third assistant postmaster-generalship, both of which he refused.

On the twenty-third of May, 1881, President Garfield appointed him register of the United States treasury. Here he showed the same wonderful executive ability which his previous life portrayed. With decision and readiness did he daily decide the perplexing questions that came before him, much to the pleasure and satisfaction of his co-workers and friends.

How truly does the life of the illustrious statesman and leader show that

> *The heights by great men reached and kept,*
> *Were not attained by sudden flight;*
> *But they, while their companions slept,*
> *Were toiling upward in the night.*

It was truly a step from slavery to this elevation, to that place where his signature made worthless paper money. A black hand to write his name across the face of paper and give it credit, not only at home but in all the nations of the earth, the hand that would have been cut off had it been found writing his name before the war. Marvelous changes. "What's in a name?" There was money in his.

Since he has retired from political life he has devoted his time to lecturing.

The Senator has named a little boy, who has come into his family, Roscoe Conkling. The following, a good reason for so doing, went the rounds of the press:

Senator Bruce has told the secret of his admiration for Senator Conkling as follows: "When I came up to the Senate I knew no one except Senator Alcorn, who was my colleague. When the names of the new Senators were called out for them to go up and take the oath, all the others except myself were escorted by their colleagues. Mr. Alcorn made no motion to escort me, but was buried behind a newspaper, and I concluded I would go it alone. I had got about half way up the aisle when a tall gentleman stepped up to me and said: 'Excuse me, Mr. Bruce, I did not until this moment see that you were without an escort. Permit me. My name is Conkling,' and he linked his arm in mine and we marched up to the desk together. I took the oath and then he escorted me back to my seat. Later in the day, when they were fixing up the committees, he asked me if any one was looking after my interests, and upon my informing him that there was not and that I was myself more ignorant of my rights in the matter, he volunteered to attend to it, and as a result I was placed on some very good committees and shortly afterwards got a chairmanship. I have always felt very kindly towards Mr. Conkling since, and always shall."

CHAPTER CIII

J. D. Bowser, Esq.
Editor of the Gate City Press—*Grain and Coal Merchant—*
Principal Lincoln School

━━━•‧•━━━

At Weldon, North Carolina, February 15, 1846, was born a son whose career as a citizen, teacher, politician and editor has been renowned. J. D. Bowser was the son of free parents, and as the opportunities for the education of the Negro in the South were very limited, when Mr. Bowser was a child of about six summers, his father removed to Chillicothe, Ohio, where the children might enjoy the benefits of the public schools of that State. There was nothing eventful in his early life.

When Mr. Bowser first went to Kansas City, wealth was his desire; his whole aim was to devote his untiring energies to the accumulation of property, and shortly after he arrived in his new home, was employed as a teacher in a school at Westport; and in 1868, when the Hon. J. Milton Turner was called to represent the United States as minister to Liberia, he succeeded him as principal of Lincoln school, where he worked for eleven years, until he removed to take charge of a school in Wyandotte, Kansas. Two years later he was appointed to a position in the mail service, where he remained for four years' until the election of Grover Cleveland.

He is an important factor in the political affairs of the State of Missouri, and a member of the Republican State Central Committee in 1885 and '86. His voice has often been heard upon the stump in behalf of the party to which he gives his support, and he has done good service in the way of making votes, controlling the colored people in that direction.

A sketch of him was recently printed in a Western journal, *The Kansas City Dispatch.* I believe Mr. Bowser is a man of wonderful reserve power, upon which he has the rare faculty to draw whenever occasion demands. As an orator he is pointed, fluent, magnetic in repose, rather unassuming and not especially prepossessing in appearance, and exigencies seem only to call out the forces within him. Whether it be in his editorial writings, or whether it be in the hustings, upon the stump before the people, Mr.

Bowser has at his immediate command a rare store-house of knowledge and he does not fail to draw upon it without reserve whenever needed. His intellectual powers are above the average, and his extensive acquaintance with literature gives him many apt illustrations, and makes him an interesting and instructive speaker.

He is the editor of the *Gate City Press,* one of the strongest papers in the United States; and it is the mouthpiece of the colored people of the West, being a strong advocate of all questions looking toward the amelioration of the condition of our race, and at the same time discussing with judicial fairness every issue before the American people. He never fails to pursue with unabated vigor any person or thing which he undertakes to antagonize. His paper thoroughly reflects the man. As a religious man his views are liberal; he believes that right, because it is right, should be a man's master. He is a most ardent defender of a cause his judgment thinks right, and nothing will make him change his honest convictions.

He is in easy financial circumstances, has a fine residence, and enjoys his wealth and social standing fully. He carries on a very lucrative trade in coal and grain, and ranks among the prominent business men of the race. In 1873, he was united in marriage to Miss Dora J. Troy of Xenia, Ohio, a cultured woman from one of the oldest and most distinguished families in that State.

JESSE FREEMAN BOULDEN

CHAPTER CIV

Rev. Jesse Freeman Boulden
Member of the Lower House of the Legislature in Mississippi
in Reconstruction Times—Agent of the American Baptist
Publication Society

The subject of this sketch was born in the State of Delaware, October 8, 1820. He was never a slave. His parents, Andrew and Theresa Boulden, were under that State law which said that "manumitted and recorded slaves" were free at the age of twenty-eight, and their children at eighteen and twenty-one, so that his parents had only one slave child out of five. This law of Delaware was a good one, for it carried with it the inspiring hopes of freedom to every slave in the State, not only to themselves but to their children; yet it did not destroy the desire of the slaveholders to perpetuate the slavery of those emancipated slaves. So when his oldest brother Benjamin was nearing his majority, they plotted to deprive him of his liberty by sending him South before his time; but the white children who had heard the old folks talk, told him, and he ran away and went to Pennsylvania. Of course his father was charged with persuading him to do this and the result was that his father, with all his family, followed the boy. In this case the Scripture seems to be verified "that a little child shall lead them." After locating in Philadelphia, they remained there for about eighteen years. When Jesse arrived at the age for schooling he enjoyed all the advantages the city afforded, through the Quakers, for several years. He was then returned to Delaware to serve an apprenticeship, the indentures specifying that he was to have schooling. He was granted a part of this and notwithstanding it was a slave State he attended a mixed school, white and colored both attended. Sometimes this was the case in those States, both in Maryland and Delaware, and in several other States of the South.

After coming to his majority he attended private school. He embraced religion in February, 1834, in the State of Maryland. In 1853 he united with the Union Baptist church at Philadelphia and became its pastor, remaining such until the autumn of 1860, when he resigned, being called to Chicago to take charge of what was known as the Zion Baptist church. After some consideration he agreed to accept the call, and entered upon his duties January 1, 1861. He found things very different from those he left behind. There were two ghosts of churches, filled with aristocracy and pride on the one hand, and ignorance and vice on the other. These, of course, are the parents of division and dissension, and there was plenty of it there. It fell to his lot under God to dissolve these two bodies and organize what has since been known as the Olivet Baptist church, which subsequently became the "Star of the West." After succeeding in this he felt it his duty to resign. He thought it best, as there were elements which did not harmonize. He thought under another's leadership they might succeed better. While he was somewhat mistaken in that, it was for the best after all, for they secured the services of Rev. R. De Baptiste, whose sketch is found elsewhere, and who appeared to be the "right man in the right place." This prepared him for an unforeseen event that was to take place that no living soul dreamed of, which was the death of Rev. J. R. Anderson of St. Louis. They had formed very friendly relations with each other. After closing his labors with the Olivet church in April, 1863, he went home to Philadelphia, leaving as he supposed Brother Anderson in the best of health, as he had just previously paid him a visit in St. Louis. Then was he suddenly called back to pay the church a visit of condolence on account of his death. After spending three months with them, they called him for their pastor and he accepted.

These were eventful times. The war was in progress, and the Union army was making its way Southward, and knowing that there was much Baptist element in the South, he felt it his duty to look after it; so he worked up a call of the Illinois State convention, through the Wood River Association, meeting at Brooklyn, Illinois, February, 1864. But few met at that time; but enough to order the call for a convention of all the Baptists in the northwest, meeting at St. Louis, in the Eighth Street Baptist church, for the purpose of considering the importance of following up the army and looking after our denomination in the southwest. This convention met, pursuant to the call, and seven States were represented. After due consideration, a northwestern and southern Baptist convention was organized, which, through its agent, Rev. William Troy, explored the Mississippi Valley from Detroit to the Gulf of Mexico. Knowing that for many years the American Baptist Missionary convention had existed in the east, and they were taking care of the east and the southeast who joined the Gulf of Savannah, Georgia, and that we, in our convention, united it at New Orleans, some of us thought that we in our western and eastern organization had the country surrounded, it would be a good thing for the two to consolidate and make one grand National body. This was effected at Richmond, Virginia, August, 1866. After the exploration of the Mississippi Valley to New Orleans, there was such a vast field open for laborers, and so few that had the disposition to enter it; notwithstanding they were in each other's way, with nothing to do, Mr. Boulden left his church in 1865, and went to work in the State of Mississippi, taking Natchez for his field. Here was organized what is now known as the Pine Street Baptist church, but then the Wall Street Baptist church. He got up the first petition that went to Congress in 1865, asking the right of franchise, and the first Emancipation celebration which took place January 1, 1866. At this celebration he delivered a lecture on the duty of the hour. After spending two years at Natchez, he very mysteriously brought up at Columbus, Mississippi, his present home. Here, like at Natchez, he found more to do than to preach to the people. He considered it his duty to give all the instruction he could to them. He was one of the leaders in forming the organization of the Republican party in the northeastern part of Mississippi. When it was organized, it fell to his lot to make the first Republican speech that was ever made in the court-house. He was a member of the first Republican convention held in the State, which met at Vicksburg, July, 1867.

When the party was preparing for election in 1869, he was brought out against his will as a candidate, and was elected to the Lower House of the Legislature. He first inquired of himself what was to be done; after looking about for some time, he concluded that one thing was to get a colored man as near the President as possible; he concluded that the United States Senate was the place for him. When the time came, he opened the fight in that direction. They met in a ten days' session to inaugurate the Governor and elect a United States Senator, and do such other things that might be necessary, preparatory to the meeting of Congress. Here he met the Honorable B. K. Bruce, whom he had known in St. Louis; he was the only one he knew that was in a position to do him any good, and he did more than any other man to get him elected sergeant-at-arms to the State Senate. This was a stepping-stone to his present position. There were three senators to be elected; one for six years, one for five and one for two; and Mr. Boulden claimed that the short term belonged to the colored people, and contended for it. After he opened the argument in the caucus, there were others to form in line, and quite a number of aspirants, and H. R. Revels was the fortunate one. He has the honor of being the first colored man that filled the speaker's position in the State of Mississippi, if not in any other State. He was appointed a trustee of the State Normal School, also of the Alcorn University. Since this, he has filled the pastorate of the Nineteenth Street Baptist church in Washington, District of Columbia.

In the year 1883 he edited the *Baptist Reflector*, at Columbus, Mississippi. Looking over an old copy of this issue, we find letters from Rev. G. W. Dupee of Kentucky; H. H. White of Little Rock, Arkansas; John Bullock, student of Alcorn University; also a poem of Mr. Boulden's composition, on the death of Elder J. R. Anderson, pastor of the Eighth Street Baptist church, St. Louis, Missouri, 1863. He is now filling a position as general agent of the American Baptist Home Mission Society for the State of New York, with duties assigned for the State of Mississippi.

CHAPTER CV

Rev. William T. Dixon
Veteran Pastor of the Concord Baptist Church, Brooklyn,
New York

The parents of this gentleman, George H. and Frances R. Dixon, were Virginians who had taken up their abode in New York City a few years previous to the birth of their son William, which occurred September 8, 1833. The death of the mother in 1836 deprived him at a very tender age of that most potent influence, maternal oversight and affection. At the age of seven he was admitted into the colored public schools, afterwards known as Colored Grammar school No. 1, of which the renowned educator, John Peterson, was master. Here he remained until he was fifteen years old. He was then employed for several years as monitor or pupil teacher, and subsequently that of assistant. In 1851 he was brought to a knowledge of saving faith, and shortly afterward united by baptism with the Abyssinian Baptist Church of New York during the pastorate of Rev. J. T. Raymond.

In 1854 he received an appointment as teacher in a school at Stonington, Connecticut, where he remained in charge for two years. Thence he removed to Baltimore to assist in the high school founded by the Rev. Chauncey Leonard. Later, Mr. Dixon established a school in the same city, which, during the short period of two years, increased in numbers from four to nearly one hundred and fifty pupils. Notwithstanding his popularity and success in Baltimore, circumstances compelled him to sever his connection with his school.

During this period he married a Miss Matilda A. Wilson. A brief space of nine years was marked by mingled joy and sorrow. The extremes of life's experience were realized and endured. The limits of the home circle expanded to include five children, but death made them motherless and deprived their father of his estimable wife. Subsequently he became united to his present faithful helpmate, formerly Mrs. A. C. Fraser of Arlington, Virginia.

From 1860 to 1863 Mr. Dixon was principal of a public school in

WILLIAM T. DIXON

Flushing, Long Island. By this time he had already taken initial steps toward entering the ministry and had received his license to preach at the hands of Rev. William Spellman. In the fall of 1863, a year memorable in many respects, he was invited to assume the charge of the Concord Church of Christ at Brooklyn, Long Island. He accepted this call, and having been ordained December 17 of that year, he entered upon the duties of his pastorate and is still actively employed discharging the same in the enlarged and manifold form into which they have gradually increased and expanded.

The career of the subject of our sketch furnishes an example and fitting illustration of the potency of that hidden stimulus, that unconscious influence, that unseen guiding principle that contributes so largely to the beautifying or distortion of human character, an influence that is none the less powerful becauses it is so often overlooked or underrated in estimating a man's worth and importance. With a full assurance of the obligation to assume the onerous duties of a minister, with enlarged views of the nature and responsibility of the sacred calling, with firm reliance on the promise of divine aid from the Master in whose service he has enlisted, he has become absorbed in the endeavor to make people better, surely wiser, and happier possibly. To this end he brings to bear an indomitable physical vigor, a keen insight into the needs and deficiencies of human nature, and steady enthusiasm, which is a matter of temperament, not of years, and which has made and is still making his later efforts as valuable and telling as the first fruits of early endeavor that were ripened by the generous fervor of ardent impulse. He habitually exercises rapidity and energy in mental action and possesses that broad and delicate sympathy that is one of the highest and most unerring of the intuitive forces that direct the activities of life. His wonderful infusing power enables him so successfully to restore the flagging energies of those who falter or grow weary in the struggle of existence, and his extraordinary power of distribution or facility in laying hold of persons, discerning the nature and extent of their moral distempers, and selecting and applying with due care and suitable caution the proper available remedies, giving to each just what is needed and at the right moment, assists immeasurably his leading disposition, to help, to elevate, to reform, to convert.

To these exceptional powers are enjoined an ability to organize, to conserve forces, to kindle and keep alive a spirit of lively enthusiasm, tempered with sterling good sense. He attaches his followers closely to himself personally, and still more closely to the truth in which he is a devout believer, and of which he is an earnest advocate. His special distinction lies in the fact that he knows he has something to give, something everybody needs and which cannot fail to do them good. He therefore occupies himself with working practical problems, not with puzzling over imaginary ones, and bravely faces human nature, striving to look at humanity as his Master regards it, with that infinite compassion so consoling to the faithful and so touchingly rebuking to the wilful and obdurate.

The history of the Concord church is the narration of the mental and moral growth of the colored people of Brooklyn. From small beginnings, its rise has been steady; its development normal and harmonious, and to-day it stands on a financial basis, with an honorable reputation and in a condition of spiritual prosperity, that does infinite credit to the organization directly, and indirectly to the great body of Christians of which it is a corporate part. It has become a centre from which civilizing, educating and elevating influences have radiated to the farthest limits of its environs. The animating spirit that under divine providence has made such a state of affairs to exist is that of the faithful pastor called to preside over the work. He has exerted personal appeal, he has given personal instruction, he has expounded and reiterated the thrilling truths of the gospel, but he has not stopped; he has seized upon all legitimate means; pressed into services all available influences to keep fresh and enduring the impressions of God, truth and eternity he has striven so zealously to effect. Thus, incidentally in the prosecution of the greater work of saving souls, he has accomplished much towards the improvement of the manners, address and homes of those in whose behalf he labors. He has lived and taught a religion designed to make people comfortable and happy in a temporal sense as well as nobler and better spiritually. That the labors of such a man should gain recognition, that he should be thoroughly identified with all the movements of reform, that he should be a leading exponent of the thought and culture of the thoughtful and cultured part of the community in which he works, is a most natural sequence.

In the affairs of public education he takes a genuine, cordial interest. Although filling no official position, he is as intimately concerned in the affairs relating to the educational welfare of colored children, his opinions are as fully respected and his advice is eagerly sought. In the temperance reform, in the literary movements, he is among those who give tone and color to public sentiment. By sympathy and tradition he naturally belongs to the Republican party, but latterly he allied himself with the Prohibitionists. Being from conviction a radical in the cause, he throws the weight of his influence on the side of those actively engaged in the suppression of the liquor traffic and in a crusade against the liquor habit. He views the subject from the high standpoint of the moral effect it has, not only in its excesses but in its more insidious, because more attractive phases.

The sister churches of the Baptist denomination hold this man in the esteem he deserves, and accord to him the honor and consideration he merits. He enjoys the confidence of his associate brethren, and the clergy at large. At one time he was appointed the preacher to deliver the introductory sermon before the noted divines comprising the Long Island Baptist Association. Formerly the president, he now holds the office of corresponding secretary of the Northeast Baptist Missionary convention. He is also the secretary of the Mount Pleasant Cemetery Association. His life full of the desire for the salvation of humanity that has enabled its possessor to perform arduous, exacting toil with patience, glad at all times for the privilege of being the humble instrument to carry the divine message to some benighted soul. The career of such a man is worthy of more than the passing limits out this sketch affords. Thousands have blessed the day he was born, and acknowledged him as the author of their hopes, and may many more days be given this beloved brother.

MATTHEW CAMPBELL

CHAPTER CVI

Rev. Matthew Campbell
One of God's Servants full of Years and Work for Christ—
A Thirty Years Pastorate—Married Two Thousand Couples

In telling of the deeds of the young men who have come to the front since slavery, and of those in the various departments of life, I have not thought it well to forget that class of old men who have created very little excitement in the world outside of their own immediate neighborhood. and yet who quietly have added to the great reservoir of good which has been accomplished. Many of these men who have done signal service have never had their names heralded in the newspapers, nor have they even filled exalted stations in their denominations, but have quietly, year after year, been the means of conversions of thousands of souls, and in the day when "Christ shall make up his jewels" then these men will shine as the brightest among them all.

As this book is to furnish examples, rather than exalt any particular individual, it would be of very little difference, as far as the purpose of the book is concerned, whether they are taken from one city or from one State. I want *examples; men of exemplary lives;* men who have labored for God; and in this respect I care very little as to whether they are graduates from colleges of learning or whether they have preached the gospel in an unlettered way. I am after results, and it may be possible too that many of these men who have had no college training and little common school training, will fill higher seats in heaven than those whose heads are filled with the classics and sciences and the "ologies" of the world.

The Rev. Campbell is the son of Jackson and Lucy Campbell, both of whom were born and reared in Madison county, Kentucky, and were slaves of one Audley Campbell. The former was born January 15, 1797, and the latter in the year 1803. Their boy "Matt" was born in Madison county, Kentucky, September 1, 1823. On September 16, 1841, he embraced religion, and was called under the influence of Rev. Edmund Martin, a colored Baptist preacher, who was the first pastor of the church over which Mr. Campbell now presides at Richmond, Kentucky.

When Mr. Campbell was converted he had no other thought than to join the Baptist church, but his master, being a Methodist, would not permit him to follow his own inclinations, neither his wife nor his children to join any other church than that to which his master belonged. He began to preach some time in August, 1842. January 21, 1843, he married Polly Woods Ballard. The following year, 1844, he was licensed to preach in the Methodist church. His late master died in 1851, and in 1856 he joined the Baptist church and was baptized by Rev. Jacob Bush, of Clark county, Kentucky, the second pastor of the church referred to above. In August, 1857, he was ordained in Lincoln county, Kentucky, in the Tates Creek Association of white Baptists. The council consisted of Rev. G. W. Broadus, and the Rev. Andrew Broadus of Louisville, and Rev. John Higgins of Lincoln, and others, all white. On the third Sunday of June, 1858, he was called to the pastorate of the Richmond church, and has been pastor of that church ever since. The membership of the church is at present seven hundred and ninety, and the value of his church property about seven thousand dollars. He also organized a church at New Liberty in 1869, and preached there for seven years. The building cost about one thousand dollars. He organized the Mt. Pleasant church in 1875, and the value of the property is about two thousand five hundred dollars. Organized two other churches, the one at Otter Creek and the other at Mt. Nebo.

He has baptized in all about three thousand since freedom, and married over two thousand couples; preached the funerals of over four thousand persons. This is a wonderful work for one man who has lived since his birth in one place, and shows that though a prophet may be without honor in his own country, that in this case the statement seems not to have been thoroughly verified. When he first embraced religion he knew nothing in the book but the alphabet, and his father bought him an old fashioned elementary spelling-book out of which he secured instruction by means of the white children to whom he applied. What a fruitful source of instruction the white children of the South were to many of our old "fathers" and "mothers." In their innocence they did not comprehend that they were putting into the minds of Negroes the mighty weapon of good. God seems to have put into the hearts of these children, who were the constant companions of slaves, the thought to assist them in their instruction. Unconsciously they were doing good, and even in the midst of bondage were preparing a great many people for freedom by teaching them to read and write. God always has a way of helping his people. Every night he would split pine knots and make a light, whereby to learn his lessons, and every Sunday he would get the white boys under his size to teach him his lessons, and he never went to school a day in his life, except a few days since freedom.

He lives in the midst of his people, honored wherever known, respected by white and colored, beloved by the members of his church, and esteemed in the highest manner as a minister of the gospel of the Lord Jesus Christ.

C. C. VAUGHN

CHAPTER CVII

Rev. C. C. Vaughn
State Grand Chief of the Independent Order of Good
Samaritans and Daughters of Samaria—Preacher and Teacher

C. C. Vaughn was born in Dinwiddie county, Virginia, December 27, 1846. His parents were slaves and were owned by Theodoric H. Grigg, who sold his plantation in 1852, and carried all his slaves to Ohio and set them free. When he was thirteen years old he was left an orphan, on the charities of the world. He lived with his cousin, who was a farmer, and whose residence was about six miles from any colored settlement or school; hence his advantages for tuition were very poor. He labored on the farm during the summer, and in the winter was sent to school this long distance. By crossing lots and going through the woods he would make this distance, five miles, but so anxious was he to learn that one winter he only lost three days during the term; one for sickness, one turkey hunting, and one from high-water which kept him at home. His relative did everything he could to furnish him with a common school education, and young Vaughn made good use of every opportunity. In 1861 and 1862 he worked in a brick-yard; the next year his relative moved to another farm, as he was poor and only a renter, and he wished to get nearer school advantages for the benefit of young Vaughn. In 1863, by the permission of his cousin, he went to work in a place near Troy, Ohio, and labored on Judge Heywood's farm during that year. In 1864 he enlisted in the army for three years, and was assigned to company F, Thirteenth regiment United States Colored Heavy Artillery. He was transferred to company A, and promoted to the position of orderly sergeant, and filled the duties of this office to the satisfaction of everybody concerned. November 27, 1865, he was mustered out of service. Returning home with a little money, he entered Liber College, Jay county, Indiana, and was the only colored student in the county. His effort was to excel for this reason, and the young man was never lacking in any of his studies. In the vacation of 1866, he was examined in Sidney, Ohio, and securing a school, taught for three months for one hundred dollars. In the fall he returned to Liber College and spent a year in hard study, at the end of which he appeared before the public on commencement day, with an oration; the subject was: "The Colored Man's Right to the Ballot," and he did credit to the subject, carrying the house by storm. His money being exhausted, he was obliged to seek a field of labor and his course was not yet completed, but the president gave him a certificate to this effect:

This is to certify that Mr. C. C. Vaughn has attended this school for several sessions; he is active, and ambitious to excel, and has made good progress in his studies. I regard him as a young man of good character and polite habits, and he is entitled to the confidence and esteem of those with whom he may have to deal.

EBENEZER TUCKER,
President Liber College, Indiana

July 11, 1867

After leaving school he worked on the farm through harvest, and in the fall he went to Washington county, in the hill region, and was examined at Marietta, Ohio, receiving a two years' certificate, and engaged to teach a six months school in Wesley township at forty dollars a month and board. Here his fame went out as a good teacher. During this time he met Dr. E. M. Cravath, who was then secretary of the Freedman's Aid Association, in Cincinnati, Ohio. April 14 he received a communication to teach in the South under the American Missionary Association, and Western Freedman's Aid Commission. His first field of labor was Cynthiana, Kentucky, a very hard place in which to stay at that time on account of the prejudice existing against Northern men; however, he remained two years, and entered school again at Berea, where he was compelled to labor very hard, chopping wood and sawing stove-wood for the halls and acting as janitor at Howard's hall. He was also a student-teacher, and by these means managed to remain in school to finish his course.

Having professed a hope in Christ in 1869, he was more able to stand the trials of life and undergo the hardships of this world. In December, 1873, having been solicited by a fellow-student, he started for Greenville, Mississippi, but was asked by Elder J. F. Thomas to stop in Russellville to teach a school at the colored Baptist church. He accepted the honor, and commenced his school January 12, 1874, and his labor was so efficient that the good people of Russellville would not give him up, and he still has charge of the public school at this writing—1887. In 1875 he became a member of the Baptist church, and was made clerk, a position he holds at the present day. He was licensed to preach the Gospel in May, 1876. Elder Moses Harding having resigned the church at Allensville, Kentucky, recommended the young preacher to the confidence of the church. He accepted the call, and has labored since the first Sunday of June, 1876. September, 1877, he was ordained at the First District Association in Hopkinsville, Kentucky, with the following elders in council: G. W. Dupee, Allen Allensworth, Moses Harding, Daniel Jones, William Howell, J. F. Thomas, E. M. Manion. Since this he has held prominent places in the association and obtained honor among the brethren. He is still pastor of the same church. In 1878 he purchased a fine piece of property, and married, January 1, 1879, settling in Russellville, Kentucky.

He has some influence in the political arena, and was elected chairman on the State Convention of Colored Men held in Louisville, in 1884, where he gained considerable reputation as a parliamentarian, being able to govern the convention better than any other convention ever held in the State. He was treasurer of the District Lodge of the Grand United Order of Odd Fellows for six years, and was elected State Grand Chief of the Independent Order of Good Samaritans and Daughters of Samaria in 1883, a position he still holds with credit and honor. At Natchez, Mississippi, in 1884, he was elected R. W. N., vice-chief of that body, and was placed on the National Executive committee.

Whenever he comes before the people, he is generally elected to all positions to which he aspires. In 1886 he was elected vice-assistant moderator of the General Association, after receiving sixty odd votes for the first place. He is a man beloved by everybody and very popular with all classes. He has led a pure life, filled many important situations, and preached a good and wholesome Gospel. He is a leader in every good work, and has the confidence of the white people in his State and community; an able and aggressive man, fearing nothing when he is right. In the defense of his people, he never spares himself; he is an intense race man, and his position on all questions touching his people is a proper one. He is a stalwart, and while he is a Republican in principles, he nevertheless demands fair treatment from those who are disposed to make differences on account of color. It may appear singular that so many colored preachers are in politics in this country; but our people being an ignorant people very largely, cannot read the newspapers and know the positions of the parties, and consequently they are dependent upon the preachers, who are without doubt the leading element among them. Their power over the people is almost unlimited, and for this reason the good man can do much good, and the bad man can do much evil. Mr. Vaughn's outspoken manner has made him very acceptable to his own people, and at the same time he has been considered rather too fast by some of the rougher elements of the white people; but no sensible man would blame him for defending his race. He has a vast influence in the southern counties of the State, and his future is hopeful and full of brightness.

HARVEY JOHNSON

CHAPTER CVIII

Rev. Harvey Johnson
Eminent Baltimore Pastor—Prominent in the Councils
of his Church

Few, if any, abler men in the church work and true representatives of the race can be found than Rev. Harvey Johnson, pastor of the Union Baptist church of Baltimore. He was born of slave parents, August 4, 1843, in Fauquier county, Virginia. His father's name was Thomas Johnson. His mother's name was Harriet Johnson. There was nothing eventful in his early life. He was always of a religious turn of mind, but was not converted until he was over twenty. He was baptized by Rev. S. W. Madden, in Alexandria, Virginia, who took him to Washington and entered him in Wayland Seminary, where he remained studying for five years, being aided in part by friends in Watertown, Massachusetts, and otherwise supporting himself by laboring during vacation as missionary and school teacher, under the Home Mission Society. The first school he attended was in Alexandria, which was taught by a gentleman by the name of Gladden, and for awhile attended a school kept by Quakers, in Philadelphia. He entered Wayland Seminary in 1868 and graduated in 1872, and in the fall of the same year was called to Union Baptist church, Baltimore, Maryland. It then had a membership of about two hundred and fifty, and now has nearly twenty-two hundred, being the largest church in the State. He has been pastor of this church about fifteen years. He has never held any political position, from the fact he never took any part in politics, except for prohibition; he has labored, however, very earnestly in trying to obtain the rights of the race as citizens, which has brought him into communication with a large number of the prominent men of the country. Some of the measures he has been interested in securing for the race are the following: Opening the bar to colored lawyers in Baltimore; assisting four of his members in a suit against the steamer "Sue." The case was won, and there has been no trouble to get proper accommodations in traveling on all boats sailing out from Baltimore. That he was the leader in these things there can be no doubt. He has been much interested in the cause of education, and especially in the young men of the race. He believes in an educated ministry and has aimed to have his church do the same; as a result, they will not license or ordain a man who will not study and prepare himself for the work. Six have been ordained and sent out.

There are others preparing for the different fields in life; four for the ministry and two for law. His church has contributed largely to the work of education and missions, raising some years over one thousand two hundred dollars for the purpose.

He is a life member of the American Baptist Home Mission Society; life director of the Publication Society; Life member of the Virginia Baptist State convention, and also of New England Baptist Missionary convention. He recently joined the Baptist Congress held in the city of Baltimore, and was made a member of its board of managers. He has been honored with different positions in the city; was elected president of Ministerial Union of this city, consisting of all denominations. He organized the Maryland Baptist State convention, and was its first president; he also organized the Mutual United Brotherhood of Liberty, wrote its constitution, and was elected president of the same. He has served for a term as vice-president of the White Baptist Minister's Conference of this city, and he is now vice-president of Maryland Baptist State convention, which is a body of white and colored churches. He has written and published several sermons, which have been commented upon in most praiseworthy terms by the public press, especially an original discourse on the "Equality of the Father and the Son." He is not a business man and claims no wealth, yet he is the owner of two fine homes, one in which he lives, valued at three or four thousand dollars; the other, a farm in Virginia, about eight miles from Richmond. He was married April 17, 1877, to Miss Amelia E. Hall, of Montreal, Canada. Their union has been blest with three children, one daughter and two sons. The following extract has appeared in prominent journals from time to time concerning his arduous labors and successful career. The Parkersburg, West Virginia *Freeman* says:

Rev. Harvey Johnson, the pastor of North Street Baptist church in this city (Baltimore), is the first representative colored man, who has cast his future political fortunes with the Prohibition party in the State of Maryland. Mr. Johnson is earnestly exerting his characteristic zeal for the upbuilding of the new party of his choice, and in an able speech a few Sunday afternoons ago, at a Prohibition meeting, said he could pledge two hundred votes for his party from his church.

In a letter to the *National Baptist*, he wrote as follows:

We feel our improper treatment keener than any tongue can tell; yes it galls me to my very soul; our friends may say, "we are to forgive our injuries;" but, my dear sir, we are not required, as I understand it, to forgive injuries that still continue to be inflicted. I understand the spirit of that Scripture to be that we are to forgive past injuries, and those that cease to be inflicted and that are repented of. Now, I hold that our injuries have neither ceased to be inflicted, nor are they repented of. Right here, in the city of Baltimore, we are not allowed to teach our own children in the colored schools. I hold that this is a gross injustice. Shall we forgive it while the injustice continues? We have separate schools, and not a single colored teacher allowed to teach, although they hold certificates qualifying them for such a position.

IRA ALDRIDGE AS 'OTHELLO'

CHAPTER CIX

Ira Aldridge
The African Tragedian—the "African Roscius"

The name of Aldridge has always been placed at the head of the list of Negro actors. He has indeed become the most noted of them, and his name is cited as standing first in his calling among all colored persons who have ever appeared on the stage. He was born at Belaire, near Baltimore, in 1804. In complexion he was dark brown, and with heavy whiskers; standing six feet in height, with heavy frame, African features, and yet with due proportions; he was graceful in his attitudes, highly polished in manners. In his early days he was apprenticed to a ship carpenter, and had his association with the Germans on the western shores of Maryland. Here he became familiar with the German language, and spoke it not only with ease but with fluency. He was brought in contact with Edmund Kean, the great actor, in 1826, whom he accompanied in his trip through Europe. His ambition to become an actor was encouraged by Kean, and receiving his assistance in the preparation, he made his appearance first at the Royalty Theatre in London, in the character of Othello. Public applause greeted him of such an extraordinary nature, that he was billed to appear at the Covent Garden Theatre, April 10, 1839, in the same character. After many years' successful appearances in many of the metropolitan cities, he appeared in the Provinces with still greater success. In Ireland he performed Othello, with Edmund Kean as Iago. In 1852 he appeared in Germany in Shakespearean characters. He was pronounced excellent, and though a stranger and a foreigner, he undertook the very difficult task of playing in English, while his whole support was rendered in the language of the country. It is said that until this time, such an experiment was not considered susceptible of a successful end, but nevertheless, with his impersonations he succeeded admirably. It is said that the King of Prussia was so deeply moved with his appearance in the character of Othello, at Berlin, that he sent him a congratulatory letter, and conferred upon him the title of chevalier, in recognition of his dramatic genius, and informed him that the lady who took the part of Desdemona was so much affected at the manner in which he played his part that she was made ill from fright and the reality with which he acted his part. I am indebted to T. Morris Chester for a sketch which he has written of the eminent tragedian, for the facts which I have presented in this article. He reports that a dramatic critic in St. Petersburg informed him that while Aldridge was great in Othello he was still greater in Shylock, which he declared was his masterpiece; but popular judgment in European cities regarded him as the ideal "Othello." Some idea of the character of his acting might be gained from the fact that the lady who played Desdemona in St. Petersburg, became very much alarmed at what appeared real passion on his part, in acting Othello; though he was never rough or indelicate in any of his acting with ladies, yet she was so frightened that she used to scream with real fear.

It is said that on another occasion, in St. Petersburg, that in the midst of his acting in scene two, act five, when he was quoting these words:

It is the cause, it is the cause, my soul;
Let me not name it to you, yon chaste stars!
It is the cause—yet I'll not shed her blood,
Nor scar that whiter skin of her's than snow,
And smooth as monumental alabaster.
Yet she must die, else she'll betray more men.
Put out the light, and then—put out the light!
If I quench thee, thou flaming minister,
I can again thy former light restore,
Should I repent me: But once put out thy light,
Thou cunning'st pattern of excelling nature;
I know not where is that Promethian heat,
That can thy light relume. When I have plucked thy rose,
I cannot give it vital growth again;
It needs must wither:—I'll smell it on the tree—(kissing her)
O balmy breath, that dost almost persuade
Justice to break her sword:—One more, one more:—
Be thus when thou art dead, and I will kill thee,
And love thee after:—One more—and this the last:
So sweet was ne'er so fatal. I must weep, but they are cruel tears: This
    sorrow's heavenly:
It strikes where it doth love."

the house was so carried away with the manner in which he rendered it, that a young man stood up and exclaimed with the greatest earnestness: "She is innocent, Othello, she is innocent," and yet so interested was he in the acting himself that he never moved a muscle but continued as if nothing had been said to embarrass him. The next day he learned, while dining with a Russian prince, that a young man who had been present had been so affected by the play that he was seized with a sudden illness and died the next day.

Mr. Aldridge was a welcome guest in the ranks of the cultured and wealthy, and was often in the "salons" of the haughty aristocrats of St. Petersburg and Moscow. Titled ladies wove, knitted and stitched their pleasing emotions into various memorials of friendship. In his palatial residence at Sydenham, near London, were collected many presents of intrinsic value, rendered almost sacred by association. Prominent among these tokens of regard was an autographic letter from the King of Prussia, transmitting the first medal of art and sciences: the Cross of Leopold, from the Emperor of Russia, and a Maltese cross received at Berne.

Mr. Aldridge played, at Belfast, in Ireland, O'Rozembo to Edmund Kean's Alban. He appeared with flattering success in Amsterdam, Brussels, Berlin, Breslau, Vienna, Pesth, The Hague, Dantzic, Konigsberg, Dresden, Berne, Frankfort-on-the-Main, Cracow, Gotha, and numerous other cities, in all of the leading parts of all the standard plays of the day. In the character of O'Rozembo, Zanga, Zorambo, Rolla, Hugo and others, suitable to his form, he was considered very fine. In all his triumphs he never lost any interest in the condition of his race. He always took an interest in everything touching their welfare, and though exalted to the companionship of those who ranked high in every department of life, yet he never in any way forgot the humble race with which he was identified, and was always solicitous for their welfare and promotion. He was an associate of the most prominent men of Paris, among whom was Alexander Dumas. When the great tragedian and great writer met they always kissed each other, and Dumas always greeted Aldridge with the words "Mon confrère." I will relate here an instance which is given by Mr. Chester:

One evening at our hotel in Paris, which was a family resort for English tourists, he was requested, after some ladies had executed several operatic selections on the piano, to give a recitation for the company, which he did in a manner that delighted and charmed the gathering. On a subsequent occasion a gathering of friends made the salon brilliant with music and wit. Aldridge was specially requested to repeat what he had before rendered. He arose and said he would give them something else. Turning down the gas to a dim twilight, upon the pretense that it was too bright for his eyes, commenced in the presence of the company to relate what seems to be a personal experience. He began in a matter-of-fact way as follows: "In my early professional struggle I met a lovely young lady in England whose name was Amelia, with whom I exchanged affections. In asking for parental consent, the father desired to know what were my means and resources. I replied that my profession was my only dependence, upon which the father declared it was too precarious to risk his daughter's happiness. I immediately communicated to Amelia, in a final interview, her father's refusal, which intensely grieved us. We then and there pledged eternal fidelity to each other, in life and in death. Some eighteen months after I was sitting in my room in a Polish hotel when the door was suddenly burst open and Amelia walked in. I had just strength enough to ring the bell when I fell unconscious to the floor. Upon my recovery there were a number of persons around applying restoratives, who asked what was the matter? The whole affair was of such a delicate nature that I shrank from entering into explanation, but simply remarked that I was seized with vertigo which prostrated me. In about ten days I received a letter informing me that Amelia had died of a broken heart on the very day and at the very hour that she had appeared in my room. I sincerely mourned her death and for a long time refused to be comforted, but my circumstances and constant change of scene produced a consoling effect. In my intercourse and associations my path crossed that of a young lady of great personal attractions and high social position. Her grace and virtue made a deep impression on my mind, sentiment and feelings, which soon became mutual and in a reasonable time we were betrothed. A happy day was appointed, and it seemed to be rapidly approaching without a cloud to mar my thrilling joy. On the afternoon previous to the designated day, my wedding attire had been brought to my room. While I was still examining it, much to my pride, and spreading the different articles out upon my bed, the door noiselessly opened and Amelia entered with a melancholy expression on her countenance and mysteriously vanished. This spiritual visit threw me into paroxysms, which confined me to my room and necessitated a postponement of the ceremonies. Some six months after, preparations were again set in motion for the event. The day came, and with it the remembrance of the past, and fear for the present. The weather was cloudy and ominous, the wedding procession formed and as we marched down the aisle of the church, I began to feel a satisfaction and pride, when I raised my eyes—Good Heavens! There she is now! Look, look! There she is!" and the tragedian struck an attitude and gave an expression of dread which infused terror into the company. There was a sensation for some seconds, but they were all surprised again when they found that he had only been declaiming the selection which they had asked for, but it was done in such a natural manner that all instinctively turned to the place to which he pointed, expecting to see Amelia as she appeared to him.

Mr. Aldridge married an English lady, who died shortly thereafter, and he married a second time, choosing for his wife a Swedish baroness of dignity and beauty. He was to sail for New York to fill an American engagement, August 16, 1867, but he died at Lodes, in Poland, August 7, 1867.

Thus from the carpenter's bench to the stage, Ira Aldridge rose to eminence, and has stamped upon the world the effects of his genius, so that he enters into the history of the race as a man of fine talent, high elocutionary powers, excellent dramatic taste, fine perception and great stage power. His talent was recognized by all the actors of his day. Much credit is due to Mr. Kean for his bravery in taking a Negro upon the stage as a partner in the principal parts, thereby assisting him to rise to the high position which he reached. Though a man may have ever so much talent, he needs, nevertheless, a helping hand from those who have succeeded in the same line or profession, to aid the beginner to lofty heights. Much praise is therefore due to Mr. Kean, and let it not be forgotten in commemorating the deeds of Mr. Aldridge that he owes his success to the distinguished Kean.

CHAPTER CX

Hon. George L. Ruffin, LL. B.
Judge of the Charlestown District, Massachusetts—From
the Barber's Chair to the "Bench"

The name most honored among the sons of Boston is not known among the living, but is a cherished name of one who, when alive, stood high in intellectual, social, legal and political affairs. He was a man of charitable, warm-hearted and generous impulses. A man whose life was a shining example of what can be done even in cultured Boston. Judge Ruffin had a distinguished, prepossessing appearance—a rich voice and charming manners—such as showed him a gentleman.

Hon. George Lewis Ruffin was born of free parents, George W. and Nancy Lewis Ruffin, in Richmond, Virginia, December 16, 1834. As the advantages for the education of the Negro in Virginia were very limited, the mother, who was anxious for the truest moral and intellectual development in her children, removed in 1853 to Boston, Massachusetts, where her family could have the benefit of the schools in that city.

George attended and graduated from the public schools in Boston, and was marked for his wonderful aptness and remarkable scholarship. He began work in a barber's shop with his book always by his side, and he daily gained information from his association with the business men of the city who came to the shop. After a few years he studied law with Messrs. Jewall & Gaston, and then entered the Harvard Law School, where he distinguished himself by completing alone the three years' course in one year and from which he graduated in 1869 with the degree of Bachelor of Laws, the second degree ever conferred by Harvard on a colored man.

From the old Sixth ward, now Ninth ward, Lawyer Ruffin was elected to the Massachusetts Legislature in 1869, and on account of his faithful services he was re-elected in 1870. This recognition was the expression of confidence in the sterling worth, exalted reputation and legal ability of this truly great citizen.

In 1872 he was a delegate to the National convention at New Orleans, and part of the time he presided over this body and delivered an eloquent speech on the life and services of Hon. Charles Sumner. Again in 1876 when he was unable to be present at the Lincoln Memorial Club of Cincinnati, where he was invited to deliver an address, his written thoughts were read for the inspiration of those present.

For many years he was a member of the Twelfth Baptist church of Boston, and for twelve years he was superintendent of its Sunday school and filled many important offices in the church. How few Christians are there while holding public position attend to their religious life and find time to give aid and counsel to the church. Let this good man's life show and thereby teach young men that political honor and a Christian life are not necessarily separable. Judge Ruffin was noted for his love of truth and his pure life. The eminent gentleman was always a consistent Republican and a member of many political conventions. For years he was a member of the Republican ward and city committee of Boston. In the year 1871 he was a Butler delegate in the famous Worcester convention, and made a telling speech for the nomination of General Butler for governor, which so won the house that had a vote then been taken, without a doubt he would have gained the day. Later, when General Butler was Governor of Massachusetts, he nominated as Judge of the District Court of Charlestown, Lawyer G. L. Ruffin, November 7, 1883, and although three nominees to this vacant judgeship were rejected, Lawyer Ruffin was unanimously confirmed by the Republican Executive Council, November 19, and General Butler himself administered the oath of office.

Whatever may be said of General Benjamin F. Butler, he is a staunch friend of the race and has always shown his fidelity to it in the person of Lawyer Ruffin. From the barber shop to the duties of a judge in Massachusetts. What a leap into fame!

In 1883 he was made consul resident for the Dominican Republic, and did what was committed to him with great care. Judge Ruffin was first president of the Wendell Phillips Club of Boston, and a member and at one time president of the Banneker Literary Club in the city. George Ruffin married a Boston lady of superior talents, who has seconded every effort of her husband in his noble career. Four children have blessed their home, all of whom have done honor to their exemplary parentage. November 19, 1886, Judge Ruffin passed away after a long protracted illness. Touching tributes of respect were paid to his memory by the many whose pleasure it had been to know him as their friend. A valiant soldier has fallen; the sheaf has been gathered into the garner. A faithful servant has gone to his reward. A truly great life has received a crown of glory.

He was elected a member of the Common Council of the city of Boston in 1875, and was re-elected in 1876. Where culture and refinement have reached so high a mark as in Boston, it was no small matter that he should be so complimented.

He was temporary chairman of a mass convention that met in Faneuil Hall during the Grant and Greeley campaign. On permanent organization was one of the vice-presidents and delivered the principal address of the convention, urging the election of Grant and Wilson. This was the second convention of the kind ever held in New England by the colored people.

A few years after, when vice-president Wilson died, the mayor of Boston called a meeting, and prominent among the speakers, Mayor Cobb, Governor Gaston, General W. P. Banks, Judge Hoar, Charles Francis Adams and John D. Long, stood Hon. George L. Ruffin. Does not this array of names show his powers as an orator and that his views as a patriot were acknowledged by those high in authority?

CHAPTER CXI

*Professor D. Augustus Straker, LL. B., LL. D.
Dean of Law Department—Lawyer—Orator and Stenographer*

In the year 1842, to John and Margaret Straker was born D. Augustus Straker, in the Islands of Barbadoes, West Indies. He was not a slave, but like many others, had felt the cruel shafts of prejudice and injustice. His father died when he was only eleven months old. He was, therefore, reared by his mother, who was a poor hard-working woman. She, having faith in the boy's future, was deeply interested in his education, and placed him in school at the age of seven years. After attending the Dame School until he was about eleven years old, he was put to a private teacher for two years; then he entered the Central Public school of the Island, whose principal was Robert P. Elliott of England. Here he completed the English course, and having been put to learn the tailor's trade and disliking it, induced his mother, through the assistance of friends interested in him, to withdraw him from his calling and permit him to pursue his studies, which he did, giving attention to French and Latin under the instruction of Rev. Joseph N. Durant, one of the most celebrated linguists in the world. His studies were carried on mainly through instruction by lectures delivered by R. R. Rawle, principal of Codrington College, who at that time was preparing students to become school teachers. At the age of seventeen he was appointed principal of St. Mary's School, one of the largest and most advanced schools of the Island, and filled the position of school teacher of St. Amis' and St. Giles' school in said Island. In the year 1868 the Rev. B. B. Smith, Episcopal Bishop of the Protestant Church of America, wrote to the principal of Codrington College, inquiring if there were any colored men and women who, having received the blessings of an education, were desirous of coming to the States to assist in the work of educating the lately emancipated of their race. This inquiry reached Mr. Straker and others by means of a sermon preached by the Dean of the college, on the topic of slavery and its evils. He was moved to compassion for his brethren in America, and although at that time many kind friends, regarding him as one disposed to the profession

D. AUGUSTUS STRAKER

of law, had voluntarily raised a good sum of money, looking to send him to England to study law, there being but one colored lawyer on the island at that time who had been similarly educated for that profession, and who is now chief-justice of the Islands of Barbadoes and other islands, he revoked his promise to go to England and came to America for the purpose spoken of, notwithstanding the kind proffer which he had already received. He arrived here in 1868 and began teaching school under the auspices of the Episcopal church and the Freedmen's Bureau, in Louisville, Kentucky. He was induced, while so engaged, to study for "Orders" in the Episcopal church and did so; but at the time when ready for said "Orders," refused to receive them if the proscriptions shown his race as a layman, was to be his lot as a clergyman. Not being assured of any different treatment, he abandoned any further preparation for the ministry. At this time, the Honorable John M. Langston was traveling through the South, informing the colored youth of that section of the country of the law school of Howard University. This man's earnestness and eloquence and deep interest for his race so moved upon Mr. Straker that he concluded to enter the law school of that University, which he did in 1870, six months after the class he entered was started. He graduated with distinguished honor in June, 1871, and among his classmates were the Honorable John H. Smythe, ex-minister to the Republic of Liberia; Moses W. Moore, now teacher in Paris, France, in the Polytechnique Academy.

While a student of law he was appointed stenographer for General O. O. Howard, in his office as head of Freedman's Bureau. He was also appointed teacher in the Normal and Preparatory Department of the University. In September, 1871, he was married at Detroit, Michigan, to Ann, daughter of Thomas and Julia Carey. In 1871 he was appointed first class clerk in the sixth auditor's office of the United States Treasury Department, Washington, District of Columbia. By due examination he was promoted to a second class clerkship, having charge of the postal accounts between the United States and all countries by treaty in postal relationship with the United States. This position he held until 1875. He was then appointed by Secretary Bristow as Inspector of Customs at the port of Charleston, South Carolina. In 1876 he entered upon the practice of his profession as a lawyer, in Orangeburg county, South Carolina, and was elected to the Legislature from said county that same year. He was ejected from his seat in the Legislature by the usurpation of the Democrats, known as the "Hampton House," with Wallace as speaker, as distinguished from the Republican House known as the "Chamberlin House," with Honorable E. W. Mackey as speaker. He engaged in fierce debates in the session in the Dual House, but was finally ejected. He was again returned by the electors of Orangeburg county, but his seat was denied him again. He was a third time elected in 1878, and still he was denied his seat. He then formed a law partnership with Honorable R. B. Elliott, ex-Speaker of the House of Representatives of South Carolina and late attorney general of the State, and with T. McCants Stewart, Esq., now practicing in New York City. In 1880 he was appointed special Inspector of Customs under said R. B. Elliott; special agent of the Treasury Department, Washington, District of Columbia, by Secretary Sherman, and assigned headquarters at Charleston, South Carolina. In 1882 he was called to the deanship and professorship of law, by the trustees of Allen University, in the city of Columbia, South Carolina, said institution being founded by the Right Rev. William Fisher Dickerson, D.D., now deceased. From said law school have been graduated seven colored youths in two classes. These young men were, subsequent to their examination in the law school by him, examined also by the Supreme Court of the State and secured praise from members of the court and the press of the State. Most of these are now in active practice.

Professor Straker himself has been giving strict attention to his profession for about ten years, winning many important suits. As a criminal lawyer he is astute, learned, persuasive and shrewd. He has a high conception of the duties and obligations of a lawyer.

He has appeared in several important law cases, notably in the case of murder by one James Coleman. The plea of insanity having been set up, he won the case. The report of this case can be found in the records of the Supreme Court, under the head of appeals from the Fifth Circuit, the State being respondent against James Coleman, defendant, appellant, R. G. Bonham, solicitor, and D. A. Straker for the defendant. He also had two important cases against Bethel A. M. E. church in Columbia, South Carolina, one of them against property, and one by reason of the trustees locking the door against the appointed minister. In both of these cases he was associated with white lawyers of prominence and won the cases. This case is recorded in the Court of Common Pleas in the October term of the Fifth Judicial Circuit, Hon. C. B. Presley, presiding judge; J. W. Morris *et al.*, plaintiffs *vs.* S. B. Wallace, *et al.*, defendants.

Mr. Straker has played a prominent part in many educational conventions, notably the one held at Louisville in 1883. He has done much literary work. He delivered the address at the opening of the colored department of the New Orleans Exposition. He has written several articles for the *A. M. E. Review,* which has attracted considerable attention and shows his scholastic learning, and his deep interest in the promotion of those things of vital interest to the race. We give here the names of these articles:

1. "Are we more influenced by opinion than fact?"—April, 1885, number of the *A. M. E. Review.*
2. "Does color unfit a man to fill positions that involve master minds or trained hands?" "The advantage of beginning trades schools in our colleges." —In the July number *A. M. E. Review*, 1886.
3. "The Congo Valley, its redemption."—in January number, 1886.

He has also written and delivered many lectures mainly on the subject of "Universal Industrial Education;" "Capital and Labor, and the True Relationship of Colored Citizens to all Labor Organizations;" "Marriage and Divorce;" "Shams in Life;" "The Necessity for a Broader and Higher Education in the South;" "Do or Do Not, or Useful Hints;" "Ireland and the Irish Question."

He delivered a eulogy on the life, character and public services of Robert Brown Elliott, which showed a high appreciation for his former law partner.

In 1885 Mr. Straker visited Detroit, Michigan, and was courteously received by the bench and the bar of the city. He spoke on the occasion of the memorial exercises of Lawyer Romeyn, deceased, in the courthouse, and was highly complimented. Subsequently Judge Jennison, circuit judge, and Judge J. L. Chapman of the Superior Court, united with others in inviting him to deliver a lecture under their auspices. This lecture was delivered in Merril Hall, in the city of Detroit; subject, "The New South." It was very highly commended by the press of both parties in the State, and it has been delivered in Boston since, under the auspices of the William Lloyd Garrison Club, in Charles Street A. M. E. church. The meeting was presided over by the late Judge G. L. Ruffin. It has also been delivered in New York, in Bleeker Hall. He also delivered an oration before the North Carolina Fair Association, in 1883. In addition to his political career mentioned above, he was nominated for Lieutenant-Governor of South Carolina by the Republican State convention, held in 1884. He wrote a letter accepting and discussing the needs of the party. The ticket was subsequently abandoned and not put before the people by a cowardly State executive committee. Professor Straker was one of the three colored men who stood at the bedside of Charles Sumner when he died, the other two being George T. Downing and James Wormley. Mr. Straker is now a member of the A. M. E. church, though he claims to hold no special denominational views. In addition to the LL.B., the title which he received on graduation from the Law Department, he has received LL.D. from the trustees of Selma University, when it was presided over by the Rev. E. M. Brawley, D.D.

Mr. Straker has great faith in the future of the colored man, but would desire to see him taught in the practical life-sustaining industries, rather than in the fanciful ideas of an education which please and entertain while they are unable to furnish a loaf of bread. In his article, "Does Color Unfit a Man?" he says:

Are we not to-day presented with the conditions in our social relationship which show that, despite the few colored persons who are capable of performing skilled workmanship in the industrial arts, these are yet denied the privilege in many places in the North as well as in the South? When we shall have taught our youth telegraphy, printing, engineering, carpentry, navigation and ship building, are we assured that they will receive employment in like manner as the white citizens? If not, what shall we do? I venture the opinion that the work is not only with the colored man, but with the American white citizen, North and South. The American white citizen's mind, in its belief of the Negro and his rights, needs conversion as well as conviction. It is ours by diligence, industry, intellectual development, economy and moral rectitude to do the work of convincing our opponents of our capacity. What shall we do to convince the oppressor that we have rights as men and as citizens of a common country?

Attempt the end and never stand to doubt,
Nothing's so hard but search will find it out.

The end of the discrimination and distinction among the races in America must come sooner or later, or the Nation will fall into decay. It must be remembered that freedom, liberty, justice and right flourished and decayed with the rise and fall of both the Grecian and Roman empires; such is inevitable. Let America beware. Professor Straker is in the prime of life, and his future, if judged by the past, will be even more successful, and his fame more extended as an orator, and his good name largely increased by his many acts of beneficence.

CHAPTER CXII

Rev. John Hudson Riddick
Preacher—Councilman—Deputy Marshal

Was born near Sunbury, Gates county, North Carolina, on the first day of April, 1848, where he lived until 1857, when he moved to Norfolk, Virginia. He was a slave and owned by Rev. Isaac Hunter of Virginia.

During the war he was in both armies as body servant. He was first with his young master in the Rebel army and afterwards with the hospital steward of the Seventh New York Independent battery, until 1864, when he served in the custom-house of Norfolk, Virginia, under Major J. H. Hudson, special collector appointed by President Lincoln. Major Hudson was removed by President Andrew Johnson, and Mr. Riddick removed to northeast Pennsylvania, where he was converted and began the study of theology under Dr. Samuel G. Ortor. He afterward spent four years in Boston, Massachusetts, where he worked days for support and studied theology and medicine at night, with a view of going into missionary work in some foreign country. He returned to Virginia in 1869 and practiced medicine for a short time, but soon gave it up to enter upon the active duties of a gospel minister, which he did July 4, 1869. He served as a missionary under Bishop A. W. Waymen, by whom he was ordained deacon in 1871, and in 1872 he was elected to the city council of Norfolk and also appointed United States deputy marshal in that city at the Grant and Greeley election. He has been school teacher among the freedmen in the South and served in the following Methodist Conferences as a minister of the gospel: Virginia A. M. E., Washington, Newark and Delaware M. E., and has had charge of some of the most prominent churches at the following places: Staunton, Virginia; Baltimore, Maryland, and Philadelphia, where he is now stationed. At the Zoar M. E. church he was ordained elder by Bishop E. R. Ames.

Mr. Riddick has always been noted for his loyalty to his race and courage for the right and honesty of purpose. When a number of our people were murdered at the Danville riot, he was the first to lift his voice among all colored men in the State in a strong address against the murderers at Staunton, Virginia, and their sympathizers. Five thousand copies were published and distributed by request of the people.

J. C. PRICE

CHAPTER CXIII

Rev. J. C. Price, A. B.
President of Livingstone College—Great Temperance Orator

The subject of our sketch is without doubt one of the most popular colored men in the United States. Largely endowed by nature with rare talent and more than ordinary ability, by industry and perseverance he has gained for himself a national reputation and has been the means of doing inestimable good for his race.

Joseph C. Price was born in Elizabeth City, North Carolina, February 10, 1854. Notwithstanding his father was a slave, his mother was a free woman, and according to the regulations of the "peculiar institution," the child followed the fortunes of the mother. When nine years old he went with his mother to New Berne, North Carolina, where he has spent the largest part of his life. He was nearly twelve years old when his mother, though unlettered herself, determined—since at this time the surrender of the Southern armies made it possible for Negro children to study books—to do her part through toil and selfdenial to procure for the boy the rudiments of knowledge. It was at the above stated age when he began and mastered the alphabet, and soon he learned to read fluently and to spell well. Subsequently he attended the St. Cyprian Episcopal school, one under the control of the Boston Society, known as the Lowell Normal School of New Berne. In 1871 he began the life of a pedagogue, and was successful as a teacher in the public school of Wilson, North Carolina, which he held four years; then entered Shaw University, Raleigh, North Carolina, in 1873, remaining five months. Here he experienced faith in Christ. Returning to New Berne he connected himself with the A. M. E. Zion church, and feeling that he was called to the gospel ministry was granted license to preach in less time than two years. Desiring to better qualify himself to discharge ministerial duties, he entered Lincoln University in Pennsylvania. His previous preparation enabled him to enter the Freshman class. His genial disposition, modesty and retiring manners soon made him a favorite in college. His powers of speech and eloquence in delivery gained for him the sobriquet of "Lion of the Lyceum." In the oratorical contest for the Freshman prizes he took the first medal, and also gained the first in the Junior contest for prize orations. In 1879 he graduated with the valedictory. During his senior year in the Classical Department he took up the studies of the Junior Theological year, thereby gaining a year. From this department he graduated in 1881. Before his graduation, however, he was ordained an elder and went as a delegate to the General Conference held at Montgomery, Alabama, in 1880. It was at this Conference that Mr. Price's ability as a ready debater, his sound scholarship and matchless eloquence were first brought to the notice of the general church, and made his name favorably considered as a worthy representative of the church to the Ecumenical Conference in London, to which he was accordingly delegated. The meeting was held September, 1881. He distinguished himself in this Council, and made one of the happiest efforts of his life in perhaps the shortest speech he ever made.

Remaining in England and on the Continent one year in the interest of the Zion Wesley Institute, he succeeded in collecting nearly ten thousand dollars, with which the trustees purchased the beautiful grounds and buildings now known as Livingstone College, in Salisbury, North Carolina. As president of the school, Mr. Price has guided with an unerring hand an able corps of eight teachers and nearly two hundred students. In the early part of 1881, previous to the trip to the Old World, he lectured in nearly every important town in North Carolina, in the interest of Prohibition, and proved to be one of the most convincing orators of the campaign. As a platform speaker Mr. Price has few superiors. Rev. Dr. Cuyler of New York says: "J. C. Price of North Carolina is a fair match for Douglass in culture and eloquence." He has a style peculiarly his own—not much of the dash and show, but his first sentences pleasingly captivate his audience, and his "wit and wisdom," with a combination of rhetoric and logic, poured forth in such masterly strains of eloquence, chains his hearers as if influenced by magic or under some peculiar spell.

The New York Evangelist of January, 1887, says of Mr. Price:

On the evening of January 19 he addressed a crowded assembly in Lafayette Avenue church, and for an hour held their closest attention to a well-reasoned address, full of argument, and red-hot with earnest emotion. . . . Mr. Price's rich, resonant voice is a fortune to any public speaker, and his flow of admirable language is strong and rapid as a mill-race. On the following evening a reception was tendered him in the parlors of the Broadway Tabernacle, when Dr. William M. Taylor was one of the speakers. The rooms were crowded by prominent ministers, laymen and ladies. President Price's speech had a Websterian dignity and power in it. . . . which astonished his audience. If he could be spared from the higher work of the pulpit and the college he would be an admirable representative of our colored fellow countrymen in the Senate Chamber.

As a preacher he is no less acceptable. He has occupied and satisfactorily filled the pulpits of some of the most influential churches in the country, from Massachusetts to California, and in England, Scotland and Ireland. He was the first colored preacher to occupy the pulpit of Henry Ward Beecher.

He was delegated by the Committee of Zion church as a representative to the Centenary Conference which met in Baltimore in 1884, and responded to the opening address by Bishop Andrews of the M. E. church. He was also elected chairman of the board of commissioners for Zion church on "Organic Union" between the A. M. E. and A. M. E. Zion, which met in Washington, District of Columbia, in 1875, to map out a basis for the union of these two bodies.

Mr. Price headed the delegation from North Carolina, which conveyed the congratulations of the colored citizens of the State to his excellency, President Garfield, shortly after his inauguration. In 1885 he visited California and succeeding in raising eight thousand eight hundred dollars, which, with the five thousand dollars pledged by the Hon. William Dodge, he erected Dodge and Hopkins' halls on the grounds of Livingstone College. He is still young—just thirty-three years old—strong, healthy and vigorous; weighs about two hundred and sixty-six pounds, is genial in disposition, plain and unassuming. He is a success as president; a good disciplinarian, yet not severe. The students regard him in the light of a loving brother or father. It has been prophesied that Livingstone College is destined to be the "Harvard" for the colored people in the South.

PINCKNEY BENTON STEWART PINCHBACK

CHAPTER CXIV

*Hon. Pinckney Benton Stewart Pinchback
Governor—Lieutenant Governor—United States Senator—
Lawyer—His Daring "Railroad Race"—Eminent Politician—
Wealthy Gentleman*

―――――•◆•―――――

May 10, 1837, the subject of this sketch was born. His father, Major William Pinchback (white) was a planter in Holmes county, Mississippi. His mother, Eliza Stewart, was of mixed blood and known as a mulatto, though she claimed to have Indian blood in her veins. She died at the ripe age of seventy, in 1884. In girlhood she was a slave, the property of Major Pinchback, who became enamored of her and for whom she bore ten children, all of whom are dead except Pinckney. He was the eighth child. In 1835, 1836, or near that time, Major Pinchback went to Philadelphia with his slave wife and manumitted her. Though freed, she did not abandon the father of her children but returned with him to his home, which was then in Virginia. It was while in transit from Virginia to Mississippi, in 1837, that the governor was born. He was ostensibly free. In 1846, in company with his brother Napoleon, who was seven years his senior, Pinckney was sent by his father to Cincinnati to attend Gilmore's High School. In 1848 they returned home. This same year his father died and his mother with five children, Napoleon, Mary, Pinckney, Adeline and the baby girl, was sent to Cincinnati by the administrator of his father's estate. They were hastily sent away, he acknowledged, to prevent any attempt to enslave them by the white heirs to the estate, who ruthlessly robbed them of their right inheritance of a goodly fortune. Napoleon, the mainstay of the family, lost his mind in Cincinnati. This misfortune compelled Pinckney at the tender age of only twelve years to start out into the world on his own responsibility. He secured work as a cabin boy at eight dollars a month on a canal boat on the Miami canal, running from Cincinnati to Toledo, Ohio. In this respect he resembles the lamented Garfield. Several years were spent in canal boating on the Miami, and also the Fort Wayne and Toledo canals. In the meantime he made a considerable stay at Terre Haute, Indiana. From 1854 to 1861 he followed steamboating on the Red, Missouri and the Mississippi rivers and had reached the highest position, that of a steward, attainable by a colored man, when the war interrupted that business. May 10, 1862, in Yazoo City, Mississippi, he abandoned the steamer "Alonzo Childs," of which he was steward, ran the Confederate blockade and arrived in New Orleans two days after. May 16, 1882, he had a serious difficulty with his brother-in-law, John Keppard, who was wounded in the encounter. The civil authorities arrested him but he gave bail. While awaiting trial, the military authorities rearrested, speedily tried and convicted him for assault with attempt to murder and sentenced him to two years in the workhouse. This was an unfortunate point in his career, but he has bravely outlived the high temper characteristic of the Southern youth. May 25, 1862, he was committed and August 18, 1862, released to enlist in the First Louisiana Volunteer infantry. A few days after enlistment he was detailed to assist in recruiting the Second Louisiana infantry. While engaged in this service, Major General Benjamin F. Butler, commanding the department of the Gulf, issued his celebrated order No. 62, calling upon free men of color of Louisiana to take up arms in the defense of the Union.

This order at once opened a more congenial and prolific field, and he at once made application for and was assigned to duty August 27, 1862. He opened an office for recruiting colored soldiers, on the corner of Bienville and Vilere streets, New Orleans, and by September 6, 1862, had a company ready for muster. But it was not mustered into service until October 6, 1862, owing to some dissatisfaction with the arrangement of the companies in the first regiment. October 12, 1862, the second regiment Louisiana Native Guards, with Captain Pinchback in command of Company A, was mustered into the service of the United States. His career in the army was short, but stormy and eventful from his entry into the service until his retirement. He strove manfully and heroically to maintain the dignity of his own position and the rights and privileges of the men under his command. For this Mr. Pinchback is especially noted, and though so fair that he could readily pass for a white man, he is known to stand up for his race. The Federal soldiery, rank and file, in the main were as hostile as the bitterest rebel. In his efforts to maintain the manhood and equality of rights of the colored soldiery, Captain Pinchback was often placed in great peril. His struggles with the street car companies of the city of New Orleans are ever memorable. His bravery gave such courage to Louisiana Negroes that to-day they are the most fearless body of politicians in this country, and knowing how to assert their rights in securing a part of the patronage that comes from adherence to political parties' fortunes, do not tamely submit to any and everything that may be thrust upon them. In those days it was not an uncommon sight to see squares of cars blockaded on account of his insistance upon his right to ride upon a car not designated for his people by having a star painted upon it. This was manhood and pluck. His boldness always excited admiration, and many have wondered that he did not lose his life; but a brave man is respected even by his enemies.

Early in his army career he had a difficulty with his colonel on account of unjust treatment of his men. The task of fighting the army prejudice was too heavy, however, and after all his brother officers had resigned, despairing of accomplishing any good result, he resigned on September 3, 1863. Bitter and disappointing as his experience had been in the army, he disliked to give up the work. After resting a few weeks he obtained an interview with General N. P. Banks, and impressed him so favorably that the general issued a special authorization to him to recruit a company of colored cavalry. In a very short time the company was raised and tendered the government, but the energetic originator of the command was refused his commission as captain on the grounds of his being a colored man. The action of General Banks in refusing to commission Captain Pinchback was based upon the fact that no authority existed then for the employment of colored persons in any other capacity than that of privates, citizens and non-commissioned officers. This great injustice induced Captain Pinchback to abandon any further effort in Louisiana to serve his country in the army. In 1865, accompanied by Captain H. C. Carter, he went to Washington with a hope of obtaining from President Abraham Lincoln authority to raise a regiment of colored men in Ohio and Indiana, but the end of the war and the assassination of Mr. Lincoln, which occurred while he was in that city, rendered his trip useless. After a while he returned South, and in the latter part of 1865, at Montgomery, Selma and Mobile, made speeches to assemblies of the colored people, denunciating the unjust treatment they were receiving at the hands of the lawless and vicious in that State. Soon after the enactment by Congress of the reconstruction acts, he returned to New Orleans. On April 9, 1867, he made his first move in the political field, upon which he afterward won such enduring honors by organizing the Fourth Ward Republican Club. From that time until now he has filled a large place and many important positions. The organization last referred to elected him a member of the Republican State committee, of which body he has been a member almost continuously up till the present day. The first civil appointment for which he held a warrant was Inspector of Customs, made by the Hon. William P. Kellogg, May 22, 1867. Mr. Kellogg was at that time collector of the port of New Orleans, but the position was declined. At the election held September 27 and 28, 1867, on the question of a convention "for the purpose of establishing a constitution and civil government for the State of Louisiana, loyal to the Union," he was elected a delegate, and the record attests that he was an influential member of that body. He introduced in it and succeeded in securing the adoption by the convention of the thirteenth article of the Constitution, which guarantees civil rights to all the people of the State. April 17 and 18, 1868, at the election held to ratify the Constitution, and for the election of officers thereunder, he was elected a State Senator from the Second Senatorial district composed of the Fourth, Fifth and Sixth wards of the city of New Orleans. He made a strong, valuable Senator, and was the author of several important legislative measures now on the statute books of the State, notably, an act to enforce the thirteenth article of the Constitution. The Republican State convention of 1868 elected him a delegate at large to the Republican National convention held at Chicago, May 20, 1868.

He was also a delegate to the Soldiers' and Sailors' convention which met at the same time and place. April 19, 1869, he was appointed by President Grant, and confirmed by the United States Senate, register of the land office at New Orleans, Louisiana, but preferring to remain in the State Senate he declined the office. In November, 1869, he established a commission and cotton factorage business under the name and style of Pinchback & Antoine. This was a very important movement and if his attention had not been attracted from it by political work there is no doubt that he would have established a business which would have been worth hundreds of thousands of dollars to-day. December 25, 1870, he started the publication of the *New Orleans Louisianian*, published semi-weekly for two or three years, and afterwards weekly. At first it was owned by a stock company in which Mr. Pinchback had a controlling number of shares. In a short time he bought all the stock and ran the paper for about eleven years with credit to himself and advantage to the race, whose cause he always championed manfully. In the same year he endeavored to establish the Mississippi River Packet company. He secured an act of incorporation by the State Legislature in which an appropriation of twenty-five thousand dollars was made to aid the organization, but the money could not be obtained owing to the State debt exceeding the constitutional limits.

March 18, 1871, he was appointed by the State Board of Education School Director of the city of New Orleans, and served as such until March, 1877. December 6, 1871, he was elected president pro tem. of the State Senate, and lieutenant-governor to fill the vacancy caused by the death of Hon. Oscar J. Dunn. This position made him ex-officio president of the Board of Metropolitan Police, practically the head of the police force in the city of New Orleans. August 25, 1872, he was nominated by a large and enthusiastic Republican State convention for Governor of the State of Louisiana, with a complete State ticket. The "Federal officials" in the State had placed another State ticket in the field, headed by William P. Kellogg. The Democrats also had a ticket in the field, and the election of the latter seemed imminent unless a compromise could be effected between the Republicans. Mr. Pinchback, though undoubtedly the choice of the majority of the Republicans of the State, fearing that the triangular contest might result in a Democratic victory, accepted a compromise with the Kellogg ticket, which resulted in one Republican ticket composed of four nominees of the custom-house faction and three nominees of the Pinchback ticket. This ticket was headed by Hon. William Pitt Kellogg for Governor, and Mr. Pinchback was placed upon it for Congress from the State-at-large. It was victorious at the election, November, 1872. In September of 1872 he ran the great railroad race with Governor Warmouth, being lieutenant-governor and acting governor in the absence of the governor from the State. His object was to reach the capital and sign two acts of the Legislature which had been passed at the session of 1871 and 1872, and which deprived the governor of the control and redistribution of election officers of the State. It was a desperate undertaking and the largest stake ever run for before. It involved the control of the State and possibly the National government. December 6, 1872, the Legislature that was elected in November (half of the Senate and all of the House) was convened in extraordinary session. Its organization was a question of momentous importance. Both Democrats and Republicans claimed a majority of members in the Senate. The returning board had given certificates of election to a sufficient number of Republicans to constitute a quorum in both houses, but many of the seats were claimed by Democrats. The Republicans, constituting a majority of the Senate holding over, and who were in sympathy with Governor Warmouth, who had gone over to the Democrats, met in caucus the day before with Lieutenant-governor Pinchback presiding, and decided that in organizing the Senate the next day the President should only swear in the Senators whose seats were not contested. To remove any possible doubt of the President adhering to the decision caucus, the governor of the State called at his house late at night on the fifth and made him a tempting offer to carry out its decision. Mr. Pinchback told Governor Warmouth that he would sleep on the matter and call at the St. Charles hotel the next morning with the answer. Before daylight he repaired to the Senate chamber and remained there until he had organized the Senate by swearing in, *in solido*, every members whose election was certified to by the returning board. This action required more than ordinary courage and saved the Senate to the Republicans and perpetuated the Republican rule four years longer than it would have existed in Louisiana had Mr. Pinchback proceeded in any other course.

Three days after the organization of the Legislature, he became acting Governor by the impeachment of Governor Warmouth, and was actually Governor until January 13, 1873, when the term expired and the Kellogg government was inaugurated. The brief period he occupied the gubernatorial chair was the stormiest ever witnessed in the history of any State in the Union; but the Governor was equal to the emergency and displayed administrative capacity of a high order. January 15, 1873, he was elected by the Legislature United States Senator for the term of six years from March 4, 1873. This election gave him the extraordinary distinction of being the member-elect of both houses of Congress. In accordance with law his credentials for the House were sent to the clerk of said House, and in due time his credentials for the Senate were laid before that body by the sitting Senator from Louisiana. The Senate met in extra session, March 4, 1873, and its first duty was the second inaugural of General U. S. Grant. Leading Republican Senators advised the Senators-elect from Alabama and Louisiana whose seats were contested, to refrain from presenting themselves to be sworn in until the inaugural ceremonies were over, as it might prejudice their case to precipitate the contest at such an important junction. Consequently neither the Senator from Alabama nor the Senator from Louisiana presented themselves to be sworn in. Two days later Mr. Spencer from Alabama presented himself, and objection was made to his taking the oath. The question was debated at considerable length, but he was seated March 7, 1873. It required only two days to settle his case. He was white. It was two years later before Mr. Pinchback could get his case brought before the Senate. Friday, March 5, 1875, Mr. Oliver P. Morton, the gallant son of Indiana, introduced two resolutions, the first to recognize the Kellogg government, the second in these words: "Resolved, that P. B. S. Pinchback be admitted as a Senator from the State of Louisiana to the term of six years, beginning March 8, 1873." March 13, 1875, Edmunds, the "iceberg" of Vermont, moved to amend by inserting the word "not" before "admitted." The amendment and resolution was not disposed of until March 8, 1876, when the amendment was adopted by thirty-two yeas and twenty-nine nays. The record shows that eleven Republican Senators opposed his admission to his seat in the Senate, a seat to which he was legally and justly entitled. This unjust and most extraordinary action of the Senate was a wrong to the State of Louisiana, which was deprived of her just representation in that body for over three years; an outrage upon the loyal Republicans of Louisiana, who stood by their party through storm and carnage without a parallel in political history; an injury to the rejected Senator which time cannot heal. Four months later, July 5, 1876, the Senate passed a resolution allowing Mr. P. B. S. Pinchback and Francis W. Sykes, out of the contingent fund of the Senate, an amount equal to the pay and mileage of the Senator for the term for which they were respectively contestants up to the period of the termination of their respective contests by the Senate. This gave Mr. Pinchback $16,666. It was the foundation for the competency which he now enjoys, but he says with great feeling, even now, that he would rather have died a pauper than to have been denied the right to represent his people in the Senate of the Nation.

The following interesting article appeared in the *New York Commercial Advertiser*, as written by their Washington correspondent during the vote in the Senate. It is worthy to be preserved.

Pinchback's case was brought up yesterday, but its discussion was interrupted by the obsequies of Hooper. To-day, on motion of Senator Morton, the Senate have agreed to go at "Pinch," *pro* and *con*, and sit without intermission until they have made him a skylark in the air or a turtle in the mud. The contest will be fierce, but briefer than the civil rights fight in the House. The Senators lack the fire and youthful vigor of the lower body. Their old bones won't stand the strain of cramped-up desks and sofas, and spasmodic snoozes in the cloak room. McCreery, Senator from Kentucky, declares, privately, in that pastoral phraseology proverbially peculiar to blue grass Democrats, that he "will give that nigger some sleepless nights before he gets his seat." McCreery, though an able man, is probably the laziest man in the Senate, and about the fiftieth roll-call, or the fourth hour of Maryland Hamilton's speech, would probably, with Kentucky impulsiveness, give his own seat to Downing sooner than stand any more of it. Pinchback glides around the Chamber like a bronze Mephistopheles, smiling sardonically, and buzzing his supporters.

He is a trained politician, and if he does not prove to be a statesman, and has "counted noses" until he avers himself certain of eleven majority on a full vote—and he is too good a "whip" not to have all his friends on hand when it comes to a vote. In fact the mad abstinacy and devilish cruelties of the White League in the South recently, have made Pinchback's support a party measure, and unless indisputable evidences of fraud are brought against him by better authority than New Orleans pimps, thugs and traitors, the North will assuredly accept the loyal Negro in preference to the possibility of a white rebel. Aside from the political view of the question, Pinchback's presence in the United States Senate is not open to the smallest objection, except the old Bourbon war-whoops of color. He is about thirty-seven years of age, not darker than an Arab, less so than the Kanaka. Like Lord Tomnoddy, "his hair is straight but his whiskers curl." His features are regular, just perceptibly African, his eyes intensely black and brilliant, with a keen, restless glance. His most repellent point is a sardonic smile which, hovering continuously over his lips, gives him an evil look, undeniably handsome as the man is. It seems as though the scorn which must rage within him, at sight of the dirty ignorant men from the South who affect to look down upon him on account of his color, finds play imperceptibly about his lips.

His manner is reserved but polite, exhibiting a modesty rarely seen in a successful politician—a model indeed of good breeding to those Texas and Louisiana Yahoos who shout "nigger, nigger, nigger," in default of common sense or logic. Mr. Pinchback is the best dressed Southern man we have had in Congress from the South since the days when gentlemen were Democrats; and were he to walk into Delmonico's *café* he would be mistaken by even so experienced an eye as Admiral Wenberg's for a wealthy creole island planter educated abroad. It is a curious fact that while Welcker and other leading *restaurateurs* here have been avowing their purpose to become Alpine monks, and go to making "Benedictine" sooner than cater to colored people, they have been permitted as guests at Delmonico's in Democratic New York, for years. The only requirements in that most fastidious of restaurants, kept by gentlemen for gentlemen, are propriety of demeanor, decency in personal attire, and a reasonable alacrity in the settlement of accounts. Yet any ardent son of the South who accused the Delmonico's of being "nigger" worshipers would find few believers.

The seat in the House of Representatives was given to his contestant in the last hours of its session, after the most extraordinary conduct on the part of the Republicans of that body. No fair-minded person can read the proceedings of the two Houses of Congress and the credentials of Mr. Pinchback without concluding that a conspiracy existed to keep him out of both Houses. April 24, 1873, he was appointed Commissioner to the Vienna Exposition from the State of Louisiana, by Governor Kellogg, and sailed from Boston for that city about one month later. He was abroad three months and visited England, France, Italy, Austria and Switzerland. January 13, 1875, the Legislature of the State of Louisiana, to cure the objections raised against the Legislature of 1873, re-elected him United States Senator as in case of vacancy. The Republican State convention, held in 1876, elected him a delegate from the State-at-large to the Republican National convention, held in Cincinnati, June 14, 1876. When it assembled he was still knocking at the door of the Senate. To demonstrate to that body that he was the unquestionable choice of the majority of the Republicans of Louisiana, his friends at the assembling of the Republican State convention placed him in nomination for temporary chairman. Kellogg, Packard & Co., backed by the combined patronage of the Federal and State governments, opposed him. But on a *viva voce* vote he was elected after one of the most exciting contests ever witnessed in preliminary organization. On the permanent organization he was elected president of the convention, and the following resolution was adopted by it with great unanimity and enthusiasm.

Resolved, that we re-affirm our unalterable allegiance to, and confidence in the Honorable P. B. S. Pinchback, United States Senator-elect, from Louisiana, and while we regret that he has not been seated we have every faith that the Senate of the United States will, in due time, honor his credentials as one of the representatives of the sovereign State of Louisiana. But in case it should be deemed necessary for the General Assembly of Louisiana at its next session to ratify his credentials as United States Senator, we hereby nominate and re-indorse the Honorable P. B. S. Pinchback as our unanimous choice and only candidate for United States Senator from this State, and direct all the Republicans, members of the General Assembly, to put in force and to execute this declaration of the deliberate wisdom of the Republican party in convention assembled.

In nearly every parish of the State the resolution was indorsed by the Republican voters. It will be seen therefore that every Republican member of the Legislature, and indeed the entire Republican party of the State, were solemnly pledged to his re-election to the United States Senate. In the face of this fact it was plainly manifest on the assembling of the Legislature that Kellogg, Packard and their party did not intend to allow Mr. Pinchback to be elected if they could prevent it. Kellogg was governor and Packard governor-elect, and of course their power was great, and both were experts in the corrupt uses of patronage and money. They worked upon the members day and night, to disregard their instructions from the convention and the people to vote for Mr. Pinchback, and support Kellogg instead; and long before the day for balloting arrived it was generally known they had succeeded in capturing a sufficient number to accomplish their purpose. It is said to have cost them over nineteen thousand dollars, besides all the promises of offices they could make to control the Senate.

During the time this nefarious business was going on, Mr. Pinchback was advised of its progress by true and trusted friends; and he knew better than any one could tell him that, notwithstanding he had ever been loyal and true to his race and party and had rendered both services of the highest importance, he was doomed to be slaughtered in the house of his friends. In such an hour, what must have been the bitterness of his feelings? Who can measure the depths of his wound? Betrayed and deserted by the party and men who would have been driven from power in the State four years before if it had not been for his integrity and bravery. Is it any wonder that he took advantage of a fortuitous circumstance—the co-operation of the four Republican Senators who stood by him and went over to the Nicholls government? To a man of his temperament, who has never failed to strike when struck, it was the most natural thing in the world. Kellogg and Packard were warned of the danger, but they laughed at the idea of a Negro daring to revolt against the Republican party, as they termed it. They learned better when it was too late. In 1877 he was appointed a member of the State Board of Education by Governor Nicholls. February 8, 1879, he was appointed by Commissioner Green B. Raum, internal revenue agent. March 5, 1879, he was elected delegate from Madison Parish to the Constitutional convention of the State of Louisiana, and he resigned his internal revenue agency to take his seat in that body. In 1880 he was elected by the Republican State convention from the State-at-large, to the Republican National convention, held at Chicago, June 3 to 8, 1880. February 24, 1882, he was appointed surveyor of customs for the port of New Orleans by President Chester A. Arthur, and confirmed unanimously by the Senate without reference to the committee. In 1883 he was appointed member of the Board of Trustees of the Southern University by Governor S. T. McEnry. This institution, the finest and best in the State for the education of colored people, was made under the constitutional requirement by the State convention of 1879, through an article introduced in that body by Mr. Pinchback. In 1884 he was elected a delegate from the State-at-large to the Republican National convention held at Chicago from June 1 to June 6, 1884, inclusive. 1885 he was re-appointed by Governor McEnry, member of the Board of Trustees of the Southern University. July 2, 1885, he resigned the surveyor's office.

He was married in 1860, and his wife has borne him six children, four boys and two girls. Two, a boy and a girl, died. The remaining give promise of being useful members of society. The oldest boy, Pinckney Napoleon, after obtaining a fair English education entered the College of Pharmacy, Philadelphia, Pennsylvania, and graduated from said institution March 18, 1887. His father is very proud of his success, as very large numbers of that institution fail to pass the examination.

Governor Pinchback has been a prudent, economical financier, and has accumulated a very handsome fortune. His income is about ten thousand dollars a year from stocks and bonds. In the fall of 1885 Governor Pinchback entered the Law School of the State University, and owing to his familiarity with the general principles of law and especially the laws of Louisiana, he passed a successful examination at the close of the first term of the class, and was admitted to the bar, April 10, 1886.

This short sketch is hardly a fair outline of his present mode of living. He has wedged his name so firmly in the affairs of the "Pelican State," that its history cannot be written without his romantic life making several leading chapters. He has held more offices than any other colored man in the United States. Let me close with the hope that he will yet be United States Senator from Louisiana.

I here give an account of "The Great Railroad Race," as told by Mr. Pinchback himself:

It was in the summer of 1872. The clouds in the political horizon were dark and lowering. I had been taking part in the campaign in the State of Maine in the interest of Mr. James G. Blaine, who was a candidate for re-election to Congress. The Republicans all over the country desired his re-election in order that he might be re-elected speaker of the House, a position he had filled with marked ability, and prominent speakers from all parts of the Union readily went to Maine and gave their services to aid his return to Congress.

General U. S. Grant had been nominated by the Republican National convention at Philadelphia, June 5, for re-election to the Presidency, and Honorable Henry Wilson of Massachusetts, for vice-president.

This ticket was opposed by Mr. Horace Greeley of New York, for President, and Mr. B. Gratz Brown of Missouri, for vice-president. These gentlemen had been placed in the field by the Liberal Republican convention at Cincinnati, May 10, and indorsed by the Democratic National convention at Baltimore, July 9. The shrewdest political calculators in the Republican party were in doubt as to the result of the contest. Some of the ablest, purest and best men in the Republican party were numbered among its membership—notably Honorable Charles Sumner—and were supporting Mr. Greeley. The situation was far from satisfactory and assuring when I arrived in New York City and entered the rooms of the Republican Committee at the Fifth Avenue Hotel, and found Honorable Henry Wilson, and Honorable William E. Chandler, secretary of the Republican National committee, in earnest consultation relative to the outlook for the party. Both gentlemen greeted me cordially and invited me to be seated. I took a seat and listened with deep interest, not unmixed with alarm, as they expressed their doubts and fears as to the result of the National election.

Turning to me Mr. Chandler asked, "What are the prospects for our carrying Louisiana?" I answered none in the world, and explained to him the character of our registration and election laws. These laws, wholesome and salutary in the hands of honest men, and designed to secure free and fair elections, could be turned into terrible engines of oppression and fraud if administered by dishonest and unscrupulous men. This fact had become so apparent by their abuse in several local contests, that the demand for their repeal among all classes was so loud and deep that the Legislature, at the close of the session of 1871 and 1872, passed new registration and election laws. These laws having passed within the last five days of the session, the governor under a provision of the constitution of the State could sign them if he so elected at any time before the assembling of the next session of the general assembly.

Through the machinations of the "Federal Officials" in Louisiana, Governor Warmouth had been driven practically out of the Republican party, and he espoused the cause of Mr. Greeley. It was not likely that he would sign these bills and deprive himself of the great power they conferred upon him. At the conclusion of my explanation Mr. Chandler said: "Governor Warmouth is here in New York, at this very hotel, and it would be a grand thing if you would go home and sign those bills." Mr. Wilson concurred in the opinion and asked me if I dared to undertake the perilous performance. I replied, "If the success of the Republican party is at stake, I dare do anything that will save it." Both gentlemen declared it was their opinion that the electoral vote of Louisiana might be necessary to secure the success of the National ticket. I was lieutenant-governor, and, in the absence of the governor from the State, my position made me acting governor, and I could legally exercise all the power of the governor. If I could reach the State and sign those laws while the governor was outside its borders, they would be valid laws, and the entire machinery of registration and elections would be changed, and the chances of the Republicans carrying the State doubly multiplied. The control of the government of Louisiana, and possibly that of the Federal government was involved in the issue.

I resolved to start at once for Louisiana. The time was propitious. It was Saturday. If I left that night I would have twenty-four hours the best of the start in any contingency, as there were no trains leaving New York for the South, Sunday morning.

Unfortunately for the success of my undertaking, I had an engagement with Governor Warmouth to join him at a bird supper that very evening. It was my failure to appear at that supper which aroused his suspicion that something was up. I suspected as much, and endeavored to allay any suspicion my absence from the supper might create by leaving my trunk (my name was on the cover) in the hall of the hotel where he could see it. I also left my secretary, Mr. Henry Corbin, at the hotel with instructions to see Governor Warmouth early Sunday morning and offer him some reasonable excuse for my disappointing him. Mr. Chandler assured me he would keep me posted on Governor Warmouth's movements, and should he start home, would notify me by telegram, as he would know just where, to reach me by the schedule time of the railroad.

With everything arranged as satisfactorily as it could be done in such a short time, at nine o'clock that Saturday night I left New York via the

Pennsylvania Railroad. Next morning I arrived at Pittsburgh and was much annoyed to find that a delay of six hours was before me on account of no trains running on Sunday. At Cincinnati the train missed connection and I lost six hours more, but as I heard nothing from Mr. Chandler I thought I was all right.

In order to attract as little attention as possible, on leaving Cincinnati I took a seat in the smoking car. About eleven o'clock at night when the train arrived at Canton, Mississippi, I was aroused from a deep sleep by a rude shake, and opening my eyes I saw a man with a lantern in his arm, who, I think, was the conductor of the train, standing in front of me. As soon as he saw I was awake he asked, "Are you Governor Pinchback?" And without waiting for an answer said, "There is a telegram in the telegraph office for you."

Remembering Mr. Chandler's promise to wire me should Governor Warmouth become apprised of my movements, I rushed out of the car into the telegraph office to get what I had been expecting—a dispatch from Mr. Chandler. Before I had finished the inquiry for the dispatch I knew by the *manner* of the man in the office that something was wrong. He seemed to be in no hurry to hand me the pretended dispatch, and his face had a sinister expression upon it. On reaching the door in my attempt to return to the train I found it closed and locked on the outside. This confirmed the suspicion already aroused, and I made a desperate attempt to regain the train by bolting through the window. It was too late. I saw only the rear end of the train disappearing around the curve in the road fully a mile distant.

I had lost the largest stake ever ran for in this or any other country— a State and possibly the National Government. It is needless for me to state that I was the victim of a conspiracy. Governor Warmouth had learned of my departure from New York by the Pennsylvania road, through one of its agents, who saw me board the train in Jersey City and divined the cause. He instantly put the telegraph wires to work and started after me on the next train (Sunday night) and arrived at Humbolt on time, only twelve hours behind me. At that point he took a "special" and came rattling along at the rate of forty, fifty, and even sixty miles an hour where the road would stand it. Under any circumstances it would have been a close finish between us at New Orleans, but he and his allies could not afford to take any chances. The money and intelligence, the telegraph and railroads of the entire section of country through which I had to pass after leaving the Ohio river, were on his side. These things considered, it will be seen at a glance that it was next to impossible for me to reach New Orleans in advance of the governor."

I shall never forget the triumphant expression upon his face as I saw him standing upon the front platform of his special car as it came lumbering into the town of Canton that morning, and the haughty, taunting manner in which he exclaimed, "Hello, old fellow, what are you doing here?" I replied with the best grace I could command, "I am on my way home what are you doing here?" He said, "I am after you." "Well, you have caught me," was my reply, "and if you have no objections I will go on with you the balance of the journey."

He consented, but the railroad people required me to sign a contract exempting the road from all responsibility, as the "special" was traveling outside of schedule and lawful time. The news of my capture had been telegraphed all along the line of the road, and great crowds were assembled at each station as the train rolled by. And oh! how they did yell. I dare say the howlers were hoarse for days afterwards.

In closing this account of my railroad race, I must state in all seriousness, that it was a desperate and most hazardous adventure. The moment my purpose was suspected and I crossed Mason and Dixon's line, my life was not worth a pin's fee. I have been told by one of the men who helped entrap me at Canton, that every railroad entering New Orleans from the North was picketed for miles from the State line and the orders were to prevent my entrance into the State in advance of the governor if it required the sacrifice of my life.

CHAPTER CXV

Alexander Petion
President of Hayti—Skilful Engineer—Education
at the Military School of France

Alexander Petion, already alluded to in our *Glance at the History of St. Domingo*, was one of the first presidents of the Republic of Hayti. He was a Mulatto, but of a very dark complexion, and received his education in the military school of France. Being a man of cultivated understanding and attractive manners, and moreover, well instructed in the art of war, he served in the French, and afterwards in the Haytian armies with success and reputation. He was in high esteem as a skilful engineer, in which capacity he rendered the most essential service to Toussaint and Desalines. Petion was a man of fine talents, acute feelings and honorable intentions, but not fully adapted for the station he was called upon to fill. The Haytians, just liberated from absolute slavery, without education, habits of thought, moral energy and perfect rectitude of character so necessary in a government perfectly republican, stood in need of a ruler less kind, gentle and humane than Petion. In consequence of this, his people relaxed in their attention to agriculture, his finances became disorganized and his country impoverished. The unfortunate Petion, disheartened at a state of things which he saw no means of remedying, sunk into a state of despondency which ended, it is said, in voluntary death. Petion was, perhaps, less beloved in his lifetime than his memory has been venerated since his death. High mass is said every year for his departed soul, with great pomp and circumstance, according to the rites of the Romish church; and the people appear to look back upon him with more than a common feeling of kindness and regard, as the father and friend of his country. His body, encased in a coffin, lies in an open cenotaph fronting the government house, and by the side of it that of his only daughter; both coffins are occasionally decorated with simple native offerings. "There is no doubt," says Candler, "that Petion was a patriot, and that he sincerely desired the welfare of Hayti. He was greatly averse to the shedding of blood, and had often to check the impetuosity and vengeance of the general who commanded under him. Some accounts represent him to have starved himself to death, through vexation at the slow progress of his people towards civilization; this may have been the case, as he was of a sanguine temperament, and was exceedingly thwarted in some of his plans for the public good; but a physician of Port-au-Prince assured me that such was not really the fact, and that he died of inanition from natural causes."

An interesting and pleasing trait in the character of Petion is exhibited in an anecdote related by the author above quoted, with which I shall conclude this brief sketch. "In 1815 a visit of a religious character was paid to some parts of Hayti by Stephen Grellet, a native of France, and a minister of the Society of Friends. Petion, who was at that time President of the Island, received him with great cordiality, and permitted him to preach to his soldiers from the steps of the palace, himself and his staff attending as auditors."

This sketch is taken from a work entitled *A Tribute for the Negro*, published in 1848, by Armistead.

CHAPTER CXVI

Timothy Thomas Fortune, Esq.
Editor—Author—Pamphleteer—Agitator

———◆·◆———

In Marion Township, Jackson county, Florida, lived Emanuel and Sarah Jane Fortune, in the galling bonds of slavery. To them was born a boy who was to reflect credit on their name and play an important part in the newspaper world. His father is a progressive man of great activity in local politics. His mother was a woman of much perseverance, and indelibly stamped her likeness on her eminent son, whose first birthday was October 6, 1856. The aggressive politics of the boy's father finally compelled him to move from West Florida to Jacksonville, in 1866. By this time young Fortune, through his father's influence, secured a position as page in the Florida Senate, where no doubt he early became acquainted with the tricks of politicians, which to-day shows itself in the scathing articles he writes denouncing the Democratic party and exposing the hypocrisy of the Republicans. He early began his career as a printer by taking the position as a printer's "devil" on the *Daily Union*, where he distinguished himself by attention to business. A change of owners threw him out of work, and being unable to get employment on any other paper, he entered the Staunton Institute and stood in the front ranks as a student. Soon he secured a position as office-boy in the city post office, but this was only the stepping-stone to the position of stamping and paper clerk. Inheriting his father's high spirit, he refused to take an insult even from his superior officer, and consequently he resigned on account of a disagreement with the postmaster, and again took up his "stick" at the printer's case. In 1875 he was appointed a mail route agent through the Hon. William J. Purman, Congressman from the second district of Florida. Here he met many difficulties, but he mastered them all. In 1876 he resigned with the commendations of his superior officers, and accepted a position as special inspector of customs for the first district of Delaware, to which he was appointed by Secretary B. H. Bristow, at the instance of his Congressional friend Purman. This he resigned to enter Howard University, where he remained two years preparing care-

TIMOTHY THOMAS FORTUNE

fully for his life work. The writer dates his acquaintance with Mr. Fortune from this time, and predicted for him then a brilliant and successful career, which he is magnificently fulfilling; indeed he was a hard student of history, and talked of men and things with the head of an older man. Many pleasant days did we spend together discussing our future as well as that of the race. He was an ever welcome visitor at our house, and our acquaintance has ever been pleasant and profitable to each other. His success is, therefore, not unexpected. One year he was compositor on the *New York Witness*, but his journalistic career proper dates from the year 1882, when in conjunction with George Parker and William Walter Samson, he began the publication of the *New York Globe*, which was published until November, 1884, at which time a disagreement in the partnership was caused by the introduction of other parties into the firm. This led to the suspension of the *Globe*, but did not discourage its editor; he had commenced his work with a well defined plan in view, and he was determined to continue it. He felt the need of a journal to contend for the just rights of his race, and thought that much good might be done through such an agency. He maintained that for a paper to be a power for good among his people, it must be fearless in its tone, that its editor should not fail to speak his just convictions, that he should hold himself aloof from parties and maintain his position untrammeled by parties and party bosses. In view of this he re-entered upon his journalistic work by the publication of the *New York Freeman,* November 22, 1884, a week after the suspension of the *Globe*. He is sole proprietor and editor of the journal, and continues to combat error and arraign opposers of the Negro race before the bar of public opinion.

Mr. Fortune is unusually fortunate in the selection of a very brilliant corps of correspondents from various sections of the country. He is regarded as a very brilliant editorial writer, perhaps more pointed and less polished than others, but certainly not less effective. His philippics and lampoons are sometimes of the severest sort, and strike deeper than the skin. Mr. Fortune being a practical printer, has perhaps had a better opportunity to make a newspaper a success than any of those whom we know, and no doubt he has succeeded in making a journal for the race from this fact. He has a large constituency who read his paper with interest, and perhaps no paper in the country is more widely quoted by both white and colored editors. Mr. Fortune has published one book entitled *Black and White,* and a pamphlet entitled *The Negro in Politics.* They have of course elicited much criticism, for he antagonized the positions of many who in the hurry to disagree with him failed to do justice to the work. It would pay any man to read it thoroughly. This versatile editor does not get his inspiration from others, nor does he write fulsome eulogies on knaves and tricksters who use the race for their personal aggrandizement, and no matter how much we may differ from him he should be given credit for honesty and integrity. To prove my assertion let me give a few quotations from his *Black and White*. In speaking of the blacks he says on the first page:

There is no question to-day in American politics more unsettled than the Negro question; nor has there been a time since the adoption of the Federal constitution when this question has not in one shape or another been a disturbing element, a deep rooted cancer upon the body of our society, frequently occupying public attention to the exclusion of all other questions. It appears to possess as no other question the element of perennial vitality.

Speaking of the whites he said:

It is my purpose in writing this book to show that the American government has always construed the people of African parentage to be aliens; not only when the Constitution was tortured by narrow-minded men to shield the cruel murderous slaveholder in the possession of his human property, but even now, when the panoply of citizenship is presumably all sufficient to insure to the late slave the enjoyment of full manhood rights as a sovereign citizen.

His opinion of higher education is worthy of being quoted and few seem to have been overlooked by critics in their criticisms. It is certainly worthy of note, for Mr. Fortune has a right conception of a true education. "I do not inveigh" said he "against higher education, I simply maintain that the sort of education the colored people of the South stand most in need of, is elementary and industrial. They should be instructed for the work to be done. Many a colored farmer boy or mechanic has been spoiled to make a foppish gambler or a loafer; a swaggering pedagogue or a crank. Men may be spoiled by education, even as they are spoiled by illiteracy. Education is the preparation of the mind for future work, hence men should be educated with special reference to the work." Farther on he says:

I do not hesitate to say that if the vast sums of money already expended, and now being spent in the equipment and maintenance of colleges and universities, for the so-called higher education for colored youth, had been expended in the establishment and maintenance of primary schools and schools of applied science, the race would be profited vastly more than it has, both mentally and materially, while the results would have operated far more advantageously to the State and satisfactorily to the munificent benefactors.

On the subject of the colored people's position in the South, he echoes my own opinion when he says:

I may stand alone in the opinion that the best interests of the race, and the best interests of the country will be conserved by building up a bond of union between the white people and the Negroes of the South, advocating the doctrine that the interests of the white and the interests of the blacks are one and the same. That the legislation which affects the one will affect the other; that the good which comes to the one should come to the other, and that as one people the evils which blight the hopes of the one blight the hopes of the other. I say, I may stand alone among colored men in the belief that harmony of sentiment between the blacks and the whites of the country, in so far forth as it tends to honest division and healthy opposition, is natural and necessary, but I speak that which is a conviction as strong as the stalwart idea of diversity between the black and the white which has so crystallized the opinion of the race. It is not safe in the republican form of government that clannishness should exist either by compulsory or voluntary reason. It is not good for the government and it is not good for the individual.

On the opinion as to whether the colored people will stay in the South or whether they will go away in large bodies to other sections of the country, he has this to say:

The colored man is in the South to stay there. He will not leave it voluntarily and he cannot be driven out. He had no voice in being carried into the South, but he will have a very loud voice in any attempt to put him out. The expatriation of five million to six million people to an alien country needs only to be suggested to create mirth and ridicule. The white men of the South had better make up their minds that the blacks will remain in the South just as long as corn will tassel and cotton will bloom into whiteness.

Further along he says:

That the black population cannot and will not be dispensed with, because it is so deeply rooted in the South that it is a part of it—the most valuable part—and the time will come when it will hold to its title to the land, by right of purchase, for a laborer is worthy of his hire, and is now free to invest that labor as it pleases him best.

It does seem to me that Mr. Fortune is very sensible upon these questions, and the difference of opinion has largely been in the politics of his book. Mr. Fortune has the promise of many years of active work for the race. He has often occupied the lecture platform and received the enthusiastic applause of large audiences. In religion he was tutored in the Methodist doctrine. Although he does not take an active part in religious worship, he believes that religion is the cornerstone on which we should rear our structure. His life has been one of stern reality, struggling for a foothold; he often meets difficulty and obstacles which would cause men of less fortitude to succumb; but still he battles on, believing that the race is not always to the swift, but to him who holds out to the end. Owing to his political stand he will find much to encounter, but we earnestly believe that in the long run he will have no cause to regret his course. He is still laboring with the hope that the intelligence and culture we are gaining will eventually cause the race to reach that point where it will be able to maintain itself. He sees in the future grand and glorious achievements for the scholars and thinkers of this people. He is an inveterate foe to the half-hearted who dare not stand up and take ostracism and blows for the race. He is a business man who means business, and is determined to make his paper succeed, if such a thing is possible. There are many competing for public favor, but the *Freeman* holds its own, and no matter how much newspaper disagreement there may be over first place in the newspaper world—the variety, vivacity and even impetuosity of Mr. Fortune's editorials will always give him commanding position among the lights of the fraternity.

CHAPTER CXVII

Troy Porter, Esq.
Plumber, Gas and Steam Fitter—Superintendent of Waterworks
and Town Clerk

———•◆•———

I give here a short sketch of one who has over-leaped the boundary of prejudice and compelled recognition for what he is worth. His intelligence, industry, attention to business, urbanity and general habits have attracted the attention of those of the plumbing business in his race. His competency is acknowledged. No favoritism is shown in the electing to the positions which he has held and still holds. Living among white people very largely, his career gives additional evidence of the fact that merit will win. Chances are waiting for colored men, and all they need to do is to improve them. All cannot teach nor can they preach; they must therefore go into the trades where success awaits them. If they will but pursue the methods which bring it about, success is sure.

As a son of "ole Kaintuck" he deserves credit, and Illinois, his adopted State, has honored him indeed, and may the great good done in this respect be returned to her ten fold. But let me come more particularly to the facts.

Mr. Porter first saw the light of day in the State of Kentucky, Fayette county, April 15, 1855. He spent the first ten years of his life in Kentucky and Ohio. In 1865 he removed to Illinois, and it was at this place that he began to realize the responsibilities resting upon man. He had a great desire to make his life a prosperous one, and so thought he would seek a field of labor where he might benefit himself financially and help to build up the good men of the race. At the age of eleven years, therefore, he commenced learning the trade of plumbing, gas and steam fitting, and in ten years after, November 21, 1876, he went into business for himself and at present he is still conducting it with great success. Having a great desire to become united with some honorable and benevolent organization, he joined the Grand United Order of Odd Fellows in 1877, and four years after had the honor of being elected district secretary of District Lodge No. 9, G. U. O. O. F. of Illinois, which office he held until

August, 1886. In 1883 he was appointed superintendent of the Paris Water Works by a Republican council. In 1885 was elected town clerk of Paris township by the Republican party, which latter office he is now holding, having been re-elected. He was the first colored man that was ever elected to an office in Edgar county, Illinois. He has given satisfaction in all places he has filled, and has reflected credit on the race as he so earnestly desired.

He is worth about five thousand dollars in property, all made by the labor of his own hands.

CHAPTER CXVIII

"Blind Tom" (*Thomas Green Bethune*)
The Musical Wonder of the Age—The Negro Pianist—
A Remarkable Musician

The musical world for centuries has known such great composers as Mendelssohn, Haydn, Mozart and Beethoven, but far surpassing these may be named the poor little Negro boy, Thomas Bethune, born May 25, 1849, in Columbus, Georgia. Thomas was born blind and as the beauties of nature could only be revealed to him through the sense of hearing, and retained by the power of memory and imitation, these faculties were cultivated almost to perfection.

Young Bethune is the embodiment of music, and in this art his powers know no limits. When he was four years old he had, for the first time, access to a piano; and although previously he had produced with his voice the harmonious and discordant strains that met his ears, yet his joy cannot be imagined when he could perform on the instrument the thoughts of his youthful brain. When he had exhausted his store of lessons he began to compose for himself, playing what he said "the wind said," or the trees or birds. His "Rain Storm," composed during a thunder-storm when Tom was but five years, is so perfect that the hearer instinctively looks for the lightning flash.

No one would ever undertake to teach him music, for, said one musician, "I can't teach him anything; he knows more of music than we know or can know. We can learn all that great genius can reduce to rule and put in tangible form; he knows more than that. I do not even know what it is; but I feel it is something beyond my comprehension. All that can be done for him will be to let him hear fine playing; he will work it all out by himself after awhile." The above quotation was clipped from *Music and Some Highly Musical People*, by J. M. Trotter.

Thomas Bethune received the cognomen "Blind Tom" because when he was a babe he seemed totally blind but as he grew, nature was his teacher and enabled him in time to enjoy to a limited extent the blessing

THOMAS GREEN BETHUNE

of sight. When a young child, often might he be seen with head upturned, gazing intently upon the sun, and he would thrust his fingers with such force into his eyes that they would bleed. This he continued until he became able to distinguish any very bright object and as his sight grows clearer with years it is hoped he will yet be relieved from the bondage of darkness. Says Mr. Trotter:

Considering that in early life he learned nothing, and later but little from sight, that he is possessed by an overmastering passion which so pervades his whole nature as to leave little room for interest in anything else, and the gratification of which has been indulged to the largest extent, it is not surprising that to the outside world he should exhibit but few manifestations of intellect as applicable to any of the ordinary affairs of life, or that those who see him only under its influence should conclude that he is idiotic.

The elegance, taste and power of his performance, his wonderful power of imitation, his extraordinary memory not only of names, dates and events, his strict adherence to what he believes to be right, his uniform politeness, and his nice sense of propriety, afford to those who know him well ample refutation of this opinion.

As to the musical genius of this man the testimony of eminent musicians both in America and Europe bears witness. Among his classical selections may be mentioned Andante by Mendelssohn and Sonata "Pathetique" by Beethoven.

His marches include, "Delta Kappa Epsilon," Pease; "Grand March de Concert," Wallace; "General Ripley's March," "Amazon March," "Masonic Grand March."

His imitations must not be omitted which are so perfect as often to deceive the hearer. They are imitations of the "Music Box," "Dutch Woman and Hand Organ," "Harp," "Scotch Bagpipes," "Scotch Fiddler," "Church Organ," "Guitar," "Banjo," "Douglass' Speech," "Uncle Charlie," "The Cascade," "Rain Storm," and "Battle of Manassas." The two latter, his own composition, represent his descriptive music.

It would take volumes to say all that might be said of this man. His fame is world-wide. In all the large cities of America and Europe has he entertained thousands. Doubtless more persons have flocked to see and hear him than any other living wonder.

His mother has endeavored to secure some of the benefits derived from the results of his extraordinary genius and began a lawsuit which resulted in a total failure. Blind Tom is still alive and recently gave a very brilliant concert in Indiana. As he grows older he increases his list of music and performs with the vigor of youth.

Says Mr. Trotter:

No one lives, or, as far as we know, has ever lived that can at all be compared with him. Only the musical heroes of mythology remind us of him for he is

As sweet and musical
As bright Apollo's lute strung with his hair.

CHAPTER CXIX

Rev. Henry Adams
A Faithful Pastor—A good Man

Among the men who have impressed themselves most upon the people of Louisville, Kentucky, is Henry Adams, a man who in his lifetime was beloved by all who knew him. He was straightforward in all his dealings, prompt in business and faithful in the discharge of his ministerial duties. His name has become a household word with all the members of his flock, and is a constant reminder of his faithfulness. There can now be seen on a tablet in the Fifth Street Baptist church the name of Henry Adams and his period of services as pastor.

A very good sketch of this man's life can be found in the *History of Kentucky Baptists*, written by J. H. Spencer. He was a native of Franklin county, Georgia, and was born December 17, 1802. While quite young he gave very marked promise, and being early converted, about the age of eighteen, he was permitted to exercise his gifts as a preacher within the bounds of his church. In 1825 he was ordained to the full work of a minister. After preaching a few years in Georgia and South Carolina, he went to Kentucky and was settled as the pastor of the First Baptist church in Louisville in 1829. It is said that he was very proficient, not only in the English branches, but even in the dead languages. In 1842 this church, which was before a branch, was set apart with four hundred and seventy-five members as a separate organization.

During the first twenty years of his pastorate he immersed over thirteen hundred people. Out of this church many churches in Louisville have grown; in fact the direct influence of his labors has no doubt been the conversion even in his lifetime of over ten thousand souls. After freedom came, Adams was very zealous in educational work of the State. Through his instrumentality the General Association of Colored Baptists was organized August 3, 1869, in the first Baptist church in Lexington. He was elected moderator. At that time the association numbered fifty-five churches and twelve thousand six hundred and twenty members. To him is largely due the credit for establishing what is now known as the State

University. While others may have been instrumental in suggesting the beginning and promoting its progress, yet no one can doubt that Henry Adams contributed very largely to the ultimate success of the work. He did not live to see this object fully accomplished. He died on the third of November, 1872.

At one of the exercises of the students in this same institution, the following tribute was paid to Henry Adams by Rev. C. H. Parrish, A.B., and it seemed a fitting one since he was identified with the early efforts to organize the school, that this same student, being the first to graduate from the College Department of the institution, should pay this tribute. Said he:

Verily he was a lover of his people; deeply impressed with the worth of souls; an earnest and humble man. A man of faith and prayer, and above all, a man of pure life. No ministerial defection ever stained his garment: a true leader of his people in practice as well as in doctrine, his own bright life illuminated the path in which he would have the people to walk.

CHAPTER CXX

James C. Farley, Esq.
Photographer, and Prominent Citizen of Richmond, Virginia

———◆•◆———

James Conway Farley came into the world in Prince Edward county, Virginia, August 10, 1854. His parents were slaves, and he never began life until he went to Richmond with his mother in 1861. His mother was a store-room keeper at the Columbia Hotel, Richmond, Virginia. His early occupation, then, was assisting in making candles, he tying the strings and getting the molds ready for the hot grease. He went at night to an old cook at that place, who taught him from an old linen book. Later, the opportunity was given of attending a public school for three years. His mother was a poor widow, and poverty forced young Farley to strike out for himself in pursuit of education and sustenance in every way. Accordingly he was apprenticed to learn the baker's trade, but he became thoroughly disgusted with this business on account of the work entailed. He quit work at this business and entered the photographic business, being employed in the chemical department.

May, 1875, Mr. Farley having become thoroughly acquainted with the business, became an operator for G. W. Davis. In 1875 there were four white men in the gallery, Mr. Farley being the only colored operator, and they all objected to his being employed. On Saturday night they stated that they would not work if Mr. Farley was employed any longer. This miserable, contemptible color-phobia that was raised by the men who were not equal in talent was disgusting.

However, when the matter came to the contest, Mr. Davis, the proprietor, met them on a Sunday morning and they said that Mr. Farley had assumed a disagreeable disposition toward them in an indirect manner. They were injured, so they said, by Mr. Farley putting on a disagreeable air, acting with a disagreeable disposition toward them. Poor little fellows; they could not defend themselves, and the only way they could get even with one poor colored man was by asking the "boss" to discharge him. They never explained what it was that he had done that was so disagreeable, and it was left to be judged that it was simply his color that

JAMES C. FARLEY

assumed to them a disagreeable disposition. The following Monday morning the proprietor handed Mr. Farley the document containing their statement, with their names signed. Mr. Farley at once told him to keep the white men and let him go, as he did not desire to do any harm, and felt rather gratified at the manner in which Mr. Davis had acted and was disposed to release him of any embarrassment. He was very desirous of not disturbing the business relations of Mr. Davis; the four men going out of the gallery would naturally lead to complications, at least until others could be found whose competency would be beyond doubt. But Mr. Davis informed him that he had already discharged all four of them. His orders were "pull off your coat and go to work and fill their places." He ever remembers Mr. Davis' treatment in this matter, and was thankful that he had an opportunity to show what he could do, and eventually developed into a first class operator.

Mr. Davis and Mr. Farley then went to work and filled the other men's places. The business continued to improve, and Mr. Davis established a cheaper priced gallery and employed several white men to take the position Mr. Farley formerly held (that of operator), paying them enormous salaries, while he went to the business of "retouching."

One of the white men remained a week; another only a few days. Mr. Farley was again in 1879, put in the position of operator of the gallery, and since which time he has proved a complete success, and has as far as known, made more photographs in one day than any other gallery in the Southern States.

He married Miss Rebecca P. Robinson of Amelia county, December 10, 1876. The fruits of the union are five children.

Mr. Farley's work was exhibited at the Colored Industrial Fair held in Richmond, Virginia, in 1884, and received the premium. It was also placed on exhibit at the World's Exposition held at New Orleans in 1885, and received complimentary notices from the photographic journals of the country. His photographic works are greatly admired and rank with the finest in the country. Mr. Farley is polite, affable and strictly honest in all his dealings. He professed religion and joined the First Baptist church, May 18, 1878. Later he was made deacon. In the ten thousand dollar improvement of the church, he was the only one put on the committee to represent the young element. At that time the church membership was five thousand.

HENRY McNEAL TURNER

CHAPTER CXXI

Rev. Henry McNeal Turner, D. D., LL. D.
Bishop of the A. M. E. Church—Philosopher, Politician
and Orator—Eminent Lecturer—Author—Intense Race Man—
United States Chaplain

One of the most influential men in the United States is Bishop H. M. Turner, the subject of this sketch. His life is full of the most important events; he is a man of great nerve, strong character and deep convictions. Justice can hardly be done to such a man in the small space we have for these sketches; only an outline of course can be given.

He was born near Newberry Court-House, South Carolina, February 1, 1833. He is the oldest child of Howard and Sarah Turner. His father's ancestry was but little known to him, as *his* mother was a German and white; but his mother's ancestry is very familiar. She was the youngest daughter of David and Hannah Greer. His grandfather, David Greer, was the son of an African king. He was captured in colonial times while a boy on the coast of Africa, and brought to this country and sold as a slave; but owing to some British statute or law which forbade the enslavement of royal blood, he was set at liberty and declared free. He was regarded in South Carolina up to the time of his death, which occurred about the year 1819, as one of the greatest and best men of his day.

The grandmother of the bishop was not so notable for goodness and female modesty, but was regarded as a woman of fearful physical resources. She was tall and proportionately built and had a fearful temper, and was an athlete which white and black men dreaded meeting in the corporal combat. No one in the neighborhood of her dwelling ever dared to interfere with her children, animals, fences or anything that she owned, at the risk of being chased or fearfully handled, if she got within reach of them. She lived to be ninety years old. His mother is noted as a woman of good common sense, and strong mental powers, when called into requisition. She lives in Washington city with her grandson, Dr. John P. Turner.

The bishop, when young, was at one time called a "hard case." He grew up in South Carolina, amid the severity incident to colored boys in those days. Though free born, owing to the absence of a father's care he was deprived of many advantages which he would have enjoyed had he been blessed with such protection. He was bound or hired out to those who imposed upon him hard labor most of the time from a boy until he reached manhood; but at no time did he ever find an easy place. The hard labor which he performed was partly in the cotton fields of South Carolina under the meanest sort of cruel overseers, and part of the time in a blacksmith shop. He never appreciated the occupation, nor did he pursue it any longer than the four years he was serving as an apprentice. The most that can be said in this connection, with his labors in the cotton field of South Carolina and the blacksmith shop, that he generally whipped all the overseers that tried to whip him, knowing that he was free-born and could never be legally reduced to slavery. He was determined that no white man should scar his back with a lash, and from the time he was thirteen years old till he reached manhood he resented every attempt to whip him, though grown men and women were whipped around him in many instances from the rising of the sun until the going down of the same.

While but a small boy he had a very singular dream, which seriously impressed him, and became the promoter of his efforts to secure an education. He dreamed that he was standing on a small mountain, and millions of people of all sorts and sizes were standing around its base and looking to him for instruction. When he awoke, so vividly was this impressed upon his mind that he at once decided to do what he could to impart knowledge to his people.

Though but a boy he began to realize the needs of an education, for he could see no way to be a public instructor without knowing how to read and write. This he considered the height of an education; but he was puzzled how to acquire this knowledge. There were no schools for colored children and it was against the law to teach a Negro the alphabet. Only three colored men of his acquaintance could read a little in the Bible and hymn book, and they had either learned that little in Charleston, where schools for free people were tolerated in a measure, or before the law was enforced in that part of the State. He procured a spelling book, and an old white lady and a white boy with whom he played, taught him the alphabet and how to spell as far as two syllables; but one day the boy's father seeing him instructing Turner, told him that he had no right to teach a Negro, and that he was violating the law of the State is doing so, and if he undertook such a task any further he would receive severe punishment. This threat so frightened his boy teacher as to deprive him of the lessons thereafter. Many days did he weep over this, but he was compelled to submit to fate.

Soon he found an old colored man who did not know a letter but was a prodigy in sounds. The ambitious Turner would spell the words as they were syllabified, and the man could pronounce them accurately. Thus his unlettered instructor helped him to spell and pronounce words about half through the old Webster's spelling book. But another misfortune awaited him. This teacher was removed to another plantation and he was again without an instructor. He was doomed to weep more bitterly than at first.

Being in his thirteenth year, and able to understand preaching somewhat, he went to church the following Sabbath and heard a minister say, "Whatever anyone asks God for in faith would be granted." He resolved to try the virtue of asking God to help him read and write, and continued to fast and pray for the same regularly. His mother shortly afterwards, greatly to his surprise, secured the services of a white lady to give him lessons every Sabbath. But this paid assistant was soon intercepted by the indignant protests of a number of white neighbors, who threatened her with the vengeance of the law, if she continued teaching him. She naturally had to succumb to the inevitable, and he was left without a teacher again. But he continued to pray and study as best he could, believing that Providence would open another door to him in the near future. It was, however, three years before he succeeded again.

In the meantime said he:

I would study with all the intensity of my soul until overcome by sleep at night; then I would kneel down and pray, and ask the Lord to teach me what I was not able to understand myself, and as soon as I would fall asleep an angelic personage would appear with open book in hand and teach me how to pronounce every word that I failed in pronouncing while awake, and on each subsequent day the lessons given me in my dreams would be better understood than any other portions of the lessons. This angelic teacher, or dream teacher, at all events, carried me through the old Webster's spelling book and thus enabled me to read the Bible and hymn book.

I may note at this point, however, that this angelic teacher would never come to my assistance at night unless I would study the lessons with my greatest effort and kneel down and pray for God's assistance before going to sleep. So familiar did the features and general appearance of my angelic, or dream teacher become to me, that if I should meet it in the spirit world I would readily recognize it.

By the latter end of my fifteenth year I was providentially employed to wait around an office of a number of white lawyers at Abbeville court-house, where I filled the exalted station of fire making, room sweeping, boot blacking, etc. I soon won the favor of every lawyer in the office, especially the younger portion of them. My tenacious memory being such an object of curiosity, I soon attracted special attention. They thought it was marvelous that a common

Negro boy could carry any message, however many words it contained or figures it involved, and repeat them as accurately as if written upon paper. In many cases, too, these messages contained a multiplicity of the highest law terms. The sequel of this and much more night study was, those lawyers taught me, in defiance of State laws forbidding it, to read accurately, history, theology and even works on law. Also taught me arithmetic, geography, astronomy and anything I desired to know except English grammar, which I manifested no desire to study.

I shall always regard my contact with those lawyers, and the assistance given by the young lawyers of the office, as an answer to my prayer.

With the above stated advantages he continued to study at night, gathering and reading scores of books of the highest order until 1867, when he visited New Orleans and met Rev. W. R. Revels, M.D., under whom he transferred his membership from the M. E. church, South Carolina, to the A. M. E. church. He was afterwards admitted into the Missouri Conference in 1858, on motion of Dr. Revel, and was examined for admission into the ministry by Rev. Dr. John M. Brown, now bishop; John Turner, J. W. Early and B. L. Brooks, all of whom still live. Upon the adjournment of this conference, Bishop D. A. Payne, D.D., LL.D., transferred him to the Baltimore Conference and assigned him to the charge of a small mission. Here he was brought in contact with a number of much more cultured people than he had been accustomed to in South Carolina, and having been informed that a young gentleman, a member of his church, by the name of Mr. Watkins, now the Rev. George T. Watkins, D.D., had complimented his thought and oratory but had severely criticised his knowledge of grammar, he resolved at once to study English grammar and if possible ascertain what virtue there was in it. Procuring a competent teacher, he soon familiarized himself with the subject. He then studied Latin under Dr. Watkins, and for the next four years continued in the study of Latin, Greek, Hebrew, German, as well as theology, respectively, under Dr. Smith of the Presbyterian church, Dr. McCron of the Lutheran church, Dr. Dalrymple, professor of languages in the Maryland Institute; Professor D. M. Rowland, A.M., LL.D., president of Trinity College, and Rabbi Grinsburg, professor of Hebrew. His principle teacher, however, in the classics was Professor Rowland. These learned divines taught him how to read and translate all of these languages to an extent that was pronounced creditable, to say the very least. At all events he passed through most of the works included in the curriculum of Trinity College, though he did not give attention to mathematics at that time, a thing he sincerely regrets now; yet he has since given considerable study to the subject, as he could not measure the distances between the planets and other stellar orbs without a limited knowledge of trigonometry, and the study of this subject is a passion with him, as well as theology. He has been a hard student since boyhood to the present time. He read the Bible through several times before he reached manhood. His memory is wonderful, and when a young man he frequently committed fifty psalms to memory in one night before going to sleep, and then repeated them the next day between the plow handles for the entertainment of the other plowmen.

He joined the M. E. Church South in July, 1848, while but a boy, on six months probation; and he must be on probation yet, he says, as he has never been received into full membership. He was licensed to preach by Rev. Dr. Boyd of South Carolina, in 1853, at Abbeville court-house. He was admitted into the itinerant work of the A. M. E. church in St. Louis, 1858, and was ordained deacon by Bishop Payne in Georgetown, District of Columbia, in 1860; was ordained elder in Israel church in Washington, 1862, by the same bishop, and was ordained bishop in St. Louis, Missouri, by Bishops Payne and Shorter, May 20, 1880.

He has been honored with the title LL.D., by the Pennsylvania University in 1872, and the degree of D.D., by Wilberforce in 1873. He was appointed United States chaplain by President Lincoln to the First United States colored troops in the early part of 1863, and was the first commissioned colored chaplain ever appointed by a United States President. After passing through thirteen bloody battles and many skirmishes, he was mustered out with his regiment in the fall of 1865, but was recommissioned United States chaplain in the regular army by President Johnson within ten days after being mustered out, being detailed to work in Freedmen's Bureau and assigned to Georgia. After serving a short time as an officer of the bureau, and finding that the church needed his attention infinitely more than the general government, he sent in his resignation to the secretary of war and devoted his time and talents to the ministry. In that capacity he traveled, preached, lectured and organized churches and schools all over the State, and thus built up not only the largest conference in the A. M. E. church, but the largest colored conference upon the face of the globe, which has since been divided in three great annual conferences.

For several years with the appointment of the bishop of the A. M. E. Church, he was the general superintendent of church work in Georgia, and extended the same into Alabama and Tennessee. For several years more was a presiding elder, until he resigned that responsible duty and became pastor. We give an extract of his address at the time of his resignation:

And my labors have not stopped in the religious sphere, but it is well known to every one that I have done more work in the political field than any five men in the State, if you will take out Colonel Bryant. I first organized the Republican party in this State, and have worked for its maintenance and perpetuity as no other man in the State has. I have put more men in the fields, made more speeches, organized more union leagues, political associations, clubs, and have written more campaign documents, that received larger circulation, than any other man in the State. Why, one campaign document I wrote alone was so acceptable that it took four million copies to satisfy the public. And as you are well aware, these labors have not been performed amid sunshine and prosperity. I have been the constant target of Democratic abuse and venom, and white Republican jealousy. The newspapers have teemed with all kinds of slander, accusing me of every crime in the catalogue of villainy; I have even been arrested and tried on some of the wildest charges and most groundless accusations ever distilled from the laboratory of hell. Witnesses have been paid as high as four thousand dollars to swear me into the penitentiary; white preachers have sworn that I tried to get up insurrections, etc., a crime punishable with death; and all such deviltry has been resorted to for the purpose of breaking me down, and with it all they have not hurt a hair of my head, nor even bothered my brain longer than we were going through the farce of an adjudication. I never replied to their slanders nor sought revenge when it hung upon my option; nor did I even bandy words with the most inveterate and calumnious enemies I have; I invariably let them say their say and do their do; while they were studying against me, I was studying for the interest of the church, and working for the success of my party; and they would expose their own treachery and lies, and leave me to attend to my business as usual. So that up to this time my trials have been a succession of triumphs. I have enemies as is natural, but at this time their tongues are silent and their missiles are as chaff, while my friends can be counted by hundreds of thousands. And I can boast of being one of the fathers of the mammoth conference of the A. M. E. church, an honor I would not exchange for a royal diadem. Thus, having reached the goal of my ambition, I only ask now to be retired from weighty duties of the past, and given the humble and more circumscribed sphere of preacher in charge. I am perfectly willing if the bishop will consent, to let some of my sons in the gospel be my presiding elder, and I trust I shall be able to honor them as highly as they honor me, for I can say with pleasure, that with all the orders and even changes I have thought fit to make, I have yet to be resisted or questioned by a single preacher. And while I shall try to rest more regularly and comfortably in my retired relation, and enjoy life more pleasantly than I have for the last nine years, I shall, nevertheless, endeavor to be equally as useful to the church in the literary department; for I purpose to give my future days to the literary work of our grand and growing connection. Since I have been trying to preach the gospel I have had the inestimable pleasure of receiving into the church on probation, fourteen thousand three hundred and eighteen persons which I can account for, besides some three or four thousand I cannot give any definite account of. And I would guess, for I am not certain, that I have received during and since the war, about sixteen or seventeen thousand full members in A. M. E. church by change of church relation, making in all nearly forty thousand souls that I have in some manner been instrumental in bringing to religious liberty, and yet I am not quite thirty-nine years old. Hundreds of these persons have in all probability fainted by the way, and gone back to the world; but I am, on the other hand, happy to inform you that hundreds have since died in triumph and gone to heaven, while thousands are to-day pressing their way to a better land, scores among whom are preaching the gospel. I make no reference to these statistics to have you suppose that I am better than other men who have not been thus successful, for I am only a poor worthless creature, and may yet be cast away; I only mention these facts to express my profound gratitude to God for his abundant favors, which have been bestowed upon one so undeserving. If Bishops Payne and Wayman were here, I would take great pleasure in laying my gratitude at their feet for the support they gave me in the early establishment of this conference; but as they are not, I trust Bishop Brown will allow me to tender him my heartfelt thanks for the continued manifestations of respect shown me under his administration, he who has so ably presided over our conference for the last four years, and done so much to advance and elevate the members of this conference.

His request was granted.

When the Reconstruction Laws were enacted by Congress in 1867, he was appointed by the National Republican Executive Committee, Washington, District of Columbia, to superintend the organization of colored people in the State of Georgia. In this capacity he stumped the entire State of Georgia, delivered thousands of Republican speeches, and was recognized the champion orator of the State, speaking at times before thousands of people from three to five hours before taking his seat. He wrote a political document defining the status of the Republican and Democratic parties, to which reference has been made in the extract just given.

In the fall of 1867 he was elected member of the constitutional convention of the State, and served in the same. In 1868 he was elected a member of the Legislature and was re-elected in 1870, being among the colored members who were expelled from the Legislature of Georgia, solely upon the ground of color, and in making his defense he spoke from nine o'clock in the morning till about three o'clock in the afternoon. In 1869 he was appointed postmaster of Macon, Georgia, by President Grant, at a salary of four thousand dollars, but resigned in a few months on account of political persecutions. Afterwards he was appointed by President Grant coast inspector of customs and United States government detective, which position he filled for several years, and ultimately resigned to obey the demands of the church, and bore away with him the highest commendations. In 1876 he was elected by the general conference of the A. M. E. church, as general manager of the Publication Department, situated in Philadelphia, Pennsylvania, where nearly sixty thousand dollars passed through his hands as the head of this department. He directed, wrote and superintended all the papers and Sabbath school literature throughout the United States.

As an author he compiled a hymn book of the A. M. E. church, and wrote a catechism, in use by the same church, which has been published by hundreds of thousands; also a recognized standard work entitled *Methodist Polity*, defining the duties of the officers of conference and functionaries of the church, and which has been commended by the highest ecclesiastical jurists of the land; also questions and answers on Palestine or the Holy Land, and any number of printed lectures and orations. One of the finest orations which he has delivered was on the ratification of the Fifteenth Amendment and its incorporation into the United States Constitution, April 19, 1870.

Said he, among other good things:

This amendment is an ensign of our citizenship, the prompter of our patriotism, the bandage that is to blindfold justice while his sturdy hands hold the scales and weighs out impartial equity to all, regardless of popular favor or censure. It is the ascending ladder for the obscure and ignoble to rise to glory and renown; the well of living water, never to run dry; the glaring pillar of fire in the night of public commotion, and the mantling pillar of cloud by day to repel the scorching ray of wicked prejudice. Hereafter the machinery of our Government will be run by the consent of the governed, and its symmetrical operations will constitute an axiomatic weapon, for all the oppressed nations on earth to battle with for civil liberty. It is the National guaranty, as fair as the moon, clear as the sun, and terrible as an army with banners. It is the chariot of fire that is to roll us beyond the reach of our persecuting Ahabs and perfidious Jezebels. It is to be the angel in the fiery furnace warding off the burning flames. The golden debris from the high bluffs of this most preëminent country of all in the world, shall be washed by the currents of our sweet waters to the lowlands of tyrant ridden nations, to enrich their soil by spreading over them a free alluvium. The Fifteenth Amendment is the shining robe covering in immaculate grandeur the nude and exposed parts of our country, which hitherto made her fragile and vulnerable before enemies. It is the star-decked diadem covering her brow; the interjector of royal blood through every vein. It is the towering spire reaching uppermost of all natural virtues and will be like the pole to the needle, attracting men from every plain and every shore.

The Irishman, Frenchman, Chinaman, Japanese, the Hottentot, if he is here, can all return to their native lands and be to them what Wendell Phillips has been to his native land, "great reformers." All nations will, sooner or later, have missionaries from here, of their own blood and dialect, preaching manhood equality.

The sons of Africa, too, can unfettered, untrammeled and unhindered, go to the homes of our forefathers and preach a free, religious, civil and political gospel. I know some colored men chafe when they hear an expression about going to Africa. I am sorry I find no term in the vocabulary that will represent them milder than fools; for they are fools. The only reason why Africa is unpopular and ignored by some colored men is because of its unpopularity among the whites. It is the greatest country in natural resources under Heaven. But without reviewing its inexhaustible treasures, and how God is holding them in custody for the civilization of the Negro, I merely desire to remark that some of our leading men may blur and slur at Africa till their doomsday arrives. But God intends for us to carry and spread enlightenment and civilization over that land. They are ours and we are theirs. Religion, morality, economy, policy, utility, expediency, duty and every other consideration makes it our duty. We must, we shall, we will, we ought to do it.

Whatever distinction shall clothe the Negro through any future day, will be attributed to the workings of the Fifteenth Amendment, and he shall be the lily of the valley and as the rose of Sharon, in the high march of our National splendor. If ever angels congratulated saints, I fancy that Gabriel, the arch seraph, congratulated our heavenly trio, Columbus, Washington and Lincoln, on the day of its ratification, for the grand result of the Fifteenth Amendment and its concomitant blessings.

As an orator he is one of the most forcible and eloquent in the United States. His sentences weigh more than the ordinary language of most men. When speaking, he is very impressive, and carries an audience with him as easily as the wind sweeps the chaff before it. He has the power of taking hold of his audience and chaining their attention to the subject under consideration. He has been considered by many, one of the best if not the best orator of his class in the United States. Especially on great occasions has he been able to hurl such extraordinary language at his enemies as would soon annihilate them, and while enlisted in a cause which draws out his sympathies, he can be as gentle and pleasing as Demosthenes himself. He has given much attention to many of the sciences, and is never tired in investigating them, so familiar indeed is he with anatomy, physiology, phrenology, geology, astronomy, mental and natural philosophy, electricity, etc., that he can lecture upon them without special preparation. He has been honored in having his likeness printed with short sketches of his life in *Harper's Weekly, Frank Leslie's Weekly, Fowler's Phrenological Journal* and a large work entitled *New Physiology* and the *London Magazine* and other illustrated papers and pamphlets.

He was married to Miss Eliza Ann Peacher thirty years, the thirty-first of August, 1886, when he celebrated his pearl wedding anniversary in the presence of one thousand five hundred guests, having been married to the daughter of Joseph A. Peacher of Columbia, South Carolina, the wealthiest colored man in that city at that time, who afterwards went to the west coast of Africa, and did while serving out his term of mayor of Careysburg, to which he had been elected almost unanimously. The Bishop has four children living—Josephine Francis, the wife of P. W. Upshaw of Arkansas; John P. Turner, M. D., Washington, District of Columbia, who is also married; Daniel M. Turner, business manager of the *Southern Recorder and Lincolnia;* Victoria Turner, now a student of Berea College, Kentucky. These are all that are left of fourteen children.

In the life of Bishop Turner there is much to inspire any young man who is willing to labor hard to make something of himself; most assurdedly he can, if he will. The way has been opened by just such men as the Bishop, and those who don't profit by it have no one to blame but themselves.

CHAPTER CXXII

Rev. J. W. Stephenson, M. D.
Church-builder—Financier—Druggist—"His Methods"

———◆◆◆———

My personal acquaintance began with the distinguished Dr. J. W. Stephenson in 1874, when he was in charge of the church at Burlington, New Jersey. Here the winning manners of the doctor made every one his friend.

Shortly after his settlement at Trenton I visited him and assisted him in a meeting held in the opera house by playing the organ for his services. At this meeting I met for the first time Bishop T. M. D. Ward, who preached. I was a ministerial student at that time, and I remember with a great deal of merriment how friend Stephenson wanted me to fill the pulpit in the afternoon, but I stuck to the organ. He is a great, powerful, eloquent preacher, a man of magnetism, of great heart. He has published a book on *Church Financiering*, from which I take below his personal experience. It will show that he is a financier and church-builder, as I have entitled him. Before giving this, however, let me give an outline of his early life as written by his friend, Rev. W. D. Johnson, D.D., secretary of the Board of Education of the African Methodist Episcopal church, in *An Apology for African Methodism*, by Dr. B. T. Tanner.

Rev. J. W. Stephenson was born in Baltimore, Maryland, August 15, about 1836. His parents, John and Ann Stephenson, removed to Trinidad, West Indies, in 1840, taking John and five other small children. His father died in less than a year after landing on the island. His mother, becoming discontented, returned to the States, a widow with seven children, one having been born on the ocean. John was bound out to J. P. Stamly, a stove dealer in Baltimore, and sent to work on his farm near the city. His stay in this situation was very short. He was sold four different times on account of his high spirit. When eighteen years of age, he succeeded in purchasing his time with the earnings of extra labor. Having gained the precious boon, he determined to seek a more northern climate. He went to Philadelphia, and hired with a barber under the Girard House, where he remained one year. Afterward he engaged as porter in the drug store of Henry Kollock, corner of Ninth and Chestnut streets. Mr. William Kearney and his brother, clerks in the store, observing the extraordinary talent which Mr. Stephenson exhibited, commenced to instruct him in medicine. In one year he had made such progress in compounding that he was made a clerk in the store. Mr. Kollock desiring that he should become a physician for his people, sent him to Dr. Wilson, a colored physician practicing in the city, that he might receive the necessary instruction from an able doctor of his own race. It not being convenient for Dr. Wilson to take him at the time, by the influence of his friends, he was received by Professor Woodward, with whom he remained five years, engaged in his professional studies at the Philadelphia University of Medicine. While at the university he became alarmed about the salvation of his soul. After six months of deepest conviction, God delivered him out of his wretched condition. He joined the old Bethel A. M. E. church, Sixth street, where he was very active in the Sabbath school. Feeling the weight of souls heavy upon him, he was licensed to exhort in 1858, by Rev. W. D. W. Schureman. The next year he was licensed to preach by Rev. Joshua Woodlin. He became the adopted son of Bishop Campbell, from whom he drank in the very essence of the doctrine and laws of Methodism. He was soon taken into the itinerancy by Bishop Nazrey, and sent to the Westchester circuit, where he succeeded remarkably as pastor and physician. His next appointment was Freehold, New Jersey, where he was very popular in preaching and in the practice of medicine. He was one of the delegates from the general conference of 1864 to the general conference of the Zion A. M. E. church. In the same year he was ordained a deacon and sent to Oxford circuit. Lincoln University is at the head of this circuit. His church, of which many of the students were members and local preachers, being within a stone's throw of the buildings. He was a regular student in the university three years, and pursued a thorough ministerial education under the patronage of Bishop Simpson and other friends in the Methodist Episcopal church. Dr. Stephenson was one of the most prominent students in the institution, his practice of medicine being very large among them, as well as in the neighborhood. Besides these things, the doctor attended faithfully to the four points on his circuit. He is like the "iron man," Bishop Campbell, in strength and rapidity of motion. He is one of the greatest revivalists in the connection, and is likely to become the Spurgeon of the A. M. E. church, and is looked upon as being the greatest church-builder and financier of the connection, having planned and constructed the largest church among colored people in the United States, namely, the Metropolitan Church of Washington, District of Columbia. This church has a seating capacity of two thousand five hundred. He has three times in his life built two churches in the compass of eighteen months and paid for them; has been devoted to this work, and because of his extended experience in this branch of the Christian church of which he has shown himself to be so well adapted (as though especially fitted for the work by the Almighty), he has been requested and urged from time to time by bishops and ministers, both of our own and other churches, to write a book upon the subject, and give his brother pastors his successful plans of church financiering; he has at last undertaken the work, and in the book he gives his own thoughts, with as many others as he has gathered, to his brother pastors, officers and members of the church.

Speaking of personal efforts, he said:

My first experience in the art of raising money for church purposes dates back to my first appointment as pastor of a charge, in the year 1859, in Westchester, Pennsylvania, which congregation I found laboring under great embarrassment for two reasons, viz: the dilapidated state of the church building, and the still poorer location of the same. Although being very young in years, I felt that I had been called of the Lord to help carry on His work, in compliance with the command, "Go ye into all the world and preach the gospel;" and I also found that this could be done more thoroughly by and through His church, and that to be effectual it must not be crippled by financial embarrassments. I, therefore, proceeded at once to sell the old structure, bought a new lot, and started the people in the direction of a new church edifice which was afterward built. After this I removed to Freehold, from thence to Oxford, Pennsylvania, and then to Snow Hill, New Jersey; there I was successful in building two churches, and paying for them in the space of eighteen months. It was the center of a circuit that embraced three places, viz: Snow Hill, Milford and Jordantown; the first and second named having the new churches, and the remaining one being repaired at the cost of one thousand dollars. One of the leading features of raising money at this place, besides the subscriptions, was at an "ox roast," prepared and carried on by the colored people under my command, netting us one thousand dollars toward our church fund in one day. I was greatly aided at this place both with money and encouraging words by Ezra Evans, a Quaker gentleman, who gave me from his own purse one thousand dollars, and through whose influence his brother and others donated lumber and shingles and other needed material until the church was completed, showing to me that the Lord always raised up friends for us if we trust in Him. I left there at the end of two years' pastorate of hard labor—left the two churches free of debt. I then went to Delaware circuit which embraced five churches, most of which were dilapidated and suffering from mortgages and old standing debts. My headquarters were at Camden. At Dover, the capital of the State, there was no church of our connection, and considering it a good place, I proceeded at once to purchase a lot fifty by one hundred feet at a cost of one thousand dollars, which was paid for. This is all that was accomplished by me, as my time was too short to do more than lay the foundation, and leave to others who should come after me the completing of the work.

At the next conference held at Carlisle, Pennsylvania, the bishop received a communication from Wilkesbarre, Pennsylvania, saying that a man must be sent there who could save their church (which was about half completed) which had already been advertised for sale by the sheriff, and I was appointed to go. On arriving there I found a bill of sale on the church. My boarding place being with one of the stewards, I inquired what amount would be necessary to satisfy the claim, and learned that two thousand dollars would meet the emergency. I then found a white lady of wealth, Mrs. Thomas, who after hearing my plans for raising the money, although I was a stranger, immediately loaned me the money, and with it the carpenters were paid, which removed the lien; after which they proceeded at once to complete it at a cost of ten thousand dollars, and by the blessing of God I was enabled to see it out of debt within the space of two years. The agency employed was an organization of white ladies, with Mrs. Thomas as president. They arranged for suppers and concerts, and with the collections from the white churches and private subscriptions, the required amount was raised. In this church work I was greatly aided by the faithful and earnest work of my own people. One item I would like to mention: The men of the church dug the trenches for the gas pipes by moonlight, and were rewarded by the company donating the pipes and one hundred dollars in money. While engaged at work in Wilkesbarre, I received a letter requesting me to come to Bloomsburg, also. I accordingly went, and found the people had a lot selected, but no church. My first work was to visit the different pastors of the city and those in an adjoining village named Espy, where, upon invitation of the pastor of a large Methodist church, I occupied his pulpit, and after preaching, stated my purpose to build a church in Bloomsburg. A lady came to me and encouraged me by saying that it had long been needed, and if I undertook it I could rely not only upon her wealth but also upon her influence to assist in carrying the work through. Plans and specifications were immediately gotten out and the work commenced, and here I can record an experience that I have never had before nor since—the amount to pay for it was raised in one day, and that day was the dedication day!

Collections were taken in all the churches in Bloomsburg and Espy, which met the required amount, with the exception of three hundred dollars, when just at the close a bank check was sent from this same lady (to whom reference has been made), who was dying, with a message to the effect that her check must be made out to meet the deficiency that existed; and it was made out for three hundred dollars, thus clearing the church from debt. It was named "Elizabeth Mission" in honor of this Christian lady; and thus, by the blessing of God, *two* churches were built in the compass of eighteen months, and my labors were ended in Wilkesbarre. From here I was sent, in 1874, to Burlington, New Jersey, which also included "Mount Holly." At the first named place the church was remodeled at a cost of two thousand five hundred dollars, and the second at a cost of five hundred dollars, besides building through my influence a brick school-house for the children at a cost of three thousand dollars. I remained here three years, had a good harvest of souls in both churches, numbering one hundred and fifty. Thus the Lord alway honors those who trust him, and brings them off more than conquerors. My next appointment was at Trenton, New Jersey. Here I found "Old Mount Zion." Among my first friends who came to the rescue was Joseph McPherson, Chancellor Green and the Rev. Mr. Sooy. Mr. McPherson was one of the leading trustees in the State Street Methodist church, and with him were associated four other leading wealthy gentlemen, who formed a finance committee. A meeting was called for the trustees and congregation, and a resolution passed that the old structure should be taken down and replaced with a new one. Dr. John Hall, for thirty-five years pastor of the Presbyterian church, prepared an article for the papers setting forth the need of the people and called on the citizens for help; and as they saw his earnestness and zeal in the work, they too caught his inspiration and responded nobly; and I also received great assistance from the ladies of the place, and judges, and leading citizens regardless of denominations. In accordance with the resolution, the old church was taken down, and the bodies in the churchyard removed, in order to give more room for a larger structure, which was built at a cost of ten thousand dollars, and pronounced to be one of the finest churches in the State, and all paid for by subscriptions solicited myself. After the debt was paid we had a revival, and to the seventy members already in the church, three hundred were added; and the Sunday school increased from twenty to three hundred. While engaged in this work, strange as it may seem, I was impressed that I should cross the Delaware and build a chapel for my people in the village of Yardleyville. One of the members of my finance committee, Mr. H. V. B. Jacobus, went with me and purchased the ground, fifty by one hundred feet, paying for it himself. A finance committee was appointed, consisting of three gentlemen, the chairman of which was the president of the Newton Bank, Pennsylvania. Plans and specifications were drawn up, and in the short space of four months the chapel was built and paid for by the residents of the village and the surrounding farmers; some donating stone, some brick, others lumber, lime, sand and labor. As there was no organization in this place, I organized a Sabbath school with forty children and preached every Sabbath morning (during the erection of the chapel) in the Town hall. At the dedication I presented forty names for church membership, thus constituting a permanent church organization, which was presented to the next conference, and which has been supplied with a pastor ever since; and thus my work of building two churches in less than two years was accomplished.

I was then appointed presiding elder of the eastern district of the State, by Bishop Payne, D.D., my headquarters being at Trenton. My district included Princeton, Pennington, Rahway, New Brunswick, Elizabeth, Newark, Orange, Paterson, Washington, Morristown, Freehold and Jersey City. In nearly all these places I found the churches burdened with debts, many of them having been standing for years; and the spiritual life was nearly ebbed out. I gave advice to the pastors from time to time, and succeeded in removing the mortgage from the church at Rahway, and building a new chapel at Washington, New Jersey, which was paid for and dedicated. I received great assistance from Mr. Beatty, proprietor of the organ manufactory in that city. This work was accomplished in one year, when Bishop Payne received a letter from Bishop Brown requesting my transfer to the Baltimore conference to be appointed at Union Bethel church, Washington, District of Columbia, for the purpose of building a new church. The request was granted and my appointment made in 1880. Upon arriving there I found that, while it had been the desire of the bishop to have this work done, it was not the wish of the majority of the membership, and hence, in attempting it I met with great opposition; but after some discussion a resolution was passed by the trustees and members that the work should go on.

Two or three of the best ministers in the conference had been sent to Washington several years before to build what was to be known as the Metropolitan church, which was to be the representative church of our connection; but they failed for reasons for which they were not to blame, for they were good, effectual ministers of the gospel and had been successful in building churches in other places. I considered this an opportune time to try again and build the Metropolitan church, instead of Union Bethel. I therefore requested Bishop Brown to call together the bench of the bishops at his house, which he did, and they decided also the same, and commanded me to go forward with the work. I engaged an architect to draw plans for the church according to my directions, as my plans seemed to be from divine inspiration and he allowed me to guide his hand. The dimensions of the church were to be one hundred and twenty-seven by eighty-four feet, with a seating capacity of twenty-five hundred in the auditorium; with a lecture room and primary Sunday school room, and class rooms and church parlors, and a room for the meeting of the bishops. An additional lot was purchased in connection with the old site on which to place the new structure. The old building was torn down by the members of the church, and the bricks cleaned by them to be used again. By this, and by the selling of the old lumber, there was a saving of three thousand dollars, and the work began in earnest. As the membership of the church was eleven hundred, they were divided into twelve classes, the leaders of which met me from time to time to be trained in the art of raising money in their several classes.

My first plan was to issue eighty-five thousand envelopes which were given to the leaders, fifty-two for each one in his class, one for every Sunday in the year. I also prepared "shot bags" for each to keep their money in. I had all the "sinners" known as the pastor's class, and the first Sunday in every month we received a collection of one thousand dollars as the report from the shot-bags and the classes toward the building of the new church. Besides this, entertainments were given from time to time for the same fund, and every second Sunday in the month a general collection was taken for the current expenses of the church, and the glorious work went on and was completed according to the plan at a cost of over one hundred thousand dollars, and dedicated to Almighty God for divine services on May 30, 1886; and it now stands in the capital city of these United States as a monument of zeal and earnestness, which has surmounted many difficulties and which is a credit to the entire African Methodist Episcopal connection; and too much credit cannot be given to the trustees, especially John A. Sims and William Becket, and also the board of stewards, for their faithfulness and co-operation, and also the *good* members of the church. Arrangements had been previously made by the general conference that five thousand dollars should be given each year from its funds to help pay for this church, which in addition to what had been paid, and what the members were still willing to pay, would not take very long to clear the church from debt.

CHAPTER CXXIII

*Professor Joseph Carter Corbin, A. B., A. M.
State Superintendent of Public Instruction—Linguist—Master
of Latin, Greek, French, Spanish, Italian, German, Hebrew
and Danish—Profound Mathematician and Musician—
Organist—Pianist—Flutist*

Professor J. C. Corbin comes of a very distinguished and intellectual family. He was born in Richmond, Virginia, of slave parents, William and Susan Corbin, who moved to Chillicothe, Ohio, and thence to Cincinnati, where they died. They had eleven children; but of these, perhaps, it might be well said that Joseph C. Corbin is the most distinguished. He was born in Chillicothe, Ohio, March 26, 1833, and was the eldest son. He was educated in the winter schools of Chillicothe. In these schools he learned to read, write and cipher. Hon. J. M. Langston was in the school at the same time. At about fifteen years of age he went to Louisville, Kentucky, and assisted Rev. Henry Adams, whose sketch appears elsewhere, in teaching. Many of the well-known citizens of Louisville were his pupils. After teaching some years he went to the Ohio University, and by private study he had advanced sufficiently to enter the Sophomore class. Having graduated in 1853, he returned to Louisville, where his father's family were living at the time. He was employed in clerking in a mercantile agency, and then in a bank; he was clearing-house clerk for several years, and was one of the young men who conducted the colored citizens for eight years—the others being J. P. Sampson, S. W. C. Liverpool, John McLeod and Louis D. Eastin. Being engaged as a reporter for the *Arkansas Republican*, Governor Clayton's official organ, he went to Arkansas in 1872. He was afterwards chief clerk in the Little Rock post office, and then was elected State superintendent of public instruction, in which position he served two years. During his term of office the "Brooks-Baxter" war occurred and a new constitution being adopted, Mr. Corbin, with the other Republican officers, was turned out of office. For two years then he taught at Lincoln Institute of Jefferson City, Missouri, which turned out its first graduating class while he was there. He then returned

JOSEPH CARTER CORBIN

to Little Rock, for this rising teacher had not moved his residence, and while spending his vacation at home was sent for by Governor Augustus H. Garland, now attorney-general of the United States, and was engaged to go to Pine Bluff and establish the Branch Normal College. Mr. Corbin did this and opened the "College" in an old dilapidated one-storey frame house, built for a barracks in war times. The attendance at first was seven students, one or two of whom could read in the third reader. Professor Corbin has been principal ever since and the usual attendance now is about two hundred and fifty students. It had sent forth five graduating classes and a large number of colored teachers in the State. His work has been eminently successful and has received the indorsement of every administration in the State since he began operations. When it was known that he was taught during the official terms of Governors Garland, Miller, Churchill, Berry and Hughes, it is apparent he could not have expected anything from them, who were of opposite political views, except that his work itself deserved their commendation. January 12, 1887, Governor Hughes, in his message to the State Legislature, used these words:

> I call attention, with pleasure, to the very favorable mention of the efficient and faithful management of the Normal Branch of the University of Pine Bluff by Professor Corbin, in the report of the executive committee of the board of trustees, and will add my own commendation of Professor Corbin as an able and efficient principal of that school, devoted to its interests, successful in its management, which has been very careful and economical.

Of his scholastic ability very high praise has been spoken. He is a fluent reader of Greek, Latin, German, French, Spanish, Italian, Hebrew and Danish. In mathematics is especially proficient. His mathematical articles and solutions can be found in Barns' *Educational Monthly*, published at New York; *School Visitor* published in Gettysburg, Ohio; *The Mathematical Visitor*, and the *Mathematical Magazine* and *Mathematical Gazette*, Erie, Pennsylvania. Mr. Corbin is a Baptist and has been Sunday school superintendent for many years, and stands high among the brethren in all church work. He is vice-president of the Colored Industrial Fair Association. The *Weekly Gazette*, October 28, 1886 speaking of the fair said:

> In our yesterday's notes we alluded to those who, by their arduous and intelligent efforts, have materially contributed to the success of this exhibition, yet not to all, for a lack of space forbids. There was an army of subordinate workers who did their duty worthily. This may be inferred from the fact that while six days on the grounds we never heard an oath or saw a drunken man. Professor J. C. Corbin, vice-president, was here, there and everywhere, doing his duty intelligently and with rare discretion. He has that rare gift of making others pleased with themselves.

He is certainly one of the most scholastic men of the race. He is a man of solid acquirements and a hard student, a man of fine personal qualities, an agreeable companion and an eminent counselor. Such a store of knowledge as he has few men acquire without making more show. He is retiring in his nature and very modest, but such men as he who possess large stores of wisdom are generally the most quiet and amiable men. He has filled the important position of grand secretary of the Masons for thirteen years, and is an eminent commander in the Knights Templars. To his other accomplishments, he adds that of musician, performing upon the piano, organ and flute, and has attained such proficiency that he gives instruction on said instruments. During the summer he is employed by the State superintendent of public schools of the State to hold institutes for colored teachers, and has filled engagements in nearly all the important places in the State of Arkansas.

CHAPTER CXXIV

Hon. James M. Trotter
Recorder of Deeds—Author of Music and some Highly
Musical People—*Assistant Superintendent of the Registered
Letter Department, Boston, Massachusetts—Lieutenant
in the Army*

It is with no little pleasure that I take my pen to indite a few words of praise in honor of the distinguished and honored author of *Music and Some Highly Musical People*. He has become known to the literary and musical world especially for the production that does honor to himself and those whom he has made conspicuous.

Mr. Trotter has performed a very acceptable act in placing before his readers the subject of music in such a pleasant form, condensed yet highly artistic in style, judicious in matter and replete with thought. He is also to be commended for bringing to notice the musical celebrities of the race and giving them their station in the line of musical artists, and at the same time fixed their names, their abilities, their triumphs in the cold reality of type, which might well be termed vise of facts. Music is a universal language in which men, women and children join. The birds, the winds, the bells, the cataracts, all send forth music, and the "singing of the sphere," seems to betoken that the God himself takes pleasure in this art so aptly called the "Divine Art." The feelings in a man who can spend his energy of writing such a work must be of the tenderest and gentlest kind. His soul must be pure and easily moved by "a sweet concord of sounds," and indeed he has *so expressed* himself in a few lines of his preface. Speaking of music he says: "Its tones of melody and harmony require only to be heard in order to awaken in the breast emotions the most delightful." And herein he judges every soul by his own, so refined and so highly tuned to rich and cultured music, when he says: "And yet who can speak at all of an agency so charming in other than words of warmest praise." His research after facts concerning the art was rewarded in great fullness, as is shown by the following selection from the work.

JAMES M. TROTTER

But without devoting further space to the music that was in vogue prior to the Christian era, I proceed to notice that our first reliable account of it, as a system, commences with the fourth century, at which time St. Ambrose, Bishop of Milan, arranged the sacred chants that bear his name, and which were to be sung in the cathedrals. In the year 600 St. Gregory improved upon these chants, inventing the scale of eight notes. His system is the basis of our modern music.

From the close of the eleventh to the commencement of the fourteenth century, minstrels, *jongleurs,* or troubadours, were the principal devotees of music. They seemed to have been its custodians, so to speak; and to their guild many of the knights belonged. Some of the kings and nobles of the times were also, in a sense, troubadours; such as, for instance, Thibault of Navarre, and William the Ninth of Poitou. These roving musicians, who generally united the qualities of the poet, the musical composer and the performer, were treated with much favor by princes and all the nobility, and were everywhere warmly welcomed for a long period.

During the fourteenth century, music was most cultivated by the people of the Netherlands, who carried the art towards much perfection, producing several fine composers, and furnishing the leading musical instructor for the other parts of Europe. Among some of the ablest musicians of the Netherlands may be mentioned Dufay, Jan of Okenheim, and Josquin Despres, the latter being the most celebrated of contrapuntists. The Netherland musical supremacy lasted until 1563.

In the year 1400 the claims of music received the recognition of the crown in England, a charter being granted to a regularly formed musical society.

Commencing with the invention of movable type in 1502 (which invention so vastly facilitated the publication and spreading of the thoughts of the composer) and with the reformation in the sixteenth century, the noble art of music began a new, unimpeded and brilliant career among the civilized nations of the world. Dating from thence, the progress of this delightful science can be plainly traced. Unvexed and unfettered by the obscurities that attached to its antique history, we can contemplate with pleasure and profit the wonderful creations and achievements of its devotees.

To Palestrina, a learned Italian of the sixteenth century, and whose musical genius and industry were most remarkable, is due the greatest homage and gratitude of a music-loving world. Of him an eminent musical writer says: "It is difficult to overestimate his talent and influence over the art of music in his day. He was regarded as the great reformer of church music. His knowledge of counterpoint and the elevation and nobility of his style, made his masses and other compositions, of which he wrote a great number, examples for all time of what music should be."

In this century lived many notable composers, nearly all of whom distinguished themselves in the production of madrigal music. To the latter the English people were much devoted. Reading at sight was at that day, even more than now, a common accomplishment among the educated. The English Queen Elizabeth was quite fond of music, and was somewhat accomplished in the art, performing upon the lute, verginals and viol. She often charmed the attachés of and visitors to her court by her skilful performances. During her reign, and by her encouragement, the cultivation of this noble art received a new and strong impulse in England, and several composers and performers of high merit lived.

But, before proceeding farther, the writer considers it proper to remark that to give an extended description of the progress of music during the last three centuries, mentioning in detail the many creations and achievements of those who have become great, nay, in some instances he might say almost immortal in the sacred domain, would require a volume far beyond the pretensions and intended limits of this one.

Besides, the author confesses that he pauses with feelings of reverence while contemplating the mighty genius and divinely approximating achievements of Haydn, Mozart, Beethoven, Spohr and Mendelssohn, fearing that his unskilful pen might fail in an attempt at description. Nor does he feel much less embarrassed when he contemplates the accomplishments of those wonderful interpreters of the works of the noble masters, who have, either through the enchanting modulations of their voices or with skilful touch upon instruments, evolved their magic strains.

Let an abler pen than mine portray the sublime triumphs of Hasse, Mario, Wachtel, Santley, Whitney; of Albani, Malibran, Lind, Parepa Rosa, Nilsson; of Haupt, Paganini, Vieuxtemps, Ole Bull, Rubinstein, Liszt and Von Bulow.

Justin D. Fulton, D.D., editor of the *Baptist Outlook*, New York, said:

It should find a welcome to every library. It traverses a field hitherto untrodden, and the results are placed before us in a manner that will surprise and delight the reader. Mr. Trotter wields the pen with great care. There is before him an open door to a bright future in the world of letters.

The *Literary World*, Boston, Massachusetts, speaking of this same work, said:

Music and Some Highly Musical People—We were disposed to give this book a generous reception before reading it, for its author's sake; and now, after reading, we give it a hearty commendation for its own. It is a well-conceived and well-constructed essay, in an entirely new direction, combining some really useful qualities in a truly clever way. Mr. Trotter is an African by race, now occupying (we believe) a position in the Boston post office; and his aim in this work is to show what is being done by his people in the musical profession. Of its three parts, the first—an essay proper, critical and historical —and the third—a collection of musical compositions by different hands— are of the least value. The second, which is by far the larger portion of the volume, comprising biographical and critical sketches of a large number of "highly musical (colored) people," brings together a mass of curious, interesting and valuable information, which it would probably be impossible to duplicate in any one place elsewhere.

J. O. Freeman, professor of music, Charleston, Massachusetts, wrote as follows:

> The few pages devoted to music, its beauty, its power, uses, etc., are well worth the price of the work, to say nothing of the very interesting biographies of many noted colored people, some who are still active in life, and some who have passed away. May the work have what it fully deserves; *i.e.*, a large sale; and may it be the means of bringing before the notice of the white people, that although some in this world are less favored in color, they in musical talent and intellectual ability, are fully their equals.

Of this work over seven thousand copies have been sold.

Mr. Trotter was born in Grand Gulf, Mississippi, and spent his early days in Cincinnati, Ohio, until about twelve years of age. He was born about 1844. He moved to Hamilton, Ohio, where he attended school and studied music, and took that deep interest in the art which has entered his life and became a part of his nature. He finally moved to Massachusetts, and when the war broke out he enlisted in the army as a private in the Fifty-fourth Massachusetts, and for efficiency was promoted to the position of first sergeant, then sergeant-major, and finally lieutenant. After the war the Republican party awarded him by appointing him to the position of assistant superintendent of the registered letter department in the Boston postoffice, which position he held for eighteen years and gave abundant satisfaction. He resigned in 1883 on account of color line being drawn and because he was dissatisfied with the management of the party. In politics Mr. Trotter is an Independent. He does not believe in slavishly accepting the decrees of men who care only for the votes of the Negro. With these feelings he voted for Cleveland for President, and Andrews for governor, and during the last campaign was one of the committee of one hundred in the State and was engaged at the headquarters, in distributing literature for Andrews and Foster. After the Senate of the United States had twice rejected the name of Hon. James C. Matthews as recorder of deeds, Washington, District of Columbia, the name of Mr. Trotter was sent to the Senate. This was due to the suggestion of Mr. Matthews, to whom he freely gives credit for his nomination. A full statement of this matter will be found under the name of Mr. Matthews, which will show that he was appointed first as the deputy recorder of deeds for the District of Columbia. When he was nominated by the following letter from the President on March 28, 1887, there was intense excitement in the Senate, and in fact the whole city:

To the Senate of the United States:

I hereby nominate James M. Trotter of Massachusetts, to be recorder of deeds in the District of Columbia, vice Frederick Douglass resigned.

GROVER CLEVELAND

The *Boston Daily Globe* reporter, who claims he was the first to suggest the name of Mr. Trotter for the position, and who probably got his cue from Mr. Matthews, telegraphed the following report to his paper:

Within half an hour there was not a soul between the four walls of the capitol who had not heard this entirely unexpected news, and in Washington to-night no man is so generally talked about as Lieutenant Trotter of Hyde Park. The *Evening Critic* squeezed the bare information into its forms after they had been locked, and its staid contemporary, *The Star*, set up the nomination in a double leaded two line paragraph, and issued a postscript edition. The first named paper took time to let its readers know that Mr. Matthews successor is a "colored mugwump"—an unspeakably vile combination in the eyes of the local politicians—while the *Star* inserted the bracketed word "colored," and let it go at that.

Special bulletins were quickly pasted on the windows of the newspaper offices and attracted great attention, the announcement exciting a variety of comments. I stopped before one of these boards in the evening and listened for a few minutes.

"Worse and worse," said one man, as he read aloud,

"COLORED MUGWUMPS."

While another exhausted his supply of invectives, when he had denounced the nominee as a "Bean eating nigger."

"Grover sticks," exclaimed another passer by, with mixed pleasure; while several more were heard to commend the spirit and nerve of the President; and one or two seemed to find satisfaction in the thought that the nomination of a Massachusetts colored man to the place was ramming it hard to Senator Hoar.

I am not competent to interpret the real public sentiment of Washington relative to the appointment of non-residents to offices in the District of Columbia, but it is easy to believe that this very recently developed clamor here against such nominations was incited by self-interest. There certainly is no outcry against non-residents paying half the taxes of the local government.

Indeed I do not understand that there was any general demand for such a policy until Mr. Cleveland came in, when the local politicians were encouraged somewhat by the plank.

In the Chicago platform favoring the appointment of residents to offices in the territories, the marshal of the district had always been a non-resident, and most of the recorders of deeds had been appointed from the States. The last Republican recorder was Douglass, and he was brought on from New York. When Mr. Cleveland came into office Recorder Douglass immediately tendered his resignation. Notwithstanding this, he was allowed to stay under the

Democratic administration seventeen months; for which consideration Mr. Douglass publicly expressed his gratitude.

The truth of the matter was, they were making the fight on the color line, and got whipped, since he was confirmed. His good fortune did not forsake him. The "colored troops" fought boldly. White men though senators, shrank and cringed beneath the lash of the Negroes of the country. When the fight began, it at first seemed only a little feeling about the politics of Matthews, but when the Negroes saw it was an effort of the Senate to clip the political wings of the Negro and compel him to drop in the political back yard of the Republican party, they whipped the Senate "horse, foot and dragoon," and like spoiled children who had been across their mother's knee, they whined and took their dose and swallowed it "a wiser, and it is to be hoped, a better set of men." He was confirmed March 4, 1887, with only eleven votes against him. Senator Ingalls, who was now presiding over the Senate, by virtue of the resignation of Senator John Sherman from that position, left the chair and exerted his unusual powers of ridicule to shame his associates into consistency of action. It is known that he declared that the country would despise the cowardice of a change and condemn the Republicans for having drawn the color line on Matthews. He was utterly at loss to see any possible gain or virtue in taking a course that would repudiate their actions and words in the exactly parallel case.

Senator Hoar, on whom the pressure for Mr. Trotter's confirmation had been strong and continuous, said that the Senate was not to question the right of the President to nominate whomsoever he pleased for the office of recorder; the only effect of their double rejection of Matthews was to give expression to their feeling, that it was expedient to fill the place with a resident of the District. They had emphasized this objection as clearly and forcibly as was possible, and the senator thought that the people would not justify them in further obstructing the President in the exercise of the appointed power, for the good use of which he was after all solely responsible in the public mind.

Mr. Hoar said that he could not question the fitness and reputability of the nominee, and exhibited a heap of communications from Massachusetts in support of Mr. Trotter. Mr. Hoar had indeed been smoked out by the President transferring the battle ground in this war from New York to Massachusetts.

Senator Riddleberger gave the Massachusetts senator a fearful shaking up, recalling Mr. Hoar's courageous industry when a New York ox was being gored, and contrasting his attitude then with his indorsement of this new nominee, who chances to be an ox from the senator's own fields.

The Virginian insisted that he had been honest in opposing Matthews, and announced his intention of opposing Trotter for the same reasons. The talk lasted a full hour, and when the vote came the Republicans scrambled to the President's side like sheep in a thunder-storm.

While the nomination was pending it was hard for the Democrats to choose between the hope that Trotter would be served like Matthews, and the hope that the Republicans would break down; but now that action has been taken, it is easy enough to find the best side of the mouth out of which to laugh a good hearty Democratic laugh.

The proposition can now go in the arithmetics, "If two colored men can whip the United States Senate, what could a hundred do?"

The office is worth from seven thousand dollars to ten thousand dollars per year, and has much patronage attached to it. Mr. Trotter's modesty and excellent manners have made friends for him and he will serve the District of Columbia with no mean ability.

CHAPTER CXXV

Rev. Allen Allensworth, A. M.
The Great Children's Preacher of the Gospel—Chaplain
of the Twenty-fourth Infantry of the United States—
Presidential Elector—Agent of the American Baptist
Publication Society

He was born of slave parents in Louisville, Kentucky, April 3, 1843. His parents, Levi and Phyllis Allensworth, were industrious and pious; he says he owes most of the succes of his after life to his mother, who took especial pains to send him to the Sunday school of the day, which was allowed by her owners. He evidenced a thirst for knowledge at an early age. His owners becoming alarmed at the progress he was making under difficulties, concluded to quench his thirst for learning by sending him down the river to work on a tobacco farm. Henderson county, Kentucky, was selected as the place, where he could not obtain any facilities for keeping up his studies. They thought they would put him where he would get courting in his head, which would crush all desire to know more of books; then he would be brought back for service. His mother, who belonged to another person, was sick at the time, and knew nothing of the contemplated change until he was sent with the carriage driver to bid her farewell. She arose with feeble efforts from her sick-bed and asked for God's blessing to rest upon him. The mother and her youngest son parted in the spring of 1853, and met no more until 1861. The farm failing to quench his thirst for knowledge, his owners sent him South and sold him. In 1861, when Sumter fell, he was in a Negro mart in New Orleans and was sold for one thousand dollars to ride race-horses. In the summer of '61 he was brought to Kentucky by his new owner, where he met his mother. In the fall of 1862 he left Louisville with the soldiers, and obtained his freedom in the winter of 1863. After the battle of Stone River he went to Ohio. April 3, 1863, he entered the United States Navy and was soon advanced from a seaman to a petty officer, serving till April 3, 1865. He then returned to Louisville and was converted and united

ALLEN ALLENSWORTH

with the Fifth Street Baptist church, of which Elder Henry Adams was pastor.

When the Ely Normal school was established in Louisville, he was its janitor and among its first pupils, it being the first regular school he ever entered to study. While making rapid progress in the school, he was selected by the principal to go out and teach under the Freedmen's Bureau. Finding that the more he taught the less he knew, he entered the Nashville Institute, now known as the Roger Williams University. After pursuing the Normal and preacher's course in that institution he "quituated," as he is in the habit of saying, and went to teaching in Georgetown, Kentucky, and taught there until selected by the General Association of Colored Baptists to become their financial agent, from which office he was called to the pastorate of the church at Elizabethtown. Being a successful pastor, his leadership was courted by the churches and he subsequently served at Franklin, Louisville and Bowling Green, and developing into a successful Sunday school worker, the State Baptist Sunday school convention appointed him superintendent of the Sunday schools of the State, and the American Baptist Publication Society appointed him as the missionary in this field. He became eminent both at home and abroad, and was known everywhere as the "Great Children's Preacher." After four years' service in this field, he was called to take charge of the Union Baptist church in Cincinnati, where he met with unprecedented success as a pastor. It was while serving here that he was appointed by President Grover Cleveland to the chaplaincy of the Twenty-fourth United States infantry. In this new field, as in others he has been pronounced a success.

In the denomination of which he was an active member he was honored with the position of State secretary of the Sunday school convention for several years, moderator of the State Ministers' meeting, and secretary for several years of the General Association, and, besides, filled many other places of honor and trust. As a presiding officer he was impartial and ready; as a preacher he possesses the happy faculty in knowing how to express himself in the most pleasant manner; his reasoning being logical and convincing; as a lecturer he has had some success, lecturing in different churches on the subject of "Masters of the Situation," "Humbugs," and several other subjects.

His ability as a public speaker was recognized by the Republicans of Kentucky, who selected him as an elector for the State-at-large on the Garfield and Arthur ticket. Allen Allensworth is one of the shrewdest men in the whole country, for he outwitted the schemers of the district in which he lived, who had always manipulated their conventions so as to send a white man to the Presidential nominating convention which met last in Chicago, a thing no other colored man in Kentucky has succeeded in doing. He is all tact. How could a prominent Republican politician, who was a Republican elector, who had never done anything for conservatism even, be put in such a position by President Cleveland in the days of removal for offensive partisanship? Nobody could answer this but the chaplain himself. He is one of the best tempered men, and owes his success to his moderation, even in very disagreeable affairs. In debate he is always calm and wary, and is a skilful parliamentarian. As a preacher he can turn a sermon inside out and then turn it the other way for successive occasions, and make it pleasing, instructive and full of truth. His style is of the highest order; he never fails to command attention. Recognizing his success in life, and appreciating his course as a Christian gentleman and man of scholastic habits, the Roger Williams University conferred upon him the honorary degree of Master of Arts. His intellect is keen, judicial, didactic and strong. To his new field of labor he carries with him the best wishes of his friends and the prayers of all good people in the State in which he has labored so faithfully and long. Kentucky is proud of his elevation and success in the Twenty-fourth infantry, stationed now at Fort Supply, Indian Territory.

CHAPTER CXXVI

Rev. George Washington Dupee
Eminent Minister—Moderator of the General Association—
Editor—Preacher of Twelve Thousand Funeral Sermons—
Baptizer of Eight Thousand Candidates

———◆●◆———

Rev. Mr. Dupee was born July 24, 1826, in Gallatin County, Kentucky. His parents were named Cuthbert and Rachael Dupee, and were owned by Elder Joseph Taylor, a Baptist preacher, who moved to Franklin county when George was an infant. He was very small when the master sold off his slaves and moved to the State of Illinois, carrying his brother Edmund with him, whom he afterward set free. His mother having died when he was two weeks old, told the people to raise him right, for God had spared her to bring her boy into the world, whom she had named George Washington Dupee, and that this boy was for God's own purpose and that he would be useful and live to an old age. In his early days he worked at a rope and bagging factory, and also in a brickyard, and with his father and brother was hired to different parties. In 1841 he worked on the court-house in Versailles, being hired to one Mr. French, and was brought under the preaching of old "Father" David Woods, a Baptist preacher. On the second Tuesday in August, 1842, he was converted. After conversion he was impressed with the desire to preach the gospel, and he appeared before the preacher above named and brother James Evans and Charles Good and was examined to see if he was converted. He failed to give satisfaction, and they were honest enough to send him back to learn something about Christian experience. He went back to God in prayer and begged if he had done anything for his poor soul, to please to make it plain. On the following Friday his eyes were opened and his soul was filled with the love of God. On Saturday night they had a meeting at old Deacon Wingate's (white). There he told what the Lord had done for him, and was recommended to the Buck Run church. On the third Sunday he went before the church and was approved for Baptism. Pastor Kenny immersed Sister Rachael Mills, Brother Chester Fields, and G. W. Dupee, in South Elkhorn creek, a day

GEORGE WASHINGTON DUPEE

and action, as he says, never to be forgotten. The desire to preach the gospel still pressed upon his mind and he says, when speaking about the subject, "I remember to my shame until this day, of saying that if the Lord knew me as I knew myself, he would know that he could not make a preacher out of me. I have been almost puzzled since to know that God could forgive such ignorance." He did not at this time know the letters of the alphabet. Preaching left his mind. He subsequently learned the alphabet in the summer of 1844. On a rainy Wednesday in June, old Father Wood was reading in the New Testament and being weary, laid the book down, and then himself saying, "It still rains and I will lie down." After he did so Mr. Dupee took up the book wishing that he could read as he had seen Father Wood doing. He opened the book without making any effort to find a special place, at the first chapter of John. He saw the letters J-o-h-n and said, "What did that fool put those letters that way for; they don't mean anything." He had quarreled with the compositor about the arrangement of the letters of John's name, of course without knowing that there was such a character as a compositor. He paused over that name but could not pronounce it, could not spell words of four letters. Just how he got started to reading he never could tell, but he first discovered himself reading what he since learned was the third chapter of John. Surprised to find himself reading the Word of God, he went back to the first chapter and read the first three again. It still seemed a mystery. He went back again and read it over and he was in a maze. He went back again and read the first three chapters and then he recognized the fact that he could read the Holy Word of God. He pressed the open book to his breast and got down on his knees to thank the Lord for teaching him to read His precious Word. He could not speak; he cried and rolled over the floor, got up and walked about and said that his heart rejoiced, his soul magnified the Lord. He stopped and read again, and again, and then read again, and then laid down the book and went into another room to sleep. Reading had been to him but a pastime, but finally he found that he was blessed with reading the Word of God as he had never hoped to do. He was so happy that he could not keep still, but soon he was dumfounded again. For he reasoned to himself, you can read the Word of God what hinders you from preaching the gospel. He hung his head in sorrow, for he had not yet thought that God could make a preacher of him; and he refused to believe that he could or ought to preach the gospel.

He was an uncompromising Baptist, believing in "One Lord, one Faith, one Baptism." In April, 1845, he was hired to a Mr. D. C. Hamphries, in Woodford county. In June of that year he was introduced to Sister Phœbe Fields, a member of the old Big Spring Baptist church, who refused to speak to him on introduction, but gave him a very strange look that bothered him. But he passed on, and in August Sister Fields sent for him to come to her house, and to be there on a certain Sunday evening in September. This bothered him and he didn't know what to make of it, but somehow he felt impelled, and planned not to be in her presence long. So on the evening mentioned he met her, and that meeting is never to be forgotten. Arriving at her house late in the evening, she was out milking near her door, and he said, "Good evening," and told her that he heard that she wished to see him; that he had come by on that account, for he was in a great hurry to get to his brother Henry's. She said, "Go to your brother Henry's and when you get time come to see me." He was standing by a stump, and just eased himself down to wait her pleasure; but he was troubled, for what he did not know. Supper being ready he was invited to eat, but did not feel like taking any. Sister Phœbe said to him: "We are going over to old Uncle Ned Livingston's; will you go with us?" His heart said no, but his lips said yes. On the way over Sister Phœbe said to him: "Do you remember when you were introduced to me last year?" He replied: "Yes, ma'am." Then said she: "What did you think of my conduct towards you at that time?" He told her: "Very strange." Then said she, "I saw something in you that I never did in any one else. I thought I would ask you some questions and then I saw you were not honest, and I did not ask you anything, because I didn't want you to tell me a lie"; and further said that she had made his case the subject of prayer. That the Lord had shown her that he had converted him some years ago in an old field under some trees, where there were bushes, and commanded him to preach the gospel, and that he had disobeyed him, and the Lord was not pleased with him. Further, that there were many sinners in that neighborhood waiting to be called by the gospel into his service, and among them some that would preach the gospel. By that time he was nearly dead, for he began to realize the situation. He was converted in a wheat field just harvested, under an apple tree surrounded by locust bushes, but he had not told anybody about it, because he could not talk about it without feeling the pangs of his disobedience. He was completely broken down. He arrived at Livingston's, and Sister Fields and two old people and several little children were come to hold a little meeting, and called upon Sister Ailsey Fields to pray. She then went to him, took him by the arm saying: "Go about the Lord's business," and he got up but didn't know what he said. They said he made a good talk, but he was not conscious of what he was doing, for as soon as he noticed he was on his feet he sat down confused. Sister Fields sang this old hymn:

> *But when I am come to meditate,*
> *How poor, how vile I am;*
> *How can I preach the gospel true,*
> *And claim the Son of Man.*

She said to him: "You need not take this. It is for me only." After prayer and singing again she went home, and when the party arrived at the house, brother Sam Fields, her husband, expected him to go in, but she got hold of his arm and pointing to the woods near by, said: "Go and repent of your long disobedience and get ready to serve the Lord and the gospel." He often says he never shall forget the first Sunday night in September, 1845, and how he regretted that he didn't go on preaching the gospel like Paul. He repented, however, and went to work. At that time there were only two places in that neighborhood for miles around where colored people were permitted to hold meetings; but soon doors were opened and he was invited and did hold meetings on twenty-seven farms, holding night and Sunday preachings in the dining rooms, kitchens, woods and other places, and God blessed the work and many were converted. Among them were Moses Burk, David Johnson, Keene Langford, who became preachers.

An incident not to be forgotten occurred at Mr. Humphries'. One Saturday, in 1846, the most of the men living there gambled. The unmarried men occupied one room. In that room, the night referred to, Moses Burk, Simon Brown, George Washington, Harry Langford, Alfred Gaines, Lewis Allen, David Johnson, Quilla Terrior and some others were playing for tobacco. He sat near the box until late. Finally he said: "Gentlemen I gave you silent attention, if not respectful, and now I claim your silent attention while I will play my game." This greatly incensed them and they became reckless, cursing, shuffling feet and making noises on the box, at a fearful rate. However, Dupee sang a hymn, but they paid no attention to him. He sang several hymns, got down and prayed, but they didn't hear his prayer. But God did. When he got up, he sang and prayed again, then got up feeling hurt at the treatment he had received from the boys, thinking that his prayer should be answered right away. He was not done thinking before the answer came. The box on which they were sitting was near a window and all at once there came a ball of lightning, about nine inches in diameter, through that window, right about the centre of the ring, and drew itself back and struck itself at each man's face, and then passed right over his own left shoulder out of the same window. Then he felt like a giant refreshed with new wine. Brother Moses Burk took dinner with him on the tenth of January, 1887, and told him that he had never played a card since that Saturday night. The cards fell from their hands and they lay there until morning. A number of old brethren invited him to take charge of their meeting and act as a sort of pastor, which invitation he accepted. The old colored deacons of the Buck Run church had anthorized him to exercise his gifts. Father Jack Smith, the first colored preacher of Kentucky; Father David Wood, Brother James Evans and Brother Charles Good were the men. A great revival broke out and so many persons going from Woodford county to Buck Run and joining, using his name as the instrument of their going, the white pastor of the church became aroused to know who this Dupee was. The church, having appointed him deacon in old Father Jack Smith's place, didn't know him as a preacher. The church said he must be encouraged, and appointed a meeting for him to come and preach for them that he might be licensed. He thought it needless to have a license, but in obedience to the church, he went and preached the best he could. The church voted a license for him, but he never got it. Again he met Sister Fields, who impressed upon him the duty of learning to write, telling him that he would be pastor of churches sometime and that all pastors ought to read and write, and that he would be free, and have great responsibilities. She got an Irishman to set a copy for him. He soon learned that he could attend to business. He labored in Woodford, Franklin, Scott, Jessamine, Fayette, Owens and other counties for several years. He averaged four sermons a week, walking over a hundred miles to and from his preaching. He walked forty miles and preached four times in one day in 1847.

In 1848 he went to Frankfort to live with Mr. Joseph Gale, and learned the brickmaking trade. The sixteenth of November he married Mrs. Matilda Green at the Governor's Palace, Frankfort, and Father David Wood officiated. His married life did not terminate happily. He declined a proposition of the majority of the members of the Frankfort church and received the call at Georgetown, which he accepted January, 1851, and protracted a meeting, assisted by Elder James Monroe, whom he calls the best preacher he ever heard. The second Sunday in March of that year he was ordained by Rev. Reynolds D.D., president of the Georgetown College, and Rev. J. M. Frost, pastor of the white Baptist church. On the third Sunday he immersed twenty-eight persons. In 1853 he organized a church at what is called the Old Big Spring, Woodford county. In 1855 he organized a church at Paris, Kentucky, preached at Great Crossing, Stamping Grounds, Cane Run and other places with Brother James Monroe, Bias Smith, Robert Martin, Thomas Smith, Thomas Gross, Spencer Taylor, Henry Evans, Armistead Steele, John Eppison, John Osborne, George Grayson, Frederick Braxton, E. W. Green, London Ferrill, J. R. Anderson, N. G. Merry, R. V. Vandervall, and many other dear soldiers of the cross of Christ. With Elders Monroe, Green, Steele, Braxton and others, he attended the funeral of that great and good man, London Ferrill, in March, 1855. He was called to the pastorate of Pleasant Green church in Lexington, and divided time with the church at Georgetown. In December he was called the second time and signified his acceptance, but in a few days afterwards, the Honorable Richard Kendall informed him that he was advertised with his brothers, Henry and Logan D. Dupee, to be sold to the highest bidder. He reconsidered his acceptance to the call, not knowing what was to become of him. In a few days, old Father Richard Dryer, deacon of the Pleasant Green church, told him that Judge B. F. Graves of the county court of Fayette wanted to see him at the clerk's office on a certain night. Of course he thought the Negro buyers had fixed the trick up and expected to handcuff and carry him to jail. However he went down, and there met the Rev. William Pratt D.D., Judge B. F. Graves, Lawyer Drake, his brother Dr. Drake, Messrs. Plunkett, Bishop Clark, Baker, Kidd, Burbank and others. They cordially received him and finally asked him if he could read writing. He replied that he could, and they told him to read a paper which was spread out before him. There was an agreement between these gentlemen to buy him when sold, and let him pay them their money back when he could. He was not sold, and reconsidering his declination of the Pleasant Green church he accepted it, and remained until 1864. He organized a church in 1867, in Cynthiana, and did very much work in connection with Rev. Elisha W. Green, at Maysville. August, 1858, he accepted a call to the Washington Street Baptist church in Paducah as visiting pastor. He held a meeting there and, as the result, baptized eighty-one persons in fourteen minutes. In 1861 he organized the first ministers and deacons' meeting ever held by the colored people in the South or Southwestern States, in Versailles, in Elder Armistead Steeles' church. There were present Brethren James Monroe, John Oliver, R. Martin and G. Breckinridge, and they had a grand meeting. Brother A. Steele died in the fall of 1861 and Brother Dupee preached his funeral sermon, and was called to the pastorate of the church in Versailles in 1862, and divided time with the Pleasant Green church. In 1862 he baptized Rev. Reuben Lee, who came over from the Presbyterians, and, with the aid of Rev. Dr. Pratt, and Rev. J. L. Smith, ordained him. Brother Butler Harper was ordained at the same time; Reuben Lee was called to the church in Georgetown, Kentucky, and Brother Harper went to Cincinnati to see about his freedom. Mr. Dupee organized a church in Covington, building them a house of worship, and was invited to act as pastor.

In December, 1864, he declined the eleventh call to the Pleasant Green church, and having been called to locate in Paducah he moved down to Covington and remained until February, 1865. He left Brother Jack Price in charge of the Covington church and took charge of the Paducah church, frequently visiting the church at Covington. But he says: "If I could have gotten the Pleasant Green church after I had gone to Paducah, I would not have stayed in Paducah very long. The Union army and the devil had the place, and I didn't see any place for God and myself. But as I burnt the bridge behind me, I had to fight it out or surrender. The civil, religious people were gone to other places, and strangers that didn't know 'Joseph' had come in from everywhere, it seemed, but from where God had been." When he began the work, men would smoke cigars in the church, drink whiskey and curse when they were spoken to. They would curse at him fearfully when he spoke to them, so he prepared himself a hickory stick, about two inches thick and three feet long, and took it in the pulpit with him and showed it to the men and told them what he would do with it. Well, they believed him and let him alone. He has been in this place now twenty-two years, and has a fine and well-behaved congregation, as large as any in the State. He has baptized over two thousand persons there; has ordained some ten ministers in this church, some of them very able and good men. In September, 1867, with the aid of Elder S. Underwood and others, he organized the first district Baptist Association in the Washington Baptist church, and was elected moderator and has been elected ever since. He organized it with five churches, but in 1868 it had one hundred and thirty. He assisted in the organization of the General Association of Colored Baptists of Kentucky, in August, 1867. He was elected moderator of this association at its session in Danville church, August 16, 1871, and retained the position until August 17, 1881. He was a member of the American Baptist Consolidated convention which met first in Nashville, in 1867, and attended several of its sessions in different cities. He has received over 12,000 persons into the church and has baptized over 8,000 and pastored 12 churches; has married over 13,000 couples. He established and edited a religious newspaper called the *Baptist Herald*, from 1873 to 1878. He has been a Baptist for 45 years, and has been preaching for 41 years, and has been an elder for 37 years; he has preached over 12,000 funeral sermons, including the funeral sermons of the following noted ministers of the gospel: Jordan Bailey, Frederick Braxton, Armistead Steele, Reuben Lee, Emanuel Cartwright, N. G. Merry, W. W. Taylor, W. C. Dabney, Wilson Fortson and some others whose names are not here mentioned. He has given some attention to the subject of Free Masonry, and was grand senior warden of the Grand Lodge of Kentucky, and was elected two terms grand master of the State. Also was at the head of the chapter of Paducah Lodge, No. 1545, G.U.O.O.F.

Certainly no man lives in Kentucky who has done more to develop her spiritual interest. He is a man of large proportions, powerful speaker, and of a genial, sociable temperament. He has differed largely with the brethren and had his own view of matters, and has not pleased every one, nor has every one pleased him; but certain it is that there is a work done by George Dupee that cannot be undone. He is a man of a great deal of power over men.

CHAPTER CXXVII

Samuel C. Watson, M. D.
Druggist—Doctor—Member of the City Council—First
Colored Clerk of a Steamboat owned by a Colored Man

———◆●◆———

In the city of Detroit there lives a gentleman who has established himself in the drug business, and whose standing in the community makes him a fitting representative of the State of Michigan and the city of Detroit. He is acknowledged as one of the solid men of the city, and mention of his name is given on account of his success in business; for it is in this department of life that we must make successes in the future. There are orators, divines and professors in abundance, but business men are few; indeed too little attention is paid to this department of life.

The druggist is considered even more dangerous than a physician, as he is supposed to make all the mistakes in compounding medicines, and hence in this department of labor it would be expected that a colored man would refuse to enter.

His customers are, however, not separated by a color line, for the most of his sales are to those of the opposite race, who buy what they need for the price asked at any place, if only the object they seek can be obtained.

Mr. Samuel C. Watson began life in the State of South Carolina, St. James parish, in 1832. His parents died when he was about nine years old, and when a settlement of the estate was made, he was sent with two brothers and two sisters to Washington and placed in charge of a guardian, the Rev. William McLane, a Presbyterian preacher. He commenced his education before he had left the State of South Carolina. In Washington, the first school he attended was kept by Mrs. Leonard A. Grimes, wife of the distinguished Baptist minister of that place, who for many years held charge in Boston, Massachusetts, and at this time was serving a term in Richmond prison for assisting some fugitive slaves in their efforts to escape from the bonds of slavery. The next school he attended was Union Seminary, conducted by John F. Cook, a Presbyterian minister. At the age of sixteen he went of his own accord to Phillips Academy in Andover, Massachusetts, and remained there three years, one year being in the Classical Department. The future seeming dark and having but few to encourage him, meeting with prejudice on every hand he left the academy, not on account of prejudice there, but the dark future he saw pictured on every hand.

In the spring he shipped on the survey schooner, "Madison," at Brooklyn Navy Yard. The surveys extended from Delaware Bay to Portland, Maine.

Late in the fall he returned to New York and received his discharge. He was influenced perhaps, by a very great desire to know more, and because some other Washington boys had in the meantime, with his younger brother, gone to Oberlin; and learning, too, that it was about as near the colored man's paradise as any place in the country, made up his mind to commence studying again; so early in 1853 he left Washington for that city of learning.

While he was well pleased with the surroundings and the school itself, he did not fully enter into the spirit that seemed to move everything there. So in the fall he made up his mind to leave, which he did. From there he went to Ann Arbor and entered the Medical Department of the Michigan University and pursued his studies there until the fall of 1856.

After leaving the university he went to Cleveland, Ohio, and entered the Western Homeopathic College, completed his studies and graduated that winter. After leaving college he settled in Chatham, Ontario, where he practiced his profession, remaining until the fall of 1858. About that time the discovery of gold in British Columbia created quite an excitement throughout the country. He, too, was affected with the gold fever, and ambitious to better his circumstances, sought the gold fields and essayed to find that which would make him comfortable in life. But the bubble was soon pricked; gold didn't lie around waiting simply to be picked up, and so being disgusted with failure he returned the next fall.

In 1859 Mr. Whipper, a colored gentleman of Philadelphia, Pennsylvania, purchased a passenger steamboat named the "T. Whitney" and placed her on the route between Detroit and Sandusky, Ohio. Mr. Watson was requested to take a clerkship on the boat, which he did, acting also as part manager. He remained with this boat until the close of navigation, and feels gratified to-day that he had a hand in the first venture of the kind by a colored man.

In the winter of 1861 he went to Salem, Massachusetts, where he married the only daughter of Mr. Joseph Cassey of Philadelphia, Pennsylvania. He then settled in Toronto, Ontario, and resumed the practice of medicine. The Canadian laws requiring that everybody practicing there must hold a diploma from that country, he went before the board and was examined, and became a regular licentiate.

Here he remained till the spring of 1863. The rebellion in this country was going on at this time, and he was forced to return to the United States to protect the interest he had there. He went direct to Detroit, Michigan, and opened a prescription drug store and has continued in that business until the present time, now twenty-four years.

In 1875 his wife died; he has suffered the loss of three girls and a boy. One of the girls is now employed at the public library as an assistant. The other girl and boy are attending the High School.

In 1877 he married his second wife, she being the only daughter of M. F. Coleman of Philadelphia, Pennsylvania, who has borne him two children, a daughter and a son.

His public life has been marked with some degree of success, and is about as follows: In 1874, the colored people having become of some importance as a political factor, it was thought that the proper thing was to honor some one of the race with the nomination; and so Mr. Watson was nominated on the Republican ticket, but the whole ticket was defeated, and thus the honor of legislating for his people, while legislating for the State, was lost. But nothing daunted, in 1875 he was again nominated as a member of the Board of Estimates, and lost some five hundred votes by a dirty trick of misspelling his name by some gilt-edged Republicans who had bolted the regular nomination; but Mr. M. J. Mills, who was the Democratic nominee, refused to take advantage of the trick, and the aldermen voted Mr. Watson the position.

In 1876 he was again nominated for the Legislature, but the whole ticket was defeated with one exception. In 1883 without any solicitation, not being at the convention, he was nominated as a member of the city council (or the upper house) for the term of three years, and was elected by a handsome majority and served the full term. In 1884 the question of having a delegate at the Republican National convention was thoroughly discussed and defined by the *Detroit Plain Dealer*, through whose efforts the success was mainly due. At the State convention held at Grand Rapids the contest was quite bitter, the opposition coming principally from some questionable white and colored men from his own district, but he was chosen, notwithstanding opposition, as one of the four delegates-at-large. He favored Blaine until he got the nomination.

At the close of his term as councilman and twenty years' service to the party, he applied to the Republican mayor for the vacancy, with others, in the assessor's office. After promising it to him he changed his mind making Mr. Watson's color an excuse, and in the face of a Democratic council which stood ready to confirm him had he received the nomination, this cowardly act was committed.

In 1884 he was tendered by the general director of the colored department of the World's Exposition, the position of honorary commissioner for the State of Michigan. He accepted the trust and did the best he could to make a creditable showing for the States.

His success has not been through sudden or startling methods, but verifies the old adage, "If a man attends to his own business, his business will attend to him." He is still registered as a physician and has amassed a property both real and personal which would easily be valued at thirty thousand dollars.

In his religious views he says as follows: "As to church matters I generally give the Congregational denomination the preference in my attendance. I am not connected with any church, and in my religious beliefs am very liberal. I have learned to judge people more by what they practice than by what they preach."

The success of Mr. Watson should be an inspiration to others, and it is hoped that those who read this will be encouraged to undertake not simply the ordinary avocation to which colored men too often give their attention, but to the extraordinary, and in this way build up the race, making new avenues for them in which to direct their energies. The ranks of labor classed as menial or manual labor are full, and it is necessary for us to attempt new things, in order to find expression for those who are not content with the simple things in life.

RICHARD HARVEY CAIN

CHAPTER CXXVIII

Rt. Rev. Richard Harvey Cain, D. D.
Bishop A. M. E. Church—Congressman—Senator in the South
Carolina Legislature—President of Paul Quinn College

One of the brightest lights of the A.M.E. church was extinguished when Bishop Cain passed away, January 18, 1887. He was born in the "Old Dominion" in 1825, and remained there until the period of boyhood had passed, when his parents carried him to Ohio, first to Portsmouth, then to Cincinnati. The greater opportunities offered to the race in that State, and the liberal public sentiment, was an incentive to the young man to make greater efforts in securing for himself a name and in working for the upbuilding of his race.

He was converted in 1841, and though feeling that he must work for souls, continued his labors as steamboat hand until moving to Hannibal, Missouri, where he was licensed in 1844 by Rev. William Jackson of the M. E. church. Soon after this he returned to Cincinnati, and, being dissatisfied with his church relations, severed his connection with the M. E. and joined the A. M. E. His first charge was at Muscatine, Iowa.

After being ordained deacon by Bishop W. P. Quinn, in 1859, feeling a need of greater qualifications he entered Wilberforce University the following year and applied himself diligently to study. In 1861 he was transferred to the New York Conference and had charge of the Brooklyn church four years. April, 1862, he was ordained elder by Bishop Payne in Washington. In 1865 he was sent to the South Carolina Conference. This State proved to be the principal theatre of his action. Church after church sprang into existence as if by magic under his charge. Emmanuel church, having a membership of three thousand; Morris Brown church, with a membership of two thousand; besides churches in Summerville, Lincolnville, Georgetown, Marion, Sumter and other small places were organized by him. Indeed, to him is due the very large membership of the connection in Charleston, which has been quoted at ten thousand. Besides this, he felt that his people had need of him in other fields, and he accordingly interested himself in whatever touched their welfare in the State as well as in the church. He was a member of the Constitutional convention which revised the constitution of South Carolina. Served two years as State Senator from the Charleston district. In 1868 he edited a Republican newspaper, and in 1879 he was elected Republican Representative from South Carolina to the Forty-third Congress. In 1881 he was elected again to the Forty-fifth Congress, and served with distinguished and marked ability. In 1880 he was elected to his present office in the A. M. E. church and assigned to Louisiana and Texas district. His administration as president of the Paul Quinn College was acceptable to all. The title of D.D. was conferred on him by Wilberforce University, and it was borne with honor to himself and the denomination.

The whole career of the bishop excites the admiration of the thoughtful. It is a life well spent, one filled with golden deeds. At a memorial meeting held in Bethel A. M. E. church, New York, February 17, 1887, commemorating the life and services of Bishop Cain, Rev. B. W. Derrick, D.D., in a eulogy, said:

As the ministry was of divine appointment, he took the Bible as the book of his council, believing and accepting it to be the true Word of God, subordinating all other professional works to this, the greatest of all books.

Regardless of the difficulties which often cause the minister to be burdened, emanating from the pastoral work, the attendance of many kinds of meetings, the worldly-mindedness of believers, the false-heartedness of brethren, the care of loved ones, besides his studies, yet none of these things moved him. His life he counted not dear.

His relation to his church was of the most binding character; his heart and soul were deeply ingrafted into her moral and spiritual welfare; as a minister of the African Methodist Episcopal church he was able, intelligent and logical. He would often say that he considered the African Methodist Episcopal church to be an instrument, created for a special work in the civilizing and evangelizing of Africa. He considered the Bible to be the chart by which Christian mariners are guided across time's trackless ocean. Through his labors and influence, upwards of one hundred thousand souls were gathered into the African Methodist Episcopal church throughout the State of South Carolina. From among this number the church points with pride to some of her most able and educated ministers.

Death has robbed this denomination of its richest gem in the person of our deceased brother, whose influence is felt like a mantle of love from rice swamps of the South to the bleak coasts of New England. In the days when men suffered for even advocating mission work among the lowly cabins of the Negro, this brother with fearless love visited his oppressed brethren in their degradation and poverty, and filled their scanty houses with the soul-reviving truths of the Gospel, for he believed that the true mission of a minister was to better humanity and uplift the down-fallen.

The mortal remains of R. H. Cain have been consigned to an honorable and long-remembered tomb; but the memory of his Christian statesmanship, translucent in the highest degree, rises above the average, and open and faithful more than almost any of his compeers. He surely could be considered a captain of the hosts, one of the kindliest and pleasantest of Christian statesmen, a man of clear, good judgment, blended with a strong resolution and firmness which made him a master of many difficult situations in the active political career which marked with brilliant success his statesmanship.

While in Congress, with valiant loyalty to his race, he fought for the civil rights of the Negro, and in defense of the brother whom many defamers attempted to falsify, Bishop Cain made one of the most eloquent and weighty speeches of his life. To Carolina and Texas he was a brilliant star, and the Paul Quinn College, Waco, Texas, will always remember with pride her honored president. No denominational line marked the admiration and love for this brother. He was universally esteemed as one of the brightest lights of his race.

Said *The American Baptist,* February 5, 1887:

"Death loves a shining mark" has been exemplified in the taking away of so many noble men, during the last year, of the race. Amid all the disadvantages of slavery and by hard pushes, Bishop Cain elbowed himself to the front rank. Twice a Congressman; twice a State Senator; what a testimony of duty well performed! To the young men of our race and especially to the young men of the church whose Bishop he was, he has left a priceless legacy. Though gone to his eternal reward, yet the life which he lived here shows ever to them that from the humblest position in the scale of existence, they may rise to the very acme of the noblest calling known to men. Industry, truth, courage and faith, and the example he has left us, are the essentials that mark every prosperous and elevated career.

At the memorial meeting held at Quinn chapel, Louisville, Kentucky, Sunday January 30, 1887, there were delivered by two Baptists, Rev. W. J. Simmons, D.D., and W. H. Steward, Esq., and one Methodist, Rev. W. R. Harper, presiding elder, the following resolutions, which were adopted.

WHEREAS, it hath pleased Almighty God, our Heavenly Father, in the fulfillment of his Divine purposes, to remove from us our beloved Bishop, Richard Harvey Cain, D.D., we the members and congregation of Quinn chapel in memorial service assembled, do join in weeping "with those who weep" in consequence of the sad bereavement which hath befallen the whole A. M. E. church. While with profound grief we learn of the death of this distinguished man of God and deeply mourn our irreparable loss, yet realizing that this dispensation has been for the best, we bow with humble submission to the Divine will.

By the death of Bishop Cain, the Board of Bishops have lost a wise and honored colleague, the clergy a minister of vast erudition and acknowledged ability, the A. M. E. church an earnest, faithful pastor, the cause of education a teacher who delighted in progress and freely gave his time and means for the instruction of the young, and the country a just and illustrious citizen.

Full of mercy and good fruits he gave himself, and wherever he could accomplish most for the Master whom he rejoiced to serve, he was always proud. He was chaste in thought and word, and was a living epistle seen and read of all men; but he is no longer with us. He died in the Lord; "he rests from his labors; his works do follow him."

For these reasons, therefore be it

RESOLVED, That in the death of Richard Harvey Cain, D.D., late Bishop of the A. M. E. church, Christianity has lost a friend and earnest advocate, the race one of its noblest, and most highly esteemed representatives, the country, a citizen of unsullied character, of matchless worth, and the youth of the church a father whose example is worthy of imitation. And be it further

RESOLVED, That a copy of these resolutions be sent to the members of the family of the deceased as a testimony of our sympathy in this hour of loss and bereavement, and that a copy be sent to the *Christian Recorder, N. Y. Freeman*, and the *American Baptist*.

J. M. MAXWELL,
J. E. SIMPSON,
MRS. M. A. JOHNSON,
Committee

CHAPTER CXXIX

Hon. John H. Smythe, LL. B., LL. D.
United States Minister—Resident Minister—Consul General
to Liberia—Attorney at Law

One of those men reaching a high point in American history is the Hon. John H. Smythe, who began life as the first colored newsboy in Philadelphia. His parents, Sully and Ann Eliza Smythe, were born in Virginia: the first in Lynchburg, and the second in Richmond. His father died in 1857, aged sixty-seven, and his mother in 1883, aged sixty-three. July 14, 1844, this couple looked upon the face of the child who was to become so eminent in after years as to fill a large part in the affairs of the country wherein his father and mother had not been recognized. Verily the women of our race have always contributed to the greatness of their sons, and it seems that his greatness was mainly due to her energy and rare talent. He was only thirteen years old when he was left fatherless, and at that time had quit school and become errand boy in a dry goods store for a year, when he managed to return. He was known as a thorough and earnest seeker after knowledge, and had a great thirst for the stage.

The boy was early taught to read by a mulatto lady at Richmond, Virginia, between the age of five and seven. Between the age of eight and nine he was sent to the city of Philadelphia, Pennsylvania, by his parents to be educated. The writer first met young Smythe some years after in Philadelphia, where he was known as a speaker of much merit, and was generally beloved by all the boys. He attended first a Quaker school, and then a Grammar school, and lastly the Institute for Colored Youth, a Quaker institution, which he entered in the year 1859, graduating May 4, 1862. Hon. Ebenezer D. Bassett, the late minister-resident to Hayti, was then head master of said institution. During his student life he was taught drawing and painting, and was, after a year's study, admitted a member of the Academy of Fine Arts at Philadelphia, Pennsylvania. He became a fairly good landscape painter. At the time of his admission, persons of the African race were not allowed to enter this art institution,

JOHN H. SMYTHE

even as visitors. In 1864 he was employed as a laborer in the china house of Tyndale & Mitchell, Philadelphia, Pennsylvania, and he was a short time connected with the army as sutler's clerk.

Through personal inclination, and the encouraging advice of the Hon. John W. Forney and Mr. Shelton Mackenzie, histrionic critic of the *Philadelphia Press,* in the year 1865 he was induced to go to London for the purpose of preparing himself for the stage. He was furnished with letters of introduction to Mr. Samuel Phelps, then in the zenith of his fame as a tragedian, and especially to Mr. Ira Aldridge. At the time of his arrival in London, Aldridge was playing in the city of St. Petersburg and he did not get to see him. Finding himself too poor to enter on a course of study for the profession, he returned home and abandoned all thoughts of the tragic boards and entered upon a prose life.

It is interesting to note that he was willing to work at any honest labor; it cost some struggling in his breast to give up his hopes and crush the ambition of his dearest dreams. But it is always thus; we must deny ourselves for others. He has, perhaps, served his race better and been enabled to wring acknowledgment of ability and culture from his enemies. While he was engaged in manual labor, by the advice of the Negro philosopher and financier, William Whipple, he went to school—teaching at Wilkesbarre, Pennsylvania. While there he interested himself in the study of law, and in the year 1869 entered the Howard University Law School, of which Hon. J. M. Langston was dean, A. G. Riddle, Esq., professor of pleading, and Judge Knott, professor of medical jurisprudence. While a student of law he was appointed clerk in the Bureau of Refugees, Freedmen and Abandoned Lands of the War Department, by acting Assistant Adjutant-General Henry M. Whittlesey, January 12, 1870. This office he resigned about August 15, 1870, and became a clerk in the census office of the Interior Department the twentieth of the same month, and was resigned with forty-nine other clerks in 1872. He was then appointed internal revenue agent, Treasury Department, August 1, 1872; resigned the same in November, 1872, to accept the appointment of internal revenue storekeeper through the favor of Secretary Boutwell. He gave a bond of twenty thousand dollars, on which there were none but colored men. He resigned January 8, 1873, and entered the principal office of the Freedmen's Bank, Washington, District of Columbia, as a clerk, and shortly afterward was sent with the company's bank examiner, Mr. Sperry, to Wilmington, North Carolina, where there was a branch bank, to examine into its management. He became a cashier and continued to act in that capacity until the failure of the Freedmen's Bank; then he settled in Wilmington and entered upon the practice of his profession. Under the law he was required to be examined by the full bench on the

Supreme Court at the capital of the State. He passed a successful examination, and was certificated and returned to Wilmington, and on motion of Adam Empie, a distinguished lawyer, he was admitted. This gentleman, though the owner of slaves and always a Democrat, was, during his practice, his constant and sincere friend, and contributed largely to his success. Through his acquaintance with this gentleman he became known to Hon. Matthew W. Ransom, United States Senator, who subsequently wrote these terms of him to Mr. Secretary Evarts.

SENATE CHAMBER, WASHINGTON, D. C., April 23, 1878
Hon. Wm. M. Evarts, Secretary of State, U. S. A.

DEAR SIR: I have very great pleasure in commending to you for the mission of the Republic of Liberia, Mr. John M. Smythe of North Carolina. I have known Mr. Smythe for several years; he represented the county of New Hanover in the last State Convention of North Carolina. He has justly the name of an honorable man in all respects; his ability, his attainments, his promise is equal to those of any other man of his color in the country. He is esteemed in North Carolina by both races, and I am satisfied that he is fitted for the position at Liberia.

With my regards,
M. W. RANSOM

Mr. Smythe was elected a member of the third State Constitutional convention ever held in North Carolina in 1875, for the purpose of changing the constitution of the State; he took an active part in political questions, and was a prime mover in the nomination of General Grant for second term and of Mr. Hayes. He went to Washington in 1876, and practiced law for a year with considerable success. He was examined and appointed clerk in the office of the first comptroller of the treasury, where he remained during the latter part of Mr. Taylor's administration of the office and a portion of Judge Porter's administration. On the twenty-third of May, 1878, he was appointed by President Hayes minister resident and consul-general to Liberia, on the recommendation of Frederick Douglass, B. K. Bruce and M. W. Ransom. After serving a term of four years, he was recalled by President Garfield, and was subsequently reappointed by President Arthur, April 12, 1882. During his incumbency of the office of minister, by permission of his government he had charge of the German Consulate at Monrovia for a period of six months. During a vacancy in the office of the Belgian Consulate he acted in a similar capacity, and was also requested by the minister of Norway and Sweden at Washington to represent his Sovereign at Liberia.

While minister, he recommended a line of steamships to ply between New York or Baltimore and the west coast of Africa and the appointments of native gentlemen to the post of consuls and consular agents in Africa, on the ground of economy, and because of the effect such appointments would have in creating better and more intimate relations between the United States and West Central Africa. He had the honor of having made the fullest and most complete reports upon the products of Liberia that ever were made, up to the time of this appointment.

He was given the honorary degree of LL.D. by the board of trustees of Liberia College, and was appointed knight commander of the Liberian humane order of African redemption, by his excellency, H. Richard Wright Johnson, President of the Republic of Liberia, December 28, 1885; and with the appointment he is accorded the right and privilege of wearing publicly the insignia of the office. Mr. Smythe has the honor of being a member of the Atheneum Club—one of the most exclusive and distinguished in London. Mr. Smythe was recalled by President Cleveland March 25, 1885. Since his return to America he has resumed the practice of law in Washington, District of Columbia. He is a man of fine personal qualities and has many warm and devoted friends.

The career of Mr. Smythe is worthy of emulation in many respects. He lives an exemplary life, and has been a member of the Presbyterian church ever since his twenty-second year. He lives in a style befitting his station and education. He is an excellent husband and devoted father. His wife, formerly Miss Fannie Shippen, is one of the finest ladies in America and adds grace and dignity to his household.

CHAPTER CXXX

Rev. J. J. Durham, A. B., A. M., M. D.
Valedictorian in the Medical School—A Vigorous, Convincing Debater—Preacher

---

James W. Durham, a wealthy white farmer, and Dorcas Durham are the parents of the subject of this sketch, who was born April 13, 1849, near Woodruffs, Spartanburg county, South Carolina, and was held as a slave by his father.

When about ten years of age his parents removed to a farm near Cashville, in the county of his birth, and he worked until he was fifteen years of age on this farm, when he was apprenticed to learn the blacksmith's trade. Until 1870 he continued at this trade, during which time every spare moment was devoted to studying, often at night by torch light, until he learned to read and write.

In July, 1867, he was converted and joined the Pilgrim Baptist church, Greenville county, and the same year he was licensed and entered the ministry. In June, 1868, he was called to the pastorate of Foster's chapel, Spartanburg, and was ordained. He was deeply impressed with a call to the gospel ministry, yet the lack of mental preparation seemed to him a hindrance and he knew no way to remove the difficulty. At last he decided to enter the work as pastor, and do the best he could under these embarrassing circumstances.

His church was fifteen miles distant from his home, and many times he was obliged to go over rough roads, creeks and hills on mule-back or on foot. This charge he held for eighteen months and received as a compensation eighteen dollars.

After resigning this pastorate—having saved a little money from his earnings as blacksmith, Mr. Durham decided to attend school at Greenville C. H., the nearest school to his home. At this place he rented a room for $1.50 a month and boarded himself, exercising in every way the severest economy and self-denial. In this way, aided by money earned by working every Saturday and during vacations, he remained in school three years.

Twice a month he walked home to return with clothes and provisions for another fortnight. He ranked high as a scholar in his school, having passed from the lowest grades to the head of the most advanced class.

During the summer of 1873 he paid an instructor five dollars a month to teach him Latin and Algebra, with a view to entering the South Carolina College, which had been recently opened to colored students. He succeeded in entering the Senior preparatory class.

Failing to enter the Freshman class, as he had hoped to do, he could receive no aid from the State and now again he was straitened. In this difficulty he appealed to his father for help and received from him his first assistance, the sum of fifty dollars, which enabled him to remain in school during the year—coming out a little in debt.

During vacation he taught school at thirty-five dollars a month, and in October, 1874, he easily entered the Freshman class, secured a scholarship of twenty dollars a month from the State, and in this way he managed to earn enough to support himself comfortably until he completed the Sophomore class, when the State government passed into the hands of the Democratic party, which refused to make any appropriation for the institution, and in the spring of 1877 the South Carolina College closed.

In October, 1877, he entered the Junior class of Atlanta University, Atlanta, Georgia, and remained until May, 1879, when he removed to Fisk University, entering in March, 1880, and graduated the following May with the degree A. B.

After graduating he returned to Columbia, South Carolina, and took charge of a small church. This gave him an opportunity to learn something of the true condition of the Negro. Their poverty and complete ignorance of sanitary laws, lack of medical attention when sick, and inability to secure it, led him to conclude that if he knew something about medicine he might be more useful among those with whom he labored. Acting upon this desire, in October, 1880, he entered the Meharry Medical College, Nashville, Tennessee, and by vigorous application to study in two years he completed the course, graduating in March, 1882, valedictorian of his class with the degree M. D.

Again he returned to Columbia, and after remaining a short time he was called to the pastorate of Bethesda church, at Society Hill, South Carolina—one of the largest and most influential churches in the State; here, in connection with his church labors, he soon had a large and successful practice in medicine.

In October, 1883, as Dr. Durham was appointed by the American Baptist Publication Society to take charge of its work in this State, and also corresponding secretary and financial agent of the Baptist Educational Missionary and Sunday school convention in South Carolina, he was obliged to resign his pastorate and give up the practice of medicine, and since he has given his powers to this work with much success.

As an orator and debater he is said to have no equal in the schools he attended. So famed was his skill in debate that in the later years of his school life few students dared contend with him.

In Atlanta University he was appointed by the lyceum (a literary society) of the institution, to debate with Mr. Garvin, one of the best speakers in school, the question: "Which was the Greater General, Hannibal or Cæsar?" The question was Mr. Garvin's own selection, and he took Cæsar as his choice. Dr. Durham, after delivering his argument and taking his heart, was surprised to have his opponent arise and, addressing the audience, say: "Gentlemen, it is no use for me to say anything,"— and pointing to Dr. Durham, continued, "That man's *voice* is sufficient," and then take his seat.

Dr. Durham is comfortably well off—being worth about three thousand dollars, free from all encumbrances. In May, 1885, he received the degree of A. M. from Fisk University, an institution of large reputation in the South. In May, 1884, he spoke at the Baptist anniversaries which held their sessions at Detroit, Michigan, on the subject: "The Progress of the Colored People since the Emancipation," and his speech was received with great applause. His style and manner were captivating, and secured the strictest attention throughout. Dr. Durham has been a success. His struggles have made him strong, self-reliant and competent. Graduating in poverty, he is making vast strides in an upward direction, and will make a noise in the world that will yet attract the ear of the Nation. As an example of stick-to-it-iveness he is worthy of record here.

CHAPTER CXXXI

Rev. B. W. Arnett, D. D.
Financial Secretary of the A. M. E. Church—The Statistician
of this Church—Author—Editor of the Budget—Legislator—
Author of the Bill Wiping out the "Black Laws" of Ohio

To know Dr. Arnett is to know a man with royal feelings and kingly dignity. He is the prince of good men. His head is full of wisdom, his heart full of love to God and humanity, and his hands full of good deeds. I have enjoyed his acquaintance many years, and have appreciated his kind and affable ways; he gave me more encouragement in beginning this work than any man with whom I conversed. My acquaintance began in Quinn chapel, Louisville, Kentucky.

I had wandered out one morning to hear a sermon from some one beside myself, as I was tired of hearing myself talk; so when I was invited into the pulpit, I was introduced to the gentleman. He preached that morning from the subject as found in the last part of the nineteenth chapter of Exodus, comparing the wrath of God that kept the Israelites away from Him, and the blessedness of the gospel as found in the nearness of the people to Christ as he delivered that grand and inspiring "Sermon on the Mount." From that day we have been close friends. I enjoyed the hospitality of his home during my visit to Wilberforce in 1884, and I found him a loving husband, an indulgent father and a generous host.

Dr. Arnett is a man everyone loves. He is a strong man; a giant in the denomination. He is a great orator and has delivered speeches on various occasions, but they all run in an historical channel.

The jovial good-natured doctor was born in Brownsville, Fayette county, Pennsylvania, March 6, 1838. He began his public labors as a school teacher in his native town, receiving his certificate in December, 1859. He taught until 1867, ten months of that time in Washington city. He was an active member of the Pennsylvania State Equal Rights League, which had control of the educational and political interests of the race. Owing to his decided progressive views on all questions of importance to

B. W. ARNETT

his race, he soon became the acknowledged leader of the organization. He was a member of the National convention at Syracuse, N. Y., in 1864; was elected secretary of the National Convention of colored men in Washington city, in 1867; was chaplain of National convention, Louisville, September 2, 1883; was licensed to preach in the same city March 30, 1865, and April 19, 1867, took charge of the A. M. E. church at Walnut Hills, Ohio, where he soon became a great favorite of his congregation, and did much good to promote the principles of Christianity. He was the teacher of the common school of the same place. After three years of successful labor there he was sent to Toledo, Ohio—this was May 14, 1870—where he again remained for three years, or until 1873. He was again returned to Cincinnati, May 23, 1873, where his works are too well known to comment upon. From Cincinnati he was sent to Urbana, Ohio, where he remained two years, until September 3, 1878, after which he took the pastoral work of Columbus, Ohio. From this station he was elected, May, 1880, to his present position, that of histographer and financial secretary of the A. M. E. connection, and re-elected in May, 1884, for four years. This office has handled, receiving and disbursing, over one hundred and seventy nine thousand dollars within the past four years. In connection with this office Dr. Arnett edits the *Connectional Budget,* a magazine containing all interesting and historical matter of the church.

He has been grand director of the Grand Order of Odd Fellows of the United States; was the first colored foreman of a jury where all were white men (in Toledo) in 1872; he was an active member of political conventions, and several times has filled the important post of chairman of the committee on resolutions. He is the compiler of a work entitled *Negro Literature,* comprising already some ten large volumes of sermons, addresses and speeches of colored men. It is his purpose to continue these collections for the benefit of coming generations. His love for history is shown from the fact that at each place he has been stationed he has written a history of that church. He was appointed delegate to the International Convention of Sabbath schools, and also to the Y. M. C. A. at Washington city in 1872. He was appointed delegate to the Centennial Sunday school convention in London, England, 1880, but could not attend; also to the International Sunday school convention at Toronto, where he met with an ovation. Served as chaplain of the State Republican convention in Columbus in 1880; had the honorary title of Doctor of Divinity conferred upon him in June, 1883, by the trustees of Wilberforce University. It was a fit recognition of such a useful man and at the most opportune time. Mrs. Dr. Arnett is a lady of culture and polished manners. She possesses the faculty of winning friends by her lady-like appearance, and always has a good word of encouragement for those who need it. She was born in Geneva, Pennsylvania, August 1, 1838, but was reared in Uniontown. They were married May 25, 1858, by Rev. George Brown, president of Madison College, Uniontown, Pennsylvania. The children born to this happy union are Alonzo T., Benjamin W., Henry T., Annie L., Alphonso Taft, Flossy Gordon and Daniel Payne. Dr. Arnett's library is one of the finest in the State, and is composed of over two thousand volumes. His collection of distinguished men, both white and colored, is hard to excel.

Rev. Arnett has always enjoyed the implicit confidence of the persons with whom he has been associated, either in church or State; while the younger men of his race feel under many lasting obligations to him for his herculean labors to elevate his people by every good work. May he yet see many days to bless and guide his people.

In politics the doctor is a stalwart Republican, and believes that colored people will be promoted in the party by being faithful all the time, so that the leaders will know just when and where to find them. In the fall of 1885 he was elected to the Ohio Legislature from Green county, by an unprecedented vote, which showed his popularity and strength. His voice had been heard in many a campaign doing vigorous service for the Republican party, and his reward was the pay for party services. He richly deserved it—and it was generously bestowed. He realized this as the recognition of his fealty to the doctrines of the party in a speech delivered at Columbus, July 1, 1885, while a candidate; he was received with wild applause as he arose to speak. He said, "that was the principal reason why he voted the Republican ticket—because they applauded a colored man as quick as they would a white." From this he branched off into an eulogy on the character and records of the candidates, and said, "that he was proud of the greeting his standard-bearers had received; his constituency (and here he asked the pardon of everybody if he pronounced the word as if strange, because it was new) had accorded him a generous welcome, and had instructed him to use his best efforts for the success of their candidates, Foraker and Kennedy. Green county Republicans would always join hands with all their brethren, and especially in ratifying the nomination made at Springfield. Green county was the resting place for the soldiers' children, the soldiers who had gone into the war to fight the battles for his race for freedom; and all these children of the dead heroes were now in the right hands to make them follow the precepts of the Republicans. Green county, the old and steadfast stronghold of Republican principles, was green all the year, green in spring, summer, fall and winter, and each season, the green spot gave a new and fresh crop of Republicans. And these men in this county were those who demonstrated the principles of their party, by according to a black man the true recognition of his worth—his vote. To the Republicans the colored people owed all; that should give to the party who had given them freedom, and who were now going to give him (the speaker) what few colored men had obtained—an office." This speaker was interrupted many times by the cheers which would follow some characteristic remark of his, and it could plainly be seen that he was a favorite.

Once in the legislature he aimed his blows at the iniquitous "Black Laws" which had lingered like a funeral pall over the hopes of the race. After putting his hand to the plow he paused to gather power and influence, and as usual many abused him, calling him a traitor; and the man who had always done his duty was hounded by journals long since dead, and their resting places not even known. I sustained him through the *American Baptist*, and declared that we had not lost faith in him. I wrote him a letter in order to find just what was the trouble, and he told me, and said no one had asked, but they had roundly abused him. We declared our confidence in him was not and had not been shaken. The bill was finally passed in the 1887 session, with only seven votes against it. Senator Ely in the senate gave it his earnest support, and the last vestige of proscription went down by the sledge-hammer blows of the very kind of a man they were made to keep down. A jubilee meeting was held at Springfield, and the following account was reported in the *Cleveland Gazette:*

SPRINGFIELD, OHIO.—On last Monday night the large hall known as the wigwam, was packed from pit to dome with jubilant citizens over the passage of the Arnett bill, and who eagerly listened with sincere interest to the speeches made by the many distinguished orators present. The demonstration made by the people in honor of the repeal of the "Black Laws," the last remaining legislative vestige against the colored race, will live in the history of this city as one of the grandest demonstrations within the memory of its inhabitants. There were at least two thousand persons present, including the most prominent citizens among both white and colored; and when the Cadet Band played the opening strains of a march, the stage was filled by a notable gathering of local and visiting statesmen. Among the distinguished speakers on the platform were Hon. B. W. Arnett, Senators Ely and Pringle, J. Warren Keifer, Rev. James Poindexter, Professor Scarborough of Wilberforce; Mr. C. M. Nichols of the *Republic;* General Asa S. Bushnell, Rev. G. W. Zeigler, Hon. G. C. Rawlins, Mayor Goodwin, Rev. W. R. Boone, Rev. W. H. Warren, Mr. J. K. Mower, J. F. McGrew, James Buford, H. C. Smith of *The Gazette;* W. S. Newberry, D. Wilborn, C. H. Butler. The venerable patriarch, James Poindexter, led in a fervent prayer, delighting in the fact that all nations had been made of one blood, and that the eternal principles of truth were beginning to be acknowledged and recognized by all men. Rev. Wilton

R. Boone, our talented and much respected clergyman, presided as chairman.

The Hon. B. W. Arnett, the wide-famed author of the bill, was introduced and spoke in words of eloquence that took an indescribable effect upon the people. His cup seemed to be filled to overflowing with joy over the passage of his bill. His speech was a perfect shower of eloquence, and he was compelled to stop some minutes for the laughter and applause to subside. He told how Liberty's ball had rolled through succeeding years until now it had swept oppression and slavery from the land. He said that we are now equal before the law and we must take care of ourselves. And, now, since we are given an equal chance with the white brothers, if we are distanced the fault will lie in ourselves. His reference to Hon. John Sherman, predicting him for our next President, fairly took the house by storm. He spoke of how we had fought the battles of this country, and came back with a redeemed country, and every man and woman cried, "Roll on, Liberty's ball, roll on!" He said the schools are open, the churches are open, and the penitentiary is open; and if we do wrong we will be punished, and if we do right we will be honored. He said with education for our heads, religion for our hearts, and money for our pockets, we can stand up in our own innate powers. Rev. James Poindexter spoke at some length on the progress of the race, and told them to adopt the motto of Lincoln: "Root hog or die."

Extract from the speech on "The Black Laws of Ohio."

Now, in the name of the intelligence of the race, I give notice to all concerned that we do not intend to go unless it is of our own free will and accord. We cannot go without taking some of the glory of this country with us. We cannot go unless we have a settlement with this Nation. We cannot go unless we receive indemnity at the hands of the government. We would desire to take everything that belongs to us with us; and therefore we must have the bones of our fathers, the tears of our mothers, the sighs of our sisters, the groans of our brothers, the blood of the wounded and the life of the dead, in order that we may be able to carry our memories with us, and forget the wrongs of the years and the sufferings of the centuries. We must have a settlement for the years of unpaid labor in the South. We want to collect in some huge cask the tears wrung from the hearts of the bondsmen by the lash. We will not leave this country as long as there remains a bone of the soldiers of the Revolution in the soil. No, sir; we will stay here until every bone of the fugitives of other years is returned, with its flesh, to its family and friends, and the reunited families shall be honored with the blessings of the new day of freedom.

Ask us to go from this land with the record of the soldiers of the three great wars shining with glory to our race! No, sir; you might as well understand it first as last, we are NOT *going*.

While the memory of the heroes of Port Hudson and "Milliken's Bend" is being sung by our children, and while the soldiers of the war assemble around the camp fire and relate how

> *We led the Union soldier,*
>   *When fleeing from his foe;*
> *We brought him through the mountains,*
>   *Where white men dare not go.*
> *Our hoe cake and our cabbage*
>   *And pork we freely gave,*
> *That this old flag might be sustained;*
>   *Now let it brightly wave.*

Let us remember the deeds of valor of the heroes of the war, and preserve the jewel of liberty in the family of freedom.

We say unto you that, as God reigns in the world, we will not leave nor forsake you; for your country will be our country; we will feel the same pride in its mountains of iron, silver and gold as you do. We will feel as much pride in its valleys, plains, lakes, rivers, trade, commerce, institutions of learning, manufacturing interests, and in its unparalleled advantages to the husbandman; and in all of these we glory with you.

We shall say of our country, our fathers' country: Where thou dwellest, I will dwell; where thou goest to school, I will go, whether in the log school-house at the cross-roads, or the high school on the avenue: thy preacher shall be my preacher, and I will be buried in the same graveyard with you—so help me God.

GUSTAVUS VASSA

CHAPTER CXXXII

Olaudah Equiano or *Gustavus Vassa*
A Virginia Slave—Purchases his Freedom—Sails for London—
Presents a Petition to the Queen

―――――♦•♦―――――

In one of the richest and most charming provinces of the kingdom of Guinea, on the west coast of Africa, was born in 1745 Olaudah Equiano, the youngest son of a noble family. His mental and physical development was the pride of a painstaking mother. In the province of Essaka, the inhabitants were far removed from the baneful influence of a slave trade which was carried on along the coast. Surrounded by luxuriant supplies of nature and a labor-loving people, this boy lived in contentment until reaching his eleventh year, when he and his sister were kidnapped by two men and a woman, and sold into slavery. The custom was for those who traded in human flesh to go to the interior of the kingdom, steal the victims, hurry them away to the seashore, where swinging at her moorings lay the slave ship. His captors traveled night and day for six days through dense woods, with the howlings of wild beasts on every side. At last reaching their destination, Olaudah was hurried on board.

Looking around the ship he saw multitudes of black men and women of every description chained together, and wearing such expressions of misery that he was filled with anguish and fell on the deck in a dead faint. When consciousness returned the cruel faces of the white men frightened him still more. The ship sailed, and in due time landed at Barbadoes, where the slaves were crowded into a pen made for that purpose. When the day of the sale came, at a signal (the beating of a drum) the buyers rushed pell mell into the yard, each eager to make the best selections. Olaudah with a few others were sent to Virginia and sold to a planter there.

Shortly after landing he was sold again to a sea captain who sent him on board a ship called the "Industrious Bee," which was bound for England. It was here that he received the name Gustavus Vassa, and acquired some knowledge of the English language from an American lad of much culture, who saw in the poor slave a superior mind. This boy, Richard

Baker, never lost an opportunity to instruct and advise him. An intimacy sprang up between the two which was quenched only by death.

In 1757 he was taken by a press gang on a British man-of-war, and was a year in the service, both on the coast of France and of America, then returned to England and was sent to school where he learned to read and write. About this time his master was made lieutenant on a ship bound for the Mediterranean, and Gustavus accompanied him. The shipmates were so impressed with his desire for information that they instructed him at odd hours. When the ship returned to England, encouraged by the previous kindness of his master and also by a consciousness of having been a loyal slave, he asked for his freedom. For reply, in 1762, his master put him on board a ship bound for the West Indies. In a volume of three hundred and fifty pages, written by himself in 1787, he said:

At the sight of this land of bondage, a fresh horror ran through all my frame and chilled me to the heart. My former slavery now rose in dreadful review before my mind, and displayed nothing but misery, stripes, and chains; and, in the first paroxysm of my grief, I called upon God's thunder, and His avenging power, to direct the stroke of death to me rather than permit me to become a slave again, and be sold from lord to lord.

Fortune was kinder to him than he hoped. He was purchased by Mr. Robert King, a kind Quaker merchant, who lived in Philadelphia. In some way Gustavus obtained three pence which he invested, and soon gained one dollar with which he bought a Bible. A short time after, his master entrusted him with some merchandise with which to go in business for himself, promising at the same time that he should have his freedom as soon as he was able to pay for it. With this incentive Gustavus toiled without tiring, and soon accumulated the required sum to the surprise of his master, who instructed him to have the secretary of the Register office to prepare the manumission papers for his signature. That day he stood before the world a free man.

His first thoughts after getting his freedom were of old England. His heart yearned for the place where he had been treated as a man, but Mr. King's entreaties induced him to remain and enter as a sailor on one of his vessels. On the first voyage to Montserrat, when reloading the vessel to return home, Captain Doran was butted in the breast by cattle and died at once. Gustavus took his place and safely conducted the ship to port. From this he was called captain. He soon sailed for England, and with a determination to get an education; but not having sufficient money he engaged on board a ship and learned navigation. In the spring of 1773 an expedition was fitted out to explore a northwest passage to

India, conducted by the Honorable Constantine John Phipps, since Lord Mulgrave, in his majesty's sloop-of-war, "The Race-Horse." Gustavus concluded to go, and after returning to London he was engaged as steward on a ship bound from London to Cadiz. Speaking of this voyage, he said:

> In a short time after I was on board, I heard the name of God much blasphemed. I concluded to beg my bread on shore, rather than go again to sea amongst a people who feared not God, and I entreated the captain three different times to discharge me; he would not, but each time gave me greater and greater encouragement to continue with him, and all on board showed me very great civility. Notwithstanding all this, I was unwilling to embark again.
>
> When our ship was ready for sea again I was entreated by the captain to go in her once more; so I again embarked for Cadiz, in March, 1775.

Returning from the trip, Dr. Irving, an old friend who had purchased a plantation in Jamaica, also a fine sloop of 150 tons, prevailed on him to go thither. They landed January 14, but Gustavus not being satisfied returned to England in November, 1777.

In 1783 he traveled through eight counties of Wales, and the following year sailed for New York, returning to London in 1785 and found the government actively engaged in sending Africans to their native quarters. There was a special committee for the black poor, and he was asked to superintend part of the work. November, 1786, he was appointed commissary for the government. During his term his convictions of honesty were so shocked by the systematic cheating of the government on the part of the agent, that he informed the commissioners of the navy of the proceedings. Soon after he was dismissed from the service.

March 21, 1788, he presented the petition to the queen, asking for help for his fellow men in Africa.

TO THE QUEEN'S MOST EXCELLENT MAJESTY.

Your Majesty's well-known benevolence and humanity embolden me to approach your royal presence trusting that the obscurity of my situation will not prevent your Majesty from attending to the sufferings for which I plead.

Yet I do not solicit the royal pity for my own distress; my sufferings, although numerous, are in a measure forgotten. I supplicate your Majesty's compassion for millions of my African countrymen who groan under the lash of tyranny in the West Indies.

The oppression and cruelty exercised to the unhappy Negroes there have at length reached the British Legislature, and they are now deliberating on its redress; even several persons of property in slaves in the West Indies have petitioned Parliament against its continuance, sensible that it is as impolitic as it is unjust—and what is inhuman must ever be unwise.

Your Majesty's reign has hitherto been distinguished by private acts of benevolence and bounty; surely, the more extended the misery is, the greater claim it has to your Majesty's compassion, and the greater must be your Majesty's pleasure in administering to its relief.

I presume, therefore, gracious Queen, to implore your interposition, with that of your royal consort, in favor of the wretched Africans; that, by your Majesty's benevolent influence, a period may now be put to their misery; and that they may be raised from the condition of brutes to which they are at present degraded, to the rights and situation of free men, and admitted to partake of the blessings of your Majesty's happy government; so shall your Majesty enjoy the heartfelt pleasure of procuring happiness to millions and be rewarded in the grateful prayers of themselves and their posterity.

And may the All-bountiful Creator shower on your Majesty and the royal family, every blessing that this world can afford, and every fulness of joy which Divine revelation has promised us in the next.

I am your Majesty's most dutiful and devoted

Servant to command,
GUSTAVUS VASSA,
The Oppressed Ethiopian

This is a brief sketch of the great Gustavus Vessa—a man of great learning, tender sympathies, pious life and earnest zeal for the oppressed. From slavery to freedom, from an humble to an exalted freeman—he shows the genius of the native African.

CHAPTER CXXXIII

John W. Cromwell, Esq.
Editor—Distinguished English Scholar—Lawyer—President
of the Bethel Literary Society, Washington, District
of Columbia—Examiner and Register of Money Order Accounts

If you ask me for the best English scholar in the United States I would unhesitatingly refer you to John Wesley Cromwell, nor do I except any white man, woman, or child. Recently I attended a lecture, and, in the course of the speaker's remarks, he said: "The world asks a young man when he goes out of school, what can you do?" We will show you what he can do, and thus substantiate our assertion, for what man has done, man can do, and I believe he can repeat his experiences. The gentleman is so very unassuming and retiring in his disposition and manners that no one would judge, when in his presence, that there was a man with a head full of grammars, arithmetics, geographies, spellers, dictionaries, histories and other books, before him; and yet it is so. The plural is used because he is not a committer of one book, but is an analytical scholar who compares one book with another; indeed he is a walking English library and encyclopedia. On the history of his country he is thoroughly posted, and can with very little effort give the most important events, and indeed many of the minor ones, concerning the history of America. He graduated from a school which had a reputation at the time as the best in fitting persons for teachers. Under the principalship of Ebenezer D. Bassett, a race of English speaking Negroes were graduated. Such names as Shadd, Belcher, Butler, Hill, Lock and others testified to their thorough preparation in English.

Mr. Cromwell has undoubtedly reflected credit on his *alma mater*. He has maintained a character for business and honest dealing that marks him as a man of much talent, tact, and industry. His nativity begins September 5, 1846, at Portsmouth, Virginia. He was the twelfth and youngest child of Willis H. and Elizabeth Carney Cromwell. In 1851 his father had obtained the freedom of his family and moved to West Philadelphia. John W. entered the public schools there in 1851 in the lowest

JOHN W. CROMWELL

grade and remained until 1856, when he was admitted into the Preparatory Department of the Institute for Colored Youth, whose principal was Professor Ebenezer D. Bassett, since, minister to Hayti and now resident in this country, representing the Haytian government, with headquarters in the city of New York.

The day of graduation was reached in the summer of 1864, and he began the life of a school teacher at Columbia, Pennsylvania, October, 1864. When this closed he began a private school, April, 1865, at Portsmouth, Virginia, and maintained the same until the fall of the same year; then he returned to Philadelphia and was soon employed by the Baltimore Association for the moral and intellectual improvement of the colored people until May, 1866. In the month of March he was shot at and his schoolhouse subsequently burned to the ground. He returned to Virginia and was employed by the American Missionary Association and assigned to Providence church, Norfolk county. Here he took an active part in politics and engaged in the grocery business, but did not succeed in the latter enterprise and had to give it up. He was a delegate to the first Republican convention in Richmond, Virginia, April 17, 1867, and also to the celebrated "John Minor Botts" convention, held in August at the same place, after which much time was spent by him in organizing Republican clubs and councils of the Union League Association.

Mr. Cromwell was impaneled United States juror for the term at which the Hon. Jefferson Davis was to be tried, and was one of the four colored men on the jury which convicted several government officials of conspiracy to defraud the United States government. The case was pronounced by the chief-justice who presided to be the second case in the country of conviction on a similar charge. In the Constitutional convention which met in the State, he was elected clerk, and discharged the duties with especial pleasure and gratification to his friends. In 1869 he resumed teaching and organized several schools under the auspices of the Philadelphia Friends.

On the line of Richmond & Danville railroad there was a murder committed in open daylight of the Hon. Joseph R. Holmes, a member of the Constitutional convention and a candidate for the House of Delegates. This was one of the political murders which have happened in the South, and by the means of which the country has been disgraced. Mr. Cromwell was an eye witness to the murder. In the fall of 1869 and 1870 he taught at Withersville, then the highest grade school in southwest Virginia. In 1870, at Richmond, he was principal of a school held in "Dill's Bakery," one of the last pieces of confiscated property that was returned by our government to the former owners. In the summer of 1871 he taught a term in Southhampton county, near the scene of the "Nat Turner Insurrection." As a teacher he has been a marked success. His pupils rapidly advance, and he has had the pleasure of seeing many of them take exalted positions in life. In the fall of the year he went to Washington, District of Columbia, and entered Howard University Law Department, from which he graduated in March, 1874, and was, on motion of Hon. A. G. Riddle, admitted to the bar before the Supreme Court of the District of Columbia. In 1872 he entered the civil service examination in the treasury department and passed at the head of more than two hundred applicants. This of course gave him standing with the examiners and secured for him an appointment. The same week he received an appointment to teach in the public schools of the county of Washington, passing also at the head of a long list of teachers who were examined. This is a common experience with Mr. Cromwell; it makes no difference how many are in the examination, when the questions in English studies are before the candidates he always stands at the head; and in these two notable instances he gained a remarkable reputation and inspired confidence.

In 1873 and 1874 he was promoted, as a result of a competitive examination, first, to a fourteen hundred dollar clerkship, then to a sixteen hundred dollar clerkship. In the latter examination he lead the entire office, and being, with Rev. Robert William Waring, the first colored clerks to receive such an office in any of the departments. He was then appointed as chief examiner of the division of the money order department, and subsequently was register of money order accounts until the time when he retired under the Cleveland administration in 1885. In April, 1875, during the "spelling bee" excitement which traveled from one end of the country to the other like some great tidal wave, Mr. Cromwell distinguished himself for his extensive knowledge, as shown in the remarkable feat which he performed, as we now relate it. There was a spelling match arranged between the clerks of the two bureaus of the treasury department, and at both times (for the match was repeated) the office in which Mr. Cromwell was employed was successful, and he always among the fortunate ones. At the first match there remained only three, a white gentleman and lady and Mr. Cromwell, who gave color to the occasion. Referring to this spelling match, *The National Republican* for April 2, 1875, says:

Mr. J. W. Cromwell is a fine looking colored man, employed in the office of the sixth auditor. Mr. Fortune gave him some very hard words, but he maintained perfect command over himself and got through bravely, having missed but one word during the evening, and that word was *"sotto voce."*

The same year on delivering an address in the city of Richmond before the colored teachers of that city, the Virginia Educational Historical Association was organized, and he was elected its president and served continually. The last meeting was held in 1883. The Associated Press dispatch, August 4, 1875, was as follows:

J. W. Cromwell delivered an address on the difficulties surrounding the colored youth of Virginia in obtaining an education. These difficulties he thought were but financial and moral. The financial difficulties, such as the inadequacy for State and local support, and delinquency of the capitation tax, and poverty of the parents, were discussed at length. He claimed that white Southern teachers were not the best for the colored schools; that false and wicked ideas have been so widely spread, and their influences have been pernicious in the work of instruction, by limiting education, checking aspirations and shutting off opportunity for development and promotion.

These sentiments quoted twelve years ago are his sentiments to-day, and show the mental grasp of Mr. Cromwell in delineating in a very few words the true situation of the State of Virginia at that time. The views are statesmanlike, accurate and discriminating. In the *Sunday School Times* of Philadelphia, August 29, 1875, the following notice appeared:

In the published reports of the proceedings of the Colored Educational convention held at Richmond last week appears the name of J. W. Cromwell of Portsmouth, Virginia, who delivered an able address before the convention, and this address has been highly commended for its strong common sense and original ideas, and the clearness with which they were expressed. This intelligent colored man is a Philadelphian. In the old days of slavery it was the boast of the chivalry that the smartest colored men came from the South, and Fred Douglass was cited as an example of what could be accomplished by a man of no educational advantages in early life; but now times have changed, and Pennsylvania sends Virginia an intelligent, cultured and highly educated colored man who will compare with the best educated white man of the "Old Dominion."

In 1876 he organized the *People's Advocate* in the city of Alexandria, Virginia, but the next year it was removed to Washington where it is still published. As a writer, Mr. Cromwell is specific, close, logical, comprehensive. His paper is pure and is of the sort that can be put into the hands of the most virtuous, and will rather lead them to a higher life than in any way degrade them. Its weekly issue is looked for with considerable interest, as it discusses thoroughly all questions which may arise in the District of Columbia, and concerning which he expresses himself. The paper is especially notable for its typographical make up and its excellent proof reading. As would be expected, his English is plain and forcible, and his style not bombastic. He has expressed himself upon the subjects of editors and newspapers to which reference has been made by the *New York Globe* of March, 1882, from which the following is taken:

J. W. Cromwell of the *People's Advocate* remarked in a literary meeting in Washington last week that the colored newspapers and editors would compare favorably with colored colleges and colored professors. To the pioneers in this difficult field of labor, like the *Advocate* which, against pecuniary disadvantages and groveling disdain of the thoughtless and ignorant of the race, have continued to advance the interests of the race.

All praise and honor should be given him; none have worked more faithfully or unrelentingly in this field than Mr. Cromwell, and none more than he is held higher in the esteem of the colored press. To those who are outside of a newspaper office it may seem very easy to send out a paper every week, and satisfy its subscribers and secure their interest constantly; but it is indeed a trying task. Many times, persons who pay least are disposed to do the most grumbling and fault finding. The Negro editors who are not serving the people, as a rule do so at the risk of their health, personal popularity and financial prosperity. They hope against hope, and "hope deferred maketh the heart sick." Week after week, month after month, year after year, like some jack-o-lantern, just ahead, they pursued with renewed vigor the false hopes and what seems gleaming prospects. Alas! only to fail.

Mr. Cromwell has kept his paper going through these trying years and has succeeded in business, and has laid by some money for a rainy day. This is an evidence of his power to economize, and yet sustain one of the risky ventures undertaken by a colored man. Some one has compared a newspaper's financial wants to a rat hole, down which one might pour water constantly and it never seems to fill. Could his experience be given as to how he supported his newspaper in all these years, it would be like a romance. All honor to those men who have at their own expense sustained journals which have defended the cause of the people, and very often an ungrateful people. And, indeed, instead of being amused at the death of so many colored newspapers, their editors are largely to be praised, and a kind word spoken for them. They *tried*, but *failed:* it nevertheless did not detract from their intention to do good. No newspaper in the United States started by a colored man has ever had *only* a mercenary desire, but was in nearly every case started for the purpose of defending the rights of the people and defending them against the wrongs of enemies, furnish a mouthpiece for the groans and woes of a suffering people, and to proclaim abroad the injuries which have been added to the insults.

Mr. Cromwell took a prominent part in bringing this Virginia suit before the United States Supreme Court, which, with the Kentucky, West Virginia and Delaware cases, brought out the decision on the jury question. He is an orator of considerable reputation in local matters. In

Philadelphia, July 1, 1883, in the *Sunday Times*, the following notice appeared concerning his efforts made as alumni orator at the Institution for Colored Youth. It says:

In the centre sat the principal of the school, Mrs. Fannie Jackson Coppin, who conducted the exercises; and on her right hand was the orator of the occasion, Mr. J. W. Cromwell, of the class of 1864, who spoke on the subject of "The Outlook of the Colored Race in this Country." Mr. Cromwell is a brother of the famous colored caterer and well-known citizen, Mr. Levi Cromwell, and is well known among his race as a man of brains, activity and wide field of culture. His address proclaims him to be a man well booked in the issues of the day, and his fund of knowledge seems inexhaustible. He is a clear, forcible, entertaining speaker and held his audience in rapt attention. He is president of the famous "Bethel Literary" which meets weekly in the city of Washington, before which most of the prominent men of the Union have spoken. He is also an Odd Fellow and has represented his lodge in National gatherings of that fraternity, and on repeated occasions been selected as orator at the local anniversaries. He has acquired property to the amount of six thousand dollars, and is now practicing law before the district bar. He has recently connected himself with the Metropolitan A. M. E. church.

He was appointed by Hon. B. K. Bruce as one of the commissioners in the city of Washington to secure exhibits from the colored people for the Cotton Exhibition, held in New Orleans, concerning which E. Kirk in the *Southern Tribune* said:

Mr. B. K. Bruce could not have made a better selection to represent the District of Columbia if he had exhausted the city directory, or that of the floating or sojourning population, than when he appointed Mr. J. W. Cromwell honorary commissioner of the department of colored exhibits in the Cotton Centennial Exhibition at New Orleans.

Thus from one degree to another he has risen to distinction among his brethren of the newspaper fraternity, and his opinion is quoted very largely in the newspapers of the day.

E. M. BRAWLEY

CHAPTER CXXXIV

Rev. E. M. Brawley, A. B., A. M., D. D.
Editor Baptist Tribune—*President of Selma University—Sunday School Agent in South Carolina*

The work done by the subject of these remarks has brought untold good to the citizens of South Carolina and Alabama. Our acquaintance with this polished and scholarly gentleman began in 1870, when he spent a short time at Howard University, previous to his going to Lewisburg. His mild, quiet habits, added to his eminent piety, made him a beloved companion of us all. There were many South Carolina students in attendance at the time, and of them all he was the idol and pride of the number. There was O'Hear, my room-mate, who sleeps beneath the palmettoes of the old State; Morris, now president of Allen University; Dart, another who sleeps beneath the sod; McCants Stewart, an eminent lawyer in New York; Nash, the "sower of wild oats," and many others. Since those days he has grown in stature and filled important stations in the Sabbath school work as president and as editor. He began existence March 18, 1851, in Charleston, South Carolina. James M. Brawley and Ann L. Brawley were his parents. He was always free. At the early age of four years he was placed in a private school taught by an old lady. Here he remained several years and learned to read. Later he went to a school of a higher grade until the troubles occurred incidental to the uprising of John Brown, when the school was closed. In 1861, when about ten years of age, his parents sent him to Philadelphia to obtain an education. He at once entered one of the Grammar schools and remained three years, then entered the Institution for Colored Youth, Professor E. D. Bassett then being principal, and remained until 1866, when he had partly completed his preparation for college. He was now fifteen years old, and his parents thinking it best for him to learn a trade, caused him to return to Charleston and apprenticed him to a shoemaker. He served three years as an apprentice, and in 1869 returned to Philadelphia and worked as a journeyman at his trade. In April, 1865, at the age of fourteen, he had been baptized into the fellowship of the Shiloh Baptist church, Philadelphia. He early felt a call to the ministry, and became active in Sunday school work. Having concluded to enter the ministry he matriculated at Howard University in the fall of 1870, and was the first theological student regularly entered. Here he remained three months, and concluding to go through college, he left Howard and entered Bucknell University at Lewisburg, Pennsylvania, in January, 1871, being the first colored student to enter this institution. He completed his preparation and entered the College Department in the fall of 1871. At the close of his Sophomore year he was licensed to preach by the Baptist church (white) at Lewisburg, and when he graduated in 1875 he was ordained by a vote of this church by a council composed of thirty-five ministers, mainly college professors and other eminent men. He had studied theology privately during his college course. He went to Bucknell University by the advice of Rev. B. Griffith, D. D., and Mrs. Griffith gave him a scholarship, while he assisted himself by teaching vocal music to the students and others, and by preaching in vacations. On being ordained he was at once commissioned by the American Baptist Publication Society as missionary for South Carolina. His commission was dated July 1, 1875, which was the date of his ordination, (the day after his graduation, June 30, 1875). He at once entered upon his work and found but little organization among the colored Baptists in the State. There were many churches but few Sunday schools. There were also many associations, but they were doing but little work. He began at once to reorganize the associations; organized new ones, organized a Sunday school convention in every association, and then formed all these bodies into a State convention. The last was accomplished in May, 1877. He became the corresponding secretary and financial agent, and directed the work of the convention. Soon a vigorous State mission work was undertaken, a number of young men placed in the school and sustained while preparing for the ministry, many of whom are now filling important stations, and a mission work in Africa was begun and sustained for three years. Rev. Harrison N. Bouey was the missionary. His work in Africa commanded the admiration of the friends of Africa all over our land, and assisted much in creating an interest in African missions among the colored churches of the South.

Failing health compelled Rev. Mr. Brawley, after eight years of hard work in South Carolina, and against the wishes of the American Baptist Publication Society, to resign. A vacation of six months was kindly offered him, but he concluded to change his work, his physician having strongly advised it. But when he resigned there were as many Sunday schools as churches in the State, and the denomination was united and strong. While in South Carolina he raised a large amount of money not only for the State convention's work, but also for Benedict Institute.

Once in the short space of a few months he raised a special collection of one thousand dollars for the school. After having been several times invited, he accepted the position of president of the Alabama Baptist Normal and Theological school. He entered upon the work in October, 1883. In one year he reconstructed the school, graded it, put in a College Department and doubled the number of students. The name of the institution was now changed to Selma University. The first class to go out was graduated under him in May, 1884. He received his A. M., from Bucknell University (his Alma Mater) in 1878, and the honorary degree of Doctor of Divinity from State University, Louisville, Kentucky, in May, 1885. He has three times appeared as a regularly invited speaker before the American Baptist Publication Society at the National anniversaries. Some of his addresses have been printed in their minutes. He has published only a few addresses. Has received many complimentary notices, but has not preserved them. He is now writing a book on theology, entitled: *An Exposition of the Confession of Faith.* It is designed mainly for preachers with limited education. He has been Sunday school missionary, corresponding secretary, pastor and president of a university, and also edited the *Baptist Pioneer* for three years.

In January, 1877, he was married to Miss Mary W. Warrick of Virginia, a graduate of Howard University. By her he had one child, but by the close of the year both mother and child died. In December, 1879, he was married to Miss Margaret S. Dickerson of Columbia, South Carolina. She is now living. By her he has had four children, the eldest of whom is dead. He has made considerable money but spent it largely in aiding poor students. Fully one-half of his salary while president of Selma University was spent in that way. He has had various positions on boards, etc., and has been clerk of several associations. The failing health of his wife caused him to resign his position as president of Selma University, after more than three years' service, and return to South Carolina.

In January, 1887, he began the publication of the *Baptist Tribune*, a weekly denominational organ. It is one of the best papers of the South, and is a credit to his ability and earnest Christian labor.

CHAPTER CXXXV

James W. C. Pennington, D. D.
Able Presbyterian Divine—Greek, Latin and German Scholar

This, the first colored pastor of the New York Presbyterian church, was born about 1809 in Maryland. It is said by some that many men and women of the Negro race, who have stood head and shoulders above their fellow men, inherited their admirable traits of character from white ancestors; but it has been proven that there are many exceptions to this rule. The subject of our sketch was of pure African blood and descent.

Slave life in Maryland was more severe than in many of the Atlantic States, and in 1830 Mr. Pennington could no longer endure the yoke of bondage and escaped to Pennsylvania. Although twenty-one years old, he had never acquired any knowledge of letters. As soon as he was out of hearing of the slave driver's whip he applied himself earnestly to study, and in part made up for what was withheld from him in early life. In five years he had made such strides as to be able to teach a school for colored children at New Town, Long Island. Feeling that he had been called to the gospel ministry, he removed to New Haven, Connecticut, where he could enter a theological seminary and where he commanded a larger salary as teacher. After three years' earnest study he returned to his old position in New Town; was ordained and took charge of the Presbyterian church. Two years later he went to Hartford, Connecticut, and remained there teaching and preaching eight years. Dr. Pennington was five times elected a member of the "General Convention for the Improvement of the Free Colored People." If nothing more than this was said, it would speak volumes for this worker for the race.

In 1843 he was elected delegate-at-large by the State of Connecticut to attend the World's Anti-slavery convention held in London. In the same year he was delegated by the American Peace convention to represent them in the World's Peace Society, which met at the same place and in the same year. During his three visits to England he lectured in London, Paris, Brussels, and by his pulpit brilliancy won many complimentary press notices. He supplied the pulpits of the most popular ministers, and was classed with the leading theologians of his day. The degree of D. D. was conferred by the University of Heidelburg, Germany. On his return to America he was received with open arms. He was twice elected president of the Hartford Central Association of Congregational ministers, composed exclusively of white men. During his presidency two young white men presented themselves to be examined for license to preach. Dr. Pennington examined them in church history, theology, etc., and signed their certificates. It must have been a novel scene—a fugitive slave granting the sons of his oppressors (one the son of a Kentucky slave-holder) leave to preach the gospel.

In 1841 the doctor published a little book entitled, *A Text Book of the Origin and History of the Colored People;* also an "Address on West India Emancipation," and other papers. He was a life member of the American Tract Society, and many years pastor of the Shiloh church, New York. The *Rising Sun* says:

In stature he was of the common size, slightly inclined to corpulency, with an athletic frame and a good constitution. The fact that Dr. Pennington was considered a good Greek, Latin and German scholar, although his life was spent in slavery, is not more strange than that Henry Diaz, the black commander in Brazil, is extolled in all the histories of that country as one of the most sagacious and talented men and experienced officers of whom they can boast. Dr. Pennington died in 1871, his death being hastened by the excessive use of intoxicating liquors, which had impaired his usefulness in his latter days.

In the life of this man we see much to commend to the young men of the race. Copy well his earnest quest for knowledge; his love for race; but shun the vice which at the last clouded his brilliant intellect and placed him beneath the shame of a dissipate and tarnished his otherwise good name.

EDWARD WILMOT BLYDEN

CHAPTER CXXXVI

Hon. Edward Wilmot Blyden, LL. D.
Linguist—Oriental Scholar—Arabic Professor—Magazine
Writer—Minister Plenipotentiary—President of Liberia College

Without doubt the Hon. E. W. Blyden is the most learned man of the race, especially in the languages, and as such, must be acknowledged a man of a most gigantic intellect and acquisitive powers. He was born in St. Thomas, one of the Danish West Indies, August 3, 1832, but lived in the United States for some time during his youth. From this country, accompanied by his brother, he went to Liberia, landing January 26, 1851. At this time he was about nineteen years old. He was educated at Alexander High School, of which he became principal. This school was situated up the river St. Paul, about twenty miles from Monrovia. He has held many positions of honor and trust under the Liberian government. He has been twice the secretary of State of Liberia, and secretary of the interior once. For eight years he was minister plenipotentiary and envoy extraordinary to the Court of St. James. He was candidate and nominee of the Liberia Republican party, for the Presidency, in 1884, but was defeated by H. R. W. Johnson, who is now President of Liberia, and whose sketch appears elsewhere.

Dr. Blyden is a distinguished linguist and oriental scholar, and a prolific magazine writer, and has a wonderful knowledge of the Arabic language, having been professor of the said language at one time. The following notice appears in the *London Official Gazette* of August 2, and is here quoted by way of information:

A NEGRO DIPLOMATIST
THE LIBERIAN MINISTER TO THE COURT OF ST. JAMES

OSBORNE, August 3.—This day had audience of Her Majesty: Edward Wilmot Blyden, Esq., Minister Plenipotentiary from the Republic of Liberia, to deliver new credentials, to which audience he was introduced by the Marquis of Salisbury, K. G., Her Majesty's principal Secretary of State for Foreign affairs.

Dr. Blyden has the honor of being the first Negro plenipotentiary of the first Christian Negro State in Africa ever received at a court in Europe.

In 1866 he visited Palestine and Egypt, and afterward published an account of his travels in a volume, entitled *From West Africa to Palestine*. In 1871 he resigned his professorship in the college and traveled in England. On his return to Africa he accepted the appointment from Governor Kennedy of Sierra Leone, of envoy to the pagan king of the Soolima country. His report on that expedition was printed by the government and published in the proceedings of the Royal Geographical Society. In 1873 he was sent by Governor J. Pope Hennessy on another mission to a Mohammedan chief, three hundred miles northeast of Sierra Leone. In 1874 he was authorized to re-open the Alexander High School, on the St. Paul river, which is now in charge of an assistant. In 1877 he was appointed by President Payne minister to England, and President Gardner has continued the appointment.

Dr. Blyden has contributed several articles to the *Methodist Quarterly Review* in New York, and *Fraser's Magazine* in England. His local paper on "Africa and the Africans" has appeared in Fraser for August, 1878.

The twenty-sixth of July, the Liberian national anniversary, was most pleasantly spent, we are informed by Dr. Blyden, at luncheon with Dean Stanley, at a dinner at the Albion Hotel, given by the London school committee, at which the Lord Mayor presided, and in the evening at a large reception given by Mr. Samuel Gurney, where a brilliant company was assembled. He was also invited and attended the receptions held by Hon. John Welsh, American Minister, July 4 and 18, meeting at the former Bishop Holly of Hayti, and at the latter Hon. John H. Smythe, the American Minister of Liberia.

Dean Stanley, on the evening of July 24, entertained at his house a large company, to which King George of Bonny, Hon. John H. Smythe, Bishop Holly, and Dr. Blyden were invited. For the first time, it is believed, in the history of English society, have four persons of purely African descent, so freely mingled with the *élite*. Pere Hyacinth was present, having come over to England specially to meet Bishop Holly.

Dr. Blyden has been chosen an honorary member of the Atheneum Club, one of the most aristocratic and exclusive clubs in London. On the committee who elected him are such men as Sir John Lubbock, Lord Carnarvon, Herbert Spencer, Viscount Caldwell and Dean Church. The Marquis of Salisbury, the foreign secretary, is a member of the club. Dr. Blyden is probably the first Negro who has been so honored.

It is said that he is acquainted with more than forty languages and speaks all of them fluently. He has been a believer in the Christian religion, but it is now currently reported and pretty satisfactorily understood that he is an advocate of the Mohammedan faith. He has been writing a series of articles upon that topic to the *A. M. E. Review*, in which it is apparent he seeks to commend the fine points concerning the doctrines of that faith. Being brought in contact with many of the Arabic professors, he has an abundant opportunity of inquiring into the faith more practically than any one else of his color, because he gathers his information from the actual professors of that faith.

Some idea may be given of his views by a short extract from his last article in the *Review* above mentioned. He is endeavoring, I think, to prove that in the Mohammedan church there is no difference on account of color, and that the religion of the Mohammedans is more favorable to the Negro, because it has no regard in its effects and practices to or for the question of color:

In the United States there are the Methodist Episcopal church and the African Methodist Episcopal church, having the same creed, polity and language. The separation is caused by the elemental differences of race and color; evidently no fault of the Negro church, for it displays on its banner, with almost distinctness and reiteration, the sentiment of which Mohammedans do not admit the first part, but practice the second-God our Father; man our brother. The formal and continuous holding forth of this truth would be superfluous if it were universally recognized. But its presentation by the weaker—by the so-called inferior and despised party—wears to us the aspect of a humiliating appeal for recognition and sympathy. It is the "Am I not a Man and a Brother?" of the days of slavery. The excellent device of the *Christian Recorder* would have weight, it seems to us, if it were displayed by the stronger and superior with a view of attacking the weaker; but coming from the weaker it appears to us that all the desired effect is destroyed. All force is withdrawn from the strongest phrases in the language when employed by those who cannot command, but only beg. The offer of liberality is effective only when made by those who have the means to be liberal. The offer of beneficence on the part of those who have no benefits to confer is meaningless. We do not say that those who have adopted the motto have no justification for it. They have not only strong foothold in reason and common sense, but they have good ground in the gospel of Christ. We do not believe that such a brotherhood is beyond the possibilities of Christianity. We believe that the purpose and tendency of the system is to make hearts, divided by the distinctions of race, rank or intellect, clasp one another in the close embrace of a common faith. Was not this its effect in the primitive church? Our Mohammedan friends are charmed by that beautiful picture drawn by St. Luke of the simple and loving life of the Apostolic church—"And all that believed were together, and had all things common; and sold their possessions and goods, and parted them to all men as every man had need.

". . . And the multitude of them that believed were of one heart and one soul; neither said any of them that aught of the things which he possessed was his own; but they had all things common." The theory of the Church of Christ as taught by the divine founder and his immediate successors is a spiritual kingdom whose citizens are all sons of God and, therefore, brothers and sisters one of another. "For this cause," says St. Paul, "I bow my knees unto the Father of our Lord Jesus Christ, of whom the whole family on earth and Heaven is named." But alas, in a materialistic age, the noble device held forth by the *Christian Recorder* is simply "the voice of one crying in the wilderness"—*Vox lamantis in deserto.*

Mohammed appointed a Negro slave, Bilal, to call the faithful to prayer at the stated times; and from those Negro lips the beautiful sentiment first found utterance, "Prayer is better than sleep: prayer is better than sleep." It is repeated every day throughout the Mohammedan world, and the most distinguished European of whom history can boast is in Asia and Africa an unknown personage by the side of the slave Bilal. Mohammed gave this man precedence to himself in Paradise. On one occasion the prophet said to Bilal, at the time of the morning prayer, O Bilal! tell me an act of yours from which you had the greatest hopes, because I heard the noise of your shoes in front of me in Paradise in the night of my ascension.

It is said that the intellectual part of Christendom is in revolt against the renewed forms of Christianity, that there is a growing alienation from the recognized standards of belief, but among African Mohammedans the church of the people is identical with the intellect of the people. The possibilities of every individual in the nation, whatever his race or previous condition, give social stability and spiritual power to the system.

Besides the passage in the Koran which forbids the making of images, Mohammed, in private instructions, constantly impressed upon his followers the evil of such practices. The prophet said: "Those will be punished the most severely at the day of resurrection who draw likenesses of God's creation. If you must make pictures, make them of trees and things without life."

Mr. Blyden is now in Africa, and will probably spend the balance of his days there. He was formerly a Presbyterian minister, but has about abandoned the pulpit. This man's ability, scholarship and talent is a refutation of the lie that a Negro has little or no talent. His intellect towers above that of ordinary men as the church steeple above the brick chimney of the ordinary house.

CHAPTER CXXXVII

Rev. B. F. Lee, A. B., D. D.
Editor of the Christian Recorder—*President of Wilberforce*
University for Many Years

———◆◆———

Many years ago I read the following words: "President B. F. Lee, when he came to Wilberforce, was the hostler; they would not allow him to sleep with the students; but he studied, and within thirteen years of his arrival was made president of the university in which he could not sleep. Who can beat that for progress?"

It was no small leap for him, and was an evidence that true merit will not go unnoticed, but will always, as a rule, meet suitable reward.

Benjamin F. Lee, the son of Abel and Sarah Lee, was born in Gouldtown, New Jersey, September 18, 1841. His father's death occurred when he was only ten years old, and this caused him to be placed in the family of a relative. April 1, 1852, was the day when he began life's battles alone, and since then he has never spent more than six months at the old homestead where his mother still lives. His winters were spent in the country schools till he was fifteen years old. From that time till twenty-three years old, he was employed on farms and in factories. His studies in school had included algebra, and his private studies included many biographical and historical works, poetry and philosophy. Being ambitious for more learning, he entered Wilberforce University in November, 1864, where his recitations were confined to night classes for one year. In the meantime, to support himself, he labored hard at all jobs which he might secure during the day. In 1865 he entered the school as a student, completing his course in 1872, receiving the title as usual of A. B. His entire support in school was acquired by his own industry, with the exception of about one hundred and seventy-five dollars. There were but few farms within three miles of the university where he did not work, and with this means thus secured by hard labor he managed to pay his way through the school. He often walked from four to eleven miles during vacation to do a day's work in the cornfield or at harvesting. His old Greek grammar and reader, as well as his Xenophon's Anabasis, still bears the marks of the field, as with sweaty hands he would turn over its pages, gathering knowledge during some dinner hour or some other spare moment.

After becoming sufficiently advanced in studies, he spent a few months now and then teaching school. During six months he once taught school, worked on Saturdays and at other hours for his board, and kept up with his class in the college. Many times during the prosecution of his studies he was penniless, but never discouraged. On one occasion when he was keeping "bachelor's hall" or "baching" as he called it, he went to his room in the evening moneyless and crumbless. Kneeling down to pray "Give us this day our daily bread" as it is not often prayed, he was called by a voice which proved to be that of Mrs. Hannah McDonald (Aunt Mac), the sister of Mrs. Bishop Payne, whose heart had prompted her to bring food to the poor student. Verily God does not forget to feed those who trust in him: as Elijah was fed in the wilderness by the ravens, so God put it into the heart of this good woman to feed this young man, who was to fill so important a place in the affairs of his church, and add to the general aggregation of good which has been accomplished among the race. These seasons of distress and poverty have become to him the most blessed spots in his memory. Let it be here seen and read by many students seeking an education. Let mothers call the attention of their boys to this struggling student who trusted in God.

It does seem to me as if Christ himself must have felt peculiar interest in the young man at this time, for he was about to repeat the very prayer that his Master had said he should repeat, "Give us this day our daily bread." How ungrateful many of us are who get our "daily bread" without any visible effort of manual labor or spiritual devotion.

The training at home by a pious and devoted mother, God bless her! and the impressions he had from reading and observation, had led this young man to a life of trust in Christ. At the age of twenty-one he connected himself with the A. M. E. church. Having been impressed by reading and observation, he was led to adopt their views as the guide of his life. It was in 1862 when he joined the church. In 1866 he was permitted to exhort. In 1868 he was licensed to preach. In 1870 he was ordained a deacon. In 1872 he was ordained an elder. In the year 1868 he was appointed to the pastoral charge of the Salem Circuit, including Salem, Ohio, and Bridgewater, Pennsylvania. He subsequently filled several small charges as a missionary while continuing the course of study. Some were in Kentucky, others in Ohio. In 1873 he was called from the charge of Frankfort, Kentucky, to which he had been appointed at his graduation, to occupy the chair of pastoral theology, homiletics and ecclesiastical history at Wilberforce University, which position had been made vacant by the resignation of Professor T. H. Jackson. This position he held for two years when he resumed pastoral duties, taking charge of the A. M. E. church in Toledo, Ohio.

In 1876 he was called to the position of president of the university by the resignation of Bishop Payne. Here he had been gardener eleven years previous. His influence over the hundreds of young men has been far-reaching and for great good. He filled this office for eight years, when the general conference of the A. M. E. church elected him editor of the *Christian Recorder,* the official organ of that body.

He is still at this writing editor of the *Recorder,* and has given strict attention to the making it a first-class paper in every way. He was a member of the general conference of 1876 and '80 and a delegate elect to its session in Baltimore in 1884. In 1880 he was associated with Dr. J. G. Mitchell and Rev. R. A. Johnson to bear the fraternal greetings of the General Conference of the A. M. E. church to the general conference of the Methodist Episcopal church. He was also elected by the general conference of 1880 a delegate to the late Ecumenical Council of Methodists, and was chosen by the western section of the general Ecumenical committee, embracing the American continent and islands, a member of the permanent committee of arrangements. His literary productions have not been varied nor extensive. He contributed an article to the *Wesley Memorial Volume,* a work edited by Rev. J. C. A. Clark, D.D., and published by Phillips & Hunt, New York. . . . As a linguist he is the best production of the church's intellectual development, being acquainted with six different languages.

It was said of President Garfield that he went "from the towpath to the White House," and it may be said of the subject of our sketch that he went from an hostler's place to a college president's chair, where he sits the Nestor of all active, colored American Christian educators, distinguished in position, sublime in modesty.

The strong points in the life of Benjamin F. Lee are, first: that he has a tolerably correct conception of moral questions; second, he has the courage to persevere in the line of studies selected; third, he regards himself indebted to the world, not the world indebted to him; fourth, he believes in a solid growth and solid living of the individual, and of the masses in mind and in heart; fifth, he has strong confidence in the wisdom and love of God. He attributes his success in life largely to his having an intelligent mother, a good school teacher in early life, and an intelligent, faithful, Christian wife. Dr. Lee was married to Miss Mary E. Ashe of Mobile, Alabama, in 1873. She graduated with distinguished honors at Wilberforce University that year. She has very strong literary tendency, having contributed articles to the *A. M. E. Review,* chiefly poems. With black men as with white ones, good mothers and good wives are next in worth to personal excellence.

JAMES J. SPELMAN

CHAPTER CXXXVIII

Hon. James J. Spelman
State Senator—Temperance Orator—Eminent Baptist Layman

The Hon. James J. Spelman, the eldest son of the Rev. William Spelman of New York, was born in Norwich, Connecticut, January 18, 1841, and attended the public schools of that State until the family moved to New York in April, 1855. In 1859 he engaged in newspaper work, and from time to time has served in its various spheres, as carrier, dealer, reporter, editor, publisher and proprietor. On the establishment of the *Anglo-African* in New York City, he became a regular contributor to its columns, and later to the *Pine and Palm,* its successor.

When the war broke out and President Abraham Lincoln made his first call for troops, he was among the number that assembled at the Metropolitan Assembly rooms in New York City, to offer themselves to the government and were dispersed by the police of the city on the plea that the "tender of colored men to the government would exasperate the South."

When General J. C. Fremont had been removed from the department of the West, he was a member of the committee who were engaged in organizing an independent command to be known as the Fremont Legion; but in the meantime, General Fremont having been placed in command of the Mountain Department of Virginia, that hot-bed of rebellion, further efforts were abandoned. He was active in raising recruits for colored regiments, and organized from among the young men in the public schools of New York a battalion, known as the "Shaw Cadets," named after the hero of Fort Wagner, and was elected major.

Colonel Shaw's mother presented the command with a fine flag, the presentation speech being made by Professor W. Howard Day. The "cadets" gave several exhibition drills which were highly commended by the press and public. In 1868 he went to Mississippi under the auspices of the Freedmen's Bureau, and engaged actively in educational work. July, 1869, he was appointed a justice of the peace and alderman of the city of Canton, by General A. Ames, military commander, and assistant assessor of internal revenue by Secretary Boutwell, on the recommendation of General B. B. Eggleston, the assessor. In the election held for the adoption of a new constitution and the admission of the State into the Union, he was returned by a majority of one thousand eight hundred votes to the House of Representatives of the Legislature from Madison county; and in the ballot for United States senator received several votes on each ballot. He remained in the Legislature six years, serving during that period as chairman of the "Committee on Corporations," and a member of the "Judiciary" and "Ways and Means" committees. Mr. Spelman took a foremost position in the proceedings and delivered several addresses, among which was one on the Civil Rights bill and the other on the death of Senator Sumner.

The Republican Press Association was organized in 1870, and Mr. Spelman, being associated with the late Honorable James Lynch in the publication of the *Colored Citizen,* was elected to membership, and in the election of officers was chosen vice-president. He was also at that time special correspondent of the *New York Tribune.*

In 1871 the Legislature established Alcorn University, and he was appointed by Governor Alcorn a member of the Board of Trustees, and was elected secretary of the Board. He was also aide-de-camp on the staff of Governor Alcorn with the rank of lieutenant-colonel, and subsequently appointed colonel of the first regiment of militia.

In 1872 he was a delegate to the National Republican convention at Philadelphia, and was chosen a presidential elector. On the election of Governor Ames in 1873, he was appointed a member of his staff and assistant commissioner of immigration. In 1876 the Republicans of his district sent him to the National Republican convention at Cincinnati, and there he served on the committee on rules. He was among the number who voted for Secretary Benjamin H. Bristow, and finally for Rutherford B. Hayes.

Senator Bruce secured his appointment from President Hayes as consul to Port au Platte, San Domingo, which he declined; and was afterwards appointed a special agent of the post office department, with headquarters at St. Louis. In this service he remained until a change was made in the office of collector of internal revenue, when he accepted the position of office deputy to the new collector. In 1881 he was nominated by the Republicans for the office of secretary of State for Mississippi, and was counted out by the Democrats. In 1884 he was made superintendent of education by the American Baptist Home Mission Society, for its work in Mississippi; and remained in that field until called by Senator Bruce to the charge of the department of colored exhibits in the World's Exposition at New Orleans. He was also a commissioner to the American exposition. He has been an active participant in the Prohibition elections of his State, and he made an effective and telling speech at Meridian in the exciting canvass there, which brought the colored man into line and carried the election. The National Temperance Society then commissioned him lecturer, and the Honorable John B. Finch, R. W. G. T. of the order of Good Templars, conferred upon him the honor D. R. W. G. T. He is a Mason, Odd-Fellow, Knight of Phythias and Good Templar, and is the author of a ritual for a large and prosperous organization known as the Kings of Labor. He holds high rank in the secret societies, and has presided over several grand bodies with ability. The colonel joined the Baptist church in 1853, and has been an active layman in the work of the denomination. He is president of the Baptist State Sabbath school convention, and was the first Sabbath school missionary of the American Baptist Publication Society in the State. He is recording secretary of the Foreign Mission convention and chairman of the National Baptist Temperance committee. He has always been active in educational work, and was for a number of years the secretary of the city school board of Jackson, being the unanimous choice of the board, the majority being Democrats. He married, in 1870, Miss Anna D. Lavender, a native of Jackson, Mississippi, and four children are the result of that union.

The Honorable J. J. Spelman is a consistent and earnest defender of the race, and lends unstintedly his services in their behalf. He is a true friend, a devoted and conscientious Christian and an exemplary citizen, respected and honored at home and abroad.

CHAPTER CXXXIX

Rev. Marshall W. Taylor, D. D.
Poet—Editor of the Southwestern Advocate—*Brilliant Writer*

Among the noted men in the M. E. church, the race has reason to be proud of Rev. Marshall W. Taylor, one of its prominent men. He was born free July 1, 1846, at Lexington, Fayette county, Kentucky, of parents who had been slaves and had no opportunities offered them for education, except on his mother's side. His father's name was Samuel Boyd, his mother's name was Nancy Ann Boyd, and was of African and Arabian descent. She was always anxious about the education of her children. With this in view she persuaded her husband to leave the country, where he employed his boys as farmers, and come to the city to grasp whatever opportunities might be offered, no matter how difficult to obtain them.

He received his first instruction from his mother. For a short time he attended school and then moved to Louisville with his mother and brothers, his father having died some time before. Finding no school, they continued to Ghent, where they stayed two years, obtaining instruction from little white children by stealth, who attended school. On account of some trouble they were again obliged to return to Louisville. Here young Marshall became a messenger in the law firm of J. B. Kincaid and John W. Barr. He first taught in 1866, in Breckinridge county, Kentucky, and was bitterly opposed by men to whom a Negro school was obnoxious. In 1868 Mr. Taylor was elected president of an educational convention held at Owensboro, Davies county, Kentucky. This year he was also a member of a convention at Jackson Street church, Louisville, which inaugurated the movement for the Lexington M. E. conference. The Rev. Hanson Tolbert licensed him as a local preacher this same year, at Hardinsburg. His instructors in theology were Rev. R. G. Gardiner, J. H. Lennin and Dr. R. S. Rust.

He was called to Arkansas as a missionary teacher and preacher. He preached in Texas, Indian Territory, and Missouri, returning to Kentucky in 1871, and in 1872 was ordained by Bishop Levi Scott, at Maysville, Kentucky. While in charge at Coke chapel, Louisville, he issued the *Kentucky Methodist*. After various offices in the conference, he was finally elected secretary. He was made pastor at Indianapolis, Indiana, in 1875, and elder in 1876. He was sent to Union chapel, Cincinnati, 1877-78. He received the honorary degree of a Doctor of Divinity from the faculty of Central Tennessee College, Nashville, in 1879. This same year he was made presiding elder of the Ohio District, Lexington conference. In 1881 he was appointed as a delegate from the M. E. church to the Ecumenical conference at London, England. He was the caucus nominee of the colored delegates to the General conference, in 1880, for bishop. He has written the life of Rev. George W. Downing. As a teacher he has become famous. Some of his literary productions are widely read and circulated; among these may be mentioned his revival hymns and plantation melodies. He was elected editor of the *Southwestern Christian Advocate*, which position he still holds. He resides at president in New Orleans, Louisiana.

TOUSSAINT L'OUVERTURE

CHAPTER CXL

Toussaint L'Ouverture
The Negro Soldier, Statesman and Martyr

After the eloquent words of the golden tongued orator, Wendell Phillips, it seems almost profanity to undertake the sketch of the distinguished San Domingo chief, who rose from a slave to the position he occupies in history. The Negro race cannot be spoken of without mentioning among its great men the subject of this sketch. He is, perhaps, the most eminent Negro that has ever lived in the world. This I state with some caution; but when it is remembered that he has played an important part in the three characters which I have here mentioned at the head of this sketch, it can easily be seen that none can be mentioned who has so ably filled at least the two former positions. It is a fact that statesmen are failures as soldiers, and soldiers are failures as statesmen; it is also a fact that statesmen can talk much, but rarely become martyrs. A soldier cannot be called a martyr, for as a rule he hires himself to the government for pay for the very purpose of being shot at. He expects to die either in the hospital or in battle; beforehand he calculates concerning wounds and sickness. Then, too, in general, fighting men are not singled out, but are many times shot down in the crowd. Moreover, in tactics of recent days, generals or leaders have their places in the rear, rather than in the lead, assuming that an officer of high rank could not be well spared and that the common soldiery could easily be supplied, but the general commands the battle must be protected in order that his life may be longer for the purpose of direction. But aside from these reflections, I desire to present a few facts in regard to this man's life.

The date of the birth of Toussaint L'Ouverture is not known, but it is supposed to have been about the twentieth of May, 1743, though from his name it might be November 1, as that is "All Saints' Day" with the French. For several years he was so feeble and slender that he was called the little "lath," but as he grew to the age of twelve he was much stronger, and played, frolicked, jumped and ran races with boys. His disposition was kind, and his manner frank and open. He differed from the boys of his age in his careful and gentle treatment of all animals committed to his care. It should be mentioned here that, as a boy he tended the flocks and herds. His real name was Toussaint Breda, from the name of the estate on which he worked, and M. Bayou De Libertas was so pleased with him that he made him his coachman, a situation that was highly prized by slaves as it brought them in contact with the master, and if he happened to be kind, it gave them less drudgery. Performing his duties well in this respect, he was afterwards promoted to the office of steward of the sugar house. He finally married a widow named Susan, who had a little son named Placide. They were married according to the rites of the Catholic church, and lived peaceably and happily. He learned to read, contrary to the usual custom; but though he read very little, what he did read he understood thoroughly.

There was a French author called Abbé Raynal who was much opposed to slavery. One of his books fell into the hands of Toussaint and made a deep impression upon him. The question was discussed in that book, what should be done to overthrow slavery, and these words were used in connection with the question:

Self-interest alone governs kings and nations; we must look elsewhere; a courageous chief is all the Negroes need; where is he? Where is that great man whom nature owes to her vexed, oppressed and tormented children? He will doubtless appear; he will come forth and raise the sacred standard of liberty. This venerable signal will gather around him his companions in misfortune. More impetuous than the torrents, they will elsewhere leave the indelible trace of their just resentment. Everywhere people will bless the name of the hero who shall have re-established the rights of the human race.

These words, no doubt, sank deep into the heart of the reader, and as he pondered them they more and more impressed upon his mind, and indeed the prophecy seemed fitted to him to such an extent, that it was without doubt the keynote to his success. At the time when he arose from obscurity to fame a revolution was going on in France, and the friends of liberty were growing bolder every day and gave encouragement to three classes of persons who were on the island of San Domingo, and upon whom liberty would have a great effect. There were at the time 30,000 whites and 20,000 free mulattoes and 500,000 black slaves. Contrary to the American custom, the slaves in San Domingo followed the condition of the father and were free as far as the body was concerned. He was permitted to own property and amass all the wealth he could, but was not permitted political privileges. In America the child followed the condition of the mother, and no matter if they had a white father, the progeny was a slave. The white planters of course had many children by their slaves, and these mulattoes referred to were a very powerful class.

They were neither allowed in the church, nor could they be buried in the same graveyard. This class of people despised the Negroes, though they themselves felt, perhaps, more keenly their degradation than did the slaves, because they might be insulted by a white man and could not retaliate with a blow, for had they dared to do such a thing the right hand would be cut off. They were not allowed to be lawyers, doctors or priests; they could not attend school with the white boys; they could not intermarry; while they had nominal freedom, and many had been sent to France and educated, and had the advantage of culture and refinement. The distinction that was drawn between themselves and the white people was always like a knife in their hearts. This ought to have made them feel more kindly to those who were on the plantation and who had less of the enjoyments of life, but it seemed only to make them more forgetful of their brethren. About this time, feeling that their numbers and wealth entitled them to more considerations than they had, they sent a deputation to France, asking the convention to grant civil rights, a thing for which Negroes have contended so bravely in America. They carried with them a gift of 6,000,000 francs, and pledged one-fifth of their annual rental towards payment of the national debt, and only asked in return that the yoke of civil and social contempt should be taken away. The convention issued a decree at once saying that all freeborn were equal before the law. The representative of this opinion, Oge, carried the petition to the Island of San Domingo and laid it before the General Assembly of the island, and one old planter seized it and tore it into pieces and trampled it under his feet, and swore by all the gods that he would rather see the island sink than to have their bastards made their equals. They took Oge and broke his limbs on a wheel, and cut off his head as a warning to all those whom he represented. His body was cut in four pieces and hung in the four principal parts of the cities of the island. This caused the mulattoes much anxiety, and there was a class of what would be called in this country "poor whites" who sought every opportunity to inflame their anger, and make them feel their disappointments by insulting them and inflicting cruelties and outrages upon them. The white planters having thus outraged the decree which had been passed in the convention, sought the aid of the English against their own country, offering to make the island over to Great Britain in case of success.

In the meantime, they had refused to take the oath of allegiance to France; the Negroes had suffered along with the mulattoes, but they did not understand what was the cause of the extra whippings and murdering of the patriots. But when they came to understand it, on the twenty-second of August, 1791, they rose with a determination of defending themselves and gaining liberty. Toussaint L'Ouverture was at this time working on the plantation when he heard that the planters had called for aid of the English, and four thousand Negroes had risen in insurrection. Jean Francois was the leader of these armed Negroes. When the French governor in the Island called on him with his troops to lay down his arms, he replied:

We have never been failing in respect or duty we owe to the representatives of the King of France. The king has beheld our lot and broken our chains, but those who should have proven fathers to us have been tyrants, monsters unworthy the fruits of our labors. Do you ask the sheep to throw themselves into the jaws of the wolf? To prove to you, excellent sir, that we are not so cruel as you think, we assure you that we wish for peace with all our souls; but on the condition that all the whites, without a single exception, leave the cape. Let them carry with them their gold, their jewels; all we seek is liberty; but victory or death for freedom is our profession of faith, and we will maintain it to the last drop of our blood.

The slaveholders mounted the English cockade and entered into alliance with Great Britain, while their revolted slaves joined the Spanish who were on the eastern part of San Domingo, and had become allies of the King of France. It was in this state of things that Toussaint L'Ouverture came to the front. He joined the black soldiers and occupied himself as physician, trying to heal the wounded and take care of the sick. His disposition made him dislike war, and even when he became their leader he would never permit any cruelties if he knew it. The Negroes having suffered some defeats, desired a leader of more intelligence than the one they had, and they made Toussaint aide-de-camp of Biassou, under the title of brigadier. Commissioners came from France for the purpose of negotiating peace, and the blacks sent deputies to the colonial assembly to help the French commissioners; but the planters would yield nothing and finally lost all. History repeated itself in the American conflict; for when the peace commissioners met and overtures were made to the South, they refused every overture. Concession of Congress and profession of kindness on the part of Abraham Lincoln were all refused; and in their perversity the South lost everything, just as the planters in San Domingo had.

Speaking of him as a soldier, Wendell Phillips has said:

Cromwell manufactured his own army; Napoleon at the age of twenty-seven was placed at the head of the best troops that Europe ever saw. They were both successful. "But," says Macaulay, "with such disadvantages the Englishman showed the greatest genius. Whether you will allow the inference or not, you will at least grant it is a fair mode of measurement; apply it to Toussaint. Cromwell never saw an army until he was forty. This man never saw a soldier until he was fifty. Cromwell manufactured his own army, out of what? Englishmen—the best blood in Europe out of the middle classes of Englishmen—the best blood of the Island. And with it he conquered what? Englishmen—their equals. This man manufactured his army out of what? Out of what you class a despicable race of Negroes, debased and demoralized by two hundred years of slavery. One hundred thousand of them imported into the Island within four years, unable to speak a dialect intelligible even to each other. Yet out of this mixed, as you say despicable mass, he forged a thunderbolt, and hurled it at what? At the proudest blood of Europe, the Spaniards, and sent him home conquered; at the most warlike blood in Europe, the French, and put them under his feet. At the pluckiest blood in Europe, the English, and they skulked home to Jamaica." The soldiers were proud of their general and under his guidance performed miracles. It seems as if he never slept. The title "L'Ouverture" was given him because an officer said that wherever Toussaint goes he always makes an opening, the word means "the opening."

However, Toussaint finally cleared the island of all foreign enemies and restored peace and prosperity. With a view of establishing friendship between the planters and the former slaves, he offered five years' work for their masters on the condition that they received one-fourth of the produce out of which the cost of their subsistence was to be defrayed. He encouraged agriculture, and impressed upon the Negroes that the permanence of their freedom depended in a great measure upon their becoming owners and cultivators of the soil. Fugitives were invited to come back again, and the discipline of the army was so strict that some accused him even of security. They assumed perfect order under his regulations and he was the first ruler in the world to establish free trade by opening all the ports to the commerce of the world. He favored the white people more than the blacks from fear that he might be considered partial. On one occasion he assembled a court-martial to try his nephew, who was accused of indecision in quelling a riot, and the court-martial having adjudged him guilty, Toussaint ordered him to be shot. Everything was moving along peaceably on the island, which had again been restored to peace and prosperity by the beneficent laws which he established, when the news reached San Domingo that Bonaparte had issued a decree in May, 1801, restoring slavery in the island. This wicked measure was carried by a vote of two hundred and twelve against sixty-five. Toussaint's soul was fired with rage that vented itself in such words as these: "I took up arms for the freedom of my color; France proclaimed it and she has no right to nullify it. Our liberty is no longer in her hands; it is in our own; we will defend it or perish." In January, 1802, General LeClerc sailed with sixty ships and thirty thousand of the best troops under Bonaparte's command; "they were soldiers who had never met their equal and whose tread, like Cæsar's," say Phillips, "had shaken Europe; soldiers who had scaled and planted the French banners on the walls of Rome." Toussaint was dismayed, for the moment, as he saw the fleets coming in the waters of San Domingo, and exclaimed, "All France is coming to enslave San Domingo. We must perish." He then saw that he had trusted Bonaparte who had turned traitor to him. He then went to his people and said to them "Burn the cities, destroy the harvests, tear up the roads with cannon and poison the wells. Show the white man the hell he comes to make." General LeClerc did not find it so easy to deceive Toussaint with the fair promise which he made, for Toussaint had already been much deceived by Napoleon and had no faith in any other white man who represented any sort of peace and freedom. Messengers were sent for a conference with Toussaint, and many assurances of freedom and protection were given and he was even promised the position of colleague with LeClerc in the government of the island, and that his officers would still retain their rank in the army. But none of these things deceived him. Finally LeClerc sent word that he was about to land at Cape City, and received the reply, that "Toussaint is governor of this island. You send to him for permission. If the French soldiers set foot on shore I will burn the town and fight over the ashes." Disregarding this he undertook to land. Christophe set fire to the splendid palace which the French architect had just finished for him, and in forty hours the place was in ashes. After having been defeated and having made many promises, Toussaint yielded in obedience, as he said, to the orders of the first consul, for he said he himself desired to live in retirement, but that he would accept favorable terms for his people and the army.

LeClerc had won over by intrigue and bribes all of his generals except Christophe, Dessalines and his own brother Pierre. He took the oath of allegiance to be a faithful citizen, and on the same crucifix LeClerc swore that he should be faithfully protected and the island should be free.

Of Toussaint, Hermona, a Spanish general said: "He was the purest soul God ever put in a body. He never broke his word." Finally, on the tenth of June, he was arrested, his papers were seized, his house rifled and burned, and his wife and children captured, and at midnight he was taken on board the French ship "Hero," to be borne to France as a prisoner of state. He was chained like a common criminal and locked in a cabin and guarded by soldiers with fixed bayonets—not even allowed to commune with his family. As he was leaving San Domingo he looked upon her beautiful mountains for the last time, and said they had cut down the tree of liberty, but the roots are many and deep and it will sprout again. From the vessel he was carried to the Castle Joux, near the borders of Switzerland. He was placed in a deep dungeon from the walls of which the water continually dropped, and was allowed four shillings a day for food; and the faithful servant, who had accompanied the family from San Domingo, was allowed to remain with him. It is believed Napoleon hated the Negro general because the people called him the "Black Napoleon," and because he had addressed a letter once to Napoleon addressed: "From the Black Napoleon to the White Napoleon." Several times while in prison he addressed letters to Bonaparte, but no answer was given to his appeals. He finally died of apoplexy in April, 1803, after having been in the dungeon about eight months, and when he was a little more than sixty years of age. His body was buried in the chapel under the castle. His wife became enfeebled and her mind wandered. She died in the year 1816. When the power of Napoleon was overthrown she was granted a pension for her support, and her sons released her from prison.

No richer words can close this sketch than those of Phillips:

I would call him Napoleon, but Napoleon made his way to empire over broken oaths and a sea of blood. This man never broke his word. "No Retaliation" was his great motto and the rule of his life; and the last words uttered to his son in France were these: "My boy, you will one day go back to San Domingo: forget that France murdered your father." I would call him Cromwell, but Cromwell was only a soldier, and the state he founded went down to him into his grave; I would call him Washington, but the great Virginian held slaves. This man risked his empire rather than permit the slave trade in the humble village of his dominions. You think me fanatic to-night, for you read history not with your eyes but with your prejudices. But fifty years hence, when truth gets a hearing, the muse of history will put Phocion for the Greeks, Brutus for the Romans, Hampton for England, Fayette for France, choose Washington as the bright consummate flower of our earlier civilization, and John Brown as the ripe fruit of our noon-day; then, dipping her pen in the sunlight, will write in the clear blue, above them all, the name of the soldier, the statesman, the martyr, Toussaint L'Ouverture.

CHAPTER CXLI

Hon. Hiram R. Revels, D. D.
First Negro United States Senator—President of Alcorn
University, Rodney, Mississippi—Secretary of State—Preacher
of the A. M. E. Church—Retired Farmer

———•◆•———

Honorable Hiram R. Revels, United States Senator from Mississippi, was born in Fayetteville, Cumberland county, North Carolina, September 1, 1822. Desiring to obtain an education, which was denied in his native state to those of African descent, he removed to Indiana and spent some time at the Quaker Seminary, in Union county, after which he went to Dark county, Ohio. He graduated at Knox College, Galesburg, Illinois. After his graduation he entered the ministry as a preacher of the gospel in the M. E. church. He was now twenty-five years of age, and was called to take charge of a church in Indiana. After spending some years there, he went to Missouri, Maryland, Kentucky and Kansas, in the cause of the A. M. E. church. He was in Maryland in 1861 at the breaking out of the civil war, and did much in forming in that State the first colored regiment. In 1863 and 1864 he taught school in St. Louis, Missouri, and then went to Vicksburg, where he assisted the provost marshal in managing the affairs of the Freedmen. He followed the army to Jackson, organizing churches, lecturing and trying to organize schools. His health failing him, he went north again until the close of the war. Returning he located in Natchez, where he preached to a large congregation regularly. He was also appointed by General Ames, then military governor, to the position of alderman, and in 1869 was elected to the State Senate of Mississippi. In January 1870, he was the first colored man sent to the United States Senate. Dr. Revels was selected to fill the place of Jefferson Davis, which selection took the country by surprise, and as the time drew near for the Negro to take his seat, the interest became intense. The Nation stood with its mouth wide open, and the world stood still in silent amazement at this new phase of American life. The bottom rail is on top; the newly emancipated unfranchised citizen enters upon the dignified position of United States Senator, to mingle his voice with the lawmakers and to cast his vote in behalf of God and his country. He served in Congress from February 25, 1870, to March 3, 1871. Says Wells Brown, in the *Rising Sun:*

Salisbury had done his best to turn backward the wheels of progress; Davis fought in vain, declaring he would "resist at every step" this unconstitutional measure, giving illustrations, dissertations, execrations, and recommendations of and for the "Negro" and his Republican friends; Stockton, in the interest of law and precedent, begged that the subject should go to the judiciary committee, but the party of freedom moved on in solid phalanx of unanimity to the historic results. Mr. Sumner, who had not taken part in the debate, raised his voice with impressiveness and power, comprehending the whole question in a short speech, just before the vote.

After his senatorial term had closed, he was called to the exalted position of president of Alcorn University, Rodney, Mississippi, at a salary of two thousand five hundred dollars per annum. Governor Powers appointed him secretary of the State, which position he held for several months only. Rev. H. R. Revels makes his home near the city of Natchez, Mississippi, where he leads the quiet life of a farmer, having served his God and his country to the best of his ability. As the first Negro Senator he stands the solitary figure in history that marks the ascent of the race; and it seemed one of the revenges of history, too, for the black man sat in the seat of Jefferson Davis the president of the Southern Confederacy. The Negro was no longer chattels, beast of burden, but a Senator mingling with the exalted in exalted stations and attracting the attention of the world. The irrepressible Negro is hard to "keep in his place." He succeeds persistently in getting some white man's place, or his own held wrongfully so long by another.

HARRISON N. BOUEY

CHAPTER CXLII

Rev. Harrison N. Bouey
Missionary to Africa—Agent American Baptist Publication
Society—District Secretary

The above named gentleman was born in Columbia county, Georgia, August 4, 1849, and was reared in Augusta, Georgia. In early life he was apprenticed to the painter's trade and worked at it two years, during which time he attended night school where he received his elementary education. He made such progress in his studies that he was soon enabled to pass an examination for a teacher's certificate. He then taught two years in the public schools of Augusta, Georgia. In April, 1870, he was converted and became a member of the Springfield Baptist church. Soon after his baptism he entered the Baptist Theological school at Augusta, now the Atlanta Baptist Seminary. In the spring of 1873 he completed his studies, and desiring to be of service to his race, he went to Ridge Springs, South Carolina, where he became principal of a school of one hundred and fifty pupils. Such was his prominence that after teaching two years he was elected by the Republican party as probate judge of Edgefield county, South Carolina. In the fall of 1876 he was elected sheriff of his county, but was counted out. Without any solicitation on his part, the Macedonia Baptist church of Edgefield Court House, South Carolina, called him to ordination, he having connected himself with this body. The church did not even desire to have him work as a licensed minister, so acceptable had been his services in the general church work, and so evident was his divine call. He then became general missionary for the State of South Carolina, continuing in this service over a year. At this time the colored Baptists of South Carolina, under the leadership of Rev. E. M. Brawley, D.D., concluded to begin a mission work in Africa. Unanimous choice was made of Rev. Bouey. He responded to the call. He sailed from New York April 11, 1879, for Monrovia, Africa, *via* Liverpool. In this foreign work he remained nearly three years, and was remarkably successful. He thoroughly traveled over Liberia, stirring up the churches and directing the energies of the brethren. He organized two associations and a National Baptist convention, of which he became the corresponding secretary and financial agent. Feeling that he ought more thoroughly to enlist the American colored Baptists in the work of African missions, he resolved to return home. This he did and became the general agent of the Liberian convention.

In April, 1882, he was married to Miss Laura P. Logan of Charleston, South Carolina. In March, 1882, he was commissioned by the American Baptist Publication Society as Sunday school missionary for Alabama, and at once entered upon his work. He served in this office four years, during part of which time he was the financial agent of Selma University and the corresponding secretary of the State Mission Board of Alabama. But such was the strain upon his health that he resigned these positions in January, 1886, in order to seek rest. He was at once chosen associate editor of the *Baptist Pioneer* and business manager. He filled this office one year. He is a member of the Board of Trustees of Selma University and of the State Mission Board of Alabama. He is now secretary of the Foreign Mission Convention of the United States for the Third District.

CHAPTER CXLIII

Colonel James Lewis
Surveyor-General—Colonel of the Second Regiment State
Militia—Collector of the New Orleans Port—Naval Officer—
Superintendent of the United States Bonded Warehouses

The native place of Colonel James Lewis is Woodville, Wilkinson county, Mississippi. He was born in the year 1832. When he was fifteen years of age his real life work began on the river. By his steadiness of purpose, strict integrity and indomitable courage and energy, he worked himself up to a highly honorable and conspicuous station in life. When the war broke out it found Mr. Lewis steward on board the Confederate Transport, "De Soto," and at the fighting about Columbus Island, No. 10, and New Madrid, where the first news of emancipation reached him. Gladdened by the hope of the liberation of his race, knowing that the cause of freedom needed all its friends, Mr. Lewis made his way by a dangerous route to New Orleans, over which the flag of the Union had just been planted. He at once resolved to be a soldier, and, with some other colored men, petitioned the commanding officer for permission to raise what he maintains proved to be the first regiment of colored troops that entered the United States army, September, 1862. Of this there seems some doubt, as George W. William's *History of the Negro Race,* page 278, Vol. II, says General Hunter employed "Negroes as soldiers, in the *spring* of 1862, directed the organization of a regiment of blacks. He secured the best white officers for the regiment, and it soon obtained a fine condition of discipline. The news of a Union Negro regiment in South Carolina completely surprised the people at Washington." We leave this matter to the future historians; the one may have been formed first, but the other was recorded first. Mr. Lewis raised two companies of colored infantry and at the head of one of these he was mustered into the First Louisiana volunteer native guards as captain of Company K.

After the Bank Expedition up the Red River in 1864, Captain Lewis resigned his commission, returned to the city and became a permit and custom-house broker, until the opening of the coast trade and the coming

JAMES LEWIS

of reconstruction. He received the appointment of traveling agent of the educational department of the Freedman's Bureau, and devoted his whole time, talent and energy to the establishment of schools for the instruction and elevation of his down-trodden race. In this capacity he traveled all over the State, establishing schools wherever he went. This position was not, however, an enviable one, as his life was in constant peril, and in many places he moved about in the very jaws of death. He was captured on one occasion in North Louisiana, and nothing but the interposition of some friendly Masons saved his neck; but the seeds he planted, the love of learning he instilled, brought forth good fruit. When the business of the Freedmen's Bureau closed, Colonel Lewis received a high compliment from the commanding officer for his worth and daring zeal in the cause of education. At the time Honorable William P. Kellogg became collector of the port at New Orleans, he appointed the first colored man to a civil position in the Federal service in Louisiana, when he made Colonel Lewis United States inspector of customs. This place he held up to the time that Perry Fuller turned him out because he refused to vote for Seymour and Blair in 1869. Colonel Lewis became sergeant of the Metropolitan police, and discharged his duties with such fidelity, impartiality and integrity, that he was soon promoted to the position of captain of the police in recognition of his service in this capacity. He extorted even the admiration of the Democrats, a thing most difficult for a colored man to do at any time. In 1870 Governor Warmouth appointed Mr. Lewis colonel of the Second regiment State militia, and in the same year he was elected administrator of police for two years, at a salary of six thousand dollars per annum. In 1872 he was nominated by the State convention for Congress-at-large, and was also chairman of the Louisiana delegation to the Philadelphia National Republican convention. On returning home, finding that a breach had occurred in the party ranks, he boldly stepped forward and placed his nomination in the hands of his friends, who tendered it to the Honorable P. B. S. Pinchback, and by this unselfish action all party differences became harmonized. He had entered the canvass with the Honorable Wm. P. Kellogg, gubernatorial candidate, and during his absence from New Orleans was nominated and elected administrator of public improvements, defeating General G. T. Beauregard for the most important office in the city government.

Hon. Louis A. Wiltz, mayor, in his annual message to the city council for the year 1873, paid Colonel Lewis a graceful and well-merited compliment. In speaking of the office of administrator of improvements, he said:

> It will be observed that economical and judicious management in this department has resulted in one year in a saving to the city, $541,415, to-wit: $2,207 in the administrator's office; $269,895 in the Bureau of Streets; $73,-

389 in the Bureau of Wharves and Landings, and $195,924 in the Bureau of Drainage. Facts like these require no commendatory comments. Colonel Lewis has devoted himself to his duties with great energy and industry, having constant care that every dollar expended should benefit the city.

It will be remembered that Colonel Lewis was the only Republican in that city government. In the fall of 1876 he was one of the most active and untiring advocates the Republicans had in the State. He canvassed the entire State with Governor Packard, a task very few men, white or colored, would desire to undertake. On the assembling of the Legislature, he was elected a United States Senator for the short term. Seeing Louisiana and two other Southern Republican States turned over to the Democrats, he refused to press his claim.

President Hayes in 1877 appointed Colonel Lewis naval officer of the port at New Orleans, which place is only second to that of collector of customs. He held this position up to the time of the National Republican convention at Chicago, 1880, casting his lot with the old guard of "306," at the sacrifice of his official head, which followed after his return home in the same month. Colonel Lewis had retired to private life when Judge Folger, secretary of the treasury, called him to public life again by his appointment to the position of superintendent of the United States bonded warehouse in New Orleans. The following appeared in the *Louisiana Standard,* January 19, 1884:

We note with pleasure the confirmation of Colonel James Lewis as surveyor-general of Louisiana, by the Senate last Tuesday. Colonel Lewis has, during the course of a busy, active, political life, filled many important State and Federal positions, notably those of administrator of police and administrator of improvements of this great city, and naval officer at this port, with credit and honor to himself, his party and his race. His confirmation by the Senate is but a just recognition of his services as a Republican and his worth as a citizen, and is heartily approved by the masses of the people.

During all the vicissitudes of his active political life, he has always found time to attend to his Masonic duties. He is a past master, past grand master, past eminent commander, sublime prince of the royal secrets or thirty-second degree, A. A. S. R., and is the present very eminent grand captain general of Ohio and its jurisdiction. Very few public men in this country can show a more brilliant record, either personally, masonically or officially, than Colonel James Lewis.

CHAPTER CXLIV

Rev. E. H. Lipscombe
President of the Western Union Institute—Professor
of Rhetoric and Moral Philosophy—Preacher—Editor
of the Mountain Gleaner

It is with pleasure that I speak of this young man, who had the nerve and the moral courage to do severe and arduous labor with his own hands for the rising generation.

The Western Union Institute will always be a monument to the brilliant professor. I wish we had a hundred thousand such men, who would slay the trees, dig up the roots and set up an educational light-house.

Professor Edward Hart Lipscombe, came into this busy world, September 29, 1858, in Orange county, North Carolina, near the now famous town of Durham, the city of the "great Durham tobacco."

In 1868 he was taken to Raleigh and put in school under the Rev. William Warrick of Philadelphia and his teachers, among whom were his daughter Louisa and son Charles. He soon loved his teachers and his studies. In 1870 he was taken back to help his mother. In 1871 he returned to Raleigh and resumed his studies, but was forced to return again to the farm. In the spring of 1873 Rev. Augustus Shepperd of Raleigh came for him to join the North Carolina Jubilee Singers, then practicing at Raleigh, under Miss Nettie M. Sage, preparatory to going on a tour in the interest of Shaw University. She pronounced his voice one of remarkable sweetness. This concert troupe, under the musical direction of Miss Sage and general management of President H. M. Tupper, traveled through the New England States, in Canada and Nova Scotia. From its entertainments eight thousand dollars or ten thousand dollars were realized for the institution. Returning from this tour, he entered Shaw Collegiate Institute, now Shaw University, where he remained until graduation in 1879. He was the youngest member of his class.

At the age of nineteen the professor was associated with Dr. H. M. Tupper and Professor N. F. Roberts in founding and editing the *African Expositor*. In 1879 he was elected the professor of mathematics and langauges in Shaw University. In 1881, while only twenty-three years old, he was elected principal of the Washington graded school of Raleigh, having an attendance of 500 scholars and the largest school in the city. In 1882 he was appointed by the Baptist State Convention of North Carolina one of the editors of the *Baptist Standard*, the then organ and property of the convention. In 1883 he resigned the principalship of the school to accept the professorship of rhetoric and moral philosophy in Shaw University, where he was again connected with the *African Expositor*, editing the temperance department. In 1884 he was the chairman of the committee of prominent colored men of the South, which issued an address to temperance Republicans, protesting against the action of certain politicians in attempting to ally the Republican party with the politically organized whisky interest.

In the fall of 1884 he was strongly urged by many to accept the nomination as candidate for the General Assembly of North Carolina by Wake county, but he declined to have his name used. This same year he was elected principal of the Durham graded school, but soon resigned to accept the principalship of Dallas Academy, located at Dallas, Gaston county, and under the auspices of the Western Baptist Missionary Union. He began this school from the start in October, 1884, and made it a success, drawing students from many counties of North Carolina and from South Carolina, old and young, married and single, enrolling over one hundred in each of the two years that the school was carried on in Dallas. In 1886 he was made educational adviser for the county of Gaston, by the North Carolina State Teachers' Association. This year he took part in the formation of the Prohibition party in Gaston county, and then and there joined the National Prohibition party. Previously he had been a sort of local optionist, but he is now for prohibition, local or national, wherever it is an issue.

In 1886 the Union moved the school to Ashville and changed its name to Western Union Institute, of which he is now president, with students from North Carolina, South Carolina and Tennessee. He has erected one good building since it started from nothing in 1884. While doing this he has lead his students into the woods and cut and hauled saw-logs by the hundreds to aid in supplying the needed lumber. He has been sneered at and ridiculed by some for trying to establish a school in this poor, wild, ignorant part of North Carolina; but he has accomplished his aim, and the school has a property valued at from six thousand dollars to eight thousand dollars, with some of the best men of the South acting as trustees. The professor's religious views are those of the Baptists. He received his A. M. from Shaw University in 1882. He delivered a literary address before the society of Shaw University in 1883, and was chosen by the citizens of Wake county to deliver the oration in the city hall at Raleigh in January, 1884. He also delivered, in 1886, a literary address at the commencement of the State Normal school at Salisbury; many white persons who were present pronounced the speech as the best they ever heard by a colored man, and one of the editors in that town in a printed reference delivered himself in these words: "He is one of the ablest men of the 'Old North State.'"

He was also appointed by the people of Buncombe county as the emancipation orator for January 1, 1887.

He is the oldest of four children, and was married in 1882 to Miss Lizzie L. Taylor of Lynchburg, Virginia. Four children have been born to them, three boys and one girl, only one of whom, the girl, the youngest, is now living.

Professor Lipscombe is somewhat of a poet and has written several poems which have been published in the *African Expositor*. The titles of some of them are as follows: "Graves on Old Plantations;" "Panther Lake;" "Birth of my Adelaide;" "Life's Storms." He is now at work on a poem called "The Wind Song," which he announces shall be the most complete and extended of all his poetical compositions.

His religious life might be condensed in a few statements. He professed religion in 1877. He was baptized by Rev. H. C. Ransome, and united with the Blount Street Baptist church of Raleigh, and served it as their clerk for seven years. In 1883 he was ordained to the ministry, and the same year he was elected clerk to the Baptist State Convention of North Carolina. In 1884 with others he established the *Light-house,* and was its editor-in-chief, until it was changed in 1886 to the *Mountain Gleaner,* of which he is the editor and half owner.

He has filled a very important place in the affairs of North Carolina and is worthy of mention on account of the excellent life which he lives, and the vigorous, praiseworthy energy displayed in all matters which he has undertaken. He is a true type of the sturdy earnest North Carolinian.

JAMES C. MATTHEWS

CHAPTER CXLV

Honorable James C. Matthews
Lawyer and Recorder of Deeds, Washington, District of Columbia

---

William W. Matthews and his wife, Esther Ann, resided in New Haven, Connecticut. November 6, 1846, the gentleman who has figured so conspicuously in American Congressional affairs recently, was born. It was on this day and date that his star ascended above the horizon. Soon after this his parents moved to Albany, New York, where their children could get the advantages of schooling. The schools of that city were famed for their excellence, and had no color line; so the children entered without objections being made. There was a colored school in town, however. In 1856 an effort was made to get all the colored children out of the white schools, and they succeeded. But young Matthews succeeded, through a Democratic member, in regaining admission. They would have gotten him out again, only his teacher, Professor Steele, plead for him, saying that he was so very bright and he did not want to lose him.

In the boys' academy he competed, in 1860, for a scholarship; and among three who passed was James C. Matthews. This was a surprise, indeed. Again objections were made by the canting hypocrites in the Republican fold; but singular to say, Honorable William A. Rice, a Democratic members of the Board of Instruction, sustained him, and he was admitted.

In 1861 he lost both parents, but was kindly cared for by Mrs. Phebe Jones and Miss Lydia Mott. He graduated June 30, 1864, gaining the first prize for the best English essay, and the Beck literary medal. After leaving school, he kept books for several firms in Albany, and finally entered the law office of J. Wirner, one of the ablest lawyers in the State. After completing his course he was admitted to the bar, May, 1870, and afterwards to the United States Court. The Young Men's Association of Albany, in order to encourage literary pursuits, offered annually a medal for the best essay. He had tried several times for this, and on one occasion there were two so near alike in excellence, that the committee failed to agree as to which was the better; finally it was decided by opening the envelopes containing the names, and it was given to a white young man. But when he tried again, the medal was conceded to him by the general excellence of his production. A fictitious name was given on the essay, but accompanied by an envelope containing the true name. When it was revealed, July 4, 1869, it was James C. Matthews, and he secured the medal. This same society once invited Wendell Phillips to lecture before them, and he refused to do so because the colored people were not allowed to attend their meetings. Mr. Matthews cast his first vote for General U. S. Grant, and was a supporter of that party till 1872. I here quote his sentiments as given by Judge Andrew Hamilton, who knew him well:

For a long time he had seen that a division of the colored vote was essential, not alone to the advancement of his people, but to the welfare of the Nation. He had grown up to the belief that there should be neither color nor latitude in politics. His own experience, the warm friends he had found, the hearty encouragement he had met with, and almost entirely in Democratic circles, impressed him that if the colored people had not gained the Democratic co-operation, it was because they had avoided it. In keeping with these ideas, and influenced by the patriotic motives which drove so many of the best men from the Republican party in 1872, he joined the Liberal movement in that year, and attended the Liberal National convention as a delegate. When the two conventions came together and formed the Democratic-Liberal Republican convention, Mr. Matthews, at the request of Honorable Samuel J. Tilden, delivered the congratulatory speech to a surprised and electrified audience.

In 1872 he proceeded against the Republican School Board of Albany, by mandamus, to compel them to admit the colored children of Mr. William A. Deitz to the public schools. He succeeded, and wiped out the color line.

His address on Henry Highland Garnet, and his speech on July 4, 1880, in the capitol, Albany, were highly commended.

In 1875 he married Miss Adele Duplessis of New York City, at the residence of Professor Charles L. Reason. He has four sisters.

It will be of interest to record here in this work a brief outline of the nomination and rejection of James C. Matthews of New York, when he was nominated by President Grover Cleveland for the position of recorder of deeds in the District of Columbia, a position which was held by the gifted Frederick Douglass. Mr. Matthews is one of the rising young men of this generation, and having seen fit to ally himself to the Democratic party, it is no more than right that the Democratic party, through its President, should place him in a position of honor and trust. It is my desire not to give so much my opinion on the matter before us, but to give the record that it might live in history in a place where it might be read more constantly than it would be if buried in the records of the United States. The space given to this subject cannot possibly be wasted, for it shows how a colored man might become so prominent in the affairs of the Nation as to attract such considerable attention, and marks, indeed, in my opinion, the beginning of a new state of affairs; when it is remembered that the Democratic party, as a party, has always been against the Negro, it is a matter for very great consideration that the President, who is supposed at least to be the embodiment of the principles and practices of that party, has been so bold as to nominate, not once, but twice, a colored man to so prominent an office in his gift. It also marks the moral heroism of the Negro in being able and willing to cut loose from a party to which so many of his race have given their support for so long a period unquestioned. It does honor also to Mr. Matthews' foresight, that he could look down the ranks of liberalism and independency, and at the right time ally himself with the Democratic party and become so prominent as to attract the attention of a Democratic President and arouse the ire of a Republican Senate, and bring to his support nearly every Negro journal in the United States, though nineteen out of every twenty of them are stalwart Republicans. This we consider quite an achievement for a man of Mr. Matthews' age and experience, and, indeed, marks him as a statesman of no ordinary calibre. But now for the record:

EXTRACTS FROM THE EXECUTIVE JOURNAL OF THE SENATE

TUESDAY, March 9, 1886

The following message was received from the President of the United States:

To the Senate of the United States:

I nominate James C. Matthews of New York, to be recorder of deeds in the District of Columbia, *vice* Frederick Douglass, who has resigned.

GROVER CLEVELAND

Executive Mansion, Washington, March 4, 1886.

Ordered, that the nomination of James C. Matthews be referred to the committee on the District of Columbia.

EXTRACTS FROM THE COMMITTEE ON THE DISTRICT OF COLUMBIA

March 12, 1886

The nomination of James C. Matthews to be recorder of deeds for the District of Columbia was considered, but final action was deferred.

March 19, 1886

The nomination of James C. Matthews to be recorder of deeds for the District of Columbia was considered, and on a motion to confirm, the roll was called thereon, absent members being counted as their views were known, as follows:

For confirmation: Messrs Ingalls, Brown, Palmer, Pike (4).
Against confirmation: Messrs Harris, Blackburn, Riddleberger, Vance (4).
Absent: Mr. Miller of California (1).

The vote being a tie, Mr. Blackburn was instructed to report the nomination back unfavorably to the Senate.

EXTRACTS FROM THE EXECUTIVE JOURNAL OF THE SENATE

March 22, 1886

Mr. Blackburn, from the committee on the District of Columbia, to whom was referred, the 9th inst., the nomination of James C. Matthews, report adversely thereon.

MONDAY, March 22, 1886

The president *pro tem.* presented a memorial of the Jefferson Democratic Association of the District of Columbia protesting against the confirmation of James C. Matthews to be recorder of deeds in the District of Columbia, which was ordered to lie on the table.

March 29, 1886

The Senate proceeded to consider the nomination of James C. Matthews.
On motion of Mr. Harris, ordered that the said nomination be recommitted to the committee on the District of Columbia.

April 5, 1886

Mr. Sewell presented a petition of citizens of Camden, New Jersey, praying for the confirmation of James C. Matthews to be recorder of deeds in the District of Columbia. Referred to the committee on the District of Columbia.

EXTRACTS FROM MINUTES OF COMMITTEE

April 9, 1886

On motion, the consideration of the nomination of James C. Matthews to be recorder of deeds for the district, which has been recommitted, was postponed for one week.

On April 16, 1886, the following letter was addressed to James C. Matthews, by Thomas J. White, clerk of the committee on the District of Columbia:
The committee on the District of Columbia, United States Senate:

WASHINGTON, D. C., April 16, 1886

SIR: I am directed by the Honorable Isham G. Harris, as a Senator and as a member of the committee on the District of Columbia, to request that you will state the position which you have heretofore occupied and the views which you at present entertain upon the subject of mixed or separate schools for colored and white children; also state what, if any, action you have taken upon this question in the State of New York or elsewhere.

An early reply will oblige. Respectfully,

THOMAS J. WHITE
Clerk to Committee on District of Columbia

James C. Matthews, 334 Clinton avenue, Albany, New York.

To which Mr. Matthews sent the following reply.

ALBANY, April 20, 1886

MY DEAR SIR: Yours of the 17th inst., written under the direction of Hon. Isham G. Harris, Senator, and a member of the committee on the District of Columbia, was received this A. M., and in answer to which I have to say:

An effort was made in the City of New York, in this State, in 1884, to close the colored schools in that city, and the proper school authorities directed the same to be done, to take effect at the close of the school term, to wit, July 1, 1884, which action threw out of employment a large number of educated and cultivated ladies and gentlemen, thus closing the main avenue open for the employment of the educated. I was solicited by some, personally interested of course, and more not so (for there exists among the prominent thinking colored men of this country a great diversity of opinion as to the advisability of abolishing schools and institutions designated as colored schools and institutions, thus throwing out of employment all colored teachers and professors), to assist in protecting their rights and what they believed to be the interest of the children, and so I was instrumental in securing the passage of an act which became a law and of which the enclosed is a copy, and which embodies my view and action so far as they have been formulated upon the subject matter of your letter of inquiry.

Very respectfully,

JAMES C. MATTHEWS

Thomas J. White, Esq., clerk to committee on District of Columbia

(Chapter 248—An act in relation to public education in the city of New York —passed May 5, 1884, three-fifths being present.)

People of the State of New York, represented in Senate and assembly, do enact as follows:

SECTION 1. The colored schools in the city of New York, now existing and in operation, shall hereafter be classed and known and be continued as ward schools and primaries, with their present teachers, unless such teachers are removed in the manner provided by law, and such schools shall be under the control and management of the school officers of the respective wards in which they are located, in the same manner and to the same extent as other ward schools, and shall be open for the education of pupils for whom admission is sought, without regard to race or color.

SECTION 2. All acts or parts of acts inconsistent with the provisions of this act are hereby repealed.

SECTION 3. This act shall take effect immediately.

EXTRACTS FROM MINUTES OF COMMITTEE

April 30, 1886

The subject of the confirmation of James C. Matthews to be recorder of deeds for the District of Columbia was taken up for consideration, a protest and charges having been made and filed.

Mr. Riddleberger moved that a sub-committee of three be appointed to investigate the charges made of intimidation and bribery of votes in Albany, New York, which motion prevailed by the following vote:

Ayes: Harris, Blackburn, Spooner, Vance and Riddleberger (5).

Nays: Ingalls, Brown, Palmer and Pike, (4).

Mr. Harris suggested that the sub-committee be instructed to report at the next meeting such information as may be derived by such action as they may adopt. The chair appointed the following as the sub-committee: Messrs. Riddleberger, Brown and Spooner.

Whereupon the following letter was addressed to Mr. Matthews by Senator Riddleberger:

COMMITTEE ON THE DISTRICT OF COLUMBIA, UNITED STATES SENATE

WASHINGTON, DISTRICT OF COLUMBIA, April 30, 1886

J. C. Matthews, Esq., Albany, New York:

DEAR SIR: At a meeting of the committee on the District of Columbia, held this morning, your nomination was considered and all the papers relating thereto were laid before it. Among these was one paper, numerously signed, preferring charges against you, which, in the opinion of the committee, is proper to be inquired into. For this purpose a sub-committee of three, composed of myself and Senators Brown and Spooner, was appointed. I enclose a copy of the charges, together with a copy of the paragraph from the *Troy Times*, that you may be fully informed of the scope of our investigation.

It is not possible to fix a day of meeting just now, but if you will indicate the notice you desire to have, we will endeavor to so arrange as to give it to you.

For the present we can determine nothing definitely, but you can be assured there will be no unnecessary delay.

H. H. RIDDLEBERGER, Chairman Sub-Committee

On May 5, 1886, the following letter was addressed to W. H. Johnson of Albany, New York, by Mr. Riddleberger:

COMMITTEE ON THE DISTRICT OF COLUMBIA, UNITED STATES SENATE

WASHINGTON, DISTRICT OF COLUMBIA, May 5, 1886

W. H. Johnson, Esq., Albany, New York:

DEAR SIR: Under date of April 23, 1886, a communication was addressed to the Senate, signed by yourself and others, protesting against the confirmation of J. C. Matthews as recorder of deeds for this district, in which, among other things you say:

"The unrefuted but well-attested fact that Mr. Matthews, at the recent municipal election in this city, in keeping with his old practice, went into a ward other than his own, and by threats, intimidation and bribery, sought to coerce colored Republicans to vote the Democratic ticket, has brought down upon his head the just indignation of all good citizens, regardless of politics."

The investigation of the charge here made of intimidation and bribery of electors has been intrusted to a sub-committee, of which I am chairman, and by which I am instructed to call upon you for specifications, giving names of persons intimidated or sought to be intimidated, bribed or sought to be bribed, with names of witnesses. We wish to go thoroughly into the matter, but we wish only definite information, which can be sworn to by witnesses. We desire to prevent any unnecessary delay, and request your immediate attention to this matter.

Respectfully yours,
H. H. Riddleberger,
Chairman Sub-Committee

EXTRACTS FROM MINUTES OF COMMITTEE

May 7, 1886

On motion of Mr. Palmer the subject of the confirmation of James C. Matthews was postponed for one week.

May 14, 1886

The matter of the nomination of James C. Matthews was considered, but Mr. Riddleberger not having the reply of Mr. W. H. Johnson of Albany, New York, with him, no action was taken.

May 21, 1886

The Matthews nomination was called up and discussed, and, in response to inquiry, Mr. Riddleberger stated that while he had received a reply from W. H. Johnson of Albany, New York, he did not have it with him, and stated his determination to vote against the confirmation on general principles. (It does look like he did not want to have that letter there.)

Mr. Spooner moved that the sub-committee charged with the investigation of the charges against Matthews be discharged; which motion was carried.

Mr. Spooner moved that another sub-committee of three, with the chairman of the committee as its chairman, be appointed to investigate preliminarily for future report to the committee the charges of intimidation and bribery in connection with the elections made by Mr. Johnson of Albany against Mr. Matthews.

Mr. Harris moved to reconsider the vote of the committee by which the previous sub-committee was discharged, and to instruct that sub-committee to proceed as rapidly as possible, so that the committee may obtain whatever information is obtainable by the next meeting, with a view to a final disposition of the case.

Mr. Spooner thereupon withdrew his motion.

The motion of Mr. Harris was adopted, Mr. Riddleberger alone voting in the negative.

Messrs Riddleberger, Spooner and Brown each declined to serve longer upon the sub-committee.

Mr. Brown moved that Messrs Ingalls, Harris and Blackburn be appointed a sub-committee to continue the investigation; but, after discussion, it was deemed best to leave the latter with the full committee. Mr. Spooner stated that he was not ready to vote for or against the confirmation in face of the charges, whereupon Mr. Riddleberger was requested to produce for the information of the committee the reply from Mr. Johnson, which, on leaving the committee room, he promised to do.

It was suggested that Messrs Ingalls and Harris take all necessary action in the Matthews case as soon as Mr. Riddleberger files the papers called for. (It takes a hard pull to get that letter.)

EXTRACT FROM EXECUTIVE JOURNAL OF THE SENATE

Friday, May 28, 1886

Mr. Ingalls submitted the following resolution, which was considered by unanimous consent and agreed to:

Resolved: That the committee on the District of Columbia, or the sub-committee thereof, having under consideration the nomination of James C. Matthews to be recorder of deeds for the District of Columbia, be, and it hereby is, authorized to send for persons and papers, and sit during the session of the Senate, and to employ a stenographer.

Resolved: That the expenses arising under the foregoing resolution be paid out of the appropriation for the contingent fund of the Senate upon vouchers to be approved by the chairman of said committee.

Under the above resolution, witnesses were subpoenaed and the testimony was taken.

After taking over twenty-one pages of closely written testimony from many persons who had been summoned, on July 4, 1886, the special committee to whom this matter of the investigation had been referred, Messrs Ingalls and Harris, reported to the full committee that they had taken the testimony of witnesses *and there was no evidence to sustain the charges made against James C. Matthews.* Yet we find in the record of the minutes of the committee the following:

June 11, 1886

The nomination of James C. Matthews was considered, but further deferred for a week.

June 25, 1886

The nomination of James C. Matthews to be recorder of deeds of the Dis-

trict of Columbia, was considered, and on an adverse report to the Senate ordered by the following on the question of, "Shall the nomination be favorably reported?"
Ayes:—Harris, Brown.
Nays:—Ingalls, Blackburn, Palmer, Chase, Vance, Pike, Spooner.

Mr. Riddleberger resigned as a member of the committee of the District of Columbia, and Mr. Chace was appointed in his place, June 4, 1886; that accounts for his being on the committee. We furnish now the extract from the executive journal of the Senate, which shows the action taken thereon. It will be seen that the Republicans voted against Mr. Matthews, even the members from his own State. But let us here give the record again:

July 3, 1886

Mr. Blackburn, from the committee on the District of Columbia, to whom was recommitted, the twenty-ninth of March, the nomination of James C. Matthews, reported adversely thereon.

July 31, 1886

The Senate proceeded to consider the nomination of James C. Matthews, and after debate on the question, "Will the Senate advise and consent to the appointment of James C. Matthews?" it was determined in the negative—yeas fourteen; nays thirty-eight.

On motion by Mr. Brown, the yeas and nays being desired by one-fifth of the Senators present, those who voted in the affirmative are: Messrs Brown, Call, Camden, Hampton, Harris, Hearst, Jones of Arkansas, McPherson, Payne, Van Wick, Vest, Voorhees, Walthall, and Whitthorn.

Those voting in the negative are: Messrs Aldrich, Berry, Blackburn, Blair, Coke, Conger, Cullom, Dawes, Dolph, Edmunds, Eustis, Evarts, Frye, Harrison, Hawley, Hoar, Ingalls, Jones of Nevada, McMillan, Mahone, Manderson, Maxey, Miller, Mitchell of Oregon, Palmer, Plumb, Ransom, Riddleberger, Salisbury, Sawyer, Sewell, Sherman, Spooner, Stanford, Tellar, Vance, and Wilson of Iowa. So it was

Resolved, That the Senate do not advise and consent to the appointment of James C. Matthews to be recorder of deeds in the District of Columbia.

During the roll call the following pairs were announced: Mr. Colquitt, in the affirmative, with Mr. Chace in the negative. Mr. George, in the affirmative, with Mr. Gorman in the negative. Mr. Kenna, in the affirmative, with Mr. Sabin in the negative. Mr. Brown submitted a motion that the injunction of secrecy be removed from the vote last taken.

Monday, August 2, 1886

The Senate proceeded to consider the motion submitted by Mr. Brown to remove the injunction of secrecy from the vote by which the Senate refused to advise and consent to the appointment of James C. Matthews to be recorder of deeds from the District of Columbia.

Mr. Edmunds proposed to amend by adding thereto the following words: "And from the reports of all committees, and votes upon all nominations acted upon during the present session."

Mr. Butler proposed, as a further amendment, the following words: "And that all Senators be allowed to publish their remarks thereon."

On motion by Mr. Butler, and by unanimous consent,

Ordered, That the resolution of the Senate of the thirty-first of July that the Senate do not advise and consent to the appointment of James C. Matthews, be transmitted forthwith to the President of the United States.

However, August 9, the day after the Senate adjourned, the President stood by his appointee, and commissioned him recorder of deeds for the city of Washington, and he was privileged, therefore, to act in that capacity until the Senate should meet again in December, after the summer vacation. The rejection of Mr. Matthews occasioned very great excitement among the colored people, and arrayed, as we have already said, in his behalf the Negro press, which has become a very powerful factor in the affairs pertaining to the race. Space will not permit us to give selections from the journals of the day, but on investigation it will be found as said. The Washington journals were very active *pro* and *con*. The *Washington Bee*, being very pronounced against the action of the members of the Senate, bitterly denounced them. Delegations from all parts of the country were constantly calling on Senator Ingalls who was the chief antagonist of Mr. Matthews, on the ground that a Negro had no right to be a Democrat; but to this the Negroes took exceptions saying, that in this country any man had a right to think as he pleased; that the Republicans were not the keepers of the Negro conscience, nor should they be the suppressor of any man's opinion. Men who had been life-long Republicans and who were still stalwart in their convictions and who were political antagonists of Mr. Matthews, nevertheless came to his rescue, believing that he was honest, sincere in his convictions and was entitled to the protection of his race; and that it was their bounden duty to see that he was not crushed because he chose to be a Democrat. There were many who opposed him professedly on the ground, that he was not a resident of the District. This pretext was very flimsy, for scores of men had been appointed in territories where they did not live. The Democratic party had agreed in their platform, upon which Mr. Cleveland was elected, to appoint residents of the District of Columbia to the offices therein, and while a man may not be bound by the general outlines of the platform, he cannot be compelled to stay close to the minutiae thereon; and President Cleveland, desirous to encourage the Negroes, saw fit to select this very competent and excellent gentleman to fill the place in the city of Washington, which had already been filled by Frederick Douglass, who was a resident of New

York City. He therefore renominated him on the reassembling of Congress, in the letter which we here give.

TUESDAY, December 21, 1886

The following message was received from the President of the United States:

To the Senate of the United States:

I nominate James C. Matthews of New York, to be recorder of deeds in the District of Columbia, in the place of Frederick Douglass, resigned.

This nomination was submitted to the Senate at its last session upon the retirement of the previous incumbent, who for a number of years had held the office to which it refers. In the last days of the session the Senate declined to confirm the nomination.

Opposition to the appointment of Mr. Matthews to the office for which he was named was developed among the citizens of the District of Columbia, ostensibly on the ground that the nominee was not a resident of the District, and it is supposed that such opposition, to some extent at least, influenced the determination of the question of his confirmation.

Mr. Matthews has now been in occupancy of the office to which he was nominated for more than four months, and he has in the performance of the duties thereof won the approval of all those having business to transact with such office, and has rendered important service in rescuing the records of the District from loss and illegibility.

I am informed that his management of this office has removed much of the opposition to his appointment which heretofore existed.

I have ventured, therefore, in view of the demonstrated fitness of this nominee, and with the understanding that the objections heretofore urged against his selection have to a great extent subsided, and confessing a desire to cooperate in tendering to our colored fellow-citizens just recognition and the utmost good faith, to again submit this nomination to the Senate for confirmation, at the same time disclaiming any intention to question its previous action in the premises.

GROVER CLEVELAND

Executive Mansion, December 21, 1886

Upon which the following action was taken:

ORDERED, that the nomination of James C. Matthews be referred to the committee on the District of Columbia.

EXTRACTS FROM MINUTES OF THE COMMITTEE

January 14, 1887.—The nomination of Mr. James C. Matthews was then taken up, and Mr. Brown moved to postpone its consideration for one week, which was lost by the following vote:

Ayes—Harris, Brown (2).
Nays—Ingalls, Palmer, Chace, Cheney, Vance, Spooner (6).
Absent—Blackburn (1).

Mr. Blackburn (having since the former vote entered the committee room) was then instructed to report the nomination back to the Senate adversely, by the following vote on the question: "Shall the nomination be favorably reported for confirmation?"

Ayes—Harris, Brown (2).

Nays—Ingalls, Blackburn, Palmer, Chace, Vance, Cheney, Spooner (7).

EXTRACTS FROM THE EXECUTIVE JOURNAL OF THE SENATE

WEDNESDAY, January 19, 1887

Mr. Blackburn from the committee on the District of Columbia, to whom was referred, the twenty-first December last, the nomination of James C. Matthews, reported adversely thereon.

WEDNESDAY, January 26, 1887

The Senate proceeded to consider the nomination of James C. Matthews, and after debate on the question, "Will the Senate advise and consent to the appointment of James C. Matthews?" it was determined in the negative. Yeas—17; nays—31.

On motion, by Mr. Dawes, yeas and nays being desired by one-fifth of the Senators present, those who voted in the affirmative are: Messrs Beck, Blair, Brown, Call, Cockrell, Colquitt, Farwell, Gibson, Hampton, Harris, Jones of Arkansas, McPherson, Mitchell of Oregon, Payne, Vest, Walthall and Whitthorn.

Those who voted in the negative are: Messrs Allison, Blackburn, Bowen, Chace, Coke, Conger, Cullom, Dawes, Edmunds, Eustis, Evarts, Gorman, Hawley, Hoar, Ingalls, Jones of Nevada, McMillan, Mahone, Morgan, Palmer, Plumb, Pugh, Ransom, Salisbury, Sawyer, Sewell, Sherman, Spooner, Vance, Williams, and Wilson of Iowa.

So it was

Resolved, That the Senate do not advise and consent to the appointment of James C. Matthews to be recorder of deeds in the District of Columbia.

During the roll call the following pairs were announced:

Mr. Butler with Mr. Cameron.

Mr. Berry with Mr. Tellar.

Mr. Camden with Mr. Stanford.

Mr. Gray with Mr. Manderson.

Mr. Kenna with Mr. Miller.

SATURDAY, January 29, 1887

Mr. Ingalls submitted the following in the nature of a resolution to accompany the resolution of the Senate of the 26th inst., rejecting the nomination of James C. Matthews to be recorder of deeds for the District of Columbia:

James C. Matthews of New York was nominated March 9, 1886, to be recorder of deeds in the District of Columbia in place of Frederick Douglass, resigned. This nomination was rejected by the Senate July 21, 1886.

Immediately after the adjournment of the Senate, to wit: August 9, 1886, the President appointed James C. Matthews to the office for which he had been rejected by the Senate, and he continued in the discharge of its duties during the recess of Congress.

On the twenty-first day December, 1886, the President again nominated James C. Matthews of New York to be recorder of deeds in the District of Columbia, in place of Frederick Douglass, resigned.

In his message to the Senate of March 1, 1886, relative to papers on file and other information touching suspensions from and appointments to office, the President, among other things, said:

Upon a refusal to confirm I shall not assume the right to ask the reasons for the action of the Senate, nor question its determination. I cannot think that anything more is required to secure worthy incumbents in public office than a careful and independent discharge of our respective duties within their well defined limits.

The nomination of Matthews being apparently not strictly in accord with these declarations of the President, and being the only instance of a person rejected by the Senate who has been reappointed and again nominated for the same office under this administration, the President considered the event of sufficient consequence to accompany the transmission of the nomination with the following statement in justification of his action: (See President's letter.)

The Senate does not consider that it is required either to admit or to deny the propriety or the correctness of the conjecture of the President as to the reasons by which it was guided in declining to confirm the original nomination.

The President attempts to justify the renomination of Matthews by stating,

1. That the fitness of the nominee has been demonstrated.

2. That the previous opposition to his appointment among the citizens of the District has largely subsided.

3. That he desires in this way to tender just recognition and good faith toward our colored fellow citizens.

It is sufficient answer to the first two reasons alleged to say that neither could have been applicable when Matthews was appointed in August, immediately after the adjournment of the Senate, for at that time his fitness had not been demonstrated, nor had there been any interval for local opposition to subside.

Until suggested by the President, the Senate was not aware that the question of "just recognition or good faith to our colored fellow citizens" was involved in the question; and it has never before been urged that a person's nomination for an office should be confirmed or rejected because he is black or because he is white.

This classification has been abolished by the suppression of the Rebellion, and by the Amendments of the Constitution, and is no longer properly to be recognized in dealing with public affairs. The Senate, however, in view of the message of the President, cannot forbear to apprise him, since he has raised the race issue, that Frederick Douglass was, it is understood, requested to resign the office of recorder of deeds in the District of Columbia, in order that James C. Matthews might be appointed to the place. Without doubt, Frederick

Douglass is the most distinguished representative of the colored race, not in this country only but in the world. "Just recognition" would have been tendered to our colored fellow citizens by the retention of Frederick Douglass, rather than by his enforced retirement, in order to reward an unknown and obscure partisan who had never been a slave, and therefore represented the enfranchised race only by the accident of color. The devotion of the President to the political and civil advancement of the colored race might have been equally attested, and "good faith" might have been as strongly evinced by the retention of Douglass in the office whose duties he was discharging to the satisfaction of the people, unless it is to be understood that "just recognition" is to be tendered only to those members of that race who are supposed to entertain particular political opinions. In such a case the issue of race disappears, and the test is politics.

The Senate has no official information, other than that contained in the message of the President, whether Matthews is white or black. He is admitted to be a citizen of New York. The office to which he is nominated is strictly local. The compensation for the performance of its duties is not paid by the Government, but mainly by citizens of the district having papers to be recorded therein.

His confirmation is opposed with substantial unanimity by the citizens of the district without regard to color, politics or occupation.

The just principles of self-government, as well as the declaration of both political parties, justify their desire that the duties of the office of recorder of deeds should be performed by some resident of the district acceptable to those whose property is to be affected by his acts, and who pay the entire expense of its administration.

It can readily be seen that the threat on the part of the Senate answering the President, was really a political document addressed to the colored people of the United States; and there was cowardice in the Senate in not doing just what they meant to do. Complimenting Frederick Douglass and directing the President whom he should choose, was a piece of impudence that has not its equal in the political or senatorial action.

It would be as well before closing up this testimony, to select a passage from the Congressional record, February 23, 1887. This passage shows that secrecy was removed from all the papers and matters, and that Senator Isham G. Harris boldly declared in open meeting that all the charges made against Mr. Matthews were false. But here let us give the record:

MR. HARRIS. I shall have something to say when the Senator is through, but not now.

MR. RIDDLEBERGER. Lest I should not give the Senator time before two o'clock, I am almost inclined to say that I have about finished now. I think I have about given the facts of this case. If I have not, when there shall come a response to the resolution the facts will be sent out.

JAMES C. MATTHEWS

Mr. Harris. Mr. President, I shall most cheerfully vote for the resolution of the senator from Virginia. He does not desire more than I do that every fact connected with the nomination of J. C. Matthews and the report of the committee and the action of the Senate should go to the public.

It is due to the truth of history, however, inasmuch as the senator has emphasized the fact that certain charges were filed before the committee on the District of Columbia against James C. Matthews, that some other facts should be stated in that connection. It is true that charges were made, but it is equally true that the chairman of the committee [Mr. Ingalls], the Senator who now occupies the chair, and myself were appointed a sub-committee to investigate those charges. It is equally true that we summoned from Albany, New York, every person that the man who made the charges indicated as one who could probably sustain them. We also summoned such witnesses as the accused chose to designate as having knowledge upon the subject. You and I, sir, sat for a whole day, and examined and cross-examined the various witnesses so brought to this city, under the solemn sanctions of their oaths. The evidence taken in that examination is now on file in the committee room, and I shall be glad to see every word of it go into print and go to the public. But you and I, sir, agreed and reported to the full committee that there was not the shadow of foundation in truth for any one of the charges that had been so made against James C. Matthews.

I know not what the motives were of any Senator for voting against his confirmation, nor do I choose to inquire into their motives; but if there was a member of the committee on the District of Columbia who doubted or had reason to doubt the personal respectability of the man, or his qualifications to perform the duties to that office, no such doubt was ever expressed within my hearing.

Let these facts go to the public with the statement of the senator from Virginia.

After the rejection of Mr. Matthews, James M. Trotter of Hyde Park Massachusetts, was selected to fill the position. The Republican Senators were willing to do this when they found the storm they had called up by the rejection of Mr. Matthews, and fearing, as they said, lest their action would be misunderstood, they confirmed him almost unanimously. It does seem, if they were honest and right at the time they rejected one who was not a resident of the city, they ought to have rejected another on the same grounds; and hence they lost their whole case by their action, and it stands against them either as an impeachment of integrity or complete backing down, forced by the Negroes of the country.

Mr. Matthews is also responsible for the nomination of Mr. Trotter to the position of recorder of deeds; he very wisely appointed him his deputy just before his own rejection. It was thought that he was advised to this course by the President. The appointment was made under an act of Congress, approved January 16, 1877, which says:

Be it enacted, etc., That the recorder of deeds for the District of Columbia is authorized to appoint a deputy recorder, with the full power of the recorder, and in case of a vacancy in the office of recorder, by death, resignation or other cause, the deputy recorder shall act until a recorder shall be duly appointed and qualified.

Resolved, That no additional expense shall be incurred by the district for said deputy, and no other fees shall be appointed than are now provided by law.

About the hour that the Senate was voting on his name the following paper was issued:

To all whom it may concern:

Under and by virtue of chapter twenty-three (23) of the United States Statutes at Large, approved January 16, 1877, entitled "An act authorizing the recorder of the District of Columbia to appoint an assistant with certain powers," I, James C. Matthews, recorder of deeds for the District of Columbia, do hereby make, constitute and appoint James M. Trotter, of Hyde Park, Massachusetts, deputy recorder of deeds in and for said District of Columbia.

Given under my hand and seal of office this second day of March, in the year one thousand eight hundred and eighty-seven.

[Seal]   JAMES C. MATTHEWS,
Recorder of Deeds for the District of Columbia

Of course as soon as Mr. Matthews was out of the office, this would bring Mr. Trotter in recorder anyhow; and so it was clear that the Senate would have been beaten anyway; they would have had a colored man and non-resident in the office which they labored so hard to keep him out of, and so they no doubt thought it was not worth while to be defeated in that style, and so they confirmed Mr. Trotter.

Mr. Matthews is distinguished from most leading men of his race by those characteristics that mark his career so prominently; being openhanded, frank and unacquainted with duplicity, generous, kind, not for notoriety but because he loves charity. He contributes liberally to all the deserving objects and associations, helping and encouraging wherever opportunity presents, both with his means and ability, all movements hinting at the amelioration of the race. Politically he is a clear-headed and forcing politician; one who can calculate a political complexion during a campaign down to nicety. It is this power to influence individuals that incurs for him the opposition of Republicans; they know him to be a natural orator, worthy of the best foeman's steel. His style of oratory is of that persausive, logical and argumentative kind which usually captivates the listener.

I trust that his future will be as brilliant as his past, and that he will maintain himself with honor and credit to the race.

CHAPTER CXLVI

Professor William Howard Day, D. D.
Able and Forcible Orator—Practical Printer—Veteran Editor
—Philanthropist—Agitator—Progressive Race Man

This gentleman was born in New York City. He first attended the Folsona school; then the public school, number 2, and then a celebrated private school. He prepared for college at Northampton, Massachusetts, and thoroughly learned the art of printing. His guardian, Hon. J. P. Williston, determined to teach him a trade as well as give him a liberal education. In 1842 Mr. Day was examined in Latin and Greek by Rev. Beriah Green, president of Whitestown Institute, New York. In 1843 he entered Oberlin College, Ohio, and passed a rigid private examination in Latin, Greek and algebra. He graduated in 1847, the only colored member of a class of fifty. During the term of study his effort was to pay his own bills by work in the printing office. In a short time after graduating he was appointed foreman—all the compositors were white men; but they recognized Mr. Day's fitness for the responsible position and cheerfully worked under his direction. From 1845 to 1852 he was constantly on the platform in defense of the rights of man. He was an elected representative of the colored citizens in every State or National convention. In the repeal of the "Black Laws" of Ohio, 1849, he held a prominent part, having been, with John L. Watson, elected by the colored citizens in convention assembled to address the members of the Legislature in the hall of the House of Representatives. It was unheard of presumption in that early day, on the part of the colored people, to ask for the hall of the house, but Mr. Day proposed that it be done and the result was that under God the repeal was secured. The most notable benefit derived from the repeal was the school system which was to be enjoyed by seven thousand children who, up to that time, had practically been deprived of school privileges. The influence of this worthy man at this time in Ohio was so extended that members of Congress and judges of the courts admitted their indebtedness to him for their election. This, too, was fifteen years before the Fifteenth Amendment.

In 1852 he called together at Cleveland, Ohio, the living representatives of color of the War of 1812, and brought together, for the first time in the history of the Nation, the men who fought at New Orleans under General Jackson; in Georgia, at Plattsburg, New York, and on the lakes, and for the first time the cannon of the government belched forth the praise of their heroic deeds in the early day. Mr. Day was orator of this occasion. In 1852 he was the chairman of the committee of citizens of Cleveland to address Louis Kossuth of Hungary and to present money to help to purchase muskets for Hungary's cause. He then uttered that sentence which has often since been quoted: "Liberty is one, and Despotism one, the world over." In the same year he established *The Aliened American*, a paper published once a week in the interest of his race.

In 1852 he was secretary of the National convention at Cleveland. Previously to this, he was employed as compositor in the office of the *Cleveland True Democrat*, published by Hon. Thomas Brown, with Hon. John C. Vaughan, a South Carolinian and a former slaveholder, editor. After nearly a year's work in the composing room, he was promoted to mailing clerk and local editor. In the absence of the editors he was deputed to welcome to Cleveland the representative of Georgian liberty—Professor Gottfried Kinkel. On one occasion he offered a resolution of sympathy for those struggling in the Fatherland, which did much to unite the Germans and colored citizens in bonds of friendship.

Mr. Day was also a teacher of Latin, Greek, mathematics, rhetoric, logic, vocal music, short-hand, writing and other studies. In 1857 his health failed and his physician ordered him to a farm; he went to Canada, where, while recruiting his health, he could labor for the educational development among the fugitive slaves, fifty thousand of whom had then reached the Province. In 1859, in company with Rev. William King of Canada, he visited England, Ireland and Scotland to secure means to erect a church and school-houses in the celebrated Elgia settlement at Buxton, Canada. Having been successful in raising $35,000 for that purpose, his colleague returned to Canada with the means secured, while at the earnest request of the Americans in England, Professor Day remained to give information to the British public upon the important questions connected with the stirring events of 1861–65. He was received by the General Assembly of the Presbyterian church of Ireland. In the Music Hall of Dublin he was greeted by an audience of three thousand. He sailed for Scotland and made Edinburgh his headquarters, and visited the principal towns and cities before leaving for London. All this prepared the way for public demonstrations everywhere. As if to intensify this interest, then at fever-heat, a circumstance occurred which may well be called Providential, in connection with these questions pertaining to the people of color.

In 1858 Professor Day had been elected, at Chatham, Canada, by a general convention of citizens of Canada and the United States, as president of the National Board of Commissioners of the Colored People, and had in that same year signed the papers authorizing Doctor, afterwards Major Martin R. Delaney, and others, to go to the valley of the Niger in Africa to explore it. Of the complete company assigned to that work, only two, Dr. Delaney and Professor Campbell, of the Institute for Colored Youth in Philadelphia, could go. In the meantime Professor Day sailed for Great Britain and Ireland, and from Ireland wrote to Dr. Delaney in Africa to come home by way of Great Britain. Dr. Delaney wrote back that his passage had already been arranged direct to America and the subject was dropped. But Dr. Delaney afterwards found his direct passage to America prevented, and in the same week in which Professor Day arrived at London from Scotland, Dr. Delaney and Professor Campbell arrived there also from Liverpool, and this without any understanding between them. Suffice to say, that as a result, the African Aid Society was formed and is yet in existence and doing noble work to-day.

At the Whitehall club rooms the distinguished gentleman of whom we write introduced Dr. Delaney and Professor Campbell, and addressed two hundred noblemen and gentlemen. Among them was lord bishop of Sierra Leone and by his special invitation Professor Day addressed the society of ladies for the education of West India children. At Hull he lectured in the place of Gerald Massey and wife who had failed to appear; and at Burton-on-Trent supplied the place of Father Gavarri, of European and American fame. He was a welcome guest upon the platform of the Young Men's Christian Association, and for four months regularly supplied the pulpit of a large Congregational church in Lincolnshire. He was also offered a professorship in a classical academy, which he declined. He arrived home after an absence of five years, and at the great emancipation meeting in Cooper Institute, New York City, delivered one of his stirring addresses. He was soon assigned to duty in connection with the parent Freedman's Association, and with Honorable Horace Greeley addressed meetings in behalf of the education of three white slave children, one the child of a Confederate brigadier-general and the education of a man of color who was not only a slave, but in whose forehead were branded the initials of his former master's name.

In 1866 he was appointed editor of the secular department of *Zion's Standard and Weekly Review* of New York City, a paper owned by the corporation of the A. M. E. Zion church, and of which Rev. (now Bishop)

Singleton T. Jones was the editor of the religious department. Professor Day continued in this position for more than a year, when in 1867, General E. M. Gregory, assistant commissioner of the Bureau of Refugees, Freedmen and Abandoned Lands, whose headquarters were at Baltimore, telegraphed to him to come and take charge as inspector-general of schools for Maryland and Delaware. On assuming duty Professor Day found one hundred and forty schools, one hundred and fifty teachers, and seven thousand children to superintend.

In 1869 Professor Day went to Wilmington, where he risked his life in organizing the colored citizens as voters, and was successful at the end of a year in entirely changing the representation in the lower house of Congress, a change for the first time in twenty years. In 1870 he took charge of *Our National Progress,* and for five years he fought the battle of the people. In 1872 he was appointed as clerk in the corporation department of the auditor-general's office of Pennsylvania, and for two years and a half sent out accounts from the amount of thirty cents to four thousand dollars. In 1875 upon the decease of Rev. A. Jones, secretary of the General Conference of the A. M. E. Zion connection, the Bishops united in assigning him to the position. In 1876 he served with ability in the General conference held at Louisville, Kentucky, where he was re-elected secretary.

In 1878 Professor Day, after a warm contest, was elected school director at Harrisburg, Pennsylvania. It excited no little interest, since he was the first colored man ever elected to that body. He served three years, being secretary of the committee on teachers, and occupied other important positions. He was re-elected in 1881. Professor Day declined the third election, but at the end of three years the people called for him again, and in 1887 he was elected as the Republican candidate, the Democrats refusing to nominate any one against him. On the lecture platform, either for the Grand United Order of Odd Fellows, for the Masonic fraternity representing both the York and the Scottish rite, or on general political, or economic, or literary questions, Professor Day has been, and is now, constantly in request. In 1885, at the Philadelphia and Baltimore Annual conference of the A. M. E. Zion connection, held in Washington, he was unanimously elected presiding elder of the first or Baltimore district, which he resigned in 1886 to become general missionary and intellectual instructor of the conference. Up to 1885 Professor Day had continued his connection with the Virginian conference, but in the same year was transferred to the Philadelphia and Baltimore conference, of which he is now a member. The Livingstone College, Rev. J. C. Price president, conferred on Professor William H. Day the title of D.D., at its commencement in May, 1887.

CHAPTER CXLVII

Rev. Benjamin Tucker Tanner, A. M., D. D.
Editor of the A. M. E. Review—*Twenty Years an Editor—*
For Many Years Editor of the Christian Recorder—*Author*
of Ecclesiastical Works

———•◆•———

Without doubt, one of the brightest, grandest, noblest men in the ranks of Negro Methodism is Dr. B. T. Tanner, the veteran journalist of the colored race. His fame has extended from the lakes to the gulf, and from the Atlantic to the Pacific.

He was born of Hugh and Isabella Tanner, in Pittsburgh, Pennsylvania, and was not a slave. He spent five years in study at Avery College, Allegheny City, Pennsylvania, where he paid his expenses by working at the barber's chair. At this time of life his father was dead, and his struggles were the more severe because his widowed mother needed his care. His whole nature was independent; for he might have sweetened his life some and smoothed many a road over which he passed, but he preferred to work and win. Mr. Avery, in whose honor Avery College was named, and who was its founder, offered to pay his expenses through college, but the self-reliant young man refused it. After spending one year of the five in Avery College in the College Department, he took a three years' course in the Western Theological Seminary. His birthday being December 25, 1835, he was twenty-five years old when he received his first appointment from Bishop D. A. Payne to the Sacramento station in the California conference. The appointment was not filled on account of the distance and the money to get there. So he was "supply" for the Presbyterian church of Washington, District of Columbia, for eighteen months. This was admissible on account of the liberality of the views of each denomination, and it was a magnificent compliment to his head and heart that they invited him. While here he organized the Sabbath school for Freedmen in the navy yard, by permission of Admiral Dalghren. April, 1862, he united with the Baltimore Annual conference and was appointed to the Alexander Mission, "E" street, Washington, District of Columbia. This being the first mission possible during the war, it had

BENJAMIN TUCKER TANNER

to be guarded by soldiers through the kindness of provost-marshal, General Gregory. The year 1863 found him pastor of the Georgetown, District of Columbia, church. 1866 was the date of his pastorate in "Big Baltimore" charge, and after serving to the satisfaction of all concerned he resigned the re-appointment of the charge, to become principal of the Annual Conference school at Frederickstown, Maryland. The Freedmen's Society also secured his services in organizing a common school. His fame and talents begot for him a great name. His addresses showed thought, learning and rare gifts; so that when the general conference met in the capital of the Nation, in 1868, he was not only elected chief secretary, but editor of the church organ, the *Christian Recorder,* by acclamation, and this honored position was thrust upon him in succession until he had served sixteen years. This is indeed an honor. In 1870, while the lamented Dr. Henry Highland Garnet was president of Avery College, he was given the degree of A. M., a title he richly earned by diligent literary labors. Wilberforce honored him with the degree of D.D., sometime in the seventies.

In 1881 he crossed the waters, visiting England and continental Europe, and attending the Ecumenical conference. His spare time has been spent in editing books of use to his denomination. He is the author of an *Apology for African Methodism; The Negro's Origin; and Is He Cursed of God, An Outline of our History and Government; The Negro, African and American.* In the general conference of 1884 Dr. Tanner was voted a promotion to the editorship of the *A. M. E. Review.* This is one of the most scholarly productions of the age, and its list of writers includes all classes of thinkers and writers of all denominations, male and female. Indeed, he has the rare skill of securing the ablest articles by Negro writers. It is sent out quarterly, full of matter for brain and soul. His long experience fits him to discriminate with such rare judgment that the magazine is always nicely balanced. It is the crystallization of Negro scholarship, an epitome of Negro brains, and the doctor is as unerring in hitting the mark with his own pen as the best marksman I know. He is a member of the New England Historical Society of the M. E. church, and fills many important stations in his own church. His views are in the line of Wesley's, Richard Allen and the leading lights of their faith. The affability of the doctor, added to his general worth, makes his respected everywhere. While traveling in the old world—he was sailing on Lake Geneva, Switzerland—he was called on to preside at the dinner and was also made chairman of the committee appointed to draft resolutions complimentary to Monsieur Lemoiger, who had safely piloted the party over the Alps at Chamonix.

Dr. Arnett has said of Dr. Tanner:

He has risen from a successful barber to be the king of Negro editors. His pen is sharper than his razor, and his editorial chair is finer than the barber chair. The church and race will long remember Dr. B. T. Tanner for the part he has taken in the reconstruction of the South and for his words of encouragement.

CHAPTER CXLVIII

Geoffrey L'Islet
Correspondent of the French Academy of Sciences—Versed
in the Sciences of Botany, Natural Philosophy, Zoology,
and Astronomy

Geoffrey L'Islet, a mulatto, was an officer of artillery and guardian of the depot of maps and plans of the Isle of France. In 1786 he was named a correspondent of the French Academy of Sciences, and is acknowledged as such in the "Connoisance des Temps" for 1797, to which learned society L'Islet regularly transmitted meteorological observations, and sometimes hydrographical journals. His maps of the Isle of France, delineated according to astronomical observations, were published with other plans, in 1791, by order of the minister of marine. A new edition appeared in 1802, corrected from drawings transmitted by the author. Gregoire speaks of them as the best maps of those isles that had appeared.

In the almanac of the Isle of France, several contributions of L'Islet's were inserted; among others, a description of Pitrebot, one of the highest mountains of the island. A collection of his manuscript memoirs are deposited in the archives of the Academy of Sciences. Among these is the account of a voyage of L'Islet to the Bay of St. Luce, an island of Madagascar; it is accompanied with a map of the bay and of the coast. He points out the exchangeable commodities, the resources which it presents, and which would increase, says he, if, instead of exciting the natives to war in order to obtain slaves, industry were encouraged by the prospects of advantageous commerce. The description he gives of the manners and customs of the natives of Madagascar is very curious.

L'Islet was well versed in botany, natural philosophy, geology and astronomy. He struggled more successfully than many against the prejudices attached to his race. He never visited Europe to improve his taste or acquire knowledge. Had he been able to do this in his youth, to breathe the atmosphere of the learned, it would have probably tended to the expansion of his genius and talents.

L'Islet established a scientific society in the Isle of France, of which some whites refused to become members merely because its founder was a Black. "Did they not prove by their conduct," asks Abbé Gregoire, "that they were unworthy of such an honor?" This sketch is taken from a book entitled, *A Tribute for the Negro*, written by Wilson Armistead, in 1848; published in Manchester, England.

CHAPTER CXLIX

R. C. O. Benjamin, Esq.
Lawyer—Author—Editor—Champion of the Race

R. C. O. Benjamin was born on the Island of St. Keys, March 31, 1855. Education being compulsory on the island, he was sent to school while very young, and at the age of eleven was sent to England under a private tutor, who prepared him for college. While yet a boy he entered Trinity College, Oxford, where he resided for three years, and left without taking a degree; visiting Sumatra, Java and other islands in the East Indies, then returned to England after a two years' tour. Being of a roving disposition, he soon took passage on a vessel coming to America, and arrived in the city of New York, April 13, 1869. Ten days after, the young man shipped as cabin boy on the bark "Lepanto," captain, Cyrus E. Staples, and made a six months' cruise to Venezuela, Curacoa, Demerara and West Indies. Returning to New York in the fall of the same year, he concluded to abandon the sea and settled there, working at anything he could get to do.

In the meantime he took an active part in public affairs, which brought him in close association with such prominent politicians as Dr. Henry Highland Garnet, Cornelius Vancott, Dr. Isaac Hayes, Joe Howard, Jr. The latter, then editor of the *New York Star,* employed him as a soliciting agent, and when not at his work he was assigned to office duty. In the course of a few months, business led him into the acquaintanceship of Mr. J. J. Freeman, editor of the *Progressive American,* who made him city editor of his paper. In the same year he was naturalized by the usual court on such occasions. In 1876 the Republican party nominated Rutherford B. Hayes as their standard-bearer, and the Democratic party nominated Samuel J. Tilden.

Mr. Benjamin began helping to organize Hayes and Wheeler clubs in the various wards, and then took the stump for the party making speeches at Hempstead, Long Island and other parts of the State. After the smoke of battle had passed over and Hayes was declared the choice of the people, for his services he was given a position of letter carrier in the New York post office; but finding the work too laborious, after nine months' trial he was compelled to give it up. He then went South and engaged in school teaching. Kentucky being the first State in which he began. Here he taught in several of the counties, and it was not until then that he took a notion to become a lawyer. While at Hodgensville, Larne county, Kentucky, he borrowed some law books from ex-Congressman Reed, and studied after school hours; once a week he recited lessons to Mr. Dave Smith, now State Senator, but then county attorney. From Kentucky he went to Decatur, Alabama, and was made principal of the public school and continued to read law. Next he goes to Arkansas, to Brinkley and other points, where he taught school, and made enough money to go to Memphis, Tennessee, where he put himself under Honorable Josiah Patterson, an eminent lawyer of that city. Through his influence he was soon after admitted to the bar, January, 1880.

His success has been varied as a practitioner, and the territory over which his services have been extended aggregate twelve different States. He has also owned and edited several newspapers—the *Colored Citizen*, in Pittsburgh, Pennsylvania, and the *Chronicle*, at Evansville, Indiana. He was editor of *The Negro American*, at Birmingham, Alabama.

He is a prolific writer, always selecting such subjects as will interest the people. He has written several very valuable pamphlets, the principal ones of which are *Poetic Gems; The Boy Doctor; The Defender of Obadiah Cuff; The Negro Problem Solved; Southland; The Future of the Negro; Lectures on Africa;* and also an historical chart of the colored race.

He has the credit of being one of the best speakers in the South. He has made extensive trips in lecturing in the principal cities of the United States. In 1886 he made a tour through the principal cities of Canada and lectured to large white audiences. He is a fluent conversationalist in both the French and Spanish languages. Any one reading his paper while he was editor will find that the Negroes in Birmingham, Alabama, have had an able champion in him, and one who would never fail them. His strictures on the murders and outrages on colored people by the railroad companies, in having special gates for them to pass through, show manliness; and whatever may be his faults, he stands by the race. His future is in his own hands.

CHAPTER CL

Hon. John J. Irvine
Clerk of the Circuit Court of Chattanooga, Tennessee

———•◆•———

August 3, 1852, near the village of Clarksville, in Mecklenburgh county, Virginia, the subject of our sketch was born. Clarksville at that time was quite a noted slave market, and at a very early age he began to realize that, like "Topsy," "he must just have growed," for he belonged neither to his father nor to his mother, but was in reality a part of the personal stock of one R. M. Scott.

The traits of character which he has developed had begun to show themselves in him at ten years. He showed his utter abhorrence of and rebellion against the woes of the people. Nevertheless, like others, he enjoyed the childish freedom of his times around the cabins and barnyard.

In 1866, after the death of his mother, he was hired out to a farmer for the munificent sum of twelve dollars a year and three suits of clothing, with the promise of all the education he could pick up on Saturday afternoons and at nights, but with no promise to see that he studied or improved himself in any way. He confesses now that he wasted much time in frolicking among the youth of his age, and on many a Sunday, while holding the horse while his employer and family worshiped in the church where no "nigger" dared even to look, he would have his slate, pencil, or perhaps a spelling book, and partially make up for lost time.

When he was about seven, he was ordered by his old master to work for a man named Solomon, and his mother was ordered to prepare him for departure by the next morning. This was their first separation. On the following morning, at an early hour, furnished with a small, coarse blanket, he started in charge of a boy somewhat larger than himself to what was to be his future home. Although the distance was only five miles, it seemed as if it were a hundred. His young heart was ready to break. Often when he wanted to see his mother, his companion told him he had better quit crying as he was going along the road, or the white overseer would give him something to cry about. So when he got up to the cabin he tried to control his emotions and wipe away the tears as best

JOHN J. IRVINE

he could. He was very shortly put to his duties by his new master, who was not as severe as he had expected, and when this kind-hearted man found the boy crying from homesickness, he said he would let him go home every second Sunday. But oh, how long those weeks were; and when the time came, how his little feet skipped over those five miles as though it was but a few moments' walk. Upon his arrival he found his mother at home for the day, and the welcome he received can be better imagined than described. When it was time for him to return he begged his parents not to let him go back. But all in vain. The only consolation he had was that his father agreed to take him home on the horse, thus enabling him to stay a little while longer. So mounting the horse, the father took him behind and started, giving the boy good advice all along the road, until they were within a quarter of a mile of Mr. Solomon's place, where he let him off telling him to be a good boy and save himself trouble; but his heart was too heavy to heed anything and he was overcome with a desire to return. So waiting till his father had gone a short distance, he returned and followed him even to the threshold of his mother's door; but here the thought of the consequences struck him and he was afraid to go into the house, but crawled under the house, and being very tired fell asleep almost instantly. He was suddenly awakened from his sleep by a dog which had found and knew him and was lacking his face in joy. He was discovered at home and taken back to Mr. Solomon's house with the promise that he would see that he stayed this time. He continued to labor for Mr. Solomon until the breaking out of the late civil war, when he was returned to his owner.

He now felt a great desire to be able to read; he knew his letters but dared not even hint such a thing to any of the owners. Sometimes he would get hold of the books of his young master, and in this way picked up the foundation of all the education he ever received. As emancipation dawned upon the colored people, the first thought of seriously applying himself for the purpose of getting an education entered his mind, and he determined at any sacrifice that he would learn to read and write, and from that time applied himself to that end. In 1867 a man from the North came into the settlement and proposed to open a school for the colored children. Many entertained fears for his safety and for the safety of the little school-house erected for him to teach in, which was located some eight miles from where young Irvine was then living. As soon as the first crops were gathered, the young boy determined to paddle his own canoe in search of more light.

He made arrangements with a man by the name of Moon as waiting boy, if he would teach him at night after the day's work was over; but as the gentleman was more apt at teaching him to work than the necessary branches he desired to study, he soon went to live with a Mrs. Gray, who really gave him the most of his education. When leaving her one year later, he could read and spell very well. He was now fifteen years old and hired himself to a man by the name of Turner, who agreed to give him two dollars a month and educate him; he was to furnish his own clothes and be allowed to go to school two months in the winter. At the end of eight months he applied for the small amount of money that was due him; but was met with an oath and told to go back to his work or he would teach him something. Thinking the man would do him some injury, he took up his weary search and went back to Halifax county, where he found his father, who was again working a farm on shares. After consultation they concluded to move South, where the weather would not be so severe; and on the twenty-ninth of December, 1868, the father and four sons turned their backs on the "Old Dominion State" and started for the "Sunny South." They stopped first at Marion, Alabama, where they hired to the ex-Confederate general, N. B. Forrest, to help build the Selma, Marion & Memphis railroad. Working here for about three months, at the end of which time, finding that there was no money in railroading, they again broke camp and started for a place on a large farm owned by W. N. Seldon, near Faunsdale, Marengo county, Alabama. They agreed with Mr. Seldon that the father and two younger brothers were to work in a squad of men, each of the boys to have and receive half wages, and both being entitled to the same shares as the father. John was to be employed at his house as a servant, and at the end of the year was to receive in cash the same amount each of his brothers received. Their system of work was about as follows: There were eight squads of seven men, or their equivalent in boys, employed on the place to work on shares, the landlord to find all stock, tools, etc., and to have two-thirds of the entire crops; the other one-third going to the eight different squads to be equally divided between them after their living expenses were deducted out of the proceeds of the year's crop. So they never knew exactly, but according to Mr. Seldon's figures, his brothers and himself each received nine dollars for one year's work. But as usual in such cases "kicking" only makes matters worse, and comforted by the assurance that he would make a good deal more the next year, after coaxing by his father and Mr. Seldon, he consented to try it another year, which resulted in a gain of eleven dollars on the last year's receipts.

He now became thoroughly disgusted with farming. Overcoming his father's objections to his leaving, he started to join his elder brother, who was at work on the "Alabama & Chattanooga railroad." He arrived at Carthage, Alabama, a day or so later, where he met his brother after a separation of two years. He soon procured employment at grading, which he followed for about six months, when the company failed and he with the others was left to mourn the loss of six months labor, except such provisions, clothing, etc., as he had drawn from the commissary.

By this time he was pretty well disgusted with Alabama; but being in no condition to leave, he tramped around trying to find work, and was successful after six months' efforts. The Louisville & Nashville railroad was still grading, and on it he worked and secured his pay. He was among the first selected as fireman on the road, which paid him $2.25 a day.

He stayed here about a year and having considerable taste for machinery, soon grew to take great interest in his engine and studied its every movement very closely. His next move was to Chattanooga, where he readily secured employment as stationary engineer, at which business, with the exception of about two years, spent at millwrighting, he continued until 1882. In the summer of that year he was nominated as constable of the Fourteenth civil district, Hamilton county, and was elected by a handsome majority, and entered upon the duties of the office. By careful attention to the little business entrusted to him at first, by colored men only, and by making prompt returns, he soon had all the business he could attend to, and he now began to have aspirations for reaching above the ordinary stations in life. After the two years expired he was renominated and ran much ahead of his ticket, showing he had gained the confidence of the people.

During the time he was acting as stationary engineer he conceived and patented an oil cup, which was pronounced by some of the best mechanics of the country the most complete of its kind ever gotten up. After entering upon his official duties he never pushed it any further on the market, although it brings him considerable revenue at the present time.

At the Republican county convention in 1886, he was nominated without opposition to his present position, and after a short, though excessively hot contest, was elected by 1,700 majority, with a popular Democrat and the former Republican clerk as opponents.

He married in 1875, he being at that time twenty-six years old, and probably owes much of his success to the good counsel and advice of his estimable wife. He is an active member of the Masonic fraternity. He is now deputy grand master of the State, having filled the office of secretary and worshipful master of his lodge for nine years. He is also master workman of the lodge of Knights of Labor.

He and his wife are identified with the A. M. E. church of Chattanooga. His present office pays him about three thousand dollars a year and his estimated wealth is about ten thousand.

Thus through hardships and trials he has succeeded admirably, and is given here as an example of what industry and the abstinence from the ordinary vices to which young men addict themselves, will accomplish for any young man.

CHAPTER CLI

George T. Downing, Esq.
Aggressive Politician—An Intimate Friend of Charles Sumner—
An Old Time Warrior for Free Speech and Human Rights—
A Man of Pronounced Convictions

———◆———

George T. Downing, the oldest son of Thomas and Rebecca Downing, was born December 30, 1819. His parents, who lived in Jinketig, Accomac county, Virginia, moved to New York in the early part of this century to begin life in earnest. Thomas Downing was a man of energy, perseverance and pluck, and soon developed into a successful leader in public enterprises. At an early age the subject of our sketch entered a private school taught by Mr. Charles Smith, and later attended the old Mulberry Street school, where he formed lasting ties of friendship with boys who in after years made the welkin ring for the overthrow of oppression. Among these were Philip Bell, Dr. A. Crummell, James McCune Smith, Henry Highland Garnet, and others. These boys were between the ages of fourteen and sixteen, yet they had the spirit of patriotism and bravery usually found in older persons. They organized a literary society to discuss questions pertaining to the condition of the race. At a memorable meeting of this society they adopted resolutions to refrain from celebrating the Fourth of July, giving as their reason "that the Declaration of Independence was to colored citizens a mockery."

In those days going to school was not what the boys of to-day find it. Negro children, even in the streets of New York, were jeered at and pelted with stones. It was necessary for parents or guardians to accompany the children to and from school, and then they were not safe. George Downing did not feel the need of an escort. He knew that his cause was just, and at times would fight his way through a crowd of insulting white children; at others, he would boldly lead colored boys into chasing white ones from the street. This was spirit! He had not reached manhood when he connected himself with the "Underground Railroad," and was arrested for smuggling from jail a fugitive slave. When the Antislavery society was organized he became an active member, and was one of the committee of thirteen organized after the passage of the fugitive slave law.

When the call for colored soldiers was made, he waited upon Governor John A. Andrews of Massachusetts, to ascertain whether colored soldiers would be given equal justice; and being assured that they would be treated as men and soldiers, he straightway organized several colored regiments. He went to Washington soon after this in the interest of colored troops, and was persuaded while there to take charge of the House restaurant. It was not consideration of gain which led him to make this decision, but he knew that in this position he would be brought into immediate contact with leading men of both parties. Such associations were always turned to the interest of his race. He was consulted about every important measure concerning it that was brought under discussion.

Mr. Downing never lost an opportunity to strike a blow at the color line. It is related that one day the head waiter, who had served under the former proprietor, came to him with a frightened look and said some colored people had called for dinner. Mr. Downing said in a decisive manner: "Serve them, and send to me any one who may complain." In this way he did much to break down the color line. He was instrumental in having the Senate gallery thrown open to colored people, and in putting a stop to ill treatment received by them on the Baltimore & Ohio Railroad between Washington and Baltimore.

While living in Rhode Island he fought long and well against separate schools. For twelve years he besieged the Legislature, year after year, to give all children, irrespective of color, the privilege of attending *any* school. The governor of said State commissioned him captain of a "colored" company of State militia. Mr. Downing had battled against such discrimination, so returned the commission protesting against the qualifying phrase. The governor at once made the requested change, and the next Legislature removed the proscriptive laws from the statute books concerning separate schools. Mr. Downing was intimately associated with Charles Sumner. When this great statesman was dying he reached out his hand, grasped that of Mr. Downing's and said in substance: "Don't let my civil rights bill fail." After the passage of this bill he and his wife were the first colored people to occupy boxes in the theater in Washington. In politics Mr. Downing is an Independent. He claims that the Republican party has played fast and loose with Negro voters, and advises a division in the colored vote. He also thinks the Democratic party is decidedly better than it was twenty-five years ago.

MARTIN R. DELANEY

CHAPTER CLII

*Major Martin R. Delaney, M. D.
Scientist—Ethnologist—Lecturer—Discoverer—Member
of the International Statistical Conference*

———•·•———

Martin Robinson Delaney, the son of Samuel and Pati Delaney, was born at Charlestown, Va., May 6, 1812. He was named for his godfather, a colored Baptist clergyman. His pride of birth is traceable to his maternal as well as to his paternal grandfather—native Africans—on the father's side pure Golah, on the mother's Mandingo. His grandfather was a chieftain, captured with his family in war, sold to the slavers, and brought to America. On his mother's side the father was an African prince, from the Niger valley regions of Central Africa.

Next to his pride of birth, and almost inseparable from it, is his pride of race. In a remark made once by Frederick Douglass, he said: "I thank God for making me a man simply; but Delaney always thanks him for making him a '*black* man.' " In personal appearance he was remarkable. He was of medium height, compactly and strongly built, with broad shoulders upon which rested a head seemingly inviting by its bareness, attention to the well developed organs; with eyes sharp and piercing, while will, energy and fire are alive in every feature; the whole surmounted on a groundwork of most defiant blackness. In speaking, he was most effective when in his loftiest flights. His habits were simple as well as temperate. In early youth he espoused total abstinence, conforming first from principle. It afterwards became an established habit to eschew the use of liquors and tobacco in any form. His mother was a most exemplary Christian, active and energetic, with quick preceptions and fine natural talents. She transmitted to her son great force of character.

Major Delaney was married to Kate A., youngest daughter of Charles Richards, of Pittsburgh, on the fifteenth of March, 1843. From this marriage eleven children were born. In the names of these children the specialty is again evident. The eldest, Toussaint L'Ouverture, after the first military hero and statesman of San Domingo; the second, Charles

Lennox Remond, from the eloquent declaimer; the third, Alexander Dumas, from that brilliant author of romance; the fourth, Saint Cyprian, from one of the greatest primitive bishops of the Christian Church, the fifth, Faustin Soulouque, after the late Emperor of Hayti; the sixth, Rameses Placido, from the good king of Egypt, "the everliving Rameses II.;" the seventh, the daughter, Ethiopia Halle Amelia, the country of his race, to which is given the unequalled promise that "she should soon stretch forth her hands unto God." In 1818 the first attempt was made to receive instruction. He studied from the New York primer and spelling book, which were obtained through itinerant Yankee peddlers in exchange for rags and old pewter. These peddlers always found it convenient and profitable, likewise, to whisper into the ear of a black, "You've as much right to learn to read as these whites," and always found time to give a lesson or so. It was under such covert tuition, and with such instructors, that young Martin, together with his brothers and sisters, was taught to read and write. This stealthy manner of learning made them more attentive and eager. So in harmony with the Southern rules of justice, on its discovery, his mother was so persecuted as to make her move to Chambersburg, Pennsylvania, in 1822, where she resided for fifteen years. For several years her children attended school, securing such advantages as the county schools afforded. Young Delaney's parents' means being limited he was compelled to leave school, and about two years later obtained the consent of his parents to go to Pittsburgh, where facilities for obtaining an education were superior to those of his home. He left July 29, 1831. Here, under Rev. Louis Woodson, he studied during the winter of 1831. It was commonly said by his friends at school, that his retentiveness of history was so remarkable that he seemed to have recited from the palm of his hand.

In 1834 he was actively engaged in the organization of several associations for the relief of the poor of the city, and for the moral elevation of his people. Among them was the first total abstinence society ever formed among the colored people. About 1835 or '36 he began the study of medicine under the late Dr. Andrew N. McDowell, but for some cause did not continue to completion. He resumed the study, however, in 1849. Through the influence of Drs. Joseph P. Gazzan and Francis L. Lemoyne, he was received into the Medical Department of Harvard College, having been previously refused admission, on application, to the Pennsylvania University, Jefferson College, and the Medical College of Albany and Geneva, New York. After leaving Harvard, he traveled westward and lectured on physiological subjects. He returned to Pittsburgh and entered upon the duties of a physician. His skilful treatment of the cholera, which prevailed to some extent in Pittsburgh in 1854, is still remembered. Early in 1843 he started a weekly sheet under the title of *Mystery,* devoted to the interest of his race. He was prompted to do this, because his people could get no article published in other papers in their interest. After sustaining it alone for nine months he transferred the proprietorship to a committee of six gentlemen, he, meanwhile, continuing as editor for nearly four years. The editorials of his journal elicited praises even from its enemies, and were frequently transferred to their columns. It is indisputable that to its influence originated the Avery fund. Once, while editor, a suit for libel was entered against him and after the verdict of guilty was rendered, so great was his standing among the newspaper fraternity that they made an appeal for a subscription to be raised; but about one week after the suit and before the sum could be raised, the governor remitted the fine. In 1848, when traveling through Northern Ohio, he was mobbed, it being circulated that he was an abolitionist and amalgamationist. Dr. Delaney published a call for a National emigration convention, and, it finding favor, there assembled at Cleveland, Ohio, August, 1854, many of the eminent colored men of the Northern and Western States, to discuss the question of emigration. At this convention he was made president *pro tem* to organize, and afterwards chairman of the business committee. In a speech on the Fugitive Slave Act at Allegheny City, Pennsylvania, before some of the leading white men of the time, he said:

Honorable mayor, whatever ideas of liberty I may have, have been received from reading the lives of your Revolutionary fathers. I have therein learned that a man has a right to defend his castle with his life, even unto the taking of life. Sir, my house is my castle; in that castle are none but my wife and my children, as free as the angels of heaven, and whose liberty is as sacred as the pillars of God. If any man approaches that house in search of a slave—I care not who he may be, whether constable or sheriff, magistrate or even judge of the Supreme Court—nay, let it be he who sanctioned this act to become a law, surrounded by his cabinet as his body-guard, with the Declaration of Independence waving above his head as his banner, and the Constitution of his country upon his breast as a shield—if he crosses the threshold of my door, and I do not lay him a lifeless corpse at my feet, I hope the grave may refuse my body a resting place, and righteous Heaven my spirit a home. No! he cannot enter that house and we both live.

While generally successful, he had also some failures. Two of a marked character occured about the winter of 1851–52. He had left Pittsburgh for New York to make certain arrangements necessary for obtaining a *caveat,* preparatory to an application to the department at Washington for a patent for an invention, originally his own, for the ascending and descending of a locomotive on an inclined plane, without the aid of a stationary engine. Had he succeeded in his first plan, the second would have been satisfactory.

After this failure he determined to go to Central America. Many colored men, dissatisfied with their unrecognized condition, caught this spirit. The black adventurers soon affiliated with the natives, and were made eligible to every civil right among them.

While there a new policy and future government was decided upon. It was understood that the mayor should be the highest civil municipal authority, the governor the highest civil State authority, the civil and military to be united in one person, and the governor must be commander-in-chief of the military forces. An election took place and a steamer brought the intelligence officially transmitted, that "Dr. Martin R. Delaney was duly chosen and elected mayor to Greytown, civil governor of the Mosquito reservation, and commander-in-chief of the military forces of the province." This was delivered to him by a bearer of despatches sent especially for that purpose.

In 1856 he removed to Chatham, Canada, and practiced medicine. In the early part of May, 1859, there sailed from New York, in the bark "Mendi," owned by three colored African merchants, the first colored explorers from the United States, known as the Niger Valley exploring party, at the head of which was it projector, Dr. Delaney. He traveled extensively in Africa for one year. He became acquainted with John Brown in April, prior to his departure for Africa, and Captain Brown fully revealed his design to him.

After his expedition into Central Africa, gratified at the success of his discoveries, as well as the knowledge acquired concerning the people, he departed for Europe, and arrived at Liverpool, May 12, 1860, where he remained for three days, and entered London on the evening of May 15. While in London transacting business connected with the exploration, it was Delaney's privilege to attain a distinction never before reached by a colored American under like auspices. This was when he was present in that august assembly known as the International Statistical Congress, presided over by his Royal Highness, Albert, Prince Consort of England. Shortly after his return to America the war began. At this time, too, there were endless speculations concerning the course and determined policy of Mr. Lincoln. Dr. Delaney thought he could discern, in the course then being pursued by Mr. Lincoln, a logical conclusion; he also stated that it had become inseparable from his daily existence, almost absorbing everything else, and nothing would content him but entering the service; he cared not how, provided his admission recognized the rights of his race to do so. He received the appointment of acting assistant agent, under Charles L. Remond and Charles H. Langston, Esq., for recruiting, and acting examining surgeon for the post of Chicago, from Mayor George L. Stearns, chairman of the military committee, being authorized by Governor John A. Andrew of Massachusetts. He also became commissioner for Rhode Island, New York, Pennsylvania and Ohio.

The sixth of February, 1865, found him in Washington, for the purpose of having an interview, if possible, with President Lincoln and the secretary of war. After repeated endeavors to gain the presence of Mr. Lincoln, he was at last successful. In his conversation with him he said the blacks of the South should be armed, and that they had been faithful to the duties assigned, and it follows that if they could be found of higher qualifications, they might with equal credit fill higher and more important trusts.

He proposed an army of blacks, commanded entirely by black officers, except such whites as might volunteer to serve. He received his commission as major February 8, 1865, the first of his race to be thus honored by the government. Senator Ben Wade, of Ohio, was present when he was dubbed "Gold Leaf." April 5, 1865, he was ordered to Charleston. On April 14, Major Delaney embarked to witness the ceremony on the historical steamer "Planter," with its gallant commander, Robert Smalls. Immediately after the restoration of the flag on Fort Sumter, active duty was resumed by the military at Charleston, and Delaney heartily rejoiced at the prospect of beginning his work. Before his arrival, the One Hundred and Second United States colored troops had been completed, and the One Hundred and Third had just commenced, of which regiment, according to the spirit of the order of the war department, he was entitled to the major's command; but by the request of his general, he waived his right to an officer to whom the position had been promised previous to his arrival, though he had aided in its organization, and soon began to recruit his own. After this, some of the most extraordinary messages were sent to Delaney; but finding that the "black major" could not be aroused to the extent of the danger, his enemies were disconcerted. Whatever can be said of him, it can be said that he was heroic, brave, dauntless, true to his race, and ambitious.

The hero was in the "Freedmen's Bureau" for three years after the war; a member of General Scott's staff; an inspector in the custom-house in Charleston, South Carolina, for several years; trial justice in the same city for four years. He practised medicine a short time, then went East, and remained there until March, 1884, when he was employed by a mercantile house in Boston to act as agent for the firm in Central America. He became sick and could not go. On December 28, 1884, he came home, and died January 24, 1885.

J. B. FIELDS

CHAPTER CLIII

Rev. J. B. Fields
*An Able, Eloquent Baptist Divine—Popular Historian—
Lecturer—Annihilator of Ingersollism*

The Negro race is without doubt a trustful, happy people, who never know such darkness that they cannot sing, nor such adversity that they do not pray. There are few infidels among us; what few there are, as a rule, are simply agnostics from sheer effort to be wise; but who does not see through their sham attempts to assume a learned air? And the result is they get things mixed, and go about asking "double barreled questions." It has been supposed that Ingersoll was a mountain that none could scale; that he was so powerful that none could answer; when lo, the once despised Negro came forth to the pulpit and the platform in the person of Rev. J. B. Fields, and riddled his arguments with such irresistible logic, learning and wisdom that the universal acknowledgment rose up from every source that he had succeeded in annihilating Ingersollism. And indeed it would be hard to find any man in the United States with better and more eulogistic recommendations than this gifted and eloquent preacher.

March 1, 1850, was the day of his birth in the little town of Prairieville, Pike county, Missouri. His beloved parents, Henry and Minnie Fields, were slaves and had been carried from Virginia to the State of Missouri. In 1862 the whole family fled from slavery and found a refuge in Quincy, Illinois, where they lived for many years. Finally, when the son moved to Denver, Colorado, which is his home now, the parents also moved. His father died August 27, 1883, at the age of ninety-one years.

Mr. Fields, like all other colored people in slave States, had very little opportunity for cultivating his intellect and acquiring knowledge. At Quincy he went to school two years, which was all the training he had. In 1866 he went to McCombe and learned the barber's trade. In 1870 he commenced the study of theology, and studied that and ancient history in the intervals between the calls of customers to be shaved. In 1875 he was the means of getting up a church for colored people in McCombe, and was chosen their pastor. He was converted in Quincy before he went to McCombe, and joined the Baptist church.

In October, 1869, he was married in Palmyra, Missouri, to Miss Missouri Carr of Quincy, Illinois, with whom he has lived peaceably and happily, and the result of their union has been three children, all boys. Two of these are still living.

He was ordained to the gospel ministry in McCombe, Illinois, September 25, 1878, by a regular constituted council of the Baptist denomination. In January, 1881, he was called as pastor of the Zion Baptist church, in Denver, Colorado. He at once took charge of that church, which was then in a dead condition. They worshiped in a little old frame building for several years, and there were only about twenty-five members, with scarcely any following. Since that time Mr. Fields has built for his people a very fine brick church at a cost of over eight thousand dollars. From April 8, 1881, to 1885, when he resigned, he had raised four thousand dollars on the church debt. Of this amount he himself raised in cash, donated by white people, the sum of two thousand fifty-seven dollars and fifty-one cents. The church is the finest colored church in the West. January, 1885, Mr. Fields sent in his resignation as pastor of the church, said resignation to take effect in March, and much against the wishes of the people he insisted on resigning, and gave himself to the work of a public lecturer, in which he has made a great reputation.

We furnish here a number of testimonials showing the character of his lectures and how he is appreciated by those who have heard him. The following was published in the *American Baptist,* of Louisville, Kentucky, April 23, 1886:

Rev. J. B. Fields, the celebrated lecturer of Denver, Colorado, lectured to the students Tuesday morning, subject "Mistakes of Robert Ingersoll." He is a good representative of what the Negro can do; he is the ablest, most historical, most richly prolific of truth and most complete annihilator of the infidel Ingersoll's statements I know. He is entirely biblical and backed by the sayings of the noblest minds in the world, among whom may be mentioned Josephus, Gibbons, Celsus, Horne and the encyclopedias. He has a national reputation and his lecture deserves the highest encomiums.

This certifies that for the past four years I have been personally acquainted with the Rev. J. B. Fields, pastor of Zion Baptist church, of this city, who commands the confidence and respect of the entire community and has made a high reputation as a lecturer.—Rev. Reuben Jeffery, D. D., pastor of First Baptist church, Denver, Colorado, July 28, 1884.

Elder J. B. Fields, a colored Baptist preacher, residing at McCombe, delivered a remarkable address at the Methodist Episcopal church here last Sunday afternoon. His discourse was styled, "The Bible; its Divine Origin Proven by the Fulfillment of Prophecy" etc. Our citizens will all testify who heard him, that they have not for many a day heard such copious quotations from Bible texts as on this occasion. With the book shut before him, he not only poured forth a flood of Scripture parallel passages, but quoted book, chapter and verse as well. Mr. Fields is a man of surprising memory, both in matters of sacred and profane history.—Elmwood, Illinois, *Messenger*, December 12, 1879.

The Rev. J. B. Fields, of Denver, delivered his lecture in reply to Colonel R. G. Ingersoll, on "The Bible," on Monday evening last, to a full house, at the M. E. church. His knowledge of ancient history and his different quotations from the Bible showed him to be a man possessing a very retentive memory. He handled the lives of Voltaire, Hobbs, Tom Payne, etc., the noted infidels of their day, with considerable ability.—*Colorado Miner*, Georgetown, Colorado, May 23, 1885.

Elder J. B. Fields delivered his great lecture before the Wood River Baptist Association, at its forty-first annual meeting, in the Baptist church in the city of Galesburg, September 7, 1879. The delivery of the lecture was listened to from beginning to end with the closest attention by the entire congregation. The lecture showed a comprehensive knowledge of the prophecies of the sacred Scriptures, and a corresponding acquaintance with history, both sacred and profane, and the lecture is really a strong and convincing argument in favor of the Divine origin of the Bible, and I would recommend all our pastors to arrange with Elder Field, and have him deliver it before their congregations.—R. DeBaptiste, D. D., corresponding secretary of the Wood River Baptist Association of Illinois, Chicago Illinois, 1879.

In order to show also the scope of his reading and the eloquent manner in which he speaks, I will give two extracts of speeches which he delivered upon two of the greatest minds in America:

LINCOLN

After a bondage of four hundred and thirty years, Moses was raised up and led the children of Israel away from their captors toward the promised land. On the road, when the great leader and law giver went up to Mt. Sinai to receive the law from the Deity, many of the unfettered multitude made for themselves a golden calf, and falling down adored it. The Jehovah was incensed at this act of idolatry, and their punishment was commensurate with the offense.

In August, 1620, a golden calf, the dragon and beast, was brought to this country; it was slavery, and many fell down and worshiped it and continued their adoration for upwards of two hundred and forty-three years. There were many individuals who refused to worship the idol; John Wesley said that slavery was the sum of all villainies. One of the strongest opponents of slavery was Abraham Lincoln. In his debate with Douglas, in 1858, he said that a house divided could not stand; that no Union of States could be permanent where a portion of the people was slave and the other half free. In 1860 he was nominated and elected President of the United States, and was inaugurated March 4, 1861. His paramount object was to save the Union. He elaborated this idea in a letter which he wrote to Horace Greeley. God raised Cyrus to deliver the Israelites from Babylonian captivity; the same God raised Abraham Lincoln to liberate slaves, and on the first of January, 1863, four millions of slaves were by him liberated. The slaves were raised from the lash to freedom, from sin to school, from being chattels to manhood, and from being pursued by blood-hounds and from auction blocks to the halls of Congress. He was an able lawyer and an eloquent statesman.

Greece had her Demosthenes and Pericles; Rome her Cæsar and Cicero; England her Burke, Pitt and Wilberforce; America her Patrick Henry, Henry Clay and Daniel Webster, but none of these could equal the immortal Lincoln. Major Henry Lee, in 1779, said in his great eulogy on Washington, "He was first in war, first in peace, and first in the hearts of his countrymen"; but Abraham Lincoln was the first President that ever gave the beast and dragon a deadly wound and there was no place left yet for it to languish and grow strong; it died. From the pinnacle of fame, Lincoln stepped into that country where "the wicked cease to trouble and the weary are at rest."

SUMNER

All nations have had their great men and lovers of humanity. Greece had her Pericles, Socrates and Leonidas; Rome her Servius Tullius and Cicero; England her great Wilberforce, Clarkson and Pitt; France, her Henry IV; Israel her Abraham, Daniel and Joshua; but none of these men could surpass the greatness of Charles Sumner in being a lover and defender of all mankind. Charles Sumner entered the United States Senate December 1, 1851, the beginning of his public and political life as the successor of Daniel Webster, who had been appointed Secretary of State. On the same day Henry Clay spoke his last words in the Senate and departed from the chamber never to return. In zeal and efforts in behalf of right and justice, and in his protest against the cruel and infamous Fugitive Slave law, and the great crime of African slavery, Charles Sumner spoke "as man never spake," and He that knows all things has said: "Greater love hath no man than this, that a man lay down his life for his friends." In this Charles Sumner was one who was willing to sacrifice his own life in behalf of the liberty and equality of all mankind, and for his poor and oppressed brethren of the African race. For the manly interest which was shown by him in behalf of the Negro he was assaulted and struck down in the Senate chamber on the twenty-second of May, 1856, by Brooks, pro-slavery member from South Carolina, and the blood of Sumner, like that of the righteous Abel, cried, "Freedom unto all slaves."

For thirty long years he labored and toiled for the right, and I would say he was certainly the Moses and redeemer of the colored race, and his last moments spent and words spoken were in favor of the colored man, humanity and justice. To Judge Hoar, in the last moments of earth, he said: "Do not let the Civil Rights bill fail," which was truly his adieu to earth and greeting in Heaven.

Charles Sumner was a Washington in purity, a Luther in fervor and a Cromwell in boldness. As long as American liberty shall last and patriotism shall be a virtue, the name of Charles Sumner shall be immortal.

ROBERT PELHAM, JR.

CHAPTER CLIV

Robert Pelham, Jr.
The Able Editor of the Detroit Plaindealer—*A Vigorous Writer*
—*An Active Politician*

―――――••・――――――

We are sure that among the rising and progressive men of the West, none surpass the young gentlemanly managing editor of the *Plaindealer,* the largest and ablest paper in the central Western States. That distinguished citizen, Fred Douglass, said of it: "In spirit and in letter, in method and object, in character and ability, the *Plaindealer* meets my warm approbation." Himself an editor of high standing, and a man of commanding position, his judgment on such matters can be taken as an index to the character and standing of this valuable paper.

A series of very closely written articles on "Our Relation to Labor" appeared in the *Plaindealer* columns during the past year. They attracted universal attention on account of the terse, vigorous language used, as well as the knowledge of the matter under discussion. The subject was argued with skill and ability. The *Altanta Defiance* said, when speaking of these articles: "The man who is writing those articles has a long head. The Negro of America cannot afford to fail to read them." The *Gate City Press,* in speaking of this enterprising journal, has said: "The *Detroit Plaindealer* is the model newspaper." A convention in Michigan was called through the instrumentality of the paper at Battle Creek, where resolutions were passed unanimously endorsing the course of the paper. At this convention a resolution was offered by one of its representatives that the colored people of Michigan should be recognized by the Republican party, by awarding them the delegate-at-large to the National convention to be held at Chicago. The resolution was passed and the request acceded to by the party, Dr. S. C. Watson of Detroit being honored with that position. His candidacy to the convention was managed by the *Plaindealer* staff, with Mr. Pelham at their head, easily defeating the custom-house men who opposed them.

The journal grows in favor among its readers because it is a staunch friend of the poor and oppressed of all classes. Not only does it advocate every interest of the black man, but a strong defender of all of those who are kept under the grinding heel of oppression by the capitalist or by the "bosses" in politics.

Robert Pelham, Jr., was born in Petersburg, Virginia, January 4, 1859, of free parentage. He was the second son of Robert and Frances Pelham. In the same year his parents moved northward to secure for their children, five in number, those educational advantages which the liberal minded element were extending to all classes of men. They finally settled in Detroit; here in 1868, at the age of nine, he attended a separate public school taught by Miss Fannie Richards, now a highly respected colored teacher in the mixed schools of that city. In 1871, after a long and bitter fight by the progressive element of both races, the public schools were opened to all children, irrespective of color. Robert then entered the grammar department and completed the twelve years' course offered by the city, graduating from the High school in 1877. Attached to the school at that time was a military department of which the "State Military Academy" at Orchard Lake, Michigan, is now the outgrowth. Hence in this place he was accorded a three years' military training. In 1871, while still in school, he entered the employment of the *Daily Post*, now the *Detroit Morning Tribune*, the leading Republican paper in Michigan, then owned and controlled by that vigorous exponent of early Republican principles, Zachariah Chandler. He began at the lower rounds of the ladder and has worked his way up to important positions, not only on this paper, but he is the influential editor of a Negro journal that stands in the front rank for excellence.

His habits of life have been of such a character as to give him standing in the business world and made him as a man of strict integrity and conscientious scruples, in the discharge of every duty committed to his care, as well as enabling him to profit by all the opportunities of life. He has been connected with the journal above mentioned ever since it began, filling various positions; and while at one time the only colored employee among two hundred attachés of the paper, he is now superintendent of the subscription and mailing department by contract, which is conducted entirely by colored employees.

In 1883 Mr. Pelham, together with W. H. Anderson, W. H. Stowers, Benjamin W. Pelham, started the *Plaindealer*. It was established under what might be termed almost fatal circumstances, but its success has been largely due to his early newspaper training, and to the fact that its editors and owners all held lucrative positions in three of the leading business houses in Detroit. All of them being engaged, they did not care to risk their fortunes, or what little they may have had, upon the paper with a prospect of losing it; so whatever was done, they did themselves in such hours as they were not employed. Noon, nights and holidays found each man at his post; six nights out of seven they attended to the work, planning, scheming, preparing matter, issuing circulars and procuring agents. Their appliances were crude, money scarce, and experience not what it was destined to be before they had reached several milestones on their newspaper career. But now after four years' experience, they are giving to the world one of the best papers in the country. This has not, however, been achieved without severe labor, many deprivations of pleasure, and also by a conscientious discharge of duty to the cause which they have espoused, viz., the cause of the African race.

Mr. Pelham has never held any political position, but has always taken an active part in politics and has represented his party and race in city, State and National affairs. His influence widens, and he becomes more and more able to add laurels to the fame he has already won in wielding a facile pen, conducting a noble enterprise, contributing to the great quota which the young men are making as their share toward the sum total of Negro enterprise. And he is to be congratulated because of the generous manner in which he is treated by his subscribers and the brethren of the profession. The sentiment is high toned and of the most excellent character. He never allows his columns to be abused by vituperations, criminations and recriminations. Mr. Pelham himself is a man of clear head, pure character and steady habits. I consider him one of the best business men in the country, and a man to be admired on account of his modesty, sobermindedness and intellectual character.

BOOKER T. WASHINGTON

CHAPTER CLV

Professor Booker T. Washington
Principal of the Tuskegee Normal School— A Successful Career
—A Wonderful Institution—Industrial Education

Booker T. Washington, the subject of this sketch and the present principal and founder of the Tuskegee Normal school at Tuskegee, Alabama, was born at Hale's Ford Post-office, Franklin county, Virginia, April 18, 1956. His owner was James Borroughs. His mother, Mrs. Jane Ferguson, was the cook on the slave plantation. At the close of the war he went with his mother and the rest of the family to Malden, Kanawha county, West Virginia, where he attended the common schools until 1872. Soon after going to Malden his mother died, leaving him to "paddle his own canoe," except the aid which he received from his step-father, Washington Ferguson. After the death of his mother, he was fortunate in securing a place to live with Mrs. General Lewis Ruffner, Malden, West Virginia. She paid him a small salary per month and permitted him to attend school and work night and morning. In this way he attended school at Malden till the fall of 1872, when he left to enter the Hampton Institute, at Hampton, Virginia. When he made up his mind to go to Hampton he was entirely without means; but, by the aid of money furnished him by his brother, John H. Washington, and small amounts donated by friends, he started for Hampton with enough money, as he thought, to pay traveling expenses; but reaching Richmond and counting his cash, he found himself short of means to pay for a night's lodging and to continue his journey at the same time. He compromised the matter by spending the night under the sidewalk. The next day he engaged to help unload a vessel, and thus earned money with which to continue his journey to Hampton Institute, where he arrived with but fifty cents in his pocket. The first year he worked out half of his expenses, and his brother paid the other half. During the remainder of his course at Hampton he worked out his entire expenses, as janitor. He graduated in 1875, after which he taught for several years at his home in Malden, during which time he was engaged by the State executive committee to stump the State in favor of having the capital permanently located at Charleston, West Virginia. In 1878 he entered Wayland Seminary, Washington, District of Columbia, and took a course of study. After leaving Wayland Seminary he was given a position as a teacher in the Hampton Institute, where he taught two years, having charge of the Indian boys during the last year. In 1880 the Legislature of Alabama passed an act establishing a Normal school at Tuskegee, Alabama, and the State commissioners of Alabama applied to General S. C. Armstrong, principal of Hampton Institute, to recommend some one for the principalship. He recommended Mr. Washington, who proceeded to Alabama at once, and organized the school July 4, 1881. The institution was opened on the above date, in a church and small dwelling, with thirty students and one teacher. During the first session of the school the principal and assistant principal, by the aid of friends North and South, paid for one hundred acres of land on which to permanently locate the school. This land contained several small buildings. During the same session enough money was raised to warrant their laying, at the close of the year, the corner-stone of a large hall to cost sixty-five hundred dollars. During the summer vacation Mr. Washington and the assistant principal went to Massachusetts and Connecticut where they succeeded in raising the amount necessary to complete the first building, which is called "Porter Hall." One hundred and twelve students were gathered into the school the first session from the various counties of Alabama. In the summer of 1882 Mr. Washington was married to Miss Fannie N. Smith, of West Virginia, who died after they had been married not quite two years.

At the last meeting of the Alabama State Teachers' Association he was unanimously elected president of that body.

I have great admiration for such men as Mr. Washington. On the intelligence and earnestness of such progressive giants we must lean for the purpose of securing great blessings to the race. The results of such labors as his are the greatest laurels to a rising people. It reflects not on him but through him, the light of a Negro's intellect. There are brilliant and inspiring hopes for the race when such men lend their powers in cultivating not alone the intellect but the heart and hand.

In April, 1887, the professor was invited to be the guest of the Unitarian Club of Boston, he being the first colored man so honored. At the banquet in the evening at Hotel Vendome, they were so well pleased with his remarks that they materialized their good will in such a shape that they presented the Normal school a valuable saw-mill outfit.

In August, 1886, he married Miss Oliva A. Davidson, his competent assistant. The professor is not slow to give her credit for her ability and faithfulness, for he says in a letter to the writer: "It has been largely due to Mrs. Washington's wise and earnest work that the great work done at Tuskegee has been made possible." Thus our educated women go hand in hand, side by side, with our men on the mission fields, doing work for the Master.

J. P. CAMPBELL

CHAPTER CLVI

*Right Rev. J. P. Campbell, D. D., LL. D.
Bishop of the A. M. E. Church—The Theologian
of the Denomination*

Jabez P. Campbell, the eighth Bishop of the A. M. E. church, was born in Delaware, February 6, 1815. When he was quite small his father gave a gentleman a mortgage upon him and then went away, and when the money was due the mortgage was foreclosed, and an attempt was made to sell him, but he got wind of it, and left the State of Delaware for Philadelphia, where his mother resided. He soon became an active member of the A. M. E. church. After he was licensed to preach he was appointed by Bishop Morris Brown to supply a vacancy on the Bucks county circuit, Pennsylvania. From there he was sent a missionary to the New England States. He subsequently filled Albany and New York City stations. He was then transferred to the Philadelphia conference. In 1856 he was elected editor of the *Christian Recorder,* which position he resigned, and afterward filled the Trenton, New Jersey, station, and Bethel church, Philadelphia. In 1863 he was transferred to the Baltimore conference. In the following year, May 16, 1864, he was elected bishop, and was ordained in Philadelphia, Pennsylvania, May 23, 1864.

He was the first bishop that visited California and organized that conference. In 1876 the General conference sent him as a delegate to the Wesleyan General conference in England. On his arrival he was received and treated with great Christian civility. The degree of D.D. was conferred upon him by Wilberforce University.

AS A BISHOP

Bishop Campbell has presided over conferences covering nearly all the territory occupied by the A. M. E. church. The courage and ingenuity, tact and faith, by means of which he has championed the cause of Christ, as understood in African Methodism, have rendered him a favorite on the bench of bishops.

He seems also to be a favorite among his colleagues. The late Bishop

Cain, during his illness, selected him with others, to assist him. Bishop Turner selected him to assist him in North Carolina. He has, by request, been with Bishop Shorter in all his conferences of 1886–87.

AT HOME

The Bishop is by no means obscure as a citizen. He is known in Philadelphia in the very best way as a very benevolent man, an excellent preacher, a good business man and a scholarly theologian. His social qualities are large; few men enjoy society more highly. He is practically connected with benevolent institutions in his city, in which he is known as a systematic and regular donor.

In giving to Wilberforce University one thousand dollars, to several other of our institutions from ten to fifty dollars each at different times, he has set a worthy example for others.

Bishop Campbell knew Bishop Allen well, and, of course, all others of the bishops. He possesses a wonderful store of information concerning men and things connected with the early history of African Methodism. He can entertain an audience for hours, unraveling the woven threads of our history. The only fear is that that great store of information will be largely lost to the world. Fifty years—less a half year—in the ministry, nearly twenty-three years a bishop, and for many more years a student, he has the ability to leave a legacy in the way of a book or books, that will not be left by others, but lost, unless he writes.

AS A PREACHER

Bishop Campbell is an impressive preacher; because thoughtful and logical, animated and devout, learned and eloquent. Few men among us are more popular in the pulpit. This we say without special reference to race variety.

Few men have stood so long and so eminently among the giants of the race; and whatever of good that can be said by a man has been said. The above sketch was, in the main, published in the *Christian Recorder,* and I can only add my endorsement to the truth concerning him as stated above. I know the Bishop personally, and consider him a man of *heart* and of a large soul. When a boy, I was often a visitor at his home in Philadelphia, and enjoyed his fatherly counsel. The home of the bishop is quiet and peaceful, and one finds rest for the soul there. The large experience of the bishop and the extensive and varied learning he has acquired, has made him a splendid adviser and a safe guide. He is an honor to the race and is the pride of his church.

CHAPTER CLVII

Nat Turner
Another John Brown—Insurrectionist

He was born in Southampton county, Virginia, October 2, 1800. His master was a very wealthy man and owned many slaves. His parents were very pious people. It is natural to suppose that young Nat imbibed the characteristics of his parents, their religion, their songs, their longings and their superstitions. He was a man short in stature with a very intelligent looking forehead, and possessed an inherent quality that commanded the respect of his fellowmen. He had small eyes that shone with the brightness of diamonds whenever he spoke of the Scriptures or the wrongs of his race. He was a Baptist preacher, and was ordained by his father and other preachers from the neighboring plantations. On account of the teachings and admonitions of his mother, he came to the conclusion that he, like Moses of old, was born to be the deliverer of his people from bondage. He nursed this belief and cherished it until it became the all-absorbing question of his soul. He possessed a trade, the carrying out of which kept him in the woods, and that was the making of wooden trays, bowls, etc. He became familiar with every tree, every nook, and every hiding place in Southampton county. He would come among his people on Sunday, preach the word of God and go back to the mountains to brood over the condition of his burdened people. At last his master saw that he was becoming too familiar with the slaves in the neighborhood, so he thought to hire him to a "nigger breaker" to have him tamed, or cowed down. But this soul was not born for that; it was not in his power to break the spirit of this heroic "black John Brown" of America and Spartacus of the Negro race. He was a man that never consented to an insult given by a white man. When his new master started out to break him, he caught him and tied his hands behind his back and left him on his face. Then he went to his old retreat—the mountains—and there remained thirty days.

Many white people reverenced and honored Nat Turner on account of his commanding influence. Strange to say, a man without the least knowledge of books commanded the admiration of all classes of men, both friends and enemies.

His plot for general uprising was laid in the month of February, 1831. He appointed a meeting to which he invited four friends, Sam Edwards, Hark Travis, Henry Porter and Nelson Williams. These five men met in a lonely glen and thus perfected their plans. But the general trouble was the getting of arms. Nate rose up and told them that the spirit has instructed him to slay his enemies with their own weapons. They at last decided on a plan, and then it was that "The Prophet Nat" arose and addressed them as follows:

Friends and Brothers: We are to commence a great work to-night. Our race is to be delivered from bondage, and God has appointed us as the men to do his bidding, and let us be worthy of our calling. I am told to slay all the whites we encounter without regard to age or sex. Remember we do not go forth for the sake of blood and carnage, but it is necessary that in the commencement of this revolution, all the whites we meet should die, until we have an army strong enough to carry on the war upon a Christian basis.

The blow was struck on the night of the twenty-first of August, 1831. They dealt death and destruction on all sides until the whole country was aroused and the planters armed themselves to baffle the determined actions of this bold emancipator. Yet this did not stop the onward march of this army. Those men, according to the directions of Nat Turner, spared neither men, women nor children. On their way to attack the first house they were joined by a slave belonging to a neighboring plantation, named Will, about six feet in height, a most desperate man, having been made so by the cruelty of his master. He hated him, and every white face to him was the sign of an enemy, both to himself and his race. He was overjoyed to have this opportunity to reap vengeance on those who had wronged him. He armed himself with a sharp, broad axe, under whose cruel blows many a white man fell. All night long they continued their work of death and destruction until not only the whole county of Southampton felt the stroke of that terrible blow, but the whole State of Virginia reeled on account of the boldness and persistency in action. Soldiers were dispatched to the scene of action from different parts of the State by the shortest route as soon as it became known that the blacks were in arms against their masters. Then came the real battle. The blacks fought hand to hand with the whites. Nat saw that they were compelled to be overpowered, so he and a few others escaped and sought shelter in a near swamp where they defied the patient watching of all for two months. At last he surrendered; loaded with heavy chains, with clothes all tattered and torn and besmeared with the blood of his victims, he was brought to Jerusalem, the county seat of Southampton county. Backed by his unfaltering trust in the Lord and by his belief in the justice of his cause, he stood before his judges like a modern Regulus, without flinching, with not a tremor in his whole body. When asked "guilty or not guilty" he answered straightway, "not guilty." He could not feel that he should die because he had sought to liberate his people from the yoke of slavery, no matter in what way he proceeded to accomplish his end. Nevertheless he was convicted and sentenced to be hanged. In a speech before he was hanged, he prophesied that when they hanged him that the sun would be darkened and the earth tremble in token of the justice of the cause in which he had been engaged. This made such an impression on the mind of the sheriff that he refused to have anything to do with the execution. They brought an old, drunken, broken down, white man forty miles to cut the rope of the trap.

Just as Nat Turner prophesied, at the time for the execution a black cloud came up from the east and veiled the sun; the earth was shaken by loud claps of thunder and the most severe storm followed, such as they had never before witnessed in that part of the country.

Thus died one of the greatest emancipators of the nineteenth century. Some called him a religious fanatic, no doubt because he was a black man. When men of other nations have arisen and used whatever means they had at their command to liberate their people, it has been called heroism; with the Negro, it is brutality. However civilized nations may judge Nat Turner, and however they may write about him, let it be remembered that he foresaw by his acts the career of John Brown. If the Negro was to blame, so was the white man. Nat Turner's insurrection was the upheaval of an honest heart to break, in any way possible, the chains which bound his people. If he was a brute, it must be remembered that his victims only suffered by a system which made him such. If he were a savage, the passions belonging to human nature were only whetted by the cruelties which he saw, and sharpened by the sufferings of his people. He planned in a few minutes, condensed in a few hours, and executed upon his victims in a short time only a tithe of the cruelties which had been heaped upon his own people. If his judgment was swift, it was no more severe than that which had been inflicted upon Negroes under his eyes. He had seen men whipped to death and brutally murdered by the overseers, and if his ideas of crime were of a crude standard, let it also be remembered that poor human nature is influenced by that with which it is surrounded.

CHAPTER CLVIII

*Hon. Hilery Richard Wright Johnson
President of Liberia—An Accomplished English and Classical
Scholar—A Master of German, French and Mathematics*

The president of Liberia is the son of the earliest and most distinguished Liberian, Elijah Johnson, who was born in New Jersey, and who is called "Father of Liberia." The president is about fifty-one years old, and was himself born, reared and educated in Liberia. He traveled as private secretary to President Benson, on his European tour in the latter part of the fifties, and also accompanied President Roye in a like capacity to this country. He is a thorough English and classical scholar, and speaks French and German in the most scholarly manner, and has a special aptitude for mathematics. No man in Liberia has a wider influence and he has stamped himself upon the people as a man desirous of the highest promotion, and secured for himself the affection of the people.

In the canvass of 1884 he secured the majority of votes and was elected for the presidency of the Liberian government, which position he honors and dignifies, both by his learning and his loyalty. He has filled many of the most important offices in the republic subsidiary to the presidency, and his faithfulness and earnest devotion to duty, as well as his deep interest of the welfare "of the Lone Star Republic," had prominently placed him before the people. He has given them entire satisfaction as to his course, and thereby secured their suffrage in reaching the high station in the gift of the people. When it is remembered that this republic has had quite a number of presidents, it is surprising that, hitherto, no one born on African soil has been elevated to its first position.

Mr. Johnson is the first and only native born in Liberia, who has secured the office.

The president was a professor in the Liberia College at the same time that Professors Blyden, Crummell and Freeman were professors, and Professor Joseph Jenkins Roberts was the president of the college.

The tender expressions of love for America and its people which he entertains, endears him to all on this side of the water, not only to the people at large but to his race. Born on African soil, identified with Africa's progress in the most exalted station among her people, he could but have all his interest fixed upon persons and things in that country; but, like all true Negroes, his heart is large enough to take in his brethren, and his intellect broad enough to appreciate the institutions of this country. His standing with all the eminent men both in Liberia and in this country mark him as one who has deported himself with such dignity and grace that it is a distinguished honor to have his acquaintance. It is a glorious thing for Liberia that she has at least one born on her own soil to whom she can look for future administration of her affairs.

JOHN R. LYNCH

CHAPTER CLIX

Hon. John R. Lynch
Prominent Politician—Orator—Lawyer—Congressman—
Presided at the National Republican Convention

Mr. Lynch was born in Concordia Parish, Louisiana, September 10, 1847. The bonds of slavery fastened themselves upon his young life and held him from the benefits of freedom, culture, and from developing into a full grown man, such as the peculiarity of our institutions can bring forth. Destitute by the means by which a youth is inspired to greatness, he came forth after the war naturally lacking those qualities which would make a competent statesman and a capable leader. It is astonishing, indeed, how great have been the achievements of most of the despised race when we remember that without any previous training they were called to the most important stations in American affairs; and the wonder is that they made no more mistakes than they did.

Few have succeeded in coming out of the turmoil, strife, and political contests of the past with a reputation so untarnished as that of Mr. Lynch. He remained in slavery until Abraham Lincoln, with a stroke of his pen, cut the Gordian knot and gave liberty to the bondmen.

He had no early education, but began to apply himself as soon as he was permitted to do so. A purchaser of his mother had carried her with her children to Natchez, where, when the Union troops took possession, he attended evening school for a few months. He has given diligent attention to private instructors to the acquirement of a first-class English education, and has read with considerable attention the best works published of ancient and modern literature.

He engaged in the business of photography at Natchez until 1869, when Governor Ames appointed him a justice of the peace for Adams county, Natchez, Mississippi. He held that position until the fall of the same year, when he was elected to the State Legislature from that county for the term of two years. He was re-elected in 1871, and served during the latter term as speaker of the House of Representatives. He was elected a representative from Mississippi in the Forty-third Congress as a member of the lower house, receiving fifteen thousand three hundred and ninety-one votes against eight thousand four hundred and thirty for H. Cassidy, Sr. (Democrat), and was re-elected to the Forty-fourth Congress as a Republican, defeating Roderick Seals (Democrat). He was also re-elected to the Forty-seventh Congress, but was not allowed to take his seat. It will be remembered that the contest was between Lynch and Chalmers, in what was known as the "Shoestring" district of Mississippi. When he was pleading his case in behalf of himself and constituents, he made use of the following very eloquent remarks, which, on account of the patriotism and fairness contained in them, deserve to be recorded. He said:

Both of the great political parties of the day are, no doubt, anxious to bring about the cessation of the agitation of sectionalism. They differ only as to the basis upon which this agitation shall cease. The Democrats who are in favor of upholding and defending the Bourbon system of fraudulent elections, as illustrated in this case for instance, are anxious to bring about a cessation of sectional agitation upon the basis of a violent and fraudulent suppression of the popular will.

The Republicans, on the other hand, and I am pleased to be able to say thousands of honest Democrats as well, are anxious that this agitation will cease, upon such conditions as will secure to all citizens the equal protection of the laws, and a willing acquiescence in the lawfully expressed will of the majority. As an humble member of the great Republican party, I have no hesitation in declaring it to be the unchangeable determination of that party to continue to wage a persistent war upon Bourbon methods at the South, until the right of every citizen to cast his ballot for the man or the party of his choice, and have that ballot fairly and honestly counted, shall have been acquiesced in from one end of the country to the other. [Applause on the Republican side.]

In speaking of the loyalty of the colored people to the government during the war, Mr. Lynch said:

They were faithful and true to you there; they are no less so to-day. And yet they ask no special favors as a class; they ask no special protection as a race. They feel that they purchased their inheritance, when upon the battle-fields of their country they watered the tree of liberty with the precious blood that flowed from their loyal veins. [Loud applause]. They ask no favors; they demand what they desire and must have—an equal chance in the race of life. . . .

The condition of the colored people of this country to-day is a living contradiction of the prophecies of those who have predicted that the two races could not live upon the same continent together upon terms of political equality. In spite of these predictions we are here to-day, clothed in the same rights, the same privileges, and the same immunities, with complete political assimilation; loyal to the same government, true to the same flag, yielding obedience to the same laws, revering the same institutions, actuated by the same patriotic impulses, imbued with the same noble ambition, entertaining the same hopes, seeking the same gratification and satisfaction of the same aspirations, identified with the same interests, speaking the same language, professing the same religion, worshiping the same God. The colored man asks you in this particular instance to give effect to his ballot, not for his sake alone, but for yours as well. . . . You must, then, as I am sure you will, condemn the crimes against our institutions, against law, against justice, and against public morals that were committed in this place.

In the National Republican convention at Chicago in 1884, he was elected temporary chairman over Powell Clayton, by a majority of thirty votes. Clayton was the nominee of the representatives of the Blaine interests; Mr. Lynch was nominated and supported by the different elements that were opposed to Mr. Blaine, but he also received the vote of the minority of the Blaine men. He is the first and only colored man who has ever presided over any National convention of the Republican party, and in this respect it shows very plainly that he is a man of large influence and of high standing in party councils—one who has so conducted himself as to be chosen from all the vast number of colored men who have from time to time attended these conventions, to preside over the deliberations of a convention which was fraught with so much interest and pregnant with such vast results.

The honorable gentleman has married of later years a Miss Summerville, and settled down to the quiet life of a Southern farmer, near Natchez, with a Washington, District of Columbia, residence. The time will come when he will yet play an important part in the Nation's affairs.

P. H. A. BRAXTON

CHAPTER CLX

Rev. P. H. A. Braxton
Pastor of Calvary Baptist Church, Baltimore, Maryland—
Writer—Speaker

Rev. Patrick Henry Alexander Braxton was born in slavery, in King county, Virginia, September 22, 1852, on the Canterbury farm, belonging to the Johnsons, near Whitehouse. His father and mother, Benjamin and Patsy Braxton, were both slaves. Each had been married twice. P. H. A. Braxton is the only living child by their last marriage.

By the marriage of the oldest daughter of the people to whom they belonged, Mr. Braxton's mother and all the children were carried to Staunton, Virginia, in 1860. After staying there three years, his master was killed; then he, together with his mother and half sister, was taken back to King William county, Virginia, and hired out until 1865, when the mother and children were turned out without a dollar, after working them till Christmas of that year. The oldest boy then living, that they knew anything of, was only sixteen years old. The others had been sold and died.

The mother and children started out in life to earn a livelihood by the sweat of their brows, which they did, and have lived comfortably till to-day. "Truly God cares for the widow and the fatherless." The subject of this sketch was his mother's main support; notwithstanding he was the youngest, he was also the brightest of the children. He worked on the farm and did severe labor till 1868, when a public school was started at Cat-tail church, in the aforesaid county. After several weeks in this school, August, the resting month for farmers, was over, and he had to return to work. Some weeks later a night school was started in the same building; then Alexander worked on the farm all day and walked five miles to attend. When winter set in he started to school again and continued until the spring of 1869; then went back to the farm to work. He continued to study and go to school nights and in the winter, and to a debating club on Friday evenings, until August, 1872, at which time the commencement took place, and he delivered the valedictory, from these words: "Show thyself a man, that thou mayest prosper withersoever thou goest." With the exception of having learned to spell by association with a little white boy to whose grandfather he was hired in 1863, in Staunton, Virginia, and by teaching himself at other times, he claims that if he is made at all, he is self-made.

He stopped farming and went into the stave business. Having been elected constable of the county at the May election of 1872, and having taken an active part in politics before and after, he had to give up his business. About six or eight months later, a warrant was put into his hands for the arrest of a Mr. William Virus, for assaulting a doctor. Now this "Virus" was a notorious braggadocio. He never obeyed the law and would not allow himself to be arrested. It is said that he killed a man during, or before the war, for which the officers of the law were afraid to call him to account. Braxton, in company with two other men, went to his farm, and plead in vain with him to go quietly. He refused to do so and started for his house for his firearms, swearing all the time and declaring if Braxton didn't leave he would put him under the sod. Seeing that he must capture his man to save his own life as well as to obey the injunctions of the court, he went for his victim, and after a short battle between the two, succeeded in overpowering him, and with the assistance of the other two men, bound him and put him in his own cart, and had him driven to the magistrate's court, for which he, Virus, threatened to kill Constable Braxton. The case was sent up to the county court, where he was indicted for assault and battery on the doctor; but the jury could not find any indictment against him for resisting and threatening to kill an officer of the law in the discharge of his duty. Mr. Braxton concluded that it was because he was a colored man, and thereupon resigned.

In the meantime he was studying law as opportunity offered. It was generally admitted that he did justice to his party; handled his subjects logically, manfully and eloquently, made it hard for his opponents and did credit to his race. He was always noted for his aptness to learn, good memory, thirst for knowledge, eloquence in speech, honesty, bravery and boldness in speaking his sentiments and a love of debate.

In October and November of 1874, he was a member of the United States paneled jury. He spent the latter part of 1874 and 1875 in Washington, District of Columbia, and in June, 1875, received an appointment in connection with the United States custom-house in which he was converted June 10, 1875, at Low Cedar Point, Westmoreland county, Virginia.

He was baptized the second Lord's day, October, 1875, by Rev. Silas Miles. He joined the Cat-tail Baptist church, from which he was commissioned to preach the gospel, July 9, 1876. In December, 1878, he was appointed general collecting agent of the consolidated American Baptist Missionary convention, after which he took his letter from this church and joined the Ebenezer Baptist church, Richmond, Virginia. In April, 1879, he was called to take charge of the Calvary Baptist church, Baltimore, Maryland, and was ordained June 6. He took charge of the church June 8, 1879; it was then composed of ten members, worshiping in a small old carpenter shop, corner of Preston Street and Mason alley, without any property of any kind and everything against them. They now own, and, with the exception of two thousand five hundred dollars, have paid for "the finest house of worship of any colored congregation in Baltimore."

It has a membership of five hundred and seventy-five, and was built by Rev. P. H. A. Braxton. He hired the men and built the church according to his own idea. They would not appoint a building committee but collected the money and gave it to him, so great was their confidence in him and his ability. He also collected all of the money to do it with except one thousand one hundred dollars, which was given—five hundred dollars each by Dr. G. K. Tyler and his son, Mr. Charles Tyler, and one hundred dollars by Dr. Franklin Wilson, all members of his own congregation.

The church is valued at twenty thousand dollars but he built it for ten thousand seven hundred dollars. It is located most admirably, being at the junction of three streets, Park Avenue, Howard and Biddle streets.

This church has grown from 10 to 570 members, 350 of whom composed the beautiful Mt. Sinai Baptist church, Bocas, Del-Toro, of United States of Columbia, which was received into the fellowship and fostering, July, 1876; and since his pastorate began he has collected $17,768.05.

Rev. Braxton is a radical reformer as to the manner of worshiping and preaching now carried on in many of our churches. He calls it "monkish action." He read a paper entitled "Instantaneous Conversion" (which is soon to appear in pamphlet form) before the Baptist Ministers' conference, April, 1886. We quote from the *Christian Standard* of Cincinnati, Ohio, April 24, 1886.

Yesterday one of the colored ministers (Rev. P. H. A. Braxton) read a paper on "Instantaneous Conversion" as opposed to the "mourner's bench" idea of getting religion. He took the ground that all the agonizing, shouting, ranting, howling and such other things, common enough to the world were anti-scriptural and the result of gross ignorance and unbelief on the part of both preachers and people. He struck the idea that faith is given miraculously to sinners, in answer to the prayers of the church, a blow like that of a steam hammer.

I was anxious to see how it would be received. Everybody had three minutes given to pay their respects to the paper. On one or two minor points it was criticized by some who misunderstood, and so was not fairly dealt with; in the main, though, it was endorsed most heartily. When asked for my opinion in the matter, I most thankfully added my endorsement of every important idea set forth in it. It was sound, sensible and scriptural in all its fundamentals.

The Baptist church here is very strong and has among its ministers several men of the most decided talent.

He is regarded as a fine pulpiteer and has preached able sermons before different conventions. Before the Baptist Foreign Mission Convention of the United States, he preached from the text: "Curse ye Meroz, said the angel of the Lord, curse ye bitterly the inhabitants thereof; because they came not to the help of the Lord against the mighty" (Judges 5 : 23), at the conclusion of which, the president, Rev. A. S. Jackson, said:

I have been fully converted on the secret society question this morning. I have been wearing the sheepskin and marching around as a big man in the societies, but I am done, from this moment; I will have no more to do with the things; I would not have missed this sermon this morning for a thousand dollars.

He is a life member of the Virginia State convention and of the New England Baptist Missionary convention, and of the Brotherhood of Liberty.

He was married October 18, 1881, to Miss Katie Bannister of Baltimore. He owns property in Virginia and Maryland valued at about two thousand dollars, with a library composed of some of the choicest works of the age, valued at one thousand dollars. He is much beloved and honored by the people of the republic.

CHAPTER CLXI

*Professor T. McCants Stewart, A. B., LL. B.
Attorney at Law—Professor and Author*

The subject of this sketch was born of free parents in Charleston, South Carolina, December 28, 1852. His parents were George Gilchrist Stewart and Anna Morris Stewart. Mr. Stewart says: "My mother is a woman of strong intellect, noble soul, generous nature and great energy. *I owe all I am to my mother.*" Is not this the almost universal testimony of our prominent men? McCants, while a boy, attended school in his native city, beginning when he was only five years old. In 1865 or 1866 he was chosen, on account of his popularity and good scholarship, to present a Bible to General Canby, then in command of the military department of South Carolina, as the expression of good-will and respect from the public school children of Charleston. In this he was the representative of thousands. On account of the signs of marked intelligence and future usefulness, he was sent to Howard University, Washington, District of Columbia. Here he remained from 1869 to 1873. Leaving Howard University he entered the South Carolina University from which he graduated in 1875, and received the degree of A. B.; and, graduating from the law department of the same institution the same year, he was given the title of LL. B. He entered into partnership with the Hon. R. B. Elliott, and was counsel in a murder case immediately thereafter.

After practicing law for two years, and at the same time being professor of mathematics in the State Agricultural College, in 1877 he entered Princeton College where he studied for two years; then, after ordination, he was given the pastoral charge of Bethel Methodist Episcopal church of New York City. Here he remained till 1833, when he, in company with Professor Hugh M. Brown, embarked for Africa, accepting the position of professor in the Liberia College—a post which could not be more ably filled by one of his age. On their way thither they spent a month in Scotland, England, France and Germany. They finally came to the land of their fathers and beheld it in all its glory. However, the fair prospects held out faded away and they soon became dissatisfied with the state of

T. McCANTS STEWART

affairs. He returned to America, and, after lecturing for awhile, resumed the practice of law, January, 1886.

Mr. Stewart has written a book of some merit on Africa. The writer gave the following criticism in the *American Baptist:*

LIBERIA—THE AMERICO-AFRICAN REPUBLIC.

BY T. McCANTS STEWART.

Knowing the scholarly attainments, the clear-cut reasoning powers and gifts of the author's pen, and then being an old college mate and personal friend of his, we were well prepared to read this book. Yet in this small work we scarcely expected to get such rich kernels from the African nut so many have tried to crack. The fair, honest statements in regard to the climate and his logical deductions as to the reasons, and the further profoundly sensible remarks as to the remedies, his wholesome advice to found interior cities, all challenge admiration and applause.

Mr. Stewart has retired from the ministry and gives himself wholly to the law. Added to his professional duties are the duties of presiding over the Brooklyn Literary and other educational enterprises. He is gifted as a lecturer. His manners are very attractive, his voice winning and his instructive powers well developed. He can by no means reflect credit on none but the race which he so highly honors.

E. P. McCABE

CHAPTER CLXII

Hon. E. P. McCabe
Auditor of the State of Kansas—County Clerk—
Successful Politician

The subject of this sketch was born of humble parents in Troy, New York, October 10, 1850. His parents soon after moved to Fall River, Massachusetts; remaining there a short time they settled in Newport, Rhode Island, where he attended public school. Leaving the grammar school there he went to Bangor, Maine, where he continued his studies until the death of his father compelled him to assist his widowed mother in the support of a brother and sister. Drifting to New York he was employed by Messrs. Shreve and Kendrick, 35 Wall Street. As in the case of all colored boys, he had to make various shifts from clerk to porter. Finding all avenues in the East closed to ambitious colored young men, he decided to follow Horace Greeley's advice and go West. Getting a clerkship with Potter Palmer, Hotel King, of Chicago, in 1872, he was promoted to another in the Cook county treasury, where he remained eighteen months. Tiring of metropolitan life he went to Kansas, locating in Graham county, one of the most sparsely settled of all the northwestern tier, where, in company with Abraham T. Hall, junior, of Chicago, previously the city editor of the *Conservator,* he engaged in the land business with some success.

As a reward for the valuable services rendered in the organization of the county he was appointed first county clerk, and afterwards elected to that position from which he was transferred to the auditorship of the State of Kansas, one of the most significant political successes in the upward career of the race, Kansas being one of the most prosperous of the Western States.

Long before the nomination to the auditorship, it was conceded that Mr. McCabe was the representative man of the race in Kansas, and it was also a settled fact that this element should be recognized in the selections of State officers. He was nominated and elected by what might be considered a white vote, for at no time, perhaps, had there been more than a dozen colored men in the convention. After his nomination in the fall of 1882, he was triumphantly elected and filled his office with distinguished fidelity. He had won the hearts of the people and was the admired man of all the State officers. He was a candidate for re-election to a second term. When the convention was ready to proceed with the nomination for the position of auditor, Mr. W. B. Townsend, a delegate from Leavenworth, secured the floor and with marked enthusiasm, as can be seen from the applause throughout the speech, said:

Mr. Chairman:—I desire to place in nomination for the position of auditor a young man who is not a stranger to the people of Kansas, but is well and favorably known to you all; one who is not only popular with his own race, but is exceedingly popular with the whites [great applause]; the ablest and strongest colored man from a political standpoint in the State; the recognized leader of his race in the West [applause]. That gentleman has demonstrated his fitness for the position by serving you faithfully during the past two years. His name is Edwin P. McCabe [great cheering]. Nominate him and you will please the colored element of the party and a majority of the whites. And more, Mr. Chairman, I move that the rules be suspended and Mr. McCabe be nominated by acclamation.

Mr. Townsend's motion was readily seconded and put by the chairman, and Honorable E. P. McCabe was nominated by acclamation amidst thundering applause. Men arose and swung their hats, while others stood on chairs and waved their hats and yelled for McCabe.

This shows how popular the colored candidate was with the convention, composed as it was of nearly four hundred representative Republicans of the State, and not more than six of them colored men.

Without that "influence" which in these days is so potent to obtain place and power, and comparatively unknown a few years ago, Mr. McCabe entered the State with nothing to recommend him but an Eastern education, good character, indomitable pluck, with health and energy, preferring to be a freeman on the bleak plains of the far West, rather than be an underling and political sycophant in the East, where at best our young colored men are overshadowed by hoards of young white men, who in their eagerness to obtain position often rarely secure anything worthy of their pains and labor.

Mr. McCabe's career is illustrative of the possibilities of self-made men who make their impressions upon our times by sheer force of character, and the possibilities which are open to him in life are vast and illimitable.

At the end of his term he withdrew his name which his friends were still anxious to offer for renomination for the position, and after retiring from office, spent several months in California prospecting.

We can only hope that there are great things still in store for him.

CHAPTER CLXIII

Rev. Charles Henry Parrish, A. B.
A Rising Young Man—From the Position of Janitor to the Secretaryship of a University

———◆———

He was born in Lexington, Fayette county, Kentucky, April 18, 1859. His parents were Hiram and Harriet Parrish, slaves belonging to Jeff Barr and Beverly Hicks. Hiram was a teamster and Harriet was an efficient seamtress. The father was a deacon of the First Baptist church in Lexington, when it was pastored by London Ferrill. He was a man of industry and frugality, while his wife was a woman of strong character. The Sunday school was the first gathering to which young Charles was taken. Here he was placed in the care of the late John Gillis, Esq., and was taught to spell in the old blue back spelling book his a, b, c.

He was sent to the public school in Lexington, directly after emancipation. His parents being poor, he was compelled to leave school in 1874, and went to work as a porter in the dry goods store of John O. Hodges, now city superintendent of the public schools of Lexington, where he remained for six years. During all these times, while carrying packages here and there and giving attention diligently to the store, his spare moments were spent in reading and studying. Mr. Hodges quitting the dry goods business, he went to work for another firm by the name of Cassell, Price & Company, where he remained until September, 1880. This firm was very kind to him.

At the age of twelve he joined the Baptist church. In 1872, after many years of training in the Sabbath school, he was made secretary. This position he held for eight years, at the same time filling the position of teacher, etc. He was soon elected church clerk and clerk of the deacon board. He assisted W. A. Stewart in teaching night school. His efforts to instruct others soon made him aware of his own deficiencies, and he determined by the help of God to secure a liberal education, at the cost of a life's work and study. He made it a subject of prayer, and at last prevailed with his father to let him quit work and attend the Nashville Institute. He consented, and with joy preparation was soon begun, in order that he might matriculate in September, 1878. In the midst of his

CHARLES HENRY PARRISH

joy, in the midst of his greatest expectations, he was doomed to a sore disappointment. His father died March 11, 1877. A cloud seemed to hang over his head and his way seemed hedged; but God who always listens to the earnest prayer, did not forget. Thus suddenly placed at the head of the family, a mother, sister and brother to guide, he had no time to study while working, much less think of attending school. For a season the matter was laid aside.

But troubles do not come single-handed; they sometimes seem to come in battalions, armed and fully equipped to overcome the most resolute. The greatest misfortune which befell him was on July 22, 1879, in the death of his mother. Burdened with the cares of the family, weakened by the loss of both parents, he was much discouraged.

His affections were now centered upon a little sister, thirteen years old, who was quite intelligent and promising. To educate her was his highest ambition. He put behind him all hopes for himself, and devoted himself to her culture and promotion. But here came another trouble; in June, 1880, she, too, was taken away. She left to embrace a sainted mother and father. Sickness and death had taken all his scanty earnings; harder work took the time he used to give to study; he saw no ray of hope by which he might carry out his personal plans at this critical stage of his life. Suddenly the Lord opened a way least suspected. Unconsciously, I was an agent in the hands of God in carrying out these plans, which were then unknown to me. I was the pastor of the First Baptist church at the time, and receiving a call to the State University, I resigned the church and accepted the position at Louisville, Kentucky. He accompanied me to the university and began his course of studies September 13, 1880. At this time the university was very poor indeed; it did not own a teacher's desk or any furniture of value. The character of the work which he expected to get was in the hands of another.

The young student did whatever his hands found to do, and he found friends to assist him. At one time he assisted the janitor of the Jackson Street public school. With this work, and teaching a few scholars at night, at the close of the scholastic year he was indebted to the boarding department of the institution twenty-four dollars, his expenses for the year being about ninety dollars. He went home and managed to pay the rest during vacation. September 1, 1881, he entered the second year with brighter prospects. The trustees being so well pleased with the young man's conduct, his willingness to work and his patience in doing whatever he was called upon to do, agreed to assist him with part of his expenses. This work required three-fourths of his time, yet he kept up with his class and lead it, receiving the first honor—a gold medal—in graduating from the academic course in 1882.

He entered the college course, and during the subsequent years was helped by friends North. With their assistance, coupled with the work of student-teacher, tutor, bookkeeper and several other things, he has worked his way through college, graduating May, 1886, with the title of A.B.

He has been a delegate to the Republican State convention, the Colored Educational convention, the National Convention of Colored Men, held in Louisville, and was one of those who addressed the Senatorial committee at Frankfort during the appeal of the committee at the Colored State convention for the Normal school. He was the messenger of the American National Baptist convention which held its session August 25, 1886, to the Southern Baptist convention which met in Louisville, Kentucky, from the sixth to the tenth of May, 1887. He has filled many positions wherein Christian piety was especially needed as a qualification.

During the time when the Zion Baptist church of Louisville, Kentucky, was without a pastor he served them for several months. He is a member of the Berean Baptist church, and has served as its city missionary for several years, and was superintendent of a large mission Sabbath school during the same time. He was called to six different churches while a student in school; and he finally accepted a call to the pastorate of the Calvary Baptist church, after having served it as "supply" for several months, and after ordination, January 2, 1886, was settled as its pastor, September 27, 1886. During the eighteen months in which he has served this church it has nearly doubled its membership.

After graduation, the authorities felt that his wholesome example and his exemplary life, as well as his deep interest in the work was sufficient to have his services in the institution, so he was appointed secretary and treasurer of the State University and guardian of the younger men. At the end of the year, 1886–67, he was elected professor of Greek. These positions he has ably and satisfactorily filled. From janitor to secretary —from firemaker to treasurer and professor, from poverty to honor among the faculty and fellow-students, is an achievement worthy of record. The world will yet hear more from this rising young man.

CHAPTER CLXIV

Rev. John Jasper
"The Sun do Move"

———•◆•———

The theory that "the sun do move" is no new one; but the exploded theory of the past ages and its introduction anew by Mr. Jasper is not an elaboration of a new principle of scientific deduction, but a Bible argument. It is this phase that makes his view the more puzzling to those who depend entirely on the good book for instruction. Rev. John Jasper is the son of Philip and Tina Jasper who were residents of the county of Fluvana, Virginia, and was born July 4, 1812; both dates are historical —the first because of the Declaration of Independence and the second as the year of the second war with Great Britain. Philip Jasper was a Baptist preacher of wide reputation. John, the youngest of twenty-four children, was born two months after his father's death. The mother and children were slaves to one Mr. Peachy, and for many years she was a farm hand, but soon was so broken down from the care of children that she was confined to the house, spinning and making clothes for the slaves. The young man began his slave task as a "cart boy." Next we find him promoted to a "house-boy" and dignified by being a table waiter, and in spare times he cultivated the garden. This labor was not hard and did not tax him, but he left it to be hired out to a man by the name of Peter McHenry, where he worked a year. The next year he worked with a Mr. Samuel Crosby and continued there for several years.

Had John Jasper been an educated man he would surpass Herschel, Kepler, Halley, Encke, Biela or Faye, for he is of an astronomical turn of mind, and his soul is never happier than when he revels in the beauty of the starry heavens. The great event known as the falling of the stars occurred while he was at work at this place, and John was the first among his fellows to see this magnificent sight. While to others it was a source of terror, to him it was a scene of joy.

His mistress dying, in the division of property John came to the hands of her son, John Blair Peachy, a lawyer and farmer, who went to Louisiana and died; so John was sent back to Richmond, Virginia. Fourth of

JOHN JASPER

July, 1839, he was convicted of sin and on the twenty-fifth was converted and soon went to preaching.

Rev. Mr. Jasper has been married three times; first, to Elvy Weaden, a slave in Williamsburgh, who left him and married because he could not visit her. The church permitted him to marry again. The civil law did not recognize marriages among slaves, but the colored church did. They had no children. He was a member of the old African Baptist church in Richmond. His second marriage was to Candus Jordan, in 1844, by whom he had nine children. He was divorced from her on good and justifiable grounds. His third marriage took place in 1863 to Mary Ann Cole, who died August 6, 1874.

Mr. Jasper was soon called to preach to the Third Baptist church in Petersburgh. Rev. Kean, a white minister, was opposed to his preaching, but when he heard John Jasper preach from Revelation, 6 : 2, he and many white people were in tears, and declared that he "was the only colored man God had ever called to preach." He preached many funeral sermons and was called on for miles around. During the war, John Jasper preached to the sick and wounded soldiers in the Confederate hospitals on Chimborazo Hill, and on Nineteenth and Franklin streets. He was working all these years in the factory which he left in 1859 or '60. The last sermon he preached before the fall of Richmond was down at the mills, on the second day of April, 1865, and Richmond fell April 3, 1865. At this time he had only seventy-three cents in his pocket, and was forty-two dollars in debt; but gaining his freedom, and by industry, is worth to-day about five thousand dollars.

He worked on the streets of Richmond cleaning bricks for a small compensation from April 6, 1865, to the fourth of July the same year. He was then called again to the pastorate of the Third Baptist church of Petersburgh, Virginia, December, 1866. He went back to Richmond and did missionary work till September, 1867, when he organized his present church with nine members. I come now to speak of his theory on the sun. A dispute arose between Lester Woodson and a white man about the rotation of the sun, or about the meaning of the passage found in Exodus 15 : 3: "The Lord is a man of war: the Lord is his name"; and Mr. Jasper was requested to preach upon the subject. After the sermon great excitement prevailed, and Rev. Richard Wells, of the Ebenezer Baptist church, denounced Mr. Jasper's theory, to which Mr. Jasper replied very fully, and to this day he never fails to give Rev. Wells a passing notice. He then took a trip North, lecturing in Washington, Baltimore, Philadelphia and several New Jersey cities, and he has also delivered his famous sermon before the Virginia Legislature.

I here insert an analysis of Mr. Jasper's theory, as published in the sketch of his life by Hon. E. A. Randolph, LL. B. Said sketch was written by D. B. Williams, a professor in the Virginia Normal and Collegiate Institute:

THE THEORY OF REV. JOHN JASPER CONCERNING THE SUN

The reason for the delivery of this sermon was at once simple and natural. On the sixteenth of March, 1883—a Sabbath day—I had the pleasure of listening to his noted discourse.

He somewhat minutely detailed the reason of his preaching. Two honored members of the church had discussed, with some warmth and zeal, the form of the earth and the biblical statements concerning the sun. One strongly maintained the advanced opinions of scholars, scientists and philosophers— That the earth is nearly round, and the earth rotates around the sun. The other as stoutly argued that the earth has four corners and the sun revolves around it.

Differing so widely in their respective views, they determined to submit the decision to the trusted judgment of their beloved pastor.

In this brief sketch of the theory of Rev. John Jasper, we propose to present to the reader a clear and impartial view of the opinions of Rev. Jasper, not those of himself or any other thinker. The prevailing beliefs of the cultured followers of the famed Galileo, Kepler, Herschel and Kant will be but incidentally presented.

On several occasions we availed ourselves of the rare opportunity of hearing the Reverend gentleman discuss his widely known and original sermon. On the Sabbath of the sixteenth of March, 1884, we, in company with Messrs E. D. Black and R. B. Baptiste, heard him.

The daily newspapers had duly heralded to the citizens in general that on the following Sabbath Rev. John Jasper would preach his celebrated sermon, "The Sun do Move." Arriving at the sanctuary almost an hour before service, we unexpectedly found it crowded to almost its entire capacity. The entire body of the church was filled with whites. All appeared eager and expectant. When at length the erect, commanding figure of Rev. J. Jasper promenaded the aisle toward the pulpit, all eyes were staringly fixed upon him. After devotional services he announced as his text the third verse of the fifteenth chapter of Exodus: "The Lord is a man of war: the Lord is his name."

He ably and minutely illustrated the text from the earlier history of the children of Israel. The first, second and third verses of the twelfth chapter of Genesis declared: "Now the Lord had said unto Abram, Get thee out of thy country, and from thy kindred, and from thy father's house, unto a land that I will shew thee: and I will make of thee a great nation, and I will bless thee, and make thy name great; and thou shalt be a blessing; and I will bless them that bless thee, and curse him that curseth thee; and in thee shall all the families of the earth be blessed."

In the thirteenth verse of the fifteenth chapter we learn: "And he said unto Abram, Know of a surety that thy seed shall be a stranger in a land that is not theirs, and shall serve them; and they shall afflict them four hundred years."

The fourteenth verse continues and says: "And also that nation whom they shall serve, will I judge: and afterward shall they come out with great substance." He, at some length, narrated the inhuman selling of Joseph, the providential meeting of Jacob and his supposed dead son; the growth and enslavement of the descendants of the household of Jacob, and the final deliverance of the Israelites.

It was the Lord, and not the followers of meek Moses, who overturned and destroyed the proud Egyptian host. The haughty Egyptians were strongly convinced of this themselves, for they said: "Let us flee from the face of Israel, for the Lord fighteth for them against the Egyptians."

Having more clearly illustrated the text, he attempted to show how the Lord fought for Israel, not only by encouraging them through their leader, Joshua, to go forward, but also by lengthening the day of hotly contested battle in causing the sun to stand still over Gibeon. Having come to this point in the discourse he quietly stopped and said: "I am now where you want me to come." I shall now endeavor to adduce all the scriptural evidence furnished by him that "The Sun Do Move."

This first argument is found in the twelfth and thirteenth verses of the tenth chapter of Joshua: "Then spake Joshua to the Lord in the day when the Lord delivered up the Amorites before the children of Israel, and he said in the sight of Israel, Sun, stand thou still upon Gibeon; and thou, Moon, in the valley of Ajalon; and the sun stood still, and the moon stayed, until the people had avenged themselves upon their enemies." He strenuously argued that if the sun had not been moving, Joshua would not have commanded it to stand still.

His next argument is based upon several passages of Holy Scripture, which assert the rising and setting of the sun. The first verse of the fiftieth Psalm reads: "The mighty God, even the Lord, hath spoken, and called the earth from the rising of the sun unto the going down thereof."

The third verse of the one hundred and thirteenth Psalm contains the following: "From the rising of the sun unto the going down of the same, the Lord's name is to be praised."

Again, the eighteenth verse of the fourteenth chapter of Judges reads: "And the men of the city said unto him on the seventh day before the sun went down. What is sweeter than honey? and what is stronger than a lion?" The fifth verse of the first chapter of Ecclesiastes reads: "The sun also ariseth, and the sun goeth down, and hasteth to his place where he arose."

The eleventh verse of the first chapter of Malachi proclaims: "For from the rising of the sun even unto the going down of the same my name shall be great among the Gentiles." He quoted with much fervor and force the eighth verse of the thirty-eighth chapter of Isaiah: "Behold, I will bring again the shadow of the degrees, which is gone down in the sun-dial of (King) Ahaz, ten degrees backwards. So the sun returned ten degrees, by which degrees it was gone down."

He contented, with much warmth and enthusiasm, that the sun could not have possibly returned if it had not been moving. Nor did the contradictions of philosophers and scientists, as to the distance of the sun escape his vigilance. He boldly declared that some had fixed the distance of the sun from the earth at ninety-five million of miles; others, one hundred and thirty million; and others, sixty-five million.

This, he stated, was conclusive proof of their ignorance of the sun in general.

But this much discussed sermon not only concerns the chief luminary of our solar system, but also deals with the shape of the earth. He fortifies himself from scriptural passages in the belief that the earth is flat and has four corners. The ground for this peculiar idea is found in the first verse of the seventh chapter of Revelations: "And after these things I saw four angels standing on the four corners of the earth, holding the four winds of the earth, that the winds should not blow on the earth, nor on the sea, nor on any tree." "So we are living on a four-cornered earth!" he enthusiastically exclaimed.

"They tell us," he said, "that people are living directly under us. How in the name of common sense can they walk, unless they move like flies on the wall with their feet upward."

None but an eye-witness could obtain a clean conception of the effect of this striking discourse before a promiscuous assembly of white and colored. The peculiar and unsuspected ideas advanced, answer all of the demands of wit, as set forth by Hart or Campbell. He said: "They tell us that the sun is ninety-two million of miles from the earth. How can a man take a tape line and measure from the earth to the sun."

But the great and most striking effect of this sermon is to convince the hearer of the intense earnestness of the speaker. He speaks as a man on oath. He boldly and repeatedly asserts that the Holy Bible teaches that "The Sun Do Move." He wisely and adroitly represents himself as the humble interpreter of the Scriptures. His real earnestness may be further seen from the logical conclusions which he skillfully draws from his interpretation of the Bible. He unequivocally asseverates that all who deny that "The Sun Do Move," are preaching a doctrine contrary to the Word of God. They are opposers of the Divine Word and enemies to true religion. The manly fearlessness, the fierce denunciation of opposers, the natural eleoquence, the quaint wit and the chain of Wayland-like logic, evinced in the enlargement of this idea, compel even those who differ mostly from him to be convinced of his seriousness.

This sermon has had a checkered but an interesting history from its birth to the present time. It created a lively enthusiasm among the members of his own church. Then its fame rapidly overspread Richmond. Several ministers who honestly differed from Rev. Jasper vigorously opposed the idea that the Bible inculcates that "The Sun Do Move." This led to an estrangement between Rev. Jasper and several ministers; but the name of the eloquent divine and his sermon were mentioned in scientific journals of the North.

He journeyed to Baltimore, where he preached with great success before white and colored. At Washington and Philadelphia, too, he met flattering audiences. He then returned to Richmond. Everywhere the native ability, the dignity, eloquence, wit, humor, logic, the natural gesticulation and earnestness of the preacher, were highly commended by those whose views were entirely opposite. The Mozart association succeeded in obtaining his services some time since. Mozart Hall was packed to its entire capacity. The people highly enjoyed its delivery. Few discourses have enjoyed such a continuous celebrity before learned and ignorant, rich and poor, white and colored, as this. The scientists of London, Berlin and Paris—the philosophers, scholars and students of America and Europe—have discussed orally and in print the opinions of Rev. John Jasper.

Nor is it at all strange that his opinions have aroused such a universal and profound interest. His ideas concerning the luminous orb and the opaque earth were, with rare exceptions, the belief of antiquity. That prince dialectician of Greece, the famous Aristotle, was an enthusiastic teacher of the same thing. He conceived the moon, sun and planets set in a hollow crystalline sphere, by which they were borne around the earth. Illustrious Socrates and learned Plato diligently inculcated that the earth was the centre of the solar system, and that the sun constantly revolved around it. The philosophers and scholars of Rome accepted the teachings of Greece and diligently taught it.

The great and good men of the early church were likewise convinced. Origen, Athanasius, Augustine, Clement, Ignatius, Polycarp and others simply accepted the belief of the age.

The Christian church once passed a resolution declaring "that if any person believed the earth was round and revolved around the sun, he should be expelled from the church."

The priests and teachers, the highly learned and eminent men of the church, were firmly convinced that the Holy Scriptures plainly taught that the sun moves around the earth, and that the earth is flat and has four corners.

Kiddell, in his *Elements of Astronomy*, declares: "Previous to Copernicus (1543) the general belief for more than two thousand years had been that the earth is the centre of the universe, and that all other bodies revolve around it."

Again, he says: "As late as 1633 it was deemed irreligious to believe in the motions of the earth; and Galileo, in his seventieth year was imprisoned, and finally compelled to acknowledge himself as guilty of error and heresy in teaching this astronomical truth."

It has been only two hundred years since the present prevailing opinion was advocated. The happy invention of the telescope performed a scientific revolution. Men who had been foremost in the belief that the sun moves around the earth, relinquished their opinions and advocated the contrary belief. They argued that the sun, in relation to the earth, is stationary, while the earth revolves around it.

In view of the teachings of antiquity and the apparent evidence of Scripture that the sun moves around the earth, it must not be considered strange or unprecedented that Rev. Jasper so strongly maintains his seemingly peculiar tenets. However we may differ from him in the interpretation of Scripture or the deductions of modern science, we are forced to the acknowledgement of powers of reason and eloquence as well as of his spirit of religious seriousness.

Mr. Jasper is a consecrated man, and though he has differed widely in these scientific views, he certainly can so put his arguments that you, denying them, will seem to deny the Bible. He is very earnest and a man of sound judgment and good hard sense.

CHAPTER CLXV

James E. J. Capitein
A Negro Born in Africa—Taken to Europe—Educated
in Holland—Latin Poet

James E. J. Capitein was born in Africa. He was purchased, when seven or eight years of age, on the borders of the River St. Andree, by a Negro trader who made a present of him to one of his friends.

By his new master, who proved to be his friend, he was first named Capitein; and he instructed him, baptized him and brought him to Holland, where he acquired the language of the country. He devoted his time to painting, for which he had a great inclination. He commenced his studies at the Hague, where a pious and learned lady, who was much occupied in the study of languages, is said first to have taught him Latin and the elements of Greek, Hebrew and Chaldean tongues. From the Hague he went to the University of Leyden, meeting everywhere with zealous protectors. He devoted himself to theology under able professors, with the intention of returning to Africa to preach the gospel to his countrymen.

Having studied four years, Capitein took his degree, and in 1742 was sent as a Christian minister to Elmina, on the Gold Coast. In 1802 a vague report was spread that he had abjured Christianity and embraced idolatry again. Blumenbach, however, who inserted a portrait of Capitein in his work on *The Varieties of the Human Race*, could detect no authentic information against him.

The first work of Capitein is an elegy in Latin on the death of Manger, minister at the Hague, his preceptor and his friend. It is as follows:

> *Hac autem in Batavorum gratissima sede*
> *Non primum tantum elementa linguæ Belgicoe*
> *Addidici, sed arti etiam pictorica, in quam*
> *Eram pro pensissimus, dedi operam Virum*
> *Interea tempore labente, institutioni sua.*
> *Domestica catechesios mihi interesse permisit*
> *Vir humanissimus, Joannes Phillipus Manger,*

*Cujus in obitum (cum tanti viri, tum
Solidor eruditionis, tum erga deum singularis
Pictatis, admirator semper extitis sim) flebilibus
Fatis. Cum Ecclesior Hagienis protento anno
Esset ademptus, lugubrem hanc compersui
Elegiam!*

ELEGIA

*Invida mors totum vibrat sua tela per orbem:
Et gestit quembis succubuisse sibi.
Illa, metus expers, penetrat conclavia regum;
Imperiique manu ponere sceptra jubet.
Non sinit illa diu partos spectare triumphos:
Linquere sed cogit, clara tropœa duces.
Divitis et gazas, aliis ut dividat, omnes
Mendicique casam vindicat illa sibi.
Falce senes, juvenes, nullo discriminie, dura,
Instar aristarum, demittit illa simul.
Hic fuit illa audax, nigro velamine tecta.
Limina Mangeri sollicitari domus.
Hujus ut ante domum steterat funesta cypressus,
Luctisonos gemitus nobilis Haga dedit.
Hunc, lacrymis tinxit gravivus carissima conjux,
Dum sua tundebat pectora sæpe manu
Non aliter Noami, cum te vinduata marito,
Profudit lacrymas, Elimeleche tua.
Sæpe sui manes civit gemebunda mariti,
Edidit et tales ore tremente sonos;
Condit ut obscuro vultum velamine Phœbus,
Tractibus ut terræ lumina grata neget;
O decus immortale meum, mea sola voluptas!
Sic fugis ex oculis in mea damna meis.
Non equidem invideo, consors, quod te ocyor aura
Transtulit ad lœtas œthereas que domos.
Sed quoties mando placidæ mea membra quieti,
Sive dies veniat, sum memor usque tui.
Te thalamus noster raptum mihi funere poscit,
Quis renovet nobis fœdera rupta dies?
En tua sacra deo sedes studiisque dicata,
Te propter, mæsti signa doloris habet.
Quod magis, effusas, veluti de flumine pleno,
Dant lacrymas nostri pignora cara tori.
Dentibus et misere fido pastore lupinis
Conscisso teneræ disjiciunter oves,
Aeraque horrendis, feriunt balatibus altum,
Dum scissum adspiciunt voce cientque ducem:*

Sic querulis nostras implent ululatibus œdes
Dum jacet in lecto corpus inane tuum
Succinit huic vatum viduœ pia turba querenti,
Funera quœ celebrat conveniente modo
Grande sacerdotum decus, et mea glosia cessat,
Delicium domini, gentis amorque piœ!
Clauditor os blandum sacro de fonte rigatum;
Fonte meam possum quo relevare sitim!
Hei mihi? quam subito fugit facundia linguœ,
Cœlesti dederat quœ mihi melle frui.
Nestoris eloquim veteres jactate pœtœ,
Ipso Mangerius Nestore major erat, etc.

On his admission to the University of Leyden, Capitein published a Latin dissertation on the calling of the Gentiles, "De Vocatione Ethnicorum," which he divided into three parts. From the authority of the sacred writings he establishes the certainty of the promise of the gospel, which embraces all nations, although its manifestation is only gradual. For the purpose of co-operating in this respect with the design of the Almighty, he proposes that the languages of those nations should be cultivated to whom the blessings of Christianity are yet unknown, and also that missionaries be sent among them, who, by the mild voice of persuasion, might gain their affections and dispose them to receive the truth of the gospel.

The Spaniard and Portuguese, he observes, exercise a mild and gentle treatment of their slaves, establishing no superiority of color, etc. In other countries, planters have prevented their Negroes from being instructed in a religion which proclaims the equality of men, all proceeding from a common stock and equally entitled to the benefits of a kind Providence, who is no respector of persons.

The Dutch planters, persuaded that slavery is inconsistent with Christianity, but stifling the voice of conscience, probably instigated Capitein to become the apologist of a bad cause, for he subsequently composed a politico-theological dissertation in Latin to prove that slavery is not opposed to Christian freedom. His conclusions are forced. Though poor in argument, it is rich in erudition, and translated into Dutch by Wilheur, and published with a portrait of the author in preacher's attire. This work went through four editions.

Capitein also published a small quarto volume of sermons in Dutch, preached in different towns and printed at Amsterdam in 1742.

This sketch is taken from *A Tribute for the Negro,* published in 1848 by Wilson Armistead.

D. A. PAYNE

CHAPTER CLXVI

Rev. D. A. Payne, D. D., LL. D.
Senior Bishop of the A. M. E. Church—Educator and Author—
The Scholar of the Denomination

―――――•●•―――――

His life began in the city of Charleston, South Carolina, that city of famous men. The day was an important one in that family, when the future bishop came to visit them, February 24, 1811. His father and mother were members of the M. E. church; the father had charge of two classes, the "seekers' class" and the members' class. The mother was a woman of fine feeling, a tender, loving and faithful Christian, whom the son remembers with all the reverence of his nature. Surely she impressed her own nature to the depths of his heart.

He was early taught to read and attend school supported by an organization known as the Minor's Society, which was supported by free colored men, beginning its work as early as the year 1810. What a blessing this was; they took an interest in him and paid his tuition and book bills for two years. This society was organized to take care of orphan children and give them instruction, and the limit of such aid was two years. Young Payne received the attention of the society during this period. After leaving this school he had one year's training under Thomas Bonneau. He mastered the English branches and studied also Roman and Grecian history. He paid considerable attention to mathematics, so far as to master six books of Euclid. Greek, Latin, French and kindred studies he pursued without a teacher. He came into possession of a book named the *Self-Interpreting Bible*, by Rev. John Brown, who had mastered these languages without a teacher, and Payne determined that he could do what had been done. This was a curious determination to one who had little reason to expect to attain any position of eminence in life from such a lowly station; nor did he himself have any such notion, as he had determined to become a soldier in Hayti. Rumors had come to him of the wars on that island, and he was stirred with the tales of battle and broils, and, like many young men, was lured to scenes of danger from the romance therein. He was an apprentice in the carpenter-shop of Richard Holloway, his brother-in-law, James Holloway, being the foreman.

Many a day did he ponder over his situation and long after the very things perhaps which he realized in after life. Circumscribed as he was, it is wonderful that he succeeded so admirably from such small beginnings. His warlike desires were no doubt aroused by reading the old Scottish tales which fell into his hands, and his head was full of the deeds of Wallace and Bruce.

But, like Joseph of old, he was "warned in a dream," and he changed his mind and hid forever his youthful warlike desires. At fifteen he became concerned for his soul, and was received into the class of Samuel Weston on probation, becoming a devoted seeker of the Lord Jesus Christ. Elder James O. Andrews was then in charge of the Methodist churches in the city of Charleston, and afterwards became his guide and teacher in the ways of eternal life. At fifteen he was converted, and a blessed day it was to him—a holy Sabbath day—a day of rest, when his soul found the rest it had for three years been longing. Shortly after he was impressed in a singular way to go and preach the gospel. It was on a day when at prayer he heard a voice that seemed to call him to duty which has so faithfully marked his life. Hands seemed to press upon his shoulders as if hurrying him forward to begin the work of an educator. He soon laid aside the plane and chisel, saw, spirit-level and the carpenter's apron, and went forth to chisel his name on the highest pinnacle of fame, and smooth down the rough places in the intellects of the young, and be guided by the spirit of Christ.

Herein also he was like Christ. He left the carpenter's bench to minister to the wants of others. He opened a school in the house of Cæsar Wright, having his children as his first scholars at fifty cents per month. This was in 1829, and during the year 1830 he had no more scholars than enough to make his pay about two dollars per month. Yet this was the embryo Wilberforce which he had in the sample before him. He soon gained popularity, and after six years had the largest and most successful school in the city.

But the thing was too good to last. Payne was having too much success. The white folks said the school must be broken up, and the bishop himself has told us that the people said Payne was playing "HELL" in Charleston. For Negroes to go to school was objectionable, and it was compared to the infernal regions in its results. This was not altogether out of place, it would seem, for as they had very little true religion, and among those people to destroy these schools, they felt the Negroes would rise in a generation and strike for freedom, and in so doing the white folks would get a through ticket to that place.

A sketch written by T. McCants Stewart says that they passed a law in the Legislature which made it impossible for Mr. Payne to remain any longer in the home of his birth and as an educator of his people. Before this time, however, Mr. Payne's life was embittered by what he saw of slavery. He himself had suffered. While never whipped under that system which Garrison rightly called "a league with death and a covenant in hell," he had suffered bonds and imprisonment. Standing on the street of Charleston, South Carolina, about fifty-six years ago, with a small walking cane in his hand, a white man snatched it from him and struck him, indignant at the idea of a "nigger" carrying a cane. Young Payne, full of fire and manhood, retaliated and was imprisoned. His soul was full of bitterness against oppression and the oppressor, because he saw husbands sold away from wives, he saw children, even nursing infants, torn cruelly from their parents. He saw the victims of the driver's lash and the auction block; he saw his people compelled to make bricks without mortar or straw. He heard their cries, "How long, O Lord, how long?" When, therefore, unjust and oppressive law forced him out of his native city, he resolved never to return again until slavery was destroyed.

In 1835 Mr. Payne sailed out of Charleston harbor with this determination. Strange to relate, he returned on the very day and date thirty years thereafter the bishop of the A. M. E. church, to plant the banner of that connection on the soil of South Carolina, and in the very city where thirty years before he had suffered imprisonment and oppression.

He landed in Philadelphia, where he taught school for several years. The same year of his arrival he entered the Lutheran Theological Seminary at Gettysburg, Pennsylvania, but was compelled by the weakness of his eyes to surrender his course. He was ordained an elder by the Lutherans in 1837, having entered the ministry the year before. While teaching and preaching in Philadelphia the old building, the Bethel of Richard Allen's day, was torn down, and Elder Payne assisted in laying the corner-stone of the present edifice. In 1840 he joined the Philadelphia conference as a local preacher. In 1843 he was traveling preacher in the same body. Bishop Morris Brown appointed him to the Israel Bethel church at Washington, District of Columbia. Here he remained for five years. He was then appointed to the Bethel church of Baltimore, Maryland, then to the Ebenezer church in the same city. The bishop rose from station to station because he preached the word of God and did right. May 7, 1852, the General conference met in New York City. A special sermon was to be preached and Elder Payne was selected the preacher. When he did so he easily carried off the prize. He was elected bishop and ruler of the representative of the younger and more progressive element. May 13, 1852, he was ordained bishop of the A. M. E. church, and beyond doubt has been a faithful steward.

Bishop Payne's name will stand in the history of the A. M. E. church as a founder of a system of education just as Aristotle and Bacon were founders of a system of logic. Garrison says Plato is philosophy and philosophy Plato. The A. M. E. church can freely say Bishop Payne is so of education, and the spirit of our education is embodied in Bishop Payne. Years ago Wilberforce University was offered the bishop as a school for our church. Certain parties stood ready to purchase the property at a higher figure than we could pay. The matter had to be decided on a certain day. Bishop Payne could not consult his colleagues and he would not permit the order to be given. The bishop was without a dollar and remembered the fact that the connection was not enthusiastic over Christian education; but with a firm faith in the omnipotent arm of the Jehovah, and inspired with that courage that characterized his life, he stood in the presence of the person who was to sell. Alone with Jesus and with uplifted hands, Bishop Payne cried, "In the name of God I purchase this property for the A. M. E. church, to be consecrated by them for the sacred cause of Christian education." He lived to pay every dollar of the debt which he that day incurred. This school is truly a monument to his rare foresight and earnest zeal in the cause of education, and a great desire on his part to see the ministers of the church educated.

Dr. Tanner, in speaking of him in his apology for African Methodism, says that the Wilberforce University is pre-eminently the legacy he will leave to the church and the people he loves so well. Upon it he has laid himself as a willing sacrifice; of it he thinks by day and dreams by night; of it he writes, talks and works; for it he has crossed the sea. He became the president of this college in 1863 and continued till 1876, building it up into the great and powerful school which has sent out very learned men and given many titles to its clergy and scholars. Rev. B. W. Arnett, in his centennial address on the mission of Methodism, has said of Bishop Payne that he was "the apostle of an educated ministry." He was the first president of a Negro university in the western world; the first Negro to preside over the Universal Methodist family, September 17, 1881, at the Ecumenical conference held in London, England. He has been the historian of the church since 1848 and is the author of several works.

The bishop is about to publish his recollections of men and things, which has engaged his attention for the last three score years. He has recently published a book on Domestic Education. Full of years and honor, he still continues to labor for the denomination. He received the degree of LL. D. from Lincoln University in 1880, and D. D. from Wilberforce University. He by his own exertions secured the museum to Wilberforce University, which is worth two thousand dollars; and in honor of the services which he rendered in that connection, it has been named the "Payne Museum," and, says the *Wilberforce Alumnial* of 1885:

Thus will his name be connected with the study of sciences, and as the young and rising generations tread the halls of the university, they will read the name of the noble author and disciple of knowledge, that in *our* age stands as a synonym for a Christian education, and could be transmitted from generation to generation as a worthy example of consecrated learning and a devoted love to man and God.

May his days be prolonged to do much good; but surely he will leave behind him grateful hearts and many who owe all directly to the influences which he has set in motion in the establishment of the Wilberforce University.

ISAAC M. BURGAN

CHAPTER CLXVII

Rev. Isaac M. Burgan, B. D.
President at Paul Quinn College—Educator—Pioneer

Isaac M. Burgan was born October 6, 1848, near Marion, McDowell county, North Carolina. His mother, Sylva Burgan, was one of those devoted slave mothers who allowed nothing to prevent her caring for her boy. Many times when unable to stay with him at the house, she would lead him by the hand to her work. Much of her piety was shown when they were alone. She had fine purposes and great faith. Isaac remained in slavery till the results of the late war declared him free. In his circle of associates, many of whom were older than he, all came to young Burgan for counsel and direction. When his white companions brought new lessons from school, Isaac was among the first to learn them. So at an early age, though laboring under the disadvantage of having no teacher, he could read the lessons assigned his white playmates.

While a boy he was regarded as being too knowing to make a good slave, and it was thought best to sell him for eight hundred dollars; but as he showed a disposition to use his best thoughts and energy to the advantage of his owner, when the traders returned, fifteen hundred dollars were refused and Isaac regarded as the leading hand of the field. The most he knew of slavery beyond personal privations and restrictions, was from observation; because proving himself trustworthy he enjoyed favors and privileges denied his fellow-servants. The sorest conflict of his recollection grew out of an attempt on the part of the authorities to whip his mother. When the cruel work began young Burgan hastened to the scene. Here with bare feet and tattered garments he stood merely looking on till the screams of a loving mother pierced his heart to its depths. Then seizing a large poker he struck the man a telling blow on the back of the head. The brutal arm dropped and the lash was staid. Isaac fled for his life but soon returned, and in a few days got a double portion of that from which he saved his mother.

Leaving the home of his owner he hired out for a small sum per month, most of which was required to purchase winter clothing and shoes for his mother. After working for her three years, by her consent he went to Tennessee. Here he soon made his way into the free schools by paying his tuition. This was the beginning of a long struggle, for there were none to help and but few to encourage. When school was out he found the most lucrative business to be railroading. At this employment he accumulated several hundred dollars, every cent of which he consecrated to the cause of self-education.

In December, 1869, he entered a select school in Bowling Green, Kentucky. He soon attracted the attention of his teachers and the whole school. The books of the class he entered were soon mastered and he was promoted. At the close of school the young student set out to replenish his purse. While working at Livermore, Kentucky, during the summer vacation, he met in prayer meeting a young man by the name of George Belt, who had been attending school in Evansville, and the two boys at once became friends and agreed to go to Evansville, which they did in October, 1870, and entered the public schools, taught by Rev. J. M. Townsend, D.D. Here he remained for three years, working most of the time with white families for a small sum and board. A large per cent of the money he earned was added to the sum which he had deposited in the savings bank when he arrived in the city. By one of the families he had the best of treatment, rooming a part of the time with their son, who is now a lawyer in New Orleans. But he became disgusted with the service system and sought a boarding house, declaring that he would serve no more in that manner.

It was while under Rev. Townsend's instructions he received some of his best impressions, and he gives his teacher much credit for what he is. In the fall of 1873 he entered the State Normal school at Terre Haute. There he joined a class of fifty-two, most of whom were whites and graduates of High schools. Nevertheless, he took the lead in several branches, standing pre-eminent in mathematics and philosophy. In his struggles at Terre Haute, he proved himself a man of many plans. On entering the city he and a classmate contracted for three months' board at reduced rates. The boarding master failed to comply with the contract; Mr. Beecher (the classmate) sought another boarding house, but our subject was not able to follow. So he rented a room and became cook and housekeeper. Work was soon secured which yielded ten dollars per month; but this was a dear income, for it had to be earned during the cold winters of 1873 and 1874, between five and seven o'clock in the morning. Very often this untiring student of the Normal school had to plunge into the darkness of the morning amid snow, rain and sleet, to get the post office cleaned and warmed by seven o'clock. The rush did not stop here, for hurry must be made to the baker's for a loaf of bread, and to the butcher's for his meat, and go home, make his fire, prepare his breakfast, and be at school by 8:45. But he braved it till school closed in the spring. When the session opened in the fall he secured, through the kindness of J. H. Walker, the position of assistant mail agent. The income here was board and seven dollars per month; but being assigned to night work and finding it impossible to stay awake night and day, he was driven to abandon this and make other arrangements. He found the post office department ready to receive him. He added to this other work, making his income sixteen dollars per month, and arranged to board at fifteen dollars. This gave increased work for this winter (1874–75), which was more severe, if possible, than the preceding one. The boarding house being seven squares from the post office, much of the distance had to be made in double quick time. But this winter's work proved a little too much for the resolute student. His studies had become difficult and often entertained him with an unbroken spell till a late hour at night; and then the quantity of labor required for his support compelled him to rise too early in the morning to get the requisite amount of sleep.

Spring found him exhausted physically and mentally; and impaired health compelled him to leave school a month and a half before it closed. Having no stored purse upon which to draw, he was forced to break his resolution and serve again in a family.

Having spent five terms in the Normal and being near graduation, in the fall of 1875 he went to Lost Creek, near Terre Haute, to begin teaching, a work for which time has shown him to be well adapted. It was here on account of his governing powers, his ability to teach, his wonderful tact and skill to interest and inspire his pupils, that he received the appellation of "a natural born teacher." Mr. Burgan entered Wilberforce University September, 1878, to study for the Christian ministry.

While working on the railroad in Middle Tennessee he was converted at a Baptist revival, but joined no church. In Bowling Green, Kentucky, he placed himself under the watch care of the M. E. church, and was made Sunday school superintendent and leader of the choir. In Evansville, Indiana, he joined the A. M. E. church, under Rev. A. T. Hall. His first official relation in the church of his choice was that of steward, under Rev. W. S. Lankford. He was appointed Sunday school teacher under the superintendency of Professor J. M. Townsend, and proved himself a faithful worker. From early life he had been conscious of a call to the Christian ministry; but regarding the office as being the most exalted, and feeling unprepared for the work educationally, he withstood the persuasions of friends and refused to apply for license, both at Bowling Green and Evansville. While attending the Normal, the pious life of Rev. J. Mitchem, the pastor at that place, was brought to bear, and he said he would resist the call no longer; but application for license was deferred till 1876, when his former teacher, Rev. J. M. Townsend, set a willing hand to his license to exhort. This being done he decided not to return to the Normal to graduate, but to spend the remainder of his school days in some theological school. After uniting with the church at Lost Creek, in 1877, he was licensed to preach by Rev. John Myers. Having spent three years here he parted with a host of friends to seek higher attainments and greater work.

From the time he entered college on the above date he was closely connected with all the social and religious movements of the school, and his devotion added very much to the success of the church work. While in college he was never out of office. In church he was class-leader, trustee and finally pastor of the college chapel. At commencements he represented the theological rhetorical once, the Sodalian Literary Society twice, and was honored successively with the presidency of every college society to which males were admitted. In debate Mr. Burgan was peer of the best. In every contest except two, the decision was rendered in his favor; and in one case it was thought the jury was packed, and in the other it hung. At the close of his Sophomore year he joined the Indiana Annual conference at New Albany, under Bishop J. A. Shorter, and asked for work, stating that the years of privation and hardship which he had spent in school had about worn him out, and having no means of support he could not return to school. But the fatherly bishop, who influenced him to attend Wilberforce, at first insisted that he return and finish his course; then said confidentially, "I have been requested and have concluded to appoint you pastor at the college."

While at college he held charge at Maysville, and Harveysburg, and Troy, Ohio. By his pastoral work and weekly visitations to all families regardless of church affinity, and his care for the poor and needy, he is called even to-day "The God-man." During his stay in college he was compelled to shift many ways for support. The last two years the faculty voted him a scholarship of sixty dollars per annum. With this exception and a few dollars from the Indiana conference and friends, his attainments are the results of the sacrificing life and determined efforts. His favorite studies were the sciences. His class honored him as valedictorian and editor-in-chief of the college paper. His valedictory, subject "Commencement," was pronounced the best ever delivered at the institution. His commencement oration, subject "The Christian Ministry," was a masterpiece. In a few weeks after graduating he was ordained deacon by Bishop Shorter of Indianapolis.

After he finished his long and arduous work of preparation he was appointed principal of Paul Quinn College, at Waco, Texas. On the twenty-seventh of September, 1883, he and one other teacher arrived in Waco. They were met at the depot by three of the leading trustees, who directed them to a boarding house and arranged an hour for council. At the appointed time the trustees, laboring under very great discouragements, stated that they thought it best not to open school that year, and had concluded to wait till it could be opened under more favorable circumstances. After hearing their statement of facts, etc., Burgan said, "Closing the school for one year means death for ten, and it should be announced ready for work in the face of adverse circumstance." The next day it was agreed to re-open on the conditions that the trustees be released of all financial responsibility, and the teachers be paid by the secretary with whatever might accrue from tuition. After laboring two months under this arrangement and receiving nothing in the way of compensation, the trustees saw fit to lease the school to Bishop Cain. This placed the principal in a still more awkward position, and affairs continued dark.

There were some students in attendance, and Mr. Burgan had the consciousness that he was doing good and labored on with one assistant during the greater part of the year, with no money from any source except the scant income from a few students, to pay teachers or make the necessary improvements. During this time enemies were rejoicing and friends almost quaking with fear. But the examinations during the closing exercises surpassed the highest expectations, and showed that excellent class work had been done; otherwise the condition of affairs was almost hopeless. Professor Burgan had invited the trustees to attend the closing, but none having come up to a late hour he telegraphed for Elder A. Grant, who responded by his presence. This brought others on the ground, and in their meetings (the lease having expired) it was thought that Professor Burgan was pre-eminently fitted to carry on the work, and he was elected president.

Of the buildings on the premises exclusive of the brick, there was one frame for kitchen and dining room, an office and three shed rooms for young men. The president took fresh courage and resolved to replace the shed rooms by erecting a two story frame. In this effort he was again embarrassed for the want of cooperation and encouragement, but with a disposition to yield to nothing but impossibilities he succeeded. Under these and similar discouraging and adverse circumstances he has continued his arduous labors and achieved success for the college. In his sacrificing efforts to keep employed an able corps of teachers and to continue the usefulness of the college, he has closed school (more than once) without money enough to pay his way out of Waco.

As it required all his time, energy and money to prepare for life, and as his work since preparation has demanded sacrifice of almost everything that is dear to life, this hard-working servant of God has accumulated nothing but a library of good books. These have served as his tools and companions.

Born and reared a Southerner, educated at the mother institution of the race, acquainted with the advanced work of Northern and Eastern institutions, with his physical vigor, mental ability and persevering spirit, President Burgan is destined for a still greater work among his people.

CHAPTER CLXVIII

Rev. W. J. White
Editor of the Georgia Baptist

———◆◆———

One of the most successful Baptist editors in the United States is the subject of this sketch. The *Georgia Baptist,* a twenty-eight column paper, is one of the most enterprising in the South. Its circulation does credit to the denomination. During the seven years of its existence, it has fearlessly hurled fiery darts at enemies, and carried messages of peace and love to its friends. Rev. W. J. White began his work for God and the race when quite a young man, and the experience he has gained makes him a safe and trusted counselor. Hard work and consecrated efforts have won for him the admiration not only of the State in which he resides, but beyond its borders his faithfulness is known. October 7, 1855, he was baptized and became a member of the Springfield Baptist church, Augusta, Georgia; and although he was impressed with the fact that he was called to the gospel ministry, it was not until seven years later that he was licensed to preach. April 1, 1866, he was ordained to the work of winning souls to Christ. In 1859 he organized a Sabbath school which he nourished nine years as superintendent, at which time the seed sown germinated, and the Harmony Baptist church, which he has served as pastor many years, sprang into existence. Nor did his work stop here. The Baptist family all over the State was thought of, and he assisted largely in organizing the State work. When the State convention was formed in 1870 he was elected treasurer, and for many years served in this position, besides serving as missionary agent. The Shiloh Association also elected him treasurer. The Colored Georgia Baptist Sunday school convention, organized in 1872, elected him president, and he was re-elected several times. As corresponding secretary of the Missionary Baptist convention, and of the Sunday school convention of Georgia, he has proven himself a man of much ability. At present he is chairman of the Baptist Centennial committee of Georgia. The editorial department of the *Georgia Baptist* is ably conducted. The articles are to the point and always strike home. Rev. Mr. White, in writing of his paper, says it is a newspaper now well in its seventh year and has never missed a single issue.

His services in the cause of education have marked him as a far-seeing man who knows that to patient toil and ardent work must be due the glory of the future for our people. All the school teachers of the State recognize in him a defender and advocate; nor do his views pertain only to mental development but to the training of the physical. His soul is deeply interested in the future of the young people, for they are not so readily entering the manufacturing and commercial world as he would desire. He would have artisans as well as lawyers, carpenters as well as doctors, farmers as well as school teachers.

CHAPTER CLXIX

Hon. Alexander Clark
Eminent Mason—Lawyer—Editor

———◆●◆———

Mr. Clark was born February 25, 1826. His father, John Clark, though born a slave, was emancipated in early life by his father and master, a kind-hearted Irishman. From this source Alexander Clark is said to have inherited in a great measure the genius and brilliancy which have adorned his character. From his mother, a full-blooded African, he inherited through several generations a strong, healthy constitution.

Young Clark was considered very intelligent while still a lad at school. At the age of thirteen he removed to Cincinnati, Ohio, where he attended school one year, and at the same time learned the barber business under an uncle. When but fifteen years old he left this place to go South as a hand on the steamer "George Washington." In 1842 he went to Muscatine, Iowa, and for many years conducted a barber shop with pecuniary success. After leaving this employment he invested largely in real estate, which he managed so wisely as to accumulate a neat little fortune.

In 1863 he enlisted in the First Iowa Colored volunteers and was promoted to the rank of sergeant-major, but was not permitted to muster because of a physical defect in the left ankle. This did not abate his ardor to labor for his country in her time of need. All through the West he actively busied himself gathering recruits for the Union army.

In 1869 he was a delegate from Iowa to the Colored National convention, which met at Washington, District of Columbia. This body appointed him chairman of the committee to lay before the Senate and House of Representatives the claims of colored soldiers and seamen to equal bounty and pension as that received by the whites. He was also one of the committee to wait upon President Grant and Vice-President Colfax and convey the congratulations of the colored people of the United States on their election. He acted as spokesman of the committee. As a worker in benevolent organizations. Mr. Clark has few equals. He has for years been identified with the Masonic order and has held the highest positions in its gift. In 1868 he was elected deputy grand master of the Grand Lodge of Missouri. The following year when Grand Master H. McGee

ALEXANDER CLARK

died, he was elected to succeed him as master over the States of Missouri, Iowa, Minnesota, Tennessee, Arkansas and Mississippi.

At the next session of Missouri Grand Lodge he was elected grand treasurer and delegated to attend the Most Worshipful National Grand Compact of Masons for the United States, at Wilmington, Delaware, October 9, 1869. In June of the same year he was re-elected grand master and held the position three years. In 1872 he was elected grand secretary; in 1873 was appointed chairman of the committee on foreign correspondence, and in 1874 was again elected grand master, in which position he served many years. In politics he is a stalwart Republican.

In 1869 he was elected vice-president of the Iowa State Republican convention, and in 1870 was a delegate to said body and served on the committee on resolutions. In 1872 he was elected delegate-at-large from Iowa to the convention in Philadelphia which nominated U. S. Grant President of the United States. In 1873 President Grant appointed him consul to Aux Cayes, Hayti, which position he declined because the salary was not sufficient. The State convention of colored men appointed him delegate to the Centennial Exposition at Philadelphia, Pennsylvania, for the purpose of gathering statistics and such information concerning the Negro race as would be useful in determining its true status.

In 1878 Mr. Clark's voice rang through the Northwest, urging the Negro to stand by the party. A speech made by him in Macon, at the celebration of the passage of the Fifteenth Amendment, was mentioned as follows by the *Weekly Macon Journal:*

> Mr. Clark's speech was replete with sound argument, earnest advocacy of right, and impressed all with his sound judgment. Rarely has it been the privilege of the people of Macon to listen to such words of eloquence. To attempt to reproduce it would insure failure, so we will not attempt it; suffice to say it was happy in conception, faultless in argument and delivery.

Mr. Clark, though living in the North, is full of sympathy with his people in the South. He never allows an opportunity of speaking and writing against discrimination because of color pass. Having traveled extensively through the South, he was better prepared than most men to see the wrongs suffered by our people. For many years he edited and owned the *Chicago Conservator;* he has recently sold it to other parties. While he had it, he certainly wielded a fearless pen; it was dipped in acid and driven into an enemy to his race with remorseless vigor.

He is gentlemanly and courteous, pleasant and affable, and a conversationalist of the most entertaining character. He has in his old age graduated from a law school, and is now a practicing lawyer in the city of Chicago. His wealth is quite extensive, and his good name does not diminish.

CHAPTER CLXX

Honorable John C. Dancy
Editor of the Star of Zion—*Eminent Layman in the A. M. E.*
Zion Church—Recorder of Deeds of Edgecombe County,
North Carolina

John C. Dancy was born in slavery at Tarboro, North Carolina, May 8, 1857. He was placed in school immediately after the close of the war, and instructed by able teachers from the North.

His father was a leading builder and contractor, and made it a point to keep him in school all the while. His mother also early advised and lectured him at the family fireside, and taught him the first lessons of honesty, temperance and true manhood. In school his teachers all considered him an exemplary boy, easily taught and always obedient. He always carried off the honors of his class.

In 1873 he entered the printing office of the Tarboro *Southern* as office boy, but was soon given a case by direction of the foreman, and in a few months was an acceptable "typo." The sentiment of the white newspaper fraternity of the State was soon tested, and it was unanimous against this state of things; consequently he left the office to enter Howard University, Washington, District of Columbia. His father died after he had been there a short while, and so he had to return home to care for his mother and family. He taught school for a while though only seventeen years of age, and was appointed to a position in the treasury department at Washington, District of Columbia, through the influence of Honorable John A. Hyman, then a member of Congress, and in the interim attended Howard University. He resigned his position after holding it less than a year, to take charge of the public school at Tarboro. The resignation was a great surprise to his friends in Washington, as it is said there "that few die and none resign." He continued to teach for several years.

He was secretary of the State convention of colored men in 1877, and chief secretary of the State Republican convention of 1880 and 1884. He was also president of the State convention of colored men to consider the question of placing colored men on the jury.

He was elected recorder of deeds of Edgecombe county in 1880 and 1882 by large majorities, but was defeated in 1884 by reason of a split in his own party, and a combination of other circumstances. He was chairman of the county Republican committee for eight years.

He was elected a delegate to the Chicago convention in 1884, and attracted wide attention by reason of a speech he made in that body seconding the nomination of the Honorable John A. Logan. No one knew he was to speak but himself, and he says he prepared the speech in his mind without writing a line, on going from the Palmer House to the hall. His eloquent and capital effort was greeted with a volley of hand claps and round after round of applause. He was warmly congratulated by the delegates from various States. He has been a prominent speaker in all the important campaigns since 1878, when he attained his majority. Mr. Dancy is tall, slim, and in manners very graceful, dignified and affable. He is a remarkable man and reflects credit on the race. Although a young man, being thirty years of age, he is one of the most prominent laymen in the A. M. E. Zion church. He was a lay delegate to the general conference of said church in 1880 and 1884, and took a prominent part in the debates of that august body.

He is a ripe debater and his oratory is clear, persuasive and brilliant. He is peculiarly gifted, eminently original, natural, practical and powerful as a speaker and is dashing and spicy as a writer. In short, he is a man of brains and character.

He went abroad in 1879 as a delegate to the Right Worthy Grand Lodge of Good Templars, and was elected Right Worthy Grand Marshal of that body.

He lectured extensively in England, Ireland, Scotland and Wales, and made many warm friends.

Upon his return he lectured considerably on "Scenes and Incidents Abroad," Professor J. C. Price lecturing jointly with him, the latter speaking on the topic, "One Hour with the People." They were very successful financially and otherwise. He was grand secretary of the Grand Lodge of Good Templars of North Carolina for seven years. He edited the North Carolina *Sentinel*, published at Tarboro, North Carolina, for three years, and gave it up at the request of the board of bishops of the A. M. E. Zion church, to take charge as editor and business manager of the *Star of Zion*, the organ of said church. Under his management the paper has increased wonderfully in subscription and circulation, and is now considered the equal in ability and news of any religious paper published by the race in America.

CHARLES L. REASON

CHAPTER CLXXI

Professor Charles L. Reason
A Veteran New York School Teacher—European Traveler—
One of the Giants in Anti-Slavery Days

The parents of our subject came from the scenes of revolution in the island of Hayti settled in New York, and their son, Charles Lewis Reason, was born there July 21, 1818. His parents took pains, as soon as he was of school age, to enter him as a pupil. He paid special attention to the higher arithmetic as taught in the school, and endeavored to develop all faculties that would fit him for usefulness and enlarge the tendencies of his own nature.

At the age of fourteen he had fitted himself as an instructor, and had an appointment in the school where he had been taught. With a determination to become master in his vocation, out of his scanty salary he paid for private instruction in mathematics, and in 1849 was called to be "Professor of Belles-lettres and of the French language and Adjutant-Professor of Mathematics," in the New York Central College, McGrawville, Cortlandt county, New York.

It was a perfectly consistent choice with him to accept a professorship in a college projected to sustain "The Doctrine of the Unity, Common Origin, Equality and Brotherhood of the Human Race."

Resigning his position in the college from dissatisfaction with the president, he was made, in 1852, principal of the Institute for Colored Youth, Philadelphia, which was then first opened. His experience as an instructor of youth extends over a period of more than fifty years, including three years in Philadelphia and nearly two years in Central College.

He has developed the manhood of his own youth; the qualities that endeared him to his associates in boyhood are shining now in sunlight effulgence. He has the highest regard of his fellow-pupils of the dominant class in New York City, and I am certain that in the eighteen hundred members of the Teachers' Association of the City of New York, there is no one commanding more esteem than Professor ·Charles L. Reason. Among them he stands in line with those that hold the first rank in mathematics. He has been repeatedly elected one of the delegates to the board of directors of the Teachers' Association, and is at this writing chairman of the committee on grammar school work.

As a writer there is nothing coming from under his pen but bears evidence of the utmost care as well as proof of the highest culture. He has written and delivered lectures, and written and published several poems and poetic effusions. His contributions to the public press, in the equal suffrage struggle in the State of New York, were pre-eminently effective in style and matter.

His aspiration in the cause of education brings him before us in different phases. He does not confine himself to mere mind training. He is, and ever has been the friend of industrial education—the combination of mental and physical development—not only for its own sake, but in the interest of human freedom and human progress. As early as 1854, pleading for an industrial college, he wrote:

The usefulness, the self-respect and self-dependence, the combination of intelligence and handicraft, the accumulations of the materials of wealth, all referable to such an institution, present fair claims to the assistance of the entire American people.

With the reputation distinguished for purity of life, well trained in current literature, a lover of research and thoughtful investigation, well read in history, the poets and theological investigation, he was made the choice of the vestry of St. Phillip's church as a theological student, with a view of having him enter the ministry under the auspices of that body. He commenced and pursued the studies preparatory to entering the Theological Seminary of the Protestant Episcopal church. The bishop of the diocese, however, interposed his power and forbade his entrance, except as a listener. This position Mr. Reason refused to accept, being unwilling to be a party to such sham Christianity; and as he was unsupported by any remonstrance by the vestry of the church, he resigned, and his candidacy ended.

In this effort he had been compelled to enter the same fiery furnace that had been lit up to consume the aspirations of Berry, DeGrasse and Crummell, and against which the high-toned inspirations of Rt. Rev. Bishop Doane of New Jersey had entered his solemn protest, and which, at his own request, was entered on the minutes of the trustees of the General Theological Seminary.

To say that Mr. Reason possesses poetic talent would be an expression entirely inadequate to describe that God-given gift in him. No words which I can use here would give the kind of idea that I would wish to convey to the reader as to the depth of that inspiration, which has found faint expression in the poems and composition which he has given to the readers of the press.

This is no less true in the lines written by him than in the beautiful translations made from the French of Lamartine in his "Retirement." The "Spirit Voice," "Silent Thought," etc., will speak better for themselves than any thing else that can be said here.

We get better ideas of a man's genius by reading what a man has written, and so I give two of his poems with the hope they may please my readers and furnish sufficient food for the mind. I had hoped to give more, but space compelled me refrain.

THE SPIRIT VOICE
OR LIBERTY CALL TO THE DISFRANCHISED
(State of New York)

Come! rouse ye brothers, rouse! a peal now breaks
From lowest island to our gallant lakes:
'Tis summoning you, who long in bonds have lain,
To stand up manful on the battle plain,
Each as a warrior, with his armor bright,
Prepared to battle in a bloodless fight.
Hark! How each breeze that blows o'er Hudson's tide
Is calling loudly on your birth-right pride
And each near cliff, whose peak fierce storms has stood.
Shouts back responsive to the calling flood.
List! from those heights that once with freedom rung,
And those broad fields, where Earth has oft-times sung,
A voice goes up, invoking men to prove
How dear is freedom, and how strong their love.
From every obscure vale and swelling hill
The spirit tones are mounting; louder still
From out the din where noble cities rise
On Mohawk's banks, the peal ascends the skies.
Responding sweet with morning's opening praise,
The sound commingle, far, to where the rays
Of light departing, sink to partial sleep,
'Mid caverned gems in Erie's bosomed deep.
Nor yet less heard, from inland slopes its swells,
In chiming music, with the village bells,
And mixes loud e'en with the ocean's waves,
Like shrilled voiced echo in the mountain caves.
'Tis calling you, who now too long have been
Sore victims suffering under legal sin,
To vow, no more to sleep, till raised and freed

*From partial bondage, to a life indeed
Behold ye now! here consecrate from toil
And love, your homes abide on holy soil.
To these, as sacred temples, fond you cling:
For, thence alone, life's narrow comforts spring,
'Tis here the twilight of existence broke,
The first warm throbbings of your hearts awoke.
Here first o'er you, fond mothers watch'd and pray'd,
Here friendship rose and holy vows were made.
On yon familiar height or gentle stream,
You first did mark the pleasant moonlight gleam.
Here, happy, laugh'd o'er life is cradled bloom
And here, first pensive, wept at age's tomb,
Yes; many a sire, with burnt and furrowed brow
Here died, in hope that you in freedom now
Would feel the boasted pledge your country gave,
That her defender should not be her slave.
And wherefore, round your homes has not been thrown
That guardian shield, which strangers call their own?
Why, now, do ye, as your poor fathers did,
Bow down in silence to what tyrants bid?
And sweat and bleed from early morn till eve,
To earn a dower less than beggars leave?
Why are ye pleased to delve at mammon's nod,
To buy that manhood which is yours from God,
Free choice to say who worthy is to lead
Your country's cause, to give your heart-felt meed
Of praise to him that, barring custom's rule,
Would nobly dare attack the cringing tool
That with a selfish aim and ruthless hand,
Would tear in twain love's strong and holy band:
Why can ye not, as men who know and feel
What most is needed for your nation's weal,
Stand in her forums, and with burning words
Urge on the time, when to the bleeding herds,
Whose minds are buried now in polar night,
Hope shall descend; when freedom's mellow light
Shall break, and usher in the endless day,
That from Orleans to Pass'maquoddy Bay,
Despots no more may earthly homage claim,
Nor slaves exist, to soil Columbia's name;
Then, up! awake! nor let dull slumber waste
Your soul's devotion! life doth bid you haste!
The captive in his hut, with watchful ear,
Awaits the sweet triumphant songs to hear,*

That shall proclaim the glorious jubilee
When crippled thousands shall in truth be free.

Come! rouse ye brothers, rouse! nor let the voice
That shouting, calls you onward to rejoice,
Be heard in vain! but with ennobled souls,
Let all whom now an unjust law controls,
Press on in strength of mind, in purpose bent,
To live by right; to swell the free tones sent
On Southern airs, from this, your native State,
A glorious promise for the captive's fate.
Then up! and vow no more to sleep, till freed
From partial bondage to a life indeed.

New York, July 20, 1841

SILENT THOUGHTS

Around, how joyful in the chilly air
  Sweet sounds are floating! While above, the sky,
Peopled with visions bright, seems calm and fair
  As infant smiling 'neath a mother's eye.
It is the chant of joy that fresh, sincere,
  Springs up from youthful hearts! Yet louder from that
The souls of men, to greet the laughing year
  That clothed in promise, from afar doth come,
Burdened with hope and gift unfold. 'Tis well
  The tortured feelings and the sad should rise
To hail some vision'd good, and tuneful swell
  With songs of fairy scenes that in the skies
Are forming; of the peace and glorious fame,
  And wealth and pleasure in the distance strewn.
But all must learn that song and garnished dream
  May end; that magic spells around them thrown
Will melt in air; that sweet thoughts, redolent
  As spring-time buds may droop and faint and die;
That wish and vision bright are impotent
  To clothe the mind with light; to fit the eye,
To guide the spirit's growth; to lead it on
  To triumph in the world; to gain a wreath
Of praise enduring, as those souls have won,
  Whose works do raise them from contempt and death.
'Tis thought alone, creative fervent thought!
  Earnest in life, and in its purpose bent
To uphold truth and right, that rich is fraught
  With songs unceasing, and with gleamings sent

Of sure things coming from a brighter world.
   'Tis thought alone; girt round with quickening light,
With vision lofty, and with wing unfurled
   Ready to soar, self-poised, when darkest night
Of power and of death descends, that can,
   As days flit by, and years grow old apace,
Rejoice o'er bright scenes fled, and strengthened stand
   More glorious things, singing with youthful face.

New York, January 10, 1841

CHAPTER CLXXII

Rt. Rev. John M. Brown, D. D., D. C. L.
An Active Bishop in the A. M. E. Church

———•◆•———

Bishop J. M. Brown was born in Cantwell's Bridge, now called Odessa, New Castle county, Delaware, where he remained until he was ten years of age, when he changed his home to Wilmington, Delaware, where he remained two years in the family of the Hon. William Seals, a Quaker gentleman. While at his home he attended a private day school taught by a friendly white lady, and the Sabbath school of his native town. At Wilmington his Sabbath school instruction was mixed. He attended first the Presbyterian Sunday school. The members of that church proscribed all colored children to the gallery. As young as he was, he hated proscription, and, as the natural consequence, he united with a Roman Catholic Sunday school opposite his home. He was kindly received both by the priest and his people. The priest, the Rev. Mr. Carroll, offered to educate him in the colored Catholic school in Baltimore, Maryland, but his early training had always been in the Methodist faith by his grandfather, who was a Methodist minister, and by his mother who was a Methodist "mother in Israel;" he therefore declined the offer with thanks, unwilling to forsake the religion of his ancestors. At the end of his stay in Wilmington, an older sister from Philadelphia brought him to that city, where he enjoyed the advantages of a better education than it was possible he could have received in his native town. He found a home with Dr. Emerson and Henry Chester, an attorney-at-law. While he proved serviceable to them, they, in return, did much more for him. It was while here that the foundation of an education and piety was laid. They instructed him in the rudiments of a liberal education, catechised him in the principles of religion and the doctrines of the Bible. They recommended St. Thomas' Colored Protestant Episcopal church, which he attended until 1835, and from that time until 1837 he was with Mr. Frederick H. Hinton, from whom he learned the trade of a barber, and in whose house he made a profession of religion. He united with Bethel A. M. E. church, Philadelphia, Pennsylvania, January, 1836. He attended an evening school taught by the Rev. James N. Glouster, and entered upon his study for the ministry. Mr. Hinton gave him two years of his time as an apprentice with a barber's outfit, with which he, Edward H. Ferris and A. G. Crippen left Philadelphia for Amherst, Massachusetts, where they attended a manual labor school, but soon returned home. He remained at home a short time, and left for Poughkeepsie, New York, where he attended a school conducted by Rev. Nathaniel Blount, and working between school hours at his trade with Mr. Uriah Boston. During vacation he worked in the shop with Mr. Brady in New York City, in the summer, 1838. In the fall of 1838 he became a member of the Wesleyan Academy at Wilbraham, Massachusetts, remaining two years preparing for college. The summer of 1840 his health failing, he returned to Philadelphia to recuperate. In the meanwhile he continued the study of Latin and Greek under Rev. Mr. Harris, pastor of the Presbyterian church. In the fall of 1846, apparently restored to health, he entered Oberlin College, Ohio, where he prosecuted his studies for nearly four years. It was in the fall of 1844 that he opened his first school in Detroit, Michigan, and after the death of the pastor of the African M. E. church in that city he was appointed acting pastor, which position he filled from 1844 to 1847. While there a lot was purchased and the present church edifice erected. In September, 1864, he united with the Ohio conference, and was ordained deacon. From Detroit he was sent to Columbus, Ohio, where he preached three years. In addition to his ministerial duties he was appointed principal of the Union Seminary by the Ohio conference, out of which has grown Wilberforce University. This school began with three pupils, and at the end of his administration closed with one hundred. His energies were devoted to collecting money for the erection of a permanent building. He traveled extensively with but little success. In August, 1852, he was appointed to the charge of Allen Station, Pittsburgh, from the Ohio conference; in three months Bishop Quinn called him from the Ohio to the Indiana conference, and stationed him at New Orleans.

In 1853 he was appointed by Bishop Payne to the charge of the mission in New Orleans, which consisted of Morris Brown mission, third district, Trinity mission in the first district, and oversight of all adjacent places. Morris Brown chapel was built at a cost of three thousand dollars ($3,000). The congregations in both chapels were greatly increased. He remained in New Orleans about five years, and was imprisoned once for each year; but his imprisonment was generally superinduced by the prejudice of his own color. Becoming weary of the persecutions of the police and others, he asked Bishop Payne to relieve him, and in April, 1857, the bishop stationed him at Asbury chapel, Louisville, Kentucky, where he remained one year. He was transferred from the mission into the Baltimore conference, May, 1858, to Bethel church, Baltimore, remaining in that charge three years and one month. The church was remodeled at a cost of $5,000. There were between six and seven hundred souls added to the church during that period. While pastor he became editor of the Repository of Religion, Literature, Art and Science. He also served Ebenezer of that city, from April, 1861, to December, 1863, when he was sent to Brite Street A. M. E. church as well as to superintend the organization of the A. M. E. churches in Virginia and North Carolina. At the general conference of 1864 he was elected editor of the *Christian Recorder*, which he subsequently resigned. At this time he was elected corresponding secretary of the Parent Home and Foreign Missionary Society of his church, which he held for four years, ten thousand dollars ($10,000) being raised to assist in planting schools and churches in the South; in this grand and glorious work he was assisted by Rev. James F. Sisson, William B. Derrick and William E. Matthews, Esq.

In May, 1868, he was elected and ordained to the office of bishop by the General conference which met in Washington, District of Columbia. His first district consisted of South Carolina, Georgia, Florida and Alabama, which he held until 1872. He organized the Alabama conference of the A. M. E. church in the basement of the Methodist Episcopal church, South, July 25, 1868, in Selma, Alabama. He organized the Payne Institute in South Carolina, in 1871, which has grown into the Allen University, at Columbia, South Carolina. His second district consisted of Louisiana, Texas, Arkansas and Tennessee, which he served from 1872 to 1876. He planted the school which has grown into "The Paul Quinn College" at Waco, Texas, under the presidency of the late Bishop R. H. Cain, D.D., and Bishop T. M. D. Ward. He organized the West Texas, South Arkansas, West Tennessee and Columbia (S. C.) conferences. He also assisted Bishop Ward in the organization of the North Georgia conference, in 1872. His third district consisted of the Baltimore, Virginia, North and South Carolina conferences, which he served from 1876 to 1880. His fourth district consisted of Philadelphia, New Jersey, New York and New England conferences, which he served from 1880 to 1884. His fifth district embraces Missouri, Kansas, Illinois, Iowa, North Missouri, South Kansas and California. He is president of the financial board of the A. M .E. church. From the foregoing we see that the life of Bishop Brown has been active and useful. For nearly forty years he has devoted his time and talents to the cause of Christ, and he is as faithful to his duties now as when he started. May the life of such a man be spared to the church for many years!

On February 13, 1852, he was married in Louisville, Kentucky, to Miss

Mary L. Lewis. She has been his constant companion in his travels and labor for the church of Christ. They have eight children, four of whom have completed a course of study. The eldest son, John M. Brown, Jr., M.D., completed the junior year in college, and graduated with honor from the medical course at Howard University. He is now practicing successfully his profession in Kansas City, Missouri. William L. Brown graduated from the College Department at Howard among the best in his class; was principal of the public school of Morristown, New Jersey, and is now in the ranks of educators in the West. Daniel Brown has entered the ministry. Miss Mamie L. Brown also completed a course at Howard University, graduated from the Minor Normal school, and has taught successfully in one of the public schools of Washington, District of Columbia. My personal relations with Bishop Brown have been of the most pleasant character. For a few years I lived near him in Washington, and found him a loving, fatherly gentleman, who always had a smile for young men and a generous word for the aspiring. His life is a blessing and an inspiration.

CHAPTER CLXXIII

*Professor David Abner, Jr.
A Rising Young Professor in Bishop College, Texas—
Editor—Lecturer*

David Abner, Jr., was born November 25, 1860, in Upshur county, Texas. He is the son of Hon. David Abner, Sr., and Louisa Abner. There has always been something peculiar yet pleasing about the life of this young man. When quite young he exhibited a great natural gift, and it was at once seen what this, properly cultivated, would amount to. His parents sought early to give him a good training. In 1870 they moved to Marshall, Texas, where they now live. After sending him to the best schools around there, Wiley University included, they sent him to Straight University, New Orleans, Louisiana. Here he began his course in classics. He not only stood high in his branches of study, but exerted a noble influence on the school. This institution burned while he was in attendance, and he served nobly during the fire, gathering and throwing valuables from the rooms. The faculty and people highly commended him for his bravery and invaluable service. He returned in 1877. Having attended the same institution one session, he was sent to Fisk University, Nashville, Tennessee, where he remained three successive sessions, prosecuting the higher branches with much ease. He had power to grasp and here he showed it, and was pronounced a successful student. Specimen work of his composition in Greek was put on exhibition in the Nashville Exposition. He returned home in 1881. At this time the Baptist Home Mission Society of New York had established at Marshall a grand institution known as Bishop College. He immediately connected himself with this, and in 1884 graduated from the classical course with high honors. The evening of his graduation, his father, who had filled many positions of honor for both county and State, presented him a gold-headed cane as a token of respect for his obedience and faithfulness at home and in the class-room of four institutions. He has the honor of being the first thorough colored graduate of an institution of his native State, and was an assistant teacher every year except one until he graduated; yet this by no means impeded successful work in the class-room.

DAVID ABNER, JR.

He is a strong believer of the Baptist faith and doctrine. His connection with Bishop College had become of such an intimate character, and his power to instruct so effectual, that the Baptist Home Mission Society of New York made him one of its professors the year he completed his course, which position he yet fills. The Texas and Louisiana Association, composing a membership of sixteen thousand, chose him moderator over that body in 1883, which position he still holds. That same year he was chosen by his State at the capital seat and served as delegate to represent it in the National convention of colored men, which convened in Louisville, Kentucky, September, 1883. The Baptist State Convention of Texas, representing a membership of seventy thousand in 1884, chose him corresponding secretary; in this position he has been serving every year since. In the meanwhile he edited a paper in the interest of that body, then known as the *Baptist Journal*, now *Baptist Pilot*, previously conducted by Rev. A. R. Griggs, a heart-knitted friend of his. For three years he has been serving as district master of one of the strongest fraternities in the State. He travels every summer, delivering lectures, and ably presents the claims of the great institution in which he is engaged, and the work generally of both the Baptist Home Mission Society and the State convention. He speaks with command and ease, and seldom if ever leaves an assembly unmoved. He takes hold of nothing without thought, and when he does take hold success ever attends his efforts. Though honored as he is for actual deeds done, he is wholly unselfish and without the least spirit of boastfulness. It is a saying, "That this is why he takes with others and others take to him."

Few young men are rising to true eminence faster. His future is a great one. He often contributes to some of the leading colored papers of the State, and thoroughly handles his subjects. He is not only strong in mental but also in financial resources. His estimated worth is about nine thousand dollars. It is earnestly hoped that this life, which has made such a marked beginning in the interest of humanity and God, will be so preserved that it will continue to do all that it is capable of doing.

CHAPTER CLXXIV

Rev. A. A. Whitman
Author of a Book of Poems Entitled Not a Man, and Yet a Man, *with Miscellaneous Poems, with Extracts*

 The book of poems by the subject above mentioned is worthy of perusal, and was written for a laudable purpose, that of assisting Wilberforce University, one of the finest institutions in America.

 The author of the book of poems was a native of the Green River country, Hart county, Kentucky, and was born May 30, 1857. He was a slave till made free January 1, 1863. His parents early in his life joined the redeemed in the mansion above, and the boy was left to struggle with the many adversities incidental to his condition. He was willing to toil and did so, following manual labor and teaching, and finally rose to the position of a preacher in the A. M. E. church. When he wrote in 1877, he was situated at Springfield, Ohio, and was general agent of the Wilberforce University.

 The book is largely made up of a poem entitled 'Not a Man, and Yet a Man,' running through about two hundred and thirteen pages, and thirty-eight pages of miscellaneous poems. The poet is still living in ill health in the West, in Kansas. We give first a selection from the long poem and then a humorous one, that the reader may see the bent of his genius and be persuaded to secure the work and read the whole of that thrilling slave story told in musical language.

SUSSEX VALE, CANADA

And lo! a neat cottage with windows of green,
Scarce thro' the thick boughs of yon elms is seen.
There now the free lovers that once were the slave,
The maid of the rice swamp and Rodney the brave
Are dwelling in wedlock's dear holiest ties,
The objects of comment and pride for all eyes.
The stranger who passes thro' Sussex must hear
On the lips of the cottager, far and near,
The love of these new comers pointedly told,
And telling it over, it never grows old.

He has also published a volume called *The Rape of Florida,* which has been received with great favor and highly appreciated.

SOLON STILES
(Humorous)

*To town one day rode Solon Stiles,
O'er weary roads and rocky miles
And thro' long lanes, whose dusty breath,
Did nearly smother him to death;
By ragged fences, old and brown,
And thro' great tall woods up and down.*

*Wide orchards robed in red and white,
Were singing on his left and right;
The forests carolled by his way,
The grass was chirping, green and gay,
And wild flowers, sweetest of their race,
Like country maids of bashful face,*

*Peeped thro' the briery fences nigh,
With bright hues in each timid eye.
The farm cows whisked in their cool nook,
And splashed within their peaceful brook;
And on his fence, beneath the shade,
The plow boy's pipe shrill music made.*

*Stiles saw all this, but what cared he,
When he was going the town to see?
The country he had always seen,
But into town had never been.
So on he rode, with head on high,
And great thoughts roaming thro' the sky,
Not caring what he trotted by.*

*A little mule he sat astride,
With ropes for stirrups o'er him tied,
In which huge boots, as red as clay—
Red as a fox, some folks would say—
Swung loosely down, and dangled round,
As if in hopeless search of ground.*

*At first, when from the woods he rode,
And high in sight his small mule trode ,
Rough seas of smoke rolled on his eye,
Great dizzy houses reared on high,
With steeples banging in the sky.
Then Solon stopped and said, "Umph, my!"*

And next, a river deep and wide,
With houses floating up its tide
He met, and paused again to look,
And then to move on undertook;
And spurred and spurred, but looked around,
And lo! in deep amazement found

His small mule stuck, and as he spurred
The more, the thing's ears only stirred.
"Hullo!" a swarm of blubbies cried,
"Whip on the critter's hairy side!"
At this the mule insulted grew,
Took up its ears, and fairly flew,
Till near a great white bridge it drew.

Across the bridge rode Solon Stiles,
By dusty shops and lumber piles,
And where tall houses o'er him stood,
Like cliffs within his native wood.
And furnaces with fiery tongues,
And smoky throats and iron lungs,
Like demons coughed, and howled, and roared,
And fire from out their bowels poured.

Now on and on, up Sailor street,
The donkey whirled his rattling feet,
While either sidewalk loud upon
A swarm of oaths were chorused on.
One tall boy, in this surging sea
Of rags and young profanity,
High o'er the rest, on awkward shanks,
Like stilts, led on the swelling ranks.
His deep throat like a fog horn blew,
Till lesser blasts their aid withdrew.

Then Stiles communed thus wtih his mule:
"My! listen what a cussin' school
This town lets out to fill the ears
Of God with! My! them babies swears!"
Meanwhile there came a light brigade,
To at the donkey's heels parade,
Till up before and then behind,
His honor flew and then combined
An old Dutch waltz and new quick-step,
That half a square of urchins swept,
As fast as leaves were ever seen
Brushed by a whirlwind from the green.

The tall commander now in front,
Led oathing, as his pride was wont,
The new assault, when stock still stood
The mule away not half a rood;
For lo! with tomahawk in hand,
Before a neighb'ring cigar stand,
He saw a savage, to describe
A chieftain of some bloody tribe.
At Solon straight he raised a blow
And strained with all his might to throw,
But stayed his rage, for he beheld,
That with hot rage the donkey swelled.

Ah! Solon felt his blood run cold,
For oft his gran'dad him had told
Of Indians in an early day,
Beside the backwoods cotter's way,
Skulking to on some settler fly
And scalp him ere he'd time to die.
"Throw if you dare!" aloud he cried,
And slid down at his donkey's side.
At this he saw the savage stare,
And forthwith threw his coat off there.
With club in hand, the first he found,
Then on the foe at one great bound
He flew, and hard began to pound;
When thus a broad-brimmed vender fat,
Began to interview the spat:
"Vat vas yer dun, yer grazy ding;
Schoost schtop, yer petter don't py jing!
Schoost vat yer broke my zine met, aye,
Eh! petter yer don't, yer go away!"

"Well!" Solon thought, "If this is town,
I'll give you leave to knock me down
If I ain't lost; no, this ain't me,
No, town ain't what it seems to be,
Yes, here I am, and this is me,
But town's not what it seems to be!"

CHAPTER CLXXV

E. M. Bannister, Esq.
An Artist Photographer—Gifted Painter of Providence,
Rhode Island, Who was Inspired by a Slur in the New York
Herald *Twenty Years Ago*

———•◆•———

I have read many times the story of Parrhasius, as told by N. P. Willis, wherein the poet depicts a Greek painter desirous of perpetuating his name as a great artist. A slave had been bought in order that he might be slowly put to death, and that the painter might finish a picture which he had upon the canvas, which was the picture of Prometheus

> *Chained to the cold rocks of Mt. Caucasus*
> *The vulture at his vitals, and the links*
> *Of the lame Lemnian festering in his flesh.*

Assistants were standing by racking the slave in order that he might catch his dying countenance and put it on the canvas. The feeling which the artist displayed is well expressed in the following verses:

> *So—let him writhe! How long*
>   *Will he live thus?*
> *Quick, my good pencil now!*
>   *What a fine agony works upon his brow!*
> *Ha! Gray-haired, and so strong!*
>   *How fearfully he stifles that short moan.*
> *Gods! If I could but paint a dying groan!*
>
> *Pity thee! So I do!*
>   *I pity the dumb victim at the altar—*
> *But does the robed priest for his pity falter?*
>   *I'd rack thee though I knew*
> *A thousand lives were perishing in thine—*
>   *What were ten thousand to a fame like mine?*
>
> *Yet, there's a deathless* name!
>   *A spirit that the smothering vault shall spurn,*

And like the steadfast planet mount and burn—
  And though its crown of flame
Consumed my brain to ashes as it shone,
  By all the fiery stars! I'd bind it on!

Aye—though it bid me rifle
  My heart's last fount for its insatiate thirst—
Though every life-strung nerve be maddened first—
  Though it should bid me stifle
The yearning in my throat for my sweet child,
  And taunt its mother till my brain went wild—
All—I would do it all—
  Sooner than die, like a dull worm, to rot—
Thrust foully into the earth to be forgot!

As I have often read these words and heard them declaimed, they have thrilled me with somewhat of the same feeling which the painter himself must have had as he sought to immortalize himself in this one picture. In the far off days of Greece and the story of Parrhasius, we seem almost to forget that within our neighborhood, and often within the circle of our own acquaintances, we have men who are equally ambitious to utilize their talents in such a manner as to bring glory and honor to the race; and, though not expressed in the cruel manner by racking a human being until death will give that pallor to the cheek, that quivering to the nerves, that stifling groan, which one might desire to put on canvas, yet ambition is checked simply by the surroundings and kept within the limits of reason and sound judgment.

Mr. Bannister was filled with some of this ambition; for this reason he undertook the study of art. What he has accomplished through his ambition to excel was through a desire to rebuke a slur which was passed upon the race by the New York *Herald* twenty years ago, in which it was said "that the Negro seems to have an appreciation of art, but is manifestly unable to produce it." This was said with reference to the number of colored people seen at the art exhibition; and this was the spur, the incentive, the goad that drove him to supreme effort in accomplishing such results as he has accomplished. In making himself felt and recognized as a first-class artist in a country noted for its prejudice against the Negro, and for its efforts in suppressing Negro talent, and, further, when expressed, for its efforts in many instances in keeping it from being recognized, he deserves unbounded credit.

Mr. Bannister says:

I have been sustained by an inborn love for art and accomplished all I have undertaken through the severest struggles which, while severe enough for white men, have been enhanced tenfold in my case. That I have succeeded in a measure, I can only point to the many encomiums passed upon my efforts by the leading white papers of the country.

Mr. Bannister was born in the town of Saint Andrews, New Brunswick, and was educated and grew up there. At the age of eighteen he went to Boston, Massachusetts, where he learned and worked at the photographic business for a number of years, using the only time at his disposal (nights) for the study of art, at the drawing school, at the Lowell Institute of that city. His study was, however, only elementary. That, however, is the only regular tuition, if it may be called such, that he has had, with the study of art anatomy, under Dr. Rimmer of Boston. The rest he has accomplished, as he says, "through God's help and the persistent effort on his part."

Mr. Bannister has received many notices from the very best sources in the United States, such as the New York *Herald, Tribune, Boston Globe, Traveler, Transcript,* and sketches have appeared in the *Artist of the Nineteenth Century, American Artist,* published by the Appletons of New York. He has received many medals and diplomas at important exhibitions, the most important of which he considers the first award medal from the Centennial Exhibition of 1876, where his picture was given a place of honor on the walls by a jury of European artists of eminence. He has exhibited some of his work in the Centennial Cotton Exposition held in New Orleans in 1884 and '85, to which reference has been made by the reporter of the *American Baptist,* in the issue of June 11, 1885, where it refers to his celebrated painting known as "A New England Pasture," valued at one thousand five hundred dollars.

Mr. Bannister says that to-day members of the race, which refused to receive him for instruction because of his color, would fill his room as pupils at the first sign of consent. He has endeavored to score a victory for his race in a humble way; what he has done seems to have proven to the writer of the work on "American Art," the possibility of an American artist making his own way without the aid of foreign study.

Nobody, however, appreciates the good to be derived from such study more than he; his opportunities for such have not come to him. So, with God's help, he will work within his lines and when through with it all, something left behind him may be accredited to his race, that will class him among the old masters for talent.

With such an ambition and with so laudable a purpose, may it not be hoped that he will be sustained in his aims and purposes for the race? We earnestly hope that the worthy persons among us will patronize such men as Bannister, Tanner and Stidum by purchasing their productions and placing them upon the walls of their homes, that their children may be inspired to undertake such a life, filled with such delicate and inspiring purposes as they have shown in silently and humbly working away from the multitude; not seeking applause, but in quiet studios, undertaking those things which require the very finest texture of mind and heart to show the æsthetical and the love of the beautiful in the race.

CHAPTER CLXXVI

Hon. C. C. Antoine
Lieutenant-Governor of Louisiana—State Senator—Prominent Politician

---

The ancestors of our subject transmitted to him the characteristics which are essential to the greatness of individuals as well as of nations. From his grandmother, the daughter of an African chief, he inherited intellect, industry, discretion and benevolence, and from the father, a valiant soldier in the battles about New Orleans in 1812, came the upright character and fearless advocate of human rights which made him at once a leader of his people.

Before engaging in public life, Mr. Antoine's industry and promptness in all business transactions brought him commercial success. His upright character earned the confidence of all who knew him. He worked quietly, and awaited patiently the dawn of a better day. It came, finally, with our late civil war. After the Federal troops occupied the city and colored men were admitted to the army, he devoted his energies to recruiting men for the "Native Guards." When Baton Rouge was captured by Dick Taylor, and the loyal soldiers and citizens were filled with consternation and alarm, he worked zealously until, within forty-eight hours, he had raised a colored company known subsequently as Company I, Seventh Louisiana colored regiment. As captain of this company he served at Brashear, now Morgan City, and other points in the department with credit to himself to the close of the war.

Gathering what worldly goods the war left him he removed to Shreveport, Louisiana, upon the declaration of peace, and opened a family grocery, where, with his uniform politeness, he gained many friends. With enfranchisement and reconstruction he was naturally drawn into politics. When the convention which framed the present constitution of Louisiana was called, he exerted himself in vain to induce the old citizens of Caddo to accept the new condition of affairs and permit the colored people to elect them as delegates to that convention. Time has vindicated the wisdom of his advice, which, had it been taken, would have warded off many of the disasters now complained of, but they refused to accept this olive branch of peace so magnanimously offered; they were not willing to "shake hands across the bloody chasm."

Much against his own inclination, Mr. Antoine was elected to the convention. The part he took in that body was prominent and honorable, in appreciation of which his constituents elected him to the State Senate under the new constitution. While senator, he faithfully served his State. His term expired in 1872. At the State nominating convention held at Baton Rouge, Louisiana, in August of that year, he was unanimously nominated for lieutenant-governor, a position which he filled with credit and to the entire satisfaction of his party. So great was the enthusiasm manifested at his nomination that he was carried bodily to the rostrum, when, in his usual unaffected manner, he delivered a telling address.

It has been said that few politicians escape contamination, but Hon. Antoine seems an exception. "His private and public life," says a State paper, "is exceptionable and above reproach."

In his capacity as second officer of the State of Louisiana, Lieutenant-Governor Antoine secured the admiration and confidence of his race and the respect of the whites, and his good qualities are acknowledged even by his political opponents. A man of the strictest integrity, his private character is unblemished.

He was called upon to discharge the duties of governor on several occasions, at which times he has clearly demonstrated his ability to rule by that happy medium of suavity and strength which never governs so well as when it does not appear to govern at all.

As presiding officer of the Senate he was impartial in his rulings, and an appeal was very seldom taken from his decisions. In all of his official relations he conducted himself with that modesty which so fully indicates real merit. He still lives an honored and respected citizen of Louisiana.

CHAPTER CLXXVII

*Rev. James Matthew Townsend, D. D.
Corresponding Secretay of the Parent Home and Foreign
Missionary Society of the A. M. E. Church—A Man
of Perseverance and Sound Judgment*

James Matthew Townsend, D.D., was born in Gallipolis, Ohio, August 18, 1841. He was the only son of William and Mary Ann Townsend, who were members of the A. M. E. church. From early childhood young Townsend received the most careful religious and moral training at the hands of his parents, who in the meantime had moved to Oxford, Ohio. At the age of twelve he professed religion and united with the A. M. E. church, under the pastorate of that great and good man, Rev. John Turner. He had the advantage of a common school education, and being inclined to habits of reading and thought, thus laid the foundation of future usefulness by years of careful study and research.

At the age of sixteen he was licensed for an exhorter, and two years later a local preacher. At the beginning of the rebellion he had a strong conviction that the war would result in the emancipation of his race, and therefore sought the earliest opportunity to take up arms in defense of the Union and freedom. He enlisted in the Fifty-fourth Massachusetts volunteers—the first colored regiment to enter the service—and remained on the field until the close of the war in 1865. On returning home he attended Oberlin College for two years, during which time his father died leaving him the care of the family. He secured, through the recommendation of friends, a commission from the American Missionary Board, and subsequently an appointment as principal of the colored schools of Evansville, Indiana, which position he held for four years. During this time he continued his studies, and in 1871 he was ordained deacon by Bishop A. W. Wayman. In December of this year he was married to Cornelia A., daughter of Josiah and Nancy Settle. June, 1872, he was appointed to the pastoral charge of Richmond, Indiana. After serving two years he was ordained elder by Bishop Wayman. In 1874 he was appointed to Terre Haute, Indiana. In 1876 he was elected to the general conference and was elected assistant secretary of the same. In August of the same year he was appointed to Bethel station, Indianapolis, and served two years. While here he was elected by the General Missionary Board, which met in Baltimore, Maryland, as corresponding secretary of the Parent Home and Foreign Missionary Society. He was elected by acclamation by the general conference in 1880 to the same office, which position he now holds.

He was also elected as one of the commissioners on "Organic Union," and a delegate to the Ecumenical conference held in London, England. In June of 1883 he received the degree of Doctor of Divinity from Wilberforce University. His name is prominently mentioned in all the advanced movements of his church, educationally and otherwise; and not infrequently has he been called on to participate in the public affairs of his race.

Dr. Townsend is a man of indomitable will and energy that knows no such word as fail. He has the capacity to organize, and he can execute that which he organizes. This is shown in his plan of securing an iron church for Hayti. He went to the Episcopal church mission house; they knew nothing of it; then he went to the Methodist; they could not inform him where to get one. An ordinary man would have given up and said: "If these large mission boards can give no information, I need seek no further." But he wrote to England and there received the information needed, and eventually contracted for the church, went to London, inspected, and paid for and shipped the iron church. This iron structure in Hayti will stand as a monument to the love of the A. M. E. church for the race, and will be the crystallization of the faith of the church in the possibilities of the race. It will be a shaft of beauty, exemplifying at the same time the energy, tact, skill and devotion to the mission cause—the last and greatest of the missionary societies of the A. M. E. church.

At this writing we have been unable to secure all the facts that we desired in regard to Dr. Townsend, as he is on a trip to Hayti; and so, desiring to give our readers a sketch of his life, because he is a man of push and determination, I have been compelled to take the above as found in the Budget of the A. M. E. church, edited by Rev. B. W. Arnett, D.D., for the year 1884.

I cannot omit the political career of Rev. J. M. Townsend, for his position in Indiana politics is unique, isolated and particularly eminent; for his townsmen are justly proud of him and the honorable manner in which he has borne himself. While a lover of his race, he was so moderate in his dealings with all men that he was able to secure the votes of both the white and colored members of the party, and to take off the sharp edge of Democratic spleen.

In the fall election of Wayne county, Indiana, in 1884, he was nominated and elected to the Legislature of his State, and was a very devoted member.

At this time the *Richmond Palladium*, said:

We are proud of Hon. James M. Townsend, or colored representative. No white man can object to the presence of Rev. Townsend, for he is an affable, refined, Christian gentleman, with a cultured brain.

The *Cambridge Citizen* said:

Overwise persons who were in haste to predict that, "When the *nigger* gets into the Legislature he'll see how quick they'll sit down on him," are respectfully invited to notice that Mr. Townsend has been recognized as a leading member.

Once in the Legislature, he was never forgetful of his burdened people, so he introduced a bill to wipe out the "Black Laws."

This bill was not passed, but another was, when he had returned home filled with honor, the admiration of his associates and the gratitude of the Negro race.

INDEX TO SKETCHES

Abner, David Jr. 809
Adams, Henry 561
Allain, T. T. 125
Aldridge, Ira 513
Allen, Richard 329
Allensworth, Allen 595
Amo, Anthony W. 423
Antoine, C. C. 820
Arneaux, J. A. 323
Arnett, B. W. 625
Attucks, Crispus 47
Atwood, W. Q. 449

Baltimore, J. D. 167
Banneker, Benjamin 224
Bannister, E. M. 816
Benjamin, R. C. O. 711
Bethune, T. G. 557
Blyden, E. W. 651
Bouey, H. N. 675
Boulden, J. F. 491
Bowers, T. J. 120
Bowser, J. D. 488
Brawley, E. M. 645
Braxton, P. H. A. 753
Brown, J. A. 55
Brown, John M. 805
Brown, S. G. 193
Brown, William Wells 296
Bruce, B. K. 483
Burgan, I. M. 785

Burrus, J. H. *179*

Cain, R. H. *613*
Campbell, J. P. *741*
Campbell, Matthew *501*
Capitein, J. E. J. *775*
Cardoza, F. L. *281*
Carey, Lott *342*
Chandler, H. W. *160*
Chase, W. C. *61*
Chester, T. M. *463*
Clanton, S. T. *275*
Clark, Alexander *793*
Clark, P. H. *244*
Clifford, J. R. *171*
Corbin, J. C. *583*
Council, W. H. *255*
Craig, W. F. *298*
Crogman, W. H. *480*
Cromwell, J. W. *637*
Crosby, J. O. *277*
Crummell, Alexander *357*
Cuffee, Paul *217*

Dale, Marcus *473*
Dancy, J. C. *796*
Day, William H. *701*
DeBaptiste, R. *229*
DeLaney, M. R. *721*
Derrick, W. B. *37*
Dixon, W. T. *495*
Douglass, F. *21*
Downing, George T. *718*
Dumas, Alexander *303*
Dupee, G. W. *599*
Durham, J. J. *622*

Ecton, George F. *234*
Elliott, R. B. *310*
Ensley, N. H. *237*

Farley, J. C. *563*

INDEX

Ferrill, Loudon 206
Fields, J. B. 727
Fortune, T. T. 549

Gaddie, D. A. 445
Garnet, H. H. 453
Gayles, G. W. 405
Gibbs, M. W. 407
Gibson, W. H. 369
Greener, R. T. 211
Gregory, J. M. 433
Grimes, L. A. 457
Grimke, F. J. 416

Hancock, R. M. 266
Haynes, Lemuel 467
Harlan, Robert 421
Heath, A. 108
Holmes, J. H. 460
Holmes, W. E. 384
Holland, J. 251
Hood, J. W. 70

Irvine, J. J. 713

Jasper, J. 767
Jeter, H. N. 399
Johnson, H. 509
Johnson, H. R. W. 746
Jones, Daniel 395
Jones, J. E. 145
Jones, Wiley 175

Kelly, Edmund 186

Langston, J. M. 345
Leary, J. S. 285
Lee, B. F. 655
Lewis, James 677
Lipscombe, E. H. 681
L'Islet, G. 709
L'Ouverture. T. 665

Love, E. K. *321*
Lowery, S. R, ... *77*
Lynch, J. R. *749*

Marrs, E. P. *392*
Matthews, J. C. *685*
Matthews, W. E. *153*
McAlpine, W. H. *353*
McCabe, E. P. *761*
McElwee, S. A. *335*
Miller, T. D. *162*
Mitchell, J. Jr. *201*
Morris, J. W. *91*
Murry, P. H. *43*

Page, I. E. *315*
Parrish, C. H. *763*
Payne, C. H. *241*
Payne, D. A. *779*
Pelham, Robert *733*
Pennington, J. W. C. *648*
Perry, R. L. *425*
Petion, A. *547*
Pettiford, W. R. *305*
Pinchback, P. B. S. *533*
Podd, J. A. D. *157*
Poindexter, James *259*
Porter, E. S. *287*
Porter, Troy *555*
Price, J. C. *529*
Purce, C. L. *301*
Purvis, C. B. *477*

Reason, C. L. *799*
Reeve, J. B. *118*
Revels, H. R. *672*
Riddick, J. H. *527*
Roberts, N. F. *122*
Ruffin, G. L. *518*

Scarborough, W. S. *269*
Settle, J. T. *365*

SMALLS, ROBERT	*93*
SMITH, H. C.	*115*
SMYTHE, J. H.	*617*
SPELMAN, J. J.	*659*
STEPHENSON, J. W.	*577*
STEWART, T. McC.	*757*
STEWART, W. H.	*413*
STILL, WILLIAM	*81*
STRAKER, A.	*521*
TANNER, B. T.	*705*
TANNER, H. O.	*105*
TAYLOR, BARTLETT	*430*
TAYLOR, M. W.	*662*
TAYLOR, PRESTON	*189*
TERRY, J. W.	*149*
TOLTON, AUGUSTUS	*291*
TOWNSEND, J. M.	*822*
TROTTER, J. M.	*587*
TURNER, H. M.	*567*
TURNER, NAT	*743*
VANDERVALL, R. B.	*387*
VASSA, GUSTAVUS	*633*
VAUGHN, C. C.	*505*
VEAZIE, DENMARK	*142*
WAGONER, H. O.	*469*
WALTERS, ALEXANDER	*221*
WASHINGTON, B. T.	*737*
WATSON, S. C.	*608*
WHITE, G. H.	*362*
WHITE, J. T.	*401*
WHITE, W. J.	*791*
WHITMAN, A. A.	*812*
WILLIAMS, G. W.	*371*
WILLIAMS, H. F.	*183*
WOODS, G. T.	*51*